Lecture Notes in Artificial Intelligence   11717

Subseries of Lecture Notes in Computer Science

Series Editors

Randy Goebel
University of Alberta, Edmonton, Canada
Yuzuru Tanaka
Hokkaido University, Sapporo, Japan
Wolfgang Wahlster
DFKI and Saarland University, Saarbrücken, Germany

Founding Editor

Jörg Siekmann
DFKI and Saarland University, Saarbrücken, Germany

More information about this series at http://www.springer.com/series/1244

Kazuhiro Kojima · Maki Sakamoto ·
Koji Mineshima · Ken Satoh (Eds.)

New Frontiers in Artificial Intelligence

JSAI-isAI 2018 Workshops, JURISIN,
AI-Biz, SKL, LENLS, IDAA
Yokohama, Japan, November 12–14, 2018
Revised Selected Papers

 Springer

Editors
Kazuhiro Kojima
National Institute of Advanced
Industrial Science and Technology
Ibaraki, Japan

Koji Mineshima
Ochanomizu University
Tokyo, Japan

Maki Sakamoto
University of Electro-Communications
Tokyo, Japan

Ken Satoh
National Institute of Informatics
Tokyo, Japan

ISSN 0302-9743   ISSN 1611-3349   (electronic)
Lecture Notes in Artificial Intelligence
ISBN 978-3-030-31604-4   ISBN 978-3-030-31605-1   (eBook)
https://doi.org/10.1007/978-3-030-31605-1

LNCS Sublibrary: SL7 – Artificial Intelligence

This Springer imprint is published by the registered company Springer Nature Switzerland AG
The registered company address is: Gewerbestrasse 11, 6330 Cham, Switzerland

Preface

The Japanese Society for Artificial Intelligence (JSAI) is a premier academic society that focuses on artificial intelligence (AI) in Japan and was established in 1986. The International Symposium on AI (JSAI-isAI) is supported by the JSAI and this year was the tenth edition. JSAI-isAI 2018 was successfully held during November 12–14, 2018, at Raiosha in Hiyoshi Campus of Keio University in Yokohama, Japan. In all, 160 people from 17 countries participated.

JSAI-isAI 2018 included 5 workshops, where 9 invited talks and 85 papers were presented. This volume, *New Frontiers in Artificial Intelligence: JSAI-isAI 2018 Workshops*, is the proceedings of JSAI-isAI 2018. From the five workshops (JURISIN 2018, AI-Biz 2018, SKL 2018, LENLS 15, and IDAA 2018) 33 papers were carefully selected and revised according to the comments of the workshop Program Committees. The acceptance rate was about 34%. This resulted in the excellent selection of papers that are representative of some of the topics of AI research both in Japan and in other parts of the world.

JURISIN 2018 was the 12th International Workshop on Juris-informatics. Juris-informatics is a new research area that studies legal issues from the perspective of informatics. The purpose of this workshop was to discuss both fundamental and practical issues among people from various backgrounds such as law, social science, information and intelligent technology, logic and philosophy, including the conventional "AI and law" area.

AI-Biz 2018 (Artificial Intelligence of and for Business) was the third workshop held to foster the concepts and techniques of business intelligence (BI) in AI. BI should include such cutting-edge techniques as data science, agent-based modeling, complex adaptive systems, and IoT. The main purpose of this workshop is to provide a forum for participants to discuss important research questions and practical challenges in BI, business informatics, data analysis, and agent-based modeling, to exchange the latest results, and to join efforts in solving common challenges.

SKL 2018 (the 5th International Workshop on Skill Science) aimed to internationalize research on skill sciences by organizing the meeting. Human skills involve well-attuned perception and fine motor control, often accompanied by thoughtful planning. The involvement of body, environment, and tools mediating them makes the study of skills unique among research on human intelligence.

LENLS 15 was the 15th event in the series, and it focused on the formal and theoretical aspects of natural language. LENLS (Logic and Engineering of Natural Language Semantics) is an annual international workshop recognized internationally in the formal syntax-semantics-pragmatics community. It has been bringing together for discussion and interdisciplinary communication researchers working on formal theories of natural language syntax, semantics and pragmatics, (formal) philosophy, AI, and computational linguistics. Additionally, two selected papers which were supposed to be included in the post proceedings of LENLS 14 are also included in this volume.

IDAA 2018 (the First International Workshop of Intelligent Data Analytics and Applications) began in 2018. This workshop aims to bring researchers and practitioners across different AI research and application communities together in a unique forum to present and exchange ideas, results, and experiences in AI technologies and applications. The scope of this workshop focuses on application inspired novel findings, methods, systems, and solutions which demonstrate the impact of data analytics by AI.

It is our great pleasure to be able to share some highlights of these fascinating workshops in this volume. We hope this book will introduce readers to the state-of-the-art research outcomes of JSAI-isAI 2018, and motivate them to participate in future JSAI-isAI events.

July 2018

Kazuhiro Kojima
Maki Sakamoto
Ken Satoh
Koji Mineshima

Organization

Al-Biz 2018

Chairs

Takao Terano	Chiba University of Commerce, Japan
Setsuya Kurahashi	University of Tsukuba, Japan
Hiroshi Takahashi	Keio University, Japan

Steering Committee

Reiko Hishiyama	Waseda University, Japan
Manabu Ichikawa	Shibaura Institute of Technology, Japan
Yoko Ishino	Yamaguchi University, Japan
Hajime Kita	Kyoto University, Japan
Hajime Mizuyama	Aoyama Gakuin University, Japan
Chathura Rajapaksha	University of Kelaniya, Sri Lanka
Masakazu Takahashi	Yamaguchi University, Japan
Shingo Takahashi	Waseda University, Japan
Takashi Yamada	Yamaguchi University, Japan

IDAA 2018

Chairs

Chih-Chieh Hung	Tamkang University, Taiwan
Chun-Hao Chen	Tamkang University, Taiwan
Hui-Huang Hsu	Tamkang University, Taiwan

JURISIN 2018

Chair

Katsumi Nitta	National Institute of Informatics, Japan

Steering Committee

Takehiko Kasahara	Toin Yokohama University, Japan
Makoto Nakamura	Nagoya University, Japan
Katsumi Nitta	National Institute of Informatics, Japan
Seiichiro Sakurai	Meji Gakuin University, Japan
Ken Satoh	National Institute of Informatics and Sokendai, Japan
Satoshi Tojo	Japan Advanced Institute of Science and Technology, Japan
Katsuhiko Toyama	Nagoya University, Japan

Advisory Committee

Trevor Bench-Capon	The University of Liverpool, UK
Tomas Gordon	Fraunfoher FOKUS, Germany
Henry Prakken	University of Utrecht and University of Groningen, The Netherlands
John Zeleznikow	Victoria University, Australia
Robert Kowalski	Imperial College London, UK
Kevin Ashley	University of Pittsburgh, USA

Program Committee

Thomas Agotnes	University of Bergen, Norway
Natasha Alechina	University of Nottingham, UK
Ryuta Arisaka	National Institute of Informatics, Japan
Kristijonas Cyras	Imperial College London, UK
Mehdi Dastani	Utrecht University, The Netherlands
Marina De Vos	University of Bath, UK
Juergen Dix	Clausthal University of Technology, Germany
Phan Minh Dung	Asia Institute of Technology, Thailand
Randy Goebel	University of Alberta, Canada
Guido Governatori	Commonwealth Scientific and Industrial Research Organization, Australia
Tatsuhiko Inatani	Kyoto University, Japan
Tokuyasu Kakuta	Chuo University, Japan
Yoshinobu Kano	Shizuoka University, Japan
Tetsuro Kawamoto	National Institute of Advanced Industrial Science and Technology, Japan
Mi-Young Kim	University of Alberta, Canada
Nguyen Le Minh	Japan Advanced Institute of Science and Technology, Japan
Beishui Liao	Zhejiang University, China
Brian Logan	The University of Nottingham, UK
Hatsuru Morita	Tohoku University, Japan
Yoichi Motomura	National Institute of Advanced Industrial Science and Technology, Japan
Makoto Nakamura	Niigata Institute of Technology, Japan
Yoshiaki Nishigai	Nihon University, Japan
Konatsu Nishigai	Tokyo Metropolitan University, Japan
Katsumi Nitta	National Institute of Informatics, Japan
Paulo Novais	University of Minho, Portugal
Julian Padget	University of Bath, UK
Juliano Rabelo	University of Alberta, Canada
Monica Palmirani	University of Bologna, Italy
Seiichiro Sakurai	Meiji Gakuin University, Japan
Katsuhiko Sano	Hokkaido University, Japan
Ken Satoh	National Institute of Informatics and Sokendai, Japan

Akira Shimazu	Japan Advanced Institute of Science and Technology, Japan
Fumio Shimpo	Keio University, Japan
Kazuko Takahashi	Kansei Gakuin University, Japan
Satoshi Tojo	Japan Advanced Institute of Science and Technology, Japan
Katsuhiko Toyama	Nagoya University, Japan
Rob van den Hoven van Genderen	VU University Amsterdam, The Netherlands
Leon van der Torre	University of Luxembourg, Luxembourg
Bart Verheij	University of Groningen, The Netherlands
Masaharu Yoshioka	Hokkaido University, Japan
Harumichi Yuasa	Institute of Information Security, Japan
Yueh-Hsuan Weng	Tohoku University, Japan

LENLS 2018

Chairs

Osamu Sawada (Chair)	Mie University, Japan
Daisuke Bekki (Co-chair)	Ochanomizu University and National Institute of Informatics, Japan
Koji Mineshima (Co-chair)	Ochanomizu University, Japan
Elin McCready (Co-chair)	Aoyama Gakuin University, Japan

Program Committee

Alastair Butler	Hirosaki University, Japan
Richard Dietz	University of Tokyo, Japan
Naoya Fujikawa	University of Tokyo, Japan
Yurie Hara	Waseda University, Japan
Magdalena Kaufmann	University of Connecticut, USA
Yoshiki Mori	University of Tokyo, Japan
David Y. Oshima	Nagoya University, Japan
Katsuhiko Sano	Hokkaido University, Japan
Wataru Uegaki	University of Edinburgh, UK
Katsuhiko Yabushita	Naruto University of Education, Japan
Tomoyuki Yamada	Hokkaido University, Japan
Shunsuke Yatabe	Kyoto University, Japan
Kei Yoshimoto	Tohoku University, Japan

SKIL 2018

Chair

| Tsutomu Fujinami | Japan Advanced Institute of Science and Technology, Japan |

Program Committee

Ken Hashizume	Osaka University, Japan
Kentaro Kodama	Kanagawa University, Japan
Yoshifusa Matsuura	Yokohama National University, Japan
Yuta Ogai	Tokyo Polytechnic University, Japan
Mihoko Otake	Riken, Japan
Daichi Shimizu	Tokyo University, Japan
Masaki Suwa	Keio University, Japan

Contents

LENLS 15

LENLS 14

SKL 2018

AI-Biz 2018

Artificial Intelligence of and for Business (AI-Biz 2018)

Takao Terano[1], Setsuya Kurahashi[2], and Hiroshi Takahashi[3]

[1] Chiba University of Commerce
[2] University of Tsukuba
[3] Keio University

1 The Workshop

In AI-Biz 2018 held on November 13, an excellent invited lecture and 10 cutting-edge research papers were presented with a total of about 20 participants. The workshop theme focused on various recent issues in business activities and application technologies of Artificial Intelligence (AI). The invited lecture was ``Two-Storied ELSI Guidelines: Inclusive Coverage to Individual Solutions' by Dr. Ryoju Hamada of SIIT, Thammasat University, Thailand, and President of the International Simulation and Gaming Association (ISAGA). The presentation reported on AI-oriented ELSI (Ethics, Law, and Society Implementation) problems related to guidelines authorized by academic society. He also focused on an AI-based Consensus Building Support System called COLLAGREE. AI-Biz 2018 was the third workshop hosted by the SIG-BI (Business Informatics) of JSAI and we believe that the success of the workshop can be attributed to the inclusion of very wide fields of business and AI technology for human capital, industry classifications, capturing mercurial customers, variable selection, organizational performance, traffic congestion, visualization of R&D project, credit risk, ecocars, stock price prediction, and so forth.

2 Papers

16 papers were submitted to the workshop, and 10 papers were selected for oral presentation in the workshop (a 62.5% acceptance rate). After the workshop, they were reviewed by Program Committee (PC) members again and 4 papers were finally selected (a 25% acceptance rate). Following are their synopses. Shin-Fu Chen, Goutam Chakraborty, and Li-Hua Li propose a machine learning model with feature selection to measure the credit risk of individual borrower on P2P lending. Based on their experimental results, they showed that the credit risk prediction for P2P lending can be improved using Logistic Regression in addition to proper feature selection. Yusuke Matsumoto, Aiko Suge, and Hiroshi Takahashi construct a new industrial classification system with Fuzzy C Means. This study confirmed the validity of proposed methods through composite variance and absolute prediction error.

As a result, it showed that there is a possibility to represent one company with overlapping industries. Fumiko Kumada and Setsuya Kurahashi examined the relationship of influences of a structure of diversity using the concept of faultline, which is hypothetically dividing lines that may split a group into subgroups of people based on their multiple attributes and assess diversity quantitatively. Takahiro Obata and Setsuya Kurahashi propose a new variable selection method that applies RCGA. This method contains two primary components: one is a new variable selection criterion and the other is a method for estimating the progress of RCGA optimization. The effectiveness of the selection method was confirmed through application to a nonlinear test function.

3 Acknowledgment

As the Organizing Committee chair, I would like to thank the Steering Committee members, who are leading researchers in various fields: Reiko Hishiyama (Waseda University, Japan), Manabu Ichikawa (National Institute of Public Health, Japan), Yoko Ishino (Yamaguchi University, Japan), Hajime Kita (Kyoto University, Japan), Hajime Mizuyama (Aoyama Gakuin University, Japan), Chathura Rajapaksha (University of Kelaniya, Sri Lanka), Masakazu Takahashi (Yamaguchi University, Japan), Shingo Takahashi (Waseda University, Japan), and Takashi Yamada (Yamaguchi University, Japan).

The organizers would like to thank JSAI for the financial support. Finally, we wish to express our gratitude to all those who submitted papers, the Steering Committee members, reviewers (to whom we are extremely grateful), as well as the discussant and attentive audience. We would like to thank everybody involved in the symposia organization that helped us in making this event successful.

Feature Selection on Credit Risk Prediction for Peer-to-Peer Lending

Shin-Fu Chen[1](✉), Goutam Chakraborty[1], and Li-Hua Li[2]

[1] Graduate School of Software and Information Science,
Iwate Prefecture University, 152-52 Sugo, Takizawa, Iwate Prefecture, Japan
albirtle93@gmail.com
[2] Department of Information Management, Chaoyang University of Technology,
Wufeng, Taichung City 41349, Taiwan

Abstract. Lending plays a key role in economy from early civilization. One of the most important issue in lending business is to measure the risk that the borrower will default or delay in loan payment. This is called credit risk. After Lehman shock in 2008–2009, big banks increased verification for lending operation to reduce risk. As borrowing from established financial institutions is getting harder, social lending also called Peer-to-Peer (P2P) lending, is becoming the popular trend. Because the client information at P2P lending is not sufficient as in traditional financial system, big data and machine learning become the default methods for analyzing credit risk. However, cost of computation and the problem of training the classifier with imbalance data affect the quality of result. This paper proposes a machine learning model with feature selection to measure credit risk of individual borrower on P2P lending. Based on our experimental results, we showed that the credit risk prediction for P2P lending can be improved using Logistic Regression in addition to proper feature selection.

Keywords: P2P lending · Credit risk ·
Minimum Redundancy Maximum Relevance (mRMR) ·
Least Absolute Shrinkage and Selection Operator (LASSO) ·
Logistic Regression

1 Introduction

Peer-to-Peer (P2P) lending platform is emerging as an alternative to banking system. P2P allows individual members to lend and borrow money directly without official financial institution such as banks, playing as intermediate. Since the Lehman shock in 2008–2009, customer trust in financial services declined rapidly. Regulators mandated increased safety measures to approve loans which resulted in banks tightening loan requirements. Financial institutions become more risk averse, causing a loan gap. The needs of risk seeking lenders and high-risk borrowers are not fully served by traditional financial institutions [1]. P2P lending platforms, where a lender has more flexibility to pick and choose a desired risk portfolio, is becoming more and more popular. The difference between traditional lending system and P2P lending platforms is shown in Fig. 1, where different risk taking lenders will find corresponding borrowers.

© Springer Nature Switzerland AG 2019
K. Kojima et al. (Eds.): JSAI-isAI 2018 Workshops, LNAI 11717, pp. 5–18, 2019.
https://doi.org/10.1007/978-3-030-31605-1_1

Traditional banks now work where risk is low. For new small or venture business, it is difficult to obtain loan. P2P lending works over the whole range of risk. In addition, low interest rate or risk based interest rate is an attractive option for P2P lending. Because of open playing ground, it is beneficial to both lender and borrower.

In general, financial institutions analyze customers' credit risk using linear discriminant analysis to build score card system. A reliable model requires a large number of customers' information for statistical analysis [2]. Recently, Machine Learning model has been applied in credit risk area, and shown to have a good accuracy at default prediction [1–3]. Data regarding risk related features, and a balance data, in which the number of timely paid borrowers are nearly the same as the number of default borrowers, would be able to properly train the classifier.

However, in practice, the training data contain only a few borrowers who are default, where most of the borrowers' payback in time. Training with such data, the classifier will be biased to predict all borrowers to be classified as good. This will give high overall accuracy with test data. High accuracy of prediction model doesn't mean the model is good. It predicts correctly of non-defaulting borrowers which predominate the data, wherein fails for cases where the borrower defaulted. This is due to imbalance of available data [4, 5]. Under such circumstances, the model often converges to an overtrained model biased to the predominant class of the available data. How to achieve accurate prediction for bad borrowers is crucial. In addition, compared with traditional banking system, P2P lending do not have sufficient information about customer's financial statistic and historical data. Moreover, the model is needed to be computationally light. How to find important features to reduce the cost of computing becomes another important issue. Fewer features improve the accuracy of classification and generalization, if selected properly.

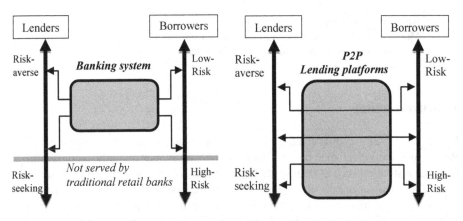

Fig. 1. The difference between traditional lending system and P2P lending platforms

In order to improve identification of credit risk on P2P lending, this research proposed machine learning model to do classification. To improve classification accuracy of both classes, we applied undersampling to deal with the problem of imbalance data. We used Minimum Redundancy Maximum Relevance (mRMR) for feature selection. This research proposed and presented comparisons of Logistic Regression (LR) and Random Forest (RF) approaches for classification. The experimental results show that LR could achieve similar performance to RF, with less computational cost.

2 Related Works

2.1 P2P Lending

The cause of Lehman shock was that the financial system took too many subprime mortgage debt, which led to the liquidity risk of the financial system [6]. Since then, the financial supervision has been strengthened. The capital adequacy requirement rules for the banking system made the bank's review of the loan stricter, to avoid predatory lending. Due to above reasons, and the development of social networking platforms, P2P Lending is popularized very rapidly [7]. It has the potential to increase economic activities and efficiency of transaction. It can replace financial institutions as a lending medium with appropriate interest rate. For example, LendingClub, one of the most popular P2P lending platform in the U.S, is enjoying a great growth at both number of loans and the total loan issuance, as shown in Fig. 2.

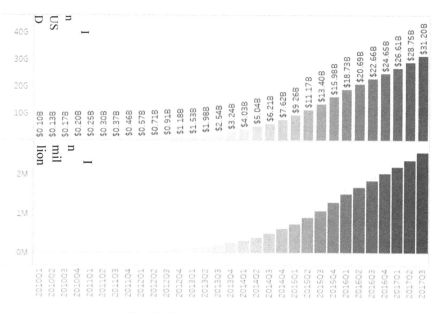

Fig. 2. The growth of LendingClub

There are some major benefits of P2P lending. Firstly, P2P lending platforms have the potential to offer lower interest rates to borrowers. Because of open market place, the interest rate would evolve to its appropriate risk value. Higher returns to investors are possible because of lower costs compared to banks through extensive use of computerization and the absence of physical store. Secondly, P2P platforms can provide a more convenient service for customers because of a transparent computerized environment for providing loan information and assessing loan risk, which can reduce the search costs of lenders. In addition, P2P lending platform can accelerate the process of lending, because there is no due diligence to borrowers. The online platform can provide faster and more convenient matchmaking mechanism [7]. However, there are a few added risk of P2P lending platform. One of the most important part is credit risk assessment quality, because platforms do not likely have the detailed information such as historical loan information of the borrower, and liabilities information. Therefore, it is not easy to assess the borrower's credibility or the amount of possible losses, making general investors less willing to bear the credit risks. This make some good borrowers with excellent plan, but with poor credit ratings, unable to get much needed fund. This study hopes to establish a better prediction model to help investors make proper risk assessments on lending, thereby increasing investor confidence in P2P platform.

2.2 Machine Learning Method

In recent years, financial institutions have begun to use machine learning in credit risk analysis. In past, researches used various machine learning models to predict the credit risk of traditional financial institutions, including Logistic Regression, Support Vector Machine (SVM), and Random Forest [2, 3, 8, 9]. However, compared to P2P lending, traditional financial institutions have more financial information about customers. They can also afford longer time for decision making. When customers apply for a loan, financial institutions can analyze the information about the customer's financial history to help them to make more appropriate decision. Relatively, P2P lending does not have financial history about borrowers, so the analysis of credit risk has been more dependent on the big data of peer borrowers.

One of the closet research to this work is by Malekipirbazari and Aksakalli [10]. They used the data set from LendingClub during the time period between 2012 and 2014, and carefully explained every feature. In their experiment, they proposed and presented comparisons of different machine learning models, and showed that the Random Forest have the best performance. To improve the classification accuracy of Random Forest model, they used a cost matrix technique that allows the model to increase costs when misclassifying bad (default) customers to good customers. However, the experiment did not use the feature selection method to retain only important features. One of the feature, namely the external credit score indicator also called FICO scores, could not be obtained in recent years' data set. Using recent data to do credit risk analysis, applying feature selection to reduce feature dimensions, and improving predictions for high-risk lending, are the focus of this research. One of the main emphasis is to remove irrelevant features. Not only they act as noise and reduce classification accuracy, they make the classifier unnecessarily complex and difficult to train with big data.

3 Methodology

Because the original data set is unbalanced, and some of the features are superfluous, we need to deal with these two problems before we train our classifier. To improve the performance of prediction, in this research we applied feature selection to select important feature in credit risk prediction. For feature selection, we tested Minimum Redundancy Maximum Relevance (mRMR) and least absolute shrinkage and selection operator (LASSO). We applied undersampling to deal with data imbalance problem. The steps of the proposed model is shown in Fig. 3.

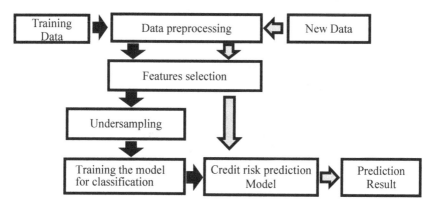

Fig. 3. Structure of the proposed model

3.1 Data Collection and Pre-processing

The original data set is collected from the LendingClub's website [11], one of the most popular P2P platform in the U.S. The period of raw data is from first quarter of 2016 to fourth quarter of 2016, contained 434,407 borrowers with 145 features. For clearing of the raw data, we follow the process: (1) feature irrelevant to the risk assessment, like location or email addresses etc., are manually deleted. (2) Features which appear for only a few numbers are deleted. By the above procedure, the number of feature were reduced to 18. Other than this, some of the borrowers have not finished their loan period yet, which is not suitable for our experiment. Therefore, we retained only the borrowers who has clear loan status, which are default, charge off, or full-pay. There are 187,192 borrowers in this dataset we could use to build our classification model. There are still some borrowers for whom does not has some important features like debt to income ratio (DTI) or revolving utilization. In this experiment, we need such information. Therefore, we omit those borrowers' data. After filtering, the data set contains 117,790 borrowers. The distribution of the loan statue was: 77% of borrowers did full-payment, 23% of borrowers were default or charge off. For this experiment, we used 80% of borrowers' data as training set to build our classification model, and used the rest 20% for model testing.

After we collected data from the website, we preprocess the data to make it suitable for the algorithm. Features are of three data types: binary, real numeric and categorized data. Binary data are used as it is, 0 or 1. Depending on the value and range, some numeric data are normalized to range 0 to 1, and for others the range in scaled down using log of the original numeric value of the feature. We did data encoding to convert categorical type variables into numeric types. For example, the feature "home ownership" has four different categories, "Rent", "Own", "Any", and "Mortgage". In this research we used binarization to generate new features, which are Home ownership (Rent), Home ownership (Own), Home ownership (Any), and Home ownership (Mortgage) to corresponding four feature descriptions. Value of these features are binary, could be 0 or 1.

3.2 Feature Selection

Feature selection is an important problem for machine learning, when there are a lot of redundant features in the dataset, it would be computationally costly to train machine learning model. The other important purpose is that feature selection can help observer to identify which features are important, out of the many possible ones. The general approach is to start with all possible features, and then remove irrelevant ones. In addition, irrelevant features act like noise and deteriorate classification results. Thus, how to reduce the number of features to minimum retaining high classification accuracy, is an important issue.

There are two main approaches, namely dimensionality reduction and feature selection. Dimensionality reduction maps the data onto a lower dimension feature space from original feature space. One of the popular method is principal component analysis (PCA). The problem with dimensionality reduction is that, features of the mapped lower dimension space do not have any physical meaning. Users will not have any idea of which real world features are important. In financial decision, it is important to retain meaningful features.

The other approach is feature selection. Feature selection method is classified into two approaches: Filter method and Wrapper method. In filter method, an individual feature is evaluated using some statistical methods like Chi squared test, information gain or correlation coefficient score. Features are selected according to their scores. In wrapper method a model is used, and a subset of feature is evaluated using the model. The model could be anything, like a regression model, K-nearest neighbor, or a neural network. Searching of optimum subset of features, could be heuristic, stochastic or forward-backward to add and remove features.

Because we want to know which feature from the original set are important, we used feature selection. We used a wrapper method with regression as model, namely absolute shrinkage and selection operator (LASSO). We also tested another statistical method namely Minimum Redundancy Maximum Relevance (mRMR).

The idea of mRMR is that in case of high-dimensional feature space, it is difficult to find which features has the largest dependency on the target class. Selecting features based on maximal relevance criterion is an option. Maximal relevance is to search features which have the approximate maximum dependency to target classes. However, maximal relevance search may select features which are redundant. When two features highly depend on each other, removing one of them would not change the class discriminative power. Therefore, minimizing redundancy could be used to select one of the mutually exclusive features [12]. The optimization criteria are as shown below:

$$\max D, D = \frac{1}{|S|} \sum_{i \in s} I(X_i, C) \tag{1}$$

$$\min R, R = \frac{1}{|S|^2} \sum_{i,j \in s} I(X_i, X_j) \tag{2}$$

$$max\ \Phi\ (D, R),\ \Phi = D - R \tag{3}$$

Where max D is the term for maximum dependency. We need to find the proper feature subset S for which the dependency on the target class C is strongest. $I(X_i, C)$ is mutual information values between individual feature X_i and class C. min R is the term for the minimum redundancy. We need to find the minimal average mutual information value between each feature in the feature subset S.

3.3 Logistic Regression Model

Our classification problem is to predict whether the borrower will default or not. We regard this as a problem of binomial classification. In this research, we used Logistic Regression (LR) as classification model. LR is one of the most widely used machine learning models for classification purposes, and the computational cost is relatively low. LR can calculate the probability that the sample belongs to 0 or 1.

LR has been used as a credit scoring model for a long time [2, 8, 9]. In LR, Sigmoid function is used for convergent. Sigmoid function is shown follows:

$$h_\theta(x) = \frac{1}{1 + e^{-x}} \tag{4}$$

Where x is the feature vector of the borrower, and θ is the set of parameter values corresponding to each feature.

The probability of this binomial classification is between 0 or 1, as calculated by function (5):

$$P(h_\theta(x) = 0, 1 | \theta_0, \cdots, \theta_N) = \frac{1}{1 + e^{-(\theta_0 + \theta_1 x1 \cdots \theta_N x_N)}} \tag{5}$$

Since logistic regression gives us a probability that the sample is closer to class 1 or 0, we must set a threshold to classify the result into 1 or 0. If the probability exceeds the threshold, we classify the sample as 1. In our experiment, we set the threshold to 0.5. The imbalance in data leads to strong inclination towards classifying to larger class of data. We use undersampling to balance the dataset. After feature selection and undersampling, we train classification model to train the credit risk prediction model.

4   Experiment and Results

The period of the data, collected from LendingClub website, is from 2016 Q1 to Q4. After data preprocessing, we have 117,790 borrowers with 18 features available for the whole dataset. Those features can be categorized into loan information, applicant information and some other information, as shown in Table 1.

In the other information part, Purpose, Home ownership and Verification status are text type features. We did binary coding to map those features to numerals, e.g., "Home ownership" – yes or no is changed to 1 or 0. After the processes, the total number of available features are 33.

Table 1. Features for the whole dataset.

Issues	Loan information	Applicant information	Other information
Features	Loan amount	Annual income	Purpose
	Term	Employment length	Public recall
	Installment	Debt to income ratio	Home ownership
	Interest rate	Total account	Verification status
		Open account	Delinquency in 2 years
		Inquire in last 6 months	Earliest credit line
		Revolving balance	
		Revolving utilization	

For feature selection we tested both mRMR and LASSO. Figure 4 is the change of feature coefficients as the value of changes, in LASSO regression. We applied cross-validation to find the best lambda, which is shown as blue dashed lines. The best lambda value after cross validation check is 0.0005467 (nature log equal to −7.51). After the selection, LASSO regression suggested to keep 27 features.

However, with LASSO regression it can only reduce 6 features from 33 to 27. As most of the feature were retained, the reduction in computational cost is not very significant. Due to that, we applied mRMR as the other feature selection method, and selected top 10 features, as shown in Table 2 below.

The ten important features selected by mRMR have 6 different type information of borrowers, they are: (1) Interest rate is the loan interest rate recommended by LC after evaluating the borrower, (2) Home ownership is the relationship between the borrower and the owner of the house in which the borrower currently resides. (3) Debt to income ratio is calculated by dividing borrower's total recurring debt by borrower's monthly income. (4) Delinquencies is the number of delinquencies for borrower in the last two years. (5) Income to payment ratio is calculate by dividing borrower's monthly income by borrower's monthly payment. (6) Inquiries in 6 months is the number of credit inquiries for borrower in the last six months.

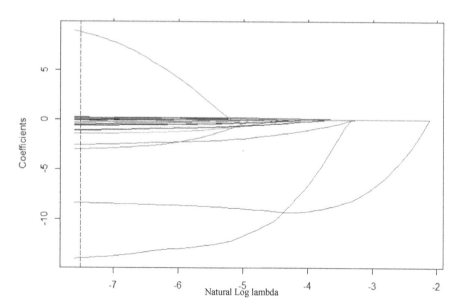

Fig. 4. The convergence changes in LASSO regression

Table 2. Selected features by mRMR

Feature	Original data type	Data manipulation
Interest rate	Numeric	Normalization-range 0 to 1
Home ownership (ANY)	Binary	None
Home ownership (RENT)	Binary	None
Loan purpose (Medical)	Binary	None
Debt to income ratio (DTI)	Numeric	Log or scale
Delinquencies	Numeric	Normalization-range 0 to 1
Loan purpose (Small business)	Binary	None
Income to payment ratio (ITP)	Numeric	Log or scale
Inquiries in last 6 months	Numeric	Normalization-range 0 to 1
Loan purpose (renewable energy)	Binary	None

Loan interest rate is the decision after the evaluation of borrower, an evaluation by LC. On the other hand, both DTI and ITP in important financial information of an applicant in the lending business, because higher is the DTI, higher is the risk that the borrower will default. This is the opposite of ITP. To observe the relationship between those important features mRMR selected, we illustrate them in Figs. 4 and 5. For the quality of data visualization, we take 0.1% of the data by random sampling from raw data, which contains data points from about 150 borrowers.

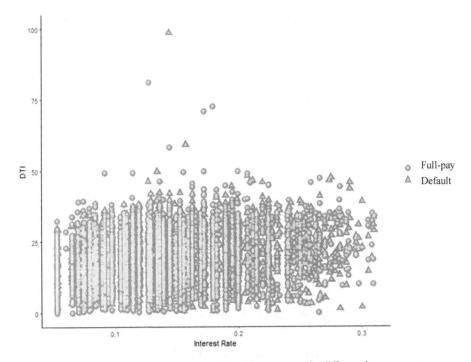

Fig. 5. Debt to income (DTI) ratio and interest rate in different loan status.

In Fig. 5, orange circles represent who fully pay back the loan. The green triangles represent default borrowers. It is clear that most of the borrowers who have both low DTI and low interest rate are full-pay borrowers. As the interest rate and DTI both getting higher, more borrowers default of their loans. This is reasonable, because higher interest represents a borrower with bad credit rating, and higher DTI also means that the borrower's debt may exceed the borrower's affordable range leading to non-payment.

In Fig. 4, it is more difficult to find the relation between ITP and loan status. Once the distribution of defaulting borrowers is closely observed, we find that, there is a high concentration of ITP lower than 0.25. This can be a reference when an investor need to be treated important goal, choose a borrower to lend money. In the financial market, both DTI and ITP can represent as credit rating. However, neither can significantly express whether the borrower will default or not. It is apparent that more information is needed for better classification of loan status at P2P lending (Fig. 6).

For classifier, we compared Logistic Regression (LR) and Random Forest (RF). In this research, we used Negative Accuracy (NA) to measure the accuracy of prediction of bad borrower, Positive Accuracy (PA) to measure the accuracy of prediction good

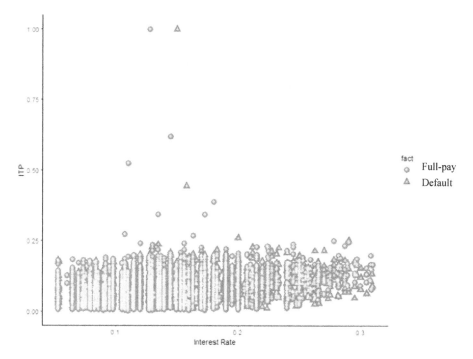

Fig. 6. Income to payment (ITP) ratio and interest rate in different loan status.

borrower, Geometric mean (GM) which is calculated by square root of PA multiplied by NA, and Total Accuracy (TA) which is the overall accuracy of the test data set. TA, PA, NA and GM are calculated by True Positive (TP), False Positive (FP), True Negative (TN), and False Negative (FN), using the following formulas.

$$TA = \frac{TP + TN}{TP + FP + TN + FN} \tag{6}$$

$$PA = \frac{TP}{TP + FP} \tag{7}$$

$$NA = \frac{TN}{FN + TN} \tag{8}$$

$$GM = \sqrt{PA * NA} \tag{9}$$

We compared results using all features and with features selected by mRMR. Experiments were done using unbalanced data and after balancing using undersampling. The results using two different classifiers, LR and RF, are shown in Table 3. Our target is to get the best GM value

Table 3. Results of comparison.

Classification model	Logistic regression				Random forest			
Experiment	NA	PA	GM	TA	NA	PA	GM	TA
No feature selection No data balance	0.160	0.957	0.391	0.751	0.153	0.956	0.382	0.748
LASSO No data balance	0.763	0.547	0.646	0.748	0.764	0.553	**0.649**	0.749
mRMR No data balance	0.154	0.957	0.384	0.749	0.104	0.973	0.313	0.748
No feature selection Balance data	0.663	0.635	0.647	0.650	0.681	0.600	0.639	0.649
mRMR Balance data	0.637	0.650	**0.649**	0.644	0.673	0.604	0.641	0.646
LASSO Balance data	0.648	0.637	0.642	0.642	0.641	0.647	0.644	0.644

It is interesting to note that without data balancing, LASSO can achieve better GM (0.649 compared to 0.3), though the model is very low at positive accuracy. This means the model is too strict, and a lot good borrowers had been classified as bad borrower. But the performance is better. So we are interested in to know which features had been filtered out as unnecessary features. They are listed below (Table 4).

Table 4. Features LASSO throw away.

No.	Features
1.	Funded amount in investment
2.	Installment
3.	Home ownership "ANY"
4.	Home ownership "OWN"
5.	Verification status "Source Verified"
6.	Purpose "credit card"

For comparison the result from different experiments, we used histogram to show the GM at from each experiment, shown in Fig. 4. LR mean Logistic Regression was used as classifier, RF means Random Forest was used classifier. The best GM outcome, 0.649, apparent twice (1) imbalance data feature selection by LASSO and classifier RF, (2) balance data with feature selection by mRMR. In additional, we can observe that GM is significantly improved after balancing the data using undersampling with or without feature selection and using mRMR for feature selection. With LASSO for feature selection, both LR and RF can reach very high GM. However, LASSO can eliminate only 6 features out of 33. With mRMR, we can reduce features from 33 to 10, leading to much more computing cost reduction for training of the classifier. On the other hand, mRMR selected only 10 featured out of 33. Even with only 10 features, high GM and TA were achieved. This means that mRMR can effectively reduce the number of features. Finally, we did not observe that Random Forest have obviously better performance than Logistic Regression, where LR is trained much faster compared to RF (Fig. 7).

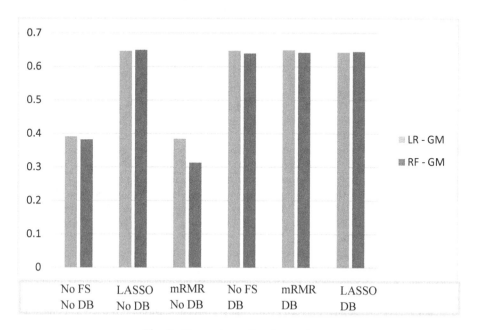

Fig. 7. Comparison of each experiment

5   Conclusion and Feature Work

In this work, we used dataset from LendingClub. The period is from 2016Q1 to 2016Q4. We applied both LASSO regression and mRMR for feature selection and compared machine learning models Random Forest and Logistic Regression, with all features and selected features.

The results show that NA and GM are poor if the data is not balanced. The training data has 33 features. LASSO selected 27 features out of 33, and achieved higher GM. We therefor conclude that those 6 feature were irrelevant for classification. mRMR on the other hand selected only 10 features out of 33, and achieved almost similar result with balanced data. When, lowering number of feature for faster training, mRMR is much effective.

For quick physical interpretation lower number of features is important. Feature selection can help investors find more meaningful indicators, to help them make right investment decisions. Also, we can observe that Logistic Regression, with much lower computational cost, can achieve similar or even better performance than Random Forest. Another important result is that, after balancing the data using undersampling, the accuracy of default borrower prediction improved significantly. However, the positive accuracy and total accuracy declined, which mean that there will be many good borrowers mistakenly judged as bad borrowers.

How to improve negative accuracy without reducing PA or total accuracy, is one of our feature works. In additional, the motivation of credit risk is not just predicting whether a customer will default or not. The total return on the loss amount is also an important parameter. We will extend our work on estimation of loss and gain on an investment.

References

1. McWaters, J., et al.: The Future of Financial Services: How Disruptive Innovations are Reshaping the Way Financial Services are Structured. Provisioned and Consumed. World Economic Forum (2015)
2. Thomas, L.C.: A survey of credit and behavioural scoring: forecasting financial risk of lending to consumers. Int. J. Forecast. 16(2), 149–172 (2000)
3. Sandberg, M.: Credit Risk Evaluation using Machine Learning (2017)
4. Birla, S., Kohli, K., Dutta, A.: Machine learning on imbalanced data in credit risk. In: 2016 IEEE 7th Annual Information Technology, Electronics and Mobile Communication Conference (IEMCON), pp. 1–6. IEEE, Vancouver (2016). https://doi.org/10.1109/iemcon.2016.7746326
5. Brown, I., Mues, C.: An experimental comparison of classification algorithms for imbalanced credit scoring data sets. Expert Syst. Appl. 39(3), 3446–3453 (2012)
6. Ashcraft, A.B., Schuermann, T.: Understanding the securitization of subprime mortgage credit. Found. Trends Finan. 2(3), 191–309 (2008)
7. Board, Financial Stability, FinTech Credit: Market Structure, Business Models and Financial Stability Implications. Financial Stability Board, Basel (2017)
8. John, C.W.: A note on the comparison of logit and discriminant models of consumer credit behavior. J. Finan. Quant. Anal. 15(3), 757–770 (1980)
9. Dong, G., Lai, K.K., Yen, J.: Credit scorecard based on logistic regression with random coefficients. Procedia Comput. Sci. 1(1), 2463–2468 (2010)
10. Malekipirbazari, M., Aksakalli, V.: Risk assessment in social lending via random forests. Expert Syst. Appl. 42(10), 4621–4631 (2015)
11. LendingClub, June 2018. https://www.lendingclub.com/info/download-data.action
12. Peng, H., Fuhui, L., Chris, D.: Feature selection based on mutual information criteria of max-dependency, max-relevance, and min-redundancy. IEEE Trans. Pattern Anal. Mach. Intell. 27(8), 1226–1238 (2005)

Capturing Corporate Attributes in a New Perspective Through Fuzzy Clustering

Yusuke Matsumoto$^{(\boxtimes)}$, Aiko Suge, and Hiroshi Takahashi

Graduate School of Business Administration, Keio University,
Hiyoshi 4-1-1, Kohoku-ku, Yokohama-shi, Kanagawa-ken, Japan
{yusukeM-aichi, aikosuge}@keio.jp,
htaka@kbs.keio.ac.jp

Abstract. Although industrial classification plays an important role in various contexts, it is rarely questioned. However, as diversification and business transformation are ongoing, it is becoming difficult to recognize company's real business. Therefore, there is not enough to allocate one type of business class to express the situation of the company, and a new type of industrial classification system is required. Through the analysis, we construct a new industrial classification system with Fuzzy C Means (FCM). This study also confirms the validity of proposed method through composite variance and absolute prediction error (APE). As the result, we present that there is a possibility that we are able to represent one company with overlapping industry, so to speak, assign one company more than two industries.

Keywords: Fuzzy C Means · Composite variance · Absolute prediction error · Industrial classification

1 Background

Industrial classification is utilized not only in practical situations but also in various research fields. For example, industrial classification is used in areas such as benchmarks for company selection criteria and financial conditions. Indicators used as criteria are set in each country. For example, in Japan, we often use the Japan Standard Industrial Classification (20 in the large classification, 99 in the meddle classification) established by the Ministry of Internal Affairs and Communications (MIC), the Nikkei classification (36 in the middle classification, 256 class in the small classification) and TOPIX Sector Indices (10 in the large classification, 33 in the meddle classification). In addition, globally, we use GICS (Global Industry Classification Standard) as international indicators established by Standard & Poor's and Morgan Stanley Capital International.

Traditionally, the existing industrial classifications constructed by various institutions give only one classification to one company, and do not permit overlapping industries. Moreover, the existing industrial classification is defined based on sales alone. However, in recent years, the business domain of companies has undergone major changes due to the increase of M&A and aggressive business transformation. Therefore, industrial identification is becoming more ambiguous than before. For example, in a diversified company, it is difficult to say that classified industrial identification accurately

© Springer Nature Switzerland AG 2019
K. Kojima et al. (Eds.): JSAI-isAI 2018 Workshops, LNAI 11717, pp. 19–33, 2019.
https://doi.org/10.1007/978-3-030-31605-1_2

reflects the enterprise when classified business is lower in sales or profits than other businesses. With these backgrounds, there is a limit to describing one company only one industry and representing the real situation of a company. Therefore, a new industrial classification is required. This paper examines whether such a new industrial classification technique can be utilized as an alternative to traditional industrial classification.

There are at least two merits to assign one company several industries. Firstly, it is easier to compare segments with other companies. How to divide the business segments shown in the securities report has been left to the discretion of each company. Therefore, when we compare the segments with other companies, we think that it is possible to compare segments among several companies on a unified scale. Secondly, there is a possibility that we can conduct empirical analysis in more detailed. Now, the existing industrial classification systems assign one type of industry to one company. However, looking at the breakdown of one company, there is a limit to using sales as the standard, as in the case of high market share even though sales are low. We think it is possible to take into account such influences and to enable more robust control of industry characteristics.

The composition of this paper is as follows: In Sect. 2, we detail the previous research. In Sect. 3, we describe data employed in this analysis. In Sect. 4, we show our method. In Sect. 5, we show our results. In Sect. 6, we select to analyze for manufacturing industry in Japan Standard Industrial Classification and show our results. Finally, we summarize this paper and describe the issues and discussion of this paper in Sect. 7. Again, the purpose of this thesis is to explore the possibility of a new industrial classification technique.

2   Related Work

There are very few research papers on industrial classification. Regarding these studies, there are mainly two areas; the reliability of the existing system and the construction of new system.

In the United States, there are several studies about the reliability of industrial classification. For example, Elton and Gruber [1] stated that there is no guarantee that existing industrial classification form homogeneous groups, and the industrial classification method constructed using statistical methods may be more accurate. Hrazdil, Trottier and Zhang [2] analyzed which index, such as Standard Industrial Classification (SIC), the North American Industry System (NAICS) or the Global Industry Classification Standard (GICS) are effective and homogeneous for the group stocks with similar operating characteristics. Weiner [3] stated that as a result of performing cluster analysis based on the company's financial information, the industrial classification constructed by himself was more accurate than the existing industrial classification. On the other hand, in Japan, there are very few studies about the reliability of industrial classification. Studies in Japan about the reliability of industrial classification have only been done by Kimura [4], Shintani [5], and Nakaoka [6].

Various methods have been proposed to address construction of a new industrial classification. For example, Sasaki and Shinno [7] and Ando and Shirai [8] have proposed a method of acquiring industry type information from web pages and classifying companies based on that information. Isogai and Dam [9] proposed methods of classifying companies based on stock price fluctuations. Peneder [10] classified the companies through the statistical cluster analysis and presented that the use of cluster analysis provided valuable tools for the industrial classification. Lee, Ma, and Wang [11] focused on "co-search" on the Internet and proposed a new method to recognize economically related peer companies.

Lewellen [12] builds an industrial classification that allows overlapping based on which companies the competitor are. There are Yang [13] and Budayan, Dikmen and Birgonul [14] as studies that classified companies using the clustering method. Yang [11] has built an industrial classification system that allowed overlapping by conducting latent class analysis for companies in Japan and Malaysia. Budayan, Dikmen and Birgonul [14] classified construction companies in Turkish by using clustering methods; K-means, self-organizing map and Fuzzy C Means. They set the number of clusters to 3 and they drew conclusions after they experimentally compare the three methods. As the result, they reported that the clustering methods such as self-organizing maps or Fuzzy C Means have a possibility to provide more valuable results.

However, in these papers, there can be pointed as three limitations. First, comparison with the existing industrial classification have not been conducted thoroughly. Second, the verification of validity of results have not been conducted thoroughly. Third, analysis using stock fluctuation depended on the heavy econometric model. Moreover, comparison with the existing industrial classification and verification of validity of results have not been conducted thoroughly. It remains to be seen whether cluster analysis that allows for overlapping can lead to more accurate results and whether reliability can be guaranteed.

The purpose of this paper is to construct a new industrial classification system that allows overlapping, and compare it with the existing industrial classification.

3   Data

We used financial data in 2016, for companies listed on the First Section of the Tokyo Stock Exchange. The number of companies analyzed is 1210. Data was obtained from Nikkei NEEDS. In this paper, we use the companies belonging to 17 industries among the large industrial classifications of the MIC. We exclude (1) companies that belong to compound service, (2) companies belonging to government except elsewhere classified, and (3) companies belonging to industries unable to classify. The reason why we exclude the three industries is that there no companies which belong to those three industries. In addition to this, we utilize the companies belonging to the manufacture industry, which is one of the 17 industries. These companies belong to the 23 industries among the middle industrial classification of the MIC. We excluded companies which belong to the manufacture of leather tanning, leather products and fur skins. The number of companies is 694.

The variables and their definitions used for performing overlapping cluster analysis and evaluating validity are in shown in Table 1 below.

Table 1. Descriptive statistics

Variable name (Variable definition)	Mean	Median	Max	Min	Number of Corp
Operating margin (Operating income ÷ Sales)	0.070	0.063	0.534	−0.376	1210
Capital adequacy ratio (Netassets ÷ total assets)	0.567	0.569	0.946	0.124	1210
Total asset turnover rats (Sales ÷ total assets)	0.904	0.848	2.705	0.264	1210
Sales growth rate (Change rate from the previous term)	0.020	0.015	0.992	−0.353	1210

We compared our new industrial classification technique by overlapping cluster analysis with the existing industrial classification. At that time, we used the Japan Standard Industry Classification (JSIC) as target industries. We obtained the data of the JSIC from Nikkei NEEDS.

4   Method

4.1   Cluster Analysis

In this paper, we adopted Fuzzy C Means (FCM) proposed by Bezdek [15] as in Eq. (1), as a way of classifying some companies. Normal cluster analyses demands that all data belongs to only one cluster. However, in FCM, by introducing a fuzzy set, it is possible to allow learning vectors to belong to two or more clusters. The centered algorithm is as follows:

$$J = \sum_{i=1}^{N} \sum_{k=1}^{K} (g_{ik})^m \| x_i - c_k \|^2 \tag{1}$$

In this paper, we set the initial value for cluster centers (K) to 17, which is larger than Budayan, Dikmen and Birgonul [14]. This number is the same as the MIC, except for three industries (financial or insurance industry, the complex service business, public service industry, and industry not classifiable). The distance ($\| x_i - c_k \|$) adopts the Euclidean distance. The degree of fuzzification (m) is 2. For the data (x_i), we selected four data; (1) operating margin which represents profitability, (2) the capital adequacy ratio which represents safety, (3) the total asset turnover which represents activity, and (4) the growth rate which represents growth. Definitions of these variables and descriptive statistics of the entire sample are shown in Table 1. As the result of the analysis, each company has a membership value (g_{ik}) for each of the 17 clusters[1]. We rearrange the clusters in descending order of membership value. We set the highest

---

[1] In this paper, FCM analysis was repeated 50 times. We used a representative one after confirming each results.

membership value as the 1st industry. So the 17th industry has the lowest membership value. We conducted standardization before analysis. (see Fig. 1).

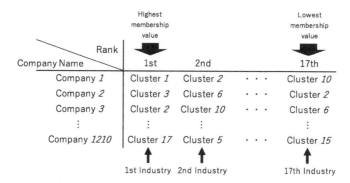

Fig. 1. Image after work

4.2 Verification Method

In Sects. 4.2 and 4.3, we propose two verification methods to confirm the validity of our proposed FCM classification. We compared the industrial classification newly created by FCM in the Sect. 4.1 with the existing industry classification. One is composite variance (Sect. 4.2), and the other is absolute prediction error (Sect. 4.3).

At first, we verified the reliability of industrial classification using the composite variance proposed in Amit and Livnat [16]. By using the composite variance, it is possible to compare the homogeneity of the group of companies.

The composite variance value (S_a) of the industry category (a) for a certain evaluation index (x) is calculated in Eq. (2).

$$S_a = \frac{\sum_{i=1}^{N_a}(n_{ai} - 1)V_{x_{ai}}}{\sum_{i=1}^{N_a}(n_{ai} - 1)} \tag{2}$$

$$\bar{X}_{ij} = \frac{1}{n_{ai}}\sum_{k=1}^{n_{ai}} X_{aik} \tag{3}$$

$$V_{x_{ai}} = \frac{1}{(n_{ai} - 1)}\sum_{k=1}^{n_{ai}} (X_{aik} - \bar{X}_{ai})^2 \tag{4}$$

Here, S_a is the composite variance value in the industry category (a), N_a is the number of business group in the industry category (a), $V_{x_{ai}}$ is the variance of the evaluation index x in the industry group i when classification of (a) is used, and n_{ai} is the number of firms in group (i) when classification (a) is used.

We calculated the ratio with the composite variance value S_b of another industrial classification (b). The dispersion ratio between S_a and S_b as shown in Eq. (5) follows the F distribution.

$$S(a, b) = \frac{S_a}{S_b} \tag{5}$$

If this ratio is statistically significantly different from 1 in the F test, we can judge that there is a difference in homogeneity in both industrial classifications. If the variance ratio is statistically significantly greater than 1, which means that the denominator S_b is statistically significantly smaller, the industry classification S_b is evaluated to be more reliable than the industry category S_a. We should remember that comparison by composite variance is not absolute but relative with respect to reliability.

In this paper, we evaluated by using the operating margin, the capital adequacy ratio, the total asset turnover, and the sales growth rate. These variables are used in FCM. We compare five of the first, second, third, fourth, and fifth industries of clusters created by FCM respectively with the JSIC. When we carried out the composite variance, we used values before standardization.

On calculating the composite variance value (S) of each evaluation index, it is greatly affected by outliers. Therefore, we calculated the composite variance value (S) by excluding outliers that are 1% above or below for each evaluation index.

4.3 Absolute Prediction Error

As the second verification method, we compared industrial classification using absolute prediction error (APE) proposed by Weiner [2]. Through the result of Sect. 4.1, we can use our industrial classification to select similar companies. We then compare the APE of these selected companies with the APE of companies selected under traditional classification. We use the APE of the enterprise value calculated using a multiple approach.

A multiple approach estimates the enterprise value of the firm by multiplying earnings with an enterprise value to EBIT multiple determined from a set of comparable companies.

The estimation for firm i's enterprise value $\widehat{EV}_i$ is given by

$$\widehat{EV}_i = median_{j \in C_i} \left(\frac{EV_j}{EBIT_j} \right) \times EBIT_i, \tag{6}$$

where C_i is the set of comparable firms based on FCM, EV_j is firm j's enterprise value, and $EBIT_j$ is the firm j's EBIT.

The valuation accuracy is calculated by the deviation between the estimated firm value and the real firm value. Therefore, we can calculate the APE_i for firm i as Eq. (7).

$$APE_i = \left| \frac{\widehat{EV}_i - EV_i}{EV_i} \right| \tag{7}$$

$\widehat{EV}_i$ is the estimated enterprise value for firm and EV_i is the observed market value for firm i. We statistically test the results by performing a Wilcoxon rank sum test on the differences between our new industrial classification system and the existing method of industrial classification. If APE_i of our industrial classification was statistically significantly smaller than that of the existing industrial classification, it would indicate that the selection of similar companies works well and is responsive to a multiple approach. This result suggests that our industrial classification shows more homogeneous.

5   Result

5.1   Analysis of Fuzzy C Means

Figure 2 displays the results of cluster analysis, plotting operating profit ratio on the horizontal axis and capital adequacy ratio on the vertical axis. Since we show the result with two axes despite analyzing with four variables, it may be difficult to understand the result. However, it turns out that cluster number 8, 13, and 14 are clearly classified.

Table 2 displays the industry to which each company belongs, with regard to using the first industry named in the FCM. We list three companies in each industry, in descending order of market capitalization in FY2016. We can observe that industry number 8 is a group of companies famous for their high capital adequacy ratio and industry number 17 is a high operating margin group. As in the above example, we specify the characteristics of some groups.

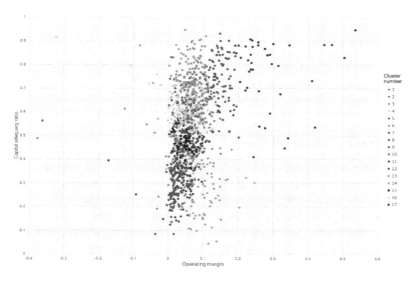

Fig. 2.   Clustering result of Fuzzy C Means

Table 2. Clustering result of Fuzzy C Means

Cluster number	Corporate name	Cluster number	Corporate name
1	Nippon Telegraph and Telephone Corp Subaru Corp Nidec Corp	10	AISIN SEIKI Co., Ltd. Sumitomo Electric Industries, Ltd. TOTO LTD.
2	DENSO Corp Eisai Co., Ltd. Uncharm Corp	11	Mitsubishi Electric Corp DAIKIN INDUSTRIES, Ltd. Kao Corp
3	Asahi Group HD NTT DATA Corp Shiseido Company	12	Dentsu Inc. Fujitsu Limited MAZDA Motor Corp
4	Daito Trust Construction Co., Ltd. NH Foods Ltd. Sundrug Co., Ltd.	13	Nintendo Co., Ltd. FUJIFILM Corp KYOCERA Corp
5	OMRON Corp Sekisui Chemical Company, Limited Hitachi High-Technologies Corp	14	Toyota Motor Corp SoftBank Corp Sony Corp
6	Mitsubishi Corp MITSUI & CO., LTD. ITOCHU Corp	15	SUZUKI MOTOR CORP YAMATO HOLDINGS CO., LTD. Nippon Express Co., Ltd.
7	Honda Motor Co., Ltd. Nissan Motor Co., Ltd. Hitachi, Ltd.	16	Canon Inc. Takeda Pharmaceutical Company Limited Bridgestone Corp
8	NTTDOCOMO, INC. KDDI CORP Shin-Etsu Chemical Co., Ltd.	17	JAPAN TOBACCO INC. KEYENCE CORP FANUC Corp
9	Marubeni Corp TOYOTA TSUSHO CORP TOYOTA BOSHOKU CORP		

(Note 1) In this paper, we treat the cluster number as industry type.
(Note 2) Three companies are listed in descending order of market capitalization in each industry.

5.2   Composite Variance Analysis

The results of comparing the reliability by the composite variance were as shown in Table 3. As a result of the analysis, all variables from the first industry S_{M1} to the third industry S_{M3} are statistically significant[2]. From Table 3, we may observe that the denominator of the classification of the newly constructed industrial classification is statistically significantly less than 1 in all four financial indicators from the first industry to the third industry. Therefore, it indicates that our new industrial classification method forms a more homogeneous group than the JSIC. However, value of the fourth industry S_{M4} and the fifth industry S_{M5} are smaller than 1 at the total asset

---

[2] $S_{M1}, S_{M2}, S_{M3}, S_{M4}$ and S_{M5} represent first industry, second industry, third industry, fourth industry and fifth industry respectively, which are newly obtained by the FCM.

turnover and the sales growth rate. It means that the composite variance at the denominator is greater than that at the numerator. In other words, homogeneity is lower than the existing industrial classification with regard to total asset turnover rate and sales growth rate.

In addition to these observations, looking at the values of the composite variance ratios in Table 3, the dispersion ratio decreases from the first industry to the fifth industry. This means that the variance of the industrial classification created by FCM, which is the denominator of the composite variance ratio, is large. Less homogeneity is observed as the number of industrial classification increases.

Table 3. The result of composite variance

First industry	$\frac{S_N}{S_{M1}}$
Operating margin	2.518***
Capital adequacy ratio	4.771***
Total asset turnover rate	2.733***
Sales growth rate	1.570***
Second industry	$\frac{S_N}{S_{M2}}$
Operating margin	1.351***
Capital adequacy ratio	3.074***
Total asset turnover rate	1.927***
Sales growth rate	1.220***
Third industry	$\frac{S_N}{S_{M3}}$
Operating margin	1.181***
Capital adequacy ratio	2.388***
Total asset turnover rate	1.303***
Sales growth rate	1.090*
Fourth industry	$\frac{S_N}{S_{M4}}$
Operating margin	1.110**
Capital adequacy ratio	2.132***
Total asset turnover rate	0.911
Sales growth rate	0.857
Fifth industry	$\frac{S_N}{S_{M5}}$
Operating margin	1.095**
Capital adequacy ratio	1.570***
Total asset turnover rate	0.911
Sales growth rate	0.857

(Note 1) The value indicates the composite variance value. The numerator S_N indicates the JSIC. Additionally, the denominator $S_{M1}, S_{M2}, S_{M3}, S_{M4}$ and S_{M5} represent the first industry, second industry, third industry, fourth industry and fifth industry respectively, which are newly constructed by the FCM.
(Note 2) Statistical significance is denoted with ***, ** and * for 1%, 5% and 10% rejection levels.

5.3   Absolute Prediction Error Analysis

We performed Wilcoxon rank sum test. Table 4 displays the result of APE. The number in the APE row shows the APE by the newly constructed industrial classification system and the APE by the JSIC. The number in the difference row means the difference between APE in each industrial classification system. A negative value indicates that our new industrial classification system has higher accuracy of corporate valuation than the JSIC. From the results, we found that the difference between the APE of our new industrial classification system and the APE of the JSIC was statistically significantly negative at the 10% level for the first industry and second industry. The APE of the first industry and second industry is smaller than that of the JSIC. Therefore, we perceived that the first industry and the second industry which we newly constructed by FCM has higher homogeneousness than industries based on the JSIC. However, it is not statistically significant after the third industry. From Table 4, we see that the *APE* of the newly constructed industrial classification increases as the number of classifications increases. In other words, this shows that homogeneity is lost as we proceed down the industry ranking.

Table 4. Result of absolute prediction error

First industry	M1	N
APE	0.279	0.311
Difference		−0.032*
Second industry	M2	N
APE	0.295	0.311
Difference		−0.016*
Third industry	M3	N
APE	0.306	0.311
Difference		−0.005
Fourth industry	M4	N
APE	0.308	0.311
Difference		−0.003
Fifth industry	M5	N
APE	0.326	0.311
Difference		0.015

(Note 1) The value in the row of *APE* are the median of the absolute prediction error of the first industry, the second industry, third industry, fourth industry and fifth industry of the newly constructed industrial classification and the median of the absolute prediction error of the JSIC.

(Note 2) Statistical significance is denoted with ***, ** and * for 1%, 5% and 10% rejection levels.

6   Manufacturing Industry

In Sect. 5, we constructed our new industrial classification and verified its validity for all industries. Next, in this chapter, we focused on the manufacturing industry in large classification of the JSIC, classified them through our FCM method, and compared the result with the existing industrial classification. In FCM, we set 23 to the number of clusters, since this number is the same number of manufacturing industry. The other settings for the parameters are the same as in Sect. 4.1. We also apply the same verification methods; composite variance method (Sect. 4.2) and absolute prediction error (Sect. 4.3).

6.1   Absolute Prediction Error Analysis

Table 5 shows the result of composite variance for manufacturing industry. From Table 5, we found that the denominator of the classification of the newly constructed industrial classification system is significantly less than 1 in all four financial indicators from the first industry to the third industry constructed by FCM. Therefore, it suggests us that the newly constructed industrial classification system provides more homogeneous groupings of firms than the existing industrial classification. However, according to sales growth rate of the fourth industry, total asset turnover rate and sales growth rate of the fifth industry, the value of them are less statistically significantly larger than 1. It means that the composite variance at the denominator is equal to the numerator. As a result, our newly constructed method is comparable to those existing classification methods.

Table 5. The result of composite variance

First industry	$\frac{S_N}{S_{MM1}}$
Operating margin	3.476***
Capital adequacy ratio	6.111***
Total asset turnover rate	3.404***
Sales growth rate	1.917***
Second industry	$\frac{S_N}{S_{MM2}}$
Operating margin	1.934***
Capital adequacy ratio	3.966***
Total asset turnover rate	1.987***
Sales growth rate	1.215***
Third industry	$\frac{S_N}{S_{MM3}}$
Operating margin	2.029***
Capital adequacy ratio	3.045***
Total asset turnover rate	1.649***
Sales growth rate	1.115*

(*continued*)

Table 5. (*continued*)

Fourth industry	$\frac{S_N}{S_{MM4}}$
Fourth industry	$\frac{S_N}{S_{MM4}}$
Operating margin	1.257***
Capital adequacy ratio	2.732***
Total asset turnover rate	1.374***
Sales growth rate	1.091
Fifth industry	$\frac{S_N}{S_{MM5}}$
Operating margin	1.191**
Capital adequacy ratio	2.112***
Total asset turnover rate	1.034
Sales growth rate	1.038

(Note 1) The value indicates the composite variance value. The numerator S_N indicates the JSIC. Additionally, the denominator $S_{MM1}, S_{MM2}, S_{MM3}, S_{MM4}$ and S_{MM5} represent the first industry, second industry, third industry, fourth industry and fifth industry respectively, which are newly constructed for manufacturing industry by the FCM.

(Note 2) Statistical significance is denoted with ***, ** and * for 1%, 5% and 10% rejection levels.

6.2 Absolute Prediction Error Analysis

We performed Wilcoxon rank sum test. Table 6 shows the result of APE for manufacturing industry. The number in the APE row shows the APE by the newly constructed industrial classification system and the APE by the JSIC. The number in the difference row means the difference between APE in each industrial classification systems. A negative value indicates that our new industrial classification system has higher accuracy of corporate valuation than the JSIC. From the result, we found that the difference between *MM1* and *N* is statistically significantly negative in the first industry. The APE of the first industry is smaller than that of the JSIC. Therefore, we perceived that our newly industrial classification system is gathering similar companies than JSIC's companies in the first industry. However, from the result of second industry to that of fifth industry, our classification system is statistically significantly positive. We confirmed that the JSIC has higher similarity than our classification system from the second to fifth industries.

Compared to the result of Sect. 5.3, the number of industries constructed by FCM, which are more homogeneous than the JSIC, has decreased from 2 to 1. However, looking at the value of APE in the first industry our newly constructed, the APE of this result is smaller than the APE of Sect. 5.3. This result suggests us that the exacter we classify the companies, the smaller the error between the actual enterprise value and the enterprise value based on multiple approach would be.

Table 6. Result of Absolute Prediction Error for manufacturing industry

First industry	MM1	N
APE	0.257	0.281
Difference		−0.024***
Second industry	MM2	N
APE	0.296	0.281
Difference		0.016***
Third industry	MM3	N
APE	0.291	0.281
Difference		0.010***
Fourth industry	MM4	N
APE	0.312	0.281
Difference		0.032***
Fifth industry	MM5	N
APE	0.306	0.281
Difference		0.025***

(Note 1) The value in the row of *APE* are the median of the absolute prediction error of the first industry, the second industry, third industry, fourth industry and fifth industry of the newly constructed industrial classification for manufacturing industry and the median of the absolute prediction error of the JSIC.
(Note 2) Statistical significance is denoted with ***, ** and * for 1%, 5% and 10% rejection levels.

7   Conclusion and Further Discussion

In this paper, we analyzed whether it is possible to construct a new industrial classification system by using FCM. The result of composite variance and APE for all industries in the .JSIC indicated that FCM is effective in making homogeneous industrial clusters. The result of analysis for the manufacturing industry in the JSIC shows us that there is a possibility of classifying companies more homogeneously by dividing them exactly. FCM is effective in constructing the new industrial classification system. Moreover, Nikkei NEEDS shows up to three industries for each company. Our three industries made by FCM are consistent with Nikkei NEEDS through composite variance analysis. As a conclusion, FCM is one of the tools to assign multiple industry to one company. Through the industrial classification with our new proposed FCM methods, it may be possible to express the company's situation and it may be useful for us to correctly perceived company's reality.

Finally, we would like to point out three limitations in this paper. Firstly, it is necessary to conduct further analysis that might enable our FCM to be more effective in wide range of clusters. Since this paper followed the methods used in previous research, the validation method is not necessarily suitable for FCM. Secondly, with regard to the cluster analysis, it is not always possible to obtain the same result each time when classifying using FCM. Therefore, it is necessary to verify the robustness of classification result by repeating it multiple times. Finally, in this paper, we classified all companies into 17 groups based on financial data. However, it is difficult to find financial features individually for each cluster, based only on the four types of financial indicators. We plan to apply other indicators to construct our classification method for a deeper understanding of economic features of each cluster.

Acknowledgements. This research was supported by a grant-in-aid from the Kayamori Foundation of Informational Science Advancement.

References

1. Elton, E.J., Gruber, M.J.: Homogeneous groups and the testing of economic hypotheses. J. Financ. Quant. Anal. **4**(5), 581–602 (1970)
2. Hrazdil, K., Trottier, K., Zhang, R.: An intra-and inter-industry evaluation of three classification schemes common in capital market research. Appl. Econ. **46**(17), 2021–2033 (2014)
3. Weiner, C.: The impact of industry classification schemes on financial research. SFB 649 discussion paper, No. 2005,062, SFB 649, Economic Risk, Berlin (2005)
4. Kimura, F.: A comparison of reliability of industrial classification in Japan. Contemp. Discl. Res. **9**, 3–42 (2009)
5. Shintani, O.: Sector classification systems: comparison of reliability between the TSE 33 (stock price index by industry <33 sectors>) and Global Industry Classification Standard (GICS) taxonomies. Secur. Anal. J. **48**(4), 77–88 (2010)
6. Nakaoka, T.: Statistical analysis on industrial classification: a comprehensive survey and a suggestion for new methods of composing homogeneous groups. J. Bus. Econ. Shokeigakuso **61**(1), 151–180 (2014)
7. Sasaki, M., Shinno H.: Industrial classification from corporate website by using document classification method. In: The Association for Natural Language Processing 12th Annual Convention Proceedings, pp. 352–355 (2006)
8. Ando, K., Shirai, K.: Extracting and classification of industry information from the corporate web pages. In: The Association for Natural Language Processing 24th Annual Convention Proceedings, pp. 1015–1018 (2018)
9. Isogai, T., Dam, H.: Building classification trees on Japanese stock groups partitioned by network clustering. IEEJ Trans. Electron. Inf. Syst. **137**(10), 1387–1392 (2017)
10. Peneder, M.: Creating industry classifications by statistical cluster analysis. Estudios de economía aplicada **23**(2), 451–464 (2005)
11. Lee, C.M., Ma, P., Wang, C.C.: Search-based peer firms: aggregating investor perceptions through internet co-searches. J. Financ. Econ. **116**(2), 410–431 (2015)
12. Lewellen S.: Firm-specific industries. Working paper (2012)
13. Sook, L.Y.: A latent class cluster analysis study of financial ratios and industry characteristics. Aust. J. Basic Appl. Sci. **7**(11), 46–53 (2013)

14. Budayan, C., Dikmen, I., Birgonul, M.T.: Comparing the performance of traditional cluster analysis, self-organizing maps and fuzzy C-means method for strategic grouping. Expert Syst. Appl. **36**(9), 11772–11781 (2009)
15. Bezdek, C., Robert, E., William, F.: FCM: the fuzzy c-means clustering algorithm. Comput. Geosci. **10**(2–3), 91–203 (1984)
16. Amit, P., Livnat, J.: Grouping of conglomerates by their segments' economic attributes: towards a more meaningful ratio analysis. J. Bus. Finance Account. **17**, 85–99 (1990)

Influences of Diversity on Organizational Performance. ~By Using Faultline Theory~

Fumiko Kumada[✉] and Setsuya Kurahashi

University of Tsukuba, 3-29-1 Otsuka Bunkyo-ku, Tokyo, Japan
s1845005@s.tsukuba.ac.jp

Abstract. The diversification of employment and work styles in organizations is inevitable to ensure a stable workforce in Japan, where a labor force is shrinking due to a declining birthrate and an aging population. Using the concept of "faultlines", which are hypothetical dividing lines that may split a group into subgroups of people based on their multiple attributes and assess diversity quantitatively, this paper examines the relationship of influences of a structure of diversity (the faultline strength and the number of subgroups) and a method of communication within an organization. It is verified by an agent-based model based on a survey of Japanese organizations. In addition, this paper demonstrates the methods of communication to enable diversification to generate a positive impact on a performance of an organization. As a result, this paper clarified that appropriate communication is related to a goal and the structure of diversity of an organization. Therefore, it is necessary for a manager to grasp a structure of diversity of an organization and to design a method of interaction along with a goal in an organization.

Keywords: Diversity · Faultline · Agent-based model

1 Introduction

It is important to ensure a stable workforce in Japan where a labor force is shrinking due to a declining birthrate and an aging population. Therefore, the acceptance of foreign workers and work style reforms are in progress. In addition, technological advancement including artificial intelligence and the Internet of Things also diversifies workers and work styles.

In the study field of diversity management, it is said that diversity can affect an organizational performance in both a positive and negative manner. Therefore, it is important to clarify the factors that diversity positively affects in Japan where it advances.

Focusing on the concept of faultlines that capture diversity quantitatively, the main objective of this paper is to clarify one of the solutions concerning how to manage a diversified organization in order to enhance the organizational performance.

© Springer Nature Switzerland AG 2019
K. Kojima et al. (Eds.): JSAI-isAI 2018 Workshops, LNAI 11717, pp. 34–49, 2019.
https://doi.org/10.1007/978-3-030-31605-1_3

2   Previous Studies

2.1   The Field of Diversity Management

Williams and O'Reilly [8] proposed the integrated model on how diversity could affect organizational performance, explaining that diversity could have both positive and negative effects; therefore, organizational diversity is referred to as a "double-edged sword."

The negative theory

- Social Categorization Theory: People categorize themselves and others with regard to demographic attributes such as age, gender, and so on. They may have conflict in their communication and relationships.
- Similarity-attraction Theory: Individuals that are highly similar feel attractiveness each other and strengthen their solidarity, while causing conflict with those who are less similar.

The positive theory

- Information and Decision-making Theory: Diversity increases knowledge and information types, providing an organization with positive effects.

The integrated model explains that the one of points that divide positive or negative influences is whether or not communicate is smooth.

2.2   Faultline Theory

Lau and Murnighan [2] proposed the concept of faultlines which are hypothetical dividing lines that split a group into subgroups based on one or more individual attributes in order to explain the causality between diversity based on attributes of organizational members and conflict within an organization. Many previous studies on faultlines have reported that faultlines increase conflict. An exceptional study was claimed that common identities (e.g., goals) or mediators could reduce conflict. As for studies focusing on subgroups, Polzer et al. [4] reported that an uneven group size could achieve high performance, and Carton and Cummings [10] conducted a field survey reporting that three or more subgroups could achieve high performance.

2.3   Conflict

A conflict has possibility that makes not only negative influence but also positive influence. Robbins [5] has shown that conflict has resulted in positive influence in the cases where it contributes to the quality of decision-making or increases the creativity of the staff. In addition, a common feature in organizations that successfully create functional conflict is that they reward dissent and punish conflict avoid.

2.4   Review of Previous Studies

Only a limited number of previous studies have been made of the faultline theory focusing on organizations in Japan. This paper carries out a survey of Japanese organizations about attributes and communication and quantifies diversity by using the faultline theory. An agent-based model (ABM) is used to examine the relationship of the diversity and communication. Many previous studies regarding the faultline theory have focused on the disfunctional conflict that negatively affects an organization. In this study, however, we employed the functional conflict leveraged by diversity into our simulation in addition to the disfunctional conflict. Through this simulation, we verified diversity from both faces, positive and negative effects.

We decided to utilize ABM because it is appropriate for verifying influence which is generated by people's actions toward the entire organization. Takahashi et al. [9] reported the relationship between diversity and organization performance using NK model and ABM. This previous research showed that an organization needed to have a certain amount of diverse members to improve the whole organizational utility under the changing environment. It also clarified the necessity of organizational diversity from the external social environment. On the other hand, this paper employs a new approach from an internal change in an organization using Faultline Theory which can show a structure of diversity.

2.5   The Faultline Measures

The previous studies proposed more than ten faultline measurement methods. Suzuki, Matsumoto, and Kitai [7] said that the rating scale for cluster analysis proposed by Meyer and Glenz [3], Average of Silhouette Width (ASW), has various advantages. For example, this rating scale can handle continuous variables as well as categorical variables and can divide target organizations into proper subgroups.

ASW is a rating scale for evaluating the cluster analysis results, which was proposed by Rousseeuw [6]. The following items are defined in Fig. 1:

– $a(i)$: average dissimilarity of i to all other objects of A.
– $d(i, C)$: average dissimilarity of i to all other objects of C.

Where the smallest value of $d(i, C)$ for all the clusters other than A is calculated as b (i) according to the above definitions, cluster B becomes adjacent to A. Equation (1) expresses the adequacy of sample i to belong to cluster A.

$$s(i) = \frac{b(i) - a(i)}{max\{a(i), b(i)\}} \tag{1}$$

Meyer and Glenz [3] defined this overall mean edge width, $\bar{s}$, as the faultline value. Where the mean edge width is $\bar{s}(k)$ when there are k clusters, k that maximums $\bar{s}(k)$ is selected. The clusters here become subgroups, while k is the number of subgroups.

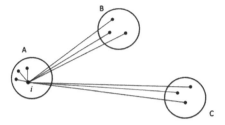

Fig. 1. Relationships of elements involved in the computation of $s(i)$, where the object i belongs to cluster A [6].

3   Model Outline

This model uses agents to resemble organizational members in order to update evaluation values based on the synergy influence generated by interactions of agents. While comparing the evaluation values for the entire organization (sum of evaluations of all agents) before and after agent interactions, this model verifies increases and decreases of this evaluation value.

3.1   Agent Attributes

Each agent has an array, consisting of 0 and 1, with six genes set. This gene array is regarded as the decision-making attitude attribute. Interactions between agents affect each agent's decision-making attitude attribute, updating the evaluation value. The decision-making attributes apply the multi-attribute attitude model in the consumer behavior theory. The multi-attribute attitude model is the concept that when the consumer evaluates the product, not only one attribute but a plurality of attributes becomes the focus and the total of the evaluations to each attribute is a comprehensive evaluation of the product. By replacing products with organizational issues on this concept, the characteristics of the approach to issues are represented by multiple attributes and the sum of the evaluation values of attributes is regarded as the comprehensive evaluation for solving the problem.

In addition, the initial array of six-gene arrays set for each agent is calculated by ASW in order to determine the faultline strength of organizations and the subgroup to which each agent belongs. Here it is assumed that the initial decision-making attitude attribute would be dependent on superficial attributes such as age and gender since the decision-making attitude attribute is free from external influence.

Initial six-gene arrays as the decision-making attitude attributes $\approx$

Demographic attributes.

A subgroup that is set based on the initial six-gene arrays can be regarded as an internal group in Social Categorization Theory which is the basis of the faultline theory. While the subgroups to which the agents belong never change during the simulation period, interactions of agents affect six-gene arrays, and the decision-making attitude attributes change. As a result, the model verifies which interaction is able to enhance the evaluation value of the entire organization.

3.2   The Utility Function

The NK model is used as the evaluation function for the decision-making attitude attributes (six-gene arrays) held by each agent. The NK model is a genetic algorithm that indicates the process by which a living organism evolves, which is utilized in various fields including technological advancement and organizational learning.

The evaluation value of the NK model is called the "fitness." The NK model is based on N genes, having 0 or 1 for their values, that are related to K genes. Figure 2 shows a specific example of N = 6, K = 2, where the evaluation value is expressed as Eq. (2).

$$W = \frac{1}{N}\sum\nolimits_{i=1}^{N} w_i \tag{2}$$

※ w_i: Fitness in the fitness function of each loci.

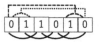

Fig. 2.   Structure of NK landscape (N = 6, K = 2)

Figure 2 shows the case of K = 2. Therefore, one evaluation value is calculated with a succession of the agent's genes and the other two genes. These are six sets of the following genes from the left: (001), (011), (110), (101), (010), and (100) (four sets in the bold line and two sets in the dashed line). The following shows the calculation result of applying the example of adequacy arrays in Table 1 based on these six sets.

{001(0.592) + 011(0.589) + 110(0.842) + 101(0.233) + 010(0.653) + 100 (0.793)}/6 = 0.617.

Table 1.   Example of fitness function (Cited from [1])

The genes	000	001	010	011	100	101	110	111
Fitness	0.141	0.592	0.653	0.589	0.793	0.233	0.842	0.916

3.3   Simulation Setting

One organization consists of 18 agents. The default six-gene array for each agent is calculated based on ASW in order to determine the faultline strength, the number of subgroups and the subgroup to which each agent belongs. Then we conducted the simulation in order to clarify whom each agent interacts with to enhance the evaluation for the entire organization. We set the following three methods by the conflict type. One simulation consists of 100 interactions, while the simulation is conducted 100 times according to each setting. Table 2 lists the simulation settings.

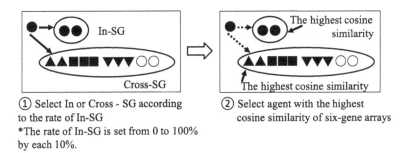

① Select In or Cross - SG according
to the rate of In-SG
*The rate of In-SG is set from 0 to 100%
by each 10%.

② Select agent with the highest
cosine similarity of six-gene arrays

Fig. 3. Similarity interaction

– Similarity interaction

The similarity interaction that reproduces Social Categorization Theory or Similarity–attraction Theory sets the percentage of agent interactions within the same subgroup (In-SG) and agent interactions in different subgroups (Cross-SG). In-SG is similar to the communication in an internal group with similar people, therefore, the percentage of In-SG is defined as the conflict size.

Figure 3 shows that the first step for determining whom to interact with is to narrow down agents to interact with according to the percentage of In-SG and Cross-SG. The second step is to select the agent with the highest cosine similarity of the six-gene arrays. In real society, this represents communication between similar people where diversity works negatively. In this state, the disfunctional conflict occurs.

– Diversity interaction

This interaction is based on Information and Decision-making theory. Here, agents with a lower cosign similarity of the six-gene arrays are selected. The counterparties to these agents are randomly selected according to the tournament size, regardless of whether they are in the same or a different subgroup, interacting with those with low similarity. In real society, this is the interaction between people with different attributes and increases the quality and the quantity of knowledge or information in an organization, while diversity works positively. In this state, the functional conflict occurs.

The tournament size indicates the number of agents that are randomly selected. Where the tournament size is four, four agents are randomly selected and interact with agents having low similarity. As the tournament size increases, the selection pressure becomes higher. This makes it easier to select agents with low similarity. Based on this feature, the tournament size is regarded as functional conflict size. When the tournament size becomes greater, the functional conflict also becomes larger while bringing about a positive influence on the organization. This simulation adopts three sizes, 2 for the minimum selection pressure, 17 for the maximum selection pressure, and 9 for the medium selection pressure (Fig. 4).

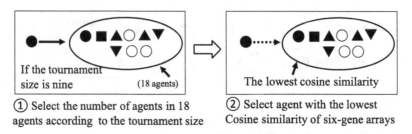

① Select the number of agents in 18   ② Select agent with the lowest
agents according to the tournament size   Cosine similarity of six-gene arrays

Fig. 4. Diversity interaction

– Random interaction

In this interaction, 18 randomly select whom to interact regardless of whether they
are in the same or a different subgroup. Here the agents interact with everybody freely
and equally; there is no conflict. This state is assumed as the organization's potential
capacity. Table 2 lists the simulation settings.

Table 2. Simulation settings

The number of agents		18
The NK model	The length of N	6
	The number of K	1
How to exchange		Single point crossover
The fitness function		(0, 1) uniform random number
The number of interactions per simulation		100
The number of simulations per setting		100

4 Simulation

4.1 Data Sets for Validation

In order to validate the model, we created six sets of validation data based on the
faultline strength and the number of subgroups (Fig. 5). We used these to conduct
simulations.

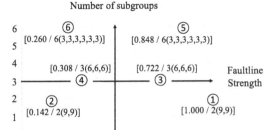

Fig. 5. Set data for the validation

4.2 Evaluation Standard

The difference in fitness of the entire organization before and after 100 interactions served as the evaluation value. Besides two evaluation standards are setting. First, it is the maximum value of 100 simulations (except outliers) as Maximum possibility. Next, it is essential for an organization to achieve stable results for every issue. For this reason, the standard deviation from 100 simulations is set as the second standard. When the standard deviation is higher, there is a lower possibility to get the maximum value. The standard deviation means Occurrence probability (Fig. 6).

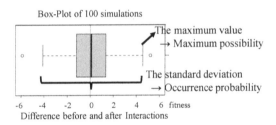

Fig. 6. Evaluation standard

Through these simulations, this paper observed how Maximum possibility and Occurrence probability change through the structure of diversity, such as the faultline strength and the number of subgroups, and interaction methods. By doing so, this paper validated the relationship between organizational diversity and performance.

Note that the values, out of those 1.5 times the interquartile range (difference between the third quartile and the first quartile) of the 100-simulation results, are considered to be outliers.

4.3 The Results of the Simulation for the Verification

Table 3 shows the correlation coefficient between the setting data, which are the faultline strength, the number of subgroups, the rate of In-SG and the tournament size,

Table 3. Correlation coefficient per the methods of interaction.

| | Correlation coefficient | | | | | | | |
| | Similarity | | | Diversity | | | Random | |
	FL	SG	Rate	FL	SG	Size	FL	SG
The maximum value	0.671***	−0.319**	−0.260*	0.449	−0.005	−0.183	0.762	0.010
The standard deviation	0.675***	−0.344**	−0.255*	0.512*	−0.262	−0.488*	0.727	−0.166

*p < .05, **p < .01, ***p < .001
※FL: Faultline Strength ※SG: Number of Subgroups ※Rate: Rate of In-SG
※Size: Tournament size.

and the evaluation standard, which are the maximum value and the standard deviation from 100 simulations.

– Similarity interaction

In this interaction method where the disfunctional conflict occurred, the faultline strength and the maximum value, as well as the standard deviation, were in a positive correlation. This result confirmed that as the faultline strength become stronger, Maximum possibility becomes higher, but Occurrence probability is decreased. The number of subgroups and the rate of In-SG worked inversely from how the faultline strength worked. Therefore, the regression analysis on the maximum value and the standard deviation as objective variables were conducted (Eqs. (3) and (4)).

Max: The maximum value
SD: The standard deviation
S: The faultline strength
N: The number of subgroups
R: The rate of In-SG

$$\text{Max} = 1.79 + 2.8S - 0.25N - 1.19R \tag{3}$$

*Coefficient of determination = 0.594, p = 8.653e-13

$$\text{SD} = 0.73 + 1.07S - 0.10N - 0.41R \tag{4}$$

*Coefficient of determination = 0.618, p = 1.348e-13

To improve Maximum possibility, the rate of In-SG is low in an organization where the faultline strength is strong and the number of subgroups is small. However, in this case, Occurrence probability is also low. In general, if the number of subgroups decreases, the rate of In-SG tends to be high. Considering this point with reference to Fig. 7, Maximum possibility is the highest in the fourth quadrant and decreases counterclockwise; conversely, Occurrence probability is the lowest in the third quadrant and increases clockwise.

– Diversity interaction

In the diversity interaction that reproduces the functional conflict, the standard deviation has a positive correlation with the faultline strength and a negative correlation with the tournament size. These results confirmed that Occurrence probability is lowered by the faultline strength and increased by the tournament size. Regression analysis was performed using the standard deviations as objective variables (see Eq. (5)). The faultline strength should be weaker and the tournament size should be larger to improve Occurrence probability:

TS: The tournament size

$$SD = 1.42 + 0.29S - 0.01TS \tag{5}$$

*Coefficient of determination = 0.433, $p = 0.006$

– The random interaction

In the random interaction that expresses an organization's potential capacity, the evaluation standards in Table 3, the maximum value and the standard deviation, could not confirm the influence of the faultline strength and the number of subgroups. This result shows that without conflict, the structure of diversity does not affect organizational performance.

Based on the above results, Fig. 7 shows the relationship between the evaluation standard (the maximum value and the standard deviation) and the structure of diversity (the faultline strength and the number of subgroups).

The simulation showed that the faultline strength and the number of subgroups, i.e., the structure of diversity, influence the results of each interaction. Furthermore, the influences are changeable according to the structure of diversity. It is especially true in the case of the similarity interaction, where the effectiveness of the diversity depends on the maximum value and the standard deviation. Therefore, to achieve organizational goals, it is important to understand the structure of the diversity and, moreover, how to manage their interaction.

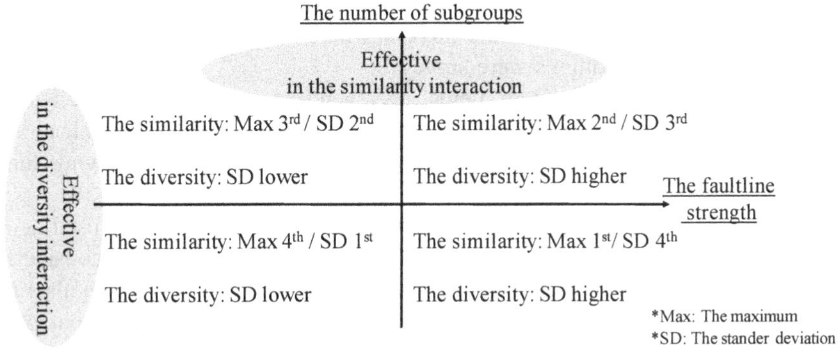

Fig. 7. Relationship between the structure of diversity and the features of each interaction

4.4   Model Validation

As for the maximum value and the standard deviation of the similarity interaction that reproduces the faultline theory, the correlation coefficients in Table 3 confirmed that an increase in the rate of In-SG (as the disfunctional conflict becomes stronger) decreases the maximum value. Additionally, Table 4 shows the result of the regression coefficient in order to see the influence of the rate of In-SG (influence of the disfunctional conflict) by the faultline strength. When the faultline strength is stronger, the absolute value of the regression coefficient becomes greater. The faultline strength makes the influence of disfunctional conflict. Therefore, this model demonstrates the phenomenon that conflicts arising from the faultline have a negative influence on an organization. This evidence validates the model.

Table 4. Regression coefficient of the rate of the In-SG

The set number	The faultline strength	The number of subgroups	The maximum value	Standard deviation
①	1.000	2	−3.495*	−0.987*
②	0.142	2	−0.545.	−0.200.
③	0.723	3	−1.079	−0.404
④	0.300	3	−0.553	−0.258
⑤	0.848	6	−0.874	−0.399*
⑥	0.260	6	−0.578	−0.215

.p < 0.1, *p < 0.05, **p < .001, ***p < 0.001

5   Fact-Finding Survey

The next simulation is based on the results of a fact-finding survey conducted targeting organizations based in Japan.

5.1   Survey Overview

Survey subjects were five companies and 14 groups in Japan (three groups of one major company, one group of one midsize company, ten groups of three joint ventures, where 126 participants responded to the survey), where the employee attributes and in-group communication conditions were surveyed.

Attribute data consisted of four items, age, gender, service years, and type of employment. Survey items consisted of two items, the frequency of communication in business with each staff members (five-stage), and the frequency of having lunch together (five-stage).

In the United States, age, gender, race, and occupation are frequently used as the attributes to calculate the faultline strength. However, in this study, while considering Japan-specific employment practices, employment status (regular or non-regular) and service years were added to the survey items in order to distinguish employees that joined the company as a new graduate and employees that joined the company by job transfer. In contrast, race and occupation were removed from the items. The reason is why many

Japanese companies hire new university graduates and cultivate them to serve as corporate generalists, so that there is less awareness in job types. By using attribute data, the structure of diversity was calculated - the faultline strength of the entire group, the number of subgroups, and the subgroups to which each staff member belongs - based on ASW. Then the percentage of communication among staff members that belong to the same subgroup was calculated, in both a business situation and at lunch.

5.2   Survey Results

The survey results in Table 5 show the structure of diversity and communication conditions. Figure 8 plots the faultline strength and the number of subgroups of the 14 groups. The results of the regression analysis on the faultline strength, the number of subgroups and the rate of In-SG is calculated below:

$$N = 0.687 + 5.721 \times S \tag{6}$$

*Coefficient of determination $= 0.522$, $p < 0.005$

$$R = 0.785 + (-0.114) \times N \tag{7}$$

*Coefficient of determination $= 0.847$, $p < 0.001$
The survey results brought about four features of the subject organizations.

- Half of the subject organizations had less diversity with a homogeneous structure because they are in the 3rd quadrant (i.e., the faultline strength is weak and the number of subgroups is low.).
- Equations (6) and (7) show tendencies where stronger faultlines increase the number of subgroups, whereas an increase in the number of subgroups decreases the rate of In-SG.
- Some major companies belonged to the 2nd quadrant with a structure where the similarity interaction and the diverse interaction were effective.
- On the other hand, organizations that belong to the 4th quadrant where the similarity interaction and the diverse interaction had little effect did not exist.

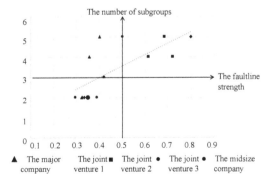

Fig. 8. Structure of diversity in 14 analyzed groups.

Table 5. Results for diversity and communication by groups.

Group		The number of staff	The faultlines strength	The number of subgroups	The number of staff per a subgroup	The percentage of agent interactions within the same subgroup	
						For business	For lunch
The major company	①	8	0.404	5	2,2,2,1,1	21%	25%
	②	7	0.357	4	3,2,1,1	28%	36%
	③	10	0.324	2	7,3	58%	71%
The Joint venture1	①	6	0.328	2	3,3	50%	43%
	②	7	0.422	3	3,2,2	35%	32%
	③	9	0.800	5	2,2,2,2,1	21%	40%
	④	6	0.336	2	3,3	49%	0%
The Joint venture2	①	10	0.686	5	3,2,2,2,1	23%	22%
	②	10	0.615	4	4,3,2,1	30%	30%
	③	19	0.722	4	11,5,2,1	42%	42%
The Joint venture3	①	4	0.297	2	1,3	61%	65%
	②	5	0.390	2	1,4	70%	71%
	③	15	0.502	5	4,3,3,3,2	21%	23%
The midsize company	①	10	0.351	2	5,5	50%	51%

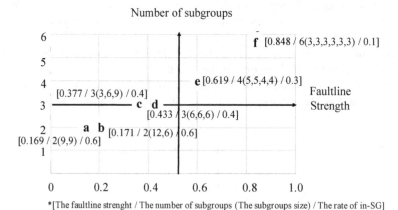

Fig. 9. Structure of diversity of six set data

Based on Eqs. (6) and (7), six new data sets (a through f) were formed and simulated. Figure 9 shows the diversity structures of the data sets. The fact-finding survey results confirmed that some groups had an imbalance in the number of subgroup members and some did not. Therefore, data sets were prepared in the case where an imbalance in the number of subgroup members with almost at the same faultline strength and the case without such an imbalance: (a:12,6 and b:9,9; c:9,6,3. and d:6,6,6).

6 Simulation Results

The simulations on three interaction methods which are Similarity, Diversity and Random were conducted. One simulation consists of 100 interactions, while the simulation was conducted 100 times according to each setting. Figure 10 shows the maximum value and the standard deviation of 100 simulations (except outliers). The maximum value shows Maximum possibility and the standard deviation shows Occurrence probability.

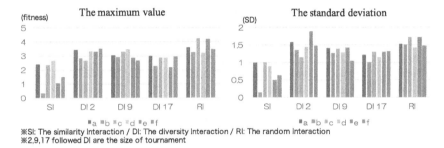

Fig. 10. Results from about 100 simulations each for method of interaction.

- In Similarity interaction, the rate of In-SG was set based on the survey. Maximum possibility became lower while Occurrence probability became higher when compared to the random interaction method. Especially in the case of (b), (e) and (f) this characteristic appeared apparently. (b) was that the faultline strength was weak, the number of subgroups was small and the number of members in the subgroup was uniform. (e) and (f) were that the faultline strength was strong and the number of subgroups was a lot.
- In (a) and (b), there were significant differences in the maximum value and the standard deviation despite the faultline strength and the number of subgroups were almost the same. This result confirmed that an imbalance in the number of subgroup members would affect the organization's performance. The previous study of Polzer et al. [4] reported in their field survey that organizations with an imbalance in the number of subgroup members tended to achieve high performance when compared to those with a uniform number of subgroup members. Comparison of the maximum value, which was higher in (a) with the imbalance than in (b), also supported this study result.
- As for the imbalance in the number of members, (a), (c), and (e) had the higher maximum value when compared with others in the random interaction method.

This confirmed that the random interaction method is not affected by the faultline strength or the number of subgroups, while being influenced by the imbalance.

- In Diversity interaction, the tendency was able to observe that is similar to the validation data sets where a greater tournament size can increase the occurrence probability (the correlation efficient is -0.55 and the p-value is significant at 5%).

7   Discussion

In this study, quantifying diversity with the faultline strength and the number of subgroups based on the faultline theory, three interaction methods based on conflict effects were simulated with ABM. Through these simulations, we validated how the relationship between organizational diversity and communication could affect organizational performance. Our simulations clarified the following points.

1. The diversity influences on organizational performance, because it occurs dysfunctional conflict and communication cannot have equality in an organization. In addition, there are different influences by the diversity structure and the method of interaction.
2. In Similarity interaction that occurs the disfunctional conflict, the faultline strength can work positively in increasing Maximum possibility; however, it causes a negative influence by decreasing Occurrence probability. The number of subgroups has an effect opposite to the faultline strength.
3. In Diversity interaction that actively leverages diversity (the functional conflict), the faultline strength has a negative influence by decreasing Occurrence probability. The functional conflict tends to work more effectively in organizations when the faultline strength is weak.
4. Therefore, there are three important things. The first is to grasp the diversity structure. The faultline theory which can analyze the diversity quantitatively is a useful tool. The second is to manage the method of interaction by assigning jobs, facilitating meetings etc. The third is to determine organizational goal-setting priorities, – whether is it more important the maximum possibility or the occurrence probability? – For example, the financial department has priority of the occurrence probability however the new business development department has priority of the maximum possibility.
5. Based on the survey of Japanese organizations, half of them have weak faultlines and few subgroups, and are uniform organizations. However, some sections of large organizations progress more than others in terms of the diversity. Also, it becomes clear that as the faultlines become strong, the number of subgroups increases.

This paper performed a simulation using the data of business communication obtained for the survey. For future research, it is necessary to use the data of frequency of the shared lunch survey and to compare it with the business communication. In addition, it is necessary to conduct the survey with more companies and sections to examine the diversity of Japanese organizations in more detail. Furthermore, there is a need to survey not only by a questionnaire but also by a digital equipment.

8   Conclusion

The purpose of this study was to clarify how to manage a diversified organization in order to enhance organizational performance. Our study obtained one solution that is to overcome the unproductive conflict by understanding the organization diversity structure, and then to form a communication mechanism that leverages diversity. It should serve as one of the management measures necessary for enhancing organizational performance.

This study made an academic contribution by reproducing the results of previous studies of the faultline theory based on ABM, clarifying part of its mechanism from the communication perspective. Additionally, on the practical contribution, this study investigated the Japanese companies with the faultline theory, clarifying a part of the diversity of Japanese organizations.

This model was based on the survey of the small organizations, and the simulation was conducted for a small group of a task execution unit. We have not verified large-scale organizations yet. Therefore, future research should be conducted in more realistic settings to understand the effect of diversification in large-scale organizations.

References

1. Iba, S.: Genetic Algorithm and Mechanism of Evolution. Iwanami Shoten, Publishers, 2-5-5 Hitotsubashi, Chiyoda-ku, Tokyo, Japan (2002)
2. Lau, D.C., Murnighan, J.K.: Demographic diversity and faultlines: the compositional dynamics of organizational groups. Acad. Manag. Rev. **23**(2), 325–340 (1998)
3. Meyer, B., Glenz, A.: Team faultline measures: a computational comparison and a new approach to multiple subgroups. Organ. Res. Methods **16**(3), 393–424 (2013)
4. Polzer, J.T., Crisp, C.B., Jarvenpaa, S.L., Kim, J.W.: Extending the faultline model to geographically dispersed teams: how collocated subgroups can impair group functioning. Acad. Manag. J. **49**(4), 679–692 (2006)
5. Robbins, S.P.: Essential of Organizational Behavior. Pearson/Prentice Hall, Upper Saddle River (2005)
6. Rousseeuw, P.: Silhouette: a graphical aid to the interpretation and validation of cluster analysis. J. Comput. Appl. Math. **20**, 53–65 (1987)
7. Suzuki, R., Matsumoto, Y., Kitai, A.: The concept and analytical techniques of faultline. J. Polit. Econ. **211**(6), 53–88 (2015)
8. Williams, K.Y., O'Reilly, C.A.: Demography and diversity in organizations: a review of 40 years of research. Res. Organ. Behav. **20**(8), 70–140 (1998)
9. Takahashi, S., et al.: Relations between partial diversity and organizational performance in an organization. SICE J. Control Meas. Syst. Integr. **6**(2), 147–156 (2013)
10. Carton, A.M., Cummings, J.N.: A theory of subgroups in work teams. Acad. Manag. Rev. **37**(3), 441–470 (2012)

A Study of New Variable Selection Method Within a Framework of Real-Coded Genetic Algorithm

Takahiro Obata$^{(\boxtimes)}$ and Setsuya Kurahashi

Graduate School of Business Science, University of Tsukuba, Tokyo, Japan
obata_takahiro@hotmail.com

Abstract. Recently, variable selection and parameter optimization are becoming increasingly important. Regarding parameter optimization, real-coded genetic algorithms (RCGA) have received attention due to their strong searching ability and flexibility. The Akaike information criterion (AIC) or Bayesian information criterion (BIC) are traditionally used as variable selection criteria. These criteria estimate the relative quality of analysis models for a given set of data, but they cannot be used to evaluate the importance of the variables themselves. This paper proposes a new variable selection method that applies RCGA. This new variable selection method contains two primary components. One is a new variable selection criterion, and the other is a method for estimating the progress of RCGA optimization. The effectiveness of this new variable selection method is confirmed through application to the sum of squares function, which is a nonlinear test function.

Keywords: Real-coded GA · Variable selection · Application of RCGA

1 Introduction

Recently, large and complex datasets have accumulated alongside the development of machine infrastructure and new measuring technologies. Additionally, the need for methods of selecting essential variables from a large dataset has been increasing. Moreover, analysis models for large and complex datasets are complicating; thus, the difficulty in parameter estimation using these models is increasing.

Regarding these complex optimization problems, real-coded genetic algorithms (RCGA) have attracted considerable attention owing to their flexibility and efficiency in performing searches. For flexibility, objective functions need not be continuous and differentiable in genetic algorithms (GA). Moreover, for variable selection problems, the Akaike information criterion (AIC) or Bayesian information criterion (BIC) is traditionally used as variable selection criteria. These criteria can be used to estimate the relative quality of analytical models

© Springer Nature Switzerland AG 2019
K. Kojima et al. (Eds.): JSAI-isAI 2018 Workshops, LNAI 11717, pp. 50–64, 2019.
https://doi.org/10.1007/978-3-030-31605-1_4

for a given dataset; however, they cannot be used to evaluate the importance of the variables themselves. When the number of variables increases with data accumulation, the number of combination increases explosively, which prevents the calculation of AIC or BIC for all combinations; hence, the order of variable selection becomes crucial.

This paper proposes a new variable selection method with a new selection criterion (based on the variances of genes in RCGA) and a new indicator to estimate the progress of optimal solution search. At the first stage of our research, we examined this new variable selection method using a linear regression model and a quadratic function model, and determined that calculating a variable criterion within the framework of RCGA is possible and that the proposed variable selection method is effective in this paper. Because the new selection criterion is calculated for each variable included in the analytical model, individual variables can be ranked based on the calculated values. Variable selection based on this ranking could be a solution to the combination explosion problem mentioned earlier. Furthermore, the proposed method could solve variable selection problems in complicated and/or discontinuous models.

The structure of this paper is as follows. Section 2 presents the previous studies on GAs and variable selection. Section 3 explains a new variable selection criterion, called the I-value, which uses the variance of genes as an indicator of variables that should be omitted. Section 4 presents the progress of solution searching in GA to determine the appropriate number of generations. Furthermore, the results of variable selection trials using the I-value and progress rate are presented in this section. Finally, Sect. 5 presents a summary of this paper.

2   Related Work

GA is an adaptive search method based on the concept of natural evolution [1]. One of the primary advantages of GA is that objective functions are not required to be continuous and differentiable; moreover, they can be used for global searching.

RCGA uses real-valued vectors to represent genes [2], and it is applicable in solving real parameter optimization problems more efficiently than those in a traditional binary-coded GA. Notably, the search performance of RCGA depends on the models that are used for crossover and generation; thus, various models for crossover and generation alteration have been proposed. According to the recent studies [3–5], the combination of adaptive real-coded ensemble crossover (AREX) (for a crossover operator) and just generation gap (JGG) (for a generation alteration model) demonstrates excellent performance. real-coded ensemble crossover (REX) is a generalized multi-parental crossover operator [6]. It uses $s + 1$ parents, where s is the dimension of the search space, and children are generated near the center of gravity of the selected $s + 1$ parents based on a probability distribution. AREX is a REX, which is combined with the following mechanisms to prevent initial convergence. One mechanism adaptively adjusts the spread of the child generation area to control group diversity, while the other one allows promising individuals to be easily generated by shifting the center of child generation in promising areas. JGG is a generation alteration model developed for multi-parental crossover operators, in which children can survive the selection while all parents selected for crossover are terminated.

It is called a variable selection problem to select the variables suitable for explaining the fluctuation of the target variable from among a large number of explanatory variables. Variable selection is also called feature selection. Especially in around 2000, research in this field became more active along with the increase in the number of dimensions of problem [7]. Variable selection methods are divided into wrapper, filter, and embedded methods. Wrapper methods include the learning algorithm as a black box algorithm to score the goodness of the subsets of the selected variables. Filter methods act as preprocessing to rank the variables, and highly ranked variables are selected into the subset. The wrapper techniques are known to be more accurate compared to the filter techniques, and they are computationally more expensive. Embedded methods are hybrid with the learning part and the feature selection part.

Researches using evolutionary computation (EC) for variable selection have also been actively conducted, and [8] comprehensively investigated and summarized them. Among ECs, there are many studies using GAs, and in particular GA is utilized as learning algorithm of wrapper methods. [9] is a research aimed at simultaneously performing variable selection and parameter optimization using GA. One of the challenges in variable selection is to select a more suitable variables while suppressing calculation cost for a large number of variable combinations; hence, the order of variable selection is important.

3   Variable Selection Using Gene Variances in RCGA

This section details the development of the proposed variable selection criterion.

3.1   Experimental Conditions

Analysis Model (Objective Function). The linear regression model in (1) below is used to analyze a model in Sect. 3.

$$y = a_0 + \sum_{i=1}^{p} a_i x_i \tag{1}$$

where y is the objective variable, x is the explanatory variable, and p is the number of explanatory variables.

A linear regression model is employed because it is important to compare the established statistical properties with the variance of genes in RCGA.

Datasets Used. We utilized two types of datasets. The first comprises data on the national strength of the United States (U.S.) and five variables: iron and steel production (irst), energy consumption (energy), military expenditure (milex), military personnel (milper), and total population (pop) per year. This dataset contained 187 samples, which was obtained from the U. S. national statistics. The second dataset comprises 17 samples of seven variables related to inflation data in Japan: food, housing (house), fuel light and water charges (util), furniture and household utensils (goods), medical care (med), transportation and communication (comm), and education as well as culture and recreation (edu). Table 1 shows the correlation matrix for each dataset. It is evident in Table 1 that some variables have high correlation, particularly in dataset 1.

The following linear regression model (2) is used for dataset 1 and model (3) is used for dataset 2. Table 2 shows the regression results for dataset 1 and Table 3 shows regression results for dataset 2.

$$pop = b_0 + b_1 \cdot irst + b_2 \cdot energy + b_3 \cdot milex + b_4 \cdot milper \tag{2}$$

$$edu = c_0 + c_1 \cdot food + c_2 \cdot house + c_3 \cdot util$$
$$+ c_4 \cdot goods + c_5 \cdot med + c_6 \cdot comm \tag{3}$$

The Settings of the RCGA. The population size and number of children were chosen based on a recommendation from the previous study [4]. The population size and number of children are ten times and four times the number of genes, respectively. We set the maximum generation to 2,000 and 1000 for dataset 1 and 2, respectively.

3.2 Variances of Genes and Fitness in RCGA

In models with several candidate explanatory variables, some objective functions are more sensitive to changes in certain variables. If the fitness value for an individual is calculated using the sum of squared residuals in RCGA, then a change in the value of the objective function is important for determining fitness. Therefore, this mechanism is expected to provide a narrower distribution of genes corresponding to coefficients of the essential variables than the other genes. Thus, this study focuses on variances of genes in RCGA.

Table 1. Correlation matrices for dataset 1 and 2.

	irst	energy	milex	milper	pop
irst	1				
energy	0.92	1			
milex	0.64	0.87	1		
milper	0.66	0.55	0.41	1	
pop	0.92	0.98	0.82	0.55	1

	food	house	util	goods	med	comm	edu
food	1						
house	0.42	1					
util	0.59	0.04	1				
goods	0.53	0.66	0.08	1			
med	0.11	−0.13	0.04	0.16	1		
comm	0.40	0.62	0.21	0.67	−0.01	1	
edu	0.74	0.77	0.34	0.83	0.13	0.62	1

Table 2. Regression results for dataset 1.

	intercept	irst	energy	milex	milper
Coefficient	3.55×10^4	-2.61×10^{-1}	1.11×10^{-1}	-2.20×10^{-4}	1.05
T statistics	20.8	1.72	11.4	-4.14	1.05

Table 3. Regression results for dataset 2.

	intercept	food	house	util	goods	med	comm
Coefficient	-1.68×10^{-1}	2.50×10^{-1}	6.64×10^{-1}	6.91×10^{-2}	6.06×10^{-1}	5.13×10^{-2}	-9.81×10^{-2}
T statistics	-0.23	1.57	2.52	0.87	2.23	0.66	-0.38

3.3 Timing of Convergence in Genes

If the importance of a variable is reflected in a gene's variance, two possibilities are conceivable. One is the possibility that the timing at which the value of a gene converges differs, and the other is the possibility that there is a difference in the spread of a gene's distribution after the optimization. Let us begin with the timing of convergence. Figure 1 shows changes in the variances of each gene for dataset 1.

From Fig. 1, it seems that genes corresponding to regression coefficients of milex and energy with large T statistics converge first, followed by the other genes. However, this timing might be affected by the scales of the parameters to be estimated, i.e., the regression coefficient shown in Table 2. In order to confirm this assertion, dataset 1 is adjusted by multiplying irst by 10^6 and dividing milex by 10^6. This adjustment changes the scales of the coefficients, while the T statistics or correlations between variables remain constant. Figure 2 shows dataset 1 after adjusting with this scale.

As shown in Fig. 2, the variance of irst initially decreases, and convergence subsequently advances in the order: energy, milper, and milex. Since this order is the same as the magnitude of the coefficients, one may conclude that the timing of gene convergence is influenced by the magnitude of the coefficient of the variable to be estimated.

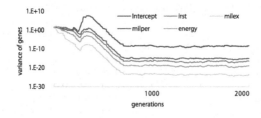

Fig. 1. Changes in the variances of genes for dataset 1.

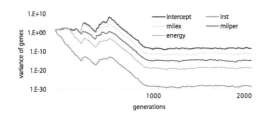

Fig. 2. Changes in the gene variances with scale-adjusted dataset 1.

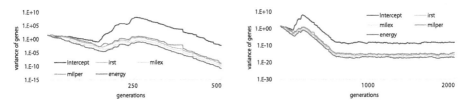

Fig. 3. Changes in gene variances with modified dataset 1.

On the other hand, there remains the possibility that the usefulness of genes might affect the timing. In order to validate this assertion, dataset 1 was modified again, in which we set the absolute value of all coefficients to 1 by multiplying each variable by its corresponding coefficient. Figure 3 shows this modified dataset 1. The left panel in Fig. 3 shows the progress from 1 to 500 generations, and the right panel in Fig. 3 shows the progress from 1 to 2000 generations in a logarithmic chart.

The left panel in Fig. 3 shows that variables with large T statistics converge first, while the right panel in Fig. 3 shows that variances of genes with large T statistics tend to be smaller in later generations.

3.4   Relation Between Variances of Genes and Standard Error

The T statistic is equal to the value obtained by dividing coefficients by standard errors. In light of the results from Subsect. 3.3, gene variances in RCGA may reflect the scales of standard errors in the corresponding parameters. We validate this assertion in this subsection.

It is desirable to compare the gene variances in a situation where gene convergence is stable because the magnitude of the estimated parameter influences the convergence of timing of gene variance. We define the variance ratio as the value obtained by dividing the variance of genes in a particular generation by the variance over the previous ten generations. The variance ratio is used as an indicator to monitor the progress of parameter optimization. Parameters approach their optimum values when the variance ratio of all parameters approaches 1, and it is observed that the variance ratio approaches 1 by the $800th$ generation. We subsequently analyzed the gene variances at the $2000th$ generation with a margin. A comparison of the standard error and the variance of genes revealed

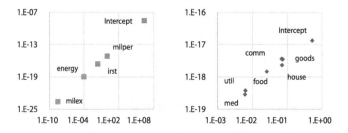

Fig. 4. Scatter plot of the squared standard errors (x-axis) and gene variances (y-axis).

Table 4. F statistics and I-value for dataset 1.

	(1)F statistics	(2)I-value	(1)/(2)
intercept	4.36×10^2	4.44×10^{17}	9.80×10^{-16}
irst	2.95×1	3.02×10^{15}	9.78×10^{-16}
energy	1.29×10	1.26×10^{17}	1.03×10^{-15}
milex	1.72×10	2.10×10^{16}	8.16×10^{-16}
milper	1.09×1	1.73×10^{15}	6.32×10^{-16}

that the order of the large and small perfectly matches with no proportional relationship. Compared with the square of standard errors in consideration that the standard error is a kind of standard deviation, gene variances are found to be proportional to the squared standard errors. Calculating the squared standard errors and dividing by the gene variances for each parameter in dataset 1 shows that these values lie in the range $(1.2 \pm 0.3) \times 10^{15}$. Performing this calculation for dataset 2 yields values lying in the range of $(2.8 \pm 1.1) \times 10^{16}$. Figure 4 shows these results with squared standard errors on the x-axis and gene variances on the y-axis. The data points lie nearly along a diagonal line.

3.5   Variable Selection Utilizing the Variances of Genes

Here, we introduce the I-value, which is defined in Eq. (4) below.

$$I_i = \frac{\nu_i^2}{V_{gi}}. \tag{4}$$

When the F statistics and I-value are in a proportional relationship, then it can be expressed as F statistics = coefficient × I-value. In the case of a perfect proportional relation, the coefficient becomes a constant value, but it is unlikely that the proportional relation becomes complete for actual data, moreover, it is assumed that a certain degree of error would occur. Tables 4 and 5 depict this scenario. In fact, the F statistics divided by the I-value for datasets 1 and 2 lie in the range $(8.2 \pm 2.0) \times 10^{-16}$ and $(3.9 \pm 2.0) \times 10^{-17}$, respectively.

Table 5. F statistics and I-value on dataset 2.

	(1)F statistics	(2)I-value	(1)/(2)
intercept	5.47×10^{-2}	2.94×10^{15}	1.86×10^{-17}
food	2.45×1	4.72×10^{16}	5.19×10^{-17}
house	6.33×1	2.61×10^{17}	2.42×10^{-17}
util	7.62×10^{-1}	1.30×10^{16}	5.86×10^{-17}
goods	5.00×1	1.24×10^{17}	4.04×10^{-17}
med	4.33×10^{-1}	1.26×10^{16}	3.43×10^{-17}
comm	1.41×10^{-1}	2.96×10^{15}	4.78×10^{-17}

Table 6. Variable selection using I-value and AIC.

Dataset 1

criterion	order of selection (frequency)
I-value	$b_4 \to b_1 \to b_3$ (5)
AIC	$b_4 \to b_1$

Dataset 2

criterion	order of selection (frequency)
I-value	$c_6 \to c_5 \to c_3 \to c_4 \to c_1$ (3)
	$c_6 \to c_3 \to c_5 \to c_4 \to c_1$ (2)
AIC	$c_6 \to c_5 \to c_3$

Variable selection by backward selection is employed here, where the I-value is utilized as a variable selection criterion. The model including all variables is considered first, and the variable with the lowest selection criterion value is omitted. Table 6 shows the results from five variable selection trials. The numerical values in parentheses indicate the frequency of occurrence.

The variable selection using I-value continues until the explanatory variable becomes the only variable remaining, while the variable deletion by AIC ends at the point when the AIC is no longer improved by deleting a variable. For this reason, these two methods have different variable selection endpoints, but when comparing the order of variable deletion until the variable deletion by AIC completes, the order of variable deletion is completely matched for dataset 1. For dataset 2, the deleted variables are the same, while the order of deletion of $c3$ and $c5$ goes back and forth in some trials. Through these trials, it was observed that the I-value could be a variable selection criterion, although limited to linear models.

4   Variable Selection Based on the Progress Rate of Optimal Solution Search

In this section, the feasibility of variable selection using I-values is demonstrated. However, the time at which variable selection should be performed was not examined. It is preferable to perform variable selection when each individual in RCGA clusters around the optimal solution, and the ranking of the variables by

I-value is not frequently changed. Taking a sufficiently large number of genera-tions increases the likelihood of achieving this condition, but the computational cost also increases. On the other hand, if the variable selection is executed dur-ing the initial search period, the likelihood of erroneously omitting a necessary variable increases. In order to manage this trade-off, an index other than ter-mination conditions used in RCGA should be utilized to decide the progress of solution search with RCGA, because these termination conditions are the mea-sures to decide if RCGA has attain the optimal solution or not. In this section, we apply a software reliability growth model (SRGM) to measure the progress of an optimal solution search with RCGA and implement variable selection based on the progress rate. To the best of our knowledge, no research has used SRGM to estimate the progress of an optimal solution search with RCGA.

4.1   Measuring of the Progress of RCGA Solution Search Using SRGM

SRGM is a method for estimating the cumulative number of remaining bugs occurring in a piece of software based on the trend from the cumulative number of bugs detected during testing. Though various SRGMs have been discussed in the literature, most of them are based on curves with typical characteristics peculiar to each model, such as an exponential-type and an S-shape. It has been shown that as a particular model is used, the accuracy of estimating the num-ber of remaining bugs decreases depending on the characteristics of the target data. Hence, an integrated model that includes other representative models is proposed as a means to solve these problems. In particular, [10] showed that parameters could be analytically estimated by taking the log of the differential equation representing the integrated model and minimizing the sum of squares in the logarithmic error from the obtained data series. The following differential equation represents the integrated model.

$$\frac{d(y + \delta)}{dt} \cdot (y + \delta)^{\gamma-1} = \alpha \cdot e^{-\beta t}, \tag{5}$$

where y is the cumulative number of bugs at time t, α is the scale factor for the y-axis, β is the scale factor for the t-axis, and δ is the parameter denoting the translation along the y-axis of the solution of the differential equation. For $\delta = 0$, Eq. (5) reduces to

$$y' \cdot y^{\gamma-1} = \alpha \cdot e^{-\beta t}. \tag{6}$$

Taking the logarithm of both sides yields

$$\ln y' + (\gamma - 1) \ln y = \ln \alpha - \beta t. \tag{7}$$

From Eq. (7), α, β, and γ are estimated by minimizing the sum of squares of the logarithmic error, which is subsequently used to calculate the cumulative number of bugs.

We used the method from [10] to estimate the solution search progress for RCGA. Herein, y' in Eq. (7) is replaced with Δy, which represents the difference between the average of fitness value for all individuals at generations $t-1$ and t, i.e., the improvement width of the average of fitness value, and y represents the cumulative of Δy.

If a solution search proceeds smoothly, the improvement width of fitness value gradually decreases and tends to reach zero in successive generations. This is analogous to the gradual decrease in the number of bugs found at each point in time as software testing progresses. Therefore, just as SRGM manages the progress of software testing by taking the ratio of the final cumulative bug number prediction at time t and the actual cumulative bug count, the progress of solution search with RCGA can be reflected by taking the ratio of the predicted to the final cumulative improvement width at generation t and the actual cumulative improvement width.

Therefore, we aim to measure progress through parameter estimation with RCGA for the sum of squares function with different weighted variables. The sum of squares function is defined in the following equation:

$$f(x) = \sum_{i=1}^{n} i \cdot (x_i - k)^2, \tag{8}$$

where n denotes the number of dimension; moreover, the larger the n, the more challenging the problem becomes. The linear models we considered in Sect. 3 have four or seven variables. To align the level of the difficulty with these models, we set n as 10. k means the optimal solutions. If k is set at 0, even when all variables are deleted, the optimum solution can be reached. So k must be more than 0. This paper set k as 5.

We chose three types of SRGMs with different shapes of curves from the representative models mentioned in [10] and used them as trial models. They comprise the exponential model in Eq. (9), the Gompertz curve in Eq. (10), and the hyper-exponential model in Eq. (11). N is the predicted cumulative improvement width. As n in Eq. (11) is 1 in this paper, the left side of Eq. (9) and the one of Eq. (11) are the same. The difference between the Eqs. (9) and (11) is whether $\gamma = 1$ or $\gamma > 1$.

$$y = N(1 - e^{-bt}) \quad where \quad \alpha = Nb, \beta = b, \gamma = 1, \tag{9}$$
$$y = N \exp(-ke^{-bt}) \quad where \quad \alpha = kb, b = \beta, \gamma = 0, \tag{10}$$
$$y = \sum_{i=1}^{n} N_i(1 - e^{-b_i t}) \quad where \quad \alpha = \frac{N^\gamma \beta}{\gamma}, \gamma > 1. \tag{11}$$

Figure 5 shows that the transition in the predicted progress rate with the Gompertz curve and the hyper-exponential model is unstable probably because of the difference between the shapes of the cumulative improvement width assumed in each model and the actual shape. In particular, while the cumulative improvement width in the Gompertz curve is supposed to be S-shaped and

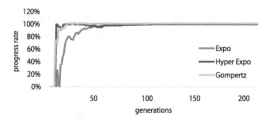

Fig. 5. Progress of solution search using RCGA in each model.

Table 7. Relation between parameter estimation and progress rate.

Generation	Parameter estimation situation	Progress rate
35	Distributed generally between 4 and 6	95.0%
70	Distributed between 4.5 and 5.5	99.0%
125	Distributed between 4.95 and 5.05	99.99%
200	Distributed between 4.995 and 5.005	99.9999%

that in the hyper-exponential model is expected to increase rapidly with a convex shape, the cumulative improvement width in RCGA is expected to increase relatively slowly with a convex shape in successive generations. Therefore, the exponential model was utilized to monitor the search progress.

Furthermore, the relation between parameter estimation and predicted progress rate is investigated. The optimal solution of this test function is 5 for all variables. Table 7 summarizes the relation between the estimation situation and progress rate. At the 35th generation, the deviation between the best individual's evaluation value and optimal solution is 20% at maximum, yielding a progress rate of 95.0%. At the 70th generation, the deviation shrinks to 10%, and the progress rate reaches 99.0%. However, even with a deviation of 20% at the 35th generation, not all genes for an individual deviate by 20%; some genes are close to their optimal values, and the average deviation of all genes does not exceed 10%. The variables in the sum of squares function are weighted differently, and it is observed that genes corresponding the variable with the larger weight are closer to the optimal solution. These points can conclude that the deviation from the optimum solution observed in all individuals is less than the average of the deviation of the individual genes; moreover, this predicted progress rate is considered to be reasonable.

4.2 Variable Selection Based on Progress Rate

Herein, we attempt variable selection using the aforementioned predicted progress rate. RCGA is initially used to search the optimal solution with all variables. When the progress rate exceeds a preset threshold, the variable with the lowest I-value is immediately omitted. Furthermore, we set the genes of all

Table 8. Order of variable omission in each trial

Threshold	90.0%					95.0%					99.0%				
Trial no.	1	2	3	4	5	1	2	3	4	5	1	2	3	4	5
x_1	2	1	3	1	1	1	1	1	1	2	2	1	1	1	2
x_2	1	2	2	2	3	2	2	2	2	3	1	3	2	2	1
x_3	3	3	4			3	3		3				3	3	
x_4	4		1	3	2			3			1	3	2		
x_5		4		4											
x_6															3
x_7, x_8, x_9, x_{10}															

individuals corresponding to the omitted variable to zero, and the fitness value of the individuals is recalculated. Subsequently, the value of the genes corresponding to the omitted variables is set to zero when new individuals are generated at crossover. Once a variable selection is executed, the numerical value relating to the progress rate is reset. In particular, the improvement width of the fitness value compared with the previous generation and the value of the cumulative improvement width are set to zero, and the progress rate is recalculated for the current generation after variable selection. This process prevents the consecutive performance of variable selection and the omission of all variables unless the progress rate calculation is reset. Additionally, as a condition for terminating searching with RCGA, either the improvement width of the fitness value reaches zero, the progress rate reaches 1, or only a single variable remains. If at least one condition is satisfied, then RCGA terminates.

Table 8 shows the variable selection results for the sum of squares function with three thresholds (90.0%, 95.0%, and 99.0%).

Regardless of the threshold level, there is a common tendency to omit variables with small weights in the sum of squares function. In particular, the top two variables in descending weight are subject to an omission in every trial, and the order of variable omission is as expected. Conversely, when the threshold was 90%, there was a tendency to delete four variables, but only three variables are deleted for the trials with thresholds of 95% and 99%. In each trial, RCGA terminates after 400 generations corresponding to one of the aforementioned termination conditions. When the threshold is high, it takes long time to omit the first variable, and the evaluation value continues to improve in the meantime. Therefore, the termination condition is applied soon after three variables are deleted, and the number of variables to be deleted decreases during the high threshold trial. Although the results are not shown in Table 8, trials with thresholds of 99.9% and 99.99% were also executed. The results revealed that only one or two variables were omitted, while the tendency to omit variables with small weights remains the same.

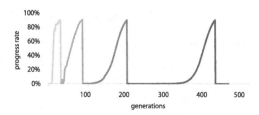

Fig. 6. Transition of progress rate.

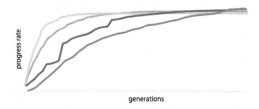

Fig. 7. Transition of cumulative improvement.

Figure 6 shows the transition in the progress rate during trial 1 with 90.0% threshold in Table 7.

As more variables are omitted, the time interval between subsequent variable selections tends to increase because the improvement width in the evaluation value gradually decreases in successive RCGA generations, which is one of the reasons. Figure 7 shows each transition in the cumulative improvement shown in Fig. 6. The scales of x-axis and y-axis have been adjusted.

Although the curves in Fig. 7 have similar shapes, where the improvement width is initially large and then gradually decreases, a difference exists in the smoothness and slope of the graph. It is expected that the progress rate can be more accurately estimated with a different calculation model based on the shape of the curve. This problem will be considered in future study.

Finally, we attempt a variable selection with the two datasets used in Sect. 3. Variables with low T statistics are often removed if the threshold is set to a sufficiently large value. Conversely, variables tend to be removed randomly if the threshold is low. Usually, processing with RCGA terminates after removing two or three variables.

Further, the improvement width of the evaluation value sometimes becomes negative, which makes it difficult to calculate the progress rate. In particular, after executing variable deletion, the optimal solution for each parameter changes from the value before variable deletion, and it seems that there are several cases where the improvement width became negative owing to the search for a renewed solution. In the case of the sum of squares function, the optimal solution for the other parameters remains unchanged at 5, even after deleting a variable. It is necessary to take an appropriate measure in the cases where the improvement width becomes negative. We will consider this point as a future subject.

5 Conclusions

Herein, a new method for variable selection in the RCGA framework is proposed. This new method comprises two main primary components: a new selection criterion using the variances of genes in RCGA and a new indicator to estimate the progress of optimal solution search. It is shown that variable selection can be performed with the nonlinear sum of squares function using this method.

Furthermore, a new variable deletion criterion called the I-value, which can be used to reflect the importance of different variables is introduced. This metric utilizes the magnitude of the genetic variance in RCGA.

SRGM can be used to monitor the search rate as RCGA progresses. This model can also be used to select variables at the appropriate time. The following areas in this study deserve attention in future: First, to examine the effect of multicollinearity on the proposed method, particularly on I-values. Notably, dataset 1 includes some variables with strong correlation, which can have an adverse effect on the stability of parameter optimization and I-values. Second, to analyze statistical property of I-values and to investigate the related works. Third, to develop processing techniques for negative improvement width. If the analytical model becomes complicated, it is highly possible that the improvement width of the evaluation value will become negative during solution search. Additionally, a progress rate calculation model suitable for the cumulative improvement depth should be considered. By addressing the challenges mentioned above, it will be possible to perform variable selection in more complicated models such as nonlinear and discontinuous models.

References

1. Goldberg, D.E.: Genetic Algorithms in Search, Optimization and Machine Learning. Addison Wesley Longman Publishing Co. Inc., Boston (1989)
2. Wright, A.: Genetic algorithms for real parameter optimization. Found. Genet. Algorithms **1**, 205–218 (1991)
3. Akimoto, Y., Hasada, R., Sakuma, J., Ono, I., Kobayashi, S.: Generation alternation model for real-coded GA using multi-parent: proposal and evaluation of just generation gap (JGG). In: Proceedings of the 19th SICE Symposium on Decentralized Autonomous Systems, vol. 19, pp. 341–346, January 2007. (in Japanese)
4. Akimoto, Y., Nagata, Y., Sakuma, J., Ono, I., Kobayashi, S.: Proposal and evaluation of adaptive real-coded crossover AREX. J. Jpn. Soc. Artif. Intell. **24**, 446–458 (2009). (in Japanese)
5. Akimoto, Y., Sakuma, J., Ono, I., Kobayashi, S.: Adaptation of expansion rate for real-coded crossovers. In: Proceedings of the 11th Annual Conference on Genetic and Evolutionary Computation (GECCO 2009), pp. 739–746 (2009)
6. Kobayashi, S.: The frontiers of real-coded genetic algorithms. J. Jpn. Soc. Artif. Intell. **24**, 147–162 (2009). (in Japanese)
7. Guyon, I., Elisseeff, A.: An introduction to variable and feature selection. J. Mach. Learn. Res. **3**, 1157–1182 (2003)
8. Xue, B., Zhang, M., Browne, W.N., Yao, X.: A survey on evolutionary computation approaches to feature selection. IEEE Trans. Evol. Comput. **20**(4), 606–626 (2016)

9. Huang, C.-L., Wang, C.-J.: A GA-based feature selection and parameters optimization for support vector machines. Expert Syst. Appl. **31**, 231–240 (2006)
10. Furuyama, T.: Analytical parameter estimation of the manifold growth model using Y - equation. J. Inf. Process. **37**(12), 2326–2333 (1996)

IDAA 2018

First International Workshop of Intelligent Data Analytics and Applications (IDAA 2018)

The International Workshop of Intelligent Data Analytics and Applications (IDAA 2018) serves as a forum for bringing researchers and practitioners across different artificial intelligent (AI) research and application communities together in a unique forum to present and exchange ideas, results, and experiences in AI technologies and applications. It welcomes researchers and practitioners to share the latest breakthroughs in analyzing data for applications in different domains by using AI techniques. These could include data science studies, data analytics applications and systems, or simulation and visualization using massive data. This workshop focused on application inspired novel findings, methods, systems, and solutions which demonstrated the impact of data analytics by AI. This year, we selected four out of nine excellent papers accepted by IDAA into the post proceeding. Zhongmin Han et al. focused on the fundamental deep learning paper where an unsupervised learning algorithm is proposed to preserve multiple features that included vertex attribute as well as network global and local topology structure; Yilang Wu et al. developed a vision sensor network (VSN) to observe and analyze viewers' visible behavior in real-time for the application scenario of deploying the VSN in an exposition spacel; Kiichi Tago et al. investigate and analyze pulse diagnosis data from a TCM doctor and a pulse diagnostic instrument (PDI) by Random Forest where subjects' vital signs and pulse diagnosis data from a TCM doctor are used as training data; and Haopeng Zhang et al. improved the gray world theory (GWT) and propose a single image dehazing method using our improved gray world theory and the dark channel prior. We hope that this workshop will inspire plenty of discussions and important follow-up research in this area. We would like to thank the authors for presenting their interesting ideas in this forum. Finally, the IDAA 2018 organizers wish to thank the JSAI-isAI organizers for their support.

April 2019

Chih-Chieh Hung
Hui-Huang Hsu
Chun-Hao Chen

Single Image Dehazing Using Improved Gray World Theory and Dark Channel Prior

Haopeng Zhang[1,3,4](✉) [iD], Bo Dong[2], and Zhiguo Jiang[1,3,4]

[1] Image Processing Center, School of Astronautics, Beihang University,
Beijing 100191, China
{zhanghaopeng,jiangzg}@buaa.edu.cn
[2] Beijing Radio Measurement Research Institute, Beijing 100854, China
bob_dongbo@yeah.net
[3] Key Laboratory of Spacecraft Design Optimization and Dynamic Simulation
Technologies, Ministry of Education, Beijing 100191, China
[4] Beijing Key Laboratory of Digital Media, Beijing 100191, China

Abstract. The images captured outdoor are usually influenced by inclement weather conditions severely, bringing a great deal of inconvenience to the automatic data processing system. The widely used dehazing method based on dark channel prior (DCP) is not effective on the image with color distortion. In order to solve this problem, we improve the gray world theory (GWT) and propose a single image dehazing method using our improved gray world theory and the dark channel prior. Experiments show that our method can restore the hazy image with color distortion effectively and outperforms the state-of-art results.

Keywords: Image dehazing · Gray world theory · Dark channel prior

1 Introduction

Image dehazing has received attracted attention for years and it is a typical ill-posed inverse problem. Previous works made use of additional information and added some constraints to avoid trivial solutions. For example, the scene structure can be estimated using the same scene of multiple images [4,8]. Recently, most methods find prior information from image itself, which can be used for image dehazing. Tan recovered the hazy image by maximizing the local contrasts of the hazy image [10]. On the assumption that the scene transmission is locally independent, Fattal [3] utilized independent component analysis to separate the haze from the scene, and then adopted Gaussian-Markov random field (GMRF)

This work was supported in part by the National Natural Science Foundation of China (Grant Nos. 61501009, 61771031 and 61371134), the National Key Research and Development Program of China (2016YFB0501300, 2016YFB0501302), and the Fundamental Research Funds for the Central Universities.

K. Kojima et al. (Eds.): JSAI-isAI 2018 Workshops, LNAI 11717, pp. 67–73, 2019.
https://doi.org/10.1007/978-3-030-31605-1_5

to adjust the transmission map. Taral and Hautiere achieved a dehazing image using non-linear filters [11]. Based on a large number of fog-free images, He [6] proposed the dark channel to remove haze. This method roughly estimated the airlight transmission using the dark channel prior, and then refined the transmission with the soft matting [6] or guided filter algorithm [5]. However, the dark channel prior is invalid to the image with color distortion. In this paper, we improve the gray world theory [1] specific to the color distortion in the hazy image and refine the dark channel prior using our improved gray world theory. Experiments show that our method can recover the hazy image and correct the color distortion effectively.

2   Our Method

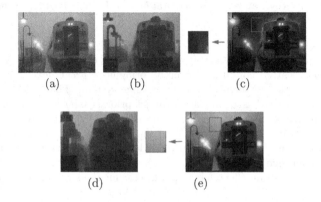

Fig. 1. Visual comparison. (a) Input hazy image. (b) Transmission map of [6]. (c) Dehazing result of [6]. (d) Our transmission map. (e) Our dehazing results.

As illustrated in Fig. 1, the dehazing method based on the dark channel prior [6] cannot appropriately dehaze the image with serious color distortion. In order to solve this problem, the color distortion needs to be corrected during dehazing. Among all of color distortion correction methods, the gray world theory has been widely used. This theory believes that the mean reflection of scene can offset chromatic aberration [2]. In this paper, we improve the gray world method specific to the hazy image with color distortion. By exploiting the statistics of the gray world theory, it can be found that the standard deviations of all three channels in the color distortion image are lower than that in the normal image. Based on this fact, the standard deviations of all three channels are calculated to determine the existence of color distortion and amend the gain coefficient. After that, we build a mapping relationship to adjust the pixel value in three color channels and obtain the corrected results. Subsequently, the dark channel prior is used to obtain the dehazing result.

2.1   Color Distortion Correction

The image can be represented in RGB channels:

$$I_i(x) = \begin{cases} R_i(x) \\ G_i(x) \\ B_i(x) \end{cases}, \tag{1}$$

where x indicates the pixel position and $I_i(x)$ is the observed intensity of pixel i. $R_i(x)$, $G_i(x)$ and $B_i(x)$ are the values of pixel i in red, green and blue channels respectively. The standard deviations of all three color channels are calculated to determine the existence of color distortion and amend the gain coefficient. Here we take blue channel as an example. Firstly, we calculate the standard deviation.

$$S_b = \sqrt{\frac{\sum_{i=1}^{N} (B_i - B_{av})^2}{N}}, \tag{2}$$

where S_b is the standard deviation of blue channel. S_r and S_g can be obtained in the same way. $B_{av} = \frac{1}{N} \sum_{i=1}^{N} B_i$. R_{av} and G_{av} can be computed in the similar manner. N represents the total quantity of pixels in the image.

According to the gray world theory [2], the gain coefficient of blue channel K_b can be calculated as:

$$K_b = \frac{R_{av} + G_{av} + B_{av}}{3B_{av}}. \tag{3}$$

However, the haze will increase the gain coefficient and lead to a false correction result. For the hazy image with color distortion, the channel with higher pixel value usually has lower standard deviation [1]. Consequently, we use the maximum and average of the standard deviation to amend the gain coefficient. The correction factor of the gain coefficient can be calculated as follow:

$$c_b = \begin{cases} \frac{S_{av}^2}{S_b \times S_{max}}, & \frac{S_{av}^2}{S_b \times S_{max}} \geq 1 \\ 1, & \frac{S_{av}^2}{S_b \times S_{max}} < 1, \end{cases} \tag{4}$$

where $S_{av} = \frac{S_r + S_g + S_b}{3}$ and $S_{max} = \max(S_r, S_g, S_b)$. We define c_b as the correction factor. And then, the gain coefficient can be amended by c_b.

$$K_{nb} = \begin{cases} 1, & c_b \times K_b \geq 1 \\ c_b \times K_b & c_b \times K_b < 1, \end{cases} \tag{5}$$

where K_{nb} is the amended gain coefficient of blue channel. R_{nb} and G_{nb} can be computed in the same way. The color distortion correction result can be obtained using the following formula:

$$I_i^{corret}(x) = \begin{cases} R_i(x) \times K_{nr} \\ G_i(x) \times K_{ng} \\ B_i(x) \times K_{nb} \end{cases}, \tag{6}$$

where $I_i^{corret}(x)$ are the correction results of pixel i.

2.2 Dehazing

Once color distortion in the hazy image has been corrected, we can use the dehazing method based on the dark channel prior to get dehazing result. As illustrated in [6], the dehazing image can be obtained using the following formula:

$$J(x) = \frac{I^{corret}(x) - A(1 - t(x))}{t(x)} = \frac{I^{corret}(x) - A}{t(x)} + A. \tag{7}$$

where $I^{corret}(x)$ is the input image with color cast correction, $J(x)$ is the dehazed image, A is the global atmospheric light which can be estimated using the method illustrated in [6], and $t(x)$ is the medium transmission. We can use $t(x)$ to describe the portion of the light which is not scattered and reaches the camera. $t(x)$ can be estimated approximately according to dark channel prior and then optimized using the guided filter algorithm.

3 Experiments

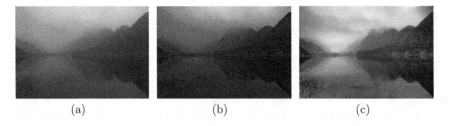

(a)   (b)   (c)

Fig. 2. Color distortion correction comparison. (a) Input hazy image. (b) Result of the gray world theory [1]. (c) Our color distortion correction result.

In this section, we compare our method with existing approaches [2,3,6,10, 11]. Comprehensive experiments are performed on real photographs with haze. Two assessment indexes are used for evaluation, including Colorfulness [9] and Global Contrast Factor (GCF) [7]. Colorfulness indicates color quality while GCF indicates the contrast of image.

Visual comparisons are shown in Figs. 1, 2 and 3. As shown in Fig. 1, there exists distinct color distortion in the result obtained by He's method [6]. In contrast, the transmission map estimated by our method is more accurate and the color distortion has been corrected in our result, thereby improving dehazing result. As can be seen from Fig. 3, our method can restore more details and textures. Especially, our method can restore the scene with large areas of background, such as the sky region, and the restored results are more natural. As shown in Fig. 2, compared with the method based the gray world theory, our method can correct the color distortion effectively.

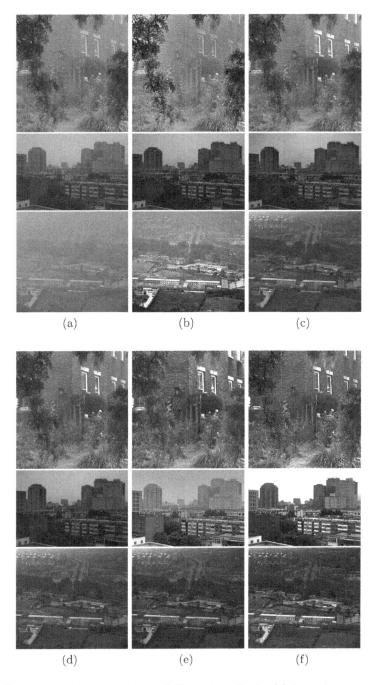

Fig. 3. Dehazing results comparison of different methods. (a) Input hazy images. (b) Tan [10]. (c) Fattel [3]. (d) Tarel [11]. (e) He [6]. (f) Ours.

Quantitative results demonstrate that our method outperforms other methods in Colorfulness and GCF, as shown in Table 1. As our method refines the dark channel using our improved gray world theory, the recovered image can preserve the color and enhance the contrast.

Table 1. Average quantitative comparison of all methods

Method	Colorfulness	GCF
Input hazy image	254.215	3.739
Tan's method [10]	293.436	5.918
Fattel's method [3]	351.093	6.415
Tarel's method [11]	461.071	6.984
He's method [6]	471.448	7.047
The gray world theory [2]	322.767	6.002
Our improved gray world theory	392.206	6.603
Our method	**605.372**	**7.943**

4 Conclusion

In this paper, we propose a single image dehazing method based on the improved gray theory and the dark channel prior. Our method can get more accurate dark channel by correcting color distortion and enlarge the applicability of the dark channel prior, which can recover the hazy image with color distortion effectively. Experiments show our method performs well in visual effect of dehazing results. As for future work, we will extend our work to handle the problem of outdoor video dehazing.

References

1. Agarwal, V., Abidi, B.R., Koschan, A., Abidi, M.A.: An overview of color constancy algorithms. J. Pattern Recogn. Res. **1**(1), 42–54 (2006)
2. Buchsbaum, G.: A spatial processor model for object colour perception. J. Franklin Inst. **310**(1), 1–26 (1980)
3. Fattal, R.: Single image dehazing. ACM Trans. Graph. **27**(3), 72 (2008)
4. Gong, C., Tang, W., He-qin, Z.: A novel physics-based method for restoration of foggy day images. J. Image Graph. **5**(13), 887–893 (2008)
5. He, K., Sun, J., Tang, X.: Guided image filtering. IEEE Trans. Pattern Anal. Mach. Intell. **35**(6), 1397–1409 (2013)
6. He, K., Sun, J., Tang, X.: Single image haze removal using dark channel prior. IEEE Trans. Pattern Anal. Mach. Intell. **33**(12), 2341–2353 (2011)

7. Matkovic, K., Neumann, L., Neumann, A., Psik, T., Purgathofer, W.: Global Contrast Factor - a New Approach to Image Contrast. In: Neumann, L., Sbert, M., Gooch, B., Purgathofer, W. (eds.) Computational Aesthetics in Graphics, Visualization and Imaging. The Eurographics Association (2005)
8. Narasimhan, S.G., Nayar, S.K.: Contrast restoration of weather degraded images. IEEE Trans. Pattern Anal. Mach. Intell. **25**(6), 713–724 (2003)
9. Sabine E. Susstrunk, S.W.: Color image quality on the internet. In: Santini, S., Schettini, R. (eds.) Proc. SPIE 5304, Internet Imaging V. vol. 5304. SPIE (2003). https://doi.org/10.1117/12.537804
10. Tan, R.T.: Visibility in bad weather from a single image. In: IEEE Conference on Computer Vision and Pattern Recognition, pp. 1–8. IEEE (2008)
11. Tarel, J.P., Hautiere, N.: Fast visibility restoration from a single color or gray level image. In: IEEE International Conference on Computer Vision, pp. 2201–2208. IEEE (2009)

Analysis of Pulse Diagnosis Data from a TCM Doctor and a Device by Random Forest

Kiichi Tago[1]([✉])(iD), Atsushi Ogihara[2](iD), Shoji Nishimura[2](iD), and Qun Jin[2](iD)

[1] Graduate School of Human Sciences, Waseda University, Tokorozawa, Japan
kiichi.tg@ruri.waseda.jp
[2] Faculty of Human Sciences, Waseda University, Tokorozawa, Japan
{aogi,kickaha,jin}@waseda.jp

Abstract. Pulse diagnosis is a typical diagnosis of Traditional Chinese Medicine (TCM). However, it is not clear if there is any relationship between the result of pulse diagnosis and other health related data. In this study, we investigate this and analyze pulse diagnosis data from a TCM doctor and a pulse diagnostic instrument (PDI) by Random Forest. Subjects' vital signs and pulse diagnosis data from a TCM doctor are used as training data. We classify vital signs which have the PDI's diagnoses labels. As a result, classification accuracies were over 60% in all cases. Our experiment results imply that better pulse diagnosis may be made with assistance of personal health data analysis.

Keywords: Health data analysis · Pulse diagnosis · Random Forest

1 Introduction

In Traditional Chinese Medicine (TCM), doctors touch a patient's wrist and diagnose his/her health conditions, which is called pulse diagnosis. It requires special training and expertise. Therefore, it is difficult to perform the diagnosis at home on a daily basis. Furthermore, it is not clear that what kinds of biological features relate with the diagnosis. By clarifying the relationship between the pulse diagnosis and personal health data, it can be helpful for health management.

In this study, we analyze pulse diagnosis data with personal health data, such as blood pressure and heart rate. In order to analyze these data, we use two kinds of diagnosis data: from a TCM doctor and from a pulse diagnostic instrument (PDI). Using vital signs which have diagnosis labels by the TCM doctor, we classify vital signs which have the PDI's diagnosis labels. In order to classify data, we adopt Random Forest method. The goal of this study is to investigate whether pulse diagnosis can be made with assistance of personal health data analysis.

This work is partly supported by 2016–2018 Masaru Ibuka Foundation Research Project on Oriental Medicine.

© Springer Nature Switzerland AG 2019
K. Kojima et al. (Eds.): JSAI-isAI 2018 Workshops, LNAI 11717, pp. 74–80, 2019.
https://doi.org/10.1007/978-3-030-31605-1_6

2 Related Work

2.1 Pulse Diagnosis

For pulse diagnosis, many studies focus on developing systems, sensors, and devices.

Grif and Ayush [1] proposed an expert system based on a Bayesian network to analyze pulse data. Their system was used for training and research purposes at higher education institutions. Duraisamy et al. [2] presented a system for performing pulse diagnosis with expertise and infrared sensors. Gong et al. [3] presented a wrist–pulse sensing system using k–nearest neighbor algorithm and verified the accuracy of detecting cirrhosis subjects. As a result, they showed that their system could detect cirrhosis subjects with an accuracy of 87%.

Yang et al. [4] developed a device for pulse diagnosis by microwave sensors. The device showed the possibility of performing pulse diagnosis in non–contact. Peng and Lu [5] developed a flexible capacitive tactile sensor for real–time pulse measurement. They miniaturized the device by integrating sensors and circuits. McLellan et al. [6] developed a device embedded three solenoids to simulate pulse diagnosis.

2.2 Random Forest

Random Forest is a kind of machine learning method [7] and used for classification. In the field of medicine and health research, this method is mainly used for detecting disease data.

Saiprasad et al. [8] used Random Forest for identifying an adrenal abnormality. Machado et al. [9] adopted Random Forest for detecting factors related with bovine viral diarrhea virus. They mentioned that this method is effective for cross–sectional studies in veterinary epidemiology and should be considered as an alternative to traditional statistical methods. Boucekine et al. [10] verified whether Random Forest is effective for potential response shift related with quality of life or not. Their results showed that the method was useful for response shift detection.

2.3 Position of This Study

As mentioned above, many devices and systems are developed for pulse diagnosis. Although some studies focus on analyzing pulse data, the relationship between pulse diagnosis and personal health data is not clear. By clarifying the relationship between the diagnosis result and personal health data analysis, it is possible to develop devices and systems with higher accuracy and effectiveness.

3 Analysis of Pulse Diagnosis Data by Random Forest

3.1 Overview of Our Approach

Figure 1 shows an overview of our approach. The approach consists of two steps: the training step and the analyzing step.

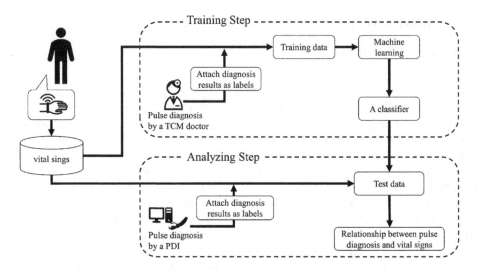

Fig. 1. Overview of our approach

1. **Training Step.** In this step, an individual's vital signs and pulse diagnosis data are collected. Vital signs are routinely acquired by wearable devices or IoT systems. The diagnosis is performed by a TCM doctor, and diagnosis result is attached to vital signs as labels. The data is used for training in machine learning, and a classifier is constructed.
2. **Analyzing Step.** In this step, an analysis for pulse diagnosis based on personal health data is performed by the classifier constructed in the training step. As test data, vital signs which have diagnosis labels given by a PDI are used. Using the classifier, the analysis is performed based on personal health data.

3.2   Data Acquisition and Preprocessing

We collected vital signs as personal health data once a day from six elderly people. In order to record vital signs, we used a wearable device[1]. Collected vital signs were systolic blood pressure, diastolic blood pressure, respiratory rate, and heart rate. The data acquisition period was from October 1, 2017 to January 31, 2018.

In this period, pulse diagnoses were performed by a TCM doctor and by a PDI[2]. The doctor diagnosed subjects at the beginning and end of the period. The PDI diagnosed subjects every two weeks.

---

[1] 37 degree bracelet, 37 Degree Technology, http://www.37c.cc/en/index.html.
[2] DS01-C Information Collection System of Pulse Condition Diagnosis (Shanghai FDA Food and Drug Administration No. 20152270429), Daosh Medical Technology Co., Ltd., http://www.daosh.com/en/.

After collecting these data, we attached labels to vital signs using pulse diagnosis data from the doctor. In this experiment, eleven categories of health conditions and physical status were given by pulse diagnosis. Therefore, we attached A–K labels, respectively. We assumed that the category result of the diagnosis was valid for five days from the day when pulse diagnosis was made.

3.3 Data Analysis by Random Forest

Random Forest is a machine learning method based on ensemble learning using multiple decision trees. In order to apply Random Forest, we prepared both the training data and test data. As the training data, we selected records which had diagnostic labels based on the TCM doctor's diagnosis. The number of training records is 21 per person. As the test data, we selected records which had only one diagnostic label given by the PDI. The number of test records is 11 per person.

In the pulse diagnosis, there is a case where a person is diagnosed with multiple categories. Therefore, some training records have multiple labels. However, in Random Forest, records with multiple labels cannot be used for the training data as it is. There are several ways to overcome this problem [11], and we adopt a method called dubbed copy–weight. In this method, $n - 1$ records are made by copying the original one (n is the number of labels). Each copied record has a single label. When we train Random Forest, these records' weights are set to $1/n$.

4 Analysis Result and Discussion

We verify the classification accuracy for each person. Furthermore, we integrate training data and test data for each gender separately and verify the classification accuracy.

The classification accuracy CA is defined as follows.

$$CA = N_{matched} \, / \, N_{total} \tag{1}$$

where N_{total} represents the total number of test data classified based on the TCM doctor's diagnosis. $N_{matched}$ represents the number of test data from which the diagnosis by the PDI matched the classification result.

The classification result is shown in Table 1. The classification accuracies were over 60% in all cases, varying from 64% to 100%. The accuracy was 64% for males, while it was 91% for females. The classification using the TCM doctor's diagnoses as training data had a similar tendency to the diagnoses by the PDI. It implies that vital signs and pulse diagnosis may have a certain relationship and the accuracy of pulse diagnosis by the PDI may be improved with assistance of personal health data analysis. Moreover, even when data was integrated for each gender, the classification accuracy did not decrease.

However, since the number of training and test data was small, it was not able to classify test data with multiple labels. Therefore, we will further improve

Table 1. Classifying result by Random Forest

Subject	Sex	Age	Labels in training data	Test data label	Accuracy (%)
No. 1	Male	69	A,B,C	A	100
No. 2	Male	73	D,E,F,G	D	100
No. 3	Male	66	A,D,H	A	64
No. 4	Female	70	D,I,J	D	91
No. 5	Female	65	D,J,K	J	82
No. 6	Female	68	D,I	D	100
Males	–	–	A,B,C,D,E,F,G,H	A or D	64
Females	–	–	D,I,J,K	J or D	91

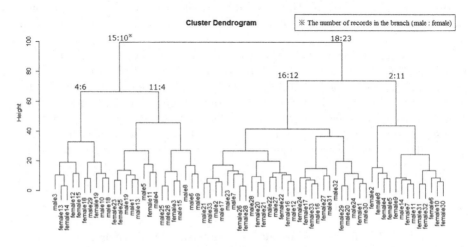

Fig. 2. Result of hierarchical cluster analysis

our approach for classifying these data. In addition, we will improve classification accuracy by increasing diagnosis data, especially these data from a TCM doctor.

In this analysis, the case for females had a higher classification accuracy than males. Based on the result, we further analyzed our data and tried to clarify whether integrating data for each gender is effective. If females' records have more similarity with each other than males' records, their records should be classified in the same or near cluster. In order to carry out the cluster analysis, we used the males' and females' test data. We attached labels as "male/female + record number" for each record, and created hierarchical clusters using four parameters: systolic blood pressure, diastolic blood pressure, respiratory rate, and heart rate. In the hierarchical cluster analysis, there are several methods to calculate a distance between each record. In this analysis, we adopted Ward's method which is a typical method [12].

Figure 2 shows the results of the hierarchical cluster analysis. In the second hierarchy, for the second branch from the left there are more records of males than that of females, and for the fourth branch there are more records of females than that of males. This result shows the possibility that these data have similar features for each gender. However, for the first branch, the difference was small. Therefore, further improvements and investigations are needed.

5 Conclusion

In this study, we analyzed pulse diagnosis data from a TCM doctor and a pulse diagnostic instrument (PDI). As a result, the classification based on vital signs and the doctor's diagnosis has a similar tendency with the PDI's diagnosis. It indicates that vital signs and diagnosis result are related and PDI may do better pulse diagnosis assisted by personal health data analysis. Furthermore, it showed the possibility that vital signs of males and females have similar features, separately.

For our future work, we will classify test data with multiple labels by improving our approach. Moreover, we will analyze pulse diagnosis based on a larger data set, apply other machine learning methods, and verify the experiment by statistical methods.

References

1. Grif, M., Ayush, Y.: Data analysis of expert systems by pulse diagnosis. In: Proceedings of the 11th International Forum on Strategic Technology (IFOST), Novosibirsk, Russia, pp. 329–332. IEEE (2016)
2. Duraisamy, R., Dinakar, S., Venkittaramanujam, V., Jeyakumar, V.: A systematic approach for pulse diagnosis based on siddha medical procedures. In: Proceedings of the 4th International Conference on Signal Processing, Communications and Netwotrking (ICSCN), Chennai, India, pp. 1–6. IEEE (2017)
3. Gong, S., Xu, B., Sun, G., Chen, M., Wang, N., Dong, C., Wang, P., Cui, J.: Accurate Cirrhosis identification with wrist-pulse data for mobile healthcare. In: Proceedings of the 2nd ACM Workshop on Mobile Systems, Applications, and Services for HealthCare, Toronto, Canada, pp. 1–6. ACM (2012)
4. Yang, C.L., Chang, T.C., Chen, Y.Y.: Microwave sensors applying for traditional Chinese medicine pulse diagnosis. In: Proceedings of the 8th International Workshop on Electromagnetics: Applications and Student Innovation Competition, London, UK, pp. 113–115. IEEE (2017)
5. Peng, J.Y., Lu, M.S.-C.: A flexible capacitive tactile sensor array with CMOS readout circuits for pulse diagnosis. IEEE Sens. J. **15**(2), 1170–1177 (2015)
6. McLellan, S., et al.: A microprocessor-based wrist pulse simulator for pulse diagnosis in traditional Chinese medicine. In: 40th IEEE Annual Northeast Bioengineering Conference (NEBEC), Boston, USA, pp. 1–2. IEEE (2014)
7. Breiman, L.: Random forests. Mach. Learn. **45**(1), 5–32 (2001)
8. Saiprasad, G., Chang, C.I., Safdar, N., Saenz, N., Siegel, E.: Adrenal gland abnormality detection using random forest classification. J. Digit. Imaging **26**(5), 891–897 (2013)
9. Machado, G., Mendoza, M.R., Corbellini, L.G.: What variables are important in predicting bovine viral diarrhea virus? A random forest approach. Vet. Res. **46**(85), 1–15 (2015)

10. Boucekine, M.: Using the random forest method to detect a response shift in the quality of life of multiple sclerosis patients: a cohort study. BMC Med. Res. Methodol. **13**(20), 1–8 (2013)
11. Tsoumakas, G., Katakis, I., Vlahavas, I.: Mining multi-label data. In: Maimon, O., Rokach, L. (eds.) Data Mining and Knowledge Discovery Handbook, pp. 667–685. Springer, Boston (2010). https://doi.org/10.1007/978-0-387-09823-4_34
12. Ward, J.R.: Hierarchical grouping to optimize an objective function. J. Am. Stat. Assoc. **58**(301), 236–244 (1963)

A Vision Sensor Network to Study Viewers' Visible Behavior of Art Appreciation

Yilang Wu[1]($\boxtimes$), Luyi Huang[1], Zhongyu Wei[2], and Zixue Cheng[1]

[1] University of Aizu, Aizu-wakamatsu, Fukushima, Japan
y-wu@ieee.org, {d8201103,z-cheng}@u-aizu.ac.jp
[2] Fudan University, Shanghai, China
zywei@fudan.edu.cn

Abstract. Since the empathic processes are essential to the aesthetic experience, the empathy-enabling technology for behavioral sensing is gaining its popularity to support the study of anonymized viewers' cognition in art appreciation. Because such behavior is highly dynamic and divergent among viewers, it is a challenge to observe the multiple dynamic features from the streaming data. In this study, we propose a vision sensor network (VSN) to support the visual interpretation of viewers' appreciation on visual arts. It firstly annotates the features in the captured frames based on CloudAPI (here the Google Cloud Vision API is used), and secondly the query on nested documents in MongoDB provides universal access to the annotated features. Comparing with the traditional approaches with subjective evidence, such as the questionnaire or social listening methods, the proposed VSN can interpret the visible behavior of viewers in real-time. In addition, it also has less selective bias because of more objective evidence being captured.

Keywords: Aesthetic empathy · Vision Sensor Network · Google Cloud Vision API · Real-time image annotation · Query on nested documents

1 Introduction

With the increasing number of travelers all over the world year by year, the study on the dynamic and interactive nature of tourist experiences [1] is gaining its importance, either from the perspectives of marketing, psychology, sociology or edutainment. The art appreciation experience is part of tourist experiences, and the expositions of visual arts or live show also attracts many visitors. The study on viewers' aesthetic appreciation is important as well to improve the quality of tourist experience. Such study requires the modeling from multiple perspectives and empirical data to complete the research [2]. It is challenging to model the dynamics and interactive nature of art appreciation experience, and collect and analyze the empirical data to support and utilize the model.

© Springer Nature Switzerland AG 2019
K. Kojima et al. (Eds.): JSAI-isAI 2018 Workshops, LNAI 11717, pp. 81–89, 2019.
https://doi.org/10.1007/978-3-030-31605-1_7

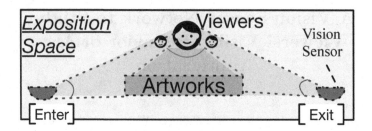

Fig. 1. Application scenario by Using Vision Sensor Network

Based on the assumption that visual arts are influential to the viewers' visible behavior, here we develop a vision sensor network (VSN) to observe and analyze viewers' visible behavior in real-time. Figure 1 shows the application scenario of deploying the VSN in an exposition space, such as a room in museum, and capturing the time-series of viewers' visible behavior. An ethical approval was not required since the study did not involve any risk or discomfort for the participants.

The rest part of this paper is organized as follows. Section 2 reviews the related work on the study of tourist experience, and focuses on the art appreciation experience in exposition. Section 3.1 introduces the implementation of real-time features annotation to the frames captured by VSN based on *CloudAPI* (here the Google Cloud Vision API, but not limit to this option [3]). In order to provide a universal access to the annotated features, Sect. 3.2 introduces the API implementation to query on nested documents (here the documents are in JSON format). As a proof of concept, Sect. 4 describes the setup of the prototype system for experimental art exposition, including the specification of the networked system and demonstration interface. And Sect. 5 summarizes the current progress and plan of future work.

2   Related Work

Since the visual arts or the live show are commonly held through exposition events, viewers' art appreciation experience can also be considered as part of the tourist experiences. Larsen [2] suggests that interactions between tourists and travel systems includes three factors in stages (expectations before the trip, perceptions during the trip, and memories after the trip), which creates the tourist experience, and may even influence other tourists' expectations. Figure 2 outlines the three factors in stages, and the related empirical data. Here we review the related study based on different empirical data collections.

Data Collection Based on Questionnaire. The questionnaire has been widely used to mainly collect volunteers' memorized experience. Sheng and Chen in [4] propose the factor and narrative analysis based on questionnaire development

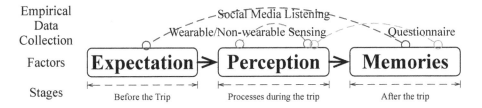

Fig. 2. Stages [2] of tourist experience and the related empirical data

and narrative text classification. However, the information collected by questionnaire is mostly subjective, and the sampling of volunteers are highly depending on their willingness of taking the questionnaire.

Data Collection Based on Social Listening. The online social media/networking services now connect people world wide into big social graph. Because the information could be quickly and widely spread over the social graph, the social sensing [5] is nowadays a new approach to understand the socio-economic environment. However, the social listening is facing the challenge of collecting the targeted object-related information from the big data of social stream, and extract the features from the ambiguous narration about the targeted object.

Data Collection Based on Wearable/Non-wearable Sensor. With the rise of empathy-enabling technology, the wearables such as fEMG and SCR have been successfully used to observe viewer's aesthetic empathy [6]. The wearable sensor is less practical to be deployed on many volunteers for the purpose of large scale data collection.

On the contrary, the non-wearable sensing technology, for example the passive sensing based on Wi-Fi signal sensor or active sensing based on TF transceiver introduced in [7], is more practical for deployment. The vision sensing or image retrieval [8] technology also a low cost and simply deployable approach.

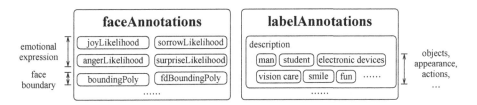

Fig. 3. Example labels in google could vision (https://cloud.google.com/vision/docs/)

In this study, we developed a sensor network to annotate the features that are related with art appreciation behavior by using the *CloudAPI*. Figure 3 shows the example labels, including the *faceAnnotations* about emotional expression and face boundary, and the *labelAnnotations* about object, appearance, and actions. A major goal of developing this system is to support the investigation on the co-occurrence between viewers' aesthetic empathy (e.g., being interested in the artworks) and the annotated labels on the captured image.

3 System Design and Implementation

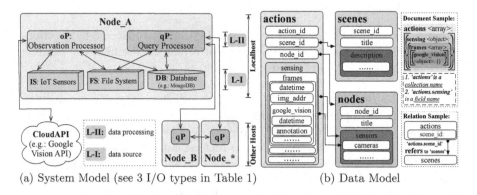

(a) System Model (see 3 I/O types in Table 1)   (b) Data Model

Fig. 4. Cross-platform system design for the Vision Sensor Network

Our current work focus on the stage of system implementation of the VSN. Figure 4 illustrates the cross-platform system design, including the system model (in Fig. 4(a)) and data model (in Fig. 4(b)). It is is advanced for its real-time image annotation (in Sect. 3.1) and query on nested documents (in Sect. 3.2).

Based on the IoT framework design, every node in the VSN is an independent Web host. Every single node is a localhost to itself, and it communicate with other hosts (other nodes in VSN or cloud servers that is hosting the *CloudAPI*) through Web socket. All nodes are designed in same architecture, taking the $node_A$ for example, there are two system layers, including the data source (L-I) and data processing (L-II). The data source components include the IoT sensors (IS) data collection, file system (FS) for storing file items, and database (DB) for storing data items. In every node of the proposed system, the vision sensor like a *Webcam* is used by IS, and the NoSQL database such as the MongoDB (https://www.mongodb.com) is used by DB. The components are implemented based on Node.js (https://nodejs.org), and their inter-communication is based on three types of I/O operations (database, disk, and Web socket in Table 1).

There are three collections in the current data model (Fig. 4(b)), named as *nodes*, *scenes*, and *actions*. Each collection is an array of data items (or instance). A *nodes*'s instance records the Web host specification of every nodes, including the field information about *Webcam*, *CloudAPI* and network configuration. A *scenes*'s instance records the field information about the set-up of the exposition space, which further descries the included artworks. A *actions*'s instance records

Table 1. Three types of IO operation among components in nodes

Communication	Node.js Modules	I/O among Components of $node_A$, $node_B$, and $node_*$	
Database I/O	'mongodb'	$node_A.oP \leftrightarrow node_A.DB$	$node_A.qP \leftrightarrow node_A.DB$
Disk I/O	'fs': File System	$node_A.oP \leftrightarrow node_A.FS$	$node_A.qP \leftrightarrow node_A.FS$
Web Socket I/O	'ws': Web Socket	$node_A.oP \leftrightarrow node_A.IS$	$node_A.qP \leftrightarrow CloudAPI$
		$node_A.qP \leftrightarrow node_B.qP$	$node_A.qP \leftrightarrow node_*.qP$

viewers' visible behavior that might be the objective reaction to *scene*, and its field information includes the image annotation output by a *nodes*'s instance based on *CloudAPI*.

3.1 Observation Processor: Real-Time Image Annotation

The observation processor (oP) automates the pipeline of image annotation, and prevent the bottleneck in pipeline for near real-time processing. The *Node.js* module '*@google-cloud/vision*' (https://cloud.google.com/vision/) and the library of *OpenCV* are integrated to oP to handle the images (in *Base64* format) that are chronologically captured by *Webcam*. To prevent the bottleneck caused by *CloudAPI* recall, the oP firstly limits the frequency ($1fps \leq feq_{frame} \leq Mfps$) of recalling *CloudAPI*. Under the frequency constrain, it secondly select the typical frame that is dissimilar with the previously selected frames.

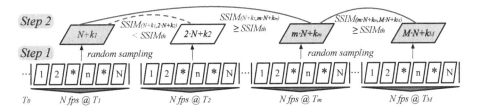

Fig. 5. Random sampling and SSIM measurement to select typical frames

Figure 5 shows the two steps of random sampling and structured similarity (SSIM) [9] measurement to select the typical frames. Step 1 randomly select M frames from the $M \cdot N$ frames that are generated from second T_1 to second T_M. Then in Step 2, given the first randomly selected frame $frame_{(N+k_1)}$ as a typical frame, $frame_{(m \cdot N+k_m)}$ is the second typical frame of which $frame_{(N+k_1, m \cdot N+k_m)}$ is detected to be above or equal to the threshold $SSIM_{th}$. If $m \geq M$, which exceeds the frequency constrain, and let $m' = arg(max(SSIM_{(N+k_1, m' \cdot N+k_{m'})}))$, then $frame_{(m' \cdot N+k_{m'})}$ will be the second typical frame. Recursively, the SSIM measure will be applied on the second typical frame to select the third one.

3.2   Query Processor: Query by Mapping Multiple Values to Multi-nested Fields

The query processor (qP) supports the query based on MongoDB by mapping the multiple values to multi-nested fields. The study on the censored behavior of viewers requires a universal data access to the annotated features that have been recorded in the collection 'actions'. However, the fields are organized in a highly nested structure (as shown in the document-oriented data model in Fig. 4(b)). It is difficult for MongoDB user to map multiple values to multi-nested fields by using the NoSQL syntax directly. Therefore, here we build an HTTP API that accepts the simple structured query input that have only a list of parameters, and the API then automatically construct NoSQL query to retrieve documents that are organized in nested structure.

Fig. 6. API sample: query by mapping multiple values to multi-nested fields

Figure 6 is a sample of recalling the query API. The array of parameters includes: (1) the HTTPS protocol in use, (2) the Web host with the address of [IP:Port] locates the query API service, (3) the query function identity, (4) the collection name, and (5) the parameters to map multiple values to multi-nested fields. Here the *find* function returns the filtered data items, the *aggregate* function returns the statistics of the filtered data items. This query example will return the statistical result of *'actions'* that are within a time interval and having the filed of *joyLikelihood* to be the value of 'UNLIKELY' or 'VERY_UNLIKELY'. The API simplifies the query composition, and provide a universal data access to the annotated features.

4   System Specification and Demonstration

As a proof of concept, we setup an exposition space for experiment (as shown in Fig. 7(a)) by using the prototype system implemented in Sect. 3. The a wooden screen, which is movable, is used to fix the painting artworks in a designed layout, and the USB LED lamps are fixed on the top of the screen to light up the artworks. There is a bounded region for the volunteers to step into, and freely view the artworks on the screen. A networked vision sensor is placed in the middle of the screen, either on the top or on the bottom, but has to be able to capture the visible behavior of viewers. An ethical approval was not required since the study did not involve any risk or discomfort for the participants. And to bring the viewers a real experience of art appreciation, a series of water color paintings [10] are used in this exposition setup.

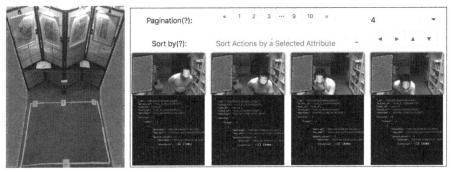

(a) Setup of Exposition Space for Experiment (b) Query Interface to Review the Captured Frames and Annotated Features of Viewers' Visible Behavior in Art Appreciation

Fig. 7. Prototype system to study viewers' visible behavior of art appreciation

Figure 7(b) demonstrates the query interface for researchers to review the capture frames and the annotated features. The four frame images shows a chronological sequence of viewer's visible behavior when he was looking at the paintings on the screen (in 7(a)). Some content in the images was blocked with privacy concern. Under each image, there is a nested-document reader for

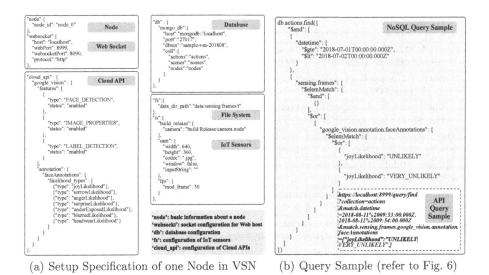

(a) Setup Specification of one Node in VSN (b) Query Sample (refer to Fig. 6)

Fig. 8. Prototype system specification and query sample

researcher to inspect the annotated features about the visible behavior the image. There are also external functions such as pagination and sorting in the query interface.

Figure 8(a) shows the setup specification of a single node in the proposed VSN system. Port 8999 is used to serve the query API, and port 8090 is used to stream the frames of captured images. The system is currently using Google Cloud Vision API, and only part of the features are targeted, mainly the 'FACE_DETECTION' (or 'fafceAnnotations'). The configuration of database, file directory, and camera is also specified in the rest blocks in Fig. 8(a). And Fig. 8(b) on the right shows the NoSQL query sentence output by the system based on the API-based query sample defined in Fig. 6. The API can greatly simplify query composition. Since the visible behavior is captured, annotated, and saved into database in real-time, the research can use the query interface to take real-time observation.

5   Summary and Future Work

In this work, we built a prototype Vision Sensor Network to study viewers' visible behavior in the scenario of art appreciation. The system is advanced for its functions of real-time image annotation and API-based query on nested documents. It can provide an automatic and scalable approach to study crowd's visible behaviors. As a future work, we plan to enhance the statistical analysis and visualization to detect the behavioral patterns; and to extend the current experiment scope by deploying the system in museums based on ethnic approval.

References

1. Ek, R., Larsen, J., Hornskov, S.B., Mansfeldt, O.K.: A dynamic framework of tourist experiences: space-time and performances in the experience economy. Scand. J. Hosp. Tour. **8**(2), 122–140 (2008)
2. Larsen, S.: Aspects of a psychology of the tourist experience. Scand. J. Hosp. Tour. **7**(1), 7–18 (2007)
3. Montelongo, S.: Comparing image tagging services: Google Vision, Microsoft Cognitive Services, Amazon Rekognition and Clarifai. https://www.reaktor.com/blog/the-rise-of-empathy-enabling-technology/. Accessed 15 May 2018
4. Sheng, C.-W., Chen, M.-C.: Tourist experience expectations: questionnaire development and text narrative analysis. Int. J. Cult. Touri. Hosp. Res. **7**(1), 93–104 (2013)
5. Liu, Y., et al.: Social sensing: a new approach to understanding our socioeconomic environments. Ann. Assoc. Am. Geogr. **105**(3), 512–530 (2015)
6. Gernot, G., Pelowski, M., Leder, H.: Empathy, einfühlung, and aesthetic experience: the effect of emotion contagion on appreciation of representational and abstract art using fEMG and SCR. Cogn. Process. **19**(2), 147–165 (2018)
7. Mokhtari, G., Bashi, N., Zhang, Q., Nourbakhsh, G.: Non-wearable human identification sensors for smart home environment: a review. Sens. Rev. **38**(3), 391–404 (2018)

8. Datta, R., Joshi, D., Li, J., Wang, J.Z.: Image retrieval: Ideas, influences, and trends of the new age. ACM Comput. Surv. (Csur) **40**(2), 5 (2008)
9. Bartra, O.: JavaScript Image Comparison. https://github.com/obartra/ssim. Accessed 15 Aug 2018
10. Huang, L.: Water Color Paintings of Mr. Cat Petter and His Cat Friends. http://cms.huangluyi.com/cn/?p=240. Accessed 05 Aug 2018

Multi-View Learning of Network Embedding

Zhongming Han[1,2](✉), Chenye Zheng[2], Dan Liu[2], Dagao Duan[1,2],
and Weijie Yang[2]

[1] Beijing Key Laboratory of Food Safety Big Data Technology, Beijing, China
Webir@163.com
[2] Beijing Technology and Business University,
No. 11 Fucheng Road, Haidian District, Beijing, China

Abstract. In recent years, network representation learning on complex information networks attracts more and more attention. Scholars usually use matrix factorization or deep learning methods to learn network representation automatically. However, existing methods only preserve single feature of networks. How to effectively integrate multiple features of network is a challenge. To tackle this challenge, we propose an unsupervised learning algorithm named Multi-View Learning of Network Embedding. The algorithm preserves multiple features that including vertex attribute, network global and local topology structure. Features are treated as network views. We use a variant of convolutional neural networks to learn features from these views. The algorithm maximizes the correlation between different views by canonical correlation analysis, and learns the embedding that preserve multiple features of networks. Comprehensive experiments are conducted on five real networks. We demonstrate that our method can better preserve multiple features and outperform baseline algorithms in community detection, network reconstruction and visualization.

Keywords: Network representation learning · Multi-view fusion ·
Convolutional neural networks · Canonical Correlation Analysis

1 Introduction

Large-scale information networks are common information carriers in real world. Mining knowledge from complex information networks can help people to understand network structure [1] or information dissemination patterns [2]. Network representation learning (NRL) [3] is a basic issue in network mining area which mainly studies how to map features of vertex in a network to a low-dimensional, continuous real-valued embedding, and the process of mapping is not only try to preserve the structural feature s, but also try to preserve the properties of the vertex. Embedding learned by NRL can be used as input feature for machine learning methods, and has important applications in the real world, such as network visualization [5], network reconfiguration [4, 6], community detection [7], link prediction [8], etc.

The traditional NRL method is similar to dimensionality reduction, such as Graph Factorization (GF) [9], Local Linear Embedding (LLE) [10] Large-scale Information Network Embedding (LINE) [11] and HOPE algorithm [12], etc. These methods use

K. Kojima et al. (Eds.): JSAI-isAI 2018 Workshops, LNAI 11717, pp. 90–98, 2019.
https://doi.org/10.1007/978-3-030-31605-1_8

single matrix to present the similarity graph structure of networks, and obtain low-dimensional embedding for networks by factorize this matrix. Matrix Factorization based Methods is unstable and incomplete because they have strong dependence on constructing single feature matrix. Our task selects multiple features from networks, and design an unsupervised fusion algorithm based on deep neural networks.

2 Related Work

With the advent of the era of big data, deep learning (DL) technology are developing rapidly. DL can discover complex structures in big data via multiple processing layers. DL brings significant results in many areas, such as computer vision, language modeling, etc. In recent years, scholars have done a lot of research on applying DL models to represent graphs or networks. Deepwalk [13] and node2vec [14] use random walk to generate sequence of nodes and adopt an unsupervised neural language model (Skip-Gram) [15] for networks embedding. SDNE [5] uses an unsupervised deep self-encoder to model the second-order proximity, the hidden layer of the deep self-encoder is the embedding of networks. In addition, convolutional neural networks (CNN) and its variants have been widely adopted in representation learning. PATCHY-SAN [16] selects fixed-length node sequence to assemble the neighborhood of nodes and directly use the original CNN model designed for Euclidean domains. GCN [17] defines the convolution in the spectral domain, and constructs a semi-supervised model for node classification task. However, networks usually contains multiple types of information, such as node attribute information, structure information, text information, etc. Existing method is incomplete because it only learns single types of information. In addition, existing method lack universality because each representation learning model is designed with a specific optimization goals.

Unlike previous approaches, we propose an unsupervised learning algorithm named multi-view of network embedding, also known as MVNE. MVNE uses multiple vertex attribute (text information, geographic location, user tags, etc.), network global topology, and local topology features as input features, and they are treated as network views. The views express the characteristics of different aspects of the network. We consider multiple localized first-order approximation spectral graph convolutions to extract features from views, and fuse features by analyzing correlation between them. The model can be applied to various network tasks because it learns representations in a fully unsupervised setting.

3 Multi-View Learning of Network Embedding

3.1 A Subsection Sample

We define a network $G = (V, E)$, $V = \{v_1, \ldots, v_i, \ldots, v_N\}$ is the collection of network vertices, where N is the number of vertices. E is the collection of network edges. $e_{ij} = (v_i, v_j) \in E$ represents an edge between v_i and v_j. A is the adjacency matrix. If there is an edge between v_i and v_j, then $A_{ij} = 1$, otherwise $A_{ij} = 0$. The vertices feature matrix X corresponding to G is a highly sparse matrix. Dimension of X is usually expressed as $|V| \times m$, where m is the feature space size of the attribute. Vertices usually have multiple attributes, such as geographic location, age, hobbies, etc. Let $Attr = \{X_1, \ldots, X_p\}$ denote the feature matrices set of network G which are treated as views of networks. In this paper, we assume that the input to our algorithm is an undirected network G and its feature matrices $Attr$. The goal of our algorithm is mapping each vertex to a low-dimensional vector $z \in \mathbb{R}^d$ by fusing the information contained in A and $Attr$, where $d \ll |V|$.

3.2 Feature Extraction Based on Graph Convolution

Convolutional neural networks (CNN) has achieved good results in areas. CNN can process Euclidean data (e.g. image data) efficiently. However, network data belongs to Graph-structured Data. In order to learn the features in Graph-structured Data, this paper use a variant of CNN which called spectral convolution to extract feature map from views in networks. The definition of spectral convolution is as shown in Eq. (1).

$$g_\theta * X = U g_\theta U^T X \tag{1}$$

$X \in \mathbb{R}^{|V| \times m}$ is a feature matrix, $g_\theta = \text{diag}(\theta)$ is a filter. Spectral convolution g_θ is generated by decomposing the normalized graph Laplacian matrix shown as Eq. (2).

$$L = I_N - D^{-\frac{1}{2}} A D^{-\frac{1}{2}} = U^T \Lambda U \tag{2}$$

D is the degree matrix, U is the matrix of eigenvectors of L, Λ is the diagonal matrix of eigenvalues of L. According to Eqs. (1) and (2), it can be seen that filter g_θ is a function of eigenvalues Λ. We can obtain the filter g_θ via the eigenvalue decomposition of L. However, in large-scale networks, eigenvalue decomposition of L is computationally expensive. So we use K^{th}-order Chebyshev polynomial to approximate $g_\theta(\Lambda)$ in Eq. (3).

$$g_{\theta'} * X = U g_{\theta'} U^T X = \sum_{k=0}^{K} \theta'_k T_k \left(U \tilde{\Lambda} U^T \right) X = \sum_{k=0}^{K} \theta'_k T_k \left(\tilde{L} \right) X \tag{3}$$

In Eq. (3), $\tilde{\Lambda} = \frac{2}{\lambda_{max}} \Lambda - I_N$, λ_{max} is the largest eigenvalue of L. $\theta' \in \mathbb{R}^K$ is a vector of Chebyshev coefficients. $T_k(\tilde{L}) = 2\tilde{L} T_{k-1}(\tilde{L}) - T_{k-2}(\tilde{L})$, with $T_0(\tilde{L}) = 1$ and $T_1(\tilde{L}) = \tilde{L}$. If $K = 2$ and $\lambda_{max} \approx 2$, we can obtain

$$g_{\theta'} * X \approx \theta'_0 X + \theta'_1 (L - I_N) X \approx \theta \left(\tilde{D}^{-\frac{1}{2}} \tilde{A} \tilde{D}^{-\frac{1}{2}} \right) X \tag{4}$$

where $\tilde{A} = A + I_N$, $\tilde{D}$ is the degree matrix of $\tilde{A}$. The equation has parameter $\theta = \theta'_0 = -\theta'_1$, and it is a matrix of filter parameters in graph convolution network. As an example, we use two-layer convolution network with different W to learn multiple views in networks. The graph convolution network can be expressed as follows:

$$z(\theta) = \text{ReLU}\left(\hat{A}\text{ReLU}\left(\hat{A}XW^0\right)W^1\right) \tag{5}$$

In Eq. (5), θ to denote the vector of all filter parameters W. $\hat{A} = \tilde{D}^{-\frac{1}{2}}\tilde{A}\tilde{D}^{-\frac{1}{2}}$ is a symmetric and sparse adjacency matrix which converges the weight information of the nodes in the first-order domain of the target node. $z(\theta)$ is the feature map learned from feature X. We will obtain multiple feature maps by multiple convolution operations. This process is shown in Fig. 1. We consider three views in network.

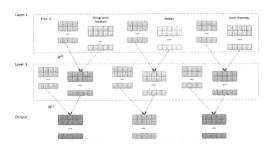

Fig. 1. A schematic of MVNE

3.3   MVNE Algorithm

Canonical Correlation Analysis (CCA) is used to mine complex relation mappings between two views $(X_1, X_2) \in \mathbb{R}^{n_1} \times \mathbb{R}^{n_2}$ by finding pairs of projections w_1, w_2 that are maximize the correlation between views. The goal of CCA is shown in Eq. (6), where Σ_{11} and Σ_{22} are covariance, Σ_{12} is cross-covariance.

$$\left(w_1^*, w_2^*\right) = \underset{w_1, w_2}{\text{argmax}}\, \text{corr}\left(w_1'X_1, w_2'X_2\right) = \underset{w_1, w_2}{\text{argmax}}\, \frac{w_1'\Sigma_{12}w_2}{\sqrt{w_1'\Sigma_{11}w_1 w_2'\Sigma_{22}w_2}} \tag{6}$$

Inspired by CCA, we fuse multi-view by finding a canonical coordinate space that maximizes correlations between the projections of views. We use $X = (x_1, x_2, \ldots, x_n) \in \mathbb{R}^{N \times m_x}$ and $Y = (y_1, y_2, \ldots, y_n) \in \mathbb{R}^{N \times m_y}$ obtained from network as an example to explain the principle of view fusion. m_x and m_y are dimensions of views. The goal of our task is learning the parameters θ in Eq. (7) for every network views, this is express as

$$\underset{\theta_1, \theta_2}{\text{argmax}}\, corr(z(X; \theta_1), z(Y; \theta_2)) \tag{7}$$

Let $Z_X = z(X; \theta_1)$ and $Z_y = z(Y; \theta_2)$ be the matrix produced by the graph convolutional layer on two views. $\Sigma_{xx} = Z_X Z_X' + r_1 I$, $\Sigma_{yy} = Z_Y Z_Y' + r_2 I$ are covariance matrices of (Z_X, Z_y), and $\Sigma_{xy} = \Sigma_{yx}' = Z_X Z_Y'$ is the cross-covariance matrices of (Z_X, Z_y). $r_1, r_2 > 0$ is the regularization constant to reduce over-fitting in training data.

We define $O = \Sigma_{xx}^{-\frac{1}{2}}\Sigma_{xy}\Sigma_{yy}^{-\frac{1}{2}}$ according to the objection in Eq. (6), then we use the traces of O to simplify the calculation of the objective function in Eq. (7)

$$\underset{\theta_1, \theta_2}{argmax} \, corr(Z_X, Z_Y) = max\, tr(O'O)^{1/2} \tag{8}$$

In order to find θ_1, θ_2 such that Eq. (8) is as high as possible, we calculate the gradient of $corr(Z_X, Z_Y)$ with respect to θ_1, θ_2, then use back propagation. Algorithm describes the multi-view fusing and embedding generation process.

Algorithm: MVNE

Input: Network $G = (V, E)$, feature views $Attr = \{X_1, ..., X_p\}$, weight matrices $W_i^k, k \in \{1 ... K\}, i \in \{1 ... p\}$
Output: node embedding
$GenerateFM(X_i)$
   $h_i = X_i$
   for $k = 1 ... K$ do:
      $h_i^k = \sigma(\widehat{A}h_i^{k-1}W_i^k)$
   $z_i = h_i^K$
   return z_i
$Z = GenerateFM(X_1)$
for $i \in \{2 ... p\}$ do:
   $z_i' = GenerateFM(X_i)$
   for e in range(epoch) do:
      $W_i^k = W_i^k - \alpha\frac{\partial}{\partial w_i^k}\{corr(Z, z_i') + \frac{\lambda}{2}\|W_i^k\|\}$
   $z_i = GenerateFM(X_i)$
   $Z = concat(Z, z_i)$

---

4   Experiments

4.1   Dataset

In order to evaluate the effectiveness of MVNE, we use community detection, network reconstruction and network visualization to evaluate different embedding generated by different methods. Table 1 gives a properties list of all real network in our experiment. We construct random walk matrix $X_R \in R^{|V| \times |V|}$ based on network to preserve local topology structure, and $X_{R_{ij}}$ denote the frequency of node v_j appearing in random walk sequence of node v_i. X_R can preserve node centrality and higher-order proximity between nodes. In addition, some networks in Table 1 contain rich information, such as region, hobbies, etc. We construct feature matrices base on attributes by one-hot coding, and use 5 layers MVNE to generate embedding.

Table 1. Experimental network basic properties.

Network	V	E	Average clustering coefficient	Label	External attribute
Karate	34	78	0.5706	√	√
Football	115	616	0.4032	√	√
Email	1133	5451	0.2202	×	×
Facebook	4039	88234	0.6005	√	√
Pokec	1632803	30622564	0.1094	×	√

4.2 Community Detection

Community detection is a basic task of network analysis. The interaction between nodes in same community is more frequent than the interaction among other communities in networks. We use K-means to classify and assign community label for every node base on embedding. Modularity can be used to evaluate the quality of community detection. Embedding with high modularity is high-quality. We report performance of eight models including our model. The result is shown in Table 2.

Table 2. Modularity result of community detection.

Model	Karate	Football	Email	Facebook	Pokec
GF	0.439	0.215	0.232	0.401	0.083
LLE	0.442	0.307	0.150	0.419	0.071
LINE	0.485	0.375	0.305	0.520	0.109
HOPE	0.497	0.412	0.320	0.546	0.103
Deepwalk	0.532	0.367	0.372	0.558	0.097
Node2vec	0.593	0.390	0.496	0.602	0.115
GCN	0.569	0.448	0.641	0.654	0.196
MVNE	0.661	0.452	0.673	0.713	0.279

We can see that MVNE has higher modularity than other benchmark algorithms. The results show that the embedding learned by MVNE is more effective because it contains multiple network information.

4.3 Network Reconstruction

The purpose of network reconstruction is to rebuild the links between nodes based on similarity of node pairs. The similarity between nodes is evaluated by the distance of their embedding. The experiment randomly selects 20% node pairs from whole pairs as a sub-network sample. We take k pairs of nodes with the highest similarity as predicted links and calculate actual link ratio to evaluate the accuracy of network reconstruction. If node embedding is effective, the accuracy will be high.

Figure 2 shows the mean and standard deviation of corresponding accuracy. Accuracy of network reconstruction decreases with increasing of k value. MVNE achieves better network reconstruction with different k values. The reconstruction precision can reach about 80% while k = 2.

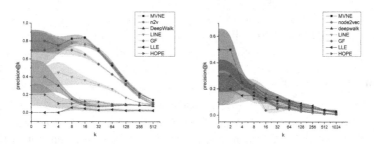

Fig. 2. Reconstruction accuracy of networks

4.4 Visualization

We can visualize embedding to make better understanding for topology and characteristics of networks intuitively. Embedding learned by different methods are different in the ability of visualization and interpretation. We compare visualization ability of embedding learned by different algorithms in Football network. Each algorithm learns 64-D embedding for nodes, and use t-SNE [4] to reduce dimension to 2-D. We color nodes to observe the basic community structure of networks. The results are shown in Fig. 3. Some nodes belonging to different communities are mixed up in HOPE, LINE and GF. The embedding generated by DeepWalk and Node2Vec can represent clear community structure, but there are still a few nodes belonging to different communities mixed. MVNE is more effective than other benchmark algorithms because nodes belonging to same communities are separated clearly.

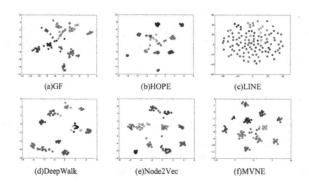

Fig. 3. Visualization of Football network

5 Future Work

In this paper, we propose a Multi-View Learning algorithm to generate embedding of networks. It fuses multiple features of networks by an unsupervised learning process. In the future, how to improve the learning efficiency of MVNE on large-scale network is a very important problem. In addition, introducing dynamic interaction information as a feature into NRL process is also worthwhile to study.

Acknowledgment. This work is supported by the National Natural Science Foundation of China (Grant No. 61170112), Beijing Natural Science Foundation (4172016), and the Scientific Research Project of Beijing Educational Committee (KM201710011006), and Key Lab of Information Network Security, Ministry of Public Security).

References

1. Zhao, D., Wang, L., Li, S., Wang, Z., et al.: Immunization of epidemics in multiplex networks. PLoS ONE **9**(11), e112018 (2014)
2. Cozzo, E., Banos, R.A., Meloni, S., et al.: Contact-based social contagion in multiplex networks. Phys. Rev. E **88**(5), 660–691 (2013)
3. Tan, S., Guan, Z., Cai, D., et al.: Mapping users across networks by manifold alignment on hypergraph. In: 28th AAAI Conference on Artificial Intelligence, vol. 1, pp. 159–165 (2014)
4. Maaten, L.v.d., Hinton, G.: Visualizing data using t-SNE. J. Mach. Learn. Res. **9**(11), 2579–2605 (2008)
5. Wang, D., Cui, P., Zhu, W.: Structural deep network embedding. In: 22nd ACM SIGKDD International Conference on Knowledge Discovery and Data Mining, pp. 1225–1234 (2016)
6. Ou, M., Cui, P., Pei, J., Zhang, Z., et al.: Asymmetric transitivity preserving graph embedding. In: 22nd International Conference on Knowledge Discovery and Data Mining, pp. 1105–1114 (2016)
7. Bhagat, S., Cormode, G., Muthukrishnan, S.: Node classification in social networks. In: Aggarwal, C. (ed.) Social Network Data Analytics, pp. 115–148. Springer, Boston (2011). https://doi.org/10.1007/978-1-4419-8462-3_5
8. Ahmed, A., Shervashidze, N., Narayanamurthy, S., et al.: Distributed large-scale natural graph factorization. In: 22nd International Conference on World Wide Web, pp. 37–48 (2013)
9. Roweis, S.T., Saul, L.K.: Nonlinear dimensionality reduction by locally linear embedding. Science **290**(5500), 2323–2326 (2000)
10. Tang, J., Qu, M., Wang, M., Zhang, M., Yan, J., Mei, Q.: LINE: large-scale information network embedding. In: Proceedings 24th International Conference on World Wide Web, pp. 1067–1077. ACM (2015)
11. Ou, M., Cui, P., Pei, J., Zhang, Z., Zhu, W.: Asymmetric transitivity preserving graph embedding. In: 22nd International Conference on Knowledge Discovery and Data Mining, pp. 1105–1114 (2016)
12. Perozzi, B., Al-Rfou, R., Skiena, S.: DeepWalk: online learning of social representations. In: 20th ACM SIGKDD International Conference on Knowledge Discovery and Data Mining, pp. 701–710. ACM (2014)

13. Grover, A., Leskovec, J.: node2vec: scalable feature learning for networks. In: 22nd ACM SIGKDD International Conference on Knowledge Discovery and Data Mining, pp. 855–864. ACM (2016)
14. Mikolov, T., Chen, K., Corrado, G., et al.: Efficient estimation of word representations in vector space. arXiv preprint arXiv:1301.3781 (2013)
15. Niepert, M., Ahmed, M., Kutzkov, K.: Learning convolutional neural networks for graphs. In: 33rd International Conference on Machine Learning, vol. 48, pp. 2014–2023 (2016)
16. Kipf, T.N., Welling, M.: Semi-supervised classification with graph convolutional networks. arXiv preprint arXiv:1609.02907 (2016)
17. Hardoon, D.R., Szedmak, S., Shawe-Taylor, J.: Canonical correlation analysis: an overview with application to learning methods. Neural Comput. **16**(12), 2639–2664 (2004)

JURISIN 2018

12th International Workshop on Juris-Informatics (JURISIN 2018)

Juris-informatics is a new research area which studies legal issues from the perspective of informatics. The purpose of the International Workshop on Jurisinformatics (JURISIN) is to discuss both the fundamental and practical issues among people from the various backgrounds such as law, social science, information and intelligent technology, logic and philosophy, including the conventional "AI and law" area. JURISIN 2018 was held in the International Symposia on AI by Japanese Society of Artificial Intelligence (JSAI-isAI). JURISIN 2018 is two-day workshop consisting of the ordinal JURISIN session and COLIEE session. COLIEE, held since 2015, stands for the Competition on Legal Information Extraction/Entailment, and consists of the following tasks:

1. The legal case retrieval task
2. The legal case entailment task
3. The statute law retrieval task
4. The legal question answering data corpus

We called for papers for both sessions, and each submitted paper was reviewed by three Program Committee members. As a result, 18 papers were selected for oral presentation. Furthermore, we invited two lectures: Harumichi Yuasa from the Institute of Information Security gave a lecture titled "Introducing Information Communication Technology into Civil Litigation in Japan" and Douglas Walton from the University of Windsor gave a lecture titled "Logical and Legal Relevance." After JURISIN 2018, according to comments of reviewers and discussion during the workshop, authors revised their papers and submitted them for the post proceedings. Each paper was reviewed again, and we selected eight excellent papers among which five papers were selected from the ordinal JURISIN session and three papers were from the COLIEE session. This volume includes these selected papers. I thank all the members of the Steering Committee, Advisory Committee, and Program Committee of JURISIN 2018, all authors who submitted papers, and all the members of Organizing Committee of JSAI-isAI.

April 2019   Katsumi Nitta

ContractFrames: Bridging the Gap Between Natural Language and Logics in Contract Law

María Navas-Loro[1]([✉]) [iD], Ken Satoh[2], and Víctor Rodríguez-Doncel[1] [iD]

[1] Ontology Engineering Group, Universidad Politécnica de Madrid, Madrid, Spain
{mnavas,vrodriguez}@fi.upm.es
[2] Principles of Informatics Research Division, National Institute of Informatics,
Tokyo, Japan
ksatoh@nii.ac.jp

Abstract. This paper introduces ContractFrames, a framework able to translate natural language texts referring to the different events related to the status of a purchase contract to logic clauses from a legal reasoning system called PROLEG. Diverse frames and rules have been developed for the extraction and storage of this event-centric information before its conversion to logic clauses. Our framework uses natural language tools and rules to extract relevant information, store it in the form of frames, and return the logic clauses of the input text. Also an ontology, called the Contract Workflow Ontology, has been developed to represent all the relevant information of the events related to a contract. The framework has been tested in a synthetic dataset, and showed promising results.

Keywords: Legal NLP · PROLEG · Contract life-cycle · Legal ontology

1 Introduction

Making machines to understand commercial contracts is a challenging and multidisciplinary task. Natural Language Processing (NLP) techniques are required to analyze different documents to extract relevant information, which can be expressed in significantly different formats and records. Once obtained, this information needs to be properly represented, via some knowledge representation system. In addition, reasoning methods are also required to extract new knowledge evaluating collected information.

This work was partially supported by JSPS KAKENHI Grant Number 17H06103 and by a project with funding from the European Union's Horizon 2020 research and innovation programme under grant agreement No. 780602. It has been also partially supported by a Predoctoral grant from the I+D+i program of the Universidad Politécnica de Madrid. This work has been done during an internship funded by the National Institute of Informatics.

K. Kojima et al. (Eds.): JSAI-isAI 2018 Workshops, LNAI 11717, pp. 101–114, 2019.
https://doi.org/10.1007/978-3-030-31605-1_9

Focusing on the legal domain, there exist different proposals for formalizing legal information in the form of logical predicates. We find among them PRO-LEG [26], a legal reasoning system able to represent and reason about contract status and derive information such as its validity or the right or reason of a rescission. Nevertheless, in spite of having all the contract law logic needed already coded, remains still open and important how to automatically transform the input text into logic facts. Currently, the translation of texts describing contract events must be manually coded, being therefore very inefficient in terms of cost and time, and remaining unsolved the fact that any ulterior change would need manual curation. A bridge between NLP and this logical system is therefore needed for automatic retrieval of all relevant facts from text to populate the PROLEG fact knowledge base.

In this paper, we propose a framework, called ContractFrames, able to translate natural language texts referring to the different status of a purchase contract into PROLEG clauses. These texts are not normative texts nor regular texts (being both types extensively studied in previous literature), but some natural language text at a mid point between regular language and pure legal language; an example of one of these texts can be found in Fig. 1, along with its translation into PROLEG. To the aim of expressing these texts in a full logical legal language, we have developed different frames[1] and rules for representing and extracting the relevant information that will feed the PROLEG reasoner. These resources are integrated into a natural language processing pipeline able to take a natural language text as an input and return its PROLEG version. Also an ontology, called the Contract Workflow Ontology, is proposed for representing the extracted information in a standard way.

'person A' bought this_real_estate from 'person B' at the price of 200000 dollars by contract0 on 1/January/2018. But 'person A' rescinded contract0 because 'person A' is a minor on 1/March/2018. However, this rescission was made because 'person B' threatened 'person A' on 1/February/2018. It is because 'person B' would like to sell this_real_estate to 'person C' in the higher price. So, 'person A' rescinded rescission of contract0 on 1/April/2018.

```
minor(personA).
agreement_of_purchase_contract(personA,personB,this_real_estate,200000,2018
    year 01 month 01 day,contract0).
manifestation_fact(rescission(contract0),personA,personB,2018 year 03 month 01 day).
fact_of_duress(personB,personA,rescission(contract0),2018 year 02 month 01 day).
manifestation_fact(rescission(rescission(contract0)),personA,personB,2018 year
    04 month 01 day).
```

Fig. 1. Example of an input text and its expected output.

The rest of this paper is as follows. Section 2 presents related work. Section 3 introduces problem and the reasoning system PROLEG, describing the clauses

---

[1] According to Minsky [19], a frame is *'a data-structure for representing a stereotyped situation'*.

on which the natural language will be translated. Section 4 analyses the main challenges. Section 5 presents how our framework tackles these problems, outlining the different steps and its main functionalities. Section 6 presents the outputs of our framework. Finally, Sect. 7 outlines the main points of our work along with some conclusions and next steps.

2 Related Work

Although the problem of extracting rules in the legal domain has been extensively tackled in literature [8,9,21,28], most efforts focus on regulations and normative text, but not on semi-formal documents dealing with the binding agreements.

The work by Biagioli et al. [3] includes for instance the idea of representing different types of provisions in normative texts as logical structures or frames; nevertheless, these frames output are XML files, not logical clauses, where each provision has some metadata arguments independent of other provisions. On the other hand, Araujo et al. [1] consider a series of legal events in Brazilian Portuguese. Using domain and linguistic knowledge, as well as ontologies, they develop rules for detecting these events via an OWL reasoner. Similarly, Wyner et al. [28] use different NLP tools and resources such as VerbNet [27] to extract events and some related roles from Regulations in English. Other approaches also use ontologies and resources such as WordNet [18] for obtaining semantic information about concepts of interest, such as *obligation, permission* and *prohibition* [8]. Although semantics is a common approach [1,8,15,28], it must be noted that not all proposals rely on NLP or semantics, such as the work by Moulin et al. [21]. Finally, the work by Nakamura et al. [22], later extended to deal with references [14], present a methodology to translate natural language Japanese law texts to logical forms following the Davidsonian Formalization.

The representation of contracts in a digital form has been made in many different forms for different purposes, but none of them matches well enough the representation of PROLEG clauses. The contract itself has been represented in different XML forms, from the well structured OASIS eContracts [16] format to the practical ebXML agreements or the RuleML based business rules [11]. Most efforts to represent the contract in a formal way lean towards defining deontic logic systems, such as Governatori's Business Contract Language intended to address contract violations [10], Daskalopulu's approach to tackle subjective visions on the contract [6] or Prisacariu's effort to consider temporal aspects [24]. However, not many efforts focus on the contract within a workflow, being among the most interesting the Kabilan's ontologies [13] and Molina's [20]. Kabilan identifies at least three perspectives under which a contract can be analyzed: the legal one, the business one, and the information systems one. From each of these perspectives, it is not trivial to abstract a common model for the representation of contracts and contract workflows. Commercial law is different from jurisdiction to jurisdiction, each organization has its own in-house business policies with respect to contract management and information systems are simply too diverse.

When it comes to representing contracts with the purpose of publishing and linking contract information, contract formats are even more scarce. LKIF [12] devotes a class to Contract[2], but provides no support to contract workflows. FrameNet [2] could be used to represent contracts to some extent (using elements such as *Documents*[3] or *Being_obligated*[4] in FrameNet), but these options do no reflect the information needed for the related PROLEG clauses. Similarly, the *Commerce_buy*[5] frame provides a lot of information on the context of the purchase, but does not consider the contract, focus of our research. The representation of contracts as RDF is not supported by any massively adopted ontology, and there are not many standards or public ontology-based specifications to choose from. One of the possible choices is the Media Contract Ontology [25], ISO standard to support the representation of contracts as RDF but nonetheless domain-specific.

Finally, the analysis of event processing and representation in the legal domain by Navas-Loro et al. [23] shows a overview of the different systems and representation options in previous literature.

3   The Problem

In this section, we will present the problem and introduce the frames developed for representing it, as well as the reasoning system PROLEG. Let us start analyzing the example exposed in Fig. 1.

In the input text, we find different events related to the status of the contract. First, the purchase is uttered via a contract; then, a rescission is claimed, adducing the fact that one of the parts was a minor. In the third sentence, a fact of duress (threatening) on one of the parts is issued. Additionally, the cause of the ending of the contract is expressed in the following sentence. Finally, in the last sentence the former rescission is rescinded, what makes the contract valid again. It must be noted that we are actually not interested in the information on the fourth sentence, since we just want information about the contract status and the 'real reasons' behind the fact of its rescission are not relevant, but just the fact of it being rescinded at some point of time. For modeling the relevant situations that can involve a contract, we developed three main frames, depicted in Fig. 2. The framework is also able to extract other relevant events to the system, such as if any of the parts involved in the contract is a minor, but most events are related to these three frames. Some examples of events involving these frames are for instance an agreement of a purchase contract, a manifestation of

---

[2] http://www.estrellaproject.org/lkif-core/norm.owl#Contract.

[3] https://framenet2.icsi.berkeley.edu/fnReports/data/frameIndex.xml?frame=Documents.

[4] https://framenet2.icsi.berkeley.edu/fnReports/data/frameIndex.xml?frame=Being_obligated.

[5] https://framenet2.icsi.berkeley.edu/fnReports/data/frameIndex.xml?frame=Commerce_buy.

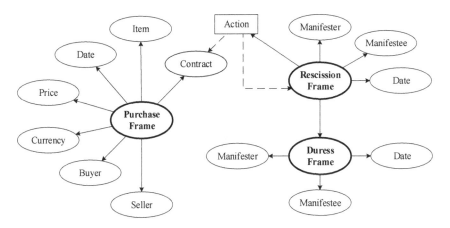

Fig. 2. The three different frames in the framework (Purchase, Rescission and Duress) and how they interact. An action can be a contract or a rescission, therefore a rescission can be of a contract or of another rescission. A duress is also necessarily attached to a rescission.

a rescission or the expression of a duress. The expected representation in PRO-LEG of the facts relevant to the contract status expressed in the example can be found in Fig. 1. With these facts and the contract law information encoded in its rule base (see Fig. 3), the PROLEG system would be able to derive legal consequences of each of the facts, leading to new conclusions such as if the buyer has the right of handling the goods purchased at some concrete point in time or if a contract or a rescission becomes invalid for some reason, such as the existence of duress or some legal incompatibility, such as one of the parts involved being a minor. The reasoning process is represented in Fig. 4.

```
right_to_handing_over_the_goods(Buyer,Seller,Object,ContractID)<=
    valid_purchase_contract(Buyer,Seller,Object,Price,Tcontract,ContractID).
valid_purchase_contract(Buyer,Seller,Object,Price,Tcontract,ContractID)<=
    agreement_of_purchase_contract(Buyer,Seller,Object,Price,Tcontract,ContractID).
exception(
    valid_purchase_contract(Buyer,Seller,Object,Price,Tcontract,ContractID),
    rescission_by_minor_buyer(Buyer,Seller,ContractID,Tcontract,Trescission)).
rescission_by_minor_buyer(Buyer,Seller,ContractID,Tcontract,Trescission)<=
    minor(Buyer),
    manifestation(rescission(ContractID),Buyer,Seller,Trescission),
    before_the_day(Tcontract,Trescission).
manifestation(Action,Manifester,Manifestee,Taction)<=
    manifestation_fact(Action,Manifester,Manifestee,Taction).
exception(
    manifestation(Action,Maniester,Manifestee,Taction),
    manifestation_by_duress(Threater,Manifester,Manifestee,Action,Taction,Tduress,Trescission)).
manifestation_by_duress(Threater,Manifester,Manifestee,Action,Taction,Tduress,Trecission)<=
    fact_of_duress(Threater,Manifester,Action,Tduress),
    before_the_day(Tduress,Taction),
    manifestation(rescission(Action),Manifester,Manifestee,Trecission).
```

Fig. 3. Rulebase of PROLEG.

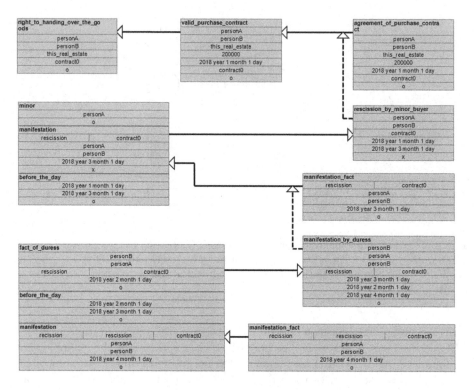

Fig. 4. Visualization of the reasoning made by PROLEG from the facts extracted by our framework.

4   Analysis of Challenges

Before explaining our framework, we will expose in this section the different difficulties found during the development of the framework. Each one has a letter assigned, so it can be referred in later paragraphs.

[A] Style of the text. Legal texts usually use patterns such as *"A sells L to B by C"*, *"Part A established a contract with Part B"*, or *"'personB' threatened 'person A'"*. In these examples, each of the letters are Named Entities that can be misleading to general NLP tools, that for instance consider *A* as a determiner, changing the whole grammar structure of the sentence. In our case, a preprocessing was done in order to distinguish among real determiners and 'A' parts, and also to eliminate misleading characters (such as ') or blank spaces.

[B] Relevance. Differently to other proposals, our aim is not to translate each sentence of the original text, but to extract just relevant facts to the PROLEG system. Therefore, not all the sentences in the text are relevant; in fact, some of them can be actually misleading.

[C] Factuality. Besides relevance, some of the sentences in the text processed do not refer to actual facts, but to possibilities, intentions or preferences (e.g., '*A would like to sell a land to B*', '*A preferred to sell it to part D*'). In these cases, some screening should be done in order to prevent these events to enter in our facts base.

[D] Paraphrasing. There are a number of different ways to express the information, both from the syntactical and semantics point of view. While in other domains a lot of semantic resources are available to palliate this phenomena, the Legal Domain presents a very specific terminology uneasy to deal with.

[E] Complexity. As already reported in the previous literature [7], texts in the legal domain tend to be more complex than texts those other domains. They have higher parse trees, more words per sentence and different POS distribution. These particularities imply an extra difficulty when extracting information from them beyond the required preprocessing previously mentioned.

[F] Coreferences and nesting. In a natural language text, a single sentence does not necessarily contain all the information of one event. Coreferences are also difficult to handle, especially when there are several manifestations of a type of event (such as a rescission). Also, some information is directly not mentioned and must be inferred using some domain knowledge information. This is the case for instance of a rescission of a contract; if we know that a *contract C* involves *part A* and *part B*, and we know there is a rescission of this contract of *part A* as manifester but it is not explicitly mentioned who is the manifestee, we can assume this role must be *Part B*. Similarly, the duress manifestation of a rescission must be coherent with the information we have of this rescission and the contract it applies to.

[G] Different information. For each of the different events processed we require different information. That is an important point that implies some ordering in the rules and preprocessing of the text. An example of this fact is the sentence like "*PersonB rescinded contract because personA was a minor on 1 March 2018.*" In PROLEG clauses, the predicate `minor()` has arity one, so there is no date attached. So even when NLP tools tend to assume that the date mentioned refers to the verb *be* and not to *rescind* (what in fact is linguistically correct and could also be the inference of a human, is an ambiguous sentence), our framework should be able to note the difference.

[H] Matching. Since some frames are dependent (e.g., a *duress* must be related to a *rescission*), they must be correctly tracked and matched, so the task is not just about extraction but also about merging.

5   ContractFrames

Our framework ContractFrames makes use of the NLP tool Stanford CoreNLP [17]. We use it for tokenization of the sentences, lemmatization, Part-of-Speech (POS) tagging, Named Entity Recognition (NER) and also for sentence dependence parsing. We also make use of the TokensRegex [4], an annotator that allows setting rules that produce customized annotations. Differently from other options, such as regex, the rules developed in the TokenRegex format are based in previous annotators output, such as POS or NER, being therefore more powerful from the semantic point of view. The steps in our framework are explained below, along with the problems exposed in the previous section that they target:

1. Preprocessing the input text: the first step in our framework deals with problems related to the style of the text and the different information (problems [A] and [G]). The objective of this step is to output a version of the text easier to be understood by the CoreNLP pipeline. To this aim, the following functionalities have been implemented, among others:
   - Algorithm to replace *A*, *'person B'*, or similar misleading expressions for the POS-tagger and the parser.
   - Replacement of appearances of relevant references like 'this_real_state', that often appear in input texts, to standard strings such as *Item1*. These replacements are eventually reversed before producing the final output.
   - Standardization of the dates, that might come as 'dd/Month/yyyy', a format that the Stanford CoreNLP temporal tagger (SUTime) is not able to detect.
   - NLP rules to detect the clause with arity one `minor(agent)`, that when found is added to the list of clauses and deleted from the text to avoid misleading parsing as the one explained in the previous section.
2. Annotation with the CoreNLP pipeline: the annotations include tokenization, sentence splitting, POS-tagging, lemmatization, NER (that includes SUTime), parse and the application of our event rules via TokensRegex. The rules developed allows our framework to detect different kind of events (establishment of contracts, purchases, sales, rescissions, duress...) both in verbal forms (*buy, sell, rescind*) or as noun events (*purchase, sale, rescission*). Each type of event is annotated consequently as a event annotation, so we find the relevant events (problem [B] in the previous section).
3. Parse sentence by sentence: we analyze each sentence separately, assigning one of each of the possible types of frame. Then we analyze the annotations of each token separately:
   (a) If the token has an event annotation, we check if it is negated in the sentence (being therefore not a fact, so we should not transform it into logic) or if it is an intention or a possibility (in this case, we should not either consider it), targeting problem [C]. Once we have verified that it is a fact, we check which type, and then apply different rules to find each its arguments (if available) and express the information as the corresponding frame of the sentence. These rules are mainly applied in the dependency

parsing of the sentence, and take into consideration not just the type of the event but also its form (if it is a noun or a verb, if it is active or passive). We cover therefore the different paraphrasing (problem [D]) that can express the information relevant for each frame. Let us analyze for instance the following sentences:

(1) *landL was sold by PartA to PartB via contractC for 20000 dollars on 13/October/2017.*

(2) *On 10/13/2017, PartB established a purchase contractC with PartA to buy landL at the price of 20000 dollars.*

(3) *PartA sold landL to PartB by contractC for 20000 dollars on October 13, 2017.*

For all of them, the same information is provided, despite of having different words and syntax; the analysis of the dependencies of each sentence is depicted in Fig. 5. Therefore, all these three different input texts imply the same frame (the establishment of a purchase contract) and their PRO-LEG output should be the following:

```
agreement_of_purchase_contract(partB,partA,landL,20000,2017 year
        10 month 13 day,contractC).
```

(b) If the token has any other relevant annotation (namely, it has been tagged as a DATE or MONEY by Stanford CoreNLP annotators or as a CONTRACT mention by our rules), we store it as relevant information in the sentence.

Once each token has been analyzed, we check if there is missing information in frames that have been initialized due to some found event. If so, we complete it with the relevant data we stored (problems [E] and [F]).

4. Once the whole sentence has been processed, we check the information stored in the frames. If there is any information missing, we look for it explicitly (for instance in the values for DATE and MONEY we stored in the previous step for the current sentence), as well as we also check if new information can complete previous frames. An example of this is the case of a duress: an expression of duress must be linked to a previous rescission, so we check previously mentioned rescissions and link it to the most suitable one (problem [H]).

5. Finally, once all the sentences have been processed, we complete the information on the final frames using some common sense. Let us imagine for instance that we have a rescission with *Manifester A* and *Manifestee B*, with a duress where *B* is the *Manifester* but with no information on the text about the threatened. Since we know the two parties in the contract, we can derive that the *Manifestee* must be *A*.

6. Last step involves just transforming the information in our frames in PRO-LEG clauses, including reversing the replacement done during the preprocessing step. Since all the relevant information has been stored as our standard frames, translation into PROLEG clauses is straightforward (each frame has one or two clauses whose arguments are among the data in the frame).

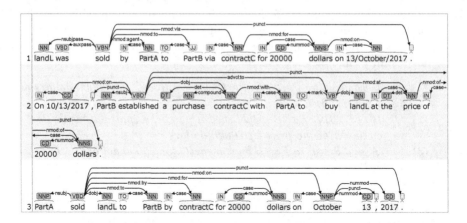

Fig. 5. CoreNLP online demo's (http://corenlp.run/) output of the enhanced dependencies of the three example sentences where the challenges of paraphrasing become evident. We can see for instance how the buyer (*PartB*) and the seller (*PartA*) play different roles in the sentence depending on the voice (*active/passive*) or the semantics of the verb expressing the purchase frame (*buy/sell/establish a contract*). Also other information can be expressed differently, such as the date.

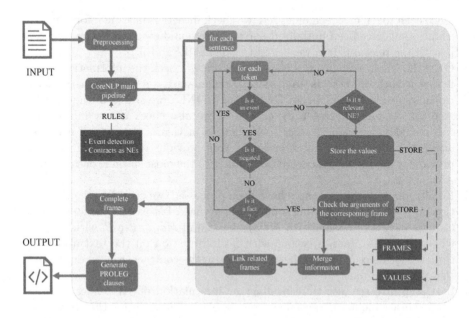

Fig. 6. The pipeline of our framework.

It must be noted that our framework's NLP pipeline does not involve the corefence annotator from CoreNLP. Although it was initially included in a first version of our framework, we detected that it presented some limitations when dealing with the same event refered both by using nouns and verbs. While it could detect that for instance that in *"The rescission of the contract was done on 1 February, 2018. This rescission was cancelled later"* there was a coreference, it did not succeed in cases such as *"A rescinded the contract with B. This rescission was cancelled later"*. We therefore developed the our own algorithm to detect previous potentially similar events and merge them, executed in step 4. Figure 6 depicts the pipeline of our framework.

6   Results

The code of ContractFrames[6] is publicly available in a GitHub repository[7]. A dataset with several different texts and their expected input is included in the repository. These texts have been generated by legal researchers, some of them taking no part in the development of the framework. The texts include different types of paraphrasing, both semantic and syntactic, such as the examples depicted in Fig. 5. Also different levels of nesting and events are represented in the dataset, that includes texts of different length explaining the workflow of a contract (the establishment of the contract, a the rescission or duress), and even surrounding facts not exploited by the system.

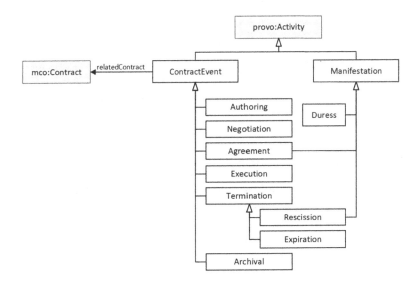

Fig. 7. The Contract Workflow Ontology.

---

[6] https://mnavasloro.github.io/ContractFrames/.
[7] https://github.com/mnavasloro/ContractFrames.

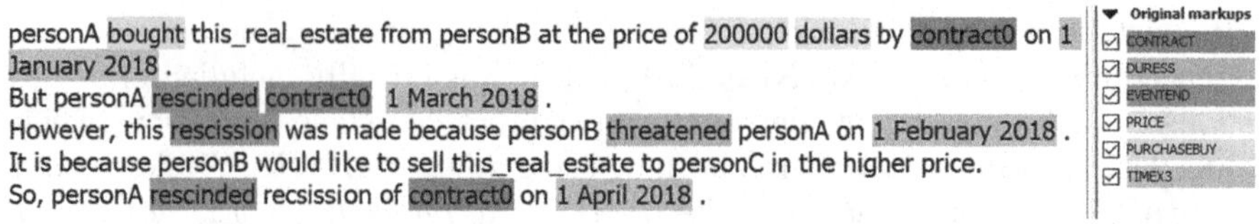

personA bought this_real_estate from personB at the price of 200000 dollars by contract0 on 1 January 2018 .
But personA rescinded contract0 1 March 2018 .
However, this rescission was made because personB threatened personA on 1 February 2018 .
It is because personB would like to sell this_real_estate to personC in the higher price.
So, personA rescinded recsission of contract0 on 1 April 2018 .

▼ Original markups
☑ CONTRACT
☑ DURESS
☑ EVENTEND
☑ PRICE
☑ PURCHASEBUY
☑ TIMEX3

Fig. 8. Visualization of our custom annotations in XML.

The code, written in Java, provides two main classes. The first allows the user to input any text and provides it in the form of PROLEG clauses. The second processes all the files in the dataset, that is also provided and can be extended by the user just by adding new files.

Besides the logic clauses output format, an ontology able to express contract has been developed. This ontology, called Contract Workflow Ontology[8], is capable of representing the different types of events processed, such as agreements and rescission, as well as others in the workflow of a general event such as negotiation. A method for generating an output in the form of triples is provided. Figure 7 shows the Contract Workflow Ontology.

Additionally, the system also generates a xml output that allows the visualization of the inner custom annotations in the text, namely events and named entities like contracts. An example of this visualization (using the tool GATE [5]) can be found in Fig. 8.

7   Conclusions

In this paper we have presented ContractFrames, a framework to process input text written in natural language including technical legal terminology and to produce as output its relevant information in the form of PROLEG logical clauses. This framework can recognize different kinds of events, can analyze if they are actual facts and can extract important related information in the form of a frame, deriving omitted information to some extent. Also, an ontology has been created as a data model to store the relevant information of the case and compound the whole contract workflow. In this way, any other logical system might also benefit of the processing and the information extracted, and would be able to generate a custom output from this knowledge representation.

Finally, although our framework has been able to successfully process all the example texts produced by legal researchers not involved in its coding, it still has some limitations that will be handled as future work. We therefore have several research lines for improving ContractFrames. For now, the framework is not able to recognize appositions nor naming statements such as *"the contract, entitled from now 'contract0', (...)"*. Despite these expressions are not very common, we consider that exploring new rules for detecting these kind of alternative paraphrasing, eventually to be added to our framework, will be useful. Also more

---

[8] https://mnavasloro.github.io/ContractFrames/datamodel.html.

frames able to represent other legal situations and rule sets for populating them will be developed, as well as common sense techniques to derive non explicit information.

References

1. Araujo, D.A., et al.: Automatic information extraction from texts with inference and linguistic knowledge acquisition rules. In: Proceedings of the 2013 IEEE/WIC/ACM International Joint Conferences on Web Intelligence and Intelligent Agent Technologies, vol. 3, pp. 151–154. IEEE Computer Society (2013)
2. Baker, C., et al.: The Berkeley FrameNet project. In: Proceedings of the 17th International ACL, vol. 1, pp. 86–90. Association for Computational Linguistics (1998)
3. Biagioli, C., et al.: Automatic semantics extraction in law documents. In: Proceedings of the 10th ICAIL, pp. 133–140. ACM (2005)
4. Chang, A.X., Manning, C.D.: TokensRegex: defining cascaded regular expressions over tokens. Technical report CSTR 2014-02, Department of Computer Science, Stanford University (2014)
5. Cunningham, H., et al.: Getting more out of biomedical documents with GATE's full lifecycle open source text analytics. PLoS Comput. Biol. $9(2)$, 1–16 (2013)
6. Daskalopulu, A., et al.: Evidence-based electronic contract performance monitoring. Group Decis. Negot. $11(6)$, 469–485 (2002)
7. Dell'Orletta, F., et al.: The SPLeT-2012 shared task on dependency parsing of legal texts. In: Semantic Processing of Legal Texts (SPLeT-2012) Workshop Programme, p. 42 (2012)
8. Dragoni, M., et al.: Combining NLP approaches for rule extraction from legal documents. In: 1st Workshop on MIning and REasoning with Legal Texts (MIREL 2016) (2016)
9. Francesconi, E.: Legal rules learning based on a semantic model for legislation. In: Proceedings of the LREC 2010 Workshop on the Semantic Processing of Legal Texts (SPLeT-2010), Malta, May 2010, p. 46 (2010)
10. Governatori, G., Milosevic, Z.: A formal analysis of a business contract language. Int. J. Coop. Inf. Syst. $15(04)$, 659–685 (2006)
11. Grosof, B.N.: Representing E-commerce rules via situated courteous logic programs in RuleML. Electron. Commer. Res. Appl. $3(1)$, 2–20 (2004)
12. Hoekstra, R., Breuker, J., Di Bello, M., Boer, A., et al.: The LKIF core ontology of basic legal concepts. LOAIT $\mathbf{321}$, 43–63 (2007)
13. Kabilan, V.: Contract workflow model patterns using BPMN. In: Proceedings of the 10th International Workshop on EMMSAD (2005)
14. Kimura, Y., Nakamura, M., Shimazu, A.: Treatment of legal sentences including itemized and referential expressions – towards translation into logical forms. In: Hattori, H., Kawamura, T., Idé, T., Yokoo, M., Murakami, Y. (eds.) JSAI 2008. LNCS (LNAI), vol. 5447, pp. 242–253. Springer, Heidelberg (2009). https://doi.org/10.1007/978-3-642-00609-8_21
15. Kiyavitskaya, N., et al.: Automating the extraction of rights and obligations for regulatory compliance. In: Li, Q., Spaccapietra, S., Yu, E., Olivé, A. (eds.) ER 2008. LNCS, vol. 5231, pp. 154–168. Springer, Heidelberg (2008). https://doi.org/10.1007/978-3-540-87877-3_13

16. Leff, L., Meyer, P.: eContracts 1.0 committee specification. OASIS LegalXML Technical report (2007). http://docs.oasis-open.org/legalxmlecontracts
17. Manning, C.D., et al.: The Stanford CoreNLP natural language processing toolkit. In: Proceedings of the 52nd Annual Meeting of the ACL 2014, System Demonstrations, pp. 55–60 (2014)
18. Miller, G.A.: WordNet: a lexical database for English. Commun. ACM **38**(11), 39–41 (1995)
19. Minsky, M.: A framework for representing knowledge (1975)
20. Molina-Jimenez, C., et al.: Contract representation for run-time monitoring and enforcement. In: IEEE International Conference on E-commerce, pp. 103–110 (2003)
21. Moulin, B., Rousseau, D.: Automated knowledge acquisition from regulatory texts. IEEE Expert **7**(5), 27–35 (1992). https://doi.org/10.1109/64.163670
22. Nakamura, M., Nobuoka, S., Shimazu, A.: Towards translation of legal sentences into logical forms. In: Satoh, K., Inokuchi, A., Nagao, K., Kawamura, T. (eds.) JSAI 2007. LNCS (LNAI), vol. 4914, pp. 349–362. Springer, Heidelberg (2008). https://doi.org/10.1007/978-3-540-78197-4_33
23. Navas-Loro, M., Santos, C.: Events in the legal domain: first impressions. In: Proceedings of the 2nd Workshop on Technologies for Regulatory Compliance (TeReCom) at the 31st International Conference on Legal Knowledge and Information Systems (JURIX) (2018)
24. Prisacariu, C., Schneider, G.: A dynamic deontic logic for complex contracts. J. Logic Algebraic Program. **81**(4), 458–490 (2012)
25. Rodríguez-Doncel, V., et al.: Overview of the MPEG-21 media contract ontology. Semantic Web **7**(3), 311–332 (2016)
26. Satoh, K., et al.: PROLEG: an implementation of the presupposed ultimate fact theory of Japanese civil code by PROLOG technology. In: Onada, T., Bekki, D., McCready, E. (eds.) JSAI-isAI 2010. LNCS (LNAI), vol. 6797, pp. 153–164. Springer, Heidelberg (2011). https://doi.org/10.1007/978-3-642-25655-4_14
27. Schuler, K.K.: Verbnet: A broad-coverage, comprehensive verb lexicon (2005)
28. Wyner, A.Z., Peters, W.: On rule extraction from regulations. In: JURIX. **11**, 113–122 (2011)

Reasoning by a Bipolar Argumentation Framework for PROLEG

Tatsuki Kawasaki, Sosuke Moriguchi, and Kazuko Takahashi(✉)

School of Science and Technology, Kwansei Gakuin University,
2-1, Gakuen, Sanda 669-1337, Japan
{dxk96093,ktaka}@kwansei.ac.jp, chiguri@acm.org

Abstract. We develop a system allowing lawyers and law school students to analyze court judgments. We describe a transformation from the logic programming language PROLEG to a bipolar argumentation framework (BAF) and the legal reasoning involved. Legal knowledge written in a PROLEG program is transformed into a BAF, in which the structure of argumentation in a judgment is clear. We describe two types of reasoning by the BAF: clarification of the entire structure and causality of arguments, and identification of the required evidence, and we show its applications on legal reasoning.

Keywords: Bipolar argumentation framework · PROLEG ·
Reasoning · Semantics

1   Introduction

Recently, information technology and artificial intelligence are vigorously applied in various fields, including those that have not yet been fully digitized or automated. In the context of legal reasoning, although the use of artificial intelligence has attracted a great deal of attention, higher-level and more practical support exploiting recent technological developments is required. A support for a judgment process is one of the most necessary ones. When seeking to support a judgment, it is essential to develop a system that can be easily used by lawyers who are not computer scientists; also, the system must be highly reliable and must reason accurately and rapidly. Firstly, lawyers must be able to access the system in a straightforward manner, and secondly, the system must describe both the process leading to judgment and the way in which the law was applied.

In terms of the former consideration, as law is supposed to be logical, it is reasonable to base the system on such logic and reason from that perspective. Several legal reasoning systems have adopted logic programming such as Prolog as their descriptive languages. However, it is difficult for a lawyer who is not familiar with computer science to directly write Prolog code. A PROLEG system was developed to solve this problem [17]. It was designed to support inferences based on the Japanese Presupposed Ultimate Facts Theory (termed "Yoken-jijitsu-ron" in Japanese) of the Japanese civil code, and it is currently

© Springer Nature Switzerland AG 2019
K. Kojima et al. (Eds.): JSAI-isAI 2018 Workshops, LNAI 11717, pp. 115–130, 2019.
https://doi.org/10.1007/978-3-030-31605-1_10

applied to the Japanese penal code. The theory deals with uncertainties that sometimes arise in court, where a judge must give a decision even if evidence is lacking. PROLEG is a system to reason about the theory by a Prolog-based meta-interpreter. Each presupposed ultimate fact is represented using general rules written in the form of *if-then* statements and exceptions. Exceptions of fact apply to all general rules and are used as court defenses. The use of exceptions rather than negative atoms creates a structure equivalent to that of a law, allowing lawyers to intuitively understand the program. A burden-of-proof [14] is attached to each ultimate fact to allow for decision-making even if the fact is not proven to be true. This is achieved using the negation-as-failure inference of Prolog; thus, for a given goal, a general rule is applied and the goal is true unless there is an exception.

On the other hand, in terms of legal process and application, it is appropriate to employ argumentation to describe both the judgment process and how the law was applied [1]. An argumentation system reveals both the causality in arguments (for example, how arguments interacted to create a judgment) and the influence of evidence. Argumentation is a powerful tool when used to resolve conflicts, not only formalizing the structure of the process but also incorporating any uncertainties.

In the time since Dung proposed the abstract Argumentation Framework (AF) [9], many extensions and revisions of the system have been published [15]. AF represents an argumentation by a pair of a set of arguments and a set of attacks between arguments, ignoring the contents of arguments. Several AF semantics have been defined; acceptable arguments are calculated based on these semantics. Visualization tools appropriate for argumentation systems have also been developed (e.g., [16]).

Although PROLEG facilitates the representation of a law, it is difficult to grasp the judgment process or a causal relation found in arguments from the execution trace. On the other hand, although it is possible to create an AF representing the interaction between a plaintiff and a defendant in court, it is difficult to directly write the structure of a law per se, or the part of the law used to create an argument in an AF form. Therefore, we combined the two systems.

We developed a transformation from PROLEG to a bipolar argumentation framework (BAF) [6], an extended AF, and showed its correctness [11]. More specifically, we gave a semantics for the BAF obtained as a result of the transformation, and proved that the answer set of the PROLEG program was the same as the set of acceptable arguments in BAF. However, we have not yet discussed what kind of reasoning we can do using this BAF. The objective of this paper is to show how reasoning which is difficult to emulate or understand using a PROLEG program proceeds using the BAF.

Consider the following PROLEG program representing the penal code that defines the "crime of murder."[1] The first clause indicates the general rule and the second clause an exception. The text states that if the object is a human (not

---

[1] Note that the examples shown here are simplified versions of the actual penal code; the conditions per se are simplified and the legal terminology is not precise.

a dead body) and there exists both the action of murder and the intention to murder, then the crime of murder has been committed unless there is a legitimate defense.

```
crime_of_murder <= human, action_of_murder, intention_to_murder.
exception(crime_of_murder, legitimate_defense).
```

When evidence is provided, the facts on which that evidence bears are proved, and it is then decided whether the crime_of_murder has been committed or not.

A judge should explain the judgment process to persuade those concerned with the transparency of justice. In such a legal situation, what is required is not only the outcome of judicial reasoning but also an explanation of the reasoning process or the cause-and-effect relationships of arguments used in reasoning. For example, if the crime_of_murder was adjudged to not in fact have been committed; this may be because of a lack of evidence of intention_to_murder, or because a legitimate_defense was available.

Our transformed BAF not only shows the process and structure of judgment, but also suggests a strategy by which a user can achieve a desired goal. If a plaintiff/defendant wishes to argue that a law should or should not be applied, the BAF identifies the evidence that must be presented and any counterarguments that may arise. For example, when a prosecutor wishes to charge the crime_of_murder, but finds that the lack of intention_to_murder is a complicating factor, s/he will look harder for evidence of intention_to_murder. Here, we discuss such reasoning on our BAF.

This paper is organized as follows. In Sect. 2, we briefly explain PROLEG. In Sect. 3, we describe the BAF that we use and its semantics. In Sect. 4, we describe the transformation rule from PROLEG to the BAF. In Sect. 5, we describe how the reasoning by the BAF proceeds, and in Sect. 6, we show its application. In Sect. 7, we compare our method with those of others. Finally, in Sect. 8, we offer conclusions and describe our planned future work.

2   Legal Description Language: PROLEG

The PROLEG program P is defined as a pair $\langle \mathcal{R}, \mathcal{E} \rangle$, where $\mathcal{R}$ is a finite set of rules, and $\mathcal{E}$ is a finite set of exceptions. Each rule is a Horn clause of the form $H \Leftarrow B_1, \ldots B_n$, where $H, B_1, \ldots, B_n$ are atoms. Here, n may be 0, and in this case we term such a rule *a fact rule* or simply *a fact*; when $n > 0$, we call the rule a *defining rule*, to distinguish from a fact rule. Each exception is in the form $exception(H, B)$.

A fact is something given as an evidence in a court case, whereas defining rules and exceptions describe the general case. That is, the facts are generally given in an instantiated form whereas defining rules and exceptions include variables. In the following examples, we use a proposition for simplicity.

For each rule R or exception E, we employ the functions *head* and *body* such that $head(R) = H$ and $body(R) = \{B_1, \ldots, B_n\}$ if $R = H \Leftarrow B_1, \ldots, B_n$; $head(E) = H$ and $body(E) = \{B\}$ if $E = exception(H, B)$.

An atom may have more than one defining rule. This means that there may exist distinct R_1 and R_2 such that $head(R_1) = head(R_2)$.

Example 1. The following is an example of a PROLEG program.

```
p <= q1, q2.
exception(q1, r).
q2 <=.
r <=.
```

The semantics of the PROLEG program P is defined as an answer set (a set of ground atoms). M is the *answer set* of P iff M is the minimum model of the set of Horn clauses, $\{R \in \mathcal{R} \mid \forall E \in \mathcal{E}, \text{ if } head(E) = head(R) \text{ then } body(E) \not\subseteq M\}$. The expressive power of PROLEG is the same as that of a normal logic program with an answer set [10,18].

PROLEG allows cyclic definitions. However, here, we deal with an acyclic PROLEG program, because the Japanese civil and penal codes are usually written in an acyclic manner.

3   Bipolar Argumentation Framework

First, we define an argumentation framework [9].

Definition 1 (argumentation framework). *An argumentation framework is defined as a pair $\langle AR, AT \rangle$ where AR is a set of arguments and AT is a binary relation on AR, termed an attack. If $(A, A') \in AT$, we state that A attacks A'.*

A BAF is an extension of an AF in which the two relations of attack and support are defined over a set of arguments [6]. We define a support relation between a power set of arguments and a set of arguments; this differs from the usual BAF, because the body of a defining rule generally includes more than one atom in PROLEG.

Definition 2 (bipolar argumentation framework). *A BAF is defined as a triple $\langle AR, ATT, SUP \rangle$ where AR is a finite set of arguments, $ATT \subseteq AR \times AR$ and $SUP \subseteq (2^{AR} \setminus \{\emptyset\}) \times AR$. We denote $\text{att}(B, A)$ if $(B, A) \in ATT$, and $\text{sup}(\mathbf{A}, A)$ if $(\mathbf{A}, A) \in SUP$.*

Example 2. Figure 1 is a graphical representation of a bipolar argumentation framework $\langle \{a, b, c, d, e\}, \{(b, a), (e, d)\}, \{(\{c, d\}, a)\} \rangle$. In the figure, the straight arrow indicates an attack relation and the wavy arrow a support relation.

We gave a semantics for the BAF based on labeling [5]. Usually, labeling is a function from a set of arguments to $\{in, out, undec\}$, but *undec* is unnecessary here, because the BAF is acyclic. An argument labeled *in* is considered to be an accepted argument.

Definition 3 (labeling). *For $\langle AR, ATT, SUP \rangle$, a labeling $\mathcal{L}$ is a function from AR to $\{in, out\}$.*

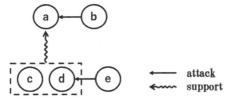

Fig. 1. Example of BAF.

Labeling of a set of arguments is denoted as follows: $\mathcal{L}(\mathbf{A}) = in$ if $\mathcal{L}(A) = in$ for all $A \in \mathbf{A}$; $\mathcal{L}(\mathbf{A}) = out$, otherwise.

We assign the label in to an argument that is neither attacked nor supported by any other argument. When an argument is both attacked and supported, the attack is supposed to be stronger than the support. We assign a label out to an argument that is attacked by another argument with the label out, and simultaneously supported by a set of arguments with the label out. Note that an argument lacking support is labeled out, even if it is attacked by an argument labeled out.

Definition 4 (complete labeling). *For* $\langle AR, ATT, SUP \rangle$, *labeling* $\mathcal{L}$ *is complete iff the following conditions are satisfied for any argument* $A \in AR$.

- $\mathcal{L}(A) = in$ *if*
  - $(\forall B \in AR, \neg \text{att}(B, A)) \wedge (\forall \mathbf{A} \subseteq AR, \neg \text{sup}(\mathbf{A}, A))$
  or
  - $(\forall B \in AR, \text{att}(B, A) \Rightarrow \mathcal{L}(B) = out) \wedge (\exists \mathbf{A} \subseteq AR, \text{sup}(\mathbf{A}, A) \wedge \mathcal{L}(\mathbf{A}) = in)$.
- $\mathcal{L}(A) = out$, *otherwise.*

Figure 2 shows the complete labeling of four BAFs.

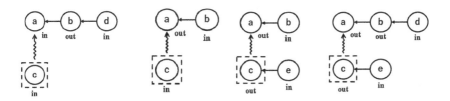

Fig. 2. Examples of complete labeling.

Example 3. For a BAF in Fig. 1, $\mathcal{L}(b) = \mathcal{L}(c) = \mathcal{L}(e) = in$ and $\mathcal{L}(a) = \mathcal{L}(d) = \mathcal{L}(\{c, d\}) = out$.

The following theorem holds [11].

Theorem 1. *For any acyclic BAF, there is exactly one complete labeling.*

Note that we distinguish the case in which an argument is supported by a set of arguments from that in which it is supported by multiple arguments separately.

Example 4. Consider two BAFs baf_1 and baf_2 shown in Fig. 3. Formally, baf_1 is represented as $\langle\{a, b, c, d\}, \{(d, c)\}, \{(\{b, c\}, a)\}\rangle$ and baf_2 is represented as $\langle\{a, b, c, d\}, \{(d, c)\}, \{(\{b\}, a), (\{c\}, a)\}\rangle$.

In baf_1, the argument a has one support that is a set of two arguments, whereas in baf_2, it has two supports, both of which are singletons.

Let $\mathcal{L}_1$ and $\mathcal{L}_2$ be the complete labeling of baf_1 and baf_2, respectively. In baf_1, $\mathcal{L}_1(b) = \mathcal{L}_1(d) = in$ and $\mathcal{L}_1(c) = out$ hold. It follows that $\mathcal{L}_1(\{b, c\}) = out$ holds. Therefore, $\mathcal{L}_1(a) = out$. On the other hand, in baf_2, $\mathcal{L}_2(b) = \mathcal{L}_2(d) = in$ and $\mathcal{L}_2(c) = out$ hold similarly. However, $\mathcal{L}_2(\{b\}) = in$ and $\mathcal{L}_2(\{c\}) = out$. Therefore, $\mathcal{L}_1(a) = in$.

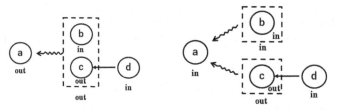

(a) baf_1: supported by a set   (b) baf_2: supported independently

Fig. 3. Two types of support.

4   Transformation

4.1   Transformation Rule

We show a transformation from a PROLEG program to a BAF. The atoms, rules, and exceptions of the PROLEG program are transformed into arguments, supports, and attacks, respectively.

We add two types of arguments to the BAF that do not appear as explicit atoms in PROLEG. One is an argument reflecting the *absence* of any rules of inference in PROLEG. In PROLEG, an atom H that does not appear in the header of any rule or exception is not in the answer set. On the other hand, arguments that are neither attacked nor supported are labeled *in*. To fill this gap, we add the argument ab(H) that attacks H. We term this argument *an absence argument*. We also add arguments showing the *existence* of fact rules. For a fact rule (i.e., a rule in the form $H \Leftarrow$), there are no arguments that support H in BAF; any support is a binary relation. Therefore, we add an argument ex(H) that supports H. We term this argument an *existence argument*.

Definition 5 (transformation rule). *Transformation from a PROLEG program $\langle \mathcal{R}, \mathcal{E} \rangle$ to a BAF $\langle AR, ATT, SUP \rangle$ is defined as follows.*

- $Atom = \bigcup_{R \in \mathcal{R}}(\{head(R)\} \cup body(R)) \cup \bigcup_{E \in \mathcal{E}}(\{head(E)\} \cup body(E))$
- $Rule = \{(body(R), head(R)) \mid R \in \mathcal{R} \wedge body(R) \neq \emptyset\}$
- $Exc = \{(B, H) \mid exception(H, B) \in \mathcal{E}\}$
- $Existence = \{H \mid H \Leftarrow \in \mathcal{R}\}$
- $ExistenceSupport = \{(\{ex(H)\}, H) \mid H \in Existence\}$
- $Absence = Atom \backslash (\{head(R) \mid R \in \mathcal{R}\} \cup \{head(E) \mid E \in \mathcal{E}\})$
- $AbsenceAttack = \{(ab(B), B) \mid B \in Absence\}$
- $AR = Atom \cup \{ex(H) \mid H \in Existence\} \cup \{ab(B) \mid B \in Absence\}$
- $ATT = Exc \cup AbsenceAttack$
- $SUP = Rule \cup ExistenceSupport$

The following theorem indicates that the semantics is preserved during transformation [11].

Theorem 2. *For PROLEG program P, let M be an answer set of P. Assume that $\mathcal{L}$ is the complete labeling of the BAF transformed from P. Then, for each atom H in P, $H \in M$ iff $\mathcal{L}(H) = in$.*

Example 5. The program in Example 1 is transformed into the following BAF:

$$\langle \{p, q_1, q_2, r, ex(q_2), ex(r)\}, \{(r, q_1)\},$$
$$\{(\{q_1, q_2\}, p), (\{ex(q_2)\}, q_2), (\{ex(r)\}, r)\} \rangle.$$

Complete labeling of the BAF is performed in the following manner. Arguments q_1 and q_2 together support argument p. The existence arguments $ex(q_2)$ and $ex(r)$ are added to support q_2 and r, respectively. Figure 4 shows a graphical representation of the BAF, with the complete labeling[2]. As $\mathcal{L}(q_1) = out$ and $\mathcal{L}(q_2) = in$, the label of the set of arguments $\mathcal{L}(\{q_1, q_2\}) = out$. Also, as p is supported by $\{q_1, q_2\}$, $\mathcal{L}(p) = out$. When we ignore the existence and absence arguments introduced during transformation, the set of arguments labeled in is $\{q_2, r\}$, which coincides with the answer set of the program in Example 1.

5   Reasoning by the BAF

We describe the two types of reasoning performed by the BAF transformed from the PROLEG program:

1. Clarification of the entire structure of judgment and the causality in the arguments.
2. Identification of the required evidence.

---

[2] Note that, in the following figures, we omit the dotted rectangle over existence arguments to avoid making a figure messy.

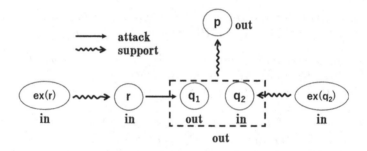

Fig. 4. BAF for the program in Example 1.

5.1   PROLEG Program

Example 6. Consider the following PROLEG program. The first set of a defining
rule and an exception states that if the object is a human (not a dead body)
and there exists both the action of murder and the intention to murder, then
the crime of murder has been committed unless there was a legitimate defense.
The second set of a defining rule and an exception states that if the accused
is infringed and takes emergent, necessary, and appropriate action to defend
himself/herself, then this is a legitimate defense, unless there was no aggressive
intention to harm the deceased. The remainder of the program deals with the
facts in evidence.

```
% rules regarding crime_of_murder
crime_of_murder <= human, act_of_murder, intention_to_murder.
exception(crime_of_murder, legitimate_defense).

legitimate_defense <=
  infringement, emergency, necessity, appropriateness,
  defense_intention.
exception(legitimate_defense, aggressive_intention_to_harm).

% facts
human <=.
act_of_murder <=.
intention_to_murder <=.
infringement <=.
emergency <=.
necessity <=.
appropriateness <=.
defense_intention <=.
```

5.2   Clarification of the Entire Structure of Judgment and Causality in the Arguments

In this case, the entire PROLEG program is transformed into a BAF using the rules shown in Sect. 4.

For each atom, rules that define it and the exceptions are transformed into the BAF. If there exists a fact, then a corresponding existence argument supporting the fact is added. If an atom does not appear in the header of any rule or exception, then a corresponding absence argument attacking the atom is added to the transformed BAF. We show a graphical representation of the transformed BAF in Fig. 5.

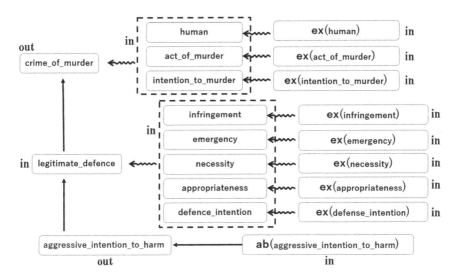

Fig. 5. Graphical representation of a transformed BAF for a murder case.

This BAF was obtained from an entire PROLEG program including facts, and shows the structure of the entire argumentation from which we can grasp the cause-and-effect relationships of the arguments.

Using this BAF, the argumentation process is explained as follows. As the label of the absence argument ab(aggressive_intention_to_harm) is *in*, that of the argument aggressive_intention_to_harm is *out* (there was no intention to harm). Therefore, the label of the argument legitimate_defense is *in* (it is a legitimate defense). The argument crime_of_murder has one attacking argument, the label of which is *in*, and one supporting set of arguments, the label of which is *in*. Hence, the label of the argument crime_of_murder is *out* (the crime of murder was not committed).

The BAF is updated as the judgment proceeds. Counter-arguments and evidences may be incrementally added as the corresponding nodes. Then, the node labels can be changed. For example, if there is another exception to a legitimate_defense argument, and this is proven, a new argument is added; legitimate_defense is attacked by this argument and its label is changed to *out*. As another example, if evidence of aggressive_intention_to_harm is given, then its absence argument is replaced by an existence argument, and attack by the absence argument is replaced by support from the existence argument. As a result, the label of the node aggressive_intention_to_harm is changed to *in*. It follows that the label of legitimate_defense is changed to *out*, and that of crime_of_murder to *in*.

5.3   Identification of Required Evidence

The BAF also identifies the evidence required to apply the law or prevent its application.

We transform a PROLEG program except for the fact part, and determine the existence arguments required to apply or not apply the law. Unlike the first type of reasoning, all available defining rules and exceptions are assumed to be represented, and no defining rules or exceptions are added.

From the definition of complete labeling, $\mathcal{L}(A) = in$ holds iff the labels of all arguments that attack A are *out* and there exists an argument that supports A, of which the label is *in*, or A is neither attacked nor supported.

Assume that a plaintiff wants to apply a law or that a defendant wants to prevent its application. Then they seek to label the corresponding argument *in* and *out*, respectively. The BAF detects the evidence required for attainment of their goals, respectively. This is achieved by repeatedly applying the following process:

Let A be an argument.

– Make $\mathcal{L}(A) = in$.
   Both of the following conditions should be satisfied.
   • (attack condition) Make $\mathcal{L}(B) = out$ for each B such that att(B, A). If there does not exist such an argument B, then the condition is satisfied.
   • (support condition) Make $\mathcal{L}(\mathbf{A}) = in$ for some $\mathbf{A}$ such that sup$(\mathbf{A}, A)$, that is, for each $A' \in \mathbf{A}, \mathcal{L}(A') = in$. If there does not exist such $\mathbf{A}$, then an existence argument $ex(A)$ and a support sup$(\{ex(A)\}, A)$ should be added.
– Make $\mathcal{L}(A) = out$.
   Either of the following conditions should be satisfied.
   • (attack condition) Make $\mathcal{L}(B) = in$ for some B such that att(B, A). If there does not exist such an argument B, then this condition is not satisfied.
   • (support condition) Make $\mathcal{L}(\mathbf{A}) = out$ for each $\mathbf{A}$ such that sup$(\mathbf{A}, A)$, that is, for some $A' \in \mathbf{A}, \mathcal{L}(A') = out$. If there does not exist such $\mathbf{A}$, then this condition is not satisfied.

As a result, a set of existence arguments, that is, a set of evidences that should be provided, is found; this allows either party to attain his/her goal no matter what evidence his/her opponent offers.

Example 7. Figure 6 shows a BAF transformed from the PROLEG program excluding the fact part of Example 6. For convenience, each node is named $a, b, \ldots, k$, respectively.

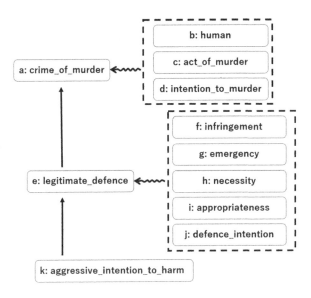

Fig. 6. Reasoning about required evidences.

– In this BAF, consider the conditions required to make $\mathcal{L}(a) = in$.
  • By attack condition for a, $\mathcal{L}(e) = out$ should be satisfied. To achieve this, attack condition for e or support condition for e should be satisfied. By attack condition for e, $\mathcal{L}(k) = in$ should be satisfied, and since k has no support, $ex(k)$ is required. By support condition for e, at least one of $\mathcal{L}(f) = out$, $\mathcal{L}(g) = out$, $\mathcal{L}(h) = out$, $\mathcal{L}(i) = out$ or $\mathcal{L}(j) = out$ holds. However, this is impossible since f, g, h, i and j are neither attacked nor supported.
  • By support condition for a, $\mathcal{L}(b) = \mathcal{L}(c) = \mathcal{L}(d) = in$ should be satisfied. To achieve this, $ex(b), ex(c)$ and $ex(d)$ are required.
  As a result, the plaintiff should provide the four evidences $ex(k), ex(b), ex(c)$ and $ex(d)$ to apply the law.
– On the other hand, consider the conditions required to make $\mathcal{L}(a) = out$.
  • By attack condition for a, $\mathcal{L}(e) = in$ should be satisfied. To achieve this, $\mathcal{L}(k) = out$ should be satisfied, but this is impossible since k is neither attacked nor supported.
  • By support condition for a, either $\mathcal{L}(b)$, $\mathcal{L}(c)$ or $\mathcal{L}(d)$ should be out, but this is impossible since b, c and d are neither attacked nor supported.
  Therefore, the defendant never prevents application of the law.

In this example, only one set of existence arguments is found to make $\mathcal{L}(a) = in$, and no argument is found to make $\mathcal{L}(a) = out$. However, in general, we may find multiple sets in both cases. For example, assume that a plaintiff wishes to make $\mathcal{L}(a) = in$ in the BAF shown in Fig. 7. The evidence required to make $\mathcal{L}(a) = in$ is one of $ex(b)$ or $ex(c)$. The evidence required to make $\mathcal{L}(f) = in$ is one of $ex(g)$ or $ex(h)$. Thus, we find four sets of required evidences.

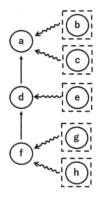

Fig. 7. Multiple sets of evidences are obtained.

6   Application of Reasoning

Here, we discuss how lawyers use the reasoning shown in Subsect. 5.3 in actual cases.

Consider an example regarding the Japanese civil code. This is a modified version of the house lease example discussed by Satoh et al. [17].

Assume that a plaintiff and a defendant have entered into a lease contract on a house. The defendant subleased a room of the house to his sister, who used the room, and the plaintiff claimed that the contract was ended by this sublease. The defendant claimed that he subleased the room for only ten days, which does not constitute abuse; however, the plaintiff argued that the neighbors complained that the sublessee played the piano, generating noise, which constituted an abuse.

The PROLEG program for this example, excluding the fact part is as follows. The first part shows that cancellation due to the sublease is effective if there was a lease contract and the house was handed over by the lessor to the lessee, there was a sublease contract and the room was handed over by the lessee to the sublessee, the sublessee used the leased item, and the lessor manifested the intention of cancelling the lease contract; however, this is effective unless the lessor granted approval for the sublease and there was no abuse of confidence. The second part shows that the lessee is considered to have obtained approval for the sublease if the lessor granted approval of the sublease before cancellation. The third part shows that there is no abuse of confidence if there is a fact supporting non-abuse unless there is an abuse of confidence. The last part shows that there is an abuse of confidence if there is a fact supporting abuse.

```
% rules regarding lease

cancellation_due_to_sublease <=
  agreement_of_lease_contract, handover_to_lessee,
  agreement_of_sublease_contract, handover_to_sublessee,
  using_leased_thing, manifestation_cancellation.
exception(cancellation_due_to_sublease,get_approval_of_sublease).
exception(cancellation_due_to_sublease,nonabuse_of_confidence).

get_approval_of_sublease <=
  approval_of_sublease, approval_before_cancellation.

nonabuse_of_confidence <= fact_of_nonabuse_of_confidence.
exception(nonabuse_of_confidence,abuse_of_confidence).

abuse_of_confidence <= fact_of_abuse_of_confidence.
```

Figure 8 shows a BAF transformed from the PROLEG program. For convenience, the nodes are named $a, a1, \ldots, a6, b, c, d, \ldots, h$, respectively.

We identified the evidences that are required for this BAF to enable the plaintiff and the defendant to achieve their respective goals using the reasoning proposed in the previous section. As a result, it is impossible for the plaintiff to make the label of a to in. Therefore, there is no way for the plaintiff to win by applying the law, depending on the defendant's behaviors. On the other hand, the defendant should provide evidences $ex(c)$ and $ex(d)$ to make the label of a to out. Then, it is possible to prevent application of the law, regardless of the evidences provided by the plaintiff.

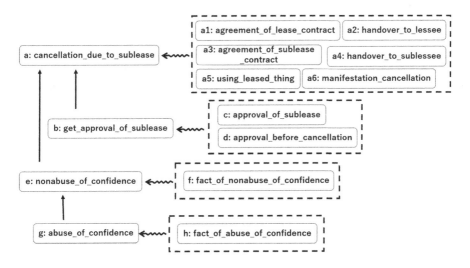

Fig. 8. BAF for a house-lease case.

In this case, what can the plaintiff do? Is there no way to achieve his/her goal? One solution is to scrutinize the evidences required for the defendant, that is, $ex(c)$ and $ex(d)$. Is it possible for the defendant (the lessee) to provide evidences for c and d, that is, approval_of_sublease and approval_before_cancellation? Mechanically, it is impossible to make either of the labels c and d to *out* if the defendant provided evidences for these nodes. But actually, these two approvals must be granted by the lessor, and the defendant may not give such evidences.

Assume that evidences for c and d are not provided. By applying the reasoning process again, the plaintiff would find that the evidences for $a1, \ldots, a6$ and h would be required to achieve his/her goal. If he/she were able to present these evidences, the defendant would not be able to prevent application of the law. Therefore, he/she will prepare these evidences. This example shows that, even if mechanical reasoning based on the BAF structure yields a solution of "impossible," it is not always impossible actually.

The reasoning proposed for the BAF supports the plaintiff's/defendant's ability to achieve his/her goals by producing the required evidences. Additionally, it helps them to check the possibility of presenting evidences that would be disadvantageous to their case and suggests the behaviors that would be to their advantage.

7 Related Works

Several works on BAF semantics have been undertaken. In almost all of them, the BAFs are given in advance or obtained by a translation from artificial logic programs. Such programs principally discuss argumentation structures that are seldom seen in actual judgments. On the other hand, we sought to apply real-world legal reasoning. A significant issue during transformation is to give BAF semantics preserving legal reasoning; no previous BAF semantics met this criterion.

Cayrol et al. investigated BAF semantics, defining several types of indirect attacks by combining attacks with supports. They also defined several types of extension [6]. Next, the concept of "coalition" (a set of arguments) was introduced and used to define a meta-AF [7,8]. The idea was to reduce a BAF to an AF by deleting the support relations between arguments in the same coalition. An argument in BAF is accepted if it is included in an accepted coalition of the meta-AF. Boella et al. pointed out that this approach does not allow use of the Dung semantics, and revised the semantics by introducing different meta-arguments and meta-supports [2]. However, if we adopt these semantics, the semantics of PROLEG and BAF do not coincide [11]. It follows that we cannot combine arguments to form a single support without considering their original relationships in PROLEG.

Noueioua et al. proposed a BAF that considered a support relation to be a "necessity" relation [12]. In this approach, each atom corresponds to each argument, similar to our approach. They proved the correspondence between a normal logic program and their BAF. The main drawback of the method is that it does not discriminate support by a set of arguments from support given by separate multiple arguments. They do not reflect the case in which a set of body goals support its head goal in a logic program.

Oren and Norman developed an evidence-based argumentation by introducing a special unique argument, corresponding to an environment, into a BAF [13]. The introduction of such a special argument is similar to that of existence and absence arguments in our method. The difference is that we add an existence or absence argument for each fact and add a support/an attack from each existence/absence argument, respectively, so that our BAF should keep a PROLEG structure.

Unlike the works cited above, Brewka et al. developed an abstract dialectical framework (ADF) as a generalization of the Dung AF [3,4]. In the ADF, each node is associated with an acceptance condition depending on the parent nodes, and each link exhibits an individual strength. A bipolar ADF is a subclass of ADF in which a link is either attacked or supported depending on the polarity of its strength. A BAF transformed from PROLEG may be considered to be an instantiation of an ADF. It would be interesting to explore whether an ADF semantics could be simply applied to a BAF transformed from PROLEG.

8 Conclusion

We have described the transformation from a PROLEG description to a BAF, and the legal reasoning using the BAF. We gave semantics to the BAF preserving the features of a PROLEG program. The BAF reflects the structure of the judgment process and causality among arguments. We have developed reasoning on the BAF, that is difficult to emulate or understand using a PROLEG program or execution trace. Our system will help lawyers and law school students to analyze judgments.

In future, we will improve reasoning by the BAF and create a graphical interface. We are also considering the combination of our reasoning method and existing causal reasoning, and we will compare our method with the existing reasoning scheme such as Abductive Logic Programming.

Acknowledgment. This work was supported by JSPS KAKENHI Grant Number JP17H06103.

References

1. Bench-Capon, T., Prakken, H., Sartor, G.: Argumentation in legal reasoning. In: Simari, G., Rahwan, I. (eds.) Argumentation in Artificial Intelligence, pp. 363–382. Springer, Boston (2009). https://doi.org/10.1007/978-0-387-98197-0_18
2. Boella, G., Gabbay, D.M., van der Torre, L., Villata, S.: Support in abstract argumentation. In: Proceedings of COMMA 2010, pp. 40–51 (2010)
3. Brewka, G., Woltran, S.: Abstract dialectical frameworks. In: Proceedings of KR 2010, pp. 102–111 (2010)

4. Brewka, G., Ellmauthaler, S., Strass, H., Wallner, J.P., Woltran, S.: Abstract dialectical frameworks revisited. In: Proceedings of IJCAI 2013, pp. 803–809 (2013)
5. Caminada, M.: On the issue of reinstatement in argumentation. In: Fisher, M., van der Hoek, W., Konev, B., Lisitsa, A. (eds.) JELIA 2006. LNCS (LNAI), vol. 4160, pp. 111–123. Springer, Heidelberg (2006). https://doi.org/10.1007/11853886_11
6. Cayrol, C., Lagasquie-Schiex, M.C.: On the acceptability of arguments in bipolar argumentation frameworks. In: Godo, L. (ed.) ECSQARU 2005. LNCS (LNAI), vol. 3571, pp. 378–389. Springer, Heidelberg (2005). https://doi.org/10.1007/11518655_33
7. Cayrol, C., Lagasquie-Schiex, M.: Coalitions of arguments: a tool for handling bipolar argumentation frameworks. Int. J. Intell. Syst. **25**, 83–109 (2010)
8. Cayrol, C., Lagasquie-Schiex, M.: Bipolarity in argumentation graphs: towards a better understanding. Int. J. Approximate Reasoning **54**, 876–899 (2013)
9. Dung, P.M.: On the acceptability of arguments and its fundamental role in non-monotonic reasoning, logic programming and n-person games. Artif. Intell. **77**, 321–357 (1995)
10. Gelfond, M., Lifschitz, V.: The stable model semantics for logic programming. In: Proceedings of ICLP, pp. 1070–1080 (1988)
11. Kawasaki, T., Moriguchi, S., Takahashi, K.: Transformation from PROLEG to a bipolar argumentation framework. In: Proceedings of SAFA 2018, pp. 36–47 (2018)
12. Nouioua, F., Risch, V.: Argumentation frameworks with necessities. In: Benferhat, S., Grant, J. (eds.) SUM 2011. LNCS (LNAI), vol. 6929, pp. 163–176. Springer, Heidelberg (2011). https://doi.org/10.1007/978-3-642-23963-2_14
13. Oren, N., Norman, T.J.: Semantics for evidence-based argumentation. In: Proceedings of COMMA 2008, pp. 276–284 (2008)
14. Prakken, H., Reed, C., Walton, D.: Dialogues about the burden of proof. In: Proceedings of ICAIL 2005, pp. 115–124 (2005)
15. Rahwan, I., Simari, G. (eds.): Argumentation in Artificial Intelligence. Springer, Boston (2009). https://doi.org/10.1007/978-0-387-98197-0
16. Reed, C., Rowe, G.: Araucaria: software for argument analysis, diagramming and representation. Int. J. AI Tools **13**, 961–980 (2004)
17. Satoh, K., et al.: PROLEG: an implementation of the presupposed ultimate fact theory of Japanese civil code by PROLOG technology. In: Onada, T., Bekki, D., McCready, E. (eds.) JSAI-isAI 2010. LNCS (LNAI), vol. 6797, pp. 153–164. Springer, Heidelberg (2011). https://doi.org/10.1007/978-3-642-25655-4_14
18. Satoh, K., et al.: On generality of PROLEG knowledge representation. In: Proceedings of JURISIN 2012, pp. 115–128 (2012)

An Empirical Evaluation of AMR Parsing for Legal Documents

Trong Sinh Vu[✉] and Le Minh Nguyen[✉]

Japan Advanced Institute of Science and Technology (JAIST), Nomi, Japan
{sinhvtr,nguyenml}@jaist.ac.jp

Abstract. Many approaches have been proposed to tackle the problem of Abstract Meaning Representation (AMR) parsing, help solving various natural language processing issues recently. In our paper, we provide an overview of different methods in AMR parsing and their performances when analyzing legal documents. We conduct experiments of different AMR parsers on our annotated dataset extracted from the English version of Japanese Civil Code. Our results show the limitations as well as open a room for improvements of current parsing techniques when applying in this non-trivial domain.

Keywords: Abstract Meaning Representation · Semantic parsing · Legal text

1 Introduction

In Natural Language Processing, semantic representation of text plays an important role and receives growing attention in the past few years. Many semantic schemes have been proposed, such as Groningen Meaning Bank [1], Abstract Meaning Representation [14], Universal Conceptual Cognitive Annotation [18]. In which, Abstract Meaning Representation (AMR) has shown a great potential and gained popularity in computational linguistics [9,11,13,25].

AMR is a semantic representation language that encodes the meaning of a sentence as a rooted, directed, edge-labeled, leaf-labeled graph while abstracting away the surface forms in a sentence. Every vertex and edge of the graph are labeled according to the sense of the words in a sentence. AMR can be represented in PENMAN notation, for a human to read and write easily, or graph structure, for a computer to store in its memory, or decomposed into conjunctions of logical triples, for calculating the difference among AMRs. Table 1 shows an example of AMR annotation for the sentence *"The boy wants to go"* with different formats mentioned above.

AMR has been applied as an intermediate meaning representation for solving various problems in NLP including machine translation [12], summarization [16], event extraction [15,22,27], machine comprehension [21]. For AMR to be useful in these problems, the AMR parsing task, which aims to map a natural language

© Springer Nature Switzerland AG 2019
K. Kojima et al. (Eds.): JSAI-isAI 2018 Workshops, LNAI 11717, pp. 131–145, 2019.
https://doi.org/10.1007/978-3-030-31605-1_11

Table 1. AMR for the sentence *"The boy wants to go"* in three formats, from left to right: logical triples, PENMAN notation and graph structure

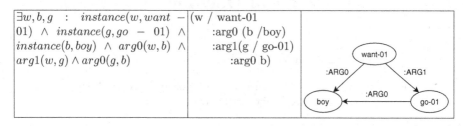

| $\exists w, b, g \; : \; instance(w, want - 01) \; \land \; instance(g, go - 01) \; \land \; instance(b, boy) \; \land \; arg0(w, b) \; \land \; arg1(w, g) \land arg0(g, b)$ | (w / want-01
  :arg0 (b /boy)
  :arg1(g / go-01)
    :arg0 b) | |

string to an AMR graph, plays a crucial role. Despite the advantages in handling semantic attributes of text, there are not many works exploring the application of AMR in analyzing legal documents. Unlike other domains, understanding legal text faces a number of challenges due to the special characteristics such as complicated structures, long sentences, domain-specific terminology.

In this paper, we investigate the potential of AMR in this interesting field. We provide an overview of main approaches in current AMR parsing techniques in Sect. 2. From each approach, we choose best systems that already published the source code to conduct our experiments. In Sect. 3, we revise the dataset **JCivilCode-1.0** introduced in 2017 by Dac Viet et al. [7] with some modifications and additional samples. We also extract sentences with various lengths from a well-known dataset LDC2017T10[1] in common domain to have more observation on the performances of each system. Our results and some discussions are provided in Sect. 4.

2   Approaches in AMR Parsing

2.1   AMR Notation

In AMRs, each node is named by an ID (variable). It contains the semantic concept, which can be a word (e.g. *boy*) or a PropBank frameset (e.g. *want-01*) or a special keyword. The keywords consist of entity type (e.g. *date-entity, ordinal-entity, percentage-entity*), quantities (e.g. *distance-quantity*), and logical conjunction (e.g. *and, or*). The edge between two vertices is labeled using more than 100 relations including frameset argument index (e.g. *":ARG0", ":ARG1"*), semantic relations (e.g. *":location", ":name"*), relations for quantities (e.g. *:quant, :unit, :scale*), relations for date-entities, relations for listing (e.g. *:op1, :op2, :op3*). AMR also provides the inverse form of all relations by concatenating -of to the original relation (e.g. :ARG1 vs :ARG1-of, :location vs :location-of). Hence, if r is a directed relation of two entities a and b, we have $R(a, b) \equiv R - of(b, a)$. This inverse relation is often used when focusing on a specific entity, e.g. in the example from Table 1, if the annotation is:

---

[1] https://catalog.ldc.upenn.edu/ldc2017t10.

(b /boy
  :arg0-of (w /want-01)
    :arg1 (g / go-01) :arg0 b)

then the entity *"boy"* is focused rather than the verb *"want-01"*, thus the corresponding sentence should be *"The boy who wants to go"*.

The task of parsing a natural language text into an AMR graph faces a lot of challenges, such as word-sense disambiguation, semantic graph construction, data sparsity. Many approaches have been proposed to tackle this problem. They can be divided into three main categories: alignment-based, grammar-based and machine-translation-based (Fig. 1).

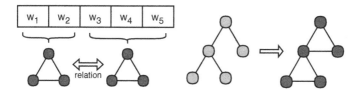

(a) Alignment-based method   (b) Grammar-based method

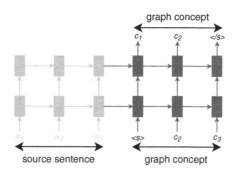

(c) Machine-translation-based method

Fig. 1. Main approaches in AMR parsing

2.2 Alignment-Based Parsing

One of the pioneer AMR parsing solutions is **JAMR** introduced by Flanigan et al. in 2014 [8], which build a two-part algorithm that first identifies concepts with an automatic aligner and then identifies the relations that it obtains between these by searching for the maximum spanning connected subgraph from an edge-labeled, directed graph representing all possible relations between the identified concepts. This method provided a strong baseline in AMR parsing.

Follow this approach, Zhou et al. [28] extended the relation identification tasks with a component-wise beam search algorithm. Lyu and Titov [5] improved this method by considering alignments as latent variables in a joint probabilistic model. They used variational autoencoding technique to perform the alignment inference and archived the state-of-the-art in AMR parsing until now. But the source code for this model has not been published completely yet. In this paper, we take the JAMR model [8] to analyze and conduct experiments.

The core idea of alignment-based methods is to construct a concept set by aligning the Propbank concepts with the words that evoke them. The authors build an automatic aligner that uses a set of rules to greedily align concepts to words. The authors use WordNet to generate candidate lemmas and a fuzzy match of a concept, defined to be a word in the sentence that has the longest string prefix match with that concept's label. For instance, the fuzzy match for **apply-01** could be aligned with *"application"* if this word is the best match in the sentence. Figure 2 shows an example of aligning words in a sentence with AMR concepts. This JAMR aligner is widely used in many later works.

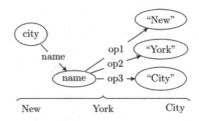

Fig. 2. Alignment of the words span "New York City" with AMR fragment [8]

In the first stage of identifying concepts, given a sentence $w = \{w_1, w_2, ..., w_n\}$, the parser segments w into subsequences, denoted $\{w_{b_0:b_1}, w_{b_1:b_2}, ..., w_{b_{k-1}:b_k}\}$, called contiguous spans. A span $\{w_{b_{i-1}:b_i}\}$ is then assigned to a concept graph fragment c_i from the concept set $clex\{w_{b_{i-1}:b_i}\}$, or to θ for words that evoke no concept. This assigning between sequence of spans b and concept graph fragment c is calculated by a score function:

$$score(b, c; \theta) = \sum_{i=1}^{k} \theta^T f(w_{b_{i-1}:b_i}, b_{i-1}, c_i), \tag{1}$$

where f is a feature vector representation of a span and one of its concept graph fragments in the sentence. The features can be fragment given words, length of the matching span, name entity recognizing or bias.

To find the highest-scoring between b and c, JAMR uses a semi-Markov model. Let $S(i)$ be the score of the first i words of the sentence $(w_{o:i})$. Then $S(i)$ is calculated recurrently via the previous scores, with the initialization $S(0) = 0$.

Obviously, $S(n)$ becomes the best score. To obtain the best scoring concept labeling, JAMR uses back-pointers method, similar to the implementation of the Viterbi algorithm [19].

The second stage is to identify the relation, which sets the edge label among the concept subgraph fragments assigned in the previous stage. The authors tackle this stage like a graph-based dependency parser problem. While the dependency parser aims to find the maximum-scoring tree over words from the sentence, the relation identifier tries to find the maximum-scoring among subgraphs that preserve concept fragments from the previous stage.

To train the two stage parser, the authors formulate the training data for concept identification and relation identification separately. In both tasks, the input must be annotated with name entities (obtained from Illinois Name Entity Tagger), part-of-speech tags and basic dependencies (obtained from Stanford Parser). The detail settings and hyper-parameters can be found in the original paper. This parser has been evaluated the first time on LDC2013E117 corpus (in 2014), archived the Smatch score (the metric to evaluate an AMR parser) of **0.58**, and the second time on LDC2015E86 corpus (in 2016), which showed great improvement with **0.67** Smatch score.

2.3   Grammar-Based Parsing

After the success of Flanigan et al. with an alignment-based approach [8], Wang et al. [24] introduced a grammar-based (or transition-based) parser called **CAMR**. The authors first use a dependency parser to generate the dependency tree for the sentence, then transform the dependency tree to an AMR graph through some transition rules. This method takes advantages of the achievements in dependency parsing, with a training set much larger than the training set of AMR parsing. Damonte et al. [17]. Brandt et al. [2], Goodman et al. [10] and Peng et al. [26] also applied the grammar-based algorithm in their works and obtained competitive results. Figure 3 shows an example of the dependency tree and the AMR graph parsed from the same sentence *"Private rights must conform to the public welfare"*.

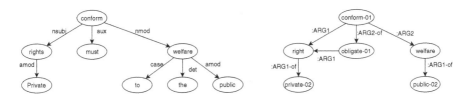

Fig. 3. Dependency tree and AMR graph generated from the sentence *"Private rights must conform to the public welfare"*

Unlike the dependency tree of a sentence, where each word corresponds to a node in the tree, in AMR graph, some words become abstract concepts or relations while other words are simply deleted because they do not contribute to the meaning. This difference causes many difficulties for aligning word tokens and the concept. In order to learn the transition from the dependency tree to AMR graph, Wang et al. [24] use the algorithm from JAMR to produce the alignment. The authors also construct a span graph to represent an AMR graph that is aligned with the word tokens in a sentence. This span graph is a directed, labeled graph $G = (V, A)$, where $V = \{s_{i,j} | i, j \in (0, n) \text{ and } j > i\}$ is a set of nodes, and $A \subseteq V \times V$ is a set of arcs. Each node $s_{i,j}$ in G is assigned a concept label from concept set L_V and is mapped with a continuous span $(w_i, ..., w_{j-1})$ in the sentence w. Each arc is also assigned a relation label from relation set L_A.

Basically, CAMR will perform three types of actions to transform the dependency tree into the AMR graph: actions performed when an edge is visited, actions performed when a node is visited, and actions used to infer abstract concepts in AMR that do not correspond to any word in the sentence. For the details of these actions, readers can refer to the original paper [23], the Boosting version [4] and the paper at Semeval2016 contest [24]. A disadvantage of this method is that it limits the parsing ability to a single sentence, because the dependency tree can cover only the structure inside a sentence.

Damonte et al. [17] developed a transition-based model called **AMREager** that also parses the AMR graph based on transition rules, but differs from CAMR which requires the full dependency tree to be obtained and then process the tree bottom-up, this parser process the sentence left-to-right. AMREager defines a stack, a buffer and a configuration to perform the transition actions, which can be: *Shift, LArc, RArc* or *Reduce*. AMREager also uses the alignment obtained from JAMR aligner to map indices from the sentence to AMR graph fragments. Although the result in Smatch score is still lower than CAMR and JAMR by a small margin, AMREager obtains best results on several subtasks such as Name Ent. and Negation (F-score on the named entity recognition and negation detection, respectively).

2.4 Machine-Translation-Based Parsing

Recently, with the achievement of the encoder-decoder architecture in deep neural networks, several supervised learning approaches have been proposed in order to deal with AMR parsing task. They attempt to linearize the AMR in Penman notation to sequences of text, at character-level [20] or at word-level [9,13], so that the parsing task can be considered as a translation task, which transforms a sentence into an AMR-like sequence. In this paper, we choose **NeuralAMR** (word-level linearization) [13] and **Ch-AMR** (character-level linearization) [20] to run our experiments.

Given an AMR graph represented in Penman notation, NeuralAMR preprocesses the graph through a series of steps: AMR linearization, anonymization, and other modifications which aim to reduce the complexity of the linearized sequences and to address sparsity from certain open class vocabulary entries, such as named entities and quantities (Table 2). Representing AMR graphs in this way, NeuralAMR takes advantage of sequence-to-sequence model by using

Table 2. AMR linearization for the sentence *"Private rights must conform to the public welfare"* in NeuralAMR - the left side is the original AMR and the right side is the linearized string

(o / obligate-01 　　:ARG1 (r / right-05 　　　　:ARG1-of (p / private-02)) 　　:ARG2 (c / conform-01 　　　　:ARG1 r 　　　　:ARG2 (w / welfare 　　　　　:ARG1-of (p2 / public-02))))	(obligate-01 :ARG1 (right-05 :ARG1-of (private-02)) :ARG2 (conform-01 :ARG1 (right-05) :ARG2 (welfare :ARG1-of (public-02))))

a stack bidirectional Long Short Term Memory (LSTM) encoder to encode the input sequence and a stacked LSTM to decode from the hidden states produced by the encoder. The output string of the model is converted back to AMR format to complete the parsing process. Since this approach requires a huge amount of labeled data, NeuralAMR uses paired training procedure to bootstrap a high-quality AMR parser from millions of unlabeled Gigaword sentences [6]. With this extra dataset, the parsing result increases significantly, from *0.55* to *0.62* in Smatch score. However, it is difficult for this linearization method to keep the structure of the original graph. In the example shown in Table 2, the distance between two nodes: *"obligate-01"* and *"conform-01"*, which are directly connected in the graph, becomes 5 (tokens) in the linearized string, as shown in Table 2. This distance can be even larger in long sentences with complicated structure, thus causing many mistakes in the annotation.

P r i v a t e *JJ* r i g h t s *NNS* m u s t *MD* c o n f o r m *VB* t o *TO* t h e *DT* p u b l i c *NN* w e l f a r e *NN*
(obligate-01 :ARG1 (right-05 :ARG1-of (private-02)) :ARG2 (conform-01 :ARG1 (right-05) :ARG2 (welfare :ARG1-of (public-02))))

Fig. 4. Preprocessing data in Ch-AMR - The sentence is converted to sequence of characters with POS tag in uppercase following each word, the AMR graph is linearized and removed all variables

Different from Kontas et al. [13], Noord and Bos [20] introduce another approach in linearizing which transforms the AMR graph to the character-level. This model removes all variables from the AMRs and duplicates co-referring nodes. The input sentences are also tokenized in character-level, along with the part-of-speech tag of the original tokens to provide more linguistic information to the decoder. An example of such a preprocessed AMR is shown in Fig. 4. Obviously, this preprocessing method causes loss of information, since the variables cannot be put back perfectly. To tackle this limitation, the authors describe an approach to restore the co-referring nodes in the output. All wikification relations present in AMRs in the training set are also removed and restored in a post-processing step. This model archives a better result, with **0.71** Smatch score.

In this section, we provided an overview about three main approaches in AMR parsing, with a brief description of five parsers belong to these approaches. Our experiments are conducted using the original models of these five parsers without any modification or retrain. Dataset information as well as experiment results will be reported in the upcoming sections.

3   Dataset and Evaluation

3.1   Dataset

The original dataset used for testing in this paper is JCivilCode-1.0, which is introduced by Dac Viet et al. in [7]. In our work, we revised JCivilCode-1.0 carefully with some modifications and extracted 48 more articles to complete the first four chapters in Part I of the Japanese Civil Code. All the AMRs are annotated by two annotators to ensure the neutrality of evaluation. Table 3 shows some statistics of this dataset after our revision.

Table 3. JCivilCode-1.0 statistic

Number of samples	128
Average length	31
Max sentence length	107
Average number of graph nodes	28
Max number of graph nodes	96
Vocabulary size	796
Number of tokens	4042

As we mentioned in Sect. 1, one of the main difficulty in analyzing legal documents is dealing with long sentences. In our experiments, we also would like to assess the performances of the five models with different lengths of the sentence. Since the current legal dataset is still small, we use extra sentences extracted from the well-known LDC2017T10 dataset, which consists of nearly 40,000 sentences in the news domain. We divide the test set of LDC2017T10 into four subsets LDC-20, LDC-20-30, LDC-30-40, LDC-40 with the lengths of the sentences in range 0–20, 21–30, 31–40 and greater than 40 words, respectively. We excluded the samples containing sub-sentences inside (annotated *"multi-sentence"* by the annotators). This exclusion guaranteed a fair comparison among the five parsers because CAMR is unable to analyze multiple sentences at the same time.

3.2   Evaluation

AMR parsers are evaluated mainly by Smatch score [3]. Given the parsed graphs and the gold graphs in the form of Penman annotations, Smatch first tries to find the best alignments between the variable names for each pair of graphs and it then computes precision, recall and F1 of the concepts and relations. In this paper, to test the performance of AMR parser on legal text, which contains sentences in complicated structures, we analyze the parsing results in a deeper measurement. Specifically, we use the test-suite introduced by Damonte et al. [17], which assesses the parsing results on various sub-scores as follow:

- *Unlabeled*: Smatch score computed on the predicted graphs after removing all edge labels (e.g., *:ARG0, :condition*)
- *No WSD*: Smatch score while ignoring Propbank senses (e.g., *perform-01* vs *perform-02*)
- *Name Entity*: F-score on the named entity recognition (:name roles)
- *Wikification*: F-score on the wikification (:wiki roles)
- *Negation*: F-score on the negation detection (:polarity roles)
- *Concepts*: F-score on the concept identification task
- *Reentrancies*: Smatch computed on reentrant edges only
- *SRL*: Smatch computed on :ARG-i roles only

In our experiment with JCivilcode-1.0, we do not include the Wikification and Name Entity criteria since there are no Wiki concepts included in this dataset, and the number of existing named entities is small.

4   Experiments and Discussion

To evaluate the performance of different parsing strategies on legal text, we conduct experiments on five models that already provided their source codes: JAMR, CAMR, AMR-Eager, NeuralAMR and Ch-AMR. While JAMR, CAMR and AMR-Eager were trained with the LDC2015E86 dataset only (the older version of LDC2017T10), NeuralAMR and Ch-AMR initialized the parser by LDC2015E86 and then used an extra corpus of 2 millions sentences extracted from a free text corpus Gigaword [6] to train the complete models[2].

We provide some statistics about LDC2015E86 as well as LDC2017T10 in Table 4. English sentences in these two datasets are collected from TV program transcriptions, web blogs and forums. Each sample in these datasets includes a pair of sentence and AMR graph corresponding.

Parsing results are summarized in Table 5 (LDC2017T10 long sentences experiments) and Table 6 (JCivilCode1.0 experiments). Overall, the Smatch score of all the parsers on JCivilCode-1.0 is still lower than on LDC2017T10 by a large margin. It can be figured out that grammar-based and alignment-based

---

[2] We keep the original trained models without retrained on the new dataset LDC2017T10.

Table 4. LDC2015E86 and LDC2017T10 number of samples

Dataset	Total	Train	Dev	Test
LDC2015E86	19,572	16,833	1,368	1,371
LDC2017T10	39,260	36,521	1,368	1,371
LDC-20	–	–	–	694
LDC-20-30	–	–	–	284
LDC-30-40	–	–	–	143
LDC-40	–	–	–	82

Table 5. Smatch scores on LDC2017T10 (different ranges of length)

	JAMR	CAMR	AMREager	NeuralAMR	Ch-AMR
LDC-20	**0.71**	0.66	0.69	0.65	0.45
LDC-20-30	**0.68**	0.62	0.64	0.59	0.43
LDC-30-40	**0.66**	0.60	0.62	0.56	0.42
LDC-40	**0.65**	0.59	0.62	0.54	0.40

Table 6. Smatch scores and sub-scores on JCivilcode-1.0

	JAMR	CAMR	AMREager	NeuralAMR	Ch-AMR
Smatch	0.45	**0.48**	0.43	0.39	0.28
Unlabeled	0.50	**0.56**	0.53	0.46	0.37
No WSD	0.47	**0.50**	0.45	0.40	0.28
Negation	0.23	0.16	0.32	**0.35**	0.19
Concepts	0.59	**0.63**	0.62	0.52	0.35
Reentrancies	0.32	**0.35**	0.31	0.29	0.22
SRL	0.43	**0.47**	0.41	0.40	0.28

methods showed promising results over MT-based method. JAMR and CAMR archieved the best score on LDC2017T10 long sentences and JCivilCode-1.0 dataset, respectively, while AMREager's performance was competitive on both tasks.

In LDC2017T10 experiments, JAMR remained the best parser in every range of sentence length. The gap between this method and the others even becomes larger when parsing longer sentences. Although grammar-based methods focus on constructing the structure of the graph based on its corresponding dependency tree, CAMR and AMREager are unable to provide better output than JAMR.

In legal text parsing experiments, CAMR outperforms the others on both the Smatch score and many sub-scores. Specifically, this method obtains best results in constructing graph topology (*Unlabeled*), predicting the Propbank sense (No

Table 7. Common errors: Incorrect concept - **Incorrect relation** - Missing concept - **Missing attribute**

Example	Private rights must conform to the public welfare (1)	No abuse of rights is permitted (2)

Gold annotation	(o / obligate-01
	  :ARG1 (r / right-05
	    :ARG1-of (p / private-02))
	  :ARG2 (c / conform-01
	    :ARG1 r
	    :ARG2 (w / welfare
	      :ARG1-of (p2 / public-02))))
		(p / permit-01
		  :polarity -
		  :ARG1 (a / abuse-01
		    :ARG1 (r / right-05)))

JAMR	(c / conform-01
	  :ARG1 (r / **right**
	    :ARG1-of (p2 / **private-03**))
	  :ARG2 (w / welfare
	    :domain-of (p / **public**)))
	
	(missing concept " **obligate-01** ")
		(p / permit-01
		  :ARG1 (a / abuse-01
		    :ARG1 (r / **right**))
		  :polarity -)

CAMR	(x2 / right-05
	  :ARG1-of (x1 / **private-03**)
	  :ARG1-of (x4 / conform-01
	  :ARG2 (x8 / welfare
	    :mod (x7 / **public**))))
	
	(missing concept " **obligate-01** ")
		(x6 / permit-01
		  :ARG1 (x2 / abuse-01
		    :ARG1 (x4 / **right**)))
		
		(missing attribute " **:polarity -** ")

AMR-Eager	(v3 / conform-01
	  :ARG1 (v2 / **right**
	    :ARG1-of (v1 / **private-03**))
	  :ARG2 (v5 / welfare
	    :mod (v4 / **public**)))
	
	(missing concept " **obligate-01** ")
		(v3 / permit-01
		  :ARG1 (v1 / abuse-01
		    polarity -
		    :ARG1 (v2 / **right**)))

Neural-AMR	(o / obligate-01
	  :arg2 (r / **rule-out-02**
	    :arg0 (r2 / **right**
	      :arg1-of (p / **private-03**))
	    :arg1 (w / welfare
	      :mod (p2 / public))))
		(p / permit-01
		  :polarity -
		  :arg1 (a / **abuse-02**
		    :arg1 (r / **right**)))

Ch-AMR	(vv1conform-01 / conform-01
	  :ARG1 (vv1person / **person**
	    :ARG1-of (vv1private-03 / **private-03**))
	  :ARG2 (vv1welfare / welfare
	    :ARG1-of **vv1**))
	
	(missing concept **"right-05"**, **"public-02"**, **"obligate-01"**)
		(vv3permit-01 / permit-01
		  :ARG1 (vv3no-abuse / **no-abuse**))
		
		(missing concept **"right-05"**)

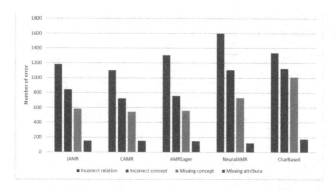

Fig. 5. Common error types statistics

WSD and SRL) as well as identifying concepts in AMR graphs (Concepts score). When parsing graphs containing cycles, CAMR also performs better, as shown in Reentrancies scores.

We analyze some common errors in parsing outputs of legal sentences, with the statistics given in Fig. 5 and the examples provided in Table 7. One of the most common errors in alignment-based and grammar-based performances is missing concept and relation related to *modal verbs*. In legal documents, modal verbs (e.g. the word "may" appears in 29%, the word "must" appears in 19% of samples in the dataset) play a crucial role in a sentence and decide whether an action is permitted or not. This differs from other domains, where these words do not often contribute a lot to the sentence meaning. As shown in example 1 in Table 7, only NeuralAMR is capable of identifying the concept *"obligate-01"* while other models totally ignore it.

Another challenge in parsing legal text is the logical complexity. In this aspect, all the parsers still show limitation when parsing negative clause. This is not too surprising as many negations are encoded with morphology (e.g., such as *"un-"* prefix in *"unless"* or *"unable"*) and cause difficulties for detection. In Table 7, we show an example of outputs from all the parsers for a sentence: *"No abuse of rights is permitted"*. NeuralAMR and JAMR succeeded in converting negation to *:polarity -*, AMREager did not put this edge in the exact position, but in this case, it does not change the meaning of the sentence. CAMR performs even worse as it skips this important information.

5   Conclusions

We conducted experiments of AMR parsing on the legal dataset JCivilCode-1.0 and news domain dataset LDC2017T10 with different ranges of sentence length to observe the abilities of five different models. The parsing outputs were evaluated by Smatch metric in several aspects including overall F-score and sub-score on specific tasks. Experimental results showed the domain adaptation of five models for the legal domain and the performance decreased by approximately

0.2 on the Smatch score. This result shows difficulties in applying AMR parsing for analyzing legal documents.

Currently, our legal dataset JCivilcode-1.0 is still too small compared to LDC2017T10. In order to improve the domain adaptation ability for current approaches as well as to obtain a fully evaluation, the legal dataset has to be enlarged. This work requires a lot of efforts from experts in both linguistic and legal domain.

Acknowledgment. This work was supported by JST CREST Grant Number JPMJCR1513, Japan.

References

1. Basile, V., Bos, J., Evang, K., Venhuizen, N.: Developing a large semantically annotated corpus. In: Proceedings of the Eighth International Conference on Language Resources and Evaluation (LREC 2012), Istanbul, Turkey, pp. 3196–3200 (2012)
2. Brandt, L., Grimm, D., Zhou, M., Versley, Y.: ICL-HD at SemEval-2016 Task 8: meaning representation parsing - augmenting AMR parsing with a preposition semantic role labeling neural network. In: Proceedings of the 10th International Workshop on Semantic Evaluation (SemEval-2016), pp. 1160–1166. Association for Computational Linguistics (2016)
3. Cai, S., Knight, K.: Smatch: an evaluation metric for semantic feature structures. In: Proceedings of the 51st Annual Meeting of the Association for Computational Linguistics, pp. 748–752. Association for Computational Linguistics (2013)
4. Wang, C., Xue, N., Pradhan, S.: Boosting transition-based AMR parsing with refined actions and auxiliary analyzers. In: Proceedings of the 53rd Annual Meeting of the Association for Computational Linguistics and the 7th International Joint Conference on Natural Language Processing, pp. 857–862. Association for Computational Linguistics (2015)
5. Lyu, C., Titov, I.: AMR parsing as graph prediction with latent alignment. In: Proceedings of the 56th Annual Meeting of the Association for Computational Linguistics, pp. 397–407 (2018)
6. Napoles, C., Gormley, M., Van Durme, B.: Annotated gigaword. In: Proceedings of the Joint Workshop on Automatic Knowledge Base Construction and Web-Scale Knowledge Extraction. Association for Computational Linguistics (2012)
7. Dac Viet, L., Trong Sinh, V., Le Minh, N., Satoh, K.: ConvAMR: abstract meaning representation parsing for legal document. In: Proceedings of the Second International Workshop on SCIentific DOCument Analysis (SCIDOCA), October 2017
8. Flanigan, J., Thomson, S., Carbonell, J., Dyer, C., Smith, N.A.: A discriminative graph-based parser for the abstract meaning representation. In: Proceedings of the 52nd Annual Meeting of the Association for Computational Linguistics (Volume 1: Long Papers), pp. 1426–1436. Association for Computational Linguistics (2014)
9. Gildea, D., Xue, N., Peng, X., Wang, C.: Addressing the data sparsity issue in neural AMR parsing. In: EACL (2017)
10. Goodman, J., Vlachos, A., Naradowsky, J.: UCL+Sheffield at SemEval-2016 Task 8: imitation learning for AMR parsing with an alpha-bound. In: SemEval@NAACL-HLT (2016)

11. Flanigan, J., Dyer, C., Smith, N.A., Carbonell, J.: Generation from abstract meaning representation using tree transducers. In: Proceedings of the 2016 Conference of the North American Chapter of the Association for Computational Linguistics, Sandiego, California, pp. 731–739 (2016)

12. Jones, B., Andreas, J., Bauer, D., Moritz Hermann, K., Knight, K.: Semantics-based machine translation with hyperedge replacement grammars. In: 24th International Conference on Computational Linguistics - Proceedings of COLING 2012: Technical Papers, pp. 1359–1376, December 2012

13. Konstas, I., Iyer, S., Yatskar, M., Choi, Y., Zettlemoyer, L.: Neural AMR: sequence-to-sequence models for parsing and generation. In: Proceedings of the 55th Annual Meeting of the Association for Computational Linguistics (Volume 1: Long Papers), pp. 146–157. Association for Computational Linguistics (2017). https://doi.org/10.18653/v1/P17-1014. http://www.aclweb.org/anthology/P17-1014

14. Banarescu, L., et al.: Abstract meaning representation for sembanking. In: Proceedings of the 7th Linguistic Annotation Workshop and Interoperability with Discourse, pp. 178–186 (2013)

15. Huang, L., et al.: Liberal event extraction and event schema induction. In: ACL (2016)

16. Liu, F., Flanigan, J., Thomson, S., Sadeh, N., Smith, N.A.: Toward abstractive summarization using semantic representations. In: NAACL, pp. 1077–1086 (2015)

17. Damonte, M., Satta, G., Cohen, S.B.: An incremental parser for abstract meaning representation. In: EACL (2017)

18. Abend, O., Rappoport, A.: Universal Conceptual Cognitive Annotation (UCCA). In: Proceedings of the 51st Annual Meeting of the Association for Computational Linguistics, pp. 228–238 (2013)

19. Rabiner, L.R.: A tutorial on Hidden Markov Models and selected applications in speech recognition. Proc. IEEE **77**(2), 257–286 (1989). https://doi.org/10.1109/5.18626

20. van Noord, R., Bos, J.: Neural semantic parsing by character-based translation: experiments with abstract meaning representations. Comput. Linguist. Neth. J. **7**, 93–108 (2017)

21. Sachan, M., Xing, E.: Machine comprehension using rich semantic representations. In: Proceedings of the 54th Annual Meeting of the Association for Computational Linguistics (Volume 2: Short Papers), pp. 486–492. Association for Computational Linguistics (2016). https://doi.org/10.18653/v1/P16-2079. http://www.aclweb.org/anthology/P16-2079

22. Rao, S., Marcu, D., Knight, K., Daum, H.: Biomedical event extraction using abstract meaning representation. In: BioNLP (2017)

23. Wang, C., Xue, N., Pradhan, S.: A transition-based algorithm for AMR parsing. In: Proceedings of the 2015 Conference of the North American Chapter of the Association for Computational Linguistics: Human Language Technologies, pp. 366–375. Association for Computational Linguistics (2015). https://doi.org/10.3115/v1/N15-1040. http://www.aclweb.org/anthology/N15-1040

24. Wang, C., Pradhan, S., Pan, X., Ji, H., Xue, N.: CAMR at SemEval-2016 Task 8: an extended transition-based AMR parser. In: Proceedings of the 10th International Workshop on Semantic Evaluation (SemEval-2016), San Diego, California, pp. 1173–1178. Association for Computational Linguistics, June 2016. http://www.aclweb.org/anthology/S16-1181

25. Wang, Y., et al.: Dependency and AMR embeddings for drug-drug interaction extraction from biomedical literature. In: Proceedings of the 8th ACM International Conference on Bioinformatics, Computational Biology, and Health Informatics, ACM-BCB 2017, pp. 36–43. ACM, New York (2017). https://doi.org/10.1145/3107411.3107426. http://doi.acm.org/10.1145/3107411.3107426
26. Peng, X., Gildea, D., Satta, G.: AMR parsing with cache transition systems. In: AAAI (2018)
27. Pan, X., Cassidy, T., Hermjakob, U., Ji, H., Knight, K.: Unsupervised entity linking with abstract meaning representation. In: Proceedings of the 2015 Conference of the North American Chapter of the Association for Computational Linguistics: Human Language Technologies, pp. 1130–1139 (2015). https://doi.org/10.3115/v1/N15-1119. http://www.aclweb.org/anthology/N15-1119
28. Zhou, J., Xu, F., Uszkoreit, H., Qu, W., Li, R., Gu, Y.: AMR parsing with an incremental joint model. In: Proceedings of the 2016 Conference on Empirical Methods in Natural Language Processing, pp. 680–689. Association for Computational Linguistics (2016). https://doi.org/10.18653/v1/D16-1065. http://www.aclweb.org/anthology/D16-1065

Legal Debugging in Propositional Legal Representation

Wachara Fungwacharakorn$^{(\boxtimes)}$ and Ken Satoh

National Institute of Informatics, Sokendai University, Tokyo, Japan
{wacharaf, ksatoh}@nii.ac.jp

Abstract. Literal interpretation on laws may produce unexpected consequences. They are difficult to be recognized unless exceptional cases were taken to the court. The court may decide a literal interpretation as exceptional, and then they have to identify which rule is a source of exception.

To assist the court, we proposed an idea called *legal debugging*, to find out which rule condition, called *a culprit*, causes unexpected consequences in such exceptional cases. We adapt the algorithmic program debugging with consideration of characteristics in reasoning in judgement, such as non-recursive stratified structures and factual propositions in order to find a culprit at last.

This paper presents legal debugging in propositional Prolog as well as PROLEG (PROlog based LEGal reasoning support system) specialized for legal reasoning. An example of legal debugging that interacts with a user and finds a culprit is also shown under the PROLEG representation of the case adapted from the real Supreme Court case.

Keywords: Legal reasoning · Legal representation · Algorithmic debugging

1 Introduction

Researchers have long been interested in representing legal knowledge in computers. Legal knowledge representation is usually divided into two types: rule-based and case-based. In rule-based legal representation, which is usually used for statutory laws, Legal rules are represented in logic programs such as Prolog [1, 2]. By formalizing the statute rules into computational logic, it provides benefits such as detecting conflicts in legal systems [3].

However, statute laws may be flawed. Even statute laws are cautiously drafted; some issues might be missing. These missing issues lead to unexpected consequences when we interpret the law literally. These issues are usually tacit, meaning that they are hard to know until such exceptional cases happen. When the cases are taken to the court, the court decided that the literal legal interpretation produces an unexpected consequence. The court has to identify which rule is a source of unexpected consequence and the court currently manually identifies such a rule so they might miss some sources of the unexpected result since exhaustive consideration might not be guaranteed.

Therefore, in this paper, we propose an idea of legal debugging, to find legal conditions that cause unexpected consequence, by imitating computer program debugging.

© Springer Nature Switzerland AG 2019
K. Kojima et al. (Eds.): JSAI-isAI 2018 Workshops, LNAI 11717, pp. 146–159, 2019.
https://doi.org/10.1007/978-3-030-31605-1_12

In contrast with legal conflicts that deal with other legal rules written explicitly, legal debugging has to deal with tacit expectations from the courts or the legal experts. This paper tries to identify the existence of unexpected consequences from those tacit expectations and propose legal debugging as a potential way to realize and solve unexpected consequences from laws.

In this paper, we report legal debugging based on algorithmic debugging, which originally proposed for tracing the difference between computation result from the program and expectation result from the user. Our technique traces the difference between a literal interpretation from the legal representation and an expected interpretation from legal experts. At this preliminary step of legal debugging development, we only focus on representation of statute laws which express the laws in written forms. This paper considers legal representations under propositional logic which is the basis of more advanced legal representations. We also take into account of characteristics of reasoning in judgements. For example, the logic rules should be stratified and not recursive so there would be only one interpretation which satisfies the rules.

This paper provides the means to find a legal bug, called a culprit, in two propositional based legal representations. The first representation in this paper is Prolog, which is more familiar to logic programmers. Although Prolog is not designed specifically for laws, a number of law formalizations have been tested in Prolog such as British Nationality Act [1] and the Income Tax Act of Canada [2]. The second representation this paper is PROLEG which stands for PROlog based LEGal reasoning support system [4]. PROLEG uses the concept of exception instead of negation which is more suitable to laws which usually separate between conditions and exceptions in legal documents. PROLEG was implemented based on the Presupposed Ultimate Fact Theory of Japanese Civil code, a legal reasoning scheme in real legal practice [5].

This paper is structured as follows. Section 2 describes propositional legal representation in logic program with negation as failure and defines a legal debugging process under the semantics. Section 3 extends the legal debugging process under the PROLEG semantics. Section 4 demonstrates a legal debugging under PROLEG using the Supreme Court case. Section 5 compares legal debugging and other related works on debugging. The final section summarizes the idea of legal debugging and its application in future works.

2   Legal Debugging Under Prolog

Prolog is a well-known logic programming based on a logic program with negation as failure. Generally, a logic program with negation as failure consists of rules in the form described as follows.

2.1   Basic Definitions

Definition 1. [Rule] A logic program with negation as failure is a finite set of rules Π which each element of Π is a rule R in the form $h \leftarrow b_1,...,b_n, not\ c_1,..., not\ c_m$ where h, b_i $(1 \leq i \leq n)$, and c_j $(1 \leq j \leq m)$ are propositions.

We denote h as $head(R)$, $\{b_1,...,b_n\}$ as $pos\_body(R)$, $\{c_1,...,c_m\}$ as $neg\_body(R)$, and $body(R)$ as $pos\_body(R) \cup neg\_body(R)$. We call a rule without a body a *fact*.

Definition 2. [Active rules] Let M be a set of propositions and Π be a logic program with negation as failure. A set of active rules of Π w.r.t. M denoted as Π^M is a set of $\{head(R) \leftarrow pos\_body(R) \mid$ for all $R \in \Pi$ such that $neg\_body(R) \cap M = \varnothing\}$.

Definition 3. [Satisfaction] Let M be a set of propositions and R be a rule. M *satisfies* R if the following condition is satisfied: if $pos\_body(R) \subseteq M$ then $head(R) \in M$.

Definition 4. [Stable Model] Let Π be a logic program and M be a set of propositions. M is a stable model of Π if M is a minimum model of Π^M.

If M satisfies every rule in Π^M, M is a *model* of Π^M. The *minimum model* of Π^M is a model of Π^M which is the minimum in the sense of set inclusion.

Example 1. The following example shows a logic program with negation as failure P.

$p \leftarrow not\, q.$
$p \leftarrow not\, f.$
$q \leftarrow not\, r.$
$r \leftarrow f.$
$f \leftarrow .$

Let M be $\{f, r, p\}$, a set of active rules of P w.r.t. M or P^M is

$p \leftarrow .$
$r \leftarrow f.$
$f \leftarrow .$

Which M satisfies every rules in P^M and M is the minimum set that can do such things according to P^M. Therefore, M is a stable model of P.

Two assumptions from legal reasoning are introduced to distinguish the propositional legal representation from general logic programs. First assumption is that, generally, legal rules are not recursive. Recursive rules are those rules whose dependency graph contains a loop (see details in [6]). For example $\{p \leftarrow p.\}$, $\{p \leftarrow not\, p.\}$, $\{p \leftarrow q.\ q \leftarrow p.\}$ are recursive, but the program in Example 1 is not recursive. It is proved in [7] that a non-recursive program consists of only one stable model.

Definition 5. [Non-recursive program] A logic program Π is non-recursive when there is a partition $\Pi = \Pi_0 \cup \Pi_1 \cup ... \cup \Pi_n$ (Π_i and Π_j disjoint for all $i \neq j$) such that, for a predicate p appears in a body of rule in Π_i then a rule with p in the head is only contained within $\Pi_0 \cup \Pi_1 \cup ... \cup \Pi_j$ where $j < i$.

Second assumption is that some legal propositions are *factual*. Their truth values are usually evidence based so the court will finalize their truth values in a phase of fact finding and shall not reverse their truth values after that. Hence, such propositions are true only when given. From Example 1, f is factual because there is no rule that implies f (except a fact $f \leftarrow .$) so its truth value cannot be changed by altering other propositions. *factual* is defined as follows.

Definition 6. [Factual] A proposition α is *factual* w.r.t. a program Π if there is no rule that implies α except a fact $\alpha \leftarrow .$, in other words, α shall be true only when given.

However, some propositions could not be true concurrently. From Example 1, if r was true, q could not be true. We could say that $\{r\}$ (or any sets that contain r) does not support q. To determine this relation between rules and a set of propositions, the idea of *support* is defined as follows.

Definition 7. [Support] A set of propositions S *support*s a proposition α w.r.t. a logic program Π if there is a rule $R \in \Pi$ such that α is the head of the rule ($\alpha = head(R)$), $pos\_body(R) \subseteq S$, and $neg\_body(R) \cap S = \varnothing$. R is called a supporting rule of α w.r.t. S.

Theorem 1. [Relation between model and support] Given Π as a non-recursive logic and M is a stable model of Π, $\alpha \in M$ if and only if M supports α w.r.t. Π. (This relation is common. For further details, please see [8].

Proof

Suppose M supports α but $\alpha \notin M$, there is a supporting rule R of α in Π.

Hence $\alpha = head(R)$, $pos\_body(R) \subseteq M$ and $neg\_body(R) \cap M = \varnothing$.
But since $\alpha \notin M$, M does not satisfy $head(R) \leftarrow pos\_body(R)$ which exists in Π^M.
It leads to contradiction with the definition of model.

Suppose M does not support α but $\alpha \in M$, then no rules are supporting α.

Thus, $M - \{\alpha\}$ must be a model because it satisfies every rule in Π^M.
It leads to contradiction with the definition of the minimum model.

2.2   Formalizing Unexpected Consequences and Culprits

When the literal interpretation gives unexpected consequences, it means that we do not agree with the current stable model. However, the intended interpretation is not known explicitly in the first place but it rather reveals proposition by proposition when we consider the truth value of each proposition together with the debugger until we find a culprit defined to be a root cause of unexpected consequences.

However, because truth values of factual propositions are already finalized, the true factual proposition would not be possible to be excluded from the stable model and the false factual proposition would not be possible to be included in the stable model.

From Example 1, we could not intend $\{p, r\}$ to be a stable model because f is already given and we could not change its truth value. In contrast, we could intend $\{p, f\}$ to be the stable model because r is not factual so we allow changing the truth value of r. Therefore, we define an intended interpretation denoted as *IM* with following definitions.

Definition 8. [Intended interpretation] An intended interpretation *IM* of a non-recursive logic program Π is a set of propositions such that a set of factual propositions in the stable model of Π and a set of factual propositions in *IM* are equal.

Consequently, if *IM* is different from the stable model, there must be a non-factual α that is not currently derived but intended to be derived or currently derived but intended not to be derived. We call such propositions as *unexpected* which is defined as follows.

Definition 9. [Unexpected proposition] A proposition α is unexpected w.r.t. an intended interpretation *IM* and a non-recursive logic program Π with a stable model M if (1) $\alpha \notin M$ but $\alpha \in IM$ or (2) $\alpha \in M$ but $\alpha \notin IM$. Factual propositions could not be unexpected due to constraints in Definition 8.

To modify the program so its stable model would become what we intend, we must work on a non-factual proposition called *culprit* defined as follows.

Definition 10. [Culprit] a non-factual proposition α will be a *culprit* w.r.t. an intended interpretation *IM* and a logic program Π if

- $\alpha \in IM$ but *IM* does not support α w.r.t. Π or
- $\alpha \notin IM$ but *IM* supports α w.r.t. Π.

Then, we get the following theorem.

Theorem 2. [Finding a culprit] Given Π as a non-recursive logic program with a stable model M and *IM* as an intended interpretation that not equal to M. If α is unexpected w.r.t. *IM* and Π and α is not a culprit w.r.t. *IM* and Π, then there is another unexpected proposition $\beta \neq \alpha$ in a body of a rule that implies α.

Proof

If $\alpha \in IM$ and α is not a culprit

Then there is a rule R supporting α w.r.t. *IM*.
Hence, $pos\_body(R) \subseteq IM$ and $neg\_body(R) \cap IM = \emptyset$.
But $\alpha \notin M$ so R is not a supporting rule of α w.r.t. M.
Thus, $pos\_body(R) \not\subseteq min(\Pi)$ or $neg\_body(R) \cap min(\Pi) \neq \emptyset$.
Because Π is non-recursive, $\alpha \notin body(R)$
Hence, there is another proposition $\beta_1 \in pos\_body(R)$ such that $\beta_1 \in IM$ and $\beta_1 \notin M$ or another proposition $\beta_2 \in neg\_body(R)$ such that $\beta_2 \notin IM$ and $\beta_2 \in M$ that could be found in a body of a rule R that implies α.

If $\alpha \notin IM$ and $\alpha \in M$, there is a rule R supporting α w.r.t. M.

Hence, $pos\_body(R) \subseteq M$ and $neg\_body(R) \cap M = \emptyset$.
And if α is not a culprit, R is not a supporting rule of α w.r.t. *IM*.
Thus, $pos\_body(R) \not\subseteq IM$ or $neg\_body(R) \cap IM \neq \emptyset$.
Because Π is non-recursive, $\alpha \notin body(R)$
Hence, there is another proposition $\beta_1 \in pos\_body(R)$ such that $\beta_1 \notin IM$ and $\beta_1 \in M$ or another proposition $\beta_2 \in neg\_body(R)$ such that $\beta_2 \in IM$ and $\beta_2 \notin M$ that could be found in a body of a rule R that implies α.

From Example 1, the stable model is $\{p, r, f\}$. Let the intended interpretation *IM* be $\{q, f\}$, p, q, and r will become unexpected, and r is a culprit according to Theorem 2 (Table 1).

From Theorem 2, if we query from any unexpected proposition and find another unexpected proposition recursively, as long as the query sequence is finite and does not loop (e.g. a finite non-recursive logic program), the query finally succeeds by finding a culprit. Therefore, we could design the finding culprit algorithm as in Table 2.

Table 1. An illustrated example of Theorem 2

Rules	Unexpected found in a head	Supporting Rule w.r.t. the stable model	Supporting Rule w.r.t. IM	Unexpected found in a body
$p \leftarrow not\ q.$	p	Supporting	-	q
$p \leftarrow not\ f.$	p	-	-	-
$q \leftarrow not\ r.$	q	-	Supporting	r
$r \leftarrow f.$	r	Supporting	Supporting	- (thus r is a culprit w.r.t. IM)
$f.$	-	-	-	-

The algorithm is only for finding one culprit. In case there are two culprits or more, the user has to repeat the same procedure again. Actually, it is safe to check that the stable model from the revised program is equal to the intended interpretation. For example, from a program $\{p \leftarrow q,\ not\ r.\ q \leftarrow f_1.\ r \leftarrow f_2\}$ with an empty set as the stable model, if an intended interpretation was $\{q\}$, we can see that only q would be unexpected hence it would be a culprit. If we resolved by just adding q as a fact, $\{p, q\}$ would become a stable model, which is not same as what we intended. In another round, p would become unexpected w.r.t. $\{q\}$ and hence p would be a culprit. If we resolved by removing the rule $p \leftarrow q,\ not\ r$ from the program, $\{q\}$ would finally become the stable model as we expected.

Table 2. Finding culprit algorithm (a - They follow directly by the definition of a culprit, Definition 10. b - These conditions are actually determined when finding a supporting rule. They are mentioned to emphasize that they are unexpected.)

Input: a finite non-recursive logic program with a stable model M, an intended interpretation IM, an unexpected proposition p

```
Find_culprit(p)
begin
   Find R as a supporting rule of p w.r.t. IM
   if p ∈ IM
     ifª there is no such R return p;
     else
         Find q ∈ pos_body(R) s.t. q ∈ IM ᵇ and q ∉ M
         if there is such q return Find_culprit(q)
         Find r ∈ neg_body(R) s.t. r ∉ IMᵇ and r ∈ M
         if there is such r return Find_culprit(r)

   if p ∉ IM
     ifª there is such R return p;
     else
         Find R' as a supporting rule of p w.r.t. M
         Find q ∈ pos_body(R') s.t. q ∉ IM and q ∈ Mᵇ
         if there is such q return Find_culprit(q)
         Find r ∈ neg_body(R') s.t. r ∈ IM and r ∉ M ᵇ
         if there is such r return Find_culprit(r)
end
```

3 Legal Debugging Under PROLEG

PROLEG (PROlog based LEGal reasoning support system) [4] is a logic programming adapted from Prolog. It reflects the legal reasoning procedures called The Japanese Presupposed Ultimate Fact Theory practiced in Japanese law schools. PROLEG is different from Prolog in manipulation of negative conditions but the representation power of PROLEG is the same as Prolog [9]. In this section, we provide definitions for PROLEG and extend the legal debugging under PROLEG. First, these are basic definitions of PROLEG.

Definition 11. [PROLEG] A PROLEG program P is a pair $\langle H, E \rangle$ where

- H is a set of rules R of the from $h \leftarrow b_1,\ldots,b_n$. where h and b_i ($1 \leq i \leq n$) are propositions (note that there are no negations in the rule). We denote h as *head* (R) and $\{b_1,\ldots,b_n\}$ as *body*(R).
- E is a set of exceptions of the form *exception*(h, e) where h and e be propositions (note that e is a proposition, not a set of propositions).

Definition 12. [Applicable rule] Let M be a set of propositions and $\langle H, E \rangle$ be a PROLEG program. We denote *a set of applicable rules* w.r.t. M by $H^M = \{R \in H \mid \neg\exists exception(head(R), e) \in E$ such that $e \in M\}$.

So if an exception of rule exists in M ($e \in M$) then the rule is inapplicable.

Definition 13. [Extension] A set of propositions M is an extension of a PROLEG program $\langle H, E \rangle$ if M is the minimum model of H^M ($M = \min(H^M)$).

Example 2. P' is a PROLEG program.

$p \leftarrow q.$

$q \leftarrow f_1.$

$r \leftarrow f_2.$

exception$(p, r).$

Let $M = \{r\}$, $H^M = \{q \leftarrow f_1, r \leftarrow f_2 \}$ ($p \leftarrow q$ is inapplicable here because there is an *exception* (p, r) and $r \in M$). Since $\min(H^M) = \varnothing$. M is not an extension of P'.

Let $M = \varnothing$, $H^M = \{p \leftarrow q,\ q \leftarrow f_1,\ r \leftarrow f_2 \}$. Since $\min(H^M) = \varnothing$. M is an extension of P'.

PROLEG representation is actually aligned with the logic program with negation as failure but using exception instead of negation. However, one particular different point is that if we add an exception to a condition, it applies to all rules on that condition unlike a logic program with negation as failure whose negations must be added to the rule one by one as illustrated in Table 3.

Because the representation power of PROLEG is same as the logic program with negation as failure, we can extend the same idea of supports, culprits, and finding culprit theorem by using an extension of P instead of the stable model. For example, these are definition of support (Definition 7), definition of intended interpretation (Definition 8), and definition of unexpected proposition (Definition 9) in PROLEG.

Table 3. An equivalent representation between PROLEG (left) and Prolog (right)

$p \leftarrow q.$ $p \leftarrow r.$ $exception(p, e).$	$p \leftarrow q, not\ e.$ $p \leftarrow r, not\ e.$

Definition 14. [Support in PROLEG] A set of proposition S *supports* a proposition p w.r.t. a PROLEG program P if there is a rule R such that $p = head(R)$, $body(R) \subseteq S$, and there is no *exception(p, e)* $\in E$ such that $e \in S$ We call that R is a supporting rule of p w.r.t. S and P.

Definition 15. [Intended interpretation in PROLEG] A set of propositions *IM* can be an intended interpretation of a PROLEG program P if and only if a set of factual propositions in an extension of P and a set of factual propositions in *IM* are equal.

Definition 16. [Unexpected in PROLEG] A proposition p is unexpected w.r.t. an intended interpretation *IM* and a PROLEG program P if p is not in an extension of P but in *IM* or if p is in an extension of P but not in *IM*.

We design a finding culprit algorithm in PROLEG as shown in Table 4. It is still based on recursion from an unexpected proposition according to Theorem 2. Because the input PROLEG program P is not recursive, it can be deduced that there is only one extension of P.

Table 4. Finding culprit algorithm in PROLEG

Input: a finite non-recursive PROLEG logic program $P = \langle H, E \rangle$, an intended interpretation *IM*, an unexpected proposition p

```
Find_culprit(p)
begin
    Find R as a supporting rule of p w.r.t. IM
    if p ∈ IM
        if there is no such R return p;
        else
            Find q ∈ body(R) s.t. q is not in an extension of P
            if there is such q return Find_culprit(q)
            Find e s.t. exception(p,e) ∈ E and e is in an extension of P
            if there is such e return Find_culprit(e)
    if p ∉ IM
        if there is such R return p;
        else
            Find R' as a supporting rule of p w.r.t. an extension of P
            Find q ∈ body(R') s.t. q ∉ IM
            if there is such q return Find_culprit(q)
            Find e s.t. exception(p,e) ∈ E and e ∈ IM
            if there is such e return Find_culprit(e)
end
```

4 Legal Debugging Example

In this section, we use an example of unexpected consequences adapted from this following case [10]:

1. A plaintiff made a lease contract for his house between him and the defendant.
2. When the defendant returned home for a while, he let his son use the room.
3. Then, the plaintiff claimed that the contract was ended by his cancellation for the reason that the defendant subleases without permission by literal interpretation of Japanese Civil Code Article 612 as follows.

> **Phrase 1:** A lessee may not assign the lessee's rights or sublease a leased thing without obtaining the approval of the lessor.
> **Phrase 2:** If the lessee allows any third party to make use of or take profits from a leased thing in violation of the provisions of the preceding paragraph, the lessor may cancel the contract.

When the case was taken to the court, the court decided that the literal interpretation produces an unexpected consequence. Although the cancellation is valid if we interpret the related piece of law literally, the court decided that the literal interpretation is too strict because "the third party" who makes use of the room temporally was the defendant's son and he did not harm the confidence between a lessee and a lessor, as the court mentioned the following:

> Phrase 2 is not applicable in exceptional situations where the sublease does not harm the confidence between a lessee and a lessor, and therefore the lessor cannot cancel the contract unless they prove the lessee's destructing of confidence.

The Japanese Civil Code Article 612 and the facts from the case can be represented in propositional PROLEG as in Table 5.

From this representation, `cancellation_due_to_sublease`, `effective_lease _contract`, and `effective_sublease_contract` are nonfactual predicates in the extension of the program due to the given facts entailing these proposition and no exception is executed. This reflects when we interpret the law literally. However, since the court decided that the validity of `cancellation_-due_to_sublease` is too harsh. It becomes an unexpected proposition. The legal debugger would help clarifying which legal conditions cause the unexpected consequence as well as finding the intended interpretation that supports the court reasoning. We could initiate debugging by using `cancellation_due_to_sublease` as an unexpected proposition as shown in Fig. 1.

The debugger firstly traced into the supporting rule of `cancellation_-due_to_sublease` (the first rule) to determine two conditions in the body `ef-fective_lease_contract` and `effective_sublease_contract`. The debugger asked user whether both conditions were intended to be fulfilled or not. If one of them was intended to be not fulfilled, it became a culprit because the intended interpretation would support it (situation 1 and 2). If both of them were intended to be fulfilled, the debugger retraced on `approval_of_sublease` which is an exception of `cancellation_due_to_sublease`. Then, the debugger asked user that

Table 5. Propositional PROLEG representation of Japanese Civil Code Article 612

```
cancellation_due_to_sublease <=
  effective_lease_contract,
  effective_sublease_contract,
  using_leased_thing,
  manifestation_cancellation.

effective_lease_contract <=
  agreement_of_lease_contract,
  handover_based_on_the_lease_contract.

effective_sublease_contract <=
  agreement_of_sublease_contract,
  handover_based_on_the_sublease_contract.

exception(cancellation_due_to_sublease,approval_of_sublease).


approval_of_sublease <=
  approval_of_sublease_before_the_day.
```

```
// Given Facts
  agreement_of_lease_contract.
  handover_based_on_the_lease_contract.
  agreement_of_sublease_contract.
  handover_based_on_the_sublease_contract.
  using_leased_thing.
  manifestation_cancellation.
  nonabuse_of_confidence.
```

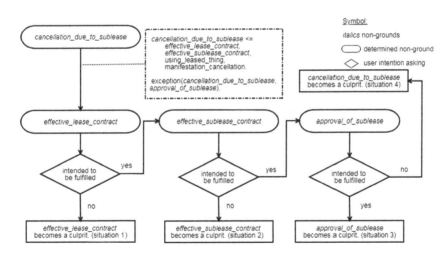

Fig. 1. Legal debugging steps from the rule base

`approval_of_sublease` was intended to be fulfilled or not. If it was intended to be fulfilled, it became a culprit because the intended interpretation would not support it (situation 3). If `approval_of_sublease` was intended to be not fulfilled, then there was no unexpected condition for `cancellation_due_to_sublease`, hence `cancellation_due_to_sublease` became a culprit itself (situation 4). The intended interpretations of each situation are illustrated in Table 6.

Table 6. Culprit and Intended Interpretation for Each Situation

Non-factual propositions in the current extension of the program: `cancellation_due_to_sublease`, `effective_lease_contract`, `effective_sublease_contract`		
Situation	Status of non-factual propositions given by the user (*IM* stands for an intended interpretation)	Found culprit
1	`cancellation_due_to_sublease` $\notin$ *IM* `effective_lease_contract` $\notin$ *IM*	`effective_lease_contract` (because it is not in *IM* but *IM* supports it w.r.t. the program)
2	`cancellation_due_to_sublease` $\notin$ *IM* `effective_lease_contract` $\in$ *IM* `effective_sublease_contract` $\notin$ *IM*	`effective_sublease_contract` (because it is not in *IM* but *IM* supports it w.r.t. the program)
3	`cancellation_due_to_sublease` $\notin$ *IM* `effective_lease_contract` $\in$ *IM* `effective_sublease_contract` $\in$ *IM* `approval_of_sublease` $\in$ *IM*	`approval_of_sublease` (because it is in *IM* but *IM* does not support it w.r.t. the program)
4	`cancellation_due_to_sublease` $\notin$ *IM* `effective_lease_contract` $\in$ *IM* `effective_sublease_contract` $\in$ *IM* `approval_of_sublease` $\notin$ *IM*	`cancellation_due_to_sublease` (because it is not in *IM* but *IM* supports it w.r.t. the program)

A culprit is considered in top-down left-to-right manner. Although the user does not consider all non-factual propositions, the debugger would return a first encountered culprit as soon as the debugger could not find any unexpected propositions. A culprit would be useful for considered rather in its resolution. Generally, the court would give an exception from extra facts of the case, such as in this case `exception(cancellation_due_to_sublease, nonabuse_of_confidence)` may be introduced to correspond to the Supreme Court decision. However, there are other possibilities to resolve one culprit so the resolution of culprits should be investigated further.

5 Discussion and Related Works

5.1 Legal Debugging in Statute Legal Practice

Statute rules are usually constructed in a top-down approach, from abstract to concrete concept. Each condition must be proved and presented to the court in the order of the list written in the procedure. For example, the case in Sect. 4 of this paper involves an issue of cancellation of a lease contract due to sublease. To claim the issue, four conditions (effective lease contract, effective sublease contract must be effective, using the less thing, and manifesting cancellation) must be proved and presented to the court in order. However, when the court decided that the case produces an unexpected consequence. The court usually identifies the top concept to be unexpected. Therefore, the legal debugging helps the court to trace in a top-down manner from the abstract concept identified by the court to the culprit that causes unexpected consequences, as well as to trace in a left-to-right manner in order of the list written in the procedure.

5.2 Application of Debugging Besides Software

"Legal debugging" is proposed for tacit expectations unlike inconsistencies [11–14] that deals with conflicts between explicit written rules. Several paradigms have been proposed to find bugs such as online-offline justifications [15] and meta-programming [16] but most debugging technique are based on algorithmic debugging [17]. Besides software, algorithmic debugging has been proposed for navigating users in a few applications [18]. Zinn [19] has applied algorithmic debugging in tutoring systems. The papers view a program as a knowledge corpus and an intended interpretation as a student expectation. A student misconception can be viewed as a bug and a wrong answer can be viewed as an unexpected answer. Algorithmic debugging has also been applied in hardware design and verification. Kuchcinski et al. [20] has worked on using algorithmic debugging in hardware design by viewing circuits as auxiliary functions and logic programs respectively to detect faulty components.

Our paper is the first work proposing legal debugging. Legal debugging has to deal with tacit expectations from legal experts and different structures of representation, such as non-stratified structure and exception separation in PROLEG, and different resolution for preventing unexpected consequences, such as using exceptions instead of adding conditions. This paper views a representation of literal interpretation as a program and a *culprit*, a rule condition which causes unexpected consequences, as a bug.

5.3 Semantics of Legal Representation on Debugging

Program semantics may affect debugging schemes [18]. For example, in answer set programming, a debugger has to treat multiple situations due to the allowance of multiple answers [21–24]. In Datalog, a debugger has to deal with non-stratified programs differently because the semantics sometimes gives an empty set instead of non-termination for some types of non-stratified programs [25].

Since this paper is the first step on legal debugging, we have focused only a stratified and non-recursive representation. This representation often reflects the structure of statutory law that expects only one interpretation. Since a stratified and non-recursive program exists only one interpretation, we can eliminate the problems mentioned above. However, it is important to consider semantics used in legal representation because they still have some effects on legal debugging. For example, separation of conditions and exceptions in PROLEG affects resolution of legal culprits due to the border scope of exceptions.

6 Conclusion and Future Works

In this paper, we have proposed the idea of *legal debugging* in legal knowledge represented by logic programming. The idea has been presented in non-recursive program which we assume that some propositions' truth values shall not be changed (called *factual proposition*). Then, we have proposed the idea of *culprit*, a rule condition that causes unexpected consequences. We begin the debugging process from an initial *unexpected* proposition. The debugger follows a sequence of unexpected propositions until it meets a culprit otherwise the initial unexpected proposition is a culprit itself. We prove the correctness of algorithm under non-recursive logic programing with negation as failure, and then we extend the algorithm to PROLEG system. In future, we will extend the algorithm for first-order logic programs with arguments and develop an interactive debugger in PROLEG system which asks user intention and steps into rule base to find culprits similarly to computer program debugging.

Acknowledgement. We appreciate Randy Goebel, Oliver Ray, and Tiago Oliveira for their comments on the paper. This research is partially supported by JSPS KAKENHI Grant No. 17H06103.

References

1. Sergot, M.J., Sadri, F., Kowalski, R.A., Kriwaczek, F., Hammond, P., Cory, H.T.: The British Nationality Act as a logic program. Commun. ACM **29**, 370–386 (1986)
2. Sherman, D.M.: A Prolog model of the income tax act of Canada. In: Proceedings of the 1st International Conference on Artificial Intelligence and Law, pp. 127–136. ACM, New York (1987)
3. Li, T., Balke, T., De Vos, M., Satoh, K., Padget, J.: Detecting conflicts in legal systems. In: Motomura, Y., Butler, A., Bekki, D. (eds.) JSAI-isAI 2012. LNCS (LNAI), vol. 7856, pp. 174–189. Springer, Heidelberg (2013). https://doi.org/10.1007/978-3-642-39931-2_13
4. Satoh, K., et al.: PROLEG: an implementation of the presupposed ultimate fact theory of Japanese civil code by PROLOG technology. In: Onada, T., Bekki, D., McCready, E. (eds.) JSAI-isAI 2010. LNCS (LNAI), vol. 6797, pp. 153–164. Springer, Heidelberg (2011). https://doi.org/10.1007/978-3-642-25655-4_14
5. Ito, S.: Lecture Series on Ultimate Facts. Shojihomu (2008). (in Japanese)
6. Ullman, J.: Principles of Database and Knowledge-Base Systems. Computer Science Press, Rockville (1988)
7. Gelfond, M., Lifschitz, V.: The stable model semantics for logic programming. In: International Conference on Logic Programming/Joint International Conference and Symposium on Logic Programming, pp. 1070–1080 (1988)
8. Fages, F.: A new fixpoint semantics for general logic programs compared with the well-founded and the stable model semantics. New Gener. Comput. **9**, 425–443 (1991)
9. Satoh, K., Kogawa, T., Okada, N., Omori, K., Omura, S., Tsuchiya, K.: On generality of PROLEG knowledge representation. In: Proceedings of the 6th International Workshop on Juris-informatics (JURISIN 2012), Miyazaki, Japan, pp. 115–128 (2012)
10. Tokyo High Court: Case to seek removal of a building and surrender of lands. 1994 (O) 693. Minshu, vol. 50, no. 9 (1996)

11. Syrjänen, T.: Debugging inconsistent answer set programs. In: Proceedings of the 11th International Workshop on Nonmonotonic Reasoning, pp. 77–83 (2006)
12. Caminada, M., Sakama, C.: On the existence of answer sets in normal extended logic programs. In: Proceedings of the 2006 Conference on ECAI 2006: 17th European Conference on Artificial Intelligence, Riva Del Garda, Italy, pp. 743–744. IOS Press, Amsterdam (2006)
13. Schulz, C., Satoh, K., Toni, F.: Characterising and explaining inconsistency in logic programs. In: Calimeri, F., Ianni, G., Truszczynski, M. (eds.) LPNMR 2015. LNCS (LNAI), vol. 9345, pp. 467–479. Springer, Cham (2015). https://doi.org/10.1007/978-3-319-23264-5_39
14. Ulbricht, M., Thimm, M., Brewka, G.: Measuring inconsistency in answer set programs. In: Michael, L., Kakas, A. (eds.) JELIA 2016. LNCS (LNAI), vol. 10021, pp. 577–583. Springer, Cham (2016). https://doi.org/10.1007/978-3-319-48758-8_42
15. Pontelli, E., Son, T.C., Elkhatib, O.: Justifications for logic programs under answer set semantics. Theor. Pr. Log. Program. **9**, 1–56 (2009)
16. Gebser, M., Pührer, J., Schaub, T., Tompits, H.: A meta-programming technique for debugging answer-set programs. In: Proceedings of the 23rd National Conference on Artificial Intelligence – vol. 1, pp. 448–453. AAAI Press (2008)
17. Shapiro, E.Y.: Algorithmic Program Debugging. MIT Press, Cambridge (1983)
18. Caballero, R., Riesco, A., Silva, J.: A survey of algorithmic debugging. ACM Comput. Surv. **50**, 60:1–60:35 (2017)
19. Zinn, C.: Algorithmic debugging for intelligent tutoring: How to use multiple models *and* improve diagnosis. In: Timm, I.J., Thimm, M. (eds.) KI 2013. LNCS (LNAI), vol. 8077, pp. 272–283. Springer, Heidelberg (2013). https://doi.org/10.1007/978-3-642-40942-4_24
20. Kuchcinski, K., Drabent, W., Maluszynski, J.: Automatic diagnosis of VLSI digital circuits using algorithmic debugging. In: Fritzson, P.A. (ed.) AADEBUG 1993. LNCS, vol. 749, pp. 350–367. Springer, Heidelberg (1993). https://doi.org/10.1007/BFb0019419
21. Fandinno, J., Schulz, C.: Answering the "why" in answer set programming – a survey of explanation approaches. Theor. Pract. Log. Program. **19**, 114–203 (2019)
22. Brain, M., De Vos, M.: Debugging logic programs under the answer set semantics. In: Answer Set Programming (2005)
23. Oetsch, J., Pührer, J., Tompits, H.: Catching the ouroboros: on debugging non-ground answer-set programs. Theor. Pract. Log. Program. **10**, 513–529 (2010)
24. Oetsch, J., Pührer, J., Tompits, H.: Stepping through an answer-set program. In: Delgrande, J.P., Faber, W. (eds.) LPNMR 2011. LNCS (LNAI), vol. 6645, pp. 134–147. Springer, Heidelberg (2011). https://doi.org/10.1007/978-3-642-20895-9_13
25. Caballero, R., García-Ruiz, Y., Sáenz-Pérez, F.: A theoretical framework for the declarative debugging of datalog programs. In: Schewe, K.D., Thalheim, B. (eds.) SDKB 2008. LNCS, vol. 4925, pp. 143–159. Springer, Heidelberg (2008). https://doi.org/10.1007/978-3-540-88594-8_8

An Agile Approach to Validate a Formal Representation of the GDPR

Cesare Bartolini[1]([⊠]), Gabriele Lenzini[1], and Cristiana Santos[2,3]

[1] Interdisciplinary Centre for Security, Reliability and Trust (SnT),
University of Luxembourg, Luxembourg, Luxembourg
{cesare.bartolini,gabriele.lenzini}@uni.lu
[2] Research Centre for Justice and Governance (JusGov), School of Law,
University of Minho, Braga, Portugal
[3] Université Toulouse Capitole, Toulouse, France
cristiana.teixeirasantos@gmail.com

Abstract. Modelling in a knowledge base of logic formulæ the articles
of the GDPR enables a semi-automatic *reasoning* of the Regulation. To
be legally substantiated, it requires that the formulæ express validly the
legal meaning of the Regulation's articles. But legal experts are usually
not familiar with logic, and this calls for an interdisciplinary validation
methodology that bridges the communication gap between formal mod-
elers and legal evaluators. We devise such a validation methodology and
exemplify it over a knowledge base of articles of the GDPR translated
into Reified I/O (RIO) logic and encoded in LegalRuleML. A pivotal
element of the methodology is a human-readable intermediate representation of the logic formulæ that preserves the formulæ's meaning, while
rendering it in a readable way to non-experts. After being applied over
a use case, we prove that it is possible to retrieve feedback from legal
experts about the formal representation of Art. 5.1a and Art. 7.1. What
emerges is an agile process to build logic knowledge bases of legal texts,
and to support their public trust, which we intend to use for a logic
model of the GDPR, called DAPRECO knowledge base.

Keywords: General Data Protection Regulation · Data protection ·
Compliance · Legal validation · Usability

1 Introduction

Artificial Intelligence (AI) applied to the legal domain can serve a number of
purposes to improve the efficiency of legal services and the predictability of the
application of the law. Some illustrative examples of legal AI applications are
evinced by existing digital services such as: search engine for retrieving legal

Bartolini and Lenzini are supported by the FNR CORE project C16/IS/11333956
"DAPRECO: DAta Protection REgulation COmpliance".

K. Kojima et al. (Eds.): JSAI-isAI 2018 Workshops, LNAI 11717, pp. 160–176, 2019.
https://doi.org/10.1007/978-3-030-31605-1_13

sources; online dispute resolution; assistance in drafting needs; predictive analysis; categorization of contracts and detection of incompatible contractual clauses; "chatbots" to support litigants; and legal reasoning and decision-making. Moreover, AI compliance tools can help to identify the laws and regulations a certain business activity is subject to, assisting undertakings in establishing legally-compliant processes, and easing the verification of compliance by auditors and enforcement bodies.

Instantiations of AI-enabled tools for legal compliance within data protection seems particularly pertinent. Notably, the new legal landscape reshaped by the General Data Protection Regulation (GDPR), coupled with the heavy fines that supervisory authorities are entitled to issue in case of data breach, calls for a need to ensure compliance for data processing activities. Herein, data controllers could use AI compliance tools designed to help them assuring accountability and compliant management processes, whilst diminishing the risks of violating provisions and incurring into fines.

A critical facet of such automation is the need to build executable rules for a computer-assisted compliance system. In previous research, the authors have proposed a complete model of the GDPR for legal reasoning and legal compliance [2, 15–17]. This model comprises three components: (i) the legal text in Akoma Ntoso format; (ii) an ontology of legal concepts concerning privacy and data protection; and (iii) a knowledge base of data protection rules. This last component, called the Data Protection Regulation Compliance (DAPRECO) Knowledge Base[1], currently under development, contains the General Data Protection Regulation (GDPR) provisions modeled in Reified Input/Output (RIO) logic [20]. Built to contain natural language interpretations of these provisions, due to the logic's defeasible nature, the DAPRECO Knowledge Base can be updated with successive and more authoritative legal interpretations [2]. Accordingly, the Knowledge Base needs to be adequately validated before it can perform in a real-world environment. Such a pragmatical stand is demanded, since "for developers, as contrasted to researchers, the issue is not whether the resulting rule base is complete or even accurate or self-modifying – but whether the rule base is sufficiently accurate to be useful" [5] when it is moved out from the research laboratory and into the marketplace [23]. However, as is widely acknowledged in literature [11,19,22], testing legal Artificial Intellingence (AI) systems is a difficult task because approaches reveal coder-dependency, and it is complex to emulate the "art-of-the-experts" [6]. With ongoing maturity in the field of AI and Law, the need for an easily accessible *interdisciplinary validation methodology* comes into play [10].

Legal Validation. The concept of validation refers to the determination of the correctness of the system with respect to user needs and requirements [22]. Legal validation is "needed to verify the correctness of the output of the system in relation to the knowledge of the legal domain it covers", "the guarantee of the one-to-one relation between analysis and representation" [12]. Such a method

---

[1] The name DAPRECO comes from DAta PRotection REgulation COmpliance, the name of the CORE-FNR project that supported this research.

would assist legal professionals framing an evaluation of an AI-legal system and help IT experts understand the validation requirements of legal professionals [11]. As "algorithmic representations of law are typically very poor as regards their transparency", "one cannot begin to devise an algorithm to apply legal provisions without determining first its intended purpose and by whom it will be used" [21]. Thus, validating a legal model requires that the formalization used is *understandable and accessible*. Consequently, the methodology should be driven by *usability* considerations in the adopted criteria, and validation tests (through user acceptance surveys or questionnaires) [22], as foreseen in the current work.

This validation quadrant also holds for our domain modeling of the GDPR. We believe that this endeavour to formalize articles in a logic formalism requires a methodology supporting its legal validation. The validation phase should not be postponed till the moment when the whole GDPR is formalized, for as detecting possible unsound conclusions at such late juncture would amount to a very expensive step, likely inspiring distrust in the whole framework. A more *agile* process is advisable and was adopted to validate the legal soundness of any formula from the moment in which they were added to the Knowledge Base, thus assisting incrementally and concomitantly the modeler.

Contribution. This paper builds on two workshop articles [3,4]. The contribution is a methodology aiming to capture *informed* feedback on the legal validity of the DAPRECO Knowledge Base's representing the meaning(s) of the articles of the GDPR. A decisive element of the methodology is a human-readable break-down of a RIO logic formula. Once the customizable human-readable representation has been assessed as understandable, increasing our confidence on it to be an eligible candidate to validate the formalized GDPR articles, we proceed further and show that the methodology is effective in gathering feedback of legal experts on the legal validity of the representation of the GDPR articles, so as to provide quality assurance of our methodology as a whole.

This paper reports fully on the study, comments on the methodology, and on the usability experiments, pointing out the limitations and future work.

2   Related Work

Some discussion within the AI and Law community [10,11,22] – specifically amidst the Proceedings of the International Conference on Artificial Intelligence and Law works (ICAIL), and later through the Journal of Artificial Intelligence and Law contributions (JAIL), – concerned qualitative evaluation methodologies suitable for legal domain systems, and the best practices through which AI and Law researchers could frame the assessment of the performance of their works, both empirical and theoretical. For example, performance evaluation is emphasized and compared to known baselines and parameters, using publicly available datasets whenever possible [8,9].

A set of six categories was compiled to define the broad types of evaluation found therefrom. They include the following assessments: i. *Gold Data*: evaluation performed with respect to domain expert judgments (e.g., classification measurements or measures on accuracy, precision, recall, F-score, etc.); ii. *Statistical*: evaluation performed with respect to comparison functions (e.g., unsupervised learning: cluster internal-similarity, cosine similarity, etc.); iii. *Manual Assessment*: performance is measured by humans via inspection, assessment, review of output; iv. *Algorithmic*: assessment made in terms of performance of a system, such as a multi-agent system; v. *Operational-Usability*: assessment of a system's operational characteristics or usability aspects; vi. *Other*: those systems with distinct forms of evaluation not covered in the categories above (task-based, conversion-based, etc.). In *our case*, we combined the following types of evaluation: gold data (i.), manual assessment (iii.) and operational-usability (v.).

Some authors [10] developed the Context Criteria Contingency-guidelines Framework (CCCF) for evaluating Legal Knowledge Based System (LKBS). Within this framework, the quadrant criteria pertinent to the purposes of this paper are herewith mentioned. The *User Credibility* quadrant refers to credibility and acceptability of a system at the individual level. It comprises three main branches associated with *user satisfaction*, *utility* (usefulness or fitness for purpose) and *usability* (ease of use). The usability branch is further decomposed into branches associated with operability, understandability, learnability, accessibility, flexibility in use, and with other human factors and human computer interface issues. The *Verification and Validation* criteria quadrant refer to knowledge base validity, including knowledge representation and associated theories of jurisprudence, inferencing, and the provision of explanations.

Validation of legal modeling by domain legal experts – driven by operational usability assessments – is also mentioned in three methodologies referring to ontological expert knowledge evaluation. For example, the Methodology for Modeling Legal Ontologies (MeLOn) [14] offers evaluation parameters, notably, completeness, correctness, coherence of the conceptualization phase and artifact reusability. Usability was considered in an experimental validation of a legal ontology by legal experts, the Ontology of Professional Judicial Knowledge (OPJK), described in [7]. This model was validated in a two-step process. First, the evaluators answered a questionnaire whereby they expressed their opinion on their level of agreement towards the ontology conceptualization and provided suggestions for the improvement thereof. Then an experimental validation based on a usability questionnaire followed, the System Usability Scale (SUS), tailored to evaluate the understandably and acceptance of the contents of the ontology. This evaluation questionnaire could offer rapid feedback and support towards the establishment of relevant agreement, shareability or quality of content measurements in expert-based ontology evaluation. An evaluation methodology based on Competency Questions (CQs) [18] was built to evaluate the transformation of legal knowledge from a semi-formal form (Semantics Of Business Vocabulary And Rules - Standard English (SBVR-SE)) [13] to a more structured formal representation (OWL 2), and to enable cooperation between legal experts and knowledge IT experts in charge of the modelling in logic formalism.

Although the framework target of this work's analysis (i.e., the DAPRECO Knowledge Base) refers to a validated ontology (i.e., the Privacy Ontology

(PrOnto)), an argument for its legal validity cannot only derive from the validity of the ontology of reference. It requires a more comprehensive analysis and we believe that both qualitative evaluation methodologies and certain criteria from the CCCF are required. Ontologies are in fact about concepts, data, and entities and any validation strategy of them is inevitably about assessing the legal qualities of those objects. Formal models for legal compliance, such as the DAPRECO Knowledge Base, model also the logical and deontic structure of a legal text, its temporal aspects and, as the used formalism yields multiple conflicting interpretations, it includes structural elements to allow defeasible reasoning. The validation assessment should take these elements into account.

Thus, the necessity of an integrated approach, which additionally should also acknowledge an operational-usability assessment, since the legal validity of the DAPRECO Knowledge Base logic formulæ have to be validated by non experts in logic.

3   DAPRECO Knowledge Base

The target of the validation methodology we propose in this work is the so called DAPRECO Knowledge Base. Currently, it contains a preliminary formalization of GDPR's provisions. Technically, the Knowledge Base stands on three interconnected components: legal text; conceptual model; deontic rules. Since it is meant to provide a semi-automated assistance to legal experts, all of the three components need to be machine-readable, and so, consolidated standards and reference formats have been used to model them.

The *legal text* is modelled in Akoma Ntoso[2]. Using ordinary XML parsers, it makes easy to navigate the document and reference specific portions of text. The *conceptual model*, specifically designed using the Web Ontology Language (OWL) language in an XML serialization, is contained in a legal ontology of privacy and data protection concepts, called PrOnto [16,17][3], which the Knowledge Base refers to. The ontology itself, has been developed following the MeLOn methodology, which is based on a glossary and a set of Competency Questions (CQs). The *deontic rules* of the GDPR are expressed in Reified Input/Output (RIO) logic [20]. It is a defeasible deontic logic that uses reification, a technique added to the logic to avoid nested obligations.

This set of RIO formulæ, their consistency and completeness are the real target of the validation task[4]. The formulæ act as a sort of *trait d'union* between the other two components, as they contain references both to ontological elements of the conceptual model and to the textual portions of the legal document expressed in Akoma Ntoso format.

---

[2] Currently stored at https://github.com/guerret/lu.uni.dapreco.parser/blob/master/resources/akn-act-gdpr-full.xml.

[3] Currently stored at https://github.com/guerret/lu.uni.dapreco.parser/blob/master/resources/pronto-v8.graphml.

[4] The formulæ are available at https://github.com/dapreco/daprecokb.

All formulæ are if-then rules in the form (x, y), such that when x is given in input, y is returned in output. When applied to the legal domain, there are three sets to which rules can belong to: C is the set of constitutive norms, which defines when something counts as something else in the domain. Every pair $(x, y) \in C$ reads as "$x \rightarrow y$", as standard first-order logic implications; O and P are respectively the set of obligations and the set of permissions of the normative system. A pair $(x, y) \in O$ reads as "given x, y is obligatory", while a pair $(x, y) \in P$ reads as "given x, y is permitted".

Both the "if" and the "then" part of each formula are composed by a conjunction of predicates. Each predicate is in the form of the predicate name followed by a list of attributes. The name can be a concept belonging to an ontology (e.g., the PrOnto ontology) or it can be a logical operator. For example, (PrOnto : PersonalDataProcessing $x\,z$) refers to a concept in the PrOnto ontology and takes two arguments. The predicate alone is incomplete, because it also needs to describe the two predicates used as arguments. If x is a controller and z some personal data of a data subject, an example may be formula 1.

$$((\mathsf{prOnto : Controller}\,x) \wedge (\mathsf{prOnto : DataSubject}\,w) \wedge$$
$$(\mathsf{prOnto : PersonalData}\,z\,w) \wedge (\mathsf{prOnto : PersonalDataProcessing'}\,x\,z)), \quad (1)$$

Furthermore, in RIO logic a predicate can be *reified* to be used as arguments for other predicates. Thus (prOnto : PersonalDataProcessing' $e_p\,x\,z$) is a new predicate, different from (prOnto : PersonalDataProcessing, $x\,z$); it represents the *possibility* that there is a processing of personal data. This allows e_p to be used as argument to another predicate.

How the DAPRECO Knowledge Base Looks Like. To make RIO formulæ machine-readable format, they were written in LegalRuleML[5], an XML markup language and a developing OASIS standard for representing the fine-grained semantic contents of legal texts [1]. In essence, each formula expressed as a LegalRuleML rule contains two parts: premise (if) and the consequence (then). The predicates (and their arguments) composing both parts are serialized as RuleML atoms (and variables). The example above, with reification added, is serialized as in Listing 1.

4   Validation Methodology

The object of the validation are the formulæ, regardless of its expressive form (logic or LegalRuleML serialization). The defeasible nature of the logic allows for many interpretations, even one superseding or contrasting with another, as typical in law. Thus, there is no correct interpretation to be validated, rather it is sought the author's checking whether a logic formula correctly represents one particular interpretation (which can be also his/her own).

---

[5] http://ruleml.org/index.html.

What we ultimately pursue is a feedback on the *legal quality* of the formulæ's expressed meaning(s). This quality can be measured at least using metrics, such as: *accuracy* (does the deontic modality expressed by a formula match the corresponding legal provisions? are the relationships among the concept accurately represented?); *completeness* (is all the required domain knowledge explicitly stated, or can it at least be inferred from the vocabulary?); *(subjective)correctness* (is the formula's meaning correct, according to your interpretation?); *consistency* (is the formula's meaning consistent with the law?); and *conciseness* (is there any amount of redundancy in the representation, or is it concise?).

Listing 1. LegalRuleML of formula 1.

```
<ruleml:Exists>
  <ruleml:Var key=":z">z</ruleml:Var>
  <ruleml:Var key=":x">x</ruleml:Var>
  <ruleml:And>
    <ruleml:Atom>
      <ruleml:Rel iri="prOnto:DataSubject"/>
      <ruleml:Var key=":w">w</ruleml:Var>
    </ruleml:Atom>
    <ruleml:Atom>
      <ruleml:Rel iri="prOnto:PersonalData"/>
      <ruleml:Var keyref=":z"/>
      <ruleml:Var keyref=":w"/>
    </ruleml:Atom>
    <ruleml:Atom>
      <ruleml:Rel iri="prOnto:Controller"/>
      <ruleml:Var key=":x">x</ruleml:Var>
      <ruleml:Var keyref=":z"/>
    </ruleml:Atom>
    <ruleml:Atom keyref=":A3">
      <ruleml:Rel iri="prOnto:PersonalDataProcessing"/>
      <ruleml:Var key=":ep">ep</ruleml:Var>
      <ruleml:Var keyref=":x"/>
      <ruleml:Var keyref=":z"/>
    </ruleml:Atom>
  </ruleml:And>
</ruleml:Exists>
```

These metrics can be empirically assessed using an *ad hoc* questionnaire, a very useful quantitative indicator of user acceptance [25]. In this case, where users are lawyers, the questionnaire was designed with the purpose of having legal feedback on the quality of the legal interpretation in the RIO formulæ, and was built around six questions reported below:

q_1	Is the deontic modality (e.g., obligation) of the formula the same as in the article?
q_2	Does the formula capture all the important legal concepts?
q_3	Does the formula capture all the important legal relations?
q_4	Is the interpretation given by the model correct?
q_5	Is the interpretation complete?
q_6	Is the interpretation to the point?

The questions have been tailored to assess Accuracy (q_1); Completeness ($q_2 - q_3$); Correctness (q_4); Consistency (q_5); and Conciseness (q_6).

However, the evaluator needs to understand what a formula states and ideally, the strain to read the formula should not overtake the effort required to provide feedback. From experience gathered in the DAPRECO project we learned that even IT experts required several and repeated explanations to understand what a specific formula expressed. Hence the need for a *human-readable* representation of the formulæ, which preserves the meaning of the machine-readable model but

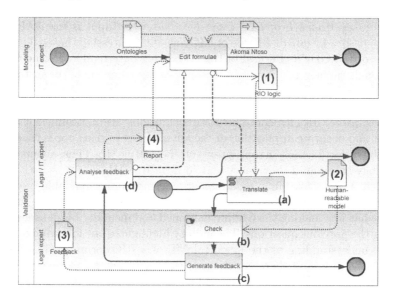

Fig. 1. Workflow of the modeling and of the validation methodology.

is understandable by non-experts in logic, ontologies, or XML. We devised one and we measured its *usability* (what the formula says is easy to understand?).

The methodology workflow is resumed in Fig. 1 on the lower portion of the diagram ("Validation"). The machine-readable version of the modelling of the legal text—in our case, the DAPRECO Knowledge Base—is the output of the modeling effort by the IT expert. That file needs to be processed and rewritten ("Translate", (a) in Figure) into a human-readable representation. The "Human-readable model" (2) is then validated ("Check", (b)) against specific measures defining if whether the modeling was correct from a legal point of view. The checking process ("generate feedback") produces a list of "Feedbacks" (3) expressing the assessment of the model's legal qualities, likely in the form of quality measures or answers of a questionnaire. The feedback is then analyzed ("Analyse feedback", (d)), e.g., the statistical significance of certain answers will be measured to compile a "Report" (4) for the IT experts and for the knowledge base builders. The report contains suggestions to review and improve their modelling. This workflow can be iterated until both parties are satisfied.

Due to space constraints, this paper will not delve into the details of each individual step, but only report on the three most critical steps in the methodology: "Translate", "Check", and "Generate Feedback".

4.1 Translate

The "Translate" step generated a representation of the formulæ that legal evaluators could read in order to give feedback about the *legal quality* of the formulæ's meaning(s). We will refer to this synthetic digest (of an otherwise specific logic formalism) as *human-readable representation of a RIO formula* and herewith we show how it was build and how we measured its understandability.

Translating LegalRuleML of RIO Logic Formulæ. Our input is the DAPRECO knowledge base, a LegalRuleML file of RIO formulæ expressing the legal meaning of articles of the GDPR. Perusal of the knowledge base rendered some difficulties, although slightly facilitated by accompanying comments. For instance, in the LegalRuleML serialization, detecting the enumerated prohibitions, obligations, reparations, exceptions was not straightforward. According to [24] "the list of [LegalRuleML] elements and their definitions are not sufficient for the consistent and accurate application of the annotations to text, nor is there clarification about how to analyse source text into LegalRuleML. Thus, an annotation methodology is required to connect text to LegalRuleML".

To elicit a set of usability requirements for the human-readable model, we performed an internal unstructured inquiry where legal experts were asked to spell out what was making the reading hardened and mentally burdensome when answering the previous questions. The inquiry highlighted the following obstacles to a clear understanding of the LegalRuleML of a RIO formula: (1) a formula has little structure, and there are many variables and cross-references between them, forcing the reader to move up and down the code; (2) external references may refer to concepts expressed in the PrOnto ontology, or to logical operators from the RIO logic; (3) the choice of the names of predicates and arguments is not driven by a clear strategy, so that the formula appears confusing; (4) whether a formula is an obligation, a permission or an entailment does not immediately stands out from its syntax, as it depends on the context, which is defined elsewhere according to LegalRuleML practices; (5) negations are hard to capture, as they are structured with two predicates, the first introducing the negation of the second predicate that is expressed positively; (6) RIO logic avoids nesting of obligations and permissions, separating the content of the deontic rule from its bearer in two distinct formulæ. This decision, motivated by the purposes of the logic, can create some confusion, as ultimately there will generally be two separate, and almost identical, formulæ, with the same premises and almost the same consequence.

We address all these problems in a two-step "Translation": the first step is a software that parses the XML, expands and reorders the predicates of the formula; this addresses obstacles 1, 4, 5 and 6. The second is hand-made, to derive an almost natural language break-up version of the formula which, we believe, removes obstacles 2 and 3.

Step One: Automatic Parsing. The output of the automatic translator[6] overcomes the problems enumerated above in the following way: (**i**) variables are substituted with the predicate (taken from PrOnto) that restricts their type; (**ii**) predicates from PrOnto are clearly highlighted in **bold**, whereas predicates from RIO logic and terms that have been introduced for readability's sake are not; (**iii**) the translation of a predicate introduces some terms to set everything into context. This technique works quite well due to a good structure of the ontology; (**iv**) the context of a formula (obligation, permission, constitutive) is carried over to the translation; (**v**) negations are treated by translating the

---

[6] Available at https://github.com/guerret/lu.uni.dapreco.parser.git.

predicates in an inline negative sentence. Additionally, when a negation is the object of an obligation, the latter is renamed into a prohibition, and its content expressed positively; **(iv)** if the parser can find another formula with the exact same IF conditions, then they are most likely the content and bearer of an obligation or permission, so the two formulæ are merged into a single translation, which includes both content and bearer.

Article 7.1 of the GDPR can serve as an example: "*Where processing is based on consent, the controller shall be able to demonstrate that the data subject has consented to processing of his or her personal data*"[7].

The (simplified) RIO formula that IT experts wrote (and later encoded in LegalRuleML) to model the provision is shown in formula 2.

$$(\, [\, (\mathsf{RexistAtTime} \ a_1 \ t_1) \, \wedge \, (\mathsf{and} \ a_1 \ e_p \ e_{hc} \ e_{au} \ e_{dp}) \, \wedge \, (\mathsf{DataSubject} \ w) \, \wedge$$

$$(\mathsf{PersonalData} \ z \ w) \wedge (\mathsf{Controller} \ y \ z) \wedge (\mathsf{Processor} \ x) \wedge (\mathsf{nominates}' \ e_{dp} \ y \ x) \wedge$$

$$(\mathsf{PersonalDataProcessing}' \ e_p \ x \ z) \wedge (\mathsf{Purpose} \ e_{pu}) \wedge (\mathsf{isBasedOn} \ e_p \ e_{pu}) \wedge$$

$$(\mathsf{Consent} \ c) \wedge (\mathsf{GiveConsent}' \ e_{hc} \ w \ c) \wedge (\mathsf{AuthorizedBy}' \ e_{au} \ e_{pu} \ c) \,] \rightarrow$$

$$[\, (\mathsf{RexistAtTime} \ e_a \ t_1) \wedge (\mathsf{AbleTo}' \ e_a \ y \ e_d) \wedge (\mathsf{Demonstrate}' \ e_d \ y \ e_{hc}) \,] \,) {\in} O \qquad (2)$$

The parser translates the formula as follows:

IF, in at least a situation,

- At time $:t_1$, the following situation exists:
  - (All of the following $(:a_1)$)
    1. **Processor** $(:x)$ does **PersonalDataProcessing** $(:e_p)$ of **PersonalData** $(:z)$
    2. **DataSubject** $(:w)$ performs a **GiveConsent** $(:e_{hc})$ action on **Consent** $(:c)$
    3. **Purpose** $(:e_{pu})$ is **AuthorizedBy** $(:e_{au})$ **Consent** $(:c)$
    4. **Controller** $(:y)$ nominates $(:e_{dp})$ **Processor** $(:x)$
- **PersonalData** $(:z)$ is relating to **DataSubject** $(:w)$
- The **Controller** $(:y)$ is controlling **PersonalData** $(:z)$
- **PersonalDataProcessing** $(:e_p)$ **isBasedOn Purpose** $(:e_{pu})$

THEN it must happen that, in at least a situation,

- At time $:t_1$, **Controller** $(:y)$ is **Obliged** to **AbleTo** $(:e_a)$
- **Controller** $(:y)$ **Demonstrate** $(:e_d)$ **GiveConsent** $(:e_{hc})$

Although the translation still requires some mental effort to be processed, it is at least understandable without having expertise in logic. The automatic processing also allowed the modeller to verify that the intended meaning has not been changed and is preserved in the translation.

Step Two: Hand Made Break-Up. The automatic translation has been further hand-processed. The output is a natural language break-up that highlights the following elements: Premises and the Conclusion of the formula; the Deontic Modality, the Ontological Concepts that can be recognized in the article, Other Ontological Concepts present in the formula but not mentioned in the article; the Contextual meaning, which is what the formula expresses but is not in the article, and the Overall Meaning of the formula. The break-up of Article 7.1 is shown in Table 1.

---

[7] The full translations for Articles 5.1 and 7.1 can be found in the repository from note 6, in the "jurisin" folder.

Table 1. Structure of the formula's meaning.

Premise	Where processing is based on consent,
Conclusion	The controller shall be able to demonstrate that the data subject has consented to processing of his or her personal data
Modality	Obligation
Ont. Concepts	Where [Processing] is based on [Consent], the [Controller] shall be [Able to] [Demonstrate] that the [Data subject] [Has consented = GiveConsent] to [Processing] of his or her [Personal data]
Other Ont. Concepts	[Purpose]; [Processor]; [IsAuthorizedBy]; [Nominates]; [IsBasedOn]; [BeAbleTo]
Context	There is a processing, which has a purpose authorized by a consent given by a data subject, and that is what a processor, whom a controller controlling the personal data nominates, does on personal data of the data of the data subject
Overall Meaning	**Whenever** there is a processing, which has a purpose authorized by a consent given by a data subject, and that is what a processor, whom a controller controlling the personal data nominates, does on personal data of the data of the data subject **then** the controller is **obliged** to able to demonstrate that "data subject gave consent"

Measuring the Usability of the Human-Readable Model. Before collect-ing feedback on the quality of the model, the human-readable model must be able to be read consistently and correctly by evaluators. Hence, our experiment consisted in requesting four legal evaluators (two with knowledge of deontic logic, two without it) to answer a few yes/no questions about their understanding of the models of two GDPR provisions. Our priority was to check the modeling of different types of legal norms into logical formulae and as such, Article 5.1(a) was elicited as it represents a constitutive rule, and Article 7.1 evinces an obliga-tion. The input is the human-readable model, but we also fed the original XML formalization and the pre-processed output as control cases, measuring (pure, not Fleiss Kappa) the average interrater agreement between the answers of the evaluators for each model. The questions, built in the wake of the ones used for the validation check (the initial questionnaire) were the following: 1. *Can you identify the formula's premise?* 2. *Can you identify the formula's conclusion(s)?* 3. *Can you identify the deontic modality (obligation, permission, other)?* 4. *Can you identify the formula's explicit ontological concepts?* 5. *Can you identify the formula's implicit ontological concepts?* 6. *Do you understand what the formula means?* 7. *Try to rewrite the formula in your own words. Did you succeed?*

We measured the average agreement over all questions and the two formulæ. The agreement on the answer 'yes', indicating readability, are shown in Table 2. The hand-processed model is where the evaluators, including the laymen in logic, agree almost unanimously over answering 'yes' to all questions, thus indicating high understandability; the control item, the XML file, is where instead there is a major consensus on not being understandable. Our result also reflects that val-idators already knowledgeable on logic can somehow read the XML files, despite

Table 2. Output of the agreement 'yes' on the readability experiment.

	Commented XML	Intermediate	Human-readable
all	39.4% (yes)	40.9%(yes)	97.7%(yes)
lay	0% (yes)	45.5%(yes)	95.5%(yes)

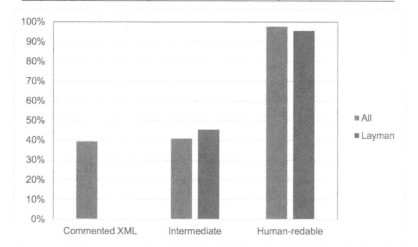

not fully; unsurprisingly, non-experts thereof could not make any sense of it. Conversely, there is no consensus on the understandability of the automatically-processed model. Supposedly, better usability scores may be attained by training the legal evaluators, but we have not explored this possibility. In this particular experiment, we did evaluated other qualities of the model, such as its correctness. Correctness has been assessed in a second experiment, see next section.

4.2   Check and Generate Feedback

We measured understandability as the inter-tester agreement: this measure can suffice to the present goal of having the human-readable model as a candidate within the methodology, although additional measures can provide a deeper evaluation of its usability. More evidence would be needed to assert that our hand-processed model is readable, but since our evaluators generally agreed on its understandability, it can already be used to collect answers to questions $q_1 - q_6$. This is what we did as next steps in the methodology, together with the analysis of the feedback collected during this research.

The starting point is the human-readable representation of Articles 5.1(a) and 7.1 of the GDPR. The "Check" action (see Fig. 1) has been implemented by gathering a set of four validators, all jurists knowledgeable on data protection law, and by asking them to answer questions $q_1 - q_6$ of the questionnaire.

Evaluators were told to compare the meaning of the formulæ, as expressed in the human-readable representation of the RIO logic, with the legal interpretation that they would convey to the articles of the GDPR. We also (re)-asked them a few questions meant to reveal how much understandable for them is the human-readable format, before they start using it. General understandability of the format was assessed already, but here the assessment is meant as a trust measure over the expert's answers. From those trusted answers, we therefore compiled a few recommendations. This is the "Generate Feedback" step in Fig. 1.

While the evaluators were requested to answer the questionnaire in reference to each of the three expressions of the formula (logic, automated translation, and manual break-up), the results are shown for brevity's sake only for the final format. Feedbacks on the less-readable formats have been used to refine the two steps of the translation. Additionally, the multiple feedbacks helped detect the exact location of errors, whether in the formula, in the automated translation, or in the manual break-up.

Questions $q_1 - q_6$ are yes/no questions but we invited our checkers to motivate the answers and to pinpoint whatever observation they valued meaningful. We collected eight documents (four reviewers, two articles) with such written answers and comments which we reviewed and summarized. The following table resumes the findings, wherein we report the comments whenever the answer to the question was 'no', indicating that someone found some issue pertinent.

Table 3. Feedback collected

	Art 5.1a	Art. 7.1
Accuracy	✓	✓
Completeness	It was complex to capture the legal concepts within the structure of the formula; It is missing the obligation: "the processing must be fair, lawful, transparent"	It was complex to capture the legal concepts within the structure of the formula;
Consistency	Interchanged roles for the controller and the processor; The interpretation is complex. It refers to the implementation and description of a measure that it is hard to understand; I can read/understand the model, but I think it does not faithful to the article's meaning;	The reference to consent should be enhanced, namely regarding the requirements concerning the burden of the proof; "Shall" is not captured;
Conciseness	The formula mentions "implement" "describe" not expressed in the article; "implement measure" is not expressed in the article; "Obliged to be able" sounds weird;	It is redundant and restates concepts already present at previous articles;

Table 3 shows that legal experts were able to give feedback on all the factors about the quality of the legal interpretation in the logic formalization of the articles. Even if the input to provide to the IT expert is not yet straightforward, a few highlights clearly emerge.

For instance, all experts easily understood and confirmed the deontic modality and agreed that the formulæ captured all the legal concepts and relations (see Table 4). But is from the analysis conferred to the provided comments that we are able to offer a broader spectrum, for they refer to the above surveyed

Table 4. Inter-evaluators agreement on answering 'yes' to the questions

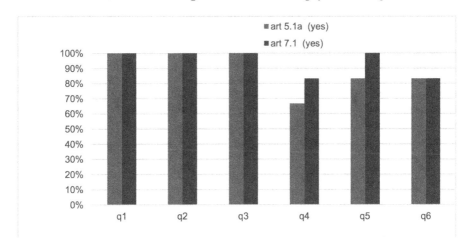

criteria and also to other (non-surveyed) related criteria. Comments – in Completeness like "it was complex to capture the legal concepts within the structure of the formula"; comments in Consistency like "It refers to the implementation and description of a measure that it is hard to understand; "It is redundant and restates concepts already present at previous articles", and comments in Conciseness like "'Obliged to be able to' sounds weirds" – clearly show uneasiness about how formula have been structured; such comments may lead to a better formalization, for instance, stating certain contextual facts as a common premise valid for all the GDPR's articles without repeating them each time.

One evaluator, in particular, has mentioned "Interchanged roles for the controller and the processor" in Consistency. Even if that is stated in the context of the human-readable table, the evaluator was probably induced in error/confused by the excess of information provided. Further analysis is of course required. Extracting from the non-structured comments valid input for the IT expert has to be left as future work, as we comment in the following section.

5 Conclusions and Future Work

This paper leverages a methodology that advocates an interdisciplinary validation of a representation of the GDPR articles in a logic formalism (i.e., RIO logic) to pursue quality, accountability, and transparency within. One important output of the methodology is the production of feedback derived from the involvement of legal experts, while assessing the quality of the legal interpretation that IT experts may instill in the formalization of the GDPR. This work has gathered evidence that such step is feasible. As a proof-of-concept, a small number of legal experts has been asked to answer six questions with the purpose of collecting comments about how two logic formulæ, modelling Articles 5.1a and

7.1 of the GDPR, are complete, accurate, concise, and consistent in reflecting the legal meaning of the articles. Several comments have been collected. Although a thorough analysis thereof requires more time – an involvement of a larger group of expert checkers is also advisable– we were able to identify a few issues of relevance which the IT expert can account in the formalization work.

Several challenges await us in the near future. We need to improve scalability in producing a human-readable representation of the RIO formulæ: it is currently done manually, starting from the pre-processed version. This is already more readable than the original LegalRuleML version and warrants us that the work to produce a natural language analysis break-up table can be automatized. This step done, a forth bringing process will consist in streamlining the validation of the RIO formalization of the GDPR as a whole. This likely requires to set up an application where the modeling of the IT expert can be suitably translated into the human-readable format and displayed, for online checking, to a group of legal testers in order to provide feedback, until a good assessment of the legal interpretations is reached.

Concomitantly, there is a need to define, together with the legal experts, a more complete set of qualities and possibly a few metrics, which we can quantify and define criteria on the legal quality of the formalization. In Sect. 2 we pointed out possible metrics, and in this paper we have assessed a few (completeness, consistency, conciseness in Sect. 4), but a wide and systematic investigation of the state-of-the-art in this topic has not been done yet. The quadrant criteria presented in [10] also merits attention. This may lead to a revision of the current human-readable model.

References

1. Athan, T., Governatori, G., Palmirani, M., Paschke, A., Wyner, A.: LegalRuleML: design principles and foundations. In: Faber, W., Paschke, A. (eds.) Reasoning Web 2015. LNCS, vol. 9203, pp. 151–188. Springer, Cham (2015). https://doi.org/10.1007/978-3-319-21768-0_6
2. Bartolini, C., Giurgiu, A., Lenzini, G., Robaldo, L.: Towards legal compliance by correlating standards and laws with a semi-automated methodology. In: Bosse, T., Bredeweg, B. (eds.) BNAIC 2016. CCIS, vol. 765, pp. 47–62. Springer, Cham (2017). https://doi.org/10.1007/978-3-319-67468-1_4
3. Bartolini, C., Lenzini, G., Santos, C.: A legal validation of a formal representation of GDPR articles. In: Proceedings of the 2nd JURIX Workshop on Technologies for Regulatory Compliance (Terecom) (2018)
4. Bartolini, C., Lenzini, G., Santos, C.: An interdisciplinary methodology to validate formal representations of legal text applied to the GDPR. In: Proceedings of the Twelfth International Workshop on Juris-Informatics (JURISIN), November 2018
5. Berman, D.H.: Developer's choice in the legal domain. In: Proceedings of the Third International Conference on Artificial Intelligence and Law (ICAIL). ACM, June 1991
6. Boella, G., Humphreys, L., Muthuri, R., Rossi, P., van der Torre, L.W.N.: A critical analysis of legal requirements engineering from the perspective of legal practice. In: IEEE 7th International Workshop on Requirements Engineering and Law (RELAW), pp. 14–21. IEEE (2014)

7. Casellas, N.: Ontology evaluation through usability measures. In: Meersman, R., Herrero, P., Dillon, T. (eds.) OTM 2009. LNCS, vol. 5872, pp. 594–603. Springer, Heidelberg (2009). https://doi.org/10.1007/978-3-642-05290-3_73
8. Conrad, J.G., Zeleznikow, J.: The significance of evaluation in AI and law. In: Proceedings of the Fourteenth International Conference on Artificial Intelligence and Law (ICAIL), pp. 186–191. ACM, June 2013
9. Conrad, J.G., Zeleznikow, J.: The role of evaluation in AI and law. In: Proceedings of the Fifteenth International Conference on Artificial Intelligence and Law (ICAIL), pp. 181–186. ACM, June 2015
10. Hall, M.J.J., Hall, R., Zeleznikow, J.: A process for evaluating legal knowledge-based systems based upon the Context Criteria Contingency-guidelines Framework. In: Proceedings of the Ninth International Conference on Artificial Intelligence and Law (ICAIL), pp. 274–283. ACM, June 2003
11. Hall, M.J.J., Zeleznikow, J.: Acknowledging insufficiency in the evaluation of legal knowledge-based systems. In: Proceedings of the Eighth International Conference on Artificial Intelligence and Law (ICAIL), pp. 147–156. ACM, May 2001
12. Koers, A.W.: Knowledge Based Systems in Law, 1st edn. Kluwer Law and Taxation Publishers, Deventer (1989)
13. Lévy, F., Nazarenko, A.: Formalization of natural language regulations through SBVR structured English. In: Morgenstern, L., Stefaneas, P., Lévy, F., Wyner, A., Paschke, A. (eds.) RuleML 2013. LNCS, vol. 8035, pp. 19–33. Springer, Heidelberg (2013). https://doi.org/10.1007/978-3-642-39617-5_5
14. Mockus, M., Palmirani, M.: Legal ontology for open government data mashups. In: Parycek, P., Edelmann, N. (eds.) Proceedings of the 7th International Conference for E-Democracy and Open Government (CeDEM), pp. 113–124. IEEE Computer Society, May 2017
15. Palmirani, M., Martoni, M., Rossi, A., Bartolini, C., Robaldo, L.: Legal ontology for modelling GDPR concepts and norms. In: Proceedings of the 31st International Conference on Legal Knowledge and Information Systems (JURIX), December 2018 (forthcoming)
16. Palmirani, M., Martoni, M., Rossi, A., Bartolini, C., Robaldo, L.: PrOnto: privacy ontology for legal compliance. In: Proceedings of the 18th European Conference on Digital Government (ECDG), October 2018 (upcoming)
17. Palmirani, M., Martoni, M., Rossi, A., Bartolini, C., Robaldo, L.: PrOnto: privacy ontology for legal reasoning. In: Kő, A., Francesconi, E. (eds.) EGOVIS 2018. LNCS, vol. 11032, pp. 139–152. Springer, Cham (2018). https://doi.org/10.1007/978-3-319-98349-3_11
18. Ramakrishna, S., Górski, Ł., Paschke, A.: A dialogue between a lawyer and computer scientist. Appl. Artif. Intell. **30**(3), 216–232 (2016)
19. Reich, Y.: Measuring the value of knowledge. Int. J. Hum. Comput. Stud. **42**(1), 3–30 (1995)
20. Robaldo, L., Sun, X.: Reified Input/Output logic: combining Input/Output logic and reification to represent norms coming from existing legislation. J. Log. Comput. **27**(8), 2471–2503 (2017)
21. Sergot, M.: The Representation of Law in Computer Programs. The A.P.I.C. Series, Chap. 1, vol. 36, pp. 3–67. Academic Press, Cambridge (1991)
22. Stranieri, A., Zeleznikow, J.: The evaluation of legal knowledge based systems. In: Proceedings of the Seventh International Conference on Artificial Intelligence and Law (ICAIL), pp. 18–24. ACM, June 1999
23. Susskind, R.E.: Expert systems in law. Out of the research laboratory and in the marketplace. In: Proceedings of ICAIL-1987, Boston, MA, pp. 1–8. ACM (1987)

24. Wyner, A., Gough, F., Levy, F., Lynch, M., Nazarenko, A.: On annotation of the textual contents of Scottish legal instruments. In: Proceedings of the 30th International Conference on Legal Knowledge and Information Systems (JURIX), vol. 302, pp. 101–106. IOS Press, December 2017
25. Zeleznikow, J.: The split-up project. Law Probab. Risk **3**(2), 147–168 (2004)

COLIEE-2018: Evaluation of the Competition on Legal Information Extraction and Entailment

Yoshinobu Kano[6(✉)], Mi-Young Kim[1,2], Masaharu Yoshioka[4,5],
Yao Lu[2], Juliano Rabelo[2], Naoki Kiyota[6], Randy Goebel[2,3],
and Ken Satoh[7]

[1] Department of Science, Augustana Faculty, University of Alberta,
Camrose, AB, Canada
miyoung2@ualberta.ca
[2] Alberta Machine Intelligence Institute, University of Alberta,
Edmonton, AB, Canada
{yaol, rabelo, rgoebel}@ualberta.ca
[3] Department of Computing Science, University of Alberta,
Edmonton, AB, Canada
[4] Graduate School of Information Science and Technology,
Hokkaido University, N14 W9, Kita-ku, Sapporo-shi, Hokkaido, Japan
yoshioka@ist.hokudai.ac.jp
[5] Global Station for Big Date and Cybersecurity,
Global Institution for Collaborative, Research and Education,
Hokkaido University, Kita-ku, Sapporo-shi, Hokkaido, Japan
[6] Faculty of Informatics, Shizuoka University,
3-5-1 Johoku, Naka-ku, Hamamatsu-shi, Shizuoka, Japan
kano@inf.shizuoka.ac.jp, nkiyota@kanolab.net
[7] National Institute of Informatics, 2-1-2 Hitotsubashi,
Chiyoda-ku, Tokyo, Japan
ksatoh@nii.ac.jp

Abstract. We summarize the evaluation of the 5th Competition on Legal Information Extraction/Entailment 2018 (COLIEE-2018). The COLIEE-2018 tasks include two tasks in each of statute law and case law. The case law component includes an information retrieval (Task 1), and the confirmation of an entailment relation between an existing case and an unseen case (Task 2). The statute law component includes information retrieval (Task 3) and entailment/question answering (Task 4). Participation was open to any group based on any approach. 13 teams participated in the case law competition, and we received results from 7 teams where 6 submissions to Task 1 (12 runs), and 4 submissions to Task 2 (8 runs). Regarding the statute law, there were submissions of 17 runs from 8 teams (including 2 organizers' runs) for Task 3 and 7 runs from 3 teams for Task 4. We describe each team's approaches, our official evaluation, and analysis on our data and submission results. We also discuss possibilities for future competition tasks.

Keywords: COLIEE · Legal information retrieval · Legal textual entailment · Legal question answering · AI and law · Juris-informatics

© Springer Nature Switzerland AG 2019
K. Kojima et al. (Eds.): JSAI-isAI 2018 Workshops, LNAI 11717, pp. 177–192, 2019.
https://doi.org/10.1007/978-3-030-31605-1_14

1   Introduction

The Juris-informatics workshop series was created to promote community discussion on both fundamental and practical issues on legal information processing, with the intention to embrace various disciplines, including law, social sciences, information processing, logic and philosophy, including the existing conventional "AI and law" area.

Competition on Legal Information Extraction/Entailment (COLIEE) is a series of evaluation campaigns to discuss the state of the art for information retrieval and entailment using legal texts [1–3]. In the previous COLIEE 2014–2017, there were two tasks (information retrieval (IR) and entailment) using Japanese Statue Law (civil law). In COLIEE 2018, we conduct new two tasks (IR and entailment) for using Canadian case law (Task 1/2) and two tasks for using Japanese Statue Law that are same settings for the previous campaigns (Task 3/4).

Task 1 is a legal case retrieval task, and it involves reading a new case Q, and extracting supporting cases S1, S2,..., Sn from the provided case law corpus, hypothesized to support the decision for Q. Task 2 is the legal case entailment task, which involves the identification of a paragraph or paragraphs from existing cases, which entail the decision of a new case. For the information retrieval task (Task 3), based on the discussion about the analysis of previous COLIEE IR tasks [4], we modify the evaluation measure of the final results and also ask the participants to submit ranked relevant articles results to discuss the detailed difficulty of the questions. For the entailment task (Task 4), we performed categorized analyses to show different issues of the problems and characteristics of the submissions, in addition to the accuracy evaluation as same as the previous COLIEE tasks.

In the following sections, we will describe each task in detail, explain participants' systems, and assessment results.

2   COLIEE Case Law Competition Tasks

COLIEE-2018 Case Law data is drawn from an existing collection of predominantly Federal Court of Canada case law, provided by vLex Canada (http://ca.vlex.com).

2.1   Task 1: Case Law Retrieval Task

Our goal is to explore and evaluate case law retrieval technologies that are both effective and reliable. The task investigates the performance of systems that search a set of legal cases that support a previously unseen case description. The goal of the task is to accept a query and return noticed cases in the given collection. We say a case is 'noticed' with respect to a query *iff* the case supports the decision of the query case. In this task, the query case does not include a decision, because our goal is to determine how accurately a machine can capture decision-supporting cases for a new case (with no decision).

The process of executing the new query cases over the existing cases and then generating the experimental runs should be entirely automatic. In the training data, each query case is used with a pool of legal cases, and the noticed cases in the pool are produced as the answer. In test data, only query cases and a pool of case laws will be included, with no noticed case information.

The format of the COLIEE case law competition data in Task 1 is as follows:

```
<pair id="t1-1">
<query content_type="summary" description="The summary of the case created
by human expert.">
The parties to this consolidated litigation over the drug at issue brought reciprocal
motions, seeking that the opposing party be compelled to provide a further and better
affidavit of documents ... (omitted)
</query>
<query content_type="fact" description="The facts of the case created by human
expert.">
[1] Tabib, Prothonotary: The Rules relating to affidavits of documents should be well
known by litigants. Yet it seems that parties are either not following them strictly, or are
assuming that others are not ... (omitted)
</query>
<cases_noticed description="The corresponding case id in the candidate cases">
18,45,130
</cases_noticed>
<candidiate_cases description="The candidate cases indexed by id">
<candidate_case id="0"> Case cited by: 2 cases Charest v. Can. (1993)....(omitted)
</candidate_case>
<candidate_case id="1"> Case cited by: one case Chehade, Re (1994), 83 F.T.R. 154
(TD) ... (omitted)
</candidate_case>
... (omitted)
<candidate_case id="199"> Desjardins v. Can. (A.G.) (2004), 260 F.T.R. 248 (FC)
MLB headnote ... (omitted)
</candidate_case>
</candidate_cases> </pair>
```

The above is an example of Task 1 training data where query id "t1-1" has 3 noticed
cases (IDs: 18, 45, 130) out of 200 candidate cases. The test corpora will not include a
<cases_noticed> tag information. Out of the given candidate cases for each query,
participants are required to retrieve noticed cases.

2.2   Task 2: Case Law Entailment Task

Our goal in Task 2 is to predict the decision of a new case by entailment from previous
relevant cases. As a simpler version of predicting a decision, a decision of a new case
and a noticed case will be given as a query. Then a case law textual entailment system
must identify which paragraph in the noticed case entails the decision, by comparing
the extracting and comparing the meanings of the query and paragraph.

The task evaluation measures the performance of systems that identify a paragraph
that entails the decision of an unseen case. Training data consists of a triple: a query, a
noticed case, and a paragraph number of the noticed case by which the decision of the
query is allegedly entailed. The process of executing queries over the noticed cases and
generating the experimental runs should be entirely automatic. Test data will include
only queries and noticed cases, but no paragraph numbers.

The format of the COLIEE competition data in Task 2 is as following:

```
<pair id="t2-1">
<query>
<case_description content_type="summary" description="The summary of
the case created by human expert.">
The applicant owned and operated the Inn on the Park Hotel and the Holiday Inn in
Toronto ... (omitted)
</case_description>
<case_description content_type="fact" description="The facts of the case
created by human expert.">
... </case_description>
<decision description="The decision of the query case."> The applicant submits
that it is unreasonable to require the applicant to produce the information and
documentation referred to in the domestic Requirement Letter within 62 days ...
(omitted)
</decision>
<cases_noticed description="The supporting case of the basic case">
<paragraph paragraph_id="1">
[1] Carruthers, C.J.P.E.I. : This appeal concerns the right of the Minister of National
Revenue to request information from an individual pursuant to the provisions of s.
231.2(1) of the Income Tax Act , S.C. 1970-71-72, c. 63. Background
</paragraph>
<paragraph paragraph_id="2">
[2] The appellant, Hubert Pierlot, is the main officer and shareholder of Pierlot
Family Farm Ltd. which carries on a farm operation in Green Meadows, Prince
Edward Island.
</paragraph>
... (omitted)
<paragraph paragraph_id="26">
[26] I would, therefore, dismiss the appeal. Appeal dismissed. Editor: Steven C.
McMinniman/vem [End of document]
</paragraph>
</cases_noticed>
</query>
<entailing_paragraph description="The paragraph id of the entailed
case.">13</entailing_paragraph>
</pair>
```

The above is an example of Task 2 training data, and the example says that a decision in the query was entailed from the paragraph No. 13 in the given noticed case. The decision in the query does not comprise the whole decision of the case. This is a decision for a portion of the case, and a paragraph that supports the decision should be

Table 1. Baseline performances of Tasks 1 and 2

Tasks	Task 1	Task 2
Precision of term cosine similarity	0.2649	0.0405
Recall of term cosine similarity	0.4102	0.5094
F-measure of term cosine similarity	0.3219	0.0751

identified in the given noticed case. The test corpora will not include the <entailing_paragraph> tag information, and participants are required to identify the paragraph number which entails the query decision.

2.3   Evaluation Metrics and Baselines

The measures for ranking competition participants are intended only to calibrate the set of competition submissions, rather than provide any deep performance measure. The data sets for Tasks 1 and 2 are annotated, so simple information retrieval measures (precision, recall, F1-measure, accuracy) can be used to rank each submission. Task 1 calculates these measures based on number of cases for all queries, while Task 2 based on number of paragraphs for all queries. For Tasks 1 and 2, we consider the term cosine similarity as the baseline model. Table 1 presents the performances of the baseline model.

2.4   Submitted Runs and Results

In the overall case law competition, 13 teams registered, 6 teams submitted their system results in Task 1 (for a total of 12 runs), and 4 teams submitted their results in Task 2 (for a total of 8 runs). Some participants submitted multiple runs for a task. We present the results achieved by runs against the Information Retrieval and Entailment subtasks in Tables 2 and 3, respectively.

Draijer and Verberne (system id: UL) [5] used Random Forest with eight different features for Task 1. The eight features are More Like This Score on Facts, More Like This Score on Summary, Doc2vec Cosine Similarity distance to Facts, Doc2vec Cosine Similarity distance to Summary, TF-IDF Euclidean distance to Facts, TF-IDF Euclidean distance to Summary, TF-IDF Cosine similarity distance to Facts, and TF-IDF Cosine similarity distance to Summary.

Chen et al. (system id: Smartlaw) [6] proposed using association rules in both Tasks 1 and 2. They first experimented with a machine learning-based model adopting Word2Vec/Doc2Vec as features. But machine learning methods have several disadvantages for this task: first, the tasks have very limited training samples, which make current machine learning models hard to achieve good performance. Second, the space consumption of datasets and the computational cost of training exponentially increase when the size of data expands. To enhance the scalability of the solutions, they propose two association rule models: what is labelled as basic association rule model, and another co-occurrence association rule model. The basic association rule model considers only the similarity between the source document and the target document, and it does not leverage a manually labeled relevancy dictionary. The co-occurrence association rule model uses a relevancy dictionary in addition to the basic association rule model.

Tran et al. (system id: JNLP) [7] explored benefits from analyzing legal documents' summaries and logical structures for Task 1. They extended the summary of both the query and the candidates to include more attributes from fact/paragraphs. They propose to obtain document embedding information guided by the document summary. This information is used to estimate the phrasal scores for each document given their summary and paragraphs. Subsequently, they train the model with the summary acting as gold catchphrases and paragraphs acting as document sentences. After building the trained model, they generate a latent summary in continuous vector space. For the ranking of candidates, they use two selection strategies: hard top k, and flexible bound relative to score deviation.

UNCC0 applied ensemble learning using the following classifiers: logistic regression, XGBoost, Random forest, and Support Vector Machine classifier. They used resampling of input data using jnlp SMOTE for further training.

Yoshioka and Song (system id: HUKB) [8] built an IR system for the Task 1 by using the following two steps to retrieve the referred cases: first (1) they build a ranked retrieval, using an IR system to rank candidates. Since the input queries are full text case laws consisting of several parts (summary, citations, paragraph list, etc.), they experimented using different parts for building the target database and the queries. They also analyzed the effect of building one database per query (using only the given candidates for that query), and then building one database using all candidates. Their best performance was achieved when the database used all available case parts; the queries used only the summary and the database was constructed with all candidates. In their second technique (2) from a selection of the referred cases, they choose which of those cases returned in step (1) are going to be used as their system's answer. They tried two strategies: first, select the top n ranked cases (n fixed a priori), then select a variable number of cases by checking the similarity with non-related cases.

Rabelo et al. (system id: UA) [9] modeled Tasks 1 and 2 as binary classification problems. For Task 1, they constructed feature matrices by using a cosine similarity measure between paragraphs from the query case and each candidate case. Those matrices were then transformed into fixed size feature vectors via a histogram approach with pre-determined score bounds, and given to a Random Forest classifier. They also applied post processing to leverage statistical a priori knowledge. Since the dataset in Task 1 is very imbalanced, they under-sampled the dominant class and over-sampled the rarer class by synthesising samples with SMOTE. Their approach for Task 2 was also based on extracting similarity-based features from the query and noticed cases, and feeding those features to a Random Forest classifier.

Lefoane et al. (system id: UBIRLED) [10] propose an approach based on Information Retrieval and unsupervised learning to Task 1: TFIDF is used as a similarity measure between a query and candidate cases. A k-nearest neighbor search with TFIDF as a distance measure is also used. They first rank documents according to their relevance to the query, then apply filtering to exclude the lowest scoring documents from relevant cases, using a threshold value to cut off non-relevant case judgments.

In Table 2, we can see that most systems show better performance than the baseline model. The JNLP system shows the best performance combining lexical features and latent features embedding summary properties (limiting the average number of noticed cases to 10), and it achieved significant increase of the F-measure compared to other systems.

HUKB1 and HUKB2 systems extracted 194 and 191 cases as noticed cases. JNLP-r = 2.5 and JNLP-k = 10 systems extracted 412 and 399 cases. The Smartlaw system extracted 271 cases, UA, UA-postproc, and UA-smote systems extracted 203, 254, and 247 cases, UBIRLED-1, UBIRLED-2, and UBIRLED-3 systems extracted 392, 453, and 64 cases, and UL system extracted 190 cases. Even though JNLP systems extracted the most cases amongst the systems, they showed the best precision performance. In Task 1, many participants used machine learning classifiers, but the system which used more sophisticated features such as a combination of lexical features and latent features embedding summary properties showed the best performance in this year's competition.

Table 3 reports the results of Task 2, where UA and UA-500 showed the best performance, which is significantly better than the baseline performance. The UA and UA-500 systems used similarity-based features input to a Random Forest classifier with different number of estimators. Among the 8 systems, 6 systems showed better performance than the baseline model on Task 2. Task 2 was much difficult than Task 1, and even humans have difficulty in choosing the correct paragraph with the appropriate entailment relations. We can also see the task is difficult based on the low performance on all the systems.

The Tasks 1 and 2 have been newly created in this year's competition, and we think there are many rooms for improvement, such as the evaluation method of Task 2, imbalanced data set, small size set of data which have limitations in applying machine learning techniques, etc. We hope to solve these limitations step-by-step for next competition, to get more robust performances for each task.

Table 2. IR results (Task 1) on the formal run data

Run	Prec.	Recall	F-m.	Run	Prec.	Recall	F-m.
Baseline	0.2649	0.4102	0.3219	UA-postproc	0.3484	0.4038	0.3741
HUKB1	0.4974	0.3084	0.3808	UA-smote	0.3539	0.3927	0.3723
HUKB2	0.4047	0.3037	0.3470	UBIRLED-1	0.1329	0.6232	0.2191
JNLP-r = 2.5	0.5464	0.6550	0.5958	UBIRLED-2	0.1955	0.7202	0.3075
JNLP-k = 10	**0.6763**	**0.6343**	**0.6546**	UBIRLED-3	0.5614	0.1017	0.1723
Smartlaw	0.2871	0.4308	0.3446	UL	0.5638	0.3021	0.3934
UA	0.3725	0.3227	0.3458				

Table 3. Entailment results (Task 2) on the formal run data

Run	Prec.	Recall	F-m.	Run	Prec.	Recall	F-m.
Baseline	0.0405	0.5094	0.0751	UBIRLED-1	0.0484	0.8302	0.0914
Smartlaw	0.0465	0.1509	0.0711	UBIRLED-1	0.0495	0.9245	0.0940
UA	**0.2381**	**0.2830**	**0.2586**	UBIRLED-1	0.0467	0.7925	0.0881
UA-100	0.1905	0.2264	0.2069	UNCC0	0.0330	0.0566	0.0417
UA-500	**0.2381**	**0.2830**	**0.2586**				

3   COLIEE Statute Law Competition Tasks

For the statute law tasks, training and test data of the legal questions are collected from the civil law short answer (multiple choice) part of the Japanese legal bar exam. All questions and Japanese civil law articles (total 1056 articles) are provided in two languages; Japanese and English. English version of the Law articles and questions are provided by the organizers. The organizers provides data set used for previous campaigns [1–3] as training data (651 questions) and new questions selected from bar exam on 2017 as test data (69 questions both for Task 3 and Task 4 individually).

3.1   Task 3: Statute Law Information Retrieval Task

Task 3 is a task to retrieve articles to decide the appropriateness of the legal question. The participants are asked to submit relevant articles for the questions using Japanese or English data. Each participant can submit at most 3 runs for Task 3. Since most of the system returns only 1 article for each question, the numbers of relevant article(s) for the question affect the system performance. Followings are numbers of questions classified by the number of relevant article.

3.1.1   Submitted Runs

Following 8 teams (alphabetical order except organizers' team for baseline) submitted the results. Since all team can submit at most three runs, there are 17 runs in total. Three teams (HUKB, JNLP, and UA) have an experience on submitting results in previous campaign and four teams (Smartlaw, SPABS, UB and UE) are new to the campaign.

HUKB (2 runs) [8] use structural analysis results (condition, decision) of the article and questions and use Indri [11] to calculate similarity measure among different parts. SVM-rank [12] is used to aggregate such similarity measure. HUKB1 decides the number of returned articles based on the analysis of IR retrieval difficulty. HUKB2 returns only 1 article for each question.

JNLP (2 runs) [7] uses structural analysis results (requisite and effectuation) of articles, uses TF-IDF based vector space model for calculating similarity among them. JNLP1 uses similarity between query and articles only for article ranking. JNLP2 calculate final similarity value as a linear combination of similarity used for JNLP1 and similarity between query and article effectuation part. Both runs returns two articles for all questions based on the analysis of training data.

Smartlaw (3 runs) [6] calculate the similarity of a question and an article by checking the similarity between (1–4) gram sets extracted from the question and the article. Based on the experimental analysis, they submit three runs whose setting for constructing (1–4) gram sets are different; Smartlaw, Smartlaw 2 gram, and Smartlaw 3 gram use bigram+trigram, bigram and trigram, respectively.

SPABS (3 runs) uses recurrent neural network to calculate similarity between question and articles. For training word embedding they use English legal documents with Word2Vec. SPABS bm25 is their baseline results using BM25.

UA (1 run) [13] uses same system for COLIEE 2017 for Task 3. This system uses TF-IDF model of Lucene (https://lucene.apache.org/).

UB (3 runs) uses Terrier 4.2 (http://terrier.org/) with PL2 term weighting model as IR platform. UB3 use TagCrowd (https://tagcrowd.com/) to select important keywords from each question and use them as a query of the IR platform. UB2 uses query expansion after UB3 retrieval, and UB1 uses word embeddings.

UE (1 run) uses rule based method to retrieve relevant documents.

ORG (2 runs) uses Indri [11] with simple setting (use question as query and each articles with title are indexed as a document) [7].

Teams who participated previous COLIEE propose an extension or equivalent system for Task 3, and new teams propose methods that are different from previous ones.

3.1.2 Evaluation of Submitted Runs

Table 4 shows the evaluation results of submitted runs including organizer runs. Official evaluation measures are F2 measure, precision (Prec.), recall (Rec.). "ret.", and "rel." represent number of return articles and number of returned relevant articles, respectively. Columns after MAP will be explained later. There are two differences on evaluation measure used in the task compared to the former campaigns:

1. F2 measure, $F2 = (5 \times Prec \times Rec)/(4 \times Prec + Rec)$, is used instead of F1 measure. F2 measure is a variation of f-measure that weights recall higher than precision. If we assume IR task is a preprocess to provide relevant article(s) to the entailment system, it is requested to provide a set of candidate article(s) including relevant article(s) to the entailment system.
2. Macro average is used instead of micro average (Average of evaluation measures are calculated based on the aggregated numbers of relevant articles, returned articles, and returned relevant articles for all questions) used in the former campaigns. Micro average is not so appropriate for the case with different numbers of relevant articles. For example, for analyzing the recall, questions with multiple relevant articles is more important than one with one relevant article. In addition, when the system returns many articles for one query due to the uncertainty of the returned results, this seriously deteriorates the precision of micro average. However, using macro average (Each evaluation measure is calculated based on the numbers of relevant articles, returned articles, and returned relevant articles for each question. After calculating evaluation measure for each question, average of such measure over all questions are calculated), we can reduce the effect of such different characteristics among all retrieved results.

In the previous campaigns, since most of the teams submit only one or two articles for each question, we can only evaluate the topic difficulties based on the number of systems that can return such articles as relevant one. However, it is almost impossible to estimate the reason of the problem. For example, some questions have difficulties to rank the relevant articles higher due to the vocabulary mismatch, and some questions have difficulties to select appropriate one from similar articles (relevant articles are ranked higher but not 1st rank). Therefore, we decide to ask participants to submit long ranking list (100 articles) in addition to the selected relevant article candidate list.

This list provides information that can discuss the type of difficulties to retrieve relevant articles. For the long list, mean average precision (MAP), recall at using top k rank documents as returned documents (R_k) are used for the evaluation measure.

Table 4 also shows information about the evaluation measure for long rank list. However, UE does not submit this long list, values are described as "-".

Table 4. Evaluation of submitted runs (Task3) and organization run

Run id	Language	Ret.	Rel.	F2	Prec.	Rec.	MAP	R$_5$	R$_{10}$	R$_{30}$
UB3	E	69	54	**0.6964**	**0.7826**	0.6860	**0.7988**	0.7978	0.8539	**0.9551**
UA	E	69	50	0.6602	0.7246	0.6522	0.7451	0.7303	0.7528	0.8539
ORGE1	E	69	49	0.6368	0.7101	0.628	0.7381	0.7528	0.809	0.8989
UB2	E	69	47	0.6232	0.6812	0.6159	0.7542	**0.7978**	**0.8652**	**0.9551**
JNLP1	E	138	57	0.6118	0.413	**0.7126**	0.7398	0.764	0.8202	0.9213
Smartlaw	E	138	57	0.6042	0.413	0.7005	0.7036	0.7079	0.764	0.8315
JNLP2	E	138	56	0.5997	0.4058	0.6981	0.7296	0.7528	0.809	0.9101
SPABS_bm25	E	138	55	0.5821	0.3986	0.6739	0.707	0.7753	0.8202	0.9101
UE	E	69	34	0.4516	0.4928	0.4469	–	–	–	–
Smartlaw_3 gram	E	69	34	0.4387	0.4928	0.4324	0.47	0.4494	0.4607	0.5056
UB1	E	69	31	0.4171	0.4493	0.413	0.5355	0.573	0.7191	0.8202
Smartlaw_2 gram	E	141	34	0.3421	0.3023	0.4275	0.4594	0.4382	0.4831	0.5169
SPABS_rnnen	E	138	19	0.215	0.1377	0.2536	0.2638	0.3371	0.4494	0.573
SPABS_rnnsq	E	138	17	0.1957	0.1232	0.2319	0.2662	0.3483	0.4494	0.6067
HUKB2	J	69	53	0.6859	0.7681	0.6763	0.7805	0.7865	0.8427	0.9326
HUKB1	J	74	53	0.6826	0.7536	0.6763	0.7805	0.7865	0.8427	0.9326
ORGJ1	J	69	51	0.6633	0.7391	0.6546	0.7703	0.7753	0.8427	0.9326

Based on the comparison of ORGJ1 and ORGE1, we confirm there is not so big difference between English and Japanese data.

Since average of the relevant articles per query is 1.29 (89/69), the performance of systems that return 2 articles for each question are worse than one that return 1 article only. The best performance system is UB3 that uses tag cloud algorithm to select appropriate keywords for constructing query and use Terrier IR platform to retrieve final results. Teams that have participated in the previous campaigns have almost similar scores except JNLP that returns 2 articles for each question. The performances of new teams except UB are worse than baseline system.

We discuss the difficulties of the questions based on the averaged evaluation measure among team top run results for each language (8 results; HUKB2, JNLP1, SPABS bm25, UB3, UA, Smartlaw, ORGJ, and ORGE). For the questions that have 1 relevant article, 28 out of 51 questions have average MAP = 1.0. It means those questions are easy questions and none of the system made mistake to rank relevant articles as 1st article. For those questions, the system that returns two articles for each question takes bad precision score (precision = 0.5) even though the systems rank the relevant article as 1st rank article. Since those easy questions are not worthwhile to discuss in detail, we only focus on the non-easy questions.

Figure 1 shows averages of MAP, R5, R10 for the non-easy questions (23 questions) with single relevant article. Most of the cases, all of the system find the articles as higher ranked articles (14 questions have R5 = 1 and 2 questions have R5 = 0.875 that means only 1 system cannot rank the articles in top 5). There are few questions that have difficulties to rank relevant articles higher.

Figure 2 shows averages of precision, recall, MAP, R5, R10 for questions with multiple relevant article (2 questions H29-28-E and H29-35-I have three relevant articles and 16 other questions have two relevant articles). There are few questions where both 1st and 2nd ranked articles are relevant articles (MAP = 1). In other cases, there are many questions whose contents is similar to one of the relevant article, but the other is not so similar.

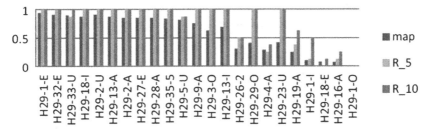

Fig. 1. Averages of MAP, R5, R10 for the non-easy questions with single relevant article

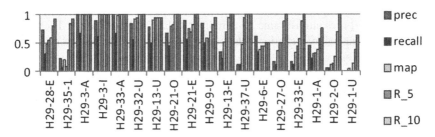

Fig. 2. Averages of precision, recall, MAP, R5, R10 for the non-easy questions with single relevant article

3.1.3 Discussion
Since we have conducted series of campaigns to retrieve relevant articles to entail the questions of Japanese bar exam, most of the system succeed to retrieve relevant articles of the simple questions that have only one relevant article and higher vocabulary (phrase) overlap between question and the relevant article. However, retrieval performance of the questions with vocabulary mismatch is not so good semantic matching technique including RNN approach may be a good approach to tackle this type of problem. But in order to avoid the side effect of degrading the retrieval performance of easy question, preprocessing would be useful to select whether it is necessary to use such semantic matching technique.

For the questions with multiple answers, there are many questions that contents based similarity is not good enough to find out 2nd or 3rd supplemental relevant articles. Information about relationship among articles may be a candidate information resource that are not well utilized at this moment, but further discussion is necessary to tackle this type of the problem.

3.2   Task 4: Statute Law Entailment/Question Answering Task

Task 4 is a task to determine entailment relationships between a given problem sentences and article sentences. Participants should answer yes or no regarding the given problem sentences. There were pure entailment tasks hold until COLIEE 2016, where t1 (relevant article sentences) and t2 (problem sentence) were given. Due to the limited number of available problems, COLIEE 2017 and 2018 did not hold this style of task. In Task 4 of COLIEE 2018, t1 (relevant articles) is not given, participants should find the relevant articles by themselves.

3.2.1   Submitted Runs and Evaluation Results

Following 3 teams submitted the results. Since a team submitted five runs, there are 7 runs in total. Two teams (KIS and UA) have experiences on submitting results in previous tasks and a team (UE) is new to our tasks.

KIS (3 runs) [14] analyze Japanese sentences linguistically, use predicate argument structures to determine similarities. [15] uses frame information to calculate similarity between predicates. Their final results were ensemble of these different modules by SVM.

UA (1 run) [9] uses almost same system of COLIEE 2017 for Task 4. Their system uses condition/conclusion/exception detection rules, and negation dictionaries created manually.

UE (1 run) combined deep neural network with additional features, and word2vec to gain the corresponding civil law articles.

Table 5 shows an evaluation results of submitted runs. Official evaluation measures used in this task is accuracy.

Table 5. Evaluation results of submitted runs (Task 4) and baseline result

Team	Language	Correct Answers (69 questions in total)	Accuracy
BaseLine	N/A	35 (answers No to all)	0.5072
UA	?	44	0.6377
KIS_Frame	Japanese	39	0.5652
KIS_mo3	Japanese	38	0.5507
KIS_dict	Japanese	37	0.5362
KIS_SVM	Japanese	36	0.5217
KIS_Frame2	Japanese	35	0.5072
UE	English	33	0.4783

The best system was UA, which accuracy was 0.6377. The baseline was almost 0.5, because this task is a binary classification, with 35/69 questions are No. Effect of language difference is unclear. In our statue law tasks, the Japanese legal bar exam is the original data, which is translated into English manually. Team UA used translation system and Korean parser internally. Translation process might have absorbed ambiguities and paraphrases.

Because an entailment task is essentially a complex compositions of different subtasks, we manually categorized our test data into categories, depending on what sort of technical issues are required to be resolved. Table 6 shows our categorization results. As this is a compositional task, overlap is allowed between categories. Our categorization is based on the original Japanese version of the legal bar exam.

We have summarized the results of the COLIEE-2018 competition. Two tasks for Case Law, Task 1: retrieving noticed cases (information retrieval), and Task 2: extracting paragraphs of relevant case which entail the conclusion of a new case. Other two tasks for Statute Law, Task 3: information retrieval, and Task 4: entailment/question answering. There were 13 teams who participated in this competition, and we received results from 7 teams. There were 6 submissions to Task 1 (for a total of 12 runs), and 4 submissions to Task 2 (for a total of 8 runs). There are 17 run submissions from 8 teams (including 2 organizers' run) for Task 3 and 7 run submissions from 3 teams for Task 4.

A variety of methods were used for Task 1: combining lexical features and latent features embedding summary properties, creating queries from the summaries of cases, and building an information retrieval system to extract noticed cases, co-occurrence association model, pairwise paragraph similarity computation, K-NN, TF-IDF, and a Random forest classifier. Various features were also proposed: features from summary properties, Word2Vec, Doc2Vec, More Like This Score, cosine similarity, Euclidean distance, etc. For Task 2, co-occurrence association model, similarity-based features fed to a random forest classifier, and ensemble machine learning with SMOTE resembling techniques were used. Even though most systems outperformed baseline, all the performances are low, and the task didn't make it easy to identify relevant useful attributes. For future competitions, we will need to expand the data sets in order to improve the robustness of results. We also need to more deeply investigate how to extract good features for Task 2.

For Task 3, we found there are three types of problem in the test data; i.e., easy question, difficult questions with vocabulary mismatch, and questions with multiple answers. Most of the submission systems are good at retrieving relevant answers for easy questions, but it is still difficult to retrieve relevant articles with other question types. It may be necessary to focus on such question types to improve the overall performance of the IR system. For Task 4, overall performance of the submissions is still not sufficient to use their systems for the real application. However, detailed analysis could capture the characteristics of the submitted systems. We found this task is still a challenging task to discuss and develop deep semantic analysis issues in the real application, and natural language processing in general.

3.2.2   Discussion

Our categorization shown in the previous section suggests several issues and analyses. The largest number among these categories was for the conditions. UA, the best team, was better in this condition category. Their condition detection should have successfully performed. KIS Frame2, which used the frame information, was good in case roles, person relations, and person roles. Their frame relation would have certain effect in these deep semantic issues.

Table 6. Technical category statistics of questions, and correct answers of submitted runs for each category. Team names stand for their number of correct answers for corresponding category.

Category	# of questions	UA	Accuracy	UE	Accuracy	KIS_mo3	Accuracy	KIS_dict	Accuracy	KIS_SVM	Accuracy	KIS_Frame2	Accuracy	KIS_Frame	Accuracy
Itemized	3	1	0.33	2	0.67	1	0.33	1	0.33	1	0.33	1	0.33	2	0.67
Numerical priority	3	2	0.67	2	0.67	1	0.33	1	0.33	2	0.67	1	0.33	2	0.67
Entailment	5	2	0.4	2	0.4	1	0.2	1	0.2	4	0.8	2	0.4	2	0.4
Dependency	5	3	0.6	1	0.2	2	0.4	2	0.4	3	0.6	0	0	4	0.8
Article search	5	3	0.6	2	0.4	3	0.6	3	0.6	1	0.2	1	0.2	4	0.8
Paraphrase	5	2	0.4	4	0.8	3	0.6	3	0.6	2	0.4	3	0.6	3	0.6
Negation	7	5	0.71	3	0.43	5	0.71	5	0.71	2	0.29	1	0.14	7	1
Legal terms	7	4	0.57	2	0.29	2	0.29	2	0.29	3	0.43	4	0.57	3	0.43
Normal terms	9	5	0.56	5	0.56	4	0.44	4	0.44	5	0.56	6	0.67	4	0.44
Predicate argument	9	8	0.89	3	0.33	5	0.56	5	0.56	5	0.56	4	0.44	5	0.56
Verb paraphrase	13	7	0.54	6	0.46	7	0.54	7	0.54	7	0.54	7	0.54	4	0.31
Case role	15	8	0.53	6	0.4	9	0.6	9	0.6	6	0.4	11	0.73	6	0.4
Ambiguity	17	9	0.53	7	0.41	8	0.47	8	0.47	8	0.47	10	0.59	9	0.53
Anaphora	20	13	0.65	5	0.25	12	0.6	11	0.55	8	0.4	8	0.4	13	0.65
Morpheme	25	18	0.72	16	0.64	20	0.8	19	0.76	10	0.4	16	0.64	16	0.64
Person relationship	26	14	0.54	11	0.42	13	0.5	13	0.5	13	0.5	18	0.69	10	0.38
Person role	27	16	0.59	12	0.44	14	0.52	14	0.52	14	0.52	18	0.67	13	0.48
Conditions	31	19	0.61	9	0.29	13	0.42	12	0.39	16	0.52	11	0.35	16	0.52

Because the distribution of yes/no answers is quite diverse between submissions, an ensemble could performs better results if we could capture meaningful information for each submission.

4 Conclusion

We have summarized the results of the COLIEE-2018 competition. For the case law, Task 1 retrieves noticed cases (information retrieval), Task 2 extracts paragraphs of relevant case which entail the conclusion of a new case. Task 3 is a task to retrieve articles to decide the appropriateness of the legal question and Task 4 is a task to entail whether the legal question is correct or not. 13 teams participated in the case law competition, and we received results from 7 teams where 6 submissions to Task 1 (for a total of 12 runs), and 4 submissions to Task 2 (for a total of 8 runs). Regarding the statute law, there were 17 run submissions from 8 teams (including 2 organizers' run) for Task 3 and 7 run submissions from 3 teams for Task 4.

A variety of methods were used for Task 1: combining lexical features and latent features embedding summary properties, creating queries from the summaries of cases, and building an information retrieval system to extract noticed cases, co-occurrence association model, pairwise paragraph similarity computation, K-NN, TF-IDF, and a Random forest classifier. Various features were also proposed: features from summary properties, Word2Vec, Doc2Vec, More Like This Score, cosine similarity, Euclidean distance, etc. For Task 2, co-occurrence association model, similarity-based features fed to a random forest classifier, and ensemble machine learning with SMOTE resembling techniques were used. Even though most systems outperformed baseline, all the performances are low, and the task didn't make it easy to identify relevant useful attributes. For future competitions, we will need to expand the data sets in order to improve the robustness of results. We also need to more deeply investigate how to extract good features for Task 2.

For Task 3, we found there are three types of problem in the test data; i.e., easy question, difficult questions with vocabulary mismatch, and questions with multiple answers. Most of the submission systems are good at retrieving relevant answers for easy questions, but it is still difficult to retrieve relevant articles with other question types. It may be necessary to focus on such question types to improve the overall performance of the IR system. For Task 4, overall performance of the submissions is still not sufficient to use their systems for the real application. However, detailed analysis could capture the characteristics of the submitted systems. We found this task is still a challenging task to discuss and develop deep semantic analysis issues in the real application, and natural language processing in general.

Acknowledgements. This research was supported by Alberta Machine Intelligence Institute (AMII), National Institute of Informatics, Shizuoka University and Hokkaido University. Thanks to Colin Lachance from vLex for his constant support in the development of the case law data set, and to support from Ross Intelligence and Intellicon. This work was partially supported by JSPS KAKENHI Grant Number 16H01756, 18H0333808, 17H06103, and JST CREST.

References

1. Kim, M.Y., Goebel, R., Satoh, K.: COLIEE-2015: evaluation of legal question answering. In: Ninth International Workshop on Juris-Informatics (JURISIN 2015) (2015)
2. Kim, M.Y., Goebel, R., Kano, Y., Satoh, K.: COLIEE-2016: evaluation of the competition on legal information extraction/entailment. In: Tenth International Workshop on Juris-Informatics (JURISIN 2016) (2016)
3. Kano, Y., Kim, M.Y., Goebel, R., Satoh, K.: Overview of COLIEE 2017. Epic Ser. Comput. **47**, 1–8 (2017)
4. Yoshioka, M.: Analysis of COLIEE information retrieval task data. In: Arai, S., Kojima, K., Mineshima, K., Bekki, D., Satoh, K., Ohta, Y. (eds.) New Frontiers in Artificial Intelligence, pp. 5–19. Springer, Cham (2018). https://doi.org/10.1007/978-3-319-93794-6_1
5. Draijer, W., Verberne, S.: Case law retrieval with doc2vec and elastic search. In: Twelfth International Workshop on Juris-Informatics (JURISIN 2018), 2018
6. Chen, Y., Zhou, Y., Lu, Z., Sun, H., Yang, W.: Legal information retrieval by association rules. In: JURISIN 2018 (2018)
7. Tran, V., Truong, S.N., Le Nguyen, M.: JNLP group: legal information retrieval with summary and logical structure analysis. In: International Workshop on Juris-Informatics (JURISIN 2018) (2018)
8. Yoshioka, M., Song, Z.: HUKB at COLIEE2018 information retrieval task. In: International Workshop on Juris-Informatics (JURISIN 2018) (2018)
9. Rabelo, J., Kim, M.Y., Babiker, H., Goebel, R., Farruque, N.: Legal information extraction and entailment for statute law and case law. In: JURISIN 2018 (2018)
10. Lefoane, M., Koboyatshwene, T., Narasimhan, L.: KNN clustering approach to legal precedence retrieval. In: Twelfth International Workshop on Juris-Informatics (JURISIN 2018) (2018)
11. Strohman, T., Metzler, D., Turtle, H., Croft, W.B.: Indri: a language-model based search engine for complex queries. In: Proceedings of the International Conference on Intelligent Analysis, pp. 2–6 (2005)
12. Joachims, T.: Optimizing search engines using clickthrough data. In: Proceedings of the Eighth ACM SIGKDD International Conference on Knowledge Discovery and Data Mining, pp. 133–142 (2002)
13. Kim, M.Y., Goebel, R.: Two-step cascaded textual entailment for legal bar exam question answering. In: 16th International Conference on Artificial Intelligence and Law (ICAIL 2017), 2017
14. Hoshino, R., Taniguchi, R., Kiyota, N., Kano, Y.: Question answering system for legal bar examination using predicate argument structure. In: Twelfth International Workshop on Juris-Informatics (JURISIN 2018) (2018)
15. Taniguchi, R., Hoshino, R., Kano, Y.: Legal question answering system using framenet. In: Twelfth International Workshop on Juris-Informatics (JURISIN 2018) (2018)

Legal Question Answering System Using FrameNet

Ryosuke Taniguchi, Reina Hoshino, and Yoshinobu Kano[(✉)]

Informatics Course, Graduate School of Integrated Science and Technology,
Shizuoka University, 3-5-1 Johoku, Naka-ku, Hamamatsu, Japan
{rtaniguchi,rhoshino}@kanolab.net,
kano@inf.shizuoka.ac.jp

Abstract. A central issue of yes/no question answering is the usage of knowledge source given a question. While yes/no question answering has been studied for a long time, legal yes/no question answering largely differs from other domains. The most distinguishing characteristic is that legal issues require precise analysis of predicate argument structures and semantical abstraction in these sentences. We have developed a yes/no question answering system for answering questions for a statute legal domain. Our system uses a semantic database based on FrameNet, which works with a predicate argument structure analyzer, in order to recognize semantic correspondences rather than surface strings between given problem sentences and knowledge source sentences. We applied our system to the COLIEE (Competition on Legal Information Extraction/Entailment) 2018 task. Our frame based system achieved better scores on average than our previous system in COLIEE 2017, and was the second best score among participants of Task 4. We confirmed effectiveness of the frame information with the COLIEE training dataset. Our result shows the importance of the points described above, revealing opportunities to continue further work on improving our system's accuracy.

Keywords: COLIEE · Question answering · Legal bar exam · Legal information extraction · FrameNet

1 Introduction

Automatic question answering is attracting more interests recently. Due to the increasing expectation to the Artificial Intelligence (AI) technologies, people tend to regard question answering systems as a brand new technology emerged today. However, most successful systems employ rather traditional techniques of question answering which have decades of history [1–7], including series of shared tasks such as TREC [8], NTCIR [9] and CLEF [10]. This paper describes our challenge to the COLIEE 2018 legal bar exam, which asks participants to answer true or not based on the civil law Articles, given text drawn from the Japanese legal bar exam.

A variety of algorithms and systems has been proposed for question answering. Typically, these question answering systems used *big data* for answering questions [11–14]. For example, Dumais et al. [15] focused on the redundancy available in large

© Springer Nature Switzerland AG 2019
K. Kojima et al. (Eds.): JSAI-isAI 2018 Workshops, LNAI 11717, pp. 193–206, 2019.
https://doi.org/10.1007/978-3-030-31605-1_15

corpora as an important resource. They used this redundancy to simplify their algorithm and to support answer mining from returned snippets. Their system performed quite well given the simplicity of the techniques being utilized.

The now widely known IBM Watson system [16] would be considered as a typical example of such a question answering system of the big data approach. The IBM Watson system won in the Jeoperdy! Quiz TV program competing with human quiz winners. The core Watson system employed a couple of open source libraries, including the traditionally well-designed DeepQA system [17] as its skeleton of question answering processing. Because their target domain, the Jeoperdy! Quiz, could ask broad range of questions, they collected a huge amount of knowledge sources from the Internet, etc., extracting relevant knowledge by combining a couple of different natural language processing (NLP) techniques.

Answering university examinations is another example. The Todai Robot project [18] is a challenge to solve Japanese university examinations, focusing towards attaining a high score in the National Center Test for University Admissions by 2016, and passing the entrance exam of the University of Tokyo (Todai) in 2021 [19]. Although the Todai Robot project tries to achieve higher scores, their aim is rather to reveal the current performance and limitation of the existing AI technologies, using the examinations as its benchmark, similar to the COLIEE's legal bar exam task. In contrast to the COLIEE task, the challenge of Todai Robot project includes variety of subjects including Mathematics, English, Japanese, Physics, History, etc. all written in Japanese language. While solving any problem of these subjects could be considered as question answering, some problems require special technologies. For example, Mathematics and Physics require to process formula; Japanese requires to infer emotions of story characters. Solving the History subjects might be considered as rather an extension of the existing question answering issues. The Todai Robot project achieved better scores than the average of the real human applicants in their Mock Exam challenges.

Recognition of textual entailments (RTE or RITE) is another related issue. RTE has been intensively studied for recent days, including shared tasks such as RTE tasks of PASCAL [20, 21], SemEval-2012 Cross-lingual Textual Entailment (CLTE) [22], NTCIR RITE tasks [23–25], etc. In the third PASCAL RTE-3 task, contradiction relations are included in addition to entailment relations [21]. In the RTE-6 task, given a corpus and a set of candidate sentences retrieved by a search engine from that corpus, systems are required to identify all the sentences from among the candidate sentences that entail a given hypothesis. NTCIR-9 RITE, NTCIR-10 RITE2, and NTCIR-11 RITEVal Exam Search tasks [25] required participants to find an evidence in source documents and to answer a given proposition by yes or no. Research of RTE normally tries to employ logical processing.

As described above, question answering techniques could include logic, reasoning, syntactic and semantic analysis. Many previous related works tried to employ such deeper analyses. However, required techniques more or less differ depending on a target domain. Another issue is whether the knowledge source needs to be "big data" or not. Regarding the COLIEE's legal problems, required knowledge source can be limited.

In this paper, we suggest using a semantical corpus based on a Rule-based predicate argument structure analyzer in a precise way, rather than to use any machine learning methods. Due to this small data issue, supervised machine learning methods would suffer from insufficient training data. In addition, there are no "similar" problems for most of the legal bar exam problems. Therefore, a solver needs to "comprehend" the contents of the knowledge sources. Moreover, it is difficult to analyze why machine learning answers so, due to their black box architecture. Rule-based methods would make analyses less difficult and are especially effective in a limited domain like legal documents.

Based on these thoughts, we built our yes/no question answering system. Our system does not employ any machine learning. The main method of our system is a predicate argument structure analyzer using FrameNet. We integrated them and applied to COLIEE 2018 Task 4. Our frame based system achieved the second best score among participants. We compared our frame based system with our previous system as baselines, confirming effectiveness of the frame information. There are still many difficult issues remained to be solved though.

We explain about previous works and FrameNet in Sect. 2. Section 3 describes our design of the yes/no question answering system especially using FrameNet. Section 4 shows our experimental results for this COLIEE task and the comparison with previous system. We discuss our achievements and limitations comparing with previous system in Sect. 5, mentioning possible future works in Sect. 6. We conclude our paper in Sect. 7.

2 Background

2.1 COLIEE

The COLIEE shared task series is held in association with the JURISIN (Juris-informatics) workshop. The first one was the COLIEE 2014 shared task [26]. Following this, the COLIEE 2015 shared task [27], the COLIEE 2016 shared task [28], and the COLIEE 2017 [29] shared task (this time in conjunction with ICAIL) were held. This paper mainly describes our participation to the COLIEE 2018 shared task. We call COLIEE 2018 simply as COLIEE in this paper.

The COLIEE shared task consists of four tasks. Task 1 is the legal case retrieval task which involves reading a new case and extracting related cases. Task 2 is the legal case entailment task which compares the new case with related cases given by Task 1.

Task 3 of this legal question answering task involves reading a Japanese legal bar exam question and extracting a subset of Japanese Civil Code Articles. Task 4 is a legal question answering task which requires both of the legal information retrieval system and textual entailment system. Given a set of legal yes/no questions, a participant's system will retrieve relevant civil law articles. Then, answer yes/no entailment relationship between input yes/no question and the retrieved articles.

2.2   Previous Work

In COLIEE 2016 [30], our yes/no question answering system was based on case-role analyses using JUMAN [31] and KNP [32]. JUMAN is a Japanese morphological analyzer where we added a custom dictionary for legal technical terms based on a Japanese legal term dictionary ("有斐閣法律用語辞典第4版"). KNP is a Japanese dependency case structure analyzer, works on top of JUMAN. Using results of these tools, we obtained a subject and an end-of-sentence expression for each sentence. A subjective case is normally specified by particles "が (ga)" or "は (ha)", which are subjective case markers in Japanese. We regarded these cases as subjective cases. When we analyzed the civil law articles, we removed each header part "X条 (Article X)", which includes an article name and numbers. We compared the pairs of the subject and the end-of-expression between the civil law articles and the legal bar exams.

Our COLIEE 2017 [33] system was based on our COLIEE 2016 system above. We defined our own *clause* unit ("節") in order to recognize condition clauses and proposition clauses precisely, which are included in a single sentence. After recognizing condition clauses and proposition clauses in a sentence, we compared corresponding clauses between a given question and civil law articles. A clause should include a predicate as a core element of that clause. We applied a dependency parser that makes chunks ("文節") of a couple of morphemes. Starting form a chunk that includes a predicate, we aggregated neighboring chunks when a neighboring chunk does not include any predicate.

As comparing clauses, we used three modules, a precise match, a loose match and a rough match. The precise match performed exact matches for its predicate, its subject and its object. When we could not find any subject nor any object, we skip that sentence. We outputted yes if everything matched, else outputted no. When there was any negation either in problem clause or in article clause, we reversed the yes/no output. The loose match was looser version of the precise match. When comparing proposition clauses and condition clauses, we outputted yes if either subjects or objects were match in addition to matching predicates. The rough match was the loosest match. We only compared predicates of proposition clauses.

2.3   FrameNet

FrameNet [34, 35] is an English semantical lexical database based on a theory of meaning called frame semantics [36]. Basic idea of frame semantics is that people understand the meaning of words largely by frames which they evoke. Frames have some semantic roles called Frame Elements (FEs). Frame evoking words are called Lexical Units (LUs). For example, a typical situation of shopping involves *buyers, sellers, goods, money, means, rate,* and *unit.* FrameNet has ten kinds of relations (*Inheritance, Using, Perspective_on, Subframe, Precedes, Inchoactive_of, Causative_of, Metaphor, See_also,* and *ReFraming_mapping*) within frames (called Frame Relations). Figure 1 shows an example of the "Commerce-transaction" frame evoked by the shopping concept in FrameNet. There is a Japanese version of FrameNet [37]. We use LUs of Japanese FrameNet, in addition to the English version of FrameNet.

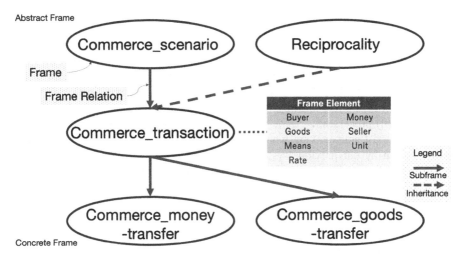

Fig. 1. An example shows a "Commerce-transaction" frame. Each node shows a frame, and an arrow between two frames shows a frame relation.

We use Japanese WordNet [38], in addition to FrameNet. Japanese WordNet is a lexical database for Japanese, where synonyms, hypernyms, hyponyms and English translation words are defined. We use WordNet to expand lexical units of FrameNet.

3 Proposed Method

We use FrameNet in addition to the previous rule-based system. A reason is that structures of civil law articles are clean. The civil law articles use only one place (snippet) for one topic. While our previous system performed textual entailments in a superficial layer, our proposed method using FrameNet could perform in a deeper level. Another reason is that we need precise analyses to solve legal issues, rather than statistically calculate rough estimate values in a superficial way. We took an unsupervised approach for the same reasons.

3.1 Previous Rule-Based System

We define two types of clauses in our previous system: proposition clauses and condition clauses. Before using FrameNet, we obtain these clauses from the previous system. We apply a Japanese dependency parser KNP with JUMAN to make the clauses including a set of a predicate, a subject, and an object. When comparing a pair of sets between civil law articles and legal bar exams, we use a *precise match* and a *loose match*. The precise match performs exact matches of strings for its predicate, its subject and its object. The loose match compares either a pair of subjects or a pair of objects, in addition to matching predicates. When our systems could not output any answer, our system answers *yes* as a default output. Additionally, when any negation appears in a clause, we reverse yes/no output.

3.2   Frame-Evoking Words

Our frame based system works like a part of semantic role labeling. Semantic Role Labeling (SRL) is a representative NLP task using FrameNet. The SRL has four processes: (i) identify a frame-evoking word, (ii) identify a frame from the frame-evoking word (frame disambiguation), (iii) estimate words, phrases, or clauses which we have to give FEs, (iv) labeling the FEs. Our frame based system corresponds to these (i) and (ii) processes.

To identify a frame-evoking word, we use a predicate in a proposition clause set which is given by our previous system. Next, we add a candidate of frame-evoking words from the predicate using Japanese WordNet to connect with a specific LU. This is because the number of frame evoking words contained in a LU is small.

We use either English LUs or Japanese LUs. When we use English LUs, we add English translation words in Japanese WordNet to the candidate of word-evoking words. When we use Japanese LUs, we add synonyms, hypernyms and hyponyms in Japanese WordNet to the candidate of word-evoking words. We select LUs which contain one of the word-evoking words. Finally, we make a candidate of frames from the selected LUs. Figure 2 shows an example of this process.

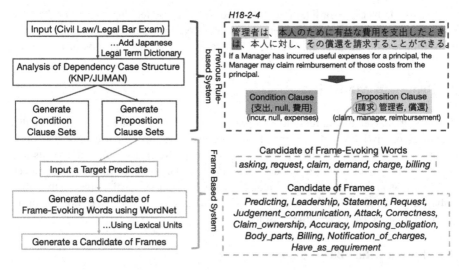

Fig. 2. An example of our frame detection process, using English LUs.

3.3   Frame Disambiguation and Metrics of Frame Confidence

We compare a pair of frame candidates in round robin. We take a pair of frames which confidence value is highest. To calculate the confidence between two frames, we use a shortest path determined by the Dijkstra Algorithm [39] from the entire graph of the frame relations. We assigned a weight value to all of the frame relation types (Table 1). These weights are determined by heuristics. When a weight value is higher between a pair of frames, then we regard this pair as more similar. The following four examples are some of the typical relations.

Table 1. Weight values of the frame relation types.

FrameRelationType	RelevanceWeignt	FrameRelationType	RelevanceWeight
Inheritance	0.95	Inchoactive_of	0.65
Perspective_on	0.9	Causative_of	0.65
Using	0.85	Metaphor	0.5
Subframe	0.8	See_also	0.5
Precedes	0.7	ReFrameing_Mapping	0.5

Inheritance is the strongest relation between frames, corresponding to is-a relationship. So, each frame element in a parent frame should correspond to a frame element in its child frame. Therefore, we set the highest value to this Frame Relation. *Using* is used in a part of a scene evoked by a child frame that refers to its parent frame; some parent frame elements might not have corresponding child frame elements. *Perspective_on* is similar to *Using*. While *Perspective_on* could treat at least two perspectivized frames (e.g. the Commercial_transaction frame specifies a complex scheme involving an exchange of subjects between a seller and a buyer). *Subframe* aggregates frames that form a complex sequence as a whole.

We define the confidence value as a multiplication by the weights of frame relations on the path (Fig. 3). As it is not easy to calculate accurate confidence value, we make a binary feature of clause similarity by setting a threshold. This binary feature is used as

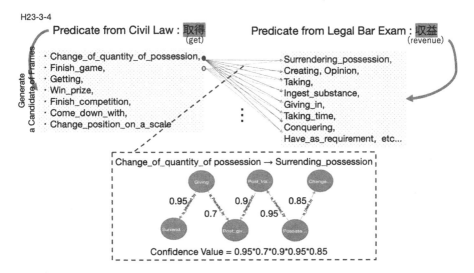

Fig. 3. An example of the confidence value, which is calculated by a multiplication by the weights of frame relations on the path.

one of the features in our yes/no question answering system. When a confidence value is beyond the threshold, we regard the corresponding pair of predicates as similar. Therefore, the lower threshold we set, the more pairs our system could compare. Then we compare the corresponding clauses of civil law articles and legal bar exams extracted by our rule based system as same as our previous system, assuming the corresponding pair of predicates is identical.

4   Experiments and Results

Experiments were conducted on the COLIEE 2018 statute law competition data corpus (Task 4). We did not use the training data except for evaluations, because our frame based system does not use any machine learning method i.e. unsupervised.

4.1   COLIEE Datasets

In this paper, we focused on Task 4. Training data of Task 4's legal questions is drawn from the Japanese legal bar exams. Relevant Japanese civil law articles were also provided. While there was an English translation version of the dataset provided, we only used the original Japanese version. Figure 4 shows an example of the COLIEE statue law competition data.

4.2   Performance Experiments

t1: (留置権の行使と債権の消滅時効) 第三百条　留置権の行使は、債権の消滅時効の進行を妨げない。 (Exercise of Rights of Retention and Extinctive Prescription of Claims)Article 300 The exercise of a right of retention shall not preclude the running of extinctive prescription of claims. t2: 留置権者が留置物の占有を継続している間であっても，その被担保債権についての消滅時効は進行する。 Even while the holder of a right to retention continues the possession of the retained property, extinctive prescription runs for its secured claim.

Fig. 4. An example of COLIEE legal bar problem which asks to answer whether t1 entails t2 or not

In order to investigate our frame based system performance, we used the COLIEE training dataset which includes the past legal bar exam problems and answers. We performed textual entailment part of Task 4, given the gold standard answer of Task 3. We compared a couple of combinations of our modules, in order to observe effects of the frame information. Because the COLIEE dataset is unbalanced, i.e. the number of yes answers and no answers are not equal. When our systems could not output any answers, we tried to fill with either all yes or all no answers as default output to normalize this unbalance. Table 2 shows the result of these performance experiments, using Japanese LUs.

Table 2. Results of performance experiments. Our FrameNet system uses Japanese LUs with 0.9 as its threshold.

Default Output	Score	PreciseMatch	PreciseMatch + FrameNet	LooseMatch	LooseMatch + FrameNet
N	Average	0.577	0.574	0.595	0.591
N	CorrectNum	378	376	390	387
Y	Average	0.522	0.525	0.533	0.542
Y	CorrectNum	342	344	349	355

Table 3 shows a distribution of scores with changing LUs and threshold values. This system is based on the loose match, and the default output is N.

Table 3. Results of performance experiments with LUs based on the loose match. "E" stands for English LU, "J" stands for Japanese LU. CorrectNum shows the number of correct answers.

LU	Threshold		H18	H19	H20	H21	H22	H23	H24	H25	H26	H27	H28	
E	0.5	Accuracy	0.543	0.381	0.533	0.536	0.553	0.585	0.692	0.621	0.532	0.486	0.714	0.573
E	0.5	CorrectNum	19	16	24	30	26	24	54	41	50	36	55	375
E	0.7	Accuracy	0.543	0.381	0.533	0.536	0.553	0.585	0.692	0.621	0.532	0.486	0.740	0.576
E	0.7	CorrectNum	19	16	24	30	26	24	54	41	50	36	57	377
E	0.9	Accuracy	0.543	0.429	0.533	0.536	0.553	0.585	0.692	0.636	0.532	0.514	0.727	0.582
E	0.9	CorrectNum	19	18	24	30	26	24	54	42	50	38	56	381
J	0.5	Accuracy	0.543	0.357	0.533	0.554	0.638	0.561	0.705	0.636	0.543	0.486	0.688	0.579
J	0.5	CorrectNum	19	15	24	31	30	23	55	42	51	36	53	379
J	0.,7	Accuracy	0.543	0.381	0.533	0.554	0.638	0.561	0.705	0.636	0.543	0.514	0.714	0.586
J	0.,7	CorrectNum	19	16	24	31	30	23	55	42	51	38	55	384
J	0.9	Accuracy	0.543	0.429	0.533	0.536	0.617	0.561	0.692	0.652	0.564	0.500	0.740	0.591
J	0.9	CorrectNum	19	18	24	30	29	23	54	43	53	37	57	387

4.3 Formal Run Experiments

Table 4 shows our formal run results in COLIEE 2018 Task 4. The results of KIS_-Frame based on the loose match, which uses English LUs with the threshold set to 0.99. The number of comparable pairs increases by using FrameNet, which becomes too many when comparing all of the civil law articles. Therefore, we restrict the possible number of the comparisons by setting larger threshold in Task 4. We changed the threshold to 0.7 from 0.99 in the performance experiments, as the possible number of comparisons is already limited. This is because we use the training datasets which include gold standard civil law articles to be compared with.

KIS_Frame2 is different from KIS_Frame in that the loose, rough and precise match modules are used together. In KIS_Frame2, we use English LUs and the threshold is 0.7.

5 Discussion

Table 4. The COLIEE 2018 formal run results. "J" is using Japanese test datasets, and "E" is English version.

Team	Language	# Correct answers (total 69 answers)	Accuracy
YA	?	44	0.6388
KIS_Frame	J	39	0.5652
KIS_mo3	J	38	0.5507
KIS_dict	J	37	0.5362
KIS_SVM	J	36	0.5217
KIS_Frame2	J	35	0.5072
UE	E	33	0.4783

Firstly, we observed similar score distribution between the baselines and our frame based systems, among examination years from H18 to H28. Our system should have added new results, rather than changing the entire answer set drastically.

Secondly, there is almost no difference between the precise match results regardless of the FrameNet's effect. These results suggest that there was a little number of clauses in the training set, which the precise match is applicable i.e. a pair of triples (subject, object and predicate) matches. On the other hand, we observed differences in the loose matches. Table 3 shows that higher threshold values result in better scores. Its reason would be that we compare the less sets when we use the higher thresholds.

In order to analyze this effect in detail, we focus on H28 (H28-3-5) as shown in Fig. 5. Our previous system cannot compare predicates when their surface strings are different, even though they have comparable similar meanings. In contrast, our frame based system can handle such predicates of similar meanings even if their string forms differ. Our frame based system could answer more problems than our previous system for this reason, which is supported by the actual results.

Thirdly, our frame based system can recognize a pair of predicates which essentially shares a same or similar meaning. However, this is not always the cases. Predicates of abstract meanings, such as "do" and "become", tend to evoke more frames, which results in higher confidence values; used frames sometimes seem not related to the legal domain; a pair of antonyms got the same frame, because they are typically used in the same situation. Figure 6 shows examples of these cases.

Fourthly, whether using English LUs or Japanese one, we observe different evoked frames. For example, from the predicate "claim (請求)", our system acquired *Predicting, Leadership, Statement, Request, Judgment_communication, Attack,*

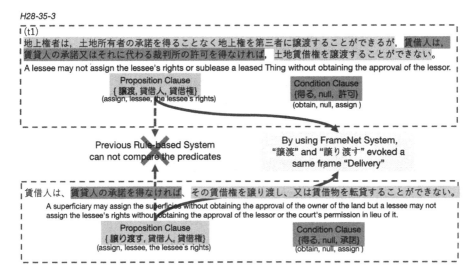

Fig. 5. An example of the effect of FrameNet.

Target Predicates	Frame Relation	Confidence
・生ずる, 生じる _(occur, occur)	Giving_birth → Giving_birth	1.0
・合意, 約する _(agreement, promise)	Documents → Documents	1.0
・成立, 定める _(occur, occur)	Creating → Creating	1.0
・拒絶, 対抗 _(reject, against)	Statement → Statement	1.0
・取り消す, 対抗 _(rescind, against)	Damaging → Confronting_problem	0.8145
・取得, 収益 _(acquire, profit)	Getting → Taking	0.95
・する, 知る _(do, know)	Touring? → Touring?	1.0
・行使, 追認 _(perform, ratification)	Ingest_substances? → Rite	0.8075
・失う, 得る _(lose, acquire)	Finish_competition → Finish_competition	1.0?

Evoked Frames which are not related to Legal Domain

A pair of Atonyms got a same Frame

Fig. 6. An example of the analysis results.

Correctness, Claim_ownership, Accuracy, Imposing_obligation, Body_parts, Billing, Notification_of_charges, and *Have_as_requirement* Frames by using English LUs, in contrast *Claime_ownership* and *Have_as_requirement* by Japanese LUs. Precise analysis between English LUs and Japanese LUs would be needed to find effects of FrameNet.

6   Future Work

Japanese text requires explicit tokenization process because there is no space between tokens. When this tokenization fails, final result could also fail. Therefore, we need to refine the tokenization process and following predicate-argument structure analysis process to be optimized with our frame based system. For example, removing an abstract word could be effective.

We heuristically defined the weights of Frame Relations and the metrics of calculating the Frame confidence. Automatic tuning of the weights with some machine learning technique would be our future work. Using relevant graph theory could also improve the system.

The core of FrameNet are frame elements, in other words, semantical roles. By using frame elements, we could identify frames more precisely, capturing deeper semantic structures.

The most difficult issue to solve in legal domain would be the logic and abstraction, and how we approach these problems using FrameNet.

7   Conclusion

Legal document processing requires a variety of issues to be solved compared with other domains. The most distinguishing characteristic is that legal issues require precise analysis of a predicate argument structure and semantical abstraction. Based on this observation, we developed a yes/no question answering system for legal domain. Our system uses a Japanese case structure analyzer and FrameNet. We applied our system to COLIEE 2018 Japanese task (Task 4). Our system achieved the second best score among Task 4 participants, the best among our systems of different module combinations. We analyzed effectiveness of our frame based system by the training dataset, confirming increase of the scores when our frame based system was used.

Acknowledgements. This work was partially supported by MEXT Kakenhi and JST CREST.

References

1. Lin, D., Pantel, P.: Discovery of inference rules for question-answering. Nat. Lang. Eng. **7** (4), 343–360 (2001)
2. Ravichandran, D., Hovy, E.: Learning surface text patterns for a question answering system. In: Proceedings of the 40th Annual Meeting on Association for Computational Linguistics, pp. 41–47 (2002)
3. Yu, H., Hatzivassiloglou, V.: Towards answering opinion questions: separating facts from opinions and identifying the polarity of opinion sentences. In: Proceedings of the 2003 Conference on Empirical Methods in Natural Language Processing, pp. 129–136 (2003)
4. Pinto, D., McCallum, A., Wei, X., Croft, W.B.: Table extraction using conditional random fields. In: Proceedings of the 26th Annual International ACM SIGIR Conference on Research and Development in Information Retrieval, pp. 235–242 (2003)

5. Cui, H., Sun, R., Li, K., Kan, M.-Y., Chua, T.-S.: Question answering passage retrieval using dependency relations. In: Proceedings of the 28th Annual International ACM SIGIR Conference on Research and Development in Information Retrieval, pp. 400–407 (2005)
6. Xue, X., Jeon, J., Croft, W.B.: Retrieval models for question and answer archives. In: Proceedings of the 31st Annual International ACM SIGIR Conference on Research and Development in Information Retrieval, pp. 475–482 (2008)
7. Bian, J., Liu, Y., Agichtein, E., Zha, H.: Finding the right facts in the crowd: factoid question answering over social media. In: Proceedings of the 17th International Conference on World Wide Web, pp. 467–476 (2008)
8. Voorhees, E.M., Harman, D.K.: TREC: Experiment and Evaluation in Information Retrieval. The MIT Press, Cambridge (2005). (Digital Libraries and Electronic Publishing)
9. Kando, N., Kuriyama, K., Nozue, T.: NACSIS test collection workshop (NTCIR-1) (poster abstract). In: Proceedings of the 22nd Annual International ACM SIGIR Conference on Research and Development in Information Retrieval, pp. 299–300 (1999)
10. Braschler, M.: CLEF 2000 — overview of results. In: Peters, C. (ed.) CLEF 2000. LNCS, vol. 2069, pp. 89–101. Springer, Heidelberg (2001). https://doi.org/10.1007/3-540-44645-1_9
11. Kwok, C.C.T., Etzioni, O., Weld, D.S.: Scaling question answering to the web. In: Proceedings of the 10th International Conference on World Wide Web, pp. 150–161 (2001)
12. Etzioni, O., et al.: Web-scale information extraction in KnowItAll: (preliminary results). In: Proceedings of the 13th International Conference on World Wide Web, pp. 100–110 (2004)
13. Jeon, J., Croft, W.B., Lee, J.H.: Finding similar questions in large question and answer archives. In: Proceedings of the 14th ACM International Conference on Information and Knowledge Management, pp. 84–90 (2005)
14. Kanayama, H., Miyao, Y., Prager, J.: Answering yes/no questions via question inversion. In: The 24th International Conference on Computational Linguistics (COLING 2012), pp. 1377–1391 (2012)
15. Dumais, S., Banko, M., Brill, E., Lin, J., Ng, A.: Web question answering: is more always better? In: Proceedings of the 25th Annual International ACM SIGIR Conference on Research and Development in Information Retrieval, pp. 291–298 (2002)
16. Ferrucci, D.: Introduction to 'This is Watson'. IBM J. Res. Dev. **56**(3.4), 1:1–1:15 (2012)
17. Ferrucci, D., et al.: Building watson: an overview of the DeepQA project. AI Mag. **31**(3), 59–79 (2010). https://doi.org/10.1609/aimag.v31i3.2303
18. Arai, N.H.: The impact of AI—can a robot get into the University of Tokyo? Natl. Sci. Rev. **2**(2), 135–136 (2015)
19. The Todai Robot Project. http://21robot.org/
20. Dagan, I., Glickman, O., Magnini, B.: The PASCAL recognising textual entailment challenge. In: Quiñonero-Candela, J., Dagan, I., Magnini, B., d'Alché-Buc, F. (eds.) MLCW 2005. LNCS (LNAI), vol. 3944, pp. 177–190. Springer, Heidelberg (2006). https://doi.org/10.1007/11736790_9
21. Giampiccolo, D., Magnini, B., Dagan, I., Dolan, B.: The third PASCAL recognizing textual entailment challenge. In: Proceedings of the ACL-PASCAL Workshop on Textual Entailment and Paraphrasing, pp. 1–9 (2007)
22. Negri, M., Marchetti, A., Mehdad, Y., Bentivogli, L., Giampiccolo, D.: Semeval-2012 task 8: cross-lingual textual entailment for content synchronization. In: Proceedings of the First Joint Conference on Lexical and Computational Semantics - Volume 1: Proceedings of the Main Conference and the Shared Task, and Volume 2: Proceedings of the Sixth International Workshop on Semantic Evaluation, pp. 399–407 (2012)
23. Shima, H., et al.: Overview of NTCIR-9 RITE: recognizing inference in TExt. In: NTCIR-9 Workshop, pp. 291–301 (2011)

24. Watanabe, Y., et al.: Overview of the recognizing inference in text (RITE-2) at NTCIR-10. In: The NTCIR-10 Workshop, pp. 385–404 (2013)
25. Matsuyoshi, S., et al.: Overview of the NTCIR-11 recognizing inference in TExt and validation (RITE-VAL) Task. In: The 11th NTCIR (NII Testbeds and Community for Information Access Research) Workshop, pp. 223–232 (2014)
26. Competition on Legal Information Extraction/Entailment (COLIEE-14), Workshop on Juris-informatics (JURISIN) 2014 (2014). http://webdocs.cs.ualberta.ca/~miyoung2/jurisin_task/index.html
27. Kim, M.-Y., Goebel, R., Ken, S.: COLIEE-2015: evaluation of legal question answering. In: Ninth International Workshop on Juris-Informatics (JURISIN 2015) (2015)
28. Kim, M.-Y., Goebel, R., Kano, Y., Ken, S.: COLIEE-2016: evaluation of the competition on legal information extraction and entailment. In: Tenth International Workshop on Juris-informatics (JURISIN 2016) (2016)
29. Kano, Y., Kim, M.-Y., Goebel, R., Ken, S.: Overview of COLIEE2017. In: International Conference on Artificial Intelligence and Law (ICAIL 2017) (2017)
30. Taniguchi, R., Kano, Y.: Legal yes/no question answering system using case-role analysis. In: Kurahashi, S., Ohta, Y., Arai, S., Satoh, K., Bekki, D. (eds.) JSAI-isAI 2016. LNCS (LNAI), vol. 10247, pp. 284–298. Springer, Cham (2017). https://doi.org/10.1007/978-3-319-61572-1_19
31. JUMAN (a User-Extensible Morphological Analyzer for Japanese). http://nlp.ist.i.kyoto-u.ac.jp/EN/index.php?JUMAN
32. Japanese Dependency and Case Structure Analyzer KNP. http://nlp.ist.i.kyoto-u.ac.jp/EN/index.php?KNP
33. Kano, Y., Hoshino, R., Taniguchi, R.: Analyzable legal yes/no question answering system using linguistic structures. In: International Conference on Artificial Intelligence and Law (ICAIL 2017) (2017)
34. Welcome to FrameNet! https://framenet.icsi.berkeley.edu/fndrupal/
35. Ruppenhofer, J., Ellsworth, M., Petruck, M.R.L., Johnson, C.R., Baker, C.F., Scheffczyk, J.: FrameNet II: Extended Theory and Practice (2016)
36. Fillmore, C.J.: Frame semantics. In: Linguistics in the Morning Calm, pp. 111–137 (1982)
37. Japanese FrameNet. http://jfn.st.hc.keio.ac.jp
38. Japanese WordNet. http://compling.hss.ntu.edu.sg/wnja/index.en.html
39. Graph Compute with Neo4j: Built-in Algorithms, Spark & Extensions. https://neo4j.com/blog/graph-compute-neo4j-algorithms-spark-extensions/

Question Answering System for Legal Bar Examination Using Predicate Argument Structure

Reina Hoshino[(✉)], Ryosuke Taniguchi[(✉)], Naoki Kiyota[(✉)],
and Yoshinobu Kano[(✉)]

Informatics Course, Graduate School of Integrated Science and Technology,
Shizuoka University, 3-5-1 Johoku, Naka-ku, Hamamatsu, Japan
{rhoshino,rtaniguchi,nkiyota}@kanolab.net,
kano@inf.shizuoka.ac.jp

Abstract. We developed a question answering system for legal bar exam, which can explain the way system solves based on underlying logical structures. We focus on the set of subject and object with their predicate, i.e. the predicate argument structure, in order to represent structures of legal documents. We implemented a couple of modules using different searching methods. Our system outputs results using these modules by learning each module's confidence value with SVM. We manually analyzed the difficulty level of the problems whether external knowledge is required or not. We created a structured synonym dictionary specialized to the legal domain, where predicates are categorized with their objects. This synonym dictionary could absorb superficial differences of predicates to solve the problems which do not require external knowledge. We confirmed that the system can solve more than 70% of simple problems. Our system achieved the second best score in Task 4 of the COLIEE 2018 shared task.

Keywords: COLIEE · Question answering · Legal bar exam · Legal information extraction · Predicate argument structure analysis

1 Introduction

Automatic question answering for legal documents is gathering attention recently. This paper describes our challenge to Task 4 of the COLIEE 2018 legal bar exam, which asks participants to answer true or not based on the Civil Law Articles, given text drawn from the Japanese legal bar exam.

The COLIEE shared task series is held in association with the JURISIN (Jurisinformatics) workshop. The first one was the COLIEE 2014 shared task [1]. Following this, the COLIEE 2015 shared task [2], the COLIEE2016 shared task [3], and the COLIEE 2017 [4] shared task (this time in conjunction with ICAIL) were held. The COLIEE shared task consists of four tasks. We challenged Task 4. Task one and Task 2 used the legal cases. Task 1 of this legal question answering task involves reading a legal bar exam question and extracting a subset of Japanese Civil Code Articles. Task 4 requires both of the legal information retrieval system and textual entailment system. Given a set of legal yes/no questions, a participant's system will

© Springer Nature Switzerland AG 2019
K. Kojima et al. (Eds.): JSAI-isAI 2018 Workshops, LNAI 11717, pp. 207–220, 2019.
https://doi.org/10.1007/978-3-030-31605-1_16

retrieve relevant civil law articles. Then answer yes/no entailment relationship between input yes/no question and the retrieved articles. The corpus of legal questions is drawn from Japanese legal bar exams, and the relevant Japanese civil law articles were also provided. While there was an English translation version of the dataset provided, we only used the original Japanese version.

Regarding question answering in general, most successful systems employ rather traditional techniques of question answering which have decades of history [5–8]. Recently, automatic answering system used machine learning by big data. The typical example is IBM Watson System [9]. The core Watson system employed a couple of open source libraries, including the traditionally well-designed DeepQA system [10] as its skeleton of question answering processing.

However, there are only hundreds of problem sentences used in COLIEE. We think that the amount of data is not enough to perform an end-to-end supervised machine learning. There are an enormous number of legal documents, many methods have been proposed to acquire knowledge from case examples [11]. However, it is difficult to use case examples directly in the legal bar exam, because we need commonsense knowledge to follow the thinking of a legal expert, not just the explicit knowledge base available. In addition, a question answering system for legal documents is required to show reasons of its decision in a human interpretable way. Our aim is to create a legal question answering system where we can trace evidences of it decision.

Reasoning is essential in understanding a legislative system. Civil law articles consist of a legal effect part and cases to state its effect. A system needs to find them from problem sentences. However, there are a couple of difficult issues to find such relevant parts.

Firstly, the legal effect is not necessarily written in the article. We conducted an experiment asking Japanese native speaker to solve the legal bar exam while showing the related articles. These native speakers have never learned legal issues. Their accuracy was about 80%, which shows that people have little knowledge of law cannot solve all problems even the related articles are given. This means that external knowledge is important to solve the problems.

Secondly, there are ambiguities in legal articles. Words used in the law articles are different from the words in problem sentence in most cases, even when they express the same situation. For example, "成立する (effect)" and "適用する (apply)" are sometimes interchangeable. We created a synonym dictionary for predicates to handle this issue. We made our synonym dictionary extracting from the past legal bar exam problems of six years (2009–2014). A predicate entry in our dictionary is structured to have a condition, what sort of object could be taken.

Thirdly, diversity of the vocabulary is a difficult issue. In the civil law, both legal technical terms and terms used in daily life are required, because civil law handles problems in daily life. We registered these words in our morphological analyzer's dictionary.

The legal bar exam includes a variety of complex linguistic issues, such as synonym, commonsense knowledge, syntax, and semantics. to be resolved to understand legal documents. In order to make our system behavior interpretable, we focus on simpler problems in this paper. We manually examined difficulty levels for tens of past years' problems.

Section 2 describes the proposed method of our question answering system. Section 3 shows results of COLIEE2018 and past years, including analyses of the difficulty levels. Section 4 concludes this paper, discussing future works.

2   System Architecture

2.1   System Design

Our question answering system consists of two parts: a related article search part, and a question answering part. These parts use predicate argument structure analysis, comparing a pair of sentences based on case roles of the arguments. The article search part searches for the related articles by searching sentences of the same structure. The question answering part compares whether each sentence represents the same event. In addition, we prepare a couple of different modules with different judgment criteria, and make modules for each criterion. Our final answer is obtained by using SVM, which selects its output from the answers of the modules and their confidence values. These confidence values are calculated from the number of articles that our predicate argument matches with the problem sentences. The datasets we used were the civil law articles, the problems of the past legal bar exam.

2.2   Dictionary

We created a legal term dictionary extracted from "有斐閣法律用語辞典第4版" (Yuhikaku legal term dictionary fourth edition).

Table 1.   Number of words used in civil bar exam

	Total	New
H18(2006)	351	–
H19(2007)	317	175
H20(2008)	322	144
H21(2009)	402	171
H22(2010)	316	87
H23(2011)	312	73
H24(2012)	484	127
H25(2013)	425	50
H26(2014)	563	144
H27(2015)	490	84
H28(2016)	441	67

We examined vocabulary using past eleven years of problems, we found that more than 300 kinds of words are used in problems per one year. More than 50 new words appeared per year when registering words from older year to newer year (Table 1). We registered these words in our morphological analyzer's dictionary.

In addition to the dictionary above, we created an additional dictionary from morphological analysis results of the problems of 7 years. This dictionary makes our analysis of predicate argument structures correct. Predicate argument structure analysis often failed because morphological analysis was not correctly performed. This failure is due to unknown words which are not listed in our Japanese dictionary nor our legal term dictionary. We added 200 new words manually.

We created our additional dictionary, extracting from source codes of PROLEG (Satoh, Asai, and Hurukawa 2011). PROLEG is a logic programming language for the legal domain based on Prolog. They systemize internal structure of the law from the civil law articles and actual cases. The PROLEG system returns a case is legally valid or not, by giving arguments such as a defendant and an object. Function names and variable names of PROLEG are named by hand. These names are necessary when reading and understanding the legal documents deeply. Therefore, we could obtain composite words not listed in the normal legal term dictionary. We extracted function names and variable names that do not use alphabets nor numbers, then added them to our additional dictionary.

2.3 Predicate Argument Structure Analysis

H24-2-1：
制限行為能力者のした契約について，<u>制限行為能力者及びその法定代理人</u>が<u>取消権を有する</u>ときは，契約の<u>相手方も取消権を有する。</u>
(With respect to contracts concluded by the person with limited capacity, if the person with limited capacity and the statutory agent have the right to rescind, the counterparty also has.)

(condition clause)
制限行為能力者及びその<u>法定代理人</u>が<u>取消権</u>を<u>有する</u>ときは，
Set:｛有する, 法定代理人, 取消権｝ （述語, 主語, 目的語）
　　{has, the counterparty, the right to rescind} (predicate , subject, object)

(proposition clause)
契約の<u>相手方</u>も<u>取消権</u>を<u>有する。</u>
Set:｛有する, 相手方, 取消権｝
　　{have, the statutory agent, the right to rescind}

Fig. 1. An example of predicate argument structure analysis

Figure 1 shows an example of predicate argument structure analysis. We defined our own clause unit ("節") in order to recognize condition clauses and main clauses precisely, which are included in a single sentence. A clause should include a single predicate as a core element of that clause. We apply a dependency parser that makes chunks ("文節") of a couple of morphemes. Starting form a chunk that includes a predicate, we aggregate neighboring chunks when a neighboring chunk does not include any predicate, until a clause unit is formed.

A predicate is not always suitable to be a core predicate of a clause. For example, "holding" in "condition holding a court" could be regarded as a predicate. However, this is not suitable as a core single predicate in a clause because we need to compare larger predicate-argument structures rather than such a noun phrase.

We define two types of special clauses: a proposition clause and a condition clause. A proposition clause includes an end of the sentence. In the Japanese language, a clause which includes an end of sentence often represents a proposition. We regard a clause as a condition clause when that clause includes specific patterns, e.g. "when...", "in case of ...", etc.

When searching related articles, we use a set of a predicate, a subject and an object as a predicate argument structure. For each sentence, we compare proposition clauses of the problem sentences and the civil law articles using these sets. The same applies for condition clauses. We use the base form of predicates for their comparison. For example, "認める (admit)" and "認めない (do not admit)" have the same meaning, sharing the same base form "認める (admit)".

Normally, a sentence consists of a proposition clause and any number of condition clauses. Because an article consists of one or more sentences, we compare sentences one by one when comparing the article sentences with the problem sentence. However, when a problem consists of a couple of sentences, we regard the whole sentences as a single sentence. This is because the last sentence tends to be most important, while other sentences tend to represent conditions of the last sentence. For this reason, we regard clauses as condition clauses except for the proposition clause of the last sentence.

A difficulty in predicate argument structure analysis is an itemized article. An itemized article first describes the effect, then cases are listed to show the effect. In such a case, we cannot understand only with the first sentence. Sometimes there are no subjects or predicates in the part of case list. There are a lot of articles that have such a structure.

As a countermeasure, we connect the case list part with the first sentence. In this case, the first sentence always contains a phrase "次に掲げる (the following things)". We delete this specific phrase and then insert the part of case list. We repeat this process for the number of items, making multiple sentences. However, the connected sentence could be syntactically invalid, causing errors in predicate argument structure analysis.

2.4 Synonym Dictionary for Predicates

We manually created a synonym dictionary for predicates. For example, "成立する (effect)" and "適用する (apply)" could have the same meaning. We used the problems of 2009 to 2006 to make our dictionary. We compared related articles and corresponding problem sentences to manually determine our synonym dictionary entries. As a result, we selected a combination of 33 verbs.

Our dictionary is structured with object conditions. For example, "果実を取得する (obtain fruits)" and "収益する (receive the profits)" have the same meaning when they have the same object (Fig. 2).

t1：
第三百五十六条　不動産質権者は、質権の目的である不動産の用法に従い、その使用及び<u>収益をする</u>ことができる。
(Pledgees of immovable property may use and receive the profits from the immovable property that is the subject matter of a pledge, in accordance with the method of its use.)

t2：
不動産質権者は，質権の目的物である不動産の用法に従いこれを使用することができるが，不動産から生じた<u>果実を取得する</u>ことはできない。
(A pledgee of immovable property may use and receive obtain fruits from the immovable property that is the subject matter of a pledge, in accordance with the method of its use, but may not collect fruits derived by the real property.)

t1: 収益する (receive the profits)
t2: 取得する (obtain) - condition: 果実 (fruits)

Fig. 2. An example of synonym dictionary

We examined difficulty levels of the problems in order to verify how many problems can be solved by a synonym dictionary. The difficulty level is classified into four levels. The first level is "very easy", corresponds to the problems which text is almost same with the article. The second level is "easy", its problem can be solved by any Japanese native speakers without external knowledge. This "easy" problem requires synonym and/or zero pronouns resolutions. The third level is "difficult", its problem requires general external knowledge but not legal expert knowledge. For example, a father's father is a grandfather, which is a common sense of external knowledge. In addition, related articles in this level could span multiple sentences, sometimes become complicated structures. The fourth level is "very difficult", its problem cannot be solved without external knowledge of the legal experts. In this level, its answer is not written in the related articles neither explicitly nor implicitly.

The "Target" column of Table 2 shows the difficulty level statistics of the problems in 2014 and 2016. The "easy" problems share around 30%. We aim to solve these "easy" problems by our synonym dictionary.

Table 2. Difficulty level statistics of the past COLIEE problems

	Very easy	Easy	Difficult	Very difficult
2014	12	10	5	5
2016	21	32	30	10

2.5 Person Estimation

Some legal bar problems ask conceptual things or ask how rights are oved using concrete stories. For example, a typical problem of concrete parable story describes persons called "A", "B", and "C". In order to answer such concrete parable stories, we implemented a person estimation feature. In our person estimation feature, our system searches for words that are actors in the sentence, i.e. words with "人 (human)" or "者 (person)", e.g. "代理人 (agent)". Predicate argument structure analysis sometimes fails to find a subject. When our system cannot find a subject, we insert a word as a subject that is found by this person estimation feature.

2.6   Question Answering Module

We created four types of question answering modules: precise match, loose match, rough match, and FrameNet modules.

Precise match module extracts civil law articles which proposition clauses match with a given proposition clause of problem sentences. For each predicate, we find a subject and an object by their case markers. We perform exact matches for the predicate, its subject and its object. When we could not find any subject nor any object, we skip that sentence. If a negative expression is detected only in one side, we reverse the corresponding Yes/No answer. Our system repeats these processes for the number of the clauses of the problem sentences. The precise match module has the highest percentage of correct answers among the four modules. However, this module cannot find answers for about 70% of problems.

Loose match module is a looser version of the precise match. When comparing proposition clauses and condition clauses, this module regards a pair of clauses as matched if either a pair of objects or a pair of subjects is matched, in addition to a pair of predicates.

For example, if a problem's clause is {結ぶ (sign), 代理人 (agent), 契約 (contract)} and if an article's clause is {結ぶ (sign), 代理人 (agent), 売買契約 (sales contract)}, then our precise match module judges that they do not have a same meaning because they do not have a same object. On the other hand, our loose match module judges that they have a same meaning as this module ignores objects in this case.

Rough match module is the loosest match in our modules. This module only compares predicates of proposition clauses and then checks whether the predicates include negative expressions or not.

Furthermore, we prepare the FrameNet module. FrameNet [12] is an English semantical lexical database based on a theory of meaning called frame semantics. The basic idea is that people understand the meaning of words largely by the frames which they evoke. Frames have some semantic roles called Frame Elements (FEs) and frame evoking words are called Lexical Units (LUs). We use LUs of Japanese FrameNet [13], in addition to the original English version of FrameNet.

We use Japanese WordNet [14], which is a lexical database for Japanese. We use Japanese WordNet to obtain synonyms, hypernyms, hyponyms and English translation words to expand FrameNet.

The FrameNet module is made by extending the loose match module. The difference of the FrameNet module from the loose match module is in comparing predicates. Using an inheritance relationship of FrameNet, we examine whether a pair of predicates represents the same meaning or not. This system measures a distance between nodes of words and regards as the same meaning if the nodes are in a near distance. We defined confidence values for each relationship type to calculate the distance.

In addition, we made more sub-modules by setting different options for these four modules. An option forces the predicate selection; when a clause includes specific condition pattern like "の場合は (in case of)" or "の時は (when)", a previous chunk is regarded as the core predicate of that clause. Another option is in the FrameNet module; we changed the confidence calculation method and/or the threshold of the confidence values.

2.7   Module Integration

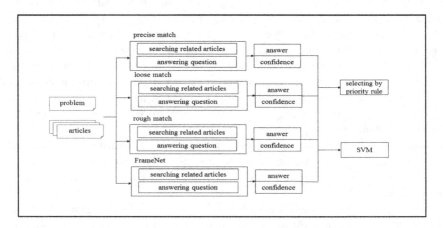

Fig. 3. Overview of our module integration

After completing the answers for each module, we decide our final answer. We pre-pared two ways for resolution (Fig. 3).

When we do not use SVM, we try applying the precise match module first. When the precise match module cannot be applied, we apply the loose match module. If the loose match module cannot be applied as well, we try applying the rough match module.

When we use SVM, we use each answer output by each module and the confidence calculated from the number of articles that matched word sets of the problem sentence for learning. The confidence is a value that decreases as more the number of the related articles. The equation of calculating the confidence is $1/n$. n is the number of the related articles when $n > 0$. The confidence is 0 when $n = 0$. However, the related articles of solving the problems are not only one, it is not necessarily true that the probability that the related articles is less and accurate is higher. The training data for SVM is the problems of 2006 to 2008.

The optimum cost and gamma value of SVM options were determined by grid search. The kernel used is a polynomial kernel. We used a kernel with a high rate of correct answers by comparing correct answer rates for each combination of functions and modules.

3   Experiment and Result

We applied our system to Task 4 of COLIEE 2018. In Task 4, only the problem sentences were provided without any additional information, asking Yes/No as answers.

3.1   Result of COLIEE 2018

Table 3. Result of COLIEE 2018 formal run

Team	Language	# Correct answers (total 69 answers)	Accuracy
YA	?	44	0.6388
KIS_Frame	J	39	0.5652
KIS_mo3	J	38	0.5507
KIS_dict	J	37	0.5362
KIS_SVM	J	36	0.5217
KIS_Frame2	J	35	0.5072
UE	E	33	0.4783

Table 3 shows the result of the COLIEE 2018 Task 4 formal run. Among these results, team names with KIS as their prefix show our results. KIS_Frame uses the FrameNet module only. KIS_mo3 uses the precise match module, the loose match module and the rough match module. We selected options of these modules to be the highest correct answer rate on the training set. KIS_dict uses the same module as KIS_mo3 while adding our synonym dictionary. KIS_SVM uses SVM for module integration; other results integrate modules in the filter based way. KIS_Frame2 uses the FrameNet module, the precise match module, the loose match module, and the rough match module. KIS_Frame was the best result among our submissions for the COLIEE 2018 formal run.

There is little difference between the results of KIS_dict and KIS_mo3, namely if synonym dictionary was used or not. Because many problems cannot be answered if the system do not handle synonyms, the effect of our synonym dictionary would have reduced due to other issues. As related articles are not given in Task 4, a huge number of combinations are compared by precise match and loose match. Our system does not have any feature to rank relevant articles. If there are many related articles, even if the correct judgment can be made by a synonym dictionary in the correct article, the result could be buried. Refining our searching meth-od for the related articles is the future work. The good result of KIS_Frame was probably because the system was able to effectively compare the predicates by the frame information.

3.2   Result of Past Years

Table 4. Result of COLIEE training data (past years's legal bar exam)

	2006	2007	2008	2009	2010	2011	2012	2013	2014	2015	2016	Total
KIS_SVM	0.54	0.57	0.60	0.66	0.51	0.65	0.53	0.62	0.60	0.52	0.53	0.57
KIS_mo3	0.57	0.57	0.60	0.60	0.48	0.63	0.51	0.63	0.57	0.52	0.55	0.56
KIS_dict	0.57	0.57	0.52	0.62	0.53	0.61	0.47	0.57	0.57	0.50	0.55	0.55
KIS_Frame	0.48	0.50	0.52	0.60	0.42	0.48	0.55	0.60	0.54	0.48	0.60	0.53
KIS_Frame2	0.51	0.59	0.62	0.58	0.46	0.53	0.44	0.44	0.53	0.50	0.42	0.51

Table 4 shows results of COLIEE training data of past years' legal bar exam. KIS_SVM, which uses SVM to mix different modules, performed best in total. However, KIS_SVM is ranked fourth in the formal run, lower than our other runs shown in the table. Its reason might be fluctuations between different year's problems. Especially, the problems of this year's formal run include many concrete stories. Moreover, this year's formal run includes problems consist of more than two sentences which were not appeared in the past problems. Because the tendency could have been different for these reasons, training model of SVM might not have fit well with the formal run data.

3.3   Comparison of Tasks to Solve the Problem

In order to understand legal documents, we need skills to understand general documents, such as paraphrase expression and the knowledge of technical terms. We manually categorized the problems by required task types to solve the problems, by defining 18 task types. Table 5 shows the list of the task types. Multiple skills may be necessary to solve even a single problem. When many task types are required to solve the problem, such a problem could be regarded as difficult.

Figure 4 shows an example of required tasks. "六箇月経過するまでの間は (until six months elapse)" shows a condition of time, so it is necessary to extract a conditional sentence. Then anaphoric analysis is required because it is necessary to know that the following two entities, the administrator of the inherited property and manager, refer to the same person. "又は (or)" and analysis of dependency is also necessary because we need parallel relations, which is sometimes more difficult to understand. In Japanese, there is a part where it is more difficult to understand parallel relations than English. All of these tasks are required to solve this problem.

We examined correct answer rates of problems for each required task. Table 6 shows the statistics of 2018 problems for each module.

Tasks such as conditional sentence extraction, person role extraction, and person relationship extraction are important to improve the overall correct answer rate, because these types are observed more frequently.

Table 5. List of the tasks to solve the problem

Task	Detail
Conditional sentence extraction	Extract each conditional sentences of problem sentences and related articles
Person role extraction	Extract which role (underage, buyer, obligor etc.) the person appearing in the problem sentences is
Person relationship extraction	Extract the positions and roles among multiple people
Morphological analysis	Include a specific case particle in order to make the sentence easier to analyze
Anaphoric analysis	Clarify what is pointing to when omitting part of the sentence
Ambiguity resolution	Analyze sentences with ambiguous expressions
Semantic role extraction	Extract whether the noun used in the problem sentence is the action principal or the object of the action or method
Verb paraphrasing	Analyze the sentences that the verb has been paraphrased
General dictionary	Analyze things used in general life that are not legal terms
Predicate argument structure	Clarify the behavior of the problem sentences
Negative interpretation	Negative form comes in and makes a true/false judgment
Legal term dictionary	Analyze the sentences that the legal term has been paraphrased. (e.g. limited ability person $\rightarrow$ minor)
Implication relation	Analyze hidden intent from sentences. (e.g. if the person request in a trial, that person is a plaintiff.)
Dependency	Focus on relation between subject and predicate or parallel relation of sentences
Refer to article	Another article is specified in the article
Paraphrase	Analyze the sentences whose the term that other than verbs has been paraphrased
Bullet	Analyze the article whose bullets are used
Digitization of priorities	Analyze the article whose priority order of effectiveness is shown in bullet points

We compared the correct answer rates for each module, by different threshold of task selections. KIS_mo3 is the best for the top 5 problems, that required important tasks observed more than 20 times. KIS_Frame2 was the best in the top 8 problems that required important tasks observed more than 10 times.

KIF_Frame, which achieved the highest correct answer rate, has a higher rate of correct answers in not frequently observed problems, probably because non-frequent problem types tend to be more difficult than others.

We implemented our system based on conditional clause and propositional clause for conditional sentence extraction. However, our analysis showed that the correct answer rate of conditional sentence extraction is lower, which is most important to improve the overall system performance in future. Especially, our method would be insufficient when comparing conditional clauses.

H29-6-U

相続財産に関しては，相続財産<u>管理人</u>が選任された場合でも，　<u>相続人が確定</u>
<u>するまでの間は</u>，時効は完成しない。

(With respect to any inherited property, even if <u>the administrator of the inherited property</u> is
appointed, the prescription shall not be completed <u>until the applicable heir is identified</u>.)

第百六十条　相続財産に関しては、相続人が確定した時、<u>管理人</u>が選任された
時又は破産手続開始の決定があった時から<u>六箇月を経過するまでの間は</u>、時効
は、完成しない。

(Article 160 :With respect to any inherited property, the prescription shall not be completed <u>until six</u>
<u>months elapse</u> from the time when the applicable heir is identified, <u>the administrator</u> is appointed, <u>or</u>
the ruling of the commencement of bankruptcy procedures is made.)

Fig. 4. An example of required tasks

Table 6. Result of the problem for each required tasks

Task	num	KIS_mo3	KIS_dict	KIS_SVM	KIS_Frame2	KIS_Frame
Conditional sentence extraction	31	0.42	0.39	0.52	0.35	0.52
Person role extraction	27	0.52	0.52	0.52	0.67	0.48
Person relationship extraction	26	0.5	0.5	0.5	0.69	0.38
Morphological analysis	25	0.8	0.76	0.4	0.64	0.64
Anaphoric analysis	20	0.6	0.55	0.4	0.4	0.65
Ambiguity resolution	17	0.47	0.47	0.47	0.59	0.53
Semantic role extraction	15	0.6	0.6	0.4	0.73	0.4
Verb paraphrasing	13	0.54	0.54	0.54	0.54	0.31
General dictionary	9	0.44	0.44	0.56	0.67	0.44
Predicate argument structure	9	0.56	0.56	0.56	0.44	0.56
Negative interpretation	7	0.71	0.71	0.29	0.14	1
Legal term dictionary	7	0.29	0.29	0.43	0.57	0.43
Implication relation	5	0.2	0.2	0.8	0.4	0.4
Dependency	5	0.4	0.4	0.6	0	0.8
Refer to article	5	0.6	0.6	0.2	0.2	0.8
Paraphrase	5	0.6	0.6	0.4	0.6	0.6
Bullet	3	0.33	0.33	0.33	0.33	0.67
Digitization of priorities	3	0.33	0.33	0.67	0.33	0.67

For example, even if there is a conditional clause in a problem sentence, its related
article may not have a corresponding conditional clause. In this case, the answer
sometimes becomes "No" due to the absence of the conditional clause in the related
article, or it may sometimes make sense by connecting with other conditional clauses.

Such cases cannot be solved by our current system. Our current logical judgement is performed only when conditional clauses match, but it would not be sufficient to express the relation of conditional clause.

3.4   Comparison of Results for Difficulty Levels

Table 7. Results for each difficulty level

	Target	Accuracy
Very easy	40	0.75
Easy	62	0.387
Difficult	44	0.522
Very difficult	21	0.380

We manually categorized problems into four difficulty levels. We wanted to be able to concentrate on solving problems that people thought as easy as possible. We divided the difficulty of the problem with the necessary tasks. For example, "very easy" problem is the case of only simple tasks such as morpheme analysis. "Easy" problem is a problem that requires extracting conditions and verb paraphrasing. "Difficult" problem is a problem that requires complex condition sentence extraction and ambiguity resolution. "Very difficult" problem is a case where a complex task is required or even if reading related texts cannot be solved without knowledge of law.

Table 7 shows analysis results of the problems in 2014 and 2016. "Very easy" problems were correctly answered by more than 70%, while "easy" problems and "difficult" problems were less than 40%. "Very easy" problems were solved well because our precise match can easily find superficially similar expressions in such problems. It was not expected that "difficult" problems were solved better than "easy" problems. Even in problems that humans feel easy, synonym and zero pronouns resolutions are required, which are very difficult issues for computers to be solved. Especially, condition sentence extraction is easy for humans to understand, but not for computers including our system. Regarding "difficult" problems, a very complicated structure could be transformed into a simple structure by predicate argument structure analysis, which is easier to solve than the "easy" problems. "Easy" and "very difficult" were far less than the random baseline (50%).

4   Conclusion and Future Work

We developed an automatic answering system for legal bar exam, which can show logical structures how the system solved a given legal problem, We focused on answering simpler problems in this paper. We confirmed that our system could correctly answer more than 70% of the simpler problems.

In order to represent structures of legal documents, we implemented a textual entailment solver, which has predicate argument structure analysis as its core part. We made a variation of different modules using different comparison methods. We used

SVM to make ensemble of these modules, using confidence values calculated from the number of related articles.

In addition, we made a legal synonym dictionary. Our synonym dictionary is structured in that as synonym of a predicate could be conditioned with its object. Unfortunately, we could not achieve a significant difference because there are too many related articles when searching relevant articles. We applied our system to the COLIEE 2018 Task 4 dataset. One of our submission achieved the second rank among participants.

The information retrieval part, which corresponds to Task 3, could be improved to increase the entire system performance in future.

Acknowledgements. This work was partially supported by MEXT Kakenhi and JST CREST.

References

1. Competition on Legal Information Extraction/Entailment (COLIEE-14). Workshop on Juris-informatics (JURISIN) 2014 (2014). http://webdocs.cs.ualberta.ca/ ~ miyoung2/jurisin_task/index.html
2. Kim, M.-Y., Goebel, R., Ken, S.: COLIEE-2015: evaluation of legal question answering. In: Ninth International Workshop on Juris-informatics (JURISIN 2015) (2015)
3. Kim, M., Goebel, R., Kano, Y., Satoh, K.: COLIEE-2016 : evaluation of the competition on legal information extraction and entailment 2. In: The Legal Question Answering Task (2016)
4. Kano, Y., Kim, M., Goebel, R., Satoh, K.: Overview of COLIEE 2017. In: ICAIL, vol. 47, pp. 1–8 (2017)
5. Lin, D., Pantel, P.: Discovery of inference rules for question answering. Nat. Lang. Eng. 7(4), 343–360 (2001)
6. Pinto, D., McCallum, A., Wei, X., Croft, W.B.: Table extraction using conditional random fields. In: Proceedings of 26th Annual International ACM SIGIR Conference on Research and Development Information Retrieval - SIGIR 2003, p. 235 (2003)
7. Ravichandran, D., Hovy, E.: Learning surface text patterns for a question answering system. In: Proceedings of the 40th Annual Meeting on Association for Computational Linguistics - ACL 2002, p. 41, July 2001
8. Yu, H., Hatzivassiloglou, V..: Towards answering opinion questions: separating facts from opinions and identifying the polarity of opinion sentences. In: Proceedings of the 2003 Conference on Empirical Methods in Natural Language Processing, pp. 129–136 (2003)
9. Ferrucci, D.A.: Introduction to 'This is Watson'. IBM J. Res. Dev. 56(3.4), 1:1–1:15 (2012)
10. Ferrucci, D., et al.: Building watson: an overview of the DeepQA project. AI Mag. 31(3), 59–79 (2010). https://doi.org/10.1609/aimag.v31i3.2303
11. Polsley, S., Jhunjhunwala, P., Huang, R.: CaseSummarizer: a system for automated summarization of legal texts. In: Proceedings of COLING 2016, 26th International Conference on Computational Linguistics System Demonstrations, pp. 258–262 (2016)
12. Welcome to FrameNet!. https://framenet.icsi.berkeley.edu/fndrupal/
13. Japanese FrameNet. http://jfn.st.hc.keio.ac.jp
14. Japanese WordNet. http://compling.hss.ntu.edu.sg/wnja/index.en.html

LENLS 15

Logic and Engineering of Natural Language Semantics (LENLS 15)

Osamu Sawada

Department of Humanities, Mie University, 1577 Kurimamachiya-cho, Tsu city,
Mie 514-8507, Japan
sawada.osamu@gmail.com

1 The Workshop

The international workshop Logic and Engineering of Natural Language Semantics (LENLS) started in 2005. Its purpose is to provide a venue for researchers working on natural language semantics and pragmatics, (formal) philosophy, logic, artificial intelligence, and computational linguistics together for discussion and interdisciplinary communication. Over the lifespan of the workshop, whose 15th iteration was held at JSAI-isAI 2018 during November 12–14, 2018, many researchers have presented their work and the workshop has become recognized internationally in the semantics-pragmatics community. LENLS 15 had 2 one-hour invited lectures and 22 thirty-minute submitted talks selected by the Program Committee. The number of participants was about 50. The invited speakers were Pauline Jacobson (Brown University, USA) and Daniel Gutzmann (University of Cologne, Germany). Professor Jacobson talked about ellipsis construction and grammatical competition principles, focusing on the case of the so-called MaxElide. Professor Gutzmann talked about an analysis of the syntactic constraints in the semantic interpretation of expressive adjectives. Topics discussed by the submitted papers raised issues from syntax and semantics of natural language, the syntax-semantics-pragmatics interface, modals and expressives in Japanese and German, event semantics, type theory, computational semantics, various logics for natural language semantics, among many others. The papers in the present volume represent a selection of the papers presented at the workshop. As the reader can see from this volume, a wide range of topics is characteristic of LENLS. All in all, the workshop was very successful and productive for both organizers and participants. We hope to keep this tradition in future to promote international researches in the semantics-pragmatics community.

2 Acknowledgements

Let me acknowledge some of those who helped with the workshop. The Program Committee and organizers, in addition to myself, were Daisuke Bekki, Elin McCready, Koji Mineshima, Alastair Butler, Richard Dietz, Naoya Fujikawa, Yurie Hara, Magdalena Kaufmann, Yoshiki Mori, David Y. Oshima, Katsuhiko Sano, Wataru

Uegaki, Katsuhiko Yabushita, Tomoyuki Yamada, Shunsuke Yatabe, and Kei Yoshimoto. I would also like to acknowledge the external reviewers for the workshop. Finally, the organizers would like to thank the JST CREST Programs "Advanced Core Technologies for Big Data Integration" for financial support and JSAI International Symposia on AI 2018 for giving us the opportunity to hold the workshop.

Against Grammatical Competition: The Case of MaxElide

Pauline Jacobson[✉]

Brown University, Providence, RI, USA
`pauline_jacobson@brown.edu`

Abstract. There have been proposed various principles of grammar which rely on competition, whereby one derivation is blocked on the basis of a competing one. This paper begins with the premise that all competition effects should be located in speaker/hearer principles, not formal grammatical principles as the latter greatly complicates the grammar. We focus on one case study: MaxElide. We show that given a variable free semantics (Jacobson 1999) the effects of this principle fall out from type rather than size competition: speakers will frame things with 'missing material' to use simpler types over more complex ones, on the assumption that the simpler types are easier for listeners to supply.

Keywords: Ellipsis · MaxElide · Variable free semantics · Competition effects · Type competition · Sluicing

1 Competition Effects

It seems likely that there are situations in which speakers and/or listeners compute competing alternatives of, for example, possible forms for expressing (roughly) the same meanings. For example, the standard (Gricean) story of scalar implicatures relies on the assumption that a listener computes an alternative (more informative) way that the speaker could have conveyed the relevant information, and assumes that the speaker was therefore not in a position to do so. (Of course not all researchers agree on this basic story; those advocating grammatical computation of implicature would not be committed to listeners' computing alternatives. Nonetheless, we will assume that there are cases of competition effects located in speakers' and hearers' abilities to compute competing ways to convey a message.)

But beginning with a number of works in the 1970s in Generative Semantics, and more recent work within Minimalism (Chomsky 1995), it is commonly assumed that the grammar itself computes competing derivations, and has principles ruling out some of these on the basis of others. Often the 'winner' is based on a notion of Economy: a derivation will be ruled out if there is a competing one which is shorter (we leave open here what constitutes the definition of the comparison class). Or, one with shorter movement paths will be preferred over one with longer movements, etc. The point of departure for the present paper is skepticism that there are *grammatically based* competition effects. Following the logic laid out in Johnson and Lappin (1997) and Jacobson (1998) (among others) I argue against grammatical competition principles. As detailed in those works, the hypothesis that the *grammar* contains principles to choose

K. Kojima et al. (Eds.): JSAI-isAI 2018 Workshops, LNAI 11717, pp. 225–239, 2019.
https://doi.org/10.1007/978-3-030-31605-1_17

one derivation over another significantly complicates how the grammar works: it not only has to compute the well-formedness and meaning of an expression via a given derivation, but it also would have to compute a set of competing derivations. Even more problematic (at least for the claim that "Economy" is the driving principle as to which wins out) is the fact that it is then entirely stipulative that the 'simplest' is what is chosen. There is no reason why that should be. Given that a set of competing derivations is computed, why should the one with the least steps (mystically) win out? Why not the most complex (most steps)? Or the second fewest steps? Since all are computed, there is nothing 'simpler' about choosing the shortest. And, even more strikingly for the case at hand, it is not even clear that there is any notion of "Economy" relevant here (although see Kimura 2013 who does give an economy-based reformulation; space precludes discussion here). The usual formulation of the requisite competition principle is completely stipulative (see also Kimura 2013 and Griffiths to appear for discussion). I therefore argue that competition is indeed at work in the case at hand but that - using the tools of variable free semantics (Jacobson 1999) - the effect can naturally be recast as a speaker/hearer based effect. In the final section 1 present empirical evidence in favor of the reformulation here.

2   MaxElide

Consider the following:

(1) a. Sally knows that Carl will endorse one of those candidates, but she doesn't know which (one).
     b.?*Sally knows that Carl will endorse one of those candidates, but she doesn't know which one he will.

(b) is highly dispreferred. Moreover, evidence that the effect is due to a competition with (a), comes from similar cases where there is no competing ellipsis are fine (additional evidence will emerge below):

(2) Sally knows which candidate Carl will endorse, but she doesn't know which one CATHY will.

In view of this and similar cases, Merchant (2001) posited a principle to the effect that when there are two competing ellipsis sites, there is a prohibition against smaller ellipsis; this has since been known as MaxElide. It is, moreover, usually taken to be a *grammatical* principle, although one might be tempted to relocate it as a speaker-based principle ("Be as lazy as possible"). The problem with that is that that would incorrectly predict that ellipsis is always obligatory when allowed (thus ruling out (3b) below. Indeed there may well be a mild preference for (3a) over (b) but the contrast is certainly not sharp like the contrasts in (1):

(3) a. Lindsay can ski that course, and Bode can too.
     b. Lindsay can ski that course, and Bode can ski that course too.

Similarly, (4) involves two competing ellipsis options. Here too there might be a mild preference for (a) over (b), but gain the contrast is not particularly sharp:

(4)   a. Bode thinks that Lindsay would win gold, and Sally also does.
      b. Bode thinks that Lindsay will win gold, and Sally also thinks she will.

To state the relevant generalization in terms often found in the literature (see especially Merchant 2008 and Takahashi and Fox 2005; hereafter T&F), I make the following assumptions (to be revised later). (1) There is silent linguistic material in the position of the 'ellipsis site'; the material is allowed to be silent under some sort of identity with some other overt expression in the discourse context. I leave open exactly what is the requisite identity for Sluicing, for convenience assume that the requisite identity for VP Ellipsis is semantic. (Most works assume also conditions on the focus structure, to simplify, I ignore this for now.) (2) Wh-movement leaves a trace which corresponds to a variable. Given this, we can follow Merchant (2008) and T&F 2005 and (roughly) state the descriptive generalization as follows: The MaxElide competition holds only when there is an unbound trace or pronoun in the ellipsis site of the smaller competitor. (The pronoun case will be motivated below).

Thus for the competition shown in (1), the representation of the ellipsis in the Sluicing case is as in (5a) (with the strikethroughs indicating the silent material, while the smaller ellipsis VPE case is as in (5b):

(5)   a. but she doesn't know which one$_i$ ~~Carl will endorse t$_i$~~
      b. but she doesn't know which one$_i$ Carl will ~~endorse t$_i$~~

But why should this be? T&F give an interesting account based on defining a "Parallelism Domain" (PD) for the licensing of ellipsis. At the risk of suppressing some of the motivation for their account as it relates to previous observations of Rooth (1992) about focus, I will just informally summarize this.

But doing so, a bit of history will help elucidate the general picture. Sag et al. (1976) first noticed the oddness of (6b) with 'little ellipsis' in comparison with (6a) with 'big ellipsis' (these are of course fine on a strict reading; the point is that (6b) does not (easily) permit a sloppy reading (readings are indicated again by the strikethrough material):

(6)   Scenario: The American presidential primary season in 2016. Each candidate in their party (Republican or Democrat) competes state by state in a primary to win the votes of the delegates from that state. Cruz and Rubio were both candidates, both hoping to win the primary in Florida.
      Speaker A: Cruz$_i$ thinks that Florida will vote for him$_i$.
      Speaker B: a. Yeah, well Rubio$_j$ also does ~~think that Florida will vote for him$_i$~~.
                   b. Yeah, well Rubio$_j$ also thinks that Florida will ~~vote for him$_j$~~.

(Actually the effect can be mitigated for some speakers especially in the right context; see Grant 2008.) This is exactly what one might expect if this is not a grammatically driven phenomenon. We will not explore here the conditions under which these can be improved.)

Sag's account of (b) here was not based on competition. We will not discuss his actual account here, but a reasonable and simple variant emerges if one also adopts one other piece of machinery from Heim (1997):

(7) <u>No meaningless coindexation</u>. Two variables (pronouns, traces) bound by different binders cannot have the same index.

Recall that we are temporarily assuming that VP Ellipsis requires semantic identity between the silenced material and some other overt VP in the discourse context. Following Sag and many others, we will also assume that the 'binding' of a pronoun within a VP happens by something akin to the Derived VP rule. Details aside, this means that in a simple case like *Every 3d grade boy called his mother* the VP has the meaning $\lambda x[x$ *called x's mother]* (i.e., it denotes the set of self's-mother-callers) and this property is argument of the subject. Given this, the composition of the first and second clauses in (6a) are as in (8); the underlined portions here represent the meanings of the elided and antecedent VPs:

(8) λx_1<u>$[x_1$ thinks Florida would vote for $x_1]$</u> (Cruz)
       λx_2<u>$[x_2$ thinks Florida would vote for $x_2]$</u> (Rubio)

The indices differ but this does not matter; the two VPs have the same meaning because the 'binding' happens at the VP and so they denote the same property. But consider the meanings of the antecedent and elided VPs in the little ellipsis case; again the relevant VPs are underlined:

(9)   (b) $\lambda x_1[x_1$ thinks Florida would <u>vote for $x_1]$</u> (Cruz)
              $\lambda x_2[x_2$ thinks Florida would <u>vote for $x_2]$</u> (Rubio)

These two VPs contain unbound variables with different indices; they thus denote different semantics objects; note that under any assignment g, $[[\text{vote for}'\, x_1]]^g$ is not necessarily the same set as $[[\text{vote for}\, x_2]]^g$. Note too that this account relies crucially on the No Meaningless Coindexation condition; were it possible to 'accidentally' use the same index in both VPs (even though they are bound from above by different things) then there would be one available analysis of (6b) where the two little VPs have the same meaning, and hence no explanation for why it is not (very) good.

But, not so fast! We cannot just stop with this explanation for the contrast, because it is quite possible to construct good cases of just this type, as was done (for a slightly different case) in Evans (1988), Jacobson (1992) and others. (Such cases were subsequently also noticed in Merchant (2001) and have gone under the rubric of 're-binding'; we show below that under the variable-free construal of these they do not deserve any special name for their existence is entirely unsurprising.) An example where little ellipsis is fine is (10) from Jacobson (1992):

(10)   Sue$_i$ asked John to water her$_i$ plants, and MARY$_j$ asked Bill to ~~water her plants~~.

The indices on the pronouns unbound within the lower VPs differ; No Meaningless Coindexation would ensure that they cannot be the same, and so the meanings must be different. The above explanation for the oddness of (6b) (and Sag's similar explanation) thus cannot be quite right.

What T&F point out is that the difference here is that (6b) competes with the larger ellipsis in (6a); that competition is absent in (10). For here there cannot be any higher ellipsis - any higher VP has no antecedent with the same meaning. This is exactly like the case of (1b) (bad) vs. (2) (good) - (1b) competes with a higher possible ellipsis and (2) does not. They thus propose that Sag's original observations reduce to MaxElide, provided that the latter is formulated in such a way as to be relevant only in cases where the little ellipsis contains an unbound pronoun or trace within it.

But why should this be? Here I cannot give full justice to the set of assumptions motivating T&F, but I will elucidate their account informally. A key property of their account is that - just as with the Sag-like account given above for (6b) - it crucially relies on No Meaningless Coindexation. With that in mind, they define the notion of a Parallelism Domain (PD) as follows:

(11) The Parallelism Domain (PD) for some ellipsis site E is the lowest node for which there is (a) some expression in the discourse context with the same meaning as E, or (b) if there is no such expression, it is the lowest node C containing within it a focused constituent which is such that the antecedent is contained with something that is within the focus value of C. (Informally: E is licensed within a domain C if there is focus somewhere in C, and there is an expression C' which is an alternative to C. This is related to the observations about ellipsis in Rooth 1992.)

Notice that in (6a) the PD for the ellipsis is itself, since its meaning is identical to the VP in the first clause. In (10) the PD is not the elided VP itself, as there is no potential antecedent with the same meaning (remember that No Meaningless Coindexation is assumed). The PD thus is the full *Mary-* clause. The badness of (6b) now follows from the following version of MaxElide:

(12) If A is an elidable constituent within some BD and B is an elidable constituent whose PD is the same as that of A, then if B contains A, ellipsis of A is bad. (Put differently: within some PD, ellipsis must target the largest elidable constituent within that same PD.)

The PD for the little ellipsis in (6b) is not itself (again because there is no VP with the same meaning, so the PD is the entire Rubio clause. Little ellipsis now fails because of MaxElide. T&F also take this as an argument against variable free semantics (to be developed below); we will return to that point.

There is an additional interesting prediction made by this account: if an ellipsis site contains within it an unbound pronoun and a larger ellipsis is available, the ellipsis will nonetheless be good *if the pronoun within the ellipsis site is co-bound with a pronoun in the antecedent.* Thus (13a) and (13b) are both possible:

(13) Every candidate$_i$ thinks that the CNN poll predicted that Iowa would vote for him$_i$ and
       (a) that the Quinnipiac poll also did ~~predict that it would vote for him~~$_i$.
       (b) that the Qunnnipiac poll also predicted that it would ~~vote for him~~$_i$.

Actually, the (b) case is a bit strange, but no worse than similar cases where there is no issue of bound pronouns:

(14) Every newscaster thinks that the CNN poll predicted that Iowa would vote for Kristen and that the Quinnipiac poll will also predict that it would.

The non deviance (or at least only mild deviance) of (13b) follows; since the unbound pronoun in the little ellipsis has the same index as the unbound pronoun in the antecedent. Therefore their meanings are the same, and the PD for ellipsis is the ellipsis site itself. There is, then, no competition with the higher ellipsis; MaxElide is irrelevant.

While T&F's definition of PDs may (or may not) be well motivated by other assumptions they make about focus and ellipsis, the fact remains that there is no obvious motivation for anything like MaxElide as a grammatical principle in the first place. Even if one is fond of Economy driven principles, there is no clear sense in which this reduces to Economy. Similar remarks are made in Kimura (2013) - who does try to account for the facts via economy considerations, and Griffiths to appear who provides a different reanalysis from the one I will give below. Unfortunately, space precludes a comparison of my account with either of these (especially since these rely on a very different set of assumptions.)

3   Recasting with a Different Set of Assumptions: Background

3.1   Ellipsis

I will frame my analysis under a view whereby there is no silent linguistic material in the position of 'ellipsis sites'. For the case of VPE, I assume that there is simply a 'missing' meaning of type <e,t> . Take the case of the dialogue in (15):

(15) Speaker A: Bode can ski that course in 5 minutes.
     Speaker B: Lindsay can too.

In the framework of variable free semantics (to be elucidated below) this means that B's utterance has the meaning represented informally as $\lambda P[bode\ can\ P]$; this is thus a function of type <<e,t >,t> and the listener supplies this to a contextually salient property (<e,t > function). (I extensionalize throughout.) Surely having been recently named is one way to for something to be salient; hence the illusion of an antecedent. There is no actual grammatical connection between the VP in A's utterance and the 'missing' meaning in B's, the connection is supplied by the listener. This is much like other cases of 'free variables'; in variable-free semantics, these are always actual argument slots. But the difference is not essential here, and the reader can think of VPE as involving a 'free variable' of the relevant type (as in, e.g., Hardt 1993) if s/he wishes. Of course, the claim that the 'missing' meaning in B's utterance is picked up from the context (where it could happen to be salient in virtue of having been named) is exactly what is argued against in Hankamer and Sag (1976): they point to examples where it is not enough to infer the meaning from the discourse context. Be that as it may, it has since been shown in numerous places that the meaning can be picked up without having been named. For recent literature with a number of attested examples see Miller and Pullum (2014). It is, however, clearly the case that it is harder to pick up an <e, t> meaning that has not been made salient by explicit naming than, say, to pick up some individual. In Jacobson (2003) (and subsequent places) I suggested that this is not an observation to be answered by the linguistic system *per se,* but rather a fact about processing. Perhaps such objects are 'fragile' - more difficult to just access and, when named, also decay more quickly than individuals. I leave open as to exactly why this is so, but some conjecture along these lines will play a role below.

There are also cases where the missing material is a 2-place relation. The analysis of Antecedent Contained Deletion (ACD) in Jacobson (1992) involved exactly this:

(16) Sarah will read every newspaper that Katie will.

Consider a similar case without ellipsis in a Categorial Grammar type analyses:

(17) Sarah will read every newspaper that Katie will read.

There is no need to posit extraction (or traces); [[read]] function composes with [[will]] (assuming that the latter takes the VP as complement) and that material in turn composes with (type lifted) [[Katie]] (i.e., with $\lambda P[P(k)]$ which gives the set of things that Katie will read. Then (16) can be similar as first noted in Cormack (1984). There is a 'missing' 2-place relation which would be picked up to function compose with *will* and the rest proceeds as above. This may sound mysterious: what does it mean to say that a meaning which is picked up from the discourse context is function composed with something else? The details are fully spelled out in Jacobson (2003) and other places. Technically we do not use function composition but rather its unary version - the "Geach" rule whereby *will* in (16) is a shifted version of lexical *will* (call it *will$_2$)* and has as its meaning $\lambda R[\lambda x[\text{will}'(R(x))]]$. The semantic composition of the whole thing, then, can be very roughly represented as in (18):

(18) $\lambda R[s \text{ will read every } [\text{newspaper} \cap \lambda x[k \text{ will } R(x)]]$

and the listener picks up the read-relation (having just been named) as the argument of this function. For full details see Jacobson (2003); Jacobson in press shows that given the more general apparatus assumed in the variable free program the availability of ACD follows immediately from the apparatus for the ordinary case of "VP Ellipsis", just as it does under the more standard account.

There are two further points worth noting about what I will henceforth call "TVP Ellipsis" (TVP standing for 'transitive verb phrase); but again one can think of this as just picking up a meaning of type <e,<e,t>>). First, Evans (1988) noticed already that this occurs (under a Categorial Grammar analysis of topicalization) in cases like (19). Rather than assuming that the second S involves a 'missing' VP-type meaning with a trace/variable within it, this is just another case where what is picked up is an <e,< e, t >> meaning (in this case, most likely [[like]]):

(19) Bagels, I like. Donuts, I don't.

Second, Jacobson (1992) showed that we get the same kind of thing in the sentences already discussed above in (10) - this too is nothing more than supplying a missing meaning of type <e,<e,t>>. This will be elucidated after we turn to variable free semantics in the next section; other cases of so-called 'rebinding' will also turn out to be nothing more than 'TVP' ellipsis.

Before leaving this, however, we do need to say something also about Sluicing, as in e.g. (1a). I will not present any kind of full analysis here, but assume that in a full wh-case (as in *she doesn't know Carl will endorse*) the post wh-constituent (*Carl will endorse*) is of type <e,t>, and is the argument of the wh-constituent *which one*. In the case of Sluicing, assume once again that there is no actual silent linguistic material, but rather a meaning of this type is picked up (in this case λx[Carl will endorse x] and supplied as argument of *which one*. There is much more to say, but space precludes a detailed discussion; see Ginzburg and Sag (2000) for a version of this.

3.2   Variable Free Semantics and 'Binding'

Since the apparatus of variable free semantics (see Jacobson 1999) plays a crucial role in my reformulation of MaxElide, a quick tutorial is in order. First, there are no variables in the semantics (and hence no assignment functions) and no indices in the syntax. The meaning of any expression which contains an unbound pronoun (or, extraction site) within it is a function from individuals to whatever type it would have if no unbound pronoun were there. So the meaning of *he lost* is λx[lost'(x)] (ignoring the contribution of the gender of the pronoun) and the meaning of *his mother* is λx[the-mother-of'(x)] (we will refer to this as 'the-mother-of' function). Note of course that I am using variables here as a tool for <u>representing</u> the meanings of expressions but they are just that and play no actual role in the theory. (One could entirely do without them by using the representations made available by Combinatory Logic.) Thus whenever in the standard theory there is an unbound variable in the meaning of some expression, here that expression just denotes a function from something. (If, in the standard view, the meaning is of type X and contains an unbound variable of some type Y, then here the meaning is a function of type <Y,X>.) Pronouns themselves are also functions from individuals; in particular they denote the identity function on individuals. (Again I ignore here the gender of the pronoun.)

Consider the composition of *his mother lost* (of type <e,t>). [[lost]] is of type <e,t>, yet the subject is of type <e,e> and is the-mother-function. In order to account for the fact that *lost* can combine with such a subject, we posit a rule (the Geach rule) allowing any expression whose meaning is a function f of type <a,b> to map into a homophonous one (call that $g(f)$) of type <<c,a>,<c,b>> such that $g(f) = \lambda X_{<c,a>}[\lambda C_c[f(X(C)]]$. Thus [[lost]] in the lexicon is of type <e,t>, but shifts by g (the "Geach rule") to be a function of type <<e,e>,<e.,t>>. The result is that *his mother lost* has the meaning λx[lost'(the-mother-of'(x)]. While this is an extra piece of machinery, it is a very simple one; the "Geach rule" is nothing more than the unary (Curry'ed) version of function composition, needed independently in the program here. While the cost might be this extra rule, the payoff is (among many other things) an elimination of the need for assignment functions and indices.

Finally, consider how 'binding' occurs in, e.g., *Every 3d grade boy$_i$ called his$_i$ mother.* (The indices here are not part of the grammar; they are being used only to indicate the relevant reading.) The 'binding' of the pronoun happens via a rule which I call **z** which maps the lexical meaning of *call* (a meaning of type <e,<e,t>>) to **z**(love') which is of type $<<e,e>,<e,t>>$ such that to $\mathbf{z}(call) = \lambda f_{<e,e>}[\lambda x[x$ call $f(x)]$. In other words, to $\mathbf{z}(call)$ some function f (of type $<e,e>$) is to be an x who calls $f(x)$. When this is applied to the meaning of *his mother* (which is the-mother-of-function) the result is the set of self-mother caller; i.e., $\lambda x[x$ called the-mother-of(x)]. This is the same as the meaning of a VP with a 'bound pronoun' under various other theories (such as ones making use of the Derived VP rule), but is accomplished without variables or indices. The VP meaning is taken as argument of the generalized quantifier [[every 3d grade boy]]. Notice, then, that when a pronoun is (loosely speaking) 'bound' within the meaning of the VP that VP has a meaning of type $<e,t>$. In (6a) for example the meaning of the VP in the first clause (which is picked up as the missing meaning) is λx [x thinks that Florida will vote for x].

Before turning to (6b), consider the case of (10). Here the meaning of *water her plants* which is supplied by the first conjunct is of type $<e,<e,t>>$ (just as in the case of ACD); this is because *her* is unbound within this VP so this is just $\lambda x[water$ x's plants]. (The full semantic composition of the second clause involves $\mathbf{z}$ on *ask* (similarly in the first clause) which allows for an $<e,<e,t>>$ type meaning to be picked up here.) There is no need for any notion of 'rebinding' - there is nothing special about these cases. They are simply instances of missing meanings of type $<e,<e,t>>$ rather than type $<e, t>$ (again see Jacobson (2003) and in press for full details showing that the existence of such cases follows automatically from the general program). Moreover, Jacobson (1992) pointed out that we get this kind of $<e,<e,t>>$ 'ellipsis' across clauses:

(20)   Sally spoke to every third grade boy. But only Jimmy wanted her to.

Cases of this type were subsequently noticed also in Merchant (2001) and are among those dubbed 'rebinding'. The overt paraphrase here would contain a pronoun (*wanted her to speak to him*) which would be bound by Jimmy. In a theory of ellipsis maintaining some sort of identity (and No Meaningless Coindexation) there is no antecedent with exact semantic identity, but if *every third grade boy* undergoes QR in the first clause then there is an antecedent VP identical modulo the different indices (the trace of QR will be indexed differently from the index on the silenced pronoun). This, however, is the kind of case which meets the definition of, e.g., T&Fs parallelism domain; ellipsis is thus allowed. Under the view here, though, there is no silent material, no indices, and no notion of 'rebinding'; the missing meaning is just [[spoke to]] (of type $<e,<e,t>>$) and *want* undergoes $\mathbf{z}$. (The observations in Merchant 2001 regarding constraints on where this is possible also follow from independent considerations about focus, but space precludes discussion here.) I also showed in earlier work that one can even get $<e,<e,t>>$ 'ellipsis' with no overt material to supply the missing relation. For example, I take a hot plate of cookies out of the oven, and Jimmy is about to grab one. I can say: *Uhuh, no. These you may* (pointing to a different tray); *those you can't - not until they've cooled down.*

4 Size Doesn't Matter; Types Do

4.1 The Basic Cases

But why is it much harder to construct cases of missing <e,<e,t>> meanings with no overt material to supply them than the run-of-the-mill VPE cases (with missing <e, t> meanings)? I would suggest that it is for the same reason that VPE itself is more difficult with no overt material to supply the meaning than is an understanding of, e.g., normal individual free pronouns: the more complex the type the harder it is to access. It seems reasonable to assume that just as <e,t> objects are less salient than individuals, 2-place relations are even less so. This of course remains to be worked out and hooked into a serious theory of processing and salience, but the fact that these types of cases (dubbed 'rebinding') and the cookie case above (with no antecedent) have been so rarely noticed lends credence to this.

But now, given the claim that (10) and (20) are good - with a missing <e,<e, t>> relation, why is the little ellipsis case in (6b) bad (or at least marginal)? Put differently, why the contrast between (6a) and (6b). Recall that the T&F explanation crucially relies on the competition between big and little ellipsis, and that its formulation crucially relies having different indices on the pronouns in the antecedent and ellipsis site in (6b). (They are, of course, assuming silent linguistic material.) That difference in indices forced the PD to look higher, and therefore MaxElide applied. As they correctly point out, there is no analogous solution in a variable free semantics. The 'antecedent' (the first clause) supplies a meaning of type <e,<e,t >> which is picked up in the second clause. The 2-place relation [[vote-for]] is understood in both clauses, there is no way to talk about anything analogous to a different index on the objects.

But there is also no need to. I will agree with T&F that the badness of (6b) is because it competes with (6a). But we need not invoke *size competition*. Rather there is a competition between the *types* of the missing material. In (6a) the missing material is of type <e,t>; *thinks* in the first clause undergoes **z** so what is picked up is the property $\lambda x[x$ thinks Florida will vote for x$]$. In (6b), however, it is only the 2-place relation [[vote-for]] that is picked up. Since we noted above that it seems plausible to assume that 2-place relations are more difficult to access and 'pick up' in this way (witness the scarcity of examples of this in the literature compared to VPE cases), it is plausible that speakers will choose an alternative that makes life simpler for the listener. The principle, then, is that when there are two possible forms - one of which involves a missing meaning of a more complex type than the other - the one with the simpler missing meaning will be chosen. More specifically, <e,t> 'ellipsis' will be chosen over <e,<e, t>> 'ellipsis'. Of course this raises the question of why ellipsis is *ever* preferred - wouldn't the easiest thing for the listener to be to have no ellipsis at all? This is a reasonable question (and one which would arise in any account given that there are pressures to facilitate the job of the listener in any case). I assume that there are a variety of competing factors; there is also a pressure to elide where possible (i.e., a pressure for speakers to say less or repeat less), and that these compete in ways which at present are not well understood. Nonetheless, as long as there is going to be an ellipsis, it is not surprising to think that <e,<e,t>> ellipsis will be avoided where possible. It is precisely in cases like (10) - where no simpler type ellipsis is allowed - that it becomes possible to have this. This, then, relocates the competition not as a grammatical principle, but as a speaker/hearer based principle.

Note that this extends directly to the Sluicing/VPE competition shown in (1), which was part of Merchant's original motivation for proposing a MaxElide principle. I have not given a full account of Sluicing here, but I assume that in the Sluicing case in (1a) what needs to be supplied is a function of type <e,t > which is taken as argument of the *wh* constituent. This is not all there is to Sluicing; the relevant <e,t> function is not any contextually salient function. Rahter, drawing on the observations of Ginzburg and Sag (2000) and AnderBois (2014), this <e,t> function must be derived from some relevant 'at issue' question (following Ginzburg and Sag I will refer to this as a Question Under Discussion (QUD) although it is not necessarily quite the same as other things that have gone under that rubric). See AnderBois and Jacobson (2018) for a related analysis of the complement of *namely*. We return to this point in 4.3. Nonetheless, in the Sluicing case the 'missing material' is of type <e,t>, whereas in the case in (1b), the missing material is again of type <e,<e,t>>. Moreover, as in T&F's account, the case in (13) - where the two pronouns are 'cobound' - will not show the competition effect. Here the two competing possibilities are both missing <e,<e,t>> meanings as the reader can verify. Moreover, cases which show no simple MaxElide effect such as (4b) are predicted to have no competition-based problem; (4a) and (4b) are both missing meanings of type <e,t>.

4.2   Further Cases

There are many other cases where our two accounts make the same prediction; some are cases where neither analysis actually accounts for a bad case, but where one can independently show that the badness is due not to competition but to something else. Consider, for example, (21b) (Merchant 2001 used this type of example for his original observation regarding a prohibition against the smaller of 2 available ellipses):

(21) a. Sally knows which candidate *The New York Times* will endorse, and Max also does.
      b. *Sally knows which candidate *The New York Times* will endorse, and Max also knows which (candidate).

T&F's's account has nothing to say about these since the smaller ellipsis - even though containing a trace in the ellipsis site - does not contain an <u>unbound</u> trace there (presumably movement of *which candidate* has the effect of λ-abstracting over that trace). The higher competitor is thus not relevant. My account says nothing about these either; both involve missing material of type <e,t>. But the badness of (21b) is independent of the competition (and note that it is quite bad). Unless the Sluiced remnant is stressed, Sluicing is not licensed by another embedded question; see AnderBois and Jacobson (2018). Thus we note bad Sluicing cases like (22) which cannot reduce to MaxElide (nor to the principle here of choosing elision of less complex types):

(22)   *John's therapist finally discovered what was bothering him, but he himself has
        yet to figure out what.

There is no higher (or less complex) competing ellipsis. Null Complement Anaphora is impossible as *figure out* does not support this, and the higher VPE is not a
competitor as the meaning is not the same. Thus (21b) is irrelevant to MaxElide. There
are other cases in the literature, which space precludes discussion of. I will note,
though, in some such cases there are independent explanations, in others the data seems
murky and in need of systematic informant work.

4.3   Where We Make Different Predictions

There are, however, three cases where the T&F's size competition account and the type
competition account make different predictions. The first is one discussed by T&F and
which - at first glance - appears to follow under T&F's version of MaxElide, but does
not follow given the type competition proposal here. However, I will show below that
the T&F generalization is incorrect and so this case actually gives no evidence for size
over type competition. The second also at first glance looks problematic for the type
competition approach. But the situation is actually more complex than first meets the
eye, and while there remain open questions about its final analysis, it is clearly a
counterexample to the proposal here. The third case, on the other hand, is one where
the type competition analysis makes the correct prediction, while T&F's account does
not.

Thus we turn first to a case discussed by T&F; the argument for their version of
MaxElide crucially relies on a QR analysis for wide scope object quantification.
Given QR, T&F point out that they correctly predict the impossibility of the wide scope
object ($\forall > \exists$) reading in (23b) as opposed to (23a); take the relevant context to be rules
governing the running of a hospital:

(23)   At least two doctors are required to examine every patient.
    (a)   But only one nurse is.
    (b)   But only one nurse is required to.

Notice that to get object wide scope at all in the frame sentence, it is necessary to
construe *require* on a kind of Raising reading; where this is a report of the rules of
hospital, not a direct obligation of the doctors. While perhaps difficult - as object wide
scope always is - this is still possible. But the wide scope reading for (23b) is more
difficult. (I am not convinced that this is impossible, but I will assume for the sake of
discussion that T&F are correct.) But this does not appear to be the consequence of a
competition effect, for the wide scope reading is not any more accessible in (24) (I
actually find it a bit more difficult)

(24)   At least two doctors are supposed to examine every patient.   But only one nurse
        is REQUIRED to.

One cannot pin the difficulty of this reading on a claim that *require* demands to be understood as a control verb (which yields a strong preference for it to be about the obligations of a single nurse), because one can get the wide scope, non-single doctor (and non control) reading in (23a). (Just why the wide scope reading correlates with a Raising reading is unclear, but the correlation seems robust.)

The second case is one the general form of which was pointed out to me by Guillaume Thomas at the LENLS conference (Keio University, Yokohama, November 2018). Consider the following (one can easily supply the requisite context):

(24) Every woman is definitely going to vote for one of those candidates
    a. but no one knows which one.
    b. ??but no one knows which one she will.

This looks at first like a problem for the type competition, since the 'missing' meaning in both cases appears to be of type $<e,<e,t>>$. Notice that he fuller paraphrase of (24a) would have as complement of *which one* the phrase *she will vote for,* and since that contains a pronouns, its meaning is of type $<e,<e,t>>$ just as is the meaning of [[vote for]] which is the missing 2-place relation in the TVP Ellipsis cases in (b). So the types would be the same, and there is no type competition explanation available for the degradation of (24b). Size competition, on the other hand, obviously makes the right prediction here.

But the reasoning above relied on an overly simplistic view of Sluicing - one in which Sluicing simply involves picking up the two place relation [[she vote for]]. (In other words, one should beware of using the non-Sluiced paraphrase as a diagnostic for the 'missing meaning'.) Recall the point above that in general the material picked up as complement of the 'remnant' *wh* in Sluicing is an $<e,t>$ function derived from some QUD - it is not just any contextually salient function. (This is similar to the analysis of the complement of *namely* developed in AnderBois and Jacobson 2018.) It is also the case that because of that requirement, an antecedent clause such as the first one in (24) which sets up the QUD generally needs wide scope on the indefinite - if there is one. But here the meaning of the first clause in (24) is quite clearly not the meaning with wide scope on *one of those candidates.* (By itself it can, of course, have that meaning, but that is not the meaning that supports Sluicing in the second clause). Hence the QUD set up here is not about the identity of some candidate. Rather, it can either be seen as a family of QUDs and/or a functional QUD: for each woman, there is a question as to who she will vote for. Put differently, the QUD set up here is a question as to the identity of the $<e,e>$ function mapping each woman to the candidate she will vote for. The understanding of the Sluiced clause, then, is that no woman z-knows the value of that function; i.e., no woman knows the value of that function applied to her. How to compositionally get this is left for future work, but it is, I believe, uncontroversial that we have to say that the QUD referenced by the Sluiced clause (once its missing material is supplied) is either a different question for each woman or, probably equivalently, a single functional QUD. Assuming the latter (that we are dealing with a functional QUD here), the argument of the *wh* word is not a 2-place relation but a one-place function (of type $<<e,e>,t>$). This is a one-place function which happens to characterize a set of $< e,e >$ functions rather than a set of individuals (as in the normal

Sluicing case, where the QUD is about an individual). If correct, there is still an open question as to why this counts as a simpler type than the missing $<e,<e,t>>$ meaning in (1b), but it is not unreasonable to think that complexity is defined by the number of argument slots for the missing function. Thus while there remain open questions as to exactly how to analyze examples of this type (and how to define the competition here), I do not think at this point any firm conclusion can be drawn from this case.]

On the other hand, there is a case where our predictions diverge, and where type competition makes the correct prediction. Note that one can take the Evans (1988) types of cases, and merely embed the topicalized constituent further as in (25):

(25) a. Bagels, I think that Sally really likes. Donuts, I also do.
　　 b. Bagels, I think that Sally really likes. Donuts, I also think she does.

There is little if any contrast here. In fact it is possible to construct ones in which the 'little ellipsis' is actually preferred due to a possible garden path effect where the larger ellipsis could (with the right prosody) could be misinterpreted in such a way that the missing meaning is just the embedded verb;

(26) a. ?The hummus, SALLY had told me Max had cooked. The pound cake, SARAH had.
　　 b. The hummus, SALLY had told me that Max had cooked. The pound cake, SARAH had told me he had.

(26b) is actually considerably better than (a) (under the relevant reading). This presumably is because of the possibility in (a) of (mis)understanding the complement of *had* as *cooked* instead of the larger [[told me he had cooked]]. But if MaxElide were a grammatical principle, this should not matter. In both cases (b) should be blocked by size competition. In the account here, however, there is no competition - both 'big' and 'little' ellipsis (missing meanings) are of the same $<e,<e,t>>$ type. (Related facts are also noted in Griffiths, to appear.)

In conclusion, a speaker/hearer based competition principle relying on type competition accounts for the basic 'MaxElide' effects, and makes the correct empirical prediction in (25)–(26). The analyses of the 'rebinding; cases falls out of the variable free apparatus with no need to be surprised at the existence of 'rebinding', and no need to invoke a stipulative No Meaningless Coindexation Condition It provides a natural account of the facts in terms of type competition. And this, in turn, can be framed as a speaker/hearer based competition effect, placing no extra burden on the grammar.

References

AnderBois, S.: The semantics of sluicing: beyond truth conditions. Language **90**(4), 887–926 (2014)

AnderBois, S., Jacobson, P.: Answering implicit questions: the case of namely. In: Maspong, S., Stefánsdóttir, B., Blake, K., Davis, F. (eds.) Proceedings of the Twenty Eighth Conference on Semantics and Linguistic Theory, Linguistic Society of America, pp. 388–408 (2018)

Chomsky, N.: The Minimalist Program. MIT Press, Cambridge (1995)

Cormack, A.: VP anaphora: variables and scope. In: Landman, F., Veltman, F. (eds.) Varieties of Formal Semantics, pp. 81–102. Foris, Dordrecht (1984)

Evans, F.: Binding into anaphoric verb phrases. In: Powers, J., deJong, K. (eds.) Proceedings of the Fifth Eastern State Conference on Linguistics, pp. 122–129. The Ohio State University, Columbus (1988)

Ginzburg, J., Sag, I.: Interrogative Investigations. University of Chicago Press, Chicago (2000)

Grant, M.: A psycholinguistic investigation of MaxElide in variable binding contexts. Talk presented at the 39th meeting of the Northeastern Linguistic Society. University of Massachusetts, Amherst (2008)

Griffiths, J.: Beyond MaxElide: an investigation of A-bar-movement from elided phrases. Linguistic Inquiry (to appear)

Hankamer, J., Sag, I.: Deep and surface anaphora. Linguist. Inquiry 7(3), 391–428 (1976)

Hardt, D.: Verb phrase ellipsis: form, meaning, and processing. Ph.D. Dissertation, University of Pennsylvania, Philadelphia (1993)

Heim, I.: Predicates or formulas? Evidence from ellipsis. In: Lawson, A. (ed.) Proceedings of Semantics and Linguistic Theory 7, pp. 197–221. CLS Publications Cornell University, Ithaca (1997)

Jacobson, P.: Antecedent contained deletion in a variable free semantics. In: Barker, C., Dowty, D. (eds.) Proceedings of Semantics and Linguistic Theory 2, pp. 193–213. The Ohio State University, Columbus (1992)

Jacobson, P.: Where (if anywhere) is transderivationality located? In: Culicover, P., McNally, L. (eds.) Syntax and Semantics 9: The Limits of Syntax, pp. 303–337. Academic Press, San Diego (1998)

Jacobson, P.: Toward a variable free semantics. Linguist. Philos. 22(2), 117–184 (1999)

Jacobson, P.: Binding without pronouns (and pronouns without binding). In: Kruiff, G.-J., Oehrle, R. (eds.) Binding and Resource Sensitivity, pp. 57–96. Kluwer, Dordrecht (2003)

Jacobson, P.: Ellipsis in categorical grammar. In: Temmerman, T., van Craenenbroeck, J., (eds.) Oxford Handbook of Ellipsis. Oxford University Press, Oxford (in press)

Johnson, D., Lappin, S.: A critique of the minimalist program. Linguist. Philos. 20(3), 273–333 (1997)

Kimura, H.: MaxElide and economy. English. Linguistics 30(1), 49–74 (2013)

Merchant, J.: The Syntax of Silence. Oxford University Press, Oxford (2001)

Merchant, J.: Variable island repair under ellipsis. In: Johnson, K. (ed.) Topics in Ellipsis 132-153. Cambridge University Press, Cambridge (2008)

Miller, P., Pullum, G.: Expophoric VP ellipsis. In: Hofmeister, P., Norcliffe, E. (eds.) The Core and the Periphery, pp. 5–32. CSLI Publications, Stanford (2014)

Rooth, M.: Ellipsis redundancy and reduction redundancy. In: Berman, S., Hestvik, A. (eds.) Proceedings of the Stuttgart Ellipsis Workshop, p. 126. IBM Heidelberg, Heidelberg (1992)

Sag, I.: Deletion and Logical Form. Ph.D. Dissertation. MIT, Cambridge (1976)

Takahashi, S., Fox, D.: MaxElide and the re-binding problem. In: Georgala, E., Howell, J. (eds.) Proceedings of Semantics and Linguistic Theory 15, pp. 223–240. CLC Publications Cornell University, Ithaca (2005)

The Dog Ate the Damn Cake!
The Syntax of Expressive Adjectives

Daniel Gutzmann[(✉)]

University of Cologne, IDSL 1, Albertus-Magnus-Platz, 50923 Cologne, Germany
mail@danielgutzmann.com

Abstract. This paper provides an analysis of the syntactic constraints for the semantic interpretation of expressive adjectives (EAs). While it will be shown that EAs differ in many respects from ordinary adjectives, the most interesting property is what is called argument extension: EAs can semantically apply to a larger constituent. For instance, an EA in object position may express an attitude towards the entire proposition. It will be shown that a pure pragmatic approach, according to which EAs can freely pick their argument, is too liberal and that there are syntactic constraints on where an EA can be interpreted. These constraints can be accounted for by upwards agreement, if the place where is the adjective is interpreted carries an interpretable expressivity feature, while the EA itself comes with an uninterpretable one.

Keywords: Expressives · Syntax · Features · Agreement

1 Introduction

Expressive adjectives (EAs) are usually the first thing that comes into mind when thinking about expressive language.

(1) a. I have seen most **bloody** Monty Python sketches! (Potts 205: 18, [10])
     b. My **friggin'** bike tire is flat again! (Potts 2005: 6, [10])

And indeed, expressive adjectives – or EAs, for short – are also the standard case used to illustrate expressive meaning in the literature, which may be the reason why they received the most attention during the recent spark in interest in expressivity. This interest, which mainly concerns their expressive semantics, lead to the development of elaborated formal analyses that seek to account for the particular semantic properties exhibited by EAs.[1] However, this strong focus on semantic

---

[1] For instance, beside type-based multidimensional systems (Potts 2007 [11], McCready 2010 [9], Gutzmann 2015 [6]), there are frameworks using continuations (Kubota and Uegaki 2011 [8], Barker, Bernardi and Shan 2010 [1]) or monads (Giorgolo and Asudeh 2011, 2012 [4,5]).

This article is a vastly appreviated version of a chapter on the same topic from my book *The Grammar of Expressivity* (Gutzmann 2019 [7]).

K. Kojima et al. (Eds.): JSAI-isAI 2018 Workshops, LNAI 11717, pp. 240–255, 2019.
https://doi.org/10.1007/978-3-030-31605-1_18

issues left the grammatical side of EAs more or less unilluminated. If current work on EAs mentions their syntax at all, it is merely stated that EAs behave just like other attributive(-only) adjectives, deeming their syntactic behavior rather uninteresting. For instance, in his extensive case study of expressives, Potts [10] concludes that "an EA plays no special role in the syntax of a nominal it appears in, beyond simply adjoining as any modifier would" and that "the contrasts between EAs and other attributive adjectives don't follow from properties of the structures they determine" (Potts 2005: 164f., [10]). In a similar vein, Frazier, Dillon and Clifton (2014: 291, [3]) state that the syntax of EAs is that of normal attributive adjectives.

But how great is the similarity between EAs and other standard attributive adjectives actually? Indeed, in many respects, they behave completely the same. However, there are many aspects in which EAs differ from ordinary descriptive adjectives in interesting ways that warrant a closer look at their syntactic properties. The most important observation we will make is that EAs license non-local readings in which they target some constituent greater than the nominal in which they occur. The following example illustrates this.

(2)   I lost my **damn** watch and I need to buy another one soon!

Examples like (1) and (2) have a reading in which the EA expresses the speaker's negative attitude towards the entire proposition; that is, the speaker is angry that they lost their watch, not about their watch.

(3)   I lost my **damn** watch. = **Damn**! I lost my watch.

Let us call this phenomenon *argument extension*. Given that the EA is part of the NP, it is rather surprising that it can extend take the entire proposition as its argument. Crucially, ordinary descriptive adjectives do not allow for such extended readings when they are nominal attributes. That is, (4) does not have a reading in which the adjective *amazing* expresses an attitude towards the entire proposition.

(4)   I finally got rid of that amazing flu. $\neq$ Amazing! I finally got rid of that flu.

As I will show in this paper, this behavior of EAs can be explained once we accept the following hypothesis.

(5)   **Hypothesis of expressive syntax**
        Expressivity does not only play a role for semantics and pragmatics, but it is a syntactic feature.

When I speak of a syntactic feature, I mean this in the technical syntactic sense. That is, I suggest that expressivity is a feature just like tense or gender. Once we assume this, we can explain argument extension.

2 The Grammar of EAs

2.1 Standard Syntax

As said in the introduction, the majority of recent work on EAs does not really delve into their grammatical properties and simply assumes that they behave like ordinary descriptive adjectives ("DAs", henceforth). And indeed, *prima facie*, EAs behave just like attributive DAs. First of all, they seem to occur in exactly the same attributive position inside the DP in which DAs occur.

(6)   [DP The {bloody/damn/fucking/...} dog] barked the whole night.

Accordingly, the most straightforward syntactic analysis for EAs would be the same as for attributive DAs. That is, they can be assumed to be simple adjuncts to the NP (see Potts 2005: 164, [10]).

(7)

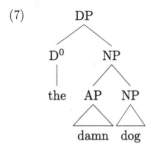

2.2 Special Syntax

Given the amount and scope of the differences between EAs and DAs that we will discuss in this section, it is a bit surprising that so little of them are even mentioned in the literature – not to speak of being looked at more closely – and that most work assumes, without further ado, that the grammar of EAs equals that of DAs. As I will argue, the fact that EAs diverge in their grammatical behavior from DAs in so plentiful and different ways renders any attempt of treating them just the same as ordinary attributive DAs very suspicious, especially if considered in conjunction with their special expressive semantics.

A first observation that we can make regarding the grammar of EAs is that they can neither surface in the comparative nor superlative form.

(8)   a.   The {damn-**er**, **more** damn} dog howled the whole night.
       b.   The {damn-**est**, **most** damn} dog howled the whole night.

Other degree expressives like *very* are also be banned from being used with EAs.

(9)   *The {very, extremly, utterly} **damn** dog barked the whole night.

EAs can also not be the target of adverbial modification which, again, is possible with DAs.

(10)   *The {presumably, probably, actually} **damn** dog barked the whole
       night.

Moreover, EAs adjectives cannot be used cannot be used predicatively, as the
following examples illustrate.

(11)   *The dog is {**damn, friggin', fucking**}.

Given all these grammatical differences between EAs and DAs (see Gutzmann
2019, [7] for many more), it is rather surprising that EAs didn't receive more
interest from a syntactic point of view; and statements saying that they do not
show any remarkable syntactic properties are even more surprising.

2.3   Argument Extension

Probably the most interesting property of EAs is the phenomenon of argument
extension. In many cases, we can observe a mismatch between the syntactic realization of an EA as a DP-internal attribute to a noun and its scope of semantic
interpretation (see Potts (2005): 18, [10]). This is already the case for the examples discussed so far. Despite its attributive position, EAs can receive a reading
in which they take the entire DP as their argument. I am using the "frownie
operator" here to represent the semantic content of the expressive as well as
an informal tower notation that puts the use-conditional content on top of the
descriptive content.

(12) $the \; \boldsymbol{damn} \; dog = \dfrac{\text{☹(the-dog)}}{\textbf{the-dog}}$

What is even more surprising is that such non-local interpretations are not
confined to the DP-level; EAs can semantically be applied to even bigger constituents. Most interestingly, they may target the entire sentence, as in the following examples.

(13)   The **damn** dog ate the cake.
       ≈   "I feel negatively about the dog!"
       ≈   "I feel negatively about the fact that the dog ate the cake!"

That is, instead of only expressing a negative attitude towards the dog, an utterance of (13) also has a reading in which the speaker is just upset about the entire
situation. Setting aside the descriptive content (that the dog ate the cake) for a
moment, (13) is therefore ambiguous between (at least) the two shown readings.
Of course, these two readings are a bit hard to disentangle, but if we alter the
example such that the EA sits on the direct object, the two readings become
more distinct.

(14)   The dog ate the **damn** cake.
       ≈   "I feel negatively about the cake!"
       ≈   "I feel negatively about the fact that the dog ate the cake!"

Taking into account the descriptive meaning and using the fraction notation, a sentence like (13) thus can give rise to (at least) the following two combinations of meaning dimensions, which differ in the size of the argument of the frownie-operator in the expressive dimension.

(15) $$\frac{\text{☹(the dog)}}{\text{the dog ate the cake}}$$ (16) $$\frac{\text{☹(the dog ate the cake)}}{\text{the dog ate the cake}}$$

We describe this behavior by saying that EAs allow what can be called *argument extension*, which basically means that they extend their scope to bigger constituents, which contain themselves. This could be, for instance, the DP or the CP. Due to the CP-level interpretation, the attribute use of EAs can lead to interpretations that are very similar to the stand-alone, interjection-like use of EAs. That is, (13) and (14) mirror (17) in their sentential reading.

(17)   **Damn!** The dog ate the cake.

What is puzzling is that such behavior is rather unheard of for attributive adjectives. To quote Potts (2005: 18, [10]) here, "syntactic movement of English attributive adjectives is contraindicated by all known syntactic tests." The same can be said for German. Moreover, most DAs certainly do not display this kind of behavior. For instance, (18a) does not have a reading in which the DA *awesome* targets the entire proposition. That is, (18a) cannot have a reading under which it is synonymous with (18b).

(18)   a.   The dog peed on the **awesome** couch.
        b.   **Awesome!** The dog peed on the ouch.

Hence, the question arises how EAs get their non-local readings and why ordinary DAs cannot receive the same range of interpretations.

3   Just Pragmatics?

As far as I know, only Frazier, Dillon and Clifton (2014) [3] provide an account for the non-local interpretation of EAs. Instead of relying on special semantic mechanisms, it is a purely pragmatic approach, without any regard to the syntax of EAs. In some sense to be elaborated below, their approach can be said to be anti-syntactic. The authors assume that EAs are, for compositional reasons, not part of the sentence they occur in at all. Instead, they base their analysis of what they dub the "speech act hypothesis" according to which "expressive like *damn* constitutes a speech act separate from the speech act of the at-issue content" and "permits the expressive to be interpreted with respect to portions of the utterance (including the entire utterance) other than its syntactic sister" (Frazier, Dillon and Clifton 2014: 299, [3]). That is, instead of being integrated into the sentence, EAs behave as if they were uttered independently and search their target from that unintegrated position in a purely pragmatics way.

From these assumptions, they derive the prediction that a sentence-internal EA gives rise to the same reading as if an EA is uttered independently before or after the sentence. This prediction corresponds to the observation we made above: minimal pairs that differ only with respect to the question of whether the EA is in subject position, object position, or used in an unintegrated, interjection-like manner all share the reading in which the EA targets the entire sentence.

(19) a. The **damn** dog ate the cake.
      b. The dog ate the **damn** cake.
      c. **Damn!** The dog ate the cake.

That is, all three variants in (18) and (19) allow for the reading in which the argument is the entire CP, even the two cases in which the EA is embedded in the subject or object DP.

However, so far, we only observed this synonymy with respect to the sentence-level interpretation of the EA. What Frazier, Dillon and Clifton's purely pragmatic speech act hypothesis allows as well is an interpretation that may completely disregard the syntactic placement of the EA, as long as pragmatics allow for it. That is, Frazier, Dillon and Clifton (2014: 295, [3]) predict that the variants should not only share the sentence interpretation, but also the subject and object interpretation. That is, an EA in subject position should be able to target just the object and *vice versa*. In addition, an EA in an unintegrated position, as in (18b) and (19c) respectively (let's call this *sentence position* henceforth), does not have to be interpreted with respect to the entire sentence, but is supposed to be able to target just the subject or object (or any other relevant constituent for that matter).

Experimental Data

Frazier, Dillon and Clifton (2014: 296, [3]) test their predictions in an experiment involving 48 undergraduate students, who had to read a sentence on a computer terminal and, after they confirmed comprehension by pressing a keyboard key, answer a question about the test sentence. The test items differed (amongst other factors) with respect to the position of the EA (subject, object, or sentence position). For the thirty critical test items (which were mixed with ninety-six items from unrelated experiments), the subjects were asked about the most likely target of the EA. The results of this experiment seem to support their two hypotheses (Frazier, Dillon and Clifton 2015: 297–299, [3]). First, they clearly show that EAs have a sentence-level interpretation, even if they are in object or subject position. They also observe a transfer in the other direction. This seems to support the speech act hypothesis, since the position of the EA does not strictly determine its place of interpretation. However, I think their findings do not entirely support the speech act hypothesis, insofar as their results are perfectly compatible with an alternative hypothesis to be discussed soon. On the other hand, the speech act hypothesis makes just some wrong predictions, as I will show now.

4   The Role of Syntax

The speech act hypothesis leads to a purely pragmatic approach to the interpretation of EA which is almost completely free from structural considerations. But the interpretation of EAs is not that free and independent of its syntactic environment.

4.1   Barries to Argument Extension

First note that Frazier, Dillon and Clifton (2014) [3] only test EAs in rather simple syntactic contexts. In order to the see the problem the speech act hypothesis faces, consider the following example in which an EA occurs in an embedded clause.

(20)   Peter said that the dog ate the **damn** cake.

Inside the embedded clause, the gEA can either target the object DP in which it occurs or the entire embedded clause itself. Speaking informally and ignoring the descriptive dimension, we can say that (20) can express a negative attitude towards the cake itself or to the fact that the dog ate the cake.

(21)   a.   ☹(the cake)
        b.   ☹(the dog ate the cake)

These are two different readings which, again, are felicitous in most likely different contexts. For instance, if the speaker dislikes the cake, she may be happy about the fact that the dog ate it. In contrast, if the speaker has a negative attitude towards the fact that the dog ate the cake, she may have a very positive picture of the cake.

The fact that an utterance of (20) allows for these two readings is very much in line with the speech acts hypothesis. The EA, performing a speech act that is independent of the remainder of the utterance, can freely target the object DP or the entire embedded sentence.

This being said, the EA inside the embedded clause can neither target the subject of the matrix clause nor the entire sentence itself. An utterance of (20) *does not* have the following two readings.

(22)   a.   *☹(Peter)
        b.   *☹(Peter said that the dog ate the cake)

That is, (20) cannot be used to express a negative attitude just toward the fact that Peter said that the dog ate the cake. Nor can it be used to express one own's disregard of Peter. If this is true, then there is a constraint at work to the effect that an EA cannot target something outside the embedded sentence. This, of course, would be a structural constraint, which in turn would mean that syntactic aspects are relevant for the calculation of the interpretational target of an EA. This is at odds with the speech act hypothesis. Moreover, the purely pragmatic approach, while perfectly able to generate the readings in (21), is unable to exclude readings like (22); it even predicts that they are available.

4.2 Experimental Evidence for Syntactic Barriers

Even though my intuitions – which I checked with a lot of informants – are pretty clear in this respect, I conducted a small empirical pilot study in order to check whether syntactic embedding actually has a kind of blocking effect on the semantic interpretation of EAs. We tested sixty undergraduate students using a Latin square design with four lists, each containing fifteen critical items, along with thirty-two fillers. The design is similar to the one used by Frazier, Dillon and Clifton (2014) [3], but we use simple questionnaires instead of reading at a computer terminal. The items vary along two factors: embedding (EA in embedded or unembedded clause) and position (EA in subject or object position). The following examples illustrate the four variants of one item (the language of the experiment was German, but I illustrate it with English here).

(23) **Simple items**
a. The damn neighbor mowed the lawn last night. (subject position)
b. The neighbor mowed the damn lawn last night. (object position)

Question: 'What does the speaker most likely judge as negative?'

    i   the neighbor
    ii   the lawn
    iii   that the neighbor mowed the lawn

(24) **Embedded items**
a. Susan said that the damn neighbor mowed the lawn. (subject position)
b. Susan said that the neighbor mowed the damn lawn. (object position)

Question: 'What does the speaker most likely judge as negative?'

    i.   the neighbor
    ii.   the lawn
    iii.   that Susan said that the neighbor mowed the lawn

We investigated the collected responses with respect to the question of whether syntactic embedding has an effect on the likelihood that the subjects choose the sentence interpretation. The prediction is that syntactic embedding should lead to a significant decrease in sentence interpretation. This prediction is confirmed by our data. In the unembedded case, the EA in subject position received 95 sentence responses compared to 120 subject or object responses. When in object position, the EA got 77 sentence responses compared to 113 subject or object responses. This is illustrated in Fig. 1(a). Compare this to the embedded case. Here, the sentence responses for the subject position dropped down to 23, while the subject/object interpretation was chosen 182 times. A similar picture arises for EAs in object position, for which 29 sentence responses were given, compared to 176 subject/object interpretations. See Fig. 1(b).

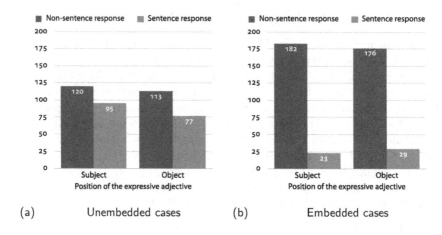

(a)   Unembedded cases   (b)   Embedded cases

Fig. 1. Number of sentence vs. non-sentence responses depending on embedding and position

We analyzed the results using a mixed-effects logistic regression model. The model computes the likelihood for a switch from a non-sentence position to a sentence-level interpretation. It contains random intercepts for subjects and items in order to "correct" for possible different preferences of subjects and items, since the data points are not completely separate from each other as several data points come from the same source. The results are given in Table 1.

Table 1. Parameters of mixed model, situation responses, syntactic embedding

	Estimate	Std. error	z value	$Pr(> |z|)$	
(Intercept)	−0.2627	0.2515	−1.045	0.296	
syn.embedded	−2.2536	0.2916	−7.728	$1.09e\text{–}14$	***
object	0.8819	0.2252	3.916	$9.02e\text{–}05$	***
syn.embedded : object	−0.4547	0.3860	−1.178	0.239	

The intercept represents the starting level (subject position, unembedded). We find an effect for embedding: syntactically embedding an EA significantly reduces the likelihood of a sentence-level interpretation (beta = −2.2536, SE = 0.2916; $p < 0.001$). In addition, we also find an effect for position: if the EA is part of the syntactic object, the likelihood of a sentence-level interpretation rises significantly (beta = 0.8819, SE = 0.2252; $p < 0.001$). The interaction between embedding and position is not significant though (beta = −0.4547,

SE $= 0.3860$, $p = 0.23$), which can be interpreted such that the blocking effect of embedding does not differ for the two positions. Overall, we can conclude that the syntactical embedding of an EA has a very strong blocking effect. The experiment thus confirms the intuitive assessment of the (un)available readings for examples like (20).

4.3   No Argument Lowering

The fact that syntactic embedding poses a barrier for getting the widest-scope reading of an EA contradicts the speech act hypothesis. If anything, the main-clause level interpretation should be the easiest to get if the EA really did perform an independent speech act. However, there is an additional, also severe problem for the speech act hypothesis. Recall that in our original investigation of the readings an EA can give rise to, we attested that they can lead to what we called *argument extension*, which described the observation that an EA can target a larger constituent which it is part of. Beyond that, the speech act hypothesis would also let us predict cases of what may be called *argument narrowing* and *argument hopping*. The former would be the case if an EA in sentence position targets only the subject (or the object, for that matter). The latter would be the case if an EA in, say, object position targets the subject; or *vice versa*. According to Frazier, Dillon and Clifton (2014, [3]) these two processes are also possible, in addition to argument extension. But is this really the case? At least the data from their experiment seems to support this assumption. However, let us again go through some reasoning to see whether the conclusion they draw from their data is really warranted. To begin, consider the following example.

(25)   **Damn!** The dog ate the cake.

At first sight, an utterance of (25) has a reading under which the EA in sentence-external position targets *the dog*, in addition to the reading under which it targets the entire proposition.

(26)   a.   ☺(the dog ate the cake)   b.   ☺(the dog)

The second reading would then be a case of *argument narrowing*, since an EA in a higher position targets only a subpart of its argument. Nevertheless, the important intuition is that, even if one interprets (25) in a way in which *damn* expresses a negative attitude towards the dog, the sentence-level interpretation is nonetheless still active. This can be tested by building a variant of (25) in which the sentence-level reading is excluded. This can be achieved, for instance, by inserting a sentence adverb of positive evaluation into the clause that would block a sentential reading. If a pure below-sentence-level interpretation of the EA were possible, such a sentence would be felicitous. However, if the sentence-level interpretation is still active, then the resulting sentence should be infelicitous or even sound contradictory. And this is indeed the case.

(27)   #**Damn**. Luckily, the dog has eaten the cake.

What is important here is that, according to the speech act hypothesis, (27) should have readings under which it is felicitous, namely those in which the EA targets just the subject or just the object, but not the entire sentence. For instance, if somebody dislikes the dog and has a vicious plan which involves the dog eating the cake so that the dog gets into trouble, then an utterance of (27) should be felicitous, just as (28) would be where the EA actually appears on the object.

(28)   Luckily, the **damn** dog ate the cake.

However, given a special context like the one just mentioned, (28) does not sound contradictory at all, in contrast to (27). The conclusion is that cases in which an EA in sentence position seems to take scope inside the sentence and seems to target only the subject or only the object are not really cases of argument narrowing. Instead, they still receive a sentence-level interpretation that remains active all the time. However, this does not exclude the possibility that due to the sentential reading of the EA, a pragmatic inference is drawn that the speaker has a negative attitude towards the subject (or object), as well.

These considerations show that EAs are not as independent as the speech act hypothesis assumes them to be. Instead, the observed constraints on the displaced interpretation of EAs shows that there are structural restrictions at work. There is only one way in which EAs can look for a place to be interpreted.

(29)   **HEADS UP!**
   a.   EAs have to look for a place to be interpreted.
   b.   They can only look up.

Together with the syntactic blocking effect we observed when EAs are put into embedded clauses, this speaks against a completely free and structurally unconstrained, purely pragmatic approach, like the one suggested by Frazier, Dillon and Clifton [3]. Instead, the data hints at a syntactic underpinning of the mechanism that drives the interpretation of EAs.

5   A Syntactic Approach to the Interpretation of EAs

The key to get a grip on the flexible though not completely unconstrained interpretation of EAs lies in the observation that the flexibility regarding their target only goes in one direction, namely upwards. That is, we can get a sentence-level interpretation from the subject or object position, but not *vice versa*. Nor can an EA in object position semantically be interpreted as just targeting the subject nor can an EA in subject position just target the object. In order to account for this restriction in direction, I employ the syntactic mechanism of agreement. More precisely, I adopt the unidirectional, upward-looking version of agreement championed by Zeijlstra (2012, [12]), which I label $\uparrow\text{Agree}_i$.

(30)   **↑Agree$_i$:**   (Zeijlstra 2012: 514, [12])
         α can ↑Agree$_i$ with β iff:

   a. α carries at least one uninterpretable feature and β carries a matching interpretable feature.
   b. β c-commands α.
   c. β is the closest goal to α.

In context of the HEADS UP! generalization from (29), the definition of upward-looking ↑Agree$_i$ is a perfect fit, as it involves uninterpretable stuff (the α) that looks up for some place of interpretation (the β). It is therefore rather straightforward to employ the ↑Agree$_i$-mechanism for the case of EAs by making the following assumptions. First, I assume that the actual interpretation of the EA is not provided by the EA itself. Rather it is a syntactic *expressivity feature, Ex,* that is what actually is semantically interpreted. However, the operator does only provide the place of interpretation, so to speak, but not the content. The content itself is instead realized by the EA. Such a configuration can, for instance be assumed for the interpretation of tense in a language like German. In this case, the interpretation of tense happens at the TP-level in T^0. However, how tense is interpreted is not determined by T^0, but rather by the features of the finite predicate in V^0, which is located lower in the syntactic structure.

Such a mismatch between the place of syntactic realization and the place of semantic interpretation is similar to the one we observed for EAs. And if assume that expressivity is a feature like tense, ↑Agree$_i$ gives us a way to connect the EA to its locus of interpretation. For this, I assume that the expressivity feature can appear in different head positions where it is interpreted, but not yet valued. It is the EA, which appears in a lower position, that provides a valued version of the expressivity feature, which cannot be interpreted though. To see how this works, let us begin with the case in which an EA in subject position targets the subject. Consulting the definition in (30) again, we see that the two *Ex*-features in (31) fulfill the conditions for ↑Agree$_i$. Therefore, as illustrated in (31), the interpretable version of the expressivity feature in D^0 can receive its value from the EA, whereas the feature, which is uninterpretable at the EA, is marked for deletion.

(31) $[_{DP} [_{D^0}$ the$_{[iEx:\; \circledcirc]}$] $[_{NP} [_{AP}$ damn$_{[uEx:\; \circledcirc]}$] $[_{NP}$ dog]]]
          |_____↑Agree$_i$_____|

The mechanism of ↑Agree$_i$ment thus provides us a means to link the EA, which realizes the expressive attitude, and the higher place of interpretation. Assuming that the expressivity feature cannot only be present in D^0, but also in C^0, we can get a sentence-level interpretation in a similar way. That is, the only difference between the DP- and sentence-level interpretation is the placement of the interpretable iEx feature that matches the uEx feature of the EA. In case of the subject interpretation, iEx is in the corresponding D^0, whereas it is C^0 in case of the sentence-level interpretation. Now that we have seen how an approach based on the syntactic mechanism of ↑Agree$_i$ment, let us investigate this approach in more detail and see how it can account for the structural constraints on the interpretation of EAs which lead us to consider a syntactic approach in the first place.

5.1   EAs Can only Look Up

The discussion regarding the mismatch between the syntactic placement of an EA and its semantic interpretation carried out in this chapter revealed that this mismatch is not of the "anything goes" kind (as assumed to by Frazier, Dillon and Clifton's [3] speech act hypothesis), but that it is rather constrained. This was formulated in the informal HEADS UP! generalization in (29). The $\uparrow\text{Agree}_i$ approach directly accounts for this restriction. Recall that in the definition in (30), only one configuration licenses $\uparrow\text{Agree}_i$; namely precisely that in which the interpretable feature c-commands the uninterpretable feature and thus is in a higher position. In case of EAs, this leads to what I called argument extension, as it is already illustrated in the configuration in (30). In contrast, argument lowering, which would correspond to an agreement configuration in which the interpretable feature is below the uninterpretable one, is not a viable configuration for $\uparrow\text{Agree}_i$.

(32) a. $[iF \ ... \ [uF]]$ *argument extension* ✓
      b. $[uF \ ... \ [iF]]$ *argument lowering* ✗

That is, the employment of $\uparrow\text{Agree}_i$ as the basis for building the link between the EA and its place of interpretation directly captures the uni-directionality of the syntax-semantics mismatch.

5.2   Syntactic Blocking

One of the main arguments against Frazier, Dillon and Clifton's [3] pragmatics-only approach (according to which EAs basically ignore the syntactic structure of the sentence they occur in all together) was the observation that EAs cannot extend out of an embedded clause. That is, if occurring in a DP in an embedded clause, they can neither target a DP in the main clause nor the entire sentence itself. To repeat the data, an utterance of (20), which I repeat here with a new number, does not have all the reading in (33).

(33) Peter said that the dog ate the damn cake.
      a. ☺(the cake)
      b. ☺(the dog ate the cake)
      c. *☺(Peter)
      d. *☺(Peter said that the dog ate the cake)

The impossible reading in (33c) is ruled out by the constraint that EAs can search for their locus of interpretation in a strictly upwards fashion, as defined in the conditions for $\uparrow\text{Agree}_i$ in (30). However, the reading in (33d) under which the EA targets the entire utterance, is unavailable as well, but the configuration of features that would lead to such an interpretation concurs with the definition of $\uparrow$Agree$_i$. The EA in the embedded clause carries an uninterpretable Ex-feature that is matched by an interpretable feature in the left periphery of the main clause.

(34)   [$_{CP}$ C$_{[iEx]}$ [$_{TP}$ Peter said [$_{CP}$ that the dog ate the **damn**$_{[uEx]}$ cake]]].

However, this configuration nevertheless does not seem to license $\uparrow$Agree$_i$ment between the higher iEx in C^0 and the EA in the embedded clause. However, it is often assumed that CPs are relevant for agreement since they constitute "phases" for agreement phenomena (Bošković 2007, [2]). Following this line of thinking, the intervening CP-boundary thus is the reason for why the EA in the embedded clause cannot $\uparrow$Agree$_i$ with an assumed iEx-feature in the main clause.

(35)

[$_{CP}$ C$_{[iEx]}$ [$_{TP}$ Peter said [$_{CP}$ that the dog ate the **damn**$_{[uEx]}$ cake]]].

~~$\uparrow$Agree$_i$~~

In a configuration like (35), the embedded CP is shipped to the interfaces before it is merged with the embedding predicate and thus the uninterpretable uEx in the embedded CP remains unchecked which makes the derivation unviable.

5.3 Multiple Agreement

Another interesting prediction made by the $\uparrow$Agree$_i$ment analysis of EAs is that it lets us expect that there are instances of multiple agreement with EAs. Multiple agreement phenomena happen if an expression bearing an interpretable feature agrees with multiple expressions downstream that all carry the corresponding uninterpretable feature. For illustration, consider the following example from Italian given by Zeijlstra (2012: 519, [12]).

(36)   Gianni non ha detto niente a   nessuno
        Gianni NEG said n-thing to   n-body
        'Gianni didn't say anything to anybody'   (Italian)

(37)   [Gianni non$_{[iNeg]}$-ha [ditto niente$_{[uNeg]}$ a nessuno$_{[uNeg]}$]]

The crucial observation is that only the highest negation bears the interpretable negative feature, while the lower n-words are all uninterpreted.

A very similar configuration can be built with EAs. Assume that we have an EA in subject as well as in object position, but no interpretable iEx-feature in the respective D-heads. Instead, we only have an iEx in C^0. Such a configuration would lead to a case of multiple agreement where both uEx-features of the two EAs agree with the higher, interpretable feature.

(38)   The damn dog ate the damn cake.

(39) $[_{CP}$ C$_{[iEx]}$ $[_{TP}$ $[_{DP}$ the damn$_{[uEx]}$ Hund] [ate $[_{DP}$ the damn$_{[uEx]}$ cake]]]].

Given this possible configuration, the ↑Agree$_i$ment-based approach predicts that a sentence like (38) has a reading under which it only expresses a negative attitude towards the fact that the dog ate the cake, and no such attitude towards the dog or the cake. And there is such a reading. This provides a syntactic explanation the well-known repeatabilty of expressives (Potts 2007, [11]).

6   Summary

Expressive adjectives are a poster child for expressive items and therefore they received a lot of attention from the semantic literature. However, the vast majority of this work (my own included) more or less ignored the syntactic side of EAs and treated them on par with descriptive adjectives. This paper has shown that this is unwarranted and that EAs differ in many and crucial ways from descriptive ones. The most interesting observation is that EAs lead to a mismatch between their syntactic placement and semantic interpretation, as they tend to take a much larger expression as their argument than the one they occur in. With the approach suggested by Frazier, Dillon and Clifton (2014, [3]), there is a first proposal how to deal with this argument extension: it is just pragmatics. However, I have shown that such a purely pragmatic approach is too liberal and overgenerates. Looking at more complex data shows that there are structural constraints on the syntax-semantics mismatch. It only goes up insofar as EAs can only be interpreted at a higher position, but neither at a lower one (nor another non-c-commanding position). This can be derived by a direct adoption of a upwards-looking agreement mechanism. Assuming that the EA comes with an uninterpretable expressivity feature, it has to look for a matching interpretable feature at a higher node, which it can valuate. This accounts for the directionality restriction and also can explain the repeatability of expressives. To conclude, with respect to the main hypothesis I put forward at the beginning of this paper, the upshot is that expressivity is a syntactic feature that can be involved in agreement, just like tense or gender.

References

1. Barker, C., Bernardi, R., Shan, C.c.: Principles of interdimensional meaning interaction. In: Proceedings of SALT, vol. 20, pp. 109–121 (2010). http://elanguage.net/journals/salt/article/view/20.109
2. Bošković, Ž.: On the locality and motivation of move and agree: an even more minimal theory. Linguist. Inq. **38**(4), 589–644 (2007). https://doi.org/10.1162/ling.2007.38.4.589

3. Frazier, L., Dillon, B., Clifton, C.: A note on interpreting damn expressives: transferring the blame. Lang. Cogn. **7**, 291–304 (2014). https://doi.org/10.1017/langcog.2014.31
4. Giorgolo, G., Asudeh, A.: Multidimensional semantics with unidimensional glue logic. In: Proceedings of the LFG11 Conference (2011)
5. Giorgolo, G., Asudeh, A.: $\langle m, \eta, \star \rangle$. Monads for conventional implicatures. In: Proceedings of Sinn und Bedeutung, vol. 16 (2012)
6. Gutzmann, D.: Use-Conditional Meaning. Oxford Studies in Semantics and Pragmatics, vol. 6. Oxford University Press, Oxford (2015)
7. Gutzmann, D.: The Grammar of Expressivity. Oxford Studies in Theoretical Linguistics, vol. 72. Oxford University Press, Oxford (2019)
8. Kubota, Y., Uegaki, W.: Continuation-based semantics for conventional implicatures. In: Cormany, E., Ito, S., Lutz, D. (eds.) Proceedings of Semantics and Linguistic Theory (SALT), vol. 19, pp. 306–323. eLanguage (2011). http://elanguage.net/journals/index.php/salt/article/view/19.18/1394
9. McCready, E.: Varieties of conventional implicature. Seman. Pragmatics **3**(8), 1–57 (2010). https://doi.org/10.3765/sp.3.8
10. Potts, C.: The Logic of Conventional Implicature. Oxford Studies in Theoretical Linguistics, vol. 7. Oxford University Press, Oxford (2005)
11. Potts, C.: The expressive dimension. Theor. Linguist. **33**(2), 165–197 (2007). https://doi.org/10.1515/TL.2007.011
12. Zeijlstra, H.: There is only one way to agree. Linguist. Rev. **29**(3), 491–539 (2012). https://doi.org/10.1515/tlr-2012-0017

Applicatives for Anaphora and Presupposition

Patrick D. Elliott[(✉)]

ZAS, Berlin, Germany
patrick.d.elliott@gmail.com

Abstract. In this paper, we construct an effectful semantic fragment using the *applicative* abstraction. Empirically, we focus primarily on the dynamics of anaphora, and secondarily on presupposition projection. We aim to show that a dynamic semantics can be constructed in a fully modular fashion with applicative functors; we don't need the full power of a monad (c.f. [4]). We take advantage of the fact that, unlike monads, applicative functors *compose* – and the result is guaranteed to be an applicative functor. Once we introduce the applicative abstraction, it turns out that the machinery necessary for dealing with the dynamics of anaphora and presupposition projection is *already implicit* in the machinery used in an orthodox static setting for dealing with *assignment sensitivity*, *scope*, and *partiality*.

Keywords: Applicative functors · Dynamic semantics · Presupposition projection · Continuation semantics

1 Overview

Applicative functors are an abstraction for dealing with *effectful* computation that emerged relatively recently in the functional programming literature [10]. Given some effectful domain defined by a type constructor F, an applicative provides a way of embedding pure computations into a pure fragment of F's effectful domain, and the peculiar way in which *application* is interpreted within that domain.

Monads are a related, and more established abstraction for dealing with effectful computation [15], and there has already been a great deal of work in the linguistics literature motivating an approach to semantic computation using monadic machinery (see, e.g., [1,4,12]). Monads are *more powerful* than applicatives – this is because the *bind* operator $\gg\!\!=$ associated with a given monad allows the result of an effectful computation to influence the choice of subsequent computations. Applicative functors don't allow this – effects don't influence the structure of computation, they just get sequenced. To quote Mcbride and Paterson [10, p. 8] "if you need a Monad, that is fine; if you need only an Applicative functor, that is even better!". It is still an open question whether or not, in order

© Springer Nature Switzerland AG 2019
K. Kojima et al. (Eds.): JSAI-isAI 2018 Workshops, LNAI 11717, pp. 256–269, 2019.
https://doi.org/10.1007/978-3-030-31605-1_19

to model natural language semantics, we require the full power of *monads*, or if applicative functors suffice.

In the present work, we construct a effectful semantic fragment using the applicative abstraction. Empirically, we focus on the dynamics of anaphora, with presupposition projection as a secondary concern. We aim to show that dynamics can be modelled with applicatives in a fully modular fashion; we don't need the full power of a monad. We take advantage of the fact that, unlike monads, applicatives *compose* – and the result is guaranteed to be an applicative. Once we introduce the applicative abstraction, it turns out that the machinery necessary for dealing with the dynamics of anaphora and presupposition projection are *already implicit* in the machinery used in an orthodox static setting for dealing with *assignment sensitivity*, *scope*, and *partiality*. In this sense, the present work bears directly on debate surrounding the explanatory power of dynamics for anaphora and presupposition projection (see, e.g., [11]).

Many of the ideas here are inspired by de Groote [6] and Charlow [4]. de Groote [6] pioneered the approach to dynamic semantics in terms of *continuations*, which will also be a necessary ingredient in the present account. Charlow's (2014) work is foundational for understanding natural language semantics, and specifically dynamics, as *effectful computation*. Unlike the present work, Charlow makes use of monadic machinery – specifically the `State.Set` monad – a technique which provides strictly more expressive power than the applicative abstraction. We'll offer an explicit comparison between the present approach and Charlow's monadic grammar in Sect. 4.

2   An Applicative for Anaphora

In this section, we begin by introducing some basic building blocks; in Sect. 2.1 we introduce *applicative functors* and the applicative functor laws. In Sect. 2.2, we introduce Charlow's (2018) account of assignment-sensitivity in terms of the applicative instance of `Reader`. In Sect. 2.2, we introduce the applicative instance of `Cont` (more frequently presented in its monadic guise), and following, e.g., Barker and Shan [2], show how it can be marshalled in order to provide a general theory of *scope* in natural language. Finally, in Sect. 2.4 we bring these pieces together in order to account for the dynamics of anaphora. Taking advantage of the fact that, unlike monads, applicatives *compose*, we show how the resources necessary for handling the dynamics of anaphora are *already implicit* in our fragment, once assignment-sensitivity and scope are brought into the picture.

2.1   Applicative Functors

Formally, an applicative functor is a tuple, consisting of a type constructor F, a function `pure` (which we'll write as π) of type $a \rightarrow \mathsf{F}a$, and a function `apply` (which we'll write as $\circledast$) of type $\mathsf{F}(a \rightarrow b) \rightarrow \mathsf{F}a \rightarrow \mathsf{F}b$. Applicative functors must obey the following laws:

(1)   Applicative laws

    a. Identity: $\mathsf{id}^\pi \circledast a = a$

    b. Composition: $\pi \circ \circledast\, a \circledast b \circledast c = a \circledast (b \circledast c)$

    c. Homomorphism: $f^\pi \circledast x^\pi = (f\ x)^\pi$

    d. Interchange: $a \circledast b^\pi = (\lambda f\ .\ f\ b)^\pi \circledast a$

Applicative functors are strictly *less powerful* than monads; a monad *is* an applicative functor together with an additional unary operation `join` of type $\mathsf{F}(\mathsf{F}\ a) \to \mathsf{F}\ a$, where the applicative's **pure** function corresponds to the monad's **return**, and **apply** corresponds to the monad's `ap` [14, 15].[1] The additional power afforded by join means that *monads* can be used to effectively reason about effectful computation, where the results of a previous computation can be used to affect the choice of another. Applicatives, on the other hand, keep the structure of computation fixed, and just sequence effects [10].

Monads have been used to great effect in the linguistic-semantics literature – see, e.g., Shan's [12] pioneering paper, although we note that almost all of the cases discussed by Shan can be recast in terms of applicative functors, and thus the additional power provided by the monadic abstraction isn't strictly speaking motivated. Charlow [4] on the other hand makes crucial use of monadic bind ($\ggg$) to account for the exceptional scope of indefinites, and therefore goes some way towards motivating a *monadic* approach to natural language semantics. We'll explicitly compare the fragment outlined here to Charlow's monadic grammar in Sect. 4.

2.2   Assignment Sensitivity

Charlow [3] provides an elegant compositional semantics for pronouns in a static setting via an applicative functor G, defined in (3). G is the type-constructor for the *assignment-sensitive* type space; g is the type of assignment functions. It is associated with two functions – π and $\circledast$, defined in (4a) and (4b) respectively.[2,3] π serves to lift a value to a trivially assignment-sensitive value.

---

[1] The monad laws are also distinct from the applicative laws, and are generally stated in terms of *monadic bind* ($\ggg$), which can be decomposed into ($\circledast$) and `join`. The details are orthogonal to our purposes here.

[2] Note that (4b) is defined in terms of *overloaded function application* A.

(2)   a. $\mathsf{A}fx := fx$ $(a \to b) \to a \to b$

       b. $\mathsf{A}xf := fx$ $a \to (a \to b) \to b$

[3] At various points, it will be important to disambiguate between, e.g., the **pure** functions associated with two different applicative functors. In this case we use a subscript, e.g., the **pure** function associated with G can be written π_G.

⊛ specifies how *application* is interpreted within the assignment-sensitive domain. Pronouns are interpreted as inherently assignment-sensitive individuals, as defined in (5). Figure 1 provides a sample derivation, for the sentence *Sally hugs her*, illustrating how π and ⊛ facilitate assignment-sensitive composition.

(3) $Ga ::= g \rightarrow a$

(4)   a. $a^\pi := \lambda g . a$ $a \rightarrow Ga$

      b. $n \circledast m := \lambda g . A (n\ g)(m\ g)$
$$\left.\begin{array}{l} G(a \rightarrow b) \rightarrow Ga \\ Ga \rightarrow G(a \rightarrow b) \end{array}\right\} \rightarrow Gb$$

(5) $pro_n = \lambda g . g_n$ Ge

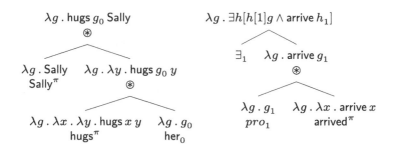

Fig. 1. Assignment-sensitive composition via π and ⊛.

It will be useful for subsequent sections to illustrate how we can define first-order quantification in terms of the machinery outlined here. First-order existential quantification is defined standardly as in (6), and first-order universal quantification in (7). Note that $h[n]g$ means that h differs *at most* from g in the value h assigns to n, which we write h_n. See Fig. 1 for a sample derivation of an existential statement such as *someone arrived*. For ease of exposition, at this stage we assume that first-order quantifiers bind silent pronominal traces.

(6) $\exists_n = \lambda p . \lambda g . \exists h[h[n]g \wedge ph]$ $Gt \rightarrow Gt$

(7) $\forall_n = \lambda p . \lambda g . \forall g'[g'[n]g \rightarrow pg']$ $Gt \rightarrow Gt$

2.3   Continuations and Scope

In this section, we will provide a basic overview of *continuation semantics* through the lens of the applicative functor K_b, defined in (8).[4] Note that, unlike our previous type-constructor G, K comes with an additional type parameter b. The definitions of the pure and apply operators associated with K are given in (9a) and (9b) respectively. pure lifts a value a to a trivially scope-taking value – in fact it is essentially a polymorphic formulation of *Montague Lift*. Again, apply specifies how function application is interpreted within the scopal domain.

(8) $K_b\, a ::= (a \rightarrow b) \rightarrow b$

(9)   a. $a^\pi := \lambda k\,.\,ka$ $\qquad\qquad\qquad\qquad\qquad\qquad\qquad\qquad a \rightarrow K\,a$

b. $n \circledast m := (\lambda k\,.\,n(\lambda n\,.\,m(\lambda m\,.\,k(A\,n\,m)))) \quad \left.\begin{array}{l} K(a \rightarrow b) \rightarrow K\,a \\ K\,a \rightarrow K(a \rightarrow b) \end{array}\right\} \rightarrow K\,b$

We can equivalently write the functions associated with K_b using Barker and Shan's *tower notation*, as in Fig. 2. We'll often take advantage of the relative succinctness of the tower notation, although bear in mind that a tower can always be expanded to a representation in the lambda calculus (see [2] for details). pure takes a value and returns a trivial tower; apply takes two towers, sequences scopal side-effects from left-to-right, and applies the inner values.

$$a^\pi := \frac{[\,]}{a} \qquad \frac{n\,[\,]}{n} \circledast \frac{m\,[\,]}{m} := \frac{n\,[\,m\,[\,]\,]}{A\,n\,m}$$

Fig. 2. The operations associated with the continuation applicative in tower notation

Within continuation semantics, quantificational DPs such as *everyone* are *continuized individuals* of type $K_t\, e$, as in (10). In order to get back from the scopal tier to an ordinary value, we'll need one final piece of machinery: a lowering function $\downarrow$, which applies a trivially continuized value of type t (since here, $b = t$) to the identity function id, as in (11). Figure 3 illustrates composition of a scopal value via K_t.[5]

(10)   everyone $:= \dfrac{\forall x[\,]}{x}$ $\qquad\qquad\qquad\qquad\qquad\qquad\qquad\qquad K_t\, e$

(11) $\downarrow t := t\,\text{id}$ $\qquad\qquad\qquad\qquad\qquad\qquad\qquad\qquad\qquad K_b\, b \rightarrow b$

---

[4] Out of necessity, our presentation of continuation semantics will presuppose a certain degree of familiarity with the framework, but see Barker and Shan [2] for a thorough introduction.

[5] It is easy to see that if we compose more than one scopal value, the resulting value will correspond to the *surface scope* reading of a given sentence. In order to derive inverse scope readings we need an additional operation – *internal lift*. This won't be relevant for our purposes, but see [2] for details.

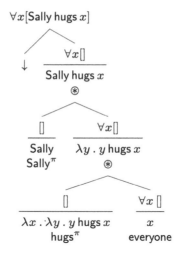

Fig. 3. Composition with a quantificational DP via K_t

2.4 The Dynamics of Anaphora

In the previous section, we parameterized our continuation type-constructor K to t, the type of *truth values*. We did this in order to account for the composition of quantificational DPs such as *everyone*. Let's shift perspective, and instead parameterize K to G t, the type of *assignment-sensitive truth values*. Due to the equivalence between characteristic functions of type a → t and sets of type { a }, we can also think of G t as the type of a *set of assignment functions*. In the following, it will be helpful to switch back and forth between characteristic function and set perspectives, although bear in mind that the underlying compositional apparatus uses functions exclusively. The **pure** operator associated with K_{Gt} lifts a value a to a scopal value of type (a → G t) → G t (Fig. 4).

Recall that one property of applicative functors is that they compose, and the result is guaranteed to be an applicative functor. The next step in the analysis is to compose K_{Gt} and our type-constructor for assignment-sensitivity G, yielding a new applicative functor, which we'll call C, defined in (12). C essentially *is* our analysis of the dynamics of anaphora, so it's worth paying attention at this point. The **pure** and **apply** operators associated with C are just the *composition*

$$a^\pi := \frac{[]}{\lambda g \cdot a} \qquad \frac{m\,[]}{m} \circledast \frac{n\,[]}{n} = \frac{m\,[n\,[]]}{\lambda g \cdot A\,(m\,g)\,(n\,g)}$$

Fig. 4. The π and $\circledast$ operators associated with C.

of those associated with $\mathsf{K_{Gt}}$ and G.[6] We've provided the partially de-sugared definition in (13) for ease of exposition.

(12) $\mathsf{C} ::= \mathsf{K_{Gt}} \circ \mathsf{G}$

(13) $\mathsf{C}\,\mathsf{a} := (\mathsf{G}\,\mathsf{a} \to \mathsf{G}\,\mathsf{t}) \to \mathsf{G}\,\mathsf{t}$

We'll be using C as our type-constructor for the domain of *contextually dynamic values*. In order to get started, let's define a function ($\uparrow$) that lifts assignment-sensitive values to trivially dynamic values.

(14) $x^{\uparrow} := \dfrac{\llbracket\,\rrbracket}{\lambda g \,.\, x\, g}$ $\qquad\qquad\qquad\qquad\qquad$ $\mathsf{G}\,\mathsf{a} \to \mathsf{C}\,\mathsf{a}$

We'll use $\uparrow$ to lift pronouns into the contextually dynamic space, as illustrated below. It turns out that in our new dynamic setting, the fundamental semantic contribution of a pronominal is no different.

(15) $\mathsf{pro}_n^{\uparrow} := \dfrac{\llbracket\,\rrbracket}{\lambda g \,.\, g_n}$

As a first attempt at a genuinely dynamic semantics for anaphora, we'll define a function $\Uparrow$, the role of which is to *dynamize* first-order operators such as $\exists$. $\Uparrow$-lifting first-order existential quantification yields *dynamic* existential quantification.

(16) $f^{\Uparrow} := \lambda p \,.\, \lambda k \,.\, (f \circ p)k$ $\qquad\qquad\qquad$ $(\mathsf{G}\,\mathsf{t} \to \mathsf{G}\,\mathsf{t}) \to (\mathsf{C}\,\mathsf{t} \to \mathsf{C}\,\mathsf{t})$

(17) $\exists_n^d := \lambda p \,.\, \lambda k \,.\, \lambda g \,.\, \exists h [h[n]g \wedge (p\,k)h]$ $\qquad\qquad$ $\mathsf{C}\,\mathsf{t} \to \mathsf{C}\,\mathsf{t}$

Once we generalize $\Uparrow$ to binary operations (details suppressed), and apply it to type-lifted static conjunction, we can derive *dynamic conjunction*. The definition of dynamic conjunction will probably look quite unfamiliar to dynamic semanticists used to theories such as Dynamic Predicate Logic [8] and Predicate Logic with Anaphora [7], but it bears some similarities to the definition given in Chierchia [5].

(18) $(\wedge^d) = \lambda q \,.\, \lambda p \,.\, \lambda k \,.\, (p \circ (\wedge_\mathsf{G}) \circ q)k$ $\qquad\qquad$ $\mathsf{C}\,\mathsf{t} \to \mathsf{C}\,\mathsf{t} \to \mathsf{C}\,\mathsf{t}$

For completeness, we define two more useful operators: *dynamic negation*, and *discourse referent introduction* (dref-intro), as in (19) and (20) respectively. Dynamic negation is defined in a reasonably standard way – the closure operator $\downarrow$ closes off the anaphoric potential of its prejacent. The dref-intro operator shifts an individual denoting expression into a dynamic binder.

---

[6] For the unary operation associated with each applicative functor this is straightforward: $\pi_{\mathsf{K_{Gt}}} \circ \pi_\mathsf{G} = \pi_\mathsf{C}$. In order to compose two curried binary operators however, we compose the composition operator with itself, i.e., $((\circ) \circ (\circ))(\circledast_{\mathsf{K_{Gt}}})(\circledast_\mathsf{G}) = (\circledast_\mathsf{C})$.

(19) $(\neg^d) = \lambda p . \uparrow (\neg(\downarrow p))$ $\mathsf{C\,t} \to \mathsf{C\,t}$

(20) $\Delta_n = \lambda x . \lambda p . \lambda k . \lambda g . (g^{[n \to x]} \circ p) \, k$ $\Delta_n := \mathsf{e} \to \mathsf{C\,t} \to \mathsf{C\,t}$

We're now in a position to derive a simple case of cross-sentential anaphora: *someone arrived and they sat down*. The full computation is illustrated in Fig. 5. Intuitively, the continuation variable k represents the *future of the discourse*. The way that dynamic conjunction passes the continuation variable from one conjunct to the next means that the scope of dynamic existential quantification extends from left-to-right automatically – the continuation variable always ends up taking scope over the right-most conjunct. In the sample derivation, the resulting continuized value is closed off via ($\downarrow$), returning a familiar assignment-sensitive value.

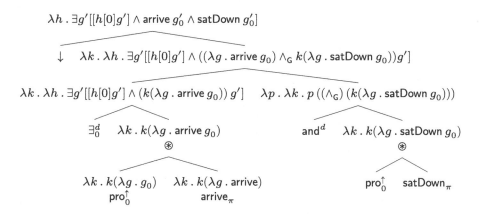

Fig. 5. Example of simple cross-sentential dynamic binding via C

One nice feature of this system is that static existential quantification and conjunction can be dynamicized in a regular way. Inherently assignment-sensitive expressions such as pronominals can be lifted into the contextually dynamic space via a simple lifter function, and every other aspect of composition is handled by the **pure** and **apply** operations associated with C. As such, this framework addresses some of the worries raised about dynamic approaches to anaphora and other phenomena, namely that they must stipulate the dynamic flow of information as part of the lexical entry of each individual expression (see, e.g., [11]).

For completeness, in Fig. 6 we show how dynamic negation roofs the scope of a dynamic existential quantifier by closing off the continuation variable before re-opening it. This directly captures the fact *nobody arrived and they sat down* is unacceptable under the intended reading.

Ultimately, we would like to extend this framework to a full compositional semantics for determiners and generalized quantification. We will leave this

$\lambda h . \neg \exists g'[[h[0]g' \wedge \text{arrive } g'_0]] \wedge \text{satDown } h_0$

$\downarrow$ $\lambda p . \lambda k . (\lambda h . \neg \exists g'[[h[0]g' \wedge \text{arrive } g'_0]]) \wedge_G (k (\lambda g . \text{satDown } g_0))$

$\lambda l . l (\lambda h . \neg \exists g'[[h[0]g'] \wedge \text{arrive } g'_0])$ $\lambda p . \lambda k . p ((\wedge_G) (k(\lambda g . \text{satDown } g_0)))$

neg $\lambda k . \lambda h . \exists g'[[h[0]g'] \wedge (k(\lambda g . \text{arrive } g_0)) g']$ and^d ...

$\exists_0$ ... $\text{pro}_0^\uparrow$ satDown_ρ

$\text{pro}_0^\uparrow$ arrive_π

Fig. 6. Dynamic negation blocks dynamic binding

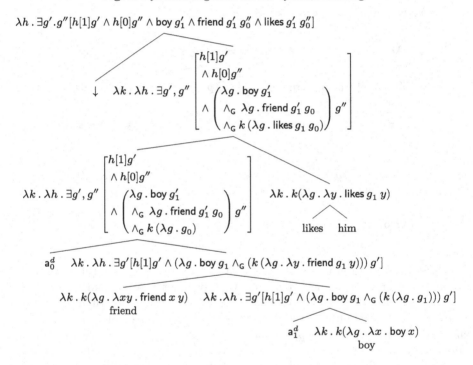

Fig. 7. Dynamic binding from out of a nominal restrictor

mostly for future work, but we do offer a sketch of an analysis of a case involving dynamic binding from out of a nominal restrictor, which relies on the dynamic denotation for the indefinite article given in (21). The computation for the sentence *a friend of a boy likes him*, where *a boy* binds *him*, is given in Fig. 7.

$$(21) \quad a_n^d = \lambda p \,.\, \lambda k \,.\, \exists_n^s ((p\, \mathsf{pro}_n^\uparrow)((\wedge_\mathsf{G})(k\, \mathsf{pro}_n))) \qquad\qquad \mathsf{C}(\mathsf{e} \to \mathsf{t}) \to \mathsf{C}\,\mathsf{e}$$

3   An Applicative for Presupposition Projection

In this section, we argue that the same technique we used to model the dynamics of anaphora can be used to model the dynamics of *presupposition projection*. This will be even more of a proof of concept than the previous section.

3.1   Back to Assignment Sensitivity

The first component we will need in order to get our analysis off the ground is a way of modelling *world-sensitivity/intensionality*. Here we follow Shan [12] in treating *intensionality* as assignment-sensitivity; We define a type-constructor S for world-sensitive meanings. The applicative operations for S are identical to those of G. Predicates are taken to be inherently world-sensitive. World-sensitive computation can be modelled as effectful computation via applicative machinery in *exactly* the same way as assignment-sensitivity. If we assume that predicates take an inner world argument, we don't even particularly need π and $\circledast$ to aid in composition.

$$(22) \quad \text{a.} \quad \mathsf{S}\,\mathsf{a} ::= \mathsf{s} \to \mathsf{a}$$

b. $\quad a^\pi := \lambda w \,.\, a$

c. $\quad n \circledast m := \lambda w \,.\, \mathsf{A}\,(n\,w)(m\,w)$

$$(23) \quad \text{a.} \quad \mathsf{arrive} ::= \mathsf{e} \to \mathsf{S}\,\mathsf{t}$$

b. $\quad \mathsf{arrive} := \lambda x \,.\, \lambda w \,.\, \mathsf{arrive}_w\, x$

3.2   Partiality

In a static setting, presuppositions are typically modelled via partiality/trivalence [9]. Unsurprisingly, there's an applicative for that: Maybe (here: P), which defines a trivalent value-space consisting of defined values $\langle a \rangle$ and an undefined value $\#$.

$$(24) \quad \text{a.} \quad \mathsf{P}\,\mathsf{a} ::= \langle \mathsf{a} \rangle \mid \#$$

b. $\quad a^\pi := \langle a \rangle$

c. $\quad m \circledast n :- \begin{cases} \langle \mathsf{A}\,x\,y \rangle & \langle x \rangle := m;\, \langle y \rangle := n \\ \# & \text{otherwise} \end{cases}$

Once we compose S with P (S$_\#$), we end up with the resources we need to model presuppositional, world-sensitive predicates in a static way, as illustrated by the lexical entry for the presuppositional predicate *stop smoking*, given in (26), which is modelled as a function from individuals to partial propositions.

(25) a. $S_\# := S \circ P$

  b. $a^\rho := \lambda w \,.\, \langle a \rangle$

  c. $f \circledast x := \lambda w \,.\, \begin{cases} \langle gy \rangle & f\,w = \langle g \rangle \wedge x\,w = \langle y \rangle \\ \text{else} & \# \end{cases}$

(26) a. $\text{stopSmoking} := e \to S_\# \, t$

  b. $\text{stopSmoking} = \lambda x \,.\, \lambda w \,.\, \begin{cases} \text{didSmoke}\,x\,w & \langle \text{notSmoke}\,x\,w \rangle \\ \text{else} & \# \end{cases}$

3.3 The Dynamics of Presupposition Projection

Famously, a static trivalent theory of presuppositions can't provide a satisfactory account of presupposition projection in complex sentences – when the presupposition of the second conjunct is entailed by the first, it fails to project [13].

(27) a. If Sally used to smoke, then she stopped smoking.

  b. Sally used to smoke, and she stopped smoking.

Here, we demonstrate that we can upgrade our existing fragment to one that accounts for the dynamics of presupposition projection by using the same technique as we used to get dynamics for anaphora - we're going to parameterize our continuation type constructor to *partial propositions*, i.e., $K_{S_\#}\, t$, and compose the result with our type constructor for presuppositional meanings $S_\#$, giving us the type constructor U, defined in (28). Again, a partially de-sugared definition is given in (29).

Just as before, we can define a lifter $\Uparrow$ to dynamicize meanings. When we apply generalized $\Uparrow$ to $\wedge^{\pi_G}$, we get the Stalnakerian update function $+$.

(28) $U := K_{S_\# \, t} \circ S_\#$

(29) $\mathsf{U}\,a := (\mathsf{S}_\#\,a \to \mathsf{S}_\#\,t) \to \mathsf{S}_\#\,t$

(30)   a. $(\Uparrow) := (\mathsf{S}\,t \to \mathsf{S}\,t) \to (\mathsf{U}\,t \to \mathsf{U}\,t)$

   b. $f^{\Uparrow} = \lambda p\,.\,\lambda k\,.\,(f \circ p)\,k$

(31) $(+) = \lambda q\,.\,\lambda p\,.\,\lambda k\,.\,(p \circ (\wedge) \circ q)k$

In Fig. 8 we demonstrate how this system derives a simple case of local satisfaction. Since the first conjunct entails the presupposition of the second, the complex sentence is effectively presuppositionless.

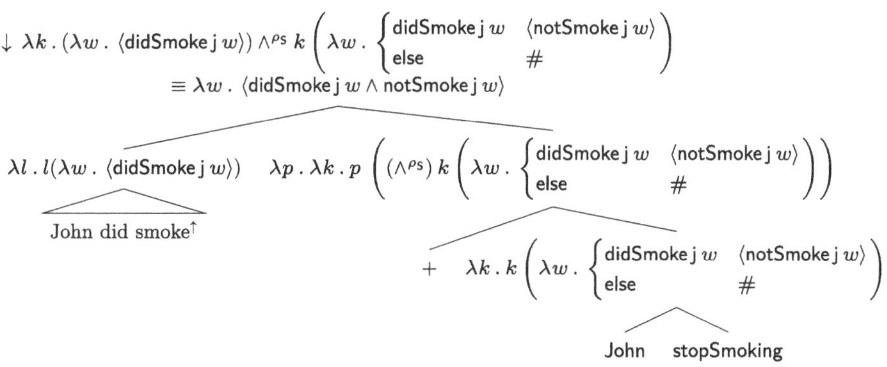

$$\downarrow \lambda k\,.\,(\lambda w\,.\,\langle \text{didSmoke}\,j\;w \rangle) \wedge^{ps} k \left(\lambda w\,.\, \begin{cases} \text{didSmoke}\,j\;w & \langle \text{notSmoke}\,j\;w \rangle \\ \text{else} & \# \end{cases} \right)$$

$$\equiv \lambda w\,.\,\langle \text{didSmoke}\,j\;w \wedge \text{notSmoke}\,j\;w \rangle$$

$$\lambda l\,.\,l(\lambda w\,.\,\langle \text{didSmoke}\,j\;w \rangle) \qquad \lambda p\,.\,\lambda k\,.\,p\left((\wedge^{ps})\,k\left(\lambda w\,.\, \begin{cases} \text{didSmoke}\,j\;w & \langle \text{notSmoke}\,j\;w \rangle \\ \text{else} & \# \end{cases}\right)\right)$$

John did smoke$^{\uparrow}$

$$+ \qquad \lambda k\,.\,k\left(\lambda w\,.\, \begin{cases} \text{didSmoke}\,j\;w & \langle \text{notSmoke}\,j\;w \rangle \\ \text{else} & \# \end{cases}\right)$$

John   stopSmoking

Fig. 8. Local satisfaction via U

4   Comparison to Charlow (2014)

Charlow's monadic grammar has a far broader empirical remit than out fairly modest goal – to decompose dynamics into scope-taking and assignment-sensitivity – allowed for. Therefore, it is difficult to compare the two directly. Nevertheless, we will attempt here to give a flavour of Charlow's approach, and point out some respects in which it differs from the applicative grammar outlined here.

One of Charlow's main goals is to provide a semantics for *indefinites* which accounts both (a) for their ability to take *exceptional scope*, and (b) their dynamic properties. At the core of Charlow's account is the `State.Set` monad, defined in (32) in terms of its `return` (32b) and `bind` (32c) functions. `State.Set` combines the `State` monad and the `Set` monad via the `StateT` monad transformer, in order to capture state-sensitivity (i.e., dynamics), and nondeterminism (i.e., indefiniteness) respectively. Indefinites are given a different semantic treatment to truly quantificational DPs – they treated as individuals with non-deterministic side-effects, as in (33). Quantificational DPs, on the other kind, must be assigned inherently scopal denotations, as in (34).

(32) a. $\text{SS}\, a ::= g \to \{\,\langle a, g\rangle\,\}$

 b. $a^\rho := \lambda g \,.\, \{\,\langle a, g\rangle\,\}$

 c. $m \ggg k := \lambda g \,.\, \displaystyle\bigcup_{\langle a, s'\rangle \in m\ s} k\, a\, s'$

(33) $\text{someone} = \lambda g \,.\, \{\, x, \widehat{gx} \mid \text{person}\ x\,\}$ $\text{SS}\ e$

(34) $\text{everyone} = \dfrac{\text{ev}\,(\lambda x [])}{x}$ $\dfrac{\text{SS}\ t}{e}$

Charlow [4] argues for a theory of *scope islands* inspired by the concept of *delimited control* in the computer science literature (see, e.g., [14]). The idea, in a nutshell, is that a scope-island is a constituent that must be completely evaluated – in other words, every continuation argument *must* be saturated. This captures the sensitivity of inherently scopal expressions, such as universals, to scope islands – the scopal side effects associated with (34) must be evaluated inside of a given scope island. Indefinites, on the other hand, trigger non-deterministic side-effects that may survive evaluation, thus capturing the ability of indefinites to take apparently exceptional scope. We suppress the details of the analysis here out of necessity.

The applicative grammar outlined here fails to make a distinction between indefinites and quantificational DPs in this respect. In fact, there is nothing to stop us from applying our *dynamicization* operator to a universal quantifier in order to yield a "dynamic" universal, as below. This must be blocked as a lexical stipulation. The exceptional status of indefinites can be considered an argument in favour of the monadic approach of Charlow [4].

(35) $\forall^d_n := \lambda p \,.\, \lambda k \,.\, \lambda g \,.\, \forall h[h[n]g \to (p\, k)h]$

5   Conclusion

In this paper, we've attempted to provide a dynamic theory of anaphora and presupposition projection that is *fully modular* in nature – in fact, the expressivity we needed to capture these phenomena was *already* implicit in our most basic applicative functors for dealing with assignment-sensitivity, scope, world-sensitivity, and partiality. We leave an elaboration of this framework to future work.

Acknowledgments. Thanks to audiences at LENLS15 and an internal ZAS workshop for their attentiveness and feedback, as well as to Simon Charlow for much useful discussion.

References

1. Asudeh, A., Giorgolo, G.: Perspectives. Semant. Pragmat. **9**, 1–57 (2016)
2. Barker, C., Shan, C.-c.: Continuations and Natural Language. Oxford University Press, Oxford (2014)
3. Charlow, S.: A modular theory of pronouns and binding
4. Charlow, S.: On the semantics of exceptional scope (2014)
5. Chierchia, G.: Dynamics of Meaning. University of Chicago Press, Chicago (1995)
6. de Groote, P.: Proceedings of SALT 16. Linguistic Society of America, pp. 1–16. Cornell University, Ithaca, NY (2006)
7. Dekker, P.: Predicate logic with anaphora. Semant. Linguist. Theory **4**, 79–95 (1994)
8. Groenendijk, J., Stokhof, M.: Dynamic predicate logic. Linguist. Philos. **14**(1), 39–100 (1991)
9. Heim, I., Kratzer, A.: Semantics in Generative Grammar. Blackwell, Malden (1998)
10. Mcbride, C., Paterson, R.: Applicative programming with effects. J. Funct. Program. **18**(1), 1–13 (2008)
11. Schlenker, P.: Local contexts. Semant. Pragm. **2**, 1–78 (2009)
12. Shan, C.-c.: Monads for natural language semantics. arXiv:cs/0205026 (2002)
13. Stalnaker, R.: Propositions. In: MacKay, A.F., Merrill, D.D. (eds.) Issues in the Philosophy of Language, pp. 79–91. Yale University Press, New Haven (1976)
14. Wadler, P.: Monads and composable continuations. LISP Symb. Comput. **7**(1), 39–55 (1994)
15. Wadler, P.: Monads for functional programming. In: Jeuring, J., Meijer, E. (eds.) AFP 1995. LNCS, vol. 925, pp. 24–52. Springer, Heidelberg (1995). https://doi.org/10.1007/3-540-59451-5_2

Switch Reference and Discourse Anaphora: Lessons from Mbyá

Guillaume Thomas[(✉)]

Department of Linguistics, University of Toronto, Toronto, ON M5S 3G3, Canada
guillaume.thomas@utoronto.ca
http://individual.utoronto.ca/gthomas

Abstract. Most analyses of Switch Reference treat it as a device that tracks the referents of pivots. Against this background, I show that Switch Reference in Mbyá (Tupí-Guaraní) can track plural discourse reference, so that its analysis must be integrated in a theory of discourse anaphora. Indeed, it appears that Same Subject marking is used when one of the pivots is a quantifier and the other refers to a set associated with the former, or both pivots are quantifiers that share the same domain. Building on these observations, I argue that Same Subject markers themselves are anaphoric to one of their pivots, and require that the other pivot introduce or retrieve a discourse referent that is identical to the value of this anaphor.

Keywords: Switch Reference ⋅ Plural discourse reference · Mbyá

1 Overview

Canonical Switch Reference indicates whether two clauses have identical or different pivots, where the pivots are prominent arguments of some sort. Although there is variation in this respect, the pivots are generally subjects, topics or agents (see [19]). Following the influential definition of Canonical Switch Reference in [11] as the marking of identity or difference of subjects, Switch Reference markers are usually called Same Subject markers (SS) or Different Subject markers (DS), regardless of the nature of the pivots.

In classical definitions of Canonical Switch Reference, identity or difference of pivots is understood as referential identity. Nevertheless, deviations from this pattern have been observed. In particular, [17,18] observe that 'Different Subject' marking may track a shift in different parameters of the events described by the two clauses, such as time, place and actuality. This phenomenon is known as Noncanonical Switch Reference. [2,16] observe that Noncanonical Switch Reference tends to be attested in coordination and clause chaining structures, while Canonical Switch Reference tends to be attested in subordination structures. [2] conclude that Canonical and Noncanonical Switch Reference might be distinct though related phenomena. In this paper, I will only discuss the former, which I will refer to simply as Switch Reference (SR).

© Springer Nature Switzerland AG 2019
K. Kojima et al. (Eds.): JSAI-isAI 2018 Workshops, LNAI 11717, pp. 270–281, 2019.
https://doi.org/10.1007/978-3-030-31605-1_20

The question that this paper addresses is that of the nature of identity and difference of pivots in SR, excluding cases of Noncanonical Switch Reference. Formally explicit theories of SR have approached pivot identity in one of three different ways. Semantically inclined analyses have treated it as identity of the pivots' referents [15,18], while syntactically inclined analyses have treated it as identity of referential indices in a syntactic representation [1,4,9] or as identity of syntactic features that entails coreference [5,20]. A third group of analyses treat SS marking as pivot sharing due to movement or VP coordination [10,12]. As we will see, this last group of analyses is not adequate for Mbyá, since two overt and lexically distinct pivots can be related by SS marking.[1] This leaves us with the first two types of analyses, and raises the question: can SS marking be analyzed as pivot co-reference?

I will argue that a coreferential analysis of SS marking is problematic, since it fails to apply to sentences where one of the pivots is a quantifier and the other is anaphoric to a set associated with the former. This configuration is illustrated in (1):

(1) Mbovy'i tekoapygua kuery o-mba'apo vy, no-mo-mba   voi-i.
     few   villager   PL   A3-work   SS   NEG-CAUS-finish quick-NEG

'Since few villagers were working, they didn't finish quickly.'

In Mbyá, the pivots of SR constructions are subjects. In example (1), the matrix subject is anaphoric to the intersection of the restriction and nuclear scope of the subordinate quantifier. The two pivots are not co-referential, since the subordinate subject does not refer. For the same reason, it cannot be said that this subject bears a referential index *stricto sensu*.

In addition, it will be shown that SR in Mbyá is sensitive to the type of plural discourse anaphora that relates the pivots. Quantificational structures $D(A)(B)$ may give rise to two types of plural discourse anaphora. A subsequent anaphor may refer to the maximal set A or to the reference set $A \cap B$. We will see that both types of anaphora may trigger SS marking in Mbyá. Studies of anaphora to quantifier sets also discuss anaphora to the complement set $A-B$, whose existence is debated. It has been argued that complement set anaphora is a form of contextually restricted anaphora to the domain set [6], or is due to an inferential process that does not depend on the introduction of discourse referents for the complement set [14]. Accordingly, we will see that reference to the complement set tends to trigger DS marking in Mbyá.

In light of such facts, I will argue that SR in Mbyá is best analyzed as tracking discourse reference. SS markers are anaphoric to one of their pivots, and require that the other pivot introduce or retrieve a discourse referent that is identical to the value of this anaphor. DS markers are used otherwise.

---

[1] In addition, if the generalization that Canonical SR is attested in subordination structure is correct, [12]'s analysis of Same Subject and Different Subject marking as vP (high) or VP (low) coordination may be valid for Noncanonical but not for Canonical Switch Reference.

Note that existing analyses of switch-reference have observed that quantifiers are attested in SR constructions [10,15]. However, previous discussions of this fact were limited to examples like (2) and (3), which can be analyzed by letting a single quantifier bind the two pivot positions. This is indeed how [10,15] analyze such examples:

(2) Háun hájél   èm   gúnmáuchè̱   èm   dáujàugù̱.
     NEG   person.INDEF [3S.RF] dance-IMP=when.SS [3S.RF] sing+act-NEG

     'Nobody₁ sang while they₁ danced.' [15]

(3) Minyma tjuta-ngku pu_nu atu-ra   nyina-nyi.
     woman many-ERG wood chop-ANT(MERG) sit-PRES

     'Many women would be sitting around making wooden artefacts.' [10]

By contrast, it will be shown that SS marking of anaphora to quantifiers in Mbyá must be analyzed as true discourse anaphora, since giving wide scope to the quantified subject would generate incorrect truth conditions. Consequently, an adequate theory of SR must be dynamic or resort to E-type anaphora. In this paper, I will pursue a dynamic analysis.

2   Switch Reference in Mbyá: Referential Pivots

Background on Mbyá. Mbyá is a Tupí-Guaraní language spoken by approximately 30,000 speakers in Argentina, Brazil and Paraguay. The data discussed in this paper come from two sources: Robert Dooley's description of SR [7], and elicitation sessions conducted by the author with four native speakers of Mbyá from Misiones (Argentina). Note that Dooley's description is based on data collected in the state of Paraná (Brazil) in the 1970s and 1980s. However, the Mbyá consultants I worked with agreed with the judgments reported in Dooley's work. Example from Dooley's work are referenced as such. All other examples were produced by the Mbyá speakers who worked with the author.

Some remarks on Mbyá grammar are in order. Verbs are not inflected for tense and aspect. In the absence of additional tense/aspect/modality markers, such 'bare verbs' have non-future temporal reference and are underspecified for viewpoint aspect. There are no definite and indefinite articles, and bare nouns may be interpreted as definite or indefinite descriptions. Subject or object arguments are cross-referenced on the verb using a split-S system known as active/inactive or active/stative. While the cross-referencing of one argument on the verb is mandatory, both null subjects and null objects are frequently attested. The reader is referred to [8] for a description of this system in Mbyá, and to [21] for its description in Paraguayan Guaraní, a closely related language.

Since I will propose that the pivots of SR in Mbyá are subjects, I should point out that some authors have argued that the grammar of Guaraní languages does not make use of the grammatical functions subject and object [21]. There is however solid evidence for a grammatically relevant opposition between subjects and objects in Mbyá, as reviewed in [8]. I will not review these arguments here, and I refer the reader to Sect. 7.1 of [8] instead.

Structure of Switch Reference. SR in Mbyá is marked by the particles *vy* (SS) and *ramo* (DS) or its reduced form *rã*, both of which occur in the right periphery of the predicate of the marked clause:

(4) Juan o-vaẽ   vy, o-mo-potĩ   ta   ng-oo.
     Juan A3-arrive SS A3-CAUS-clean PROSP REFL-house

     'When Juan$_1$ arrives, he$_{1/*2}$ will clean his$_{1/*2}$ house.'

(5) Maria o-vaẽ   rã/*vy, Juan o-mo-potĩ   ta   oo.
     Maria A3-arrive DS/SS   Juan A3-CAUS-clean PROSP house

     'When Maria arrives, Juan will clean the house.'

As these examples illustrate, there is no indication of the structural relation between the marked clause and the reference clause, beyond the presence of the SR marker itself. Furthermore, SR marking underspecifies the semantic relation between the two clauses: the marked clause may be notably interpreted as the antecedent of a conditional, as a temporal modifier (a '*when*-clause') or it may express a reason or cause of the event described by the reference clause. Dooley demonstrates that the marked clause is subordinate to the reference clause in [8], Sect. 21.2.2. In particular, Dooley observes that (i) the order of the two clauses need not reflect the order of events they describe, (ii) the marked clause verb is defective in the range of functional particles that it accepts (most tense, aspect, modality, negation and interrogation markers are unattested or have a restricted distribution in the marked clause), and (iii) SR constructions are not subject to the Coordinate Structure Constraint on question formation (Sect. 21.2.1.9).

Relation Between Pivots. [7] demonstrates that the pivots of SR in Mbyá are subjects, rather than agents or topics. Again, I refer the reader to this work for relevant examples and discussion.

Let us first put aside quantificational pivots and only consider referential ones. When the two pivots are coreferential, SS marking is used. If they have disjoint reference, DS marking is used instead. See examples (4) and (5) for illustration.

More interesting are cases of overlapping reference. [7] argues that SS marking is used when the referent of one pivot is included in that of the other one, provided the two pivots agree in person and clusivity. Example (6) from our own fieldwork appears to support this conclusion. Example (7) suggests that the two pivots must indeed agree in grammatical person:

(6) Juan ha'upei Maria o-vaẽ   vy/*rã, Juan o-mo-potĩ   oo.
     Juan and   Maria A3-arrive SS/DS   Juan A3-CAUS-clean house

     'When Juan and Maria arrived, Juan cleaned the house.'

(7) Nhande nha-vaẽ   rã/*vy, re-mo-potĩ   ta   oo.
     we.INCL A1.PL.INCL-arrive DS/SS   A2.SG-CAUS-clean PROSP house

     'When we[INCL] arrive, you[SG] will clean the house.'

However, examples like the following show that this generalization is too weak:

(8)   Context: A drunk *jurua* (non-indigenous person) caused trouble in the Guaraní village. Juan is one of the villagers who frequently represents the village in negotiations with *jurua* authorities.

I-pochy   rã/*vy tekoapygua kuery, Juan i-jayvu ta   policia pe.
B3-angry DS/SS villager   PL   Juan B3-talk PROSP police DOM

'Since the villagers are angry, Juan will talk to the police.'

Both matrix subjects have referents that are included in the denotation of the subordinate subject ('the villagers'), yet DS marking must be used. This suggests that it is not referential inclusion itself that licenses SS marking in an example like (6). Instead, one notes that in this example, the subordinate subject *Juan ha'upei Maria* makes *Juan* salient enough to serve as the antecedent of a subsequent anaphoric pronoun. By contrast, the subordinate subject in (8) does not make any particular villager salient. This phenomenon is illustrated in English by the following examples:

(9)   When Maria and Juan$_1$ arrive, he$_1$ will clean the house.

(10)   If the villagers are angry, he$_?$ will talk to the police.

In view of this fact, I would like to suggest that SS markers in Mbyá require that the referent of one of the pivots be identical to the value of an acceptable anaphoric mention of the other:

(11)   Switch Reference marking (preliminary):
        In a structure [[S$_1$ *vy/rã*] S$_0$], the SR marker *vy/rã* introduces a covert pronoun *pro$_{SR}$*. The use of SS marking is acceptable only if:
        1.   subject(S$_0$) and subject(S$_1$) agree in grammatical person and
        2.   *pro$_{SR}$* is anaphoric to subject(S$_1$) and $[\![pro_{SR}]\!]^{M,g} = [\![\text{Subject}(S_0)]\!]^{M,g}$.
        DS marking is used when SS marking is unacceptable.

In example (6), the subordinate subject conjunct *Juan ha'upei Maria* is the antecedent of *pro$_{SR}$*, which has the same denotation as the matrix subject. SS marking is acceptable since the conjoined phrase *Juan ha'upei Maria* licenses anaphoric reference to Juan. By contrast, the plural subject *tekoapygua kuery* in (8) does not provide an antecedent for the SR marker that has the same denotation as the matrix subject. The analysis correctly predicts that SS marking of partially overlapping subjects is unacceptable:

(12)   Maria ha'upei Pedro o-vaẽ   rã/*vy, Juan ha'upei Maria
        Maria and   Pedro A3-arrive DS/SS Juan and   Maria
        o-mo-potĩ   oo.
        A3-CAUS-clean house

        'When Maria and Pedro arrived, Juan and Maria cleaned the house.'

Indeed, let us assume that the SR marker in (12) is anaphoric to the subordinate subject. Its possible antecedents are Maria, Pedro and their sum. None of these individuals has a referent that is identical to the denotation of the matrix subject, which is the sum of Juan and Maria. Consequently, SS marking is unacceptable.

The proposed analysis also captures patterns of SS marking with disjunctions of referential subjects:

(13)   Context: Juan and Maria are married and each bought a lottery ticket:

Juan e'ỹvy Maria o-gana vy/*rã, Maria o-jogua ta   auto pyau.
Juan or   Maria A3-win SS/DS, Maria A3-buy PROSP car   new

'If Juan or Maria wins (the lottery), Maria will buy a new car.'

(14)   Context: Juan and Maria are married; Maria bought a lottery ticket:

Maria o-gana rã/*vy, ha'e e'ỹvy Juan o-jogua ta   auto pyau.
Maria A3-win DS/SS, 3   or   Juan A3-buy PROSP car   new

'If Maria wins (the lottery), she or Juan will buy a new car.'

The subordinate subject in (13) makes two antecedents available to the anaphoric SR marker: *Juan* and *Maria*. The latter is identical to the matrix subject, which licenses SS marking. Crucially, the disjoined subject is not referential, which supports the conclusion that the expression whose reference is compared to that of the matrix subject is the disjunct *Maria*, rather than the whole disjoined subject *Juan e'ỹvy Maria*.

Finally, [7] observes cases of SS with seemingly expletive subjects of weather predicates and verbs in the 'impersonal' voice, see examples (15a) and (15b). However, a closer look at these two classes of predicates reveals that they both have implicit subjects, which can control into purpose clauses, as illustrated in (16a) and (16b):

(15)   a.   O-mombe'u-a va'e-rã   ha'e o-japo va'e-kue hexe i-ma'endu'a
            A3-tell-IMPRS REL-FUT 3   A3-do REL-PAST 3.OBL B3-remember
            vy.
            SS

            'They will tell what she has done, remembering her.' [7]

       b.   Arai vaipa, oky-xe   vy.
            cloud much rain-DES SS

            'It's very cloudy, since it's wanting to rain.' [7]

(16)   a.   Arai oky agũã.
            cloud rain PURP

            (Lit.) 'It's cloudy in order to rain.'

       b.   Oga   o-mo-ngai-a   i-ja   pe   o-juka agũã.
            house A3-CAUS-burn-IMPRS B3-OWNER DOM A3-kill PURP

            'The house was burned to kill the owner.'

Note that the nature of the implicit subjects of weather predicates is not directly relevant to this paper; what is relevant is that they do refer. This being said, I will assume following [13] that these arguments play the role of a 'source,' similar to subjects of emission verbs.

3   Quantificational Pivots

Anaphora to Quantifier Sets. The pivots of SR constructions may be quantifiers. Importantly, SR marking of quantified subjects is not restricted to constructions where a single quantifier binds the two pivot positions. SS marking is also used when one of the pivots is anaphoric to a set associated with a quantifier that occupies the other pivot position. This is illustrated by examples (17) and (18):

(17)   Mbovy'i tekoapygua i-jayvu   kuaa español py vy, o-mba'apo tekoa
       few   villager   B3-speak know Spanish in SS A3-work   village
       py.
       in

       'Since few of the villagers can speak Spanish, they work in the village.'

(18)   Heta   tekoapygua i-jayvu kuaa español py, ha'e ...
       many villager   B3-talk know spanish in   and

       'Many villagers speak Spanish, and ...'

   a   #mbovy'i i-jayvu   kuaa español py vy o-mba'apo tekoa   py.
       few   B3-speak know spanish in SS A3-work   village in

       '#since few of them speak Spanish, they work in the village.'

   b   mbovy'i i-jayvu   kuaa va'e español py o-mba'apo tekoa   py.
       few   B3-speak know REL spanish in A3-work   village in

       'few of those who speak Spanish work in the village.'

Sentence (17) is an example of maximal set anaphora[2]. If the quantifier *mbovy'i tekoapygua* took scope over the whole sentence, (18a) should be a felicitous continuation of (18), like (18b). The fact that it isn't demonstrates that the matrix subject of example (17) is anaphoric to the subordinate quantified subject.

SS marking with quantified subjects is attested with maximal set and referent set anaphora, as illustrated respectively by examples (19) and (20):

(19)   Mava'eve tekoapygua nda-i-jayvu   kuaa-i   español py vy, (ha'e
       no   villager   NEG-B3-speak know-NEG Spanish in SS, 3
       kuery) nd-o-o-i   tetã my.
       PL   NEG-A3-go-NEG city in

       'Since none of the villagers speak Spanish, they don't go to the city.'

---

[2] This example could arguably be analyzed as a case of complement set anaphora, but we will see that clearer cases of reference to the complement set by an overt matrix subject tend to trigger DS marking, which makes it more likely that *vy* marks anaphora to the maximal set in this example.

(20) Heta tekoapygua i-jayvu   kuaa español py vy, o-i-pytyvõ   amboae
      many villager   B3-speak know Spanish in SS A3-OBJ-help other
      kuery o-mbo-jovai   aguã jurua kuery reve.
      PL   A3-CAUS-opposed PURP jurua PL   with

      'Since many villagers speak Spanish, they help the other ones deal with
      the juruas.'

By contrast, reference to the complement set of a quantificational pivot tends
to trigger DS marking.[3] This is true even with downward entailing proportional
quantifiers, which have been argued to license anaphora to complement sets in
English (see [14]):

(21) Mbovy'i kyri-ngue o-guereko telefono celular rã/*vy, nd-o-guereko-i
      few   child-PL A3-have phone cell   DS/SS NEG-A3-have-NEG
      va'e kuery o-motare'ỹ ha'e kuery pe.
      REL PL   A3-envy   3   PL   DOM

      'Since few children have a cell phone, those who don't are jealous of them.'

Finally, the following example shows that SS marking is also licensed by
cataphora to quantifier sets:

(22) Nda-i-jayvu   kuaa-i   español py vy, mbovy'i tekoapygua o-o   tetã
      NEG-B3-speak know-NEG Spanish in SS few   villager   A3-go city
      my.
      in

      'Because they don't speak Spanish, few villagers go to the city.'

Introducing Discourse Reference. The analysis of SS marking sketched in (11)
states that the covert pronoun that is anaphoric to one of the pivots must have
a referent that is identical to the denotation of the other pivot. However, SS
marking is attested in sentences with two quantificational pivots, as illustrated
in (23). This is problematic for the current analysis, since neither subject is
referential:

(23) Heta tekoapygua i-jayvu   kuaa español py vy, mbovy'i o-mba'apo
      many villager   B3-speak know Spanish in SS, few   A3-work
      tekoa py.
      village in

      'Since many villagers speak Spanish, few of them work in the village.'

In order to address this issue, I propose that SR marking is sensitive to the
discourse referents introduced or retrieved by the pivots, rather than to their

---

[3] A previous version of this work, which was based on the judgments of a single
speaker, reported that reference to the complement set could trigger SS marking.
Subsequent elicitation with four speakers of Mbyá suggests that this phenomenon is
marginal at best.

actual referents. Following [3], I assume that generalized quantifiers introduce two discourse referents. One of them corresponds to the maximal set, and the other to the reference set. By contrast, generalized quantifiers never introduce a discourse referent for their complement set (see [14]).

SR marking can now be analyzed as follows:

(24) Same Subject marking (preliminary):
      In a structure $[[\ S_1\ vy/r\tilde{a}\ ]\ S_0]$, the SR marker $vy/r\tilde{a}$ introduces a covert pronoun pro_{SR}. The use of SS marking is acceptable only if:

      1. subject(S_0) and subject(S_1) agree in grammatical person and

      2. pro_{SR} is anaphoric to subject(S_1) and the discourse referent it retrieves is identical to a discourse referent introduced or retrieved by subject(S_0).

      DS marking is used when SS marking is unacceptable.

In example (23), both quantified subjects introduce discourse referents for their maximal set and their reference set. The covert SR pronoun is anaphoric to the maximal set of the subordinate quantifier, i.e. the set of villagers. Since this set corresponds to one of the two discourse referents introduced (or, in the case of the maximal set, retrieved) by the matrix subject, SS marking is acceptable. As one expects, using disjoint restrictions for the two quantifiers prevents the use of SS marking:

(25) Mbovy'i tekoapygua i-jayvu   kuaa español py rã/*vy, heta
      few   villager   B3-speak know Spanish in DS/SS   many
      jurua   kuery ha'e kuery reve nda-i-jayvu-i.
      non.indigenous PL   3   PL   with NEG-B3-speak-NEG
      'Since few villagers speak Spanish, many juruas don't talk to them.'

Note that the constraint on SS marking introduced in (24) must be strengthened to account for the unacceptability of SS marking with partially overlapping conjoined subjects, which was illustrated in (12) and is repeated here as (26):

(26) Maria ha'upei Pedro o-vaẽ   rã/*vy, Juan ha'upei Maria
      Maria and   Pedro A3-arrive DS/SS   Juan and   Maria
      o-mo-potĩ   oo.
      A3-CAUS-clean house
      'When Maria and Pedro arrived, Juan and Maria cleaned the house.'

The conjoined phrase *Juan ha'upei Maria* introduces three discourse referents: one for Juan, one for Maria, and one for their sum. Yet, SS marking is unacceptable, which shows that the antecedent of the SR marker cannot be compared to just any discourse referent introduced by the conjuncts of the matrix subject. In order to account for this restriction, we require that the SR anaphor be compared to the discourse referent associated with the whole subject:

(27) Switch Reference marking:

In a structure $[[\ S_1\ vy/r\tilde{a}\ ]\ S_0]$, the SR marker $vy/r\tilde{a}$ introduces a covert pronoun pro_{SR}. The use of SS marking is acceptable only if:

1. subject(S_0) and subject(S_1) agree in grammatical person and

2. pro_{SR} is anaphoric to subject(S_1) and the discourse referent it retrieves is identical to the discourse referent introduced or retrieved by the maximal projection of the subject(S_0).

DS marking is used when SS marking is unacceptable.

When the subject is a conjunction of referential terms, I posit that its maximal projection introduces a discourse referent for the sum of the conjuncts. This explains the unacceptability of SS marking in (26): none of the three possible antecedents of the SR anaphor (Maria, Pedro and their sum) is identical to the sum of Juan and Maria, which is the value of the discourse referent associated with the matrix subject. When the subject is a quantifier, I hypothesize that its associated discourse referent stores its maximal set. This accounts for the acceptability of SS marking of sentences with two quantificational subjects that share the same maximal set, as illustrated in (23).

There is therefore an asymmetry in the identification of the two discourse referents that SS markers compare. One of them is retrieved by a process of anaphora, whose antecedent must be found within a domain delineated by one of the pivots. When this pivot is a conjoined phrase or a quantifier, it may introduce several discourse referents that can serve as antecedents. The other discourse referent that enters the comparison is not retrieved by anaphora. Rather, it is assumed to be the unique discourse referent that is syntactically associated with the maximal projection of the other pivot: for quantifiers, the discourse referent of their maximal set, for conjoined DPs, the discourse referent for the sum of the conjuncts.

4   Conclusion

Patterns of SS and DS marking in Mbyá present a challenge to existing analyses of SR, which tend to assume that pivot identity is a form of coreference or pivot sharing. In this paper, I showed that SS marking is sensitive to discourse anaphora. In one set of examples, SS marking is triggered when one pivot refers to the maximal set or reference set of another quantificational pivot. In another set of examples, SS marking is triggered when two quantificational pivots share the same maximal set. I sketched an analysis of these facts that may be amenable to a more rigorous implementation in dynamic semantics. The details of this analysis will be fleshed out in future research.

Acknowledgement. Many thanks to the Mbyá speakers who shared their judgments with me for this study. I am also grateful to Philippe Schlenker and Yasutada Sudo for helpful comments and suggestions. All errors are mine.

Glosses. A: cross-referenced argument, class A (active); B: cross-referenced argument, class B (inactive); CAUS: causative; DES: desiderative; DS: different subject marking; DOM: differential object marking; FUT: future temporal marking; INCL: inclusive; IMPRS: impersonal voice; NEG: negation; OBJ: object marking; OBL: oblique; PAST: past temporal marking; PL: plural; PURP: purpose; PROSP: prospective aspect; SG: singular; SS: same subject marking.

References

1. Arregui, C. Hanink E.: Switch reference in Washo as multiple subject agreement. In: NELS 48: Proceedings of the Forty-Eighth Annual Meeting of the North East Linguistic Society. GLSA, Amherst (2018, to appear)
2. Baker, M., Souza C.: Switch-reference in American languages: a synthetic overview. In: Siddiqi D., Barrie M., Coon J., Gillon C., Haugen J.D., Matthieu E. (eds.) The Routledge Handbook of North American Languages. Routledge (2017, to appear)
3. Brasoveanu, A.: Structured anaphora to quantifier domains. Inf. Comput. **208**, 450–473 (2010)
4. Broadwell, G.A.: Binding theory and switch reference. In: Bennis, H., Picaand, P., Rooryck, J. (eds.) Atomism and Binding, pp. 31–49. Foris, Dordrecht (1997)
5. Camacho, J.: On case concord: the syntax of switch-reference clauses. Nat. Lang. Linguist. Theory **28**, 239–274 (2010)
6. Corblin, F.: Quantification et anaphore discursive: la référence aux complémentaires. Langages **123**, 51–74 (1996)
7. Dooley, R.A.: Switch reference in Mbyá Guaraní: a fair-weather phenomenon. Work Papers of the Summer Institute of Linguistics, University of North Dakota Session vol. 33, pp. 93–119 (1989)
8. Dooley, R.A.: Léxico Guaraní, dialeto Mbyá, com informações úteis para o ensino médio, a aprendizagem e a pesquisa lingüística. Brazil, Cuiabá: Sociedade Internacional de Lingüística (2013)
9. Finer, D.: The syntax of switch-reference. Linguist. Inq. **16**, 35–55 (1985)
10. Georgi, D.: Switch-reference by movement. In: Weisser, P. (ed.) Perspectives on Switch-reference: Local Modeling and Empirical Distribution, pp. 1–40. Institut für Linguistik, Leipzig (2012)
11. Haiman, J. Munro P.: Introduction. In: Haiman J., Munro P. (eds.) Switch Reference and Universal Grammar, pp. ix–xv. John Benjamins, Amsterdam (1983)
12. Keine, S.: Deconstructing switch-reference. Nat. Lang. Linguist. Theory **31**(3), 767–826 (2013)
13. Levin, B.: Event encoding in a crosslinguistic perspective IV: talking about the weather. Handout of a course given at the Language Society of America Institute, Summer (2015)
14. Nouwen, R.: Plural pronominal anaphora in context. Ph.D. dissertation. UiL-OTS. Utrecht University. LOT Dissertation Series 84 (2003)
15. McKenzie, A.: The role of contextual restriction in reference tracking, Ph.D. dissertation. University of Massachusetts, Amherst (2012)
16. McKenzie, A.: A survey of switch-reference in North America. Int. J. Am. Linguist. **81**, 409–448 (2015)
17. Roberts, J.R.: Amele switch-reference and the theory of grammar. Linguist. Inq. **19**(1), 45–63 (1988)
18. Stirling, L.: Switch-Reference and Discourse Representation. Cambridge University Press, Cambridge (1993)

19. van Gijn, R.: Switch-reference: an overview. In: van Gijn, R., Hammond, J. (eds.) Switch-Reference 2.0: Typological Studies in Language, vol. 114 (2016)
20. Watanabe, A.: Feature copying and binding: evidence from complementizer agreement and switch reference. Syntax **3**(3), 159–181 (2000)
21. Velázquez-Castillo, M.: Grammatical relations in active systems. The case of Guaraní. Funct. Lang. **9**(2), 133–167 (2002)

Reconciling Inquisitive Semantics and Generalized Quantifier Theory

Ka-fat Chow$^{(\boxtimes)}$

The Hong Kong Polytechnic University, Kowloon, Hong Kong
kfzhouy@yahoo.com

Abstract. This paper proposes a new treatment of quantifiers under the theoretical framework of Inquisitive Semantics (IS). After discussing the difficulty in treating quantifiers under the existing IS framework, I propose a new treatment of quantifiers that combines features of IS and the Generalized Quantifier Theory (GQT). My proposal comprises two main points: (i) assuming that the outputs of all quantifiers given non-inquisitive inputs are non-inquisitive; and (ii) deriving a predicate X^* of type $s \rightarrow (e^n \rightarrow t)$ corresponding to each predicate X of type $e^n \rightarrow T$. By using X^*, we can then restore the traditional treatment of GQT under the IS framework. I next point out that to properly handle the pair list reading of some questions with "every", we have to revert to the old treatment of *every*. I also introduce (and prove) a theorem that shows that the new treatment of *every* is just a special case of the old treatment, and conclude that the new treatment of all quantifiers other than *every* plus the old treatment of *every* is sufficient for the general purpose of treating quantified statements and questions.

Keywords: Inquisitive Semantics · Generalized Quantifier Theory · Inquisitiveness · Pair list reading

1 Basic Notions of IS

In the 2010s, Inquisitive Semantics (IS) has risen to become an influential theory that provides a uniform treatment for declaratives and interrogatives. To facilitate subsequent discussion in this paper, I first introduce some basic notions of IS. Under IS, there are three tiers of notions that are based on possible worlds. The first tier consists of the possible worlds (hereinafter "worlds") themselves with type s. The second tier consists of information states (hereinafter "states"), which are sets of worlds, with type $s \rightarrow t$. The third tier consists of propositions, which are non-empty sets of states, i.e. sets of sets of worlds, with type $(s \rightarrow t) \rightarrow t$, that satisfy downward closure, i.e. whenever a state belongs to a proposition p, then all subsets of that state also belong to p. For convenience, the symbol T is often used as an abbreviation of the type $(s \rightarrow t) \rightarrow t$.

Let p be a proposition and let's assume that every proposition discussed in this paper consists of a finite number of states (which is a standard assumption

© Springer Nature Switzerland AG 2019
K. Kojima et al. (Eds.): JSAI-isAI 2018 Workshops, LNAI 11717, pp. 282–297, 2019.
https://doi.org/10.1007/978-3-030-31605-1_21

in the IS literature). The alternatives of p are the maximal states of p, i.e. those states that are not proper subsets of other states. We say that p is informative iff[1] $\bigcup p \neq W$, where W represents the set of all worlds. We say that p is inquisitive iff p consists of more than one alternative. Apart from the usual set operations such as $\cup$ and $\cap$, there are also two special set operations under IS, namely the relative pseudo-complement (represented by $\triangleright$) and the absolute pseudo-complement (represented by $\sim$), which can be defined as follows (in what follows, p and q are propositions, $Power(S)$ represents the power set of the set S):

$$p \triangleright q = \{i \in Power(W) : Power(i) \cap p \subseteq q\} \tag{1}$$

$$\sim p = Power(W - \bigcup p) \tag{2}$$

There are also two projection operators: the ! and ? operators, whose functions are to turn any proposition into an assertion (which is defined as a non-inquisitive proposition under IS) and a question (which is defined as a non-informative proposition under IS), respectively. These two operators can be defined as follows:

$$!p = Power(\bigcup p) \tag{3}$$

$$?p = p \cup \sim p \tag{4}$$

2 Treatment of Sub-sentential Constituents Under IS

In recent years, attempts have been made under IS to treat sub-sentential constituents. The types of these constituents are all based on the type of propositions, i.e. T. For example, the types of unary and, in general, n-ary predicates are $e{\rightarrow}T$ and $e^n{\rightarrow}T$,[2] respectively. Moreover, it is assumed under IS that all simple n-ary predicates (i.e. predicates with no internal structure) are non-inquisitive, i.e. the outputs of these functions are non-inquisitive propositions. For illustration, let's consider the following model.[3]

Model M1

$U = \{john, mary\}$
$W = \{w_1, w_2, w_3, w_4\}$
$sing = john \mapsto \{\{w_1, w_2\}, \{w_1\}, \{w_2\}, \emptyset\};$
$\quad\quad\quad mary \mapsto \{\{w_1, w_3\}, \{w_1\}, \{w_3\}, \emptyset\}$

One may check that the unary predicate $sing$ given above is a function with type $e{\rightarrow}T$. For each member x of U, this function maps x to the power set

---

[1] In this paper, I use "iff" to represent "if and only if".

[2] In this paper, I adopt the uncurried form of n-ary predicates, i.e. the input of an n-ary predicate is an n-tuple. Here I use e^n to represent the type of n-tuples of entities with type e.

[3] In what follows, the symbol $\mapsto$ is used to represent the "maps to" relation between the input and output of a function.

of the set of worlds in which "x sang" is true. Since this is the power set of a set, it contains only one alternative and is thus non-inquisitive. Now consider $?(sing(john))$, which can be used to represent the question "Did John sing?". By using the definitions given above, one can calculate

$$?(sing(john)) = \{\{w_1, w_2\}, \{w_3, w_4\}, \{w_1\}, \{w_2\}, \{w_3\}, \{w_4\}, \emptyset\} \qquad (5)$$

Note that the above result does have the form of a proposition, i.e. a non-empty set of sets of worlds satisfying downward closure. Moreover, since $\bigcup ?(sing(john)) = W$, this proposition is non-informative, i.e. a question. It has two alternatives, i.e. $\{w_1, w_2\}$, and $\{w_3, w_4\}$, which represent the two possible answers to the question "Did John sing?". For example, $\{w_1, w_2\}$ represents the answer "Yes" because w_1 and w_2 are exactly the worlds in which "John sang" is true under M1.

Quantifiers, an important subtype of sub-sentential constituents, are also treated in the recent IS literature. However, the treatment of quantifiers under IS as in [2, 3, 11] is different from the traditional treatment under the Generalized Quantifier Theory (GQT). For example, the denotation of *every* is written in [2, 3] as:

$$every = \lambda X \lambda Y \left[\bigcap_{x \in U} (X(x) \triangleright Y(x)) \right] \qquad (6)$$

which looks quite different from that given in standard GQT literature (such as [8, 10]):

$$every = \lambda X \lambda Y [X \subseteq Y] \qquad (7)$$

Of course one may argue that the difference between (6) and (7) is superficial because the denotation in (6) is in fact a "translation" of the following first order statement into the IS language: $\forall x \in U[X(x) \rightarrow Y(x)]$ (by "translating" $\forall$ and $\rightarrow$ to $\bigcap$ and $\triangleright$, respectively), which is equivalent to the set theoretic statement $X \subseteq Y$. But not all quantified statements have equivalent first order statements. Consider the denotation of the quantifier *most*:

$$most = \lambda X \lambda Y \left[\frac{|X \cap Y|}{|X|} > \frac{1}{2} \right] \qquad (8)$$

According to modern GQT studies (e.g. [10]), a quantified statement with *most* cannot be rewritten as a first order statement. Thus, it is not known under the existing IS framework how *most* should be treated. A consequence of this is that some quantifiers that have been successfully treated under GQT may not be treated in a comparably elegant way under the existing IS framework.

Moreover, there is also the issue of inquisitiveness of quantifiers. Note that the output of *every* is non-inquisitive if both of its arguments are non-inquisitive, and is in general inquisitive if at least one argument is inquisitive. This property which looks quite complicated is useful for handling the "pair list" reading of some questions with "every", which will be discussed in detail in Sect. 4.

What about the other quantifiers? As will be elaborated in more detail in Sect. 4, for constituent questions with quantifiers other than *every*, there does not exist a reading similar to the "pair list" reading in which the quantifier takes a wider scope than the WH-word. Thus, for all quantifiers other than *every*, we may assume a simpler property in terms of their inquisitiveness.

3   Proposed New Treatment of Quantifiers

3.1   The Proposal

Under the existing IS framework, the quantifier *some* is treated differently than *every* in that the output of *some* is necessarily inquisitive regardless of the inquisitiveness of its input. This property is similar to that of the propositional function *or*, whose output is also necessarily inquisitive regardless of the inquisitiveness of its input. In the current IS literature (such as [1]), the similar treatment of *or* and *some* is seen as an advantage because it provides a basis for explaining the close connection between *or* and *some* (in that a statement with *some* as quantifiers can be reformulated as a generalized disjunctive statement, e.g. $some(X)(Y) = \bigvee_{x \in X} Y(x)$) as well as the use of the same morphemes (such as Malayalam *-oo* and Japanese *ka* as recorded in [1]) in words for *or* and *some* in many languages.

While the existing treatment of *some* under IS has some advantage, it also brings in a disadvantage. Despite the close connection between *or* and *some*, these two logical operators also have an important difference in terms of the kinds of questions that they can form. On the one hand, some questions with "or" is ambiguous between an alternative question and a polar question. Consider the question "Did Mary or Susan sing?". The most prominent reading of this question is an alternative question which asks which of Mary and Susan sang. But this question can also be (less prominently) interpreted as a polar question which asks whether it was the case that either Mary or Susan sang. Both of the above readings can be represented under the existing IS framework as shown below (in what follows, the denotation of *or* is the set union operation):

$$\text{Alternative question reading: } or(sing(mary), sing(susan)) \qquad (9)$$
$$\text{Polar question reading: } ?(!(or(sing(mary), sing(susan)))) \qquad (10)$$

Note that in (9) above the sole existence of *or* is sufficient to make the whole proposition inquisitive. In (10) above, the ! operator suppresses the inquisitiveness of the proposition $or(sing(mary), sing(susan))$ and turns it into a disjunctive assertion. The ? operator then turns this assertion into a polar question about the disjunction.

On the other hand, questions with "some" does not exhibit the ambiguity as found in questions with "or". Consider the question "Did some girl sing?" (or more naturally, "Did any girl sing?" where "some" is replaced by the negative polarity item "any"). Unlike the question with "or" above, this question can only be interpreted as a polar question which asks whether there was any girl who sang, and cannot be interpreted as a constituent question which asks which of the girls in the context sang. Thus, this question can only be represented as (under the existing IS framework, the denotation of *some* is $\lambda X \lambda Y [\bigcup_{x \in U} X(x) \cap Y(x)]$):

$$?(!(some(girl)(sing)))\qquad(11)$$

and cannot be represented as

$$some(girl)(sing)\qquad(12)$$

But under the existing IS framework, there is no way to ban the above representation.

To avoid the aforesaid difficulty, I propose that we abandon the similar treatments of *or* and *some* and assume that the outputs of all quantifiers given non-inquisitive inputs are non-inquisitive. In this way, all quantifiers can be treated in a similar fashion. Note that this strategy is adequate for the usual purpose of treating quantified statements, unless we are considering the pair list reading or studying some special semantic-pragmatic aspects of some quantifiers, such as the study in [4].

But what about the connection between *or* and *some*? Note that this connection is valid only when viewed from a certain perspective. From another perspective, one will find that *some* is connected with *and* rather than *or*. After all, the denotation of *some* under GQT involves the $\cap$ rather than the $\cup$ operator. In fact, as argued in [9], if we interpret propositions as subsets of a universe comprising only one element, x say, then all true propositions and false propositions can be interpreted as $\{x\}$ and $\emptyset$, respectively, and we have $p \wedge q \equiv 1$ iff $p \cap q \neq \emptyset$. Thus, under this interpretation, $\wedge$ plays the same role as the quantifier *some*. This shows that *some* can be said to have a close connection with either *or* or *and*, depending on one's perspective. There is thus no strong reason that *or* and *some* must be treated similarly under a semantic theory, and my proposal of abandoning the similar treatments of *or* and *some* is justified[4].

Having made the aforesaid assumption, I next observe that a simple n-ary predicate under IS, whose output is the power set of a set of worlds, in fact contains a lot of redundant information. For example, in the denotation of *sing* given in Model M1 above, the output of $sing(john)$ is $\{\{w_1, w_2\}, \{w_1\}, \{w_2\}, \emptyset\}$, which contains redundant information because $\{w_1, w_2\}$ alone can tell us that John sang in w_1 and w_2. By eliminating the redundancy, we can derive predicates with a simpler type, i.e. $s \rightarrow (e^n \rightarrow t)$. More specifically, corresponding to each n-ary predicate X with type $e^n \rightarrow T$, there is a predicate X^* with type $s \rightarrow (e^n \rightarrow t)$ and the two predicates can be transformed to each other by the following formulae

---

[4] As regards the use of the same morphemes in words for *or* and *some* in many languages, I have to say that this fact cannot be explained straightforwardly under the new treatment proposed in this paper. But I am of the view that the explanation of this fact should not be considered a desideratum for the proper treatment of quantifiers. After all, this is not a universal fact. At least it is not true in English and Chinese.

(in what follows, x and w are variables of types e^n and s, respectively):

$$X^* = \lambda w[\{x : \{w\} \in X(x)\}] \tag{13}$$
$$X = \lambda x[Power(\{w : x \in X^*(w)\})] \tag{14}$$

By using X^*, the traditional treatment of GQT can then be restored under the framework of IS. For example, the denotation of *every* under IS will become

$$every = \lambda X \lambda Y[Power(\{w : X^*(w) \subseteq Y^*(w)\})] \tag{15}$$

Since X^* and Y^* have type $s \to (e \to t)$ and w is a variable with type s, $X^*(w)$ and $Y^*(w)$ have type $e \to t$, which is the type of unary predicates under GQT, and so "$X^*(w) \subseteq Y^*(w)$" in (15) is exactly parallel to "$X \subseteq Y$" in (7).

In general, let Q be a monadic quantifier[5] under GQT with n unary predicates $X_1, \ldots X_n$ each of type $e \to t$ as arguments and $C(X_1, \ldots X_n)$ be the truth condition associated with Q, i.e. Q has the denotation $\lambda X_1 \ldots \lambda X_n[C(X_1, \ldots X_n)]$. Then there is a corresponding quantifier (also denoted Q) with n unary predicates (also denoted $X_1, \ldots X_n$) each of type $e \to T$ as arguments and the denotation of Q under IS is

$$\lambda X_1 \ldots \lambda X_n[Power(\{w : C(X_1^*(w), \ldots X_n^*(w))\})] \tag{16}$$

According to (16), $Q(X_1) \ldots (X_n)$ is the power set of a set of worlds and is thus non-inquisitive because it contains only one alternative. This shows that the output of Q is non-inquisitive, which is consistent with the assumption above. By using (16), one can then write down the denotations of other quantifiers under IS. For example, the denotation of *most* under IS can be written as follows:

$$most = \lambda X \lambda Y \left[Power \left(\left\{ w : \frac{|X^*(w) \cap Y^*(w)|}{|X^*(w)|} > \frac{1}{2} \right\} \right) \right] \tag{17}$$

The proper treatment of quantifiers can help extend the empirical coverage of IS, because in natural languages there are many questions containing quantifiers. Under IS, given a declarative proposition p, the corresponding polar question can be represented as $?p$, where $?$ is the projection operator defined in (4). Similarly, under IS a constituent question "Which X is Y?", where X and Y are unary predicates, can be represented as $which(X)(Y)$, where $which$ is a non-exhaustive interrogative operator defined as follows (the context sensitivity of $which$ is ignored here)[6,7]:

---

[5] Monadic quantifiers are quantifiers all arguments of which are unary predicates. In case at least one argument is an n-ary predicate ($n > 1$), the quantifier is called polyadic.

[6] Note that the following denotation of *which* is a bit different from those given in [3,11] in that the following denotation includes a built-in $?$ operator. The inclusion of this operator is to ensure that "No X is Y" is an acceptable answer to the constituent question "Which X is Y?". In other words, I assume in this paper that *which* does not carry the existential presupposition.

[7] For unary predicates X and Y and individual x, $(X \cap Y)(x) = X(x) \cap Y(x)$.

$$which = \lambda X \lambda Y \left[? \left(\bigcup_{x \in U} (X \cap Y)(x) \right) \right] \tag{18}$$

For simplicity, only the "non-exhaustive" reading of interrogative operators is discussed in this paper. In brief, the non-exhaustive reading of the constituent question "Which X is Y?" only requires the respondent to provide at least one X that is Y or to answer that there is no X that is Y. The full list of X that is Y is not required. A discussion of the various "exhaustivity" of interrogative operators can be found in [11,12].

3.2   Worked Examples

For illustration, let's consider the following model[8].

> **Model M2**
> $U =$ $\{john, bill, mary, jane, katy\}$
> $W =$ $\{w_1, w_2, w_3\}$
> $boy =$ $john \mapsto Power(W); bill \mapsto Power(W)$
> $girl =$ $mary \mapsto Power(W); jane \mapsto Power(W); katy \mapsto Power(W)$
> $like =$ $(john, bill) \mapsto \{\{w_1\}, \emptyset\};$
> $(john, mary) \mapsto \{\{w_2\}, \emptyset\};$
> $(john, katy) \mapsto \{\{w_2\}, \emptyset\};$
> $(bill, jane) \mapsto \{\{w_2, w_3\}, \{w_2\}, \{w_3\}, \emptyset\};$
> $(bill, katy) \mapsto \{\{w_3\}, \emptyset\};$
> $(mary, jane) \mapsto \{\{w_1, w_3\}, \{w_1\}, \{w_3\}, \emptyset\};$
> $(mary, katy) \mapsto \{\{w_1\}, \emptyset\}$

$boy^* =$ $w_1 \mapsto \{john, bill\}; w_2 \mapsto \{john, bill\}; w_3 \mapsto \{john, bill\}$
$girl^* =$ $w_1 \mapsto \{mary, jane, katy\};$
        $w_2 \mapsto \{mary, jane, katy\};$
        $w_3 \mapsto \{mary, jane, katy\}$
$like^* =$ $w_1 \mapsto \{(john, bill), (mary, jane), (mary, katy)\};$
        $w_2 \mapsto \{(john, mary), (john, katy), (bill, jane)\};$
        $w_3 \mapsto \{(bill, jane), (bill, katy), (mary, jane)\}$

To simplify presentation, I adopt the following convention: if the output of a function given a particular input is $\{\emptyset\}$, then that input (and output) will not be shown. Thus, it is understood that under M2, we have $girl(john) = \{\emptyset\}$ and $like(john, john) = \{\emptyset\}$. For convenience, I have also provided the denotations of boy^*, $girl^*$ and $like^*$ above. One may check that these results can be obtained

---

[8] Note that the models M2 and M3 given in this paper are highly simplified models. They do not include all logically possible worlds (the total number of all such worlds is an astronomical number). For example, M2 does not include those worlds in which John is a girl and John likes herself. One may think that M2 and M3 are models that satisfy certain given preconditions. The satisfaction of these preconditions has greatly reduced the number of possible worlds in these two models.

by applying formula (13), and that the denotations of *boy*, *girl* and *like* can be obtained from these results by applying formula (14).

Now consider the polar question "Does some boy like most girls?". By using the ? operator and the standard GQT concepts for treating iterative quantifiers such as those in [7, 8, 10], this polar question can be formally represented as

$$?(some(boy)(most(girl)_{ACC}(like)))$$ (19)

where ACC represents the accusative case extension operator in [7] (note that "most girls" is in the accusative "semantic" case in the above polar question, hence the ACC operator). Let Q be a monadic quantifier. Then Q_{ACC} is an arity reducer that turns any binary predicate R to a unary predicate $Q_{ACC}(R)$ such that[9]

$$Q_{ACC}(R) = \lambda x[Q(\lambda y[R(x,y)])]$$ (20)

I next compute the denotation of (19) with respect to M2 step by step. To do this, I first use (20) to rewrite (19) as

$$?(some(boy)(\lambda x[most(girl)(\lambda y[like(x,y)])]))$$ (21)

I then calculate $\lambda y[like(x,y)]^*$ for each $x \in U$. For example, for $x = john$, the most straightforward way to calculate $\lambda y[like(john,y)]^*$ is to make use of $like^*$, which tells us that John likes Bill in w_1, Mary and Katy in w_2 and nobody in w_3. So we have

$$\lambda y[like(john,y)]^* = w_1 \mapsto \{bill\}; w_2 \mapsto \{mary, katy\}; w_3 \mapsto \emptyset$$

Similarly, we can calculate

$$\lambda y[like(bill,y)]^* = w_1 \mapsto \emptyset; w_2 \mapsto \{jane\}; w_3 \mapsto \{jane, katy\}$$
$$\lambda y[like(mary,y)]^* = w_1 \mapsto \{jane, katy\}; w_2 \mapsto \emptyset; w_3 \mapsto \{jane\}$$
$$\lambda y[like(jane,y)]^* = w_1 \mapsto \emptyset; w_2 \mapsto \emptyset; w_3 \mapsto \emptyset$$
$$\lambda y[like(katy,y)]^* = w_1 \mapsto \emptyset; w_2 \mapsto \emptyset; w_3 \mapsto \emptyset$$

Using the denotations of *most*, *girl** and $\lambda y[like(x,y)]^*$, I next calculate $most(girl)(\lambda y[like(x,y)])$ for each $x \in U$. For example, for $x = john$, among the three worlds, only $|girl^*(w_2) \cap \lambda y[like(john,y)]^*(w_2)|/|girl^*(w_2)| > 1/2$ is true, we thus have

$$most(girl)(\lambda y[like(john,y)]) = \{\{w_2\}, \emptyset\}$$

Similarly, we also have

$$most(girl)(\lambda y[like(bill,y)]) = \{\{w_3\}, \emptyset\}$$
$$most(girl)(\lambda y[like(mary,y)]) = \{\{w_1\}, \emptyset\}$$
$$most(girl)(\lambda y[like(jane,y)]) = \{\emptyset\}$$
$$most(girl)(\lambda y[like(katy,y)]) = \{\emptyset\}$$

---

[9] Set theoretic notation is used in [7]. In this paper, this notation is changed to λ-notation for consistency with the other parts of the paper.

Summarizing the above in the form of a unary predicate, we have

$$\lambda x[most(girl)(\lambda y[like(x,y)])] = john \mapsto \{\{w_2\}, \emptyset\};$$
$$bill \mapsto \{\{w_3\}, \emptyset\};$$
$$mary \mapsto \{\{w_1\}, \emptyset\};$$
$$jane \mapsto \{\emptyset\};$$
$$katy \mapsto \{\emptyset\}$$

Transforming the above predicate into the corresponding starred version by using formula (13), we have:

$$\lambda x[most(girl)(\lambda y[like(x,y)])]^* = w_1 \mapsto \{mary\}; w_2 \mapsto \{john\}; w_3 \mapsto \{bill\} \quad (22)$$

Using the denotations of *some*, *boy** and $\lambda x[most(girl)(\lambda y[like(x,y)])]^*$, I then calculate

$$some(boy)(\lambda x[most(girl)(\lambda y[like(x,y)])]) = \{\{w_2, w_3\}, \{w_2\}, \{w_3\}, \emptyset\} \quad (23)$$

Finally, using the definition of ?, I can then calculate

$$?(some(boy)(\lambda x[most(girl)(\lambda y[like(x,y)])])) = \{\{w_2, w_3\}, \{w_1\}, \{w_2\}, \{w_3\}, \emptyset\} \quad (24)$$

The final result above contains two alternatives corresponding to the two answers to the polar question "Does some boy like most girls?" under M2, namely $\{w_2, w_3\}$ corresponding to "Yes" and $\{w_1\}$ corresponding to "No", because it is true in w_2 and w_3 (but not w_1) that some boy likes most girls.

Next consider the constituent question "Which boy likes most girls?". By using the interrogative operator *which*, this constituent question can be formally represented as

$$which(boy)(most(girl)_{ACC}(like)) \quad (25)$$

I next compute the denotation of the above with respect to M2. As in the above example, I first use (20) to rewrite the above as

$$which(boy)(\lambda x[most(girl)(\lambda y[like(x,y)])]) \quad (26)$$

As I have already calculated the denotation of $\lambda x[most(girl)(\lambda y[like(x,y)])]$ above, what I have to do next is to use the denotations of *which*, *boy* and $\lambda x[most(girl)(\lambda y[like(x,y)])]$ to calculate the denotation of (26). To do this, I first calculate $(boy \cap \lambda x[most(girl)(\lambda y[like(x,y)])])(z)$ for every $z \in U$:

$$(boy \cap \lambda x[most(girl)(\lambda y[like(x,y)])])(john) = \{\{w_2\}, \emptyset\}$$
$$(boy \cap \lambda x[most(girl)(\lambda y[like(x,y)])])(bill) = \{\{w_3\}, \emptyset\}$$
$$(boy \cap \lambda x[most(girl)(\lambda y[like(x,y)])])(mary) = \{\emptyset\}$$
$$(boy \cap \lambda x[most(girl)(\lambda y[like(x,y)])])(jane) = \{\emptyset\}$$
$$(boy \cap \lambda x[most(girl)(\lambda y[like(x,y)])])(katy) = \{\emptyset\}$$

From the above, we have

$$\bigcup_{z\in U}(boy \cap \lambda x[most(girl)(\lambda y[like(x,y)])])(z) = \{\{w_2\},\{w_3\},\emptyset\} \qquad (27)$$

And finally we obtain the result

$$which(boy)(\lambda x[most(girl)(\lambda y[like(x,y)])]) = \{\{w_2\},\{w_3\},\{w_1\},\emptyset\} \qquad (28)$$

The final result above contains three alternatives corresponding to the three answers to the constituent question "Which boy likes most girls?" under M2, namely $\{w_2\}$ corresponding to "John", $\{w_3\}$ corresponding to "Bill" and $\{w_1\}$ corresponding to "No boy", because it is precisely John and precisely Bill who likes most girls in w_2 and w_3 respectively, whereas no boy likes most girls in w_1.

4   Pair List Reading

4.1   The Phenomenon

However, the new treatment of quantifiers proposed in this paper cannot handle the pair list reading of some questions. Consider the question "Which book did every girl read?", which is ambiguous between at least two readings: the "individual reading" and the "pair list reading"[10]. Under the individual reading, the question can be paraphrased as "Which book y is such that every girl read y?", and can thus be formally represented as

$$which(book)(every(girl)_{NOM}(read)) \qquad (29)$$

where NOM represents the nominative case extension operator in [7] (note that "every girl" is in the nominative "semantic" case in the above question, hence the NOM operator). The individual reading can be handled by the concepts and method discussed in the previous section, except that we further need the following definition of the NOM operator:

$$Q_{NOM}(R) = \lambda y[Q(\lambda x[R(x,y)])] \qquad (30)$$

---

[10] According to the literature, this question also has a third reading, namely the "functional reading" which expects a functional answer like "The book that her mother recommended". While some people may consider pair list answers as a special type of functional answers, it has been argued in [6] that pair list reading and functional reading are two different readings, one argument being that questions like "Which woman does no man love?" admit functional answers like "His mother" but no pair list answer. For this reason, I do not treat the pair list reading as a special case of the functional reading, which requires the conceptual tool of Skolem functions as argued in [6] and will not be discussed in this paper.

The individual reading will not be further discussed. What I am interested in here is the pair list reading, which can be paraphrased as "For every girl x, which book did x read?", and can thus be formally represented as[11]

$$every(girl)(which(book)_{ACC}(read)) \tag{31}$$

Under the pair list reading, *every* takes a wider scope than *which* (whereas *every* takes a narrower scope than *which* in (29)). Note that if we use the new treatment of *every* as given in (15) to handle (31), we have to transform $which(book)_{ACC}(read)$ into the starred version by using (13). But since this is a question and is thus non-informative, we would then have $which(book)_{ACC}$ $(read)^*(w) = U$ for all w. But then we would have $girl^*(w) \subseteq which(book)_{ACC}$ $(read)^*(w)$ for all w and hence $every(girl)(which(book)_{ACC}(read)) = Power$ (W) under every model, which is obviously an incorrect result. What can we do?

To properly handle the pair list reading, we have to revert to the old treatment of *every* given in (6). But there is now a question that needs to be addressed. Now that we have two treatments of *every*, i.e. the old treatment given in (6) and the new treatment given in (15), we have to make sure that (6) and (15) are consistent with each other. This is guaranteed by the following theorem (the proof of which will be given in Subsect. 4.3):

Theorem 1. *Let X and Y be non-inquisitive unary predicates. Then Power* $(\{w : X^*(w) \subseteq Y^*(w)\}) = \bigcap_{x \in U}(X(x) \rhd Y(x))$.

By comparing the right hand sides of (6) and (15), one can see that (6) is reduced to (15) when X and Y, i.e. the two arguments of *every*, are both non-inquisitive by virtue of this theorem, and so the new treatment of *every* is in fact a special case of the old treatment. When its two arguments are both non-inquisitive, one can use the reduced form (15) for convenience.

But then we have a further question: do we need to do the same for other quantifiers as we did for *every* above? The fact is that for other quantifiers, there is no similar scope ambiguity between the quantifier and a WH-word as in the case of *every*. Consider the question "Which book is recommended by some teacher?" which contains "some". Apart from the individual reading in which *some* takes a narrower scope than *which*, i.e. a reading which can be paraphrased as "Which book y is such that some teacher recommends y?", does this question also have a reading in which *some* takes a wider scope than *which*, i.e. a reading which can be paraphrased as "Name some teacher x and tell me which book x recommends"? In the literature, such a reading is called the "choice reading". According to many scholars (including [1]), "choice reading" questions do not exist in natural languages. For other quantifiers, it is even less likely that they would give rise to a reading in which the quantifier takes a wider scope than a WH-word. This means that we do not need to invoke the old treatment of these quantifiers as in the case of *every*.

---

[11] Here *which(book)* is treated as a quantifier. Note that "which men", "how many students" and the like are called "interrogative quantifiers" in [2].

In conclusion, the new treatment of all quantifiers other than *every* as proposed in this paper plus the old treatment of *every* (which in fact includes the new treatment of *every* as a special case) is sufficient for the general purpose of treating quantified statements and questions.

4.2 A Worked Example

In this subsection, I will illustrate the computation of the pair list reading. Consider the following model[12].

Model M3

$U =$ $\{john, mary, jane, RC, OT, DC\}$
$W =$ $\{w_1, w_2, w_3\}$
$boy =$ $john \mapsto Power(W)$
$girl =$ $mary \mapsto Power(W); jane \mapsto Power(W)$
$book =$ $RC \mapsto Power(W); OT \mapsto Power(W); DC \mapsto Power(W)$
$read =$ $(john, RC) \mapsto \{\{w_1\}, \emptyset\};$
           $(john, OT) \mapsto \{\{w_2, w_3\}, \{w_2\}, \{w_3\}, \emptyset\};$
           $(mary, RC) \mapsto \{\{w_1, w_2\}, \{w_1\}, \{w_2\}, \emptyset\};$
           $(mary, OT) \mapsto \{\{w_1\}, \emptyset\};$
           $(mary, DC) \mapsto \{\{w_3\}, \emptyset\};$
           $(jane, RC) \mapsto \{\{w_2\}, \emptyset\};$
           $(jane, OT) \mapsto \{\{w_1, w_2\}, \{w_1\}, \{w_2\}, \emptyset\};$
           $(jane, DC) \mapsto \{\{w_3\}, \emptyset\};$

$boy^* =$ $w_1 \mapsto \{john\}; w_2 \mapsto \{john\}; w_3 \mapsto \{john\}$
$girl^* =$ $w_1 \mapsto \{mary, jane\}; w_2 \mapsto \{mary, jane\}; w_3 \mapsto \{mary, jane\}$
$book^* =$ $w_1 \mapsto \{RC, OT, DC\}; w_2 \mapsto \{RC, OT, DC\}; w_3 \mapsto \{RC, OT, DC\}$
$read^* =$ $w_1 \mapsto \{(john, RC), (mary, RC), (mary, OT), (jane, OT)\};$
             $w_2 \mapsto \{(john, OT), (mary, RC), (jane, RC), (jane, OT)\};$
             $w_3 \mapsto \{(john, OT), (mary, DC), (jane, DC))\}$

I next compute the denotation of (31), i.e. the pair list reading of "Which book did every girl read?", with respect to M3. To do this, I first use (20) to rewrite (31) as

$$every(girl)(\lambda x[which(book)(\lambda y[read(x, y)])]) \tag{32}$$

I then calculate $which(book)(\lambda y[read(x, y)])$ for each $x \in U$. For example, for $x = john$, since $\lambda y[read(john, y)] = RC \mapsto \{\{w_1\}, \emptyset\}; OT \mapsto \{\{w_2, w_3\}, \{w_2\}, \{w_3\}, \emptyset\}$, by (18), we have

$$which(book)(\lambda y[read(john, y)]) = \{\{w_1\}, \{w_2, w_3\}, \{w_2\}, \{w_3\}, \emptyset\}$$

---

[12] In what follows, *RC*, *OT* and *DC* can be seen as abbreviations of *Robinson Crusoe, Oliver Twist* and *David Copperfield*, respectively.

Similarly, we also have

$$which(book)(\lambda y[read(mary, y)]) = \{\{w_1, w_2\}, \{w_3\}, \{w_1\}, \{w_2\}, \emptyset\}$$
$$which(book)(\lambda y[read(jane, y)]) = \{\{w_1, w_2\}, \{w_3\}, \{w_1\}, \{w_2\}, \emptyset\}$$
$$which(book)(\lambda y[read(RC, y)]) = Power(W)$$
$$which(book)(\lambda y[read(OT, y)]) = Power(W)$$
$$which(book)(\lambda y[read(DC, y)]) = Power(W)$$

Summarizing the above in the form of a unary predicate, we have

$$\lambda x[which(book)(\lambda y[read(x, y)])] = john \mapsto \{\{w_1\}, \{w_2, w_3\}, \{w_2\}, \{w_3\}, \emptyset\};$$
$$mary \mapsto \{\{w_1, w_2\}, \{w_3\}, \{w_1\}, \{w_2\}, \emptyset\};$$
$$jane \mapsto \{\{w_1, w_2\}, \{w_3\}, \{w_1\}, \{w_2\}, \emptyset\};$$
$$RC \mapsto Power(W);$$
$$OT \mapsto Power(W);$$
$$DC \mapsto Power(W)$$

Finally, to compute (32), I use (6) and (1) to rewrite (32) as

$$\bigcap_{z \in U} (i \in Power(W) : Power(i) \cap girl(z) \subseteq \lambda x[which(book)(\lambda y[read(x, y)])](z)) \quad (33)$$

To compute the above formula, I first have to find out all sets of worlds i such that $Power(i) \cap girl(z) \subseteq \lambda x[which(book)(\lambda y[read(x, y)])](z)$ for each $z \in U$. For example, in case $z = john$, since $girl(john) = \{\emptyset\}$, $Power(i) \cap girl(john)$ must be a subset of $\lambda x[which(book)(\lambda y[read(x, y)])](john)$ for any i, and so the required set of sets of worlds in this case is $Power(W)$. Similarly, in case $z = RC$, OT or DC, the required set of sets of worlds is also $Power(W)$.

In case $z = mary$, since $girl(mary) = Power(W)$ and $\lambda x[which(book) (\lambda y[read(x, y)])](mary) = \{\{w_1, w_2\}, \{w_3\}, \{w_1\}, \{w_2\}, \emptyset\}$, in order for $Power(i) \cap girl(mary)$ to be a subset of $\{\{w_1, w_2\}, \{w_3\}, \{w_1\}, \{w_2\}, \emptyset\}$, i must be a member of $\{\{w_1, w_2\}, \{w_3\}, \{w_1\}, \{w_2\}, \emptyset\}$, and every such member satisfies the requirement. Thus, the required set of sets of worlds in this case is $\{\{w_1, w_2\}, \{w_3\}, \{w_1\}, \{w_2\}, \emptyset\}$. Similarly, in case $z = jane$, the required set of sets of worlds is also $\{\{w_1, w_2\}, \{w_3\}, \{w_1\}, \{w_2\}, \emptyset\}$.

I then find the intersection of all the above sets of sets of worlds and finally obtain

$$every(girl)(which(book)_{ACC}(read)) = \{\{w_1, w_2\}, \{w_3\}, \{w_1\}, \{w_2\}, \emptyset\} \quad (34)$$

The final result above contains two alternatives corresponding to the two answers to the pair list reading of the question "Which book did every girl read?" under M3, namely $\{w_1, w_2\}$ corresponding to "Mary read RC and Jane read OT", and $\{w_3\}$ corresponding to "Both Mary and Jane read DC". Note that although the books that Mary and Jane precisely read in w_1 and w_2 are not the same (Mary also read OT in w_1 while Jane also read RC in w_2), w_1 and w_2 are grouped under the same alternative in (34) because *which* in this question has a non-exhaustive reading, i.e. "Mary read RC and Jane read OT" is an acceptable answer to the question in both w_1 and w_2.

4.3 Some Proofs

In this subsection, I will prove Theorem 1. But before doing this, I have to prove three lemmas first.

Lemma 1. *Let $p(w, x)$ be an arbitrary proposition with variables w and x. Then $Power(\{w : \forall x \in U[p(w, x)]\}) = \bigcap_{x \in U}(Power(\{w : p(w, x)\}))$.*

Proof. Let V be an arbitrary set of worlds. Then

$$V \in Power(\{w : \forall x \in U[p(w, x)]\})$$
$$\text{iff } V \subseteq \{w : \forall x \in U[p(w, x)]\}$$
$$\text{iff } \forall w \in V \, \forall x \in U[p(w, x)]$$
$$\text{iff } \forall x \in U \, \forall w \in V[p(w, x)]$$
$$\text{iff } \forall x \in U[V \subseteq \{w : p(w, x)\}]$$
$$\text{iff } \forall x \in U[V \in Power(\{w : p(w, x)\})]$$
$$\text{iff } V \in \bigcap_{x \in U}(Power(\{w : p(w, x)\}))$$

From the above, we have $Power(\{w : \forall x \in U[p(w, x)]\}) = \bigcap_{x \in U}(Power(\{w : p(w, x)\}))$. □

Lemma 2. *Let i, s and t be sets. Then $i \cap s \subseteq t$ iff $Power(i) \cap Power(s) \subseteq Power(t)$.*

Proof. (i) First assume that $i \cap s \subseteq t$. Let j be an arbitrary set and $j \in Power(i) \cap Power(s)$, i.e. $j \in Power(i) \wedge j \in Power(s)$. But this is equivalent to $j \subseteq i \wedge j \subseteq s$, i.e. $j \subseteq i \cap s$. From this we have $j \subseteq t$, i.e. $j \in Power(t)$. We have thus proved that $\forall j[j \in Power(i) \cap Power(s) \to j \in Power(t)]$, i.e. $Power(i) \cap Power(s) \subseteq Power(t)$.
(ii) Next assume that $Power(i) \cap Power(s) \subseteq Power(t)$. Let $w \in i \cap s$, i.e. $w \in i \wedge w \in s$. But this is equivalent to $\{w\} \in Power(i) \wedge \{w\} \in Power(s)$, i.e. $\{w\} \in Power(i) \cap Power(s)$. From this we have $\{w\} \in Power(t)$, i.e. $w \in t$. We have thus proved that $\forall w[w \in i \cap s \to w \in t]$, i.e. $i \cap s \subseteq t$.
Combining (i) and (ii) above, the lemma is proved. □

Lemma 3. *Let p and q be arbitrary non-inquisitive propositions. Then $p \rhd q = Power(\{w : \{w\} \in p \to \{w\} \in q\})$.*

Proof. Since p and q are non-inquisitive propositions, by the definition of inquisitiveness, each of p and q has exactly one alternative, say s and t, respectively. By the definition of alternatives, we have $p = Power(s)$ and $q = Power(t)$. From this we have

$$
\begin{aligned}
&Power(\{w : \{w\} \in p \to \{w\} \in q\}) \\
&= \{i : i \subseteq \{w : \{w\} \in p \to \{w\} \in q\}\} \\
&= \{i : i \subseteq \{w : \{w\} \in Power(s) \to \{w\} \in Power(t)\}\} \\
&= \{i : i \subseteq \{w : \{w\} \subseteq s \to \{w\} \subseteq t\}\} \\
&= \{i : i \subseteq \{w : w \in s \to w \in t\}\} \\
&= \{i : \forall v \in W[v \in i \to v \in \{w : w \in s \to w \in t\}]\} \\
&= \{i : \forall v \in W[(v \in i \land v \in s) \to v \in t]\} \\
&= \{i : i \cap s \subseteq t\} \\
&= \{i : Power(i) \cap Power(s) \subseteq Power(t)\} && \text{(by Lemma 2)} \\
&= \{i : Power(i) \cap p \subseteq q\} \\
&= p \rhd q && \text{(by (1))}
\end{aligned}
$$

Proof of Theorem 1. Let X and Y be non-inquisitive unary predicates and z be an arbitrary variable of type e. Then $X(z)$ and $Y(z)$ are non-inquisitive propositions.

$$
\begin{aligned}
&Power(\{w : X^*(w) \subseteq Y^*(w)\}) \\
&= Power(\{w : \{x : \{w\} \in X(x)\} \subseteq \{x : \{w\} \in Y(x)\}\}) && \text{(by (13))} \\
&= Power(\{w : \forall z \in U[z \in \{x : \{w\} \in X(x)\} \to \\
&\qquad z \in \{x : \{w\} \in Y(x)\}]\}) \\
&= Power(\{w : \forall z \in U[\{w\} \in X(z) \to \{w\} \in Y(z)]\}) \\
&= \bigcap_{z \in U}(Power(\{w : \{w\} \in X(z) \to \{w\} \in Y(z)\})) && \text{(by Lemma 1)} \\
&= \bigcap_{z \in U}(X(z) \rhd Y(z)) && \text{(by Lemma 3)}
\end{aligned}
$$

5   Conclusion

In this paper, I have proposed a new treatment of quantifiers. By combining features of IS and GQT, this new treatment is able to extend the coverage of IS to questions with quantifiers as well as retain the traditional truth conditions of quantifiers under GQT. I have also pointed out that the old treatment of *every* is still needed for treating the pair list reading of some questions with *every*. But apart from this, the new treatment of all other quantifiers is sufficient for the general purpose of treating quantified statements and questions. In fact, the new treatment of *every* is useful and convenient in many cases, provided that we are not treating the pair list reading. I have also shown that the new treatment of *every* is just a special case of the old treatment.

However, given the limited space, this paper has only discussed the basics of a theory of quantified statements and questions that combines IS and GQT. More specifically, regarding quantifiers, this paper has only discussed monadic quantifiers and iteration of these quantifiers. Regarding interrogatives, this paper has only discussed polar questions and constituent questions with the non-exhaustive *which*. In future studies, the coverage of this theory can be extended to non-iterated polyadic quantifiers (such as those discussed in [8,10]) and other types of questions (such as the alternative questions, open disjunctive questions, rising interrogatives and tag questions discussed in [1,5]) as well as constituent questions of other types of exhaustivity (such as the strongly exhaustive and weakly exhaustive readings discussed in [11,12]).

References

1. Ciardelli, I., Groenendijk, J., Roelofsen, F.: Inquisitive Semantics. Oxford University Press, Oxford (2019)
2. Ciardelli, I., Roelofsen, F.: An inquisitive perspective on modals and quantifiers. Ann. Rev. Linguist. **4**, 129–149 (2018)
3. Ciardelli, I., Roelofsen, F., Theiler, N.: Composing alternatives. Linguist. Philos. **40**(1), 1–36 (2017)
4. Coppock, E., Brochhagen, T.: Raising and resolving issues with scalar modifiers. Semant. Pragmatics **6**(3), 1–57 (2013)
5. Farkas, D.F., Roelofsen, F.: Division of labor in the interpretation of declaratives and interrogatives. J. Semant. **34**, 237–289 (2017)
6. Groenendijk, J., Stokhof, M.: Studies on the Semantics of Questions and the Pragmatics of Answers. Ph.D. Thesis. Universiteit van Amsterdam (1984)
7. Keenan, E.L: Semantic case theory. In: Groenendijk, J., et al. (eds.) Proceedings of the Sixth Amsterdam Colloquium, pp. 109–132. ITLI, Amsterdam (1987)
8. Keenan, E.L., Westerståhl, D.: Generalized quantifiers in linguistics and logic. In: van Ben-them, J., ter Meulen, A. (eds.) Handbook of Logic and Language, 2nd edn, pp. 859–910. Elsevier Science, Amsterdam (2011)
9. de Mey, J.: Determiner logic or the grammar of the NP. Ph.D. Thesis. University of Groningen (1990)
10. Peters, S., Westerståhl, D.: Quantifiers in Language and Logic. Clarendon Press, Oxford (2006)
11. Theiler, N.: A multitude of answers: embedded questions in typed inquisitive semantics, M.Sc. thesis, Universiteit van Amsterdam (2014)
12. Theiler, N., Roelofsen, F., Aloni, M.: A uniform semantics for declarative and interrogative complements. J. Semant. **35**, 409–466 (2018)

Solving the Individuation and Counting Puzzle with λ-DRT and MGL

If I Can Get a Book from the Library, It Saves Me from Needing to Buy It in the Bookshop

Bruno Mery[1]([⊠]), Richard Moot[2], and Christian Retoré[3]

[1] Univ. Bordeaux, CNRS, Bordeaux INP, LaBRI, UMR 5800, 33400 Talence, France
bruno.mery@u-bordeaux.fr
[2] Département Informatique, IUT de Bordeaux, Gradignan, France
richard.moot@lirmm.fr
[3] LIRMM, Univ Montpellier, CNRS, Montpellier, France
christian.retore@lirmm.fr

Abstract. Individuation and counting present an open puzzle for lexical semantics. The key challenge posed by this puzzle is that polysemous words can be counted according to different facets, using different individuation criteria for each. Several solutions have been proposed and challenged in the past, and the complexity of the responses expected makes it an interesting and pertinent test for formal theories and automated systems. We present a simple solution for this puzzle using an integrated chain of analysis from syntax to semantics and discourse, with a partial implementation that uses publicly available tools and frameworks. This clarifies the status of logical, compositional formalisms for lexical semantics regarding their ability to handle quantification and individuation. We also discuss the ability of the same formalisms to handle the resolution of discourse-level anaphora and correctly parse utterances introducing multiple lexical facets that are later referred to in the discourse.

Keywords: Individuation · Polysemy · Facets · Coercion · Quantification · Counting · Co-predication · Discourse representation theory · Discourse referents · Compositional lexical semantics

1 Compositionality, Polysemy and Counting

Type-theoretic formalisms and frameworks for compositional lexical semantics can produce logical representations for utterances that use polysemous words, based on works by [10] and [28]. These include Type Composition Logic (TCL) given in [1], Dependant Type Semantics (DTS) introduced by [4], Type Theory with Records (TTR) used in [9], Mereological Copredication detailed in [12], Modern Type Theory-based semantics (MTT) given by [20], as well as our proposed framework, the Montagovian Generative Lexicon (MGL), introduced in [3] and detailed in [30].

For our approach, and most of these frameworks, the linguistic and logical compositionality of the semantics is a prominent feature.

© Springer Nature Switzerland AG 2019
K. Kojima et al. (Eds.): JSAI-isAI 2018 Workshops, LNAI 11717, pp. 298–312, 2019.
https://doi.org/10.1007/978-3-030-31605-1_22

These approaches are often subject to criticism regarding their capacity to provide a full analysis from syntax to semantics integrating discourse and anaphora resolution; there have been several recent progresses in this area, such as [7] and [32]. One of the purposes of this paper is to show how discourse analysis can be integrated within the MGL framework; preliminary work on this issue has been presented in [17] and detailed in [18] in French, for a specialised purpose. The subtitle of the present paper[1], *If I can get a book from the library, it saves me from needing to buy it in the bookshop*, illustrates a common situation in which lexical adaptations (from the lexeme *book* to the physical object and informational content) take place, and are later referred to in the discourse; our goal is not only to extract the correct facets[2] of the lexeme, but also to correctly link their logical representations to the discourse referents, including in complex discourse structures (as the anaphora only takes place on the *informational* facet in this sentence, while the *physical* facets can be different).

Another difficulty for compositional lexical semantics is the ability of the formalisms to correctly individuate and count facets of polysemous entities. This point is illustrated by the "counting puzzle", which was introduced by [1] and is also known as the "quantification puzzle".

The puzzle arises when combining counting and co-predication on polysemous words. Logically, some predicates can select different facets of polysemous words; when the polyseme denotes a plural set of entities, the facets selected by each predicate typically have different individuation criterion, which should be modelled as different quantifications, resulting in different counts for a single referent lexeme. For instance, in utterrances such as *five books, including three copies of the same novel, were on the shelf; they all burnt, but I had already read them*, classic Montague grammar will result in both predicates being asserted on the same entities (five *books*), while taking polysemy into account should result in *burnt* applying to physical objects (five) and *read* to informational contents (three). The difficulty in producing the logical representation for this "puzzling" utterances is thus not only to extract the correct facet for each predication, but also to quantify according to each facet while keeping a single logical referent (as the predications on the different facets may be added at any point int the discourse).

We claim in [30] that the λ-calculus-based MGL framework can be easily adapted to discourse formalisms that extend DRT (presented in [14] and [5]) with Montagovian composition, such as λ-DRT detailed in [6,11,26] and [15] for a straightforward integration with tools such as the Grail syntax-semantics parser described in [25]. Other formalisms have also explored these case, with [2] reviewing discourse phenomena and their relationship with TCL and MTT, and claiming the suitability of such frameworks for this purpose.

We want to make good on these claims, detailing both the logical and computational implementation of the discourse-aware MGL mechanisms, while also presenting a simple solution to the objections pertaining to individuation, and our interpretation of the quantification puzzle.

---

[1] Example sentence found in the collaborative online translation database, tatoeba.org.

[2] The different senses, or meanings, of a single polysemous word which are logically related can be referred to as *lexical aspects*; we use the word "facet" in order to distinguish from the syntactic notion of "aspect".

1.1   Data

We need to be able to treat situations requiring anaphora resolution (as in prototypical DRT test cases) using polysemous words such as *book* which have different facets and different individuation conditions. We will be using the following example sentences and situations:

(1)   Oliver stole the books on the shelf, then read them.

(2)   If Emma finds a book that she already read, she leaves it in the store.

(3)   *On the table are two copies of van Eijck's and Unger's* Computational Semantics *and one of Pustejovsky's* The Generative Lexicon.

   Stanley read all the books on the table.

The sentences above are artificial, but such predications upon the physical and informational facets of books can be found in naturally occurring data, as illustrated by our subtitle; this sentence clearly considers a single informational referent, having two possibly different physical copies.

The lexeme *book* is in fact quite specific in presenting these possible co-predications; as discussed for example in [29], many candidates for co-predications are not productive in actual corpus data. *Books* have been used as prototypical examples with intrinsic polysemy; we have remarked that ontological subtypes such as *novels* tend to exhibit a strong bias towards their information facets. We would argue that most polysemic words have *primary* meanings (such as *events* for meals or *informational content* for most readable materials); it does not change our analysis of polysemes, but *books* will probably be the most difficult one to treat as the primary meaning is not decisively clear-cut between physical object and information content, requiring a lexical adaptation to interpret even in simple sentences.

1.2   The Quantification Puzzle

The supposed difficulty of such examples is that they can refer to entities that share a single facet (the *book-as-information*), but differ on another (the *book-as-physical object*); all while sharing a single discourse referent – the *book* lexeme, not the necessarily the same object in a model of the situation. Such sentences, combining co-predication, individuation and quantification, have been used as tests for formalisations of semantics. Paraphrasing the original from [1], the *quantification puzzle* is that a formal system, when asked the question *How many books did I read?* in the situation given in (3) should answer *two*, while correctly keeping track of the three physical objects and the relationships between the facets of the book entities. While [1] uses the quantification puzzle as an argument for preferring TCL to other formalisations of lexical semantics (including early accounts such as [27], as well as TTR and MTT), many of these other frameworks have in fact responded to the quantification puzzle; it is our belief that all basic logic frameworks can be easily adapted to handle the necessary information required to produce suitable analyses of these situations.

An early, straightforward account for these using MGL and quantification has been given in [22]; the present paper does not really depart from this first formalisation, as it incorporates all necessary mechanisms. A complete detailed formalisation built upon these examples has been made in [12] using mereology, and recent dedicated publications such as [13] and [8] abound. A common thread to all of the solutions for the quantification puzzle is to examine the distribution of the quantified sets of arguments when applied to predicates requiring different types, and to illustrate how they are individuated, and thus counted, differently. This can be done in many ways, with TCL providing different quantifiers depending upon different typing presuppositions, MGL quantifying on objects that are accessed through different lexical transformations according to their facets, [13] presenting a component-wise account, and MTT labelling each entity with a setoid, a mathematical object consisting of the pairing of a type and an individuation criterion.

Thus, every approach solves this puzzle by providing a coherent way to count polysemous terms in different ways. Yet, arguments against these accounts persist, such as [19] and [21], and we must thus consider the issue as still unsolved.

2 Anaphora, Coercions and Facets in Compositional Discourse Semantics

Our goal being to have a correct analysis of shifts in lexical meaning and their propagation through discourse references, as well as the ability for the resulting analysis to solve the counting puzzle. We present, in order, the Montagovian Generative Lexicon; its use on λ-DRT output obtained by the *GrailLight* parser; and consequences on individuation and counting.

2.1 MGL: A Montagovian Analysis for Generative Lexical Semantics

In order to compute the correct logical representations and infer the cardinalities of each predication on the different facets, MGL uses a compositional treatment chain (inspired by and extended from Montague Grammar). The syntax of the sentence is analysed using categorial grammars (here, a version of type-logical grammars), and a semantic term is computed according to Lambek calculus, yielding an output in λ-DRT suitable for anaphora resolution. The meaning shifts, known as *linguistic coercions*, that allow access to specific facets of polysemous terms (such as the informational and physical facets of *book*) and co-predications on those facets are inserted according to the mechanisms detailed in [30]:

- each lexical term is associated to a single "main" λ-term, representing its primary denotational meaning (as determined arbitrarily: *book*, being fully polysemous, is given as an entity of a generic *Readable* type),
- each lexeme might also be associated to a number of "optional" λ-terms, the *lexical transformations* that model type coercions, that might be used whenever type mismatches occur (*book* is thus associated to accessors for the two facets, modelled as transformations from *readable* to *physical* and *informational* entities respectively).

This yields logical formulæ typed using terms of a many-sorted logic ΛTY_n, distinguishing between ontological categories (the pertinent sorts in the examples are: P for people, R for readable objects including the generic *book*, I for informational content, φ for physical objects, etc). These formulæ will include *type mismatches* whenever polysemous terms are used as arguments for predicates that require a facet that is not their primary denotation (and systematically so with *book*).

The linguistic coercions that enable the disambiguation of polysemous terms are modelled by the optional terms, as transformations lexically associated to the lexemes (f_I, an accessor to the information facet, and f_φ, an accessor to the physical facet, are available for terms representing *book*; there can be many more of these terms including accessors for *qualia* so that sentences such as *The book is finished* can be analysed correctly). Inserting the optional terms in suitable positions guided by the types make the coercions apparent, and the typing of the formula correct: *a book on the shelf* will be analysed as $\exists x^R.\text{on\_shelf}(f_\varphi(x)^\varphi) \wedge \text{book}(x^R)$. Co-predication is made possible by the use of higher-order operators such as the polymorphic conjunction &: *the book is heavy and interesting* is analysed as $\exists x^R.(\& \text{ heavy}^{\varphi \to t} \text{ interesting}^{I \to t} x) \wedge \text{book}^{R \to t}(x)$, which is resolved as $\exists x^R.\text{heavy}(f_\varphi(x)) \wedge \text{interesting}(f_I(x)) \wedge \text{book}(x)$.

MGL, as its core, is a mechanism modelling the analysis methodology used in lexical semantics; a means to compute the correct logical representation with explicit lexical transformations given the relevant data. It supposes a rich database of lexical information that is challenging to obtain: most of our examples are treated by hand. Another possibility is the conversion of existing resources as described in [16], starting from an extensive crowd-sourced lexicon; however, the diverse nature of the available data makes it difficult to provide a non-supervised automated conversion. MGL provides a series of mechanisms for fixing type mismatches; the variety of types available, dependent on the granularity of the lexicon, force those mismatches to occur. If all sorts are coalesced together into the single Montagovian type **e** for entities, the classic analysis given by Montague grammar is still available – but the disambiguation of the polysemous terms do not occur at all.

Regardless of the mechanisms used to make the lexical transformations (or linguistic coercions) apparent, a common feature for all systems handling lexical semantics is that they can generate many different suitable interpretations. For example, *synecdoche* is a common language usage in which a word denoting a complex object is used to refer to a specific part. In the case of mechanical malfunctions, the word *car* can be commonly used to mean the *tire*, *motor*, *battery* or *tank* of the car (as in *my car won't start* or similar sentences). Lexical semantics predicts that there are many different coercions from vehicles to physical objects, including many parts of the vehicle as well as the vehicle itself; when making a predication on the word *car* using a predicate that take *physical objects* as its arguments, there will be many possible interpretations that should be generated. Which one of those, if any, is correct is determined by *preference*, filtering implausible meanings and scoring the possible ones. This can be done by hand, but also automatically, according to available linguistic data; this process is illustrated in [16], demonstrating how a single source of lexical data can be used both for extracting and ranking the different lexical transformations available for each lexeme.

2.2 Anaphora Resolution, Discourse Analysis and Disambiguation

In summary, the processing of the utterance starts with syntactic analysis, processes with anaphoric resolution in λ-DRT (both steps are automated using *GrailLight*); afterwards, MGL-based disambiguation is applied to the output. The following figures illustrate the processing of the example sentences, detailing first (1) (Figs. 1 and 2).

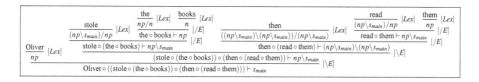

Fig. 1. Automated syntactical analysis for sentence (1) produced by GrailLight [25].

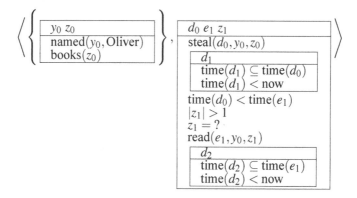

Fig. 2. Resulting DRS for sentence (1) automatically produced by GrailLight [25].

The binding process after this first discourse analysis presents interesting challenges. The anaphoric pronoun *them* (represented by the variable z_1) can safely be bound to the only plural antecedent *the books* (represented by the variable z_0). The event semantics, here given in Davidsonian fashion, summarise the relationship between the tenses of the two predicates and the succession adverb "then". Ignoring the technical sub-events d_1 and d_2 (which represent the past tense), adding missing type information (using the characteristic function to represent the set of readable objects $R \rightarrow \mathbf{t}$ for *book* and the person sort P for *Oliver*), a straightforward translation of the DRS above is:

$$\exists d_0^{\mathbf{evt}} e_1^{\mathbf{evt}} z_0^{R \rightarrow \mathbf{t}}.\text{books}(z_0) \wedge \text{steal}(d_0, \text{Oliver}^P, z_0) \wedge \text{read}(e_1, \text{Oliver}^P, z_0)$$

As we discussed in [24], the plural predications can be distributed on all members of the set by a functional coercion of the predicates, resulting in:

$$\exists d_0^{\mathbf{evt}} e_1^{\mathbf{evt}} z_0^{R \rightarrow \mathbf{t}} \forall z^R.[z_0(z) \Rightarrow \text{book}(z_0) \wedge \text{steal}(d_0, \text{Oliver}^P, z) \wedge \text{read}(e_1, \text{Oliver}^P, z)]$$

That is, the characteristic function z_0 has the property that all items z for which the function is true are books such that Oliver both stole and read them.

At this point, the type mismatch between the *book* argument (z^R) and the predicates (expecting physical and informational arguments respectively) are resolved by inserting the relevant transformations, making the coercions apparent in standard MGL fashion and solving the type mismatches.

An interesting point here is the interaction of the event semantics with the plural transformation, as the act of stealing a number of (physical) books can be done at one (or several) times, but the reading of each (informational) book will typically be accomplished one at a time; stealing and reading events can (and should) be distributed differently. As we suggested in [24], this is treated as a quantifier scope ambiguity where there is either a single stealing event d_0 in which all books z are stolen ($\exists d_0 \forall z$ reading) or there is a possibly different, event for each book ($\forall z \exists d_0$ reading). A similar scope ambiguity exists for the reading event e_1 and the universal quantifier, with the interpretations being one event for every book, and a single reading event for all of the books.

The following is the fully-typed formula for sentence (1), assuming wide scope for the existential quantifiers:

$$\exists d_0^{\text{evt}} e_1^{\text{evt}} z_0^{R \to t} \forall z^R . [z_0(z) \Rightarrow$$
$$\text{book}^{R \to t}(z) \wedge^{t \to t \to t}$$
$$\text{steal}^{\text{evt} \to P \to \varphi \to t}(e_1, \text{Oliver}^P, f_\varphi^{R \to \varphi}(z)) \wedge^{t \to t \to t}$$
$$\text{read}^{\text{evt} P \to I \to t}(d_0, \text{Oliver}^P, f_I^{R \to I}(z))]]$$

It is correctly asserted here that all physical copies of the books were arguments of *steal*, and all informational content of the same books has been read without duplication.

Example (2) should be treated with DRT-compliant mechanisms for anaphoric resolution, as it has been modelled on classic donkey sentences. The syntax-semantics-discourse analysis proceeds as previously, and there is a single (quantified) event for each predicate.

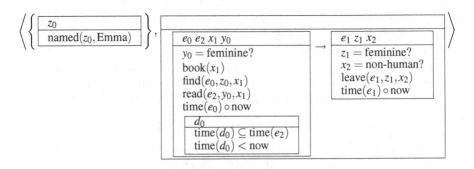

Fig. 3. Initial DRS for sentence (2).

The categorial grammar syntactic analysis ensures the object of *read* must be x_1 (the *book* in the antecedent). Anaphoric resolution binds y_0 and z_1 to the sole female human discourse referent (Emma) and x_2 to the sole non-human, non-event discourse referent x_1, transforming the initial DRS given in Fig. 3 to the structure in Fig. 4:

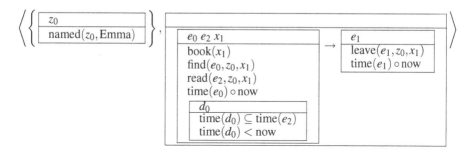

Fig. 4. DRS for sentence (2) after anaphora resolution.

The final interpretation of the sentence as a logical formula is thus:

$$\forall e_0^{\mathbf{evt}} e_2^{\mathbf{evt}} x_1^R . [[\text{book}(x_1) \ \wedge \ \text{find}(e_0, \text{Emma}^P, f_\varphi^{R \to \varphi}(x)) \wedge \text{read}(e_2, \text{Emma}^P, f_I^{R \to I}(x)))]$$
$$\Rightarrow \exists e_1^{\mathbf{evt}} . \text{leave}(e_1, \text{Emma}^P, f_\varphi^{R \to \varphi}(x))]$$

This correctly asserts that a single book has been found and left as a physical object, and that the informational content of this book has been read, but not necessarily using the same physical object as a support.

2.3 A Partial Implementation of the Treatment Chain

Several tools and frameworks are available for an automated implementation of this formalisation. We have used GrailLight for the production of both the syntactic analysis (using Type-Logical Grammars and variations of the Lambek calculus, with a small English lexicon in the same spirit as the much larger one used for the wide-coverage French parser for GrailLight) and the production of the λ-DRSs for reference resolution and anaphora binding.

Semantic disambiguation via MGL can be performed using techniques described in [23], including the distribution of collective predicates. However, event semantics are not yet implemented in MGL, and neither is scope ambiguity for event variables in GrailLight. Despite our efforts, the biggest roadblock to a fully implemented treatment chain remains the lexicon of polysemous terms with rich types, which has to be done by hand. Our treatment chain, from the text given as plain English utterances and discourse, to λ-DRSs giving a logical representation making the binding of the discourse referents apparent via a Lambek-style proof of the syntax, and then to a disambiguated logical form using MGL to insert the correct lexical transformations, is summarised in Fig. 5 below.

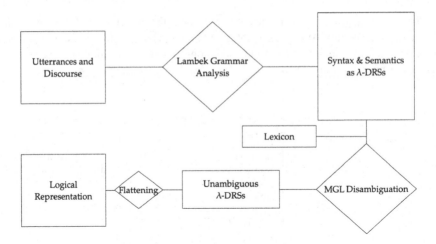

Fig. 5. Our complete treatment chain.

This process supposes that one discourse-level analysis is sufficient in order to resolve the bindings of the referents, and that lexical facets can be determined afterwards. An objection would be that some situations can require the new lexical facets that have been extracted by MGL mechanisms to act as different discourse referents afterwards; while we have no examples of this situation (co-predications being made on a single logic referent), handling it correctly would require to integrate MGL as a GrailLight component.

2.4 Individuation Criteria for Facets

The ability to analyse complex sentences with anaphoric references and co-predications, and to correctly apply lexical transformations that makes predicates access the correct facet of arguments, is sufficient to provide correct individuation criteria and to solve the quantificational puzzle. When making a co-predication on some polysemous term, such as $\lambda x^R.(P^{\varphi \to t}(f_\varphi(x)) \wedge Q^{I \to t}(f_I(x)))$ to all books, in a model in which the set of books is given as $\{b_1, b_2\}$, it is easy to have $f_I(b_1) = f_I(b_2)$ while $f_\varphi(b_1) \neq f_\varphi(b_2)$, and thus to have different cardinalities for each set of facets.

In the situation described in (3), there are two copies of van Eijck's and Unger's *Computational Semantics* $\{b_1, b_2\}$ and one of Pustejovsky's *The Generative Lexicon* $\{b_3\}$ on the table. This is modeled simply with two informational contents and three physical objects, such as:

$i_1 = f_I(b_1) = f_I(b_2)$, $i_2 = f_I(b_3)$, $p_1 = f_\varphi(i_1)$, $p_2 = f_\varphi(b_2)$, $p_3 = f_\varphi(b_3)$.

A simple representation of this situation, specifying the different individuation criteria, is given in Fig. 6 below.

Proceeding as for 1 above, we obtain the following formula:

$\exists z^{R \to t} \forall z_1^R.$

$[z(z_1) \Rightarrow [\mathrm{book}^{R \to t}(z_1) \wedge \mathrm{on\_the\_table}^{\varphi \to t}(f_\varphi(z_1)) \wedge \mathrm{read}^{P \to I \to t}(\mathrm{Stanley}^P, f_I(z_1))]]$

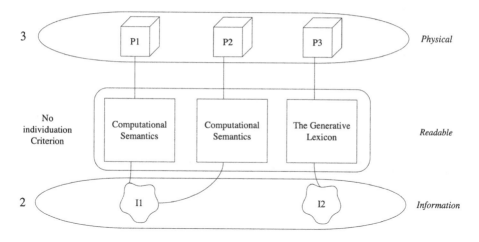

Fig. 6. Individuation summary.

The *books on the table* are the set of (physical) books defined as:

$$bt = \{p^{\varphi} \,|\, \text{on\_the\_table}(p)\}$$
$$= \{f_{\varphi}(b) \,|\, \text{on\_the\_table}(f_{\varphi}(b))\}$$
$$= \{f_{\varphi}(b) \,|\, b \in \{b_1, b_2, b_3\}\}$$
$$= \{p_1, p_2, p_3\}$$

The *books Stanley read* are the set of (informational) books such as:

$$br = \{i^{I} \,|\, \text{read}(\text{Stanley}, i\}$$
$$= \{f_{I}(b) \,|\, \text{read}(\text{Stanley}, f_{I}(b))\}$$
$$= \{f_{I}(b) \,|\, b \in \{b_1, b_2, b_3\}\}$$
$$= \{i_1, i_2\}$$

$$|bt| = 3 \qquad\qquad\qquad\qquad |br| = 2$$

The quantification puzzle is thus easily solved, as the polysemous terms (*the books*) that are common antecedents to the predicates are not counted as singular entities, but are only individuated with respect to a single, facet-specific predication that does not need to apply the same identity criterion as others.

This is made apparent by the explicit coercions f_{α}, that allow each predication and set-theoretic quantification to access the correct facet of the original term, without modifying that same term so that it can be used in any number of other predications, with or without coercions.

3   The Individuation Controversies

3.1   Books-as-parts

This does not answer all the questions raised by the quantification puzzle. A More difficult version of the quantification puzzle includes physical books that contain several informational parts labelled *books*. The *Bible* is an example, with a varying number of "books" according to different traditions, Tolkien's *Lord of the Rings* is another, being a single work of six "books" plus prologues and appendices collected as one, three or six volumes depending on the edition or translation. Other examples include collected works from an author, and single-volume compilations of several works, that can be referred to collectively as in the phrase *"three books in one"*.

We feel that such examples depend on a very specific usage of the word *book*: contemporary English speakers would use *part* or *chapter*; this use of the term is also deprecated in French. We treat these cases by associating the word *book* with coercions to *holy text*, *novel* or *work* $f_{total}^{R \to I}$ on the one hand, and to *part* $f_{part}^{R \to I}$ on the other hand.

This does not provide a single straightforward answer pertaining to the individuation condition of such multi-book books, as each of these transformations might be used in case of a type mismatch, everyone being of the same type, $R \to I$. This ties with the fact that *how-many* questions for compound works are difficult with no obvious single answer, as any coherent individuation system may be accepted.

In a situation with two copies of a Roman Catholic *Bible* (73 book-parts) and a copy of the Torah (Pentateuch, 5 book-parts included in the previous 73), possible answers to *how many books are there* include 1 (the complete holy text), 2 (different-looking books), 3 (physical volumes), 73 (books of the bible) and 78 (73+5 when considering the differences between the versions of the texts).

Formally, what happens is that we have an individuation criterion for *physical objects* (identity in the world), and a criterion for *informational content* (identity between texts), but not for polysemous *books* (readable materials should be counted one way or the other). Thus, having to resolve the type for the referent to *books* in *how many books are there*, all combinations of $f^{R \to \varphi}$, $f_{total}^{R \to I}$ and $f_{part}^{R \to I}$ can be used, yielding a number of different possible interpretation combinations.

Every single of these interpretations could be considered as correct; we do not have yet sufficient linguistic data to say which should be eliminated or which one is the "most" correct. We would not thing that a single interpretation would ever be "correct", and suppose that the specific (pragmatic) context of the utterance guides the final interpretation. Giving the list of the possible meanings is the only thing that can be done at the level of semantics, where the necessary information is absent.

3.2 Hyper-Contextuality

Such a view, developed in [19] is that, in these cases, a context can always be found that justifies *any* certain response within the possible combinations of the meanings for *book*. Our intuition is to subscribe to this view, noting that the type-matching interpretations produced by the lexical mechanisms outlined above contain all plausible responses. In our opinion, this does not prove that the meaning of words such as *book* is singular, with no polysemy; this rather illustrates the fact that such words are, as [28] put, *relationally polysemous* terms, presenting different *facets* of a single entity.

There are many possible ways to represent this fact in order to account for the specificities of individuation and quantification, with both the mereological account given by [13] and the definition of entities as setoids including type and individuation criterion given by [8] being correct. We believe that the formalisation presented here is one of the easiest ways to account for this phenomena, and would argue that this contextuality was present in MGL from the start. Including the lexical transformations as pertaining to the words, and thus the specificity of individuation criteria to be different in different contexts, allows us to relativise the identity criteria to a speaker and a situation.

The specifics of *individuation* can be refined further in type-theoretical semantics. As discussed in [31], we subscribe to a view close to Leibniz's equality, that identity and individuation are described according to properties given by predicates; thus, *books-as-information* are quantified by *the books that are the same when being read*. Predicates such as *reading* can thus provide an equivalence relation $=_r$, and, to count the books being read, one may use the *quotient type* given by the sort of readable materials R and this relation.

In one context, a person might be interested in books in general terms and assert that a book and its translation in another language count as a single book, while a translation specialist might count different translations or editions as different books. This is a matter of *preference*, not necessarily related to the *original* sense of a word: *coffee* originally denotes (part of) a plant, but is mostly used as a beverage. This may also not be a cross-linguistic phenomenon, as the French *livre* is more readily associated to the pages and bindings of a physical object, while the English *book* seems to be more polysemous and closer to the information content (or part thereof) of the term. These differences in interpretation between speakers, contexts and languages can be modelled as individuals using different lexica, with different transformations associated to words such as *book*. The basic lexicon, with "common-sense" interpretations and meaning shifts is always available, but additional lexical layers can modify this information in a given context by adding or re-ordering the preferences for some lexical transformations, accounting for the multiple different situations. This mechanism can integrate highly contextual data from the *pragmatics* level of interpretation, and be seamlessly integrated in our account, given for semantics.

As illustrated below in Fig. 7, in a situation where different copies of the same informational part, parts of the same novel and translations of such parts are collected together, different speakers may use different criteria for counting the entities in a way that is relevant to each of them.

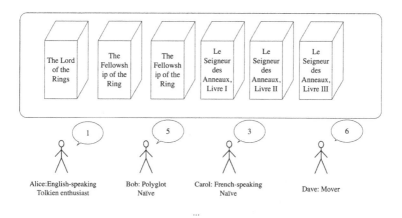

Fig. 7. A few individuals counting parts of *The Lord of the Rings* using different criteria.

4   Conclusion

Discussion – The quantification puzzle has now received responses using at least TCL, Mereology, MTT and MGL. The common elements of these responses clearly indicate that it is possible to quantify, individuate and count different facets of single, polysemous lexical items in different ways, correctly accounting for different contexts and co-predicative utterances. We argue that the differences between these formal treatments of quantifications are fundamentally very small. Our hope is that this paper provides a simple, detailed and correct answer for our framework, with a treatment chain starting from a sequence of words, utterances or sentences, and yielding the proper semantics as DRSs, that is fully mapped and mostly implemented using the Grail platform given in [25]. With this paper, we have thus given an integration of discourse representation theory, anaphora resolution and richly-typed lexical disambiguation, of which the quantification puzzle is just an illustration. Adding lexical transformations and the ability to refer to different facets of polysemous terms across the discourse is a big step towards precise, automated language understanding of real-world texts. Our processing system is quite advanced with a few elements hand-made, and most of the syntactical, semantic, discursive and lexical analysis automated. We are thankful to the LENLS organising team for providing this opportunity to present and discuss this issue, and to the reviewers of this paper for their appreciated input.

Perspectives – As part of the theoretical research on lexical semantics, we would like to explore whether a property-based individuation system, in which predicates yield their own individuations criteria by the means of quotient types as discussed in [31], can help with the more complex cases in which identity is highly dependent on context, speaker and language.

From a practical point of view, while the analysis methodology is nearly complete, we still need to acquire the rich and wide-covering lexical resources necessary for our analytical system; corpus-based approaches are beyond reach for our needs, and we can only hand-code a short lexicon. In [16], we examined suitable crowd-sourced resources to use as a starting point; the extraction of sufficient data is a challenge.

References

1. Asher, N.: Lexical Meaning in Context: A Web of Words. Cambridge University Press, Cambridge (2011)
2. Asher, N., Luo, Z.: Formalization of coercions in lexical semantics. In: Chemla, E., Homer, V., Winterstein, G. (eds.) Proceedings of Sinn und Bedeutung, vol. 17. pp. 63–80, Paris (2013)
3. Bassac, C., Mery, B., Retoré, C.: Towards a type-theoretical account of lexical semantics. J. Lang Logic Inf. **19**(2), 229–245 (2010)
4. Bekki, D.: Dependent type semantics: an introduction. In: Christoff, Z., Galeazzi, P., Gierasimczuk, N., Marcoci, A., Smet, S. (eds.) Logic and Interactive RAtionality (LIRa) Yearbook 2012, vol. I, pp. 277–300. University of Amsterdam (2014)
5. van Benthem, J., ter Meulen, A. (eds.): Handbook of Logic and Language. North-Holland Elsevier, Amsterdam (1997)

6. Bos, J., Mastenbroek, E., Mcglashan, S., Millies, S., Pinkal, M.: A compositional DRS-based formalism for NLP applications. In: In International Workshop on Computational Semantics, pp. 21–31 (1994)

7. Chatzikyriakidis, S., Luo, Z.: Proof assistants for natural language semantics. In: Amblard, M., de Groote, P., Pogodalla, S., Retoré, C. (eds.) LACL 2016. LNCS, vol. 10054, pp. 85–98. Springer, Heidelberg (2016). https://doi.org/10.1007/978-3-662-53826-5_6

8. Chatzikyriakidis, S., Luo, Z.: Identity criteria of CNs: quantification and copredication. In: CoPo 2017, Oslo, November 2017

9. Cooper, R.: Copredication, dynamic generalized quantification and lexical innovation by coercion. In: Fourth International Workshop on Generative Approaches to the Lexicon (2007)

10. Cruse, D.A.: Lexical Semantics. Cambridge University Press, New York (1986)

11. van Eijck, J., Kamp, H.: Representing discourse in context. In: van Benthem, J., ter Meulen, A.: [5], chap. 3, pp. 179–237 (1997)

12. Gotham, M.: Copredication, Quantification Individuation. Ph.D. thesis, University College London (2014)

13. Gotham, M.: Composing criteria of individuation in copredication. J. Semant. **34**(2), 333–371 (2017). https://doi.org/10.1093/jos/ffw008

14. Kamp, H., Reyle, U.: From Discourse to Logic: Introduction to Model-theoretic Semantics of Natural Language, Formal Logic and Discourse Representation Theory. Studies in Linguistics and Philosophy, vol. 42. Springer, Dordrecht (1993). https://doi.org/10.1007/978-94-017-1616-1

15. Kohlhase, M., Kuschert, S., Pinkal, M.: A type-theoretic semantics for lambda-DRT, November 1996

16. Lafourcade, M., Mery, B., Mirzapour, M., Moot, R., Retoré, C.: Collecting weighted coercions from crowd-sourced lexical data for compositional semantic analysis. In: Arai, S., Kojima, K., Mineshima, K., Bekki, D., Satoh, K., Ohta, Y. (eds.) New Frontiers in Artificial Intelligence, pp. 214–230. Springer International Publishing, Cham (2018)

17. Lefeuvre, A., Moot, R., Retoré, C., Sandillon-Rezer, N.F.: Traitement automatique sur corpus de récits de voyages pyrénéens: Une analyse syntaxique, sémantique et temporelle. In: Traitement Automatique du Langage Naturel, TALN 2012, vol. 2, pp. 43–56 (2012). http://aclweb.org/anthology/F/F12/

18. Lefeuvre-Halftermeyer, A., Moot, R., Retoré, C.: A computational account of virtual travelers in the montagovian generative lexicon. In: Aurnague, M., Stosic, D. (eds.) Advances in the Study of Motion in French, pp. 407–450. John Benjamins (2019)

19. Liebesman, D., Magidor, O.: Copredication and property inheritance. Philos. Issues **27**(1), 131–166 (2017). https://doi.org/10.1111/phis.12104

20. Luo, Z.: Contextual analysis of word meanings in type-theoretical semantics. In: Pogodalla, S., Prost, J.-P. (eds.) LACL 2011. LNCS (LNAI), vol. 6736, pp. 159–174. Springer, Heidelberg (2011). https://doi.org/10.1007/978-3-642-22221-4_11

21. Magidor, O.: Counting and copredication. In: LINGUAE Seminar. Institut Jean Nicod, Paris (2017)

22. Mery, B.: Modélisation de la Sémantique Lexicale dans le cadre de la Théorie des Types. Ph.D. thesis, Université de Bordeaux, July 2011

23. Mery, B.: Challenges in the computational implementation of montagovian lexical semantics. In: Kurahashi, S., Ohta, Y., Arai, S., Satoh, K., Bekki, D. (eds.) New Frontiers in Artificial Intelligence: JSAI-isAI 2016 Workshops, Revised Selected Papers, pp. 90–107. Springer International Publishing, Cham (2017)

24. Mery, B., Moot, R., Retoré, C.: Computing the semantics of plurals and massive entities using many-sorted types. In: Murata, T., Mineshima, K., Bekki, D. (eds.) JSAI-isAI 2014. LNCS (LNAI), vol. 9067, pp. 144–159. Springer, Heidelberg (2015). https://doi.org/10.1007/978-3-662-48119-6_11

25. Moot, R.: The grail theorem prover: type theory for syntax and semantics. In: Chatzikyriakidis, S., Luo, Z. (eds.) Modern Perspectives in Type-Theoretical Semantics. SLP, vol. 98, pp. 247–277. Springer, Cham (2017). https://doi.org/10.1007/978-3-319-50422-3_10

26. Muskens, R.: Combining montague semantics and discourse representation. Linguist. Philos. **19**, 143–186 (1996)

27. Nunberg, G.: Transfers of meaning. In: Proceedings of the 31st annual meeting on Association for Computational Linguistics, pp. 191–192. Association for Computational Linguistics, Morristown, NJ, USA (1993)

28. Pustejovsky, J.: The Generative Lexicon. MIT Press, Cambridge (1995)

29. Real, L., Retoré, C.: A case study of copredication over a deverbal that reconciles empirical data with computational semantics. In: McCready, E. (ed.) LENLS12: Logic and Engineering of Natural Language Semantics 12. Tokyo, Japan, November 2015. https://hal-lirmm.ccsd.cnrs.fr/lirmm-01311129

30. Retoré, C.: The montagovian generative lexicon lambda Tyn: a type theoretical framework for natural language semantics. In: 19th International Conference on Types for Proofs and Programs (TYPES 2013). Leibniz International Proceedings in Informatics (LIPIcs), vol. 26, pp. 202–229. Schloss Dagstuhl, Germany (2014)

31. Retoré, C., Zaradzki, L.: Individuals, equivalences and quotients in type theoretical semantics. In: Logic Colloquium 2018 (2018). https://lc18.uniud.it/slides/papers/christian-retore-quotients.pdf

32. Yoshikawa, M., Mineshima, K., Noji, H., Bekki, D.: Consistent CCG parsing over multiple sentences for improved logical reasoning. CoRR abs/1804.07068 (2018). http://arxiv.org/abs/1804.07068

Polynomial Event Semantics
Non-Montagovian Proper Treatment of Quantifiers

Oleg Kiselyov[(⊠)]

Tohoku University, Sendai, Japan
oleg@okmij.org

Abstract. We propose a simple extension of event semantics that naturally supports the compositional treatment of quantification. Our analyses require neither quantifier raising or other syntactic movements, nor type-lifting. Denotations are computed strictly compositionally, from lexical entries up, and quantifiers are analyzed in situ. We account for the universal, existential and counting quantification and the related distributive coordination, with the attendant quantifier ambiguity phenomena. The underlying machinery is not of lambda-calculus but of much simpler relational algebra, with straightforward set-theoretic interpretation.

The source of quantifier ambiguity in our approach lies in two possible analyses for the existential (and counting) quantification. Their inherent ambiguity however becomes apparent only in the presence of another, non-existential quantification.

1 Introduction

The recent paper [8] reported an application of so-called transformational semantics to textual inference within the FraCaS bank [4] – actually, only within the generalized quantifier section of FraCaS. It was left to future work to extend the approach to event semantics, so to handle tense and aspect. The present paper clears one theoretical hurdle on the road to such extension.

The major and immediate hurdle is the compositional treatment of quantifiers in event semantics, which is a well-known thorny problem: see, for example, [3,6]. The latter paper also describes two recent solutions, in the tradition of Montagovian semantics. We present an alternative, non-Montagovian treatment. Besides metatheoretic preferences, we are motivated by the goal of solving entailment problems (at first, in FraCaS) completely automatically. We hence aim not just at presenting an analysis of various quantification phenomena. Our goal is to develop a mechanical procedure, an algorithm, of hopefully low-complexity, to obtain the meaning of a sentence from its surface (or, at least, treebank-annotated) form *without any human intervention*, without any fuzzing and ad hoc adjustments.

A characteristic of [8] is the use of a first-order theorem prover to decide entailments. The meaning of sentences had to be described by first-order formulas. The careful analysis of the generated formulas shown that they fall within

© Springer Nature Switzerland AG 2019
K. Kojima et al. (Eds.): JSAI-isAI 2018 Workshops, LNAI 11717, pp. 313–324, 2019.
https://doi.org/10.1007/978-3-030-31605-1_23

a subset of first-order logic, and could in fact be represented in Description Logic (DL) [9]. DL has roots in databases and relational algebra rather than lambda-calculus, and has straightforward set-theoretic semantics (see Sect. 5 for more discussion). Thus the motivation for the present work is analyzing complex quantification phenomena within event semantics taking inspiration from DL.

Our contribution is the compositional, easily mechanizable, non-Montagovian treatment of quantified NP and adverbial phrases. In contrast to syntactic approaches – movements, raising, transformations – ours is purely semantic, based on the construction of a suitable semantic domain. We use no continuations, no monads, no lambda-calculus, and, in fact, no variables. Rather, we rely merely on sets, relations and simple algebra. We arrive at the event semantics with all of its benefits, and account for the universal, existential and counting quantification and the attendant quantifier ambiguities. Quantifiers are analyzed in situ.

In this first paper on this topic we only deal with positive polarity phrases; however, Sect. 4.3 briefly discusses handling negative polarity.

The analyses of all the examples have been mechanically verified. The accompanying source code presents the model calculations in full, and includes more examples. It is available at http://okmij.org/ftp/gengo/poly-event/.

2   Classical Event Semantics

First, we recall the 'classical' (Davidsonian) event semantics, albeit in a different notation inspired by DL [9].

Our semantic domain is comprised of *individuals* such as john and bM, of *concepts* such as Student, and of *roles* such as subj'. Individuals, identified by names, refer to entities in the domain of discourse: people, things, moments of time – and also events. Event names, such as bM, are meant to be suggestive, see Fig. 1 for the key. Concepts denote properties of individuals (that is, refer to sets of entities); concept names are always capitalized. Roles are binary relations – specifically, relations of events to individuals, which may also be events. Role names are in lower-case and end in an apostrophe. Unless stated otherwise, roles are functional relations. Figure 1 shows the sample domain to be used in running examples.

Just as in [8], our input are sentences annotated in the Penn Historical Corpora system (extensively used in [2]), such as

(1)   (IP-MAT (NP-SBJ (NPR Bill)) (VBD cut) (NP-OB1 (NPR PEMo)))

(2)   (IP-MAT (NP-SBJ (D A) (N student))
                (VBD cut) (NP-OB1 (Q every) (N class)))

Erasing the annotations gives the original plain-text sentence: "Bill cut PEMo" for (1) (where 'PEMo' is the abbreviation for 'physical education class on Monday') and "A student cut every class" for (2).

Individuals	students, classes, days of week, events
Concepts	Student : {bill , john , seth}
	Cut : events bM through sF
	Class : {peMo , peWd , peFr}
Roles	subj′, ob1′ as in the table below

event	subj	obj	event	subj	obj
bM	bill	peMo	jM	john	peMo
bW	bill	peWd	sW	seth	peWd
bF	bill	peFr	sF	seth	peFr

Fig. 1. Sample domain of student cutting classes

The meaning of (1) can be expressed by the intersection of three concepts:

$$(3) \qquad \mathsf{subj}'/\mathsf{bill} \sqcap \mathsf{Cut} \sqcap \mathsf{ob1}'/\mathsf{peMo}$$

Here subj'/x stands for the concept denoting the set of events that are related by the role subj' to the individual x: $\{y \mid \mathsf{subj}'(y, x)\}$. That is, $\mathsf{subj}'/\mathsf{bill}$ means the events in which Bill is the subject. The notation extends to concepts: $\mathsf{subj}'/\mathsf{C}$ denotes the set of events whose subjects are characterized by C. Therefore, $\mathsf{subj}'/\mathsf{bill}$ can also be written as $\mathsf{subj}'/\{\mathsf{bill}\}$ where $\{\mathsf{bill}\}$ is the singular concept, whose sole instance is the named individual. The concept Cut refers to events whose action is cutting classes. The third term of (3) is similar to the first one; it is the concept denoting events whose object is the PEMo class. The whole sentence is characterized by the intersection of the three concepts.

Formally, we call a concept (or the concept formula) like (3) a denotation of the corresponding sentence, (1) in our case. A non-empty set of events that have the property specified by the concept is a *model* for the concept. In our sample domain (world), the model of (3) is the singleton {bM}. If a sentence denotation does not have a model, then the sentence is 'false': incompatible with the record of events in the world in question.

One may think of a model as the evidence why the sentence is 'true'. The sentence (1) is true in the sample world because of the event bM that has transpired there. This point of view turns out illuminating when contemplating models of sentences with quantifiers, see Sect. 3.

One must have noticed how closely the denotation formula (3) corresponds to the structure of its sentence, (1). The correspondence will be formally defined in Sect. 4. The approach easily extends to adverbs (e.g., "deliberately" – whose denotation, Deliberately, denotes events whose action is done deliberately), temporal relations, etc. It does stumble, however, on quantification.

3 Poly-concepts

Our goal is to analyze sentences with quantifiers, such as

$$(4) \qquad \text{Bill cut every class}$$

or, annotated

(5) (IP-MAT (NP-SBJ (NPR Bill)) (VBD cut) (NP-OB1 (Q every) (N class)))

just as straightforwardly as we did (1). That is not easy, however. To account for quantification, this section refines concepts to poly-concepts, whose models are sets with some structure.

The trouble with quantification begins when trying to formulate the concept that would describe (NP-OB1 (Q every) (N class)). It cannot be ob1'/Class, because that concept admits a mere singleton $\{bM\}$ model: an event whose object is *a* class. On the other hand, an event whose object is all classes, besides physically implausible, would give too narrow interpretation of (4): After all, the sentence does not assert that Bill cut all the classes in 'one shot': the class-cutting may have been spread over time.

Let us step back and consider what should be the evidence for (4) in our sample world. It should be the events of Bill cutting the Physical Education class on Monday, Wednesday and Friday (which are all classes in our world). These events taken *together* is the evidence for (4). We call such a set of events a *group*, and write in angular brackets, for example: $\langle bM, bW, bF \rangle$. The events in a group have no particular order, temporal or causal connection – but they are all regarded as a part of a single collective of events. Thus our intuition is that sentences with quantifiers are statements about groups of events.

However, groups alone are not enough to give denotations to all quantifier phrases (QNP). Consider

(6)   Bill cut two classes.

(which we take to mean that Bill cut at least two classes). We may cite the group $\langle bM, bW \rangle$ as the evidence for (6) – or the group $\langle bW, bF \rangle$, or $\langle bM, bF \rangle$. We call a set of groups each of which could be the evidence a *factor*, notated as follows (for our example):

$$\lceil \langle bM, bW \rangle \ \langle bW, bF \rangle \ \langle bM, bF \rangle \rceil$$

The singleton set containing this factor is a model for (6). We may distribute groups to factors in a different way:

$$\{\lceil \langle bM, bW \rangle \rceil, \lceil \langle bW, bF \rangle \rceil, \lceil \langle bM, bF \rangle \rceil\}$$

This is also a model for (6), now with three alternative factors. A model is hence a set of alternative factors; once we pick one alternative ('external choice') we get a factor that contains one or more groups ('internal choice') each of which may be used as the evidence. One can see a close connection to 'alternative semantics', as we briefly discuss in Sect. 5. Later we will see that these 'external' and 'internal' choices are closely connected to the quantifier scope.

We thus generalize concepts to poly-concepts. Whereas a concept describes a property of individuals/individual events, a poly-concept describes a property of groups of individuals, with alternatives. For example, whereas Student denotes students, the poly-concept 'two students' describes groups of two students and can be used to give the meaning to 'Two students cut a class': there is a group of two students each of which cut a class (in fact, there is more than one such group to choose from). It should be clear that we take group 'loosely': we do not insists, for example, that the two students cut the class together. (Tight groups are better represented as particular individuals).

Poly-concepts are built from ordinary concepts with the $\mathcal{P}$ operation, and from the existing poly-concepts using union, intersection, the group formation ('multiplication'), and the flattening $\mathcal{N}$, as formally shown in Fig. 2. The empty poly-concept, just like the empty concept, is denoted by $\perp$.

$$
\begin{array}{lll}
\text{Concept} & c & \\
\text{Poly-concept} & x, y & ::= \quad \perp \mid \mathcal{P}c \mid \mathcal{N}x \mid x \sqcup y \mid x \sqcap y \mid x \otimes y
\end{array}
$$

Fig. 2. Poly-concepts: Syntax

Set-theoretically, a poly-concept is a set of factors; a factor is a set of groups, and a group is a set of entities. The meta-variables used to refer to groups, factors and poly-concepts, and the corresponding notation are collected below:

Individuals	i			
Concept	c	set of individuals	$\{i_1, \ldots, i_n\}$	for some $n \geq 0$
Group	g	set of individuals	$\langle i_1, \ldots, i_m \rangle$	for some $m \geq 1$
Factor	d	set of groups	$\lceil g_1 \ \ldots \ g_n \rceil$	for some $m \geq 0$
Poly-concept	x, y	set of factors	$\{d_1, \ldots, d_n\}$	for some $n \geq 0$

Groups are always non-empty. Although empty factors can come up during calculations, they are not included in a poly-concept. A poly-concept hence is a set of non-empty factors. The empty poly-concept $\perp$ is the empty set of factors. All groups within one factor have the same cardinality. We write $|d|$ for the cardinality of groups in the factor d.

$$
\begin{array}{ll}
\mathcal{P}c & = \{\lceil \langle i \rangle \rceil \mid i \in c\} \\
\mathcal{N}x & = \bigcup_{d \in x} d \\
x \sqcup y & = x \cup y \\
x \otimes y & = \{d_1 \otimes d_2 \mid d_1 \in x, d_2 \in y\} \\
d_1 \otimes d_2 & = \{g_1 \cup g_2 \mid g_1 \in d_1, g_2 \in d_2, g_1 \cap g_2 = \varnothing\} \\
x^n & = x \otimes x \ldots \otimes x \qquad n\text{-times multiplication} \\
x \sqcap y & = \{d_1 \sqcap d_2 \mid d_1 \in x, d_2 \in y\} \\
d_1 \sqcap d_2 & = d_1^{|d_2|} \cap d_2^{|d_1|}
\end{array}
$$

Fig. 3. Poly-concepts: Set-theoretic semantics. Empty factors are always suppressed when forming poly-concepts.

The (set-theoretical) meaning of the poly-concept operations is defined in Fig. 3. $\mathcal{P}c$ lifts a concept c to a poly-concept by turning each element of c into its own group, which are collected in the single factor. Empty factors are always suppressed when forming poly-concepts; therefore, $\mathcal{P}\bot$ is $\bot$, the empty set of factors. As another example, $\mathcal{P}$ Student is the poly-concept $\{\lceil \langle \text{bill} \rangle \ \langle \text{john} \rangle \ \langle \text{seth} \rangle \rceil\}$. Flattening (or narrowing) $\mathcal{N}x$ joins all factors of x into one. The poly-concept union $x \sqcup y$ is the mere set-union of x and y regarded as sets of factors.

The poly-concept multiplication $x \otimes y$ and intersection $x \sqcap y$ are interpreted as the multiplication (resp. intersection) of each factor of x with each factor of y, dropping the empty factors. Factor multiplication $d_1 \otimes d_2$ is almost as straightforward: the pairwise union of d_1's and d_2's groups – provided the groups are disjoint. Thus the result of the multiplication has bigger groups; in fact

$$(7) \qquad\qquad |d_1 \otimes d_2| = |d_1| + |d_2|$$

The disjointness condition is subtle. The table below shows the result of exponentiating $\mathcal{P}$Student (i.e., multiplying with itself several times), in our sample domain:

$(\mathcal{P} \text{ Student})^1$	$\{\lceil \langle \text{bill} \rangle \ \langle \text{john} \rangle \ \langle \text{seth} \rangle \rceil\}$
$(\mathcal{P} \text{ Student})^2$	$\{\lceil \langle \text{bill} , \text{john} \rangle \ \langle \text{john} , \text{seth} \rangle \ \langle \text{bill} , \text{seth} \rangle \rceil\}$
$(\mathcal{P} \text{ Student})^3$	$\{\lceil \langle \text{bill} , \text{john} , \text{seth} \rangle \rceil\}$
$(\mathcal{P} \text{ Student})^4$	$\bot$

In general, if c is a concept with n entities $\{i_1, \ldots, i_n\}$, then

$$\underbrace{\mathcal{P}c \otimes \mathcal{P}c \otimes \cdots \otimes \mathcal{P}c}_{m} = \begin{cases} \{\lceil \langle i_1, \ldots, i_n \rangle \rceil\} & \text{if } m = n \\ \bot & \text{if } m > n \end{cases}$$

The factor intersection $d_1 \sqcap d_2$ is even more subtle: $d_1^{|d_2|} \cap d_2^{|d_1|}$, that is, intersecting exponentiated factors. From (7) we see that the factors to intersect have the same cardinality:

$$|d_1^{|d_2|}| = |d_2^{|d_1|}| = |d_1| \, |d_2|$$

The reason the factor intersection is so complex will become clear in the next section.

4   Compositional Semantics: From a Sentence to a Poly-concept

We now describe how the poly-concept that represents the meaning of a sentence is built up, compositionally, from the concepts of lexical entries up to the tree root. Roughly, (non-functional) lexical entries contribute concepts: common nouns and adjectives are properties of individuals; verbs and adverbs are properties of the transpired events. The concepts are lifted to poly-concepts with the $\mathcal{P}$ operation. Adjoining nodes intersects the corresponding poly-concepts.

To be more precise, consider the following (simplified) grammar for the treebank annotated sentences, which we take as our input. We disregard tense and aspect and gloss plurality, which are to be dealt with in the future work.

$$
\begin{array}{lll}
\text{clause} & ::= & \text{node}_1 \ \dots \ \text{node}_n \\
\text{node} & ::= & \text{NP-SBJ np} \mid \text{NP-OB1 np} \mid \text{VB verb} \mid \text{ADV adverb} \mid \text{pp} \\
\text{np} & ::= & \text{det nom}_1 \ \dots \ \text{nom}_n \mid \text{proper-noun} \\
\text{nom} & ::= & \text{common-noun} \mid \text{pp} \mid \text{adj} \\
\text{pp} & ::= & \text{PP preposition np}
\end{array}
$$

The poly-concept describing a clause is the intersection of poly-concepts for each node. The poly-concept for (VB verb) is the concept for the verb (the set of events where the verb action took place), extended to the poly-concept with $\mathcal{P}$. Adverbs are similar. Nominals nom are described by poly-concepts, or simple concepts (for common-noun and adjectives) subsequently lifted. The poly-concept for a sequence of nominals is the intersection of poly-concepts for the members of the sequence.

What is left to define are poly-concepts for nominal phrases. NPs always appear in some role, such as NP-SUBJ, NP-OB1, or the preposition-role. Therefore, we define poly-concepts not for NPs per se but for an NP in a role. The definitions are uniform in the treatment of roles; we take subj′ for concreteness:

(8)	Proper noun	$\mathcal{P}(\text{subj}'/\{\text{properNoun}\})$
(9)	"at least" k nom	$\bigcup_{s \subset \text{CN}, |s|=k} \prod_{i \in s} \mathcal{P}(\text{subj}'/\{i\})$
(10)	"at least" k nom	$\mathcal{N}x \qquad$ where x is from (9)
(11)	"an" nom	$\bigcup_{i \in \text{CN}} \mathcal{P}(\text{subj}'/\{i\})$
(12)	"an" nom	$\mathcal{P}(\text{subj}'/\text{CN})$
(13)	"every" nom	$\prod_{i \in \text{CN}} \mathcal{P}(\text{subj}'/\{i\})$

Here, $\{\text{ProperNoun}\}$ is the concept representing the proper noun in question, and CN is the concept for the nominal nom. There are two alternative definitions for existential and counting quantifiers: they are inherently ambiguous in our approach. (The number quantification "exactly n" and "at most n" also carry negative polarity, describing events that should not take place. Negative polarity is not considered in the present paper.)

For the starting example (1) from Sect. 2, reproduced below

(14)   (IP-MAT (NP-SBJ (NPR Bill)) (VBD cut) (NP-OB1 (NPR PEMo)))

we obtain, following the just given definitions, the poly-concept denotation

(15) $\mathcal{P}(\text{subj}'/\{\text{bill}\}) \sqcap (\mathcal{P}\text{Cut} \sqcap \mathcal{P}(\text{ob1}'/\{\text{peMo}\}))$

which is the $\mathcal{P}$-lifted concept denotation (3) described in Sect. 2.

We are now in a position to compute the denotation of quantified phrases, in particular, (5) (repeated below), used as the motivation in Sect. 3:

(16)   (IP-MAT (NP-SBJ(NPR Bill)) (VBD cut) (NP-OB1 (Q every)(N class)))

The poly-concept denotation is:

$$(17) \qquad \mathcal{P}(\mathsf{subj}'/\{\mathsf{bill}\}) \sqcap (\mathcal{P}\mathsf{Cut} \sqcap \prod_{i \in \mathsf{Class}} \mathcal{P}(\mathsf{ob1}'/\{i\}))$$

To evaluate this denotation in our sample world, we compute, following Fig. 3:

$$\mathcal{P}(\mathsf{subj}'/\{\mathsf{bill}\}):$$
(18) $$\{\lceil \langle \mathsf{bM} \rangle \ \langle \mathsf{bW} \rangle \ \langle \mathsf{bF} \rangle \ \rceil\}$$

$$\mathcal{P}(\mathsf{ob1}'/\{\mathsf{peMo}\}) \otimes \mathcal{P}(\mathsf{ob1}'/\{\mathsf{peWd}\}) \otimes \mathcal{P}(\mathsf{ob1}'/\{\mathsf{peFr}\}):$$
$$\{\lceil \langle \mathsf{bM}, \mathsf{bW}, \mathsf{bF} \rangle \ \langle \mathsf{bM}, \mathsf{bW}, \mathsf{sF} \rangle \ \langle \mathsf{bM}, \mathsf{sW}, \mathsf{bF} \rangle \ \langle \mathsf{bM}, \mathsf{sW}, \mathsf{sF} \rangle$$
(19) $$\langle \mathsf{jM}, \mathsf{bW}, \mathsf{bF} \rangle \ \langle \mathsf{jM}, \mathsf{bW}, \mathsf{sF} \rangle \ \langle \mathsf{jM}, \mathsf{sW}, \mathsf{bF} \rangle \ \langle \mathsf{jM}, \mathsf{sW}, \mathsf{sF} \rangle \rceil\}$$

Taking the poly-concept intersection, we obtain the model for the entire denotation (17):
$$\{\lceil \langle \mathsf{bM}, \mathsf{bW}, \mathsf{bF} \rangle \rceil\}$$

The model shows the events that justify the truth of "Bill cut every class" in our sample world. A similar calculation shows that "Every student cut every class" does not have a model in our world.

4.1 Quantifier Ambiguity

Since the existential and counting quantifiers can be analyzed in two different ways, ambiguity arises. Indeed, consider (20) (which is (2) repeated):

(20)   (IP-MAT (NP-SBJ (D A) (N student))

              (VBD cut) (NP-OB1 (Q every) (N class)))

for which we can derive either (21) or (22), depending on whether we use (11) or (12):

$$(21) \qquad \bigcup_{i \in \mathsf{Student}} \mathcal{P}(\mathsf{subj}'/\{i\}) \sqcap (\mathcal{P}\mathsf{Cut} \sqcap \prod_{i \in \mathsf{Class}} \mathcal{P}(\mathsf{ob1}'/\{i\}))$$

$$(22) \qquad \mathcal{P}(\mathsf{subj}'/\mathsf{Student}) \sqcap (\mathcal{P}\mathsf{Cut} \sqcap \prod_{i \in \mathsf{Class}} \mathcal{P}(\mathsf{ob1}'/\{i\}))$$

In our sample world,

$$\bigcup_{i\in\mathsf{Student}} \mathcal{P}(\mathsf{subj}'\,/\,\{i\})\ (\text{``a student'' according to (11)}) :$$
$$\{\lceil\langle\mathsf{bM}\rangle\ \langle\mathsf{bW}\rangle\ \langle\mathsf{bF}\rangle\rceil,\ \lceil\langle\mathsf{jM}\rangle\rceil,\ \lceil\langle\mathsf{sW}\rangle\ \langle\mathsf{sF}\rangle\rceil\}$$
$$\mathcal{P}(\mathsf{subj}'/\mathsf{Student})\ (\text{``a student'' according to (12)}) :$$
$$\{\lceil\langle\mathsf{bM}\rangle\ \langle\mathsf{bW}\rangle\ \langle\mathsf{bF}\rangle\ \langle\mathsf{jM}\rangle\ \langle\mathsf{sW}\rangle\ \langle\mathsf{sF}\rangle\rceil\}$$

Keeping in mind (19) as the denotation for "every class" we obtain for the whole (20)

$$\text{Model of (21)} : \{\lceil\langle\mathsf{bM},\mathsf{bW},\mathsf{bF}\rangle\rceil\}$$
$$\text{Model of (22)} : \text{the same as (19)}$$

The former model demonstrates the linear reading of "a student cut every class", with the existential taking the wide scope: the sentence is true in our world because there exists one particular student (namely, Bill) who skipped every class. In contrast, the denotation (21) corresponds to the narrow-scope reading of the existential. The model has many choices for the evidence: all three classes are cut, but by generally different students.

Sentences with several existential quantifiers also have several interpretations, for example, (23):

(23)   (IP-MAT (NP-SBJ (D a) (N Student))

                        (VBD cut) (NP-OB1 (D a) (N class)))

Each of the two indefinite determiners can be analyzed either as (11) or (12), giving four possible poly-concepts for (23). They are all distinct, and have a model in our world:

$$\{\lceil\langle\mathsf{bM}\rangle\ \langle\mathsf{bW}\rangle\ \langle\mathsf{bF}\rangle\ \langle\mathsf{jM}\rangle\ \langle\mathsf{sW}\rangle\ \langle\mathsf{sF}\rangle\rceil\}$$
$$\{\lceil\langle\mathsf{bM}\rangle\ \langle\mathsf{bW}\rangle\ \langle\mathsf{bF}\rangle\rceil,\ \lceil\langle\mathsf{jM}\rangle\rceil,\ \lceil\langle\mathsf{sW}\rangle\ \langle\mathsf{sF}\rangle\rceil\}$$
$$\{\lceil\langle\mathsf{bM}\rangle\ \langle\mathsf{jM}\rangle\rceil,\ \lceil\langle\mathsf{bW}\rangle\ \langle\mathsf{sW}\rangle\rceil,\ \lceil\langle\mathsf{bF}\rangle\ \langle\mathsf{sF}\rangle\rceil\}$$
$$\{\lceil\langle\mathsf{bM}\rangle\rceil,\ \lceil\langle\mathsf{bW}\rangle\rceil,\ \lceil\langle\mathsf{bF}\rangle\rceil,\ \lceil\langle\mathsf{jM}\rangle\rceil,\ \lceil\langle\mathsf{sW}\rangle\rceil,\ \lceil\langle\mathsf{sF}\rangle\rceil\}$$

It is easy to see that the four denotation are equivalent: if one has a model, so are the others. Therefore, (23) is not really ambiguous.

Quantified adverbial modifiers like "everyday" and quantified adverbial phrases are analyzed similarly to NP-SBJ and NP-OB1 phrases. Like the latter, adverbials also describe the set of events, which occur within some time moments or places.

4.2   Counting Quantification and Ambiguity

Like existential, counting quantification can also be analyzed in two different ways, giving rise to ambiguity. Indeed, consider "Two students cut every class".

Similarly to the calculations above, we obtain two denotations; one of them has the model

$$\{\lceil\langle \mathsf{bM}, \mathsf{bW}, \mathsf{bF}, \mathsf{jM}, \mathsf{sW}, \mathsf{sF}\rangle\rceil\}$$

and the other does not, demonstrating the two readings of the sentence neither of which entails the other.

4.3 Negative-Polarity Phrases

Our approach is easily extensible to negative-polarity quantifiers such as 'no', adverbs such as 'never', and also quantifiers such as 'at most' and 'exactly'. So far, we have been computing a poly-concept that describes events that justify the sentence in question (provide the model for the sentence) – a group of events which, if occur, would make the sentence true. To deal with negative polarity, we also should compute *false conditions* – events which, if occur, will falsify the sentence. The false conditions are computed just as compositionally as truth conditions.

5 Related Work

One inspiration for this work comes from Description Logics (DL), which are subsets of C2 (first-order logic with two variables and counting quantifiers) developed for the task of knowledge representation. DL can be traced to databases and relational algebra. DL exploits the fact that the two variables in C2 formulas can be kept implicit and do not have to be named, which eliminates the whole class of problems inherent in lambda-calculus, regarding alpha-conversion, substitution and binding. The variable-free nature of DL and its roots in knowledge representation offer a different, arguably, more linguistically intuitive perspective than Montagovian semantics. Also important is that DL are developed to be decidable, and easily. The decidability/complexity of various DL are thoroughly investigated, resulting in practical decision procedures and highly optimized implementations. We refer to DL Primer [9] and the tutorial [1] for good introduction.

DL have certainly used before for computational linguistics/NLP – for example, [7], but not for theoretical linguistics, to my knowledge. The NLP applications are either at hoc or "best-effort" (or both) – neither of which is a problem for NLP since compositional treatment and building a semantic theory are not the goals there. I have not seen using DL as an alternative to Montagovian semantics, specifically, PTQ.

Our work, especially the earlier [8], have much in common with the work of Tian, Miyao et al. on Dependency-based Compositional Semantics (DCS) [5,11]. The similarity with [8] is using relation algebra semantics and representing the properties of generalized quantifiers as axioms. We share the observation that our semantic representations are essentially DL. Unlike [5], we had no problems with quantifiers like 'few', downward monotone on the first argument. The characteristic feature of the present paper is the explicit use of event semantics.

Our main difference from [5,11] is methodological: we are interested in theoretical semantics rather than NLP. Therefore, we have no use for approximately paraphrasing sentences, word sense similarity and other NLP techniques. The methodological difference leads to many technical differences. First, whereas Tian et al. semantics is coarse, ours is 'hyperfine': true sentences have distinct denotations. Therefore, the model of our denotations can be used as the evidence for the truth of the sentences.

Another distinction is our use of event semantics, and the aim to resolve problems of quantification in event semantics.

Our idea of alternative factors and alternative evidence is closely related to the alternative semantics [10]. For example, our $\mathcal{N}x$ operator also occurs in the alternative semantics.

Unlike Champollion [3] we do not try to combine Montagovian treatment of quantifiers with event semantics; we investigate the alternative to the Montagovian treatment instead.

6   Conclusions

We have outlined yet another proper treatment of quantification – this time, with no lifting, lambda calculus or even variables. Nevertheless, we are able to analyze quantifier scope (for positive polarity phrases, at the moment), quantifier ambiguity. Our semantics has straightforward set-theoretic interpretation: the models or denotations are triple-nested sets.

The future work is to fully develop the treatment of negation, only briefly hinted at in the present paper. Another item is the treatment of tense and aspect. It is intriguing to explore connections with collective readings of quantifiers.

Acknowledgments. I am grateful to anonymous reviewers for very helpful comments and the pointers to related work. I thank Yu Izumi for an inspiring conversation.

References

1. Baader, F.: Description logics. In: Tessaris, S., et al. (eds.) Reasoning Web 2009. LNCS, vol. 5689, pp. 1–39. Springer, Heidelberg (2009). https://doi.org/10.1007/978-3-642-03754-2_1

2. Butler, A.: The treebank semantics parsed corpus (2017). http://www.compling.jp/tspc/

3. Champollion, L.: The interaction of compositional semantics and event semantics. Linguist. Philos. **38**(1), 31–66 (2015)

4. Cooper, R., et al.: Using the framework. Deliverable D16, FraCaS Project (1996)

5. Dong, Y., Tian, R., Miyao, Y.: Encoding generalized quantifiers in dependency-based compositional semantics. In: Proceedings of the 28th Pacific Asia Conference on Language, Information and Computation, PACLIC 28, Cape Panwa Hotel, Phuket, Thailand, 12–14 December 2014, pp. 585–594 (2014), http://aclweb.org/anthology/Y/Y14/Y14-1067.pdf

6. de Groote, P., Winter, Y.: A type-logical account of quantification in event semantics. In: Murata, T., Mineshima, K., Bekki, D. (eds.) JSAI-isAI 2014. LNCS (LNAI), vol. 9067, pp. 53–65. Springer, Heidelberg (2015). https://doi.org/10.1007/978-3-662-48119-6_5. https://hal.inria.fr/hal-01102261
7. Gyawali, B., Shimorina, A., Gardent, C., Cruz-Lara, S., Mahfoudh, M.: Mapping natural language to description logic. In: Blomqvist, E., Maynard, D., Gangemi, A., Hoekstra, R., Hitzler, P., Hartig, O. (eds.) ESWC 2017, Part I. LNCS, vol. 10249, pp. 273–288. Springer, Cham (2017). https://doi.org/10.1007/978-3-319-58068-5_17
8. Kiselyov, O.: Transformational semantics on a tree bank. In: Arai, S., Kojima, K., Mineshima, K., Bekki, D., Satoh, K., Ohta, Y. (eds.) JSAI-isAI 2017. LNCS (LNAI), vol. 10838, pp. 241–252. Springer, Cham (2018). https://doi.org/10.1007/978-3-319-93794-6_17
9. Krötzsch, M., Simancik, F., Horrocks, I.: A description logic primer. CoRR abs/1201.4089 (2013)
10. Rooth, M.: Alternative Semantics. Oxford University Press, Oxford (2016). https://doi.org/10.1093/oxfordhb/9780199642670.013.19
11. Tian, R., Miyao, Y., Matsuzaki, T.: Logical inference on dependency-based compositional semantics. In: ACL, vol. 1, pp. 79–89. The Association for Computer Linguistics (2014). http://aclweb.org/anthology/P/P14/

The Logical Principles of Honorification and Dishonorification in Japanese

David Y. Oshima[(⊠)] [iD]

Graduate School of Humanities, Nagoya University, Nagoya 464-8601, Japan
davidyo@nagoya-u.jp
http://www.hum.nagoya-u.ac.jp/~oshima

Abstract. This work develops a comprehensive and systematic analysis of the meanings of Japanese honorifics (honorific expressions), which contrast in terms of whom they "elevate" and "lower" to what extent, and discusses some essential discourse principles regulating their usage.

Keywords: Honorification · Honorifics · Conventional implicature · Presupposition · Japanese

1 Introduction

This work develops a comprehensive and systematic analysis of the meanings of Japanese honorifics (honorific expressions), which contrast in terms of whom they "elevate" and "lower" to what extent, and discusses some essential discourse principles regulating their usage.

2 Taxonomy of Honorifics

Largely following Kikuchi (1997), I assume the following taxonomy of Japanese honorifics. The basic properties of each class will be discussed presently.

(1)   a.   **positive honorifics (honorifics$_+$)**
       i.   ARG1 honorifics
       ii.   ARG2 honorifics
       iii.   denotatum honorifics
       iv.   possessor honorifics
       v.   politeness honorifics
   b.   **negative honorifics (honorifics$_-$)**
       i.   ARG1 dishonorifics
       ii.   denotatum dishonorifics
       iii.   possessor dishonorifics

Thanks to Elin McCready, Osamu Sawada, and the reviewers and audience of LENLS 15 for valuable comments.

K. Kojima et al. (Eds.): JSAI-isAI 2018 Workshops, LNAI 11717, pp. 325–340, 2019.
https://doi.org/10.1007/978-3-030-31605-1_24

   c.   **hybrid honorifics (honorifics$_\pm$)**
      i.   courtesy honorifics

Here, honorifics are classified into three groups depending on whether (i) they positively characterize the honorability of a certain party, (ii) negatively characterize the honorability of a certain party, or (iii) do both.

Another common way to classify them is by syntactic categories, into predicative and nominal ones.

(2)   a.   **predicative honorifics**: ARG1/ARG2 honorifics, ARG1 dishonorifics, politeness honorifics, courtesy honorifics
       b.   **nominal honorifics**: denotatum/posessor honorifics, denotatum/posessor dishonorifics

Yet another is into referent-oriented honorifics and audience-oriented (addressee-oriented) honorifics (Comrie 1976). Politeness honorifics are (purely) audience-oriented. Courtesy honorifics have a dual nature in this respect (Sect. 2.3, Sect. 5). All other classes are (purely) referent-oriented, although (the three classes of) dishonorifics can be characterized as having "pseudo audience-orientation" too (Sect. 4.3).

2.1   Positive Honorifics

Positive honorifics express respect toward a certain party (an entity or a group). Corresponding to predicates belonging to what has traditionally been called *sonkeigo*, ARG1 honorifics, elevate the referent of the subject (i.e., the least oblique argument). ARG1 honorific verbs can be formed with the derivational affix -$(r)are$, as in (3b), or with the circumferential "o-V$_{stem}$(-i) ni $naru$" (-i is an epenthetic vowel) or "go-VN ni $naru$" construction, as in (3c). Literally, ni is an infinitival copula form, and NARU means 'become'.[1] VN refers to a verbal noun, a nominal that may form a verbal predicate with the light verb SURU (e.g., BENKYOO SURU 'study (lit. do study)').[2],[3]

(3)   a.   Suzuki ga   kaku.
          S.   Nom write.Prs
          'Suzuki will write (it). '
       b.   Suzuki-san ga   kak**are**ru.
          S.-Suffix   Nom write.*are*.Prs

---

[1] Here and thereafter, expressions in small capitals refer to lexemes.

[2] The abbreviations in glosses are: Acc = accusative, Attr = attributive, Cl = classifier, Cop = copula, Dat = dative, DAux = discourse auxiliary, DP = discourse particle, Evid = evidential auxiliary, Ger = gerund, Inf = infinitive, Neg(Aux) = negation/negative auxiliary, Nom = nominative, Npfv = non-perfective auxiliary, Prs = present, Pst = past, Th = thematic *wa* (topic/ground marker).

[3] The appropriate usage of suffixes like *san* and titles used as "quasi-suffixes", such as SENSEI 'teacher' and KYOOJU 'professor', has close correlation with honorification. However, with Kikuchi (1997), I will not consider them to be honorific expressions *per se*.

'Mr. Suzuki (who is honorable) will write (it).'

  c. Suzuki-san ga   **okaki** **ni naru**.
      S.-Suffix   Nom *o*.write *ni naru*.Prs
      'Mr. Suzuki (who is honorable) will write (it).'

ARG1 honorific adjectives and nominal predicates can be formed with prefix *o* or *go*.

(4) a. Suzuki ga   kuwashii.
        S.   Nom knowledgable.Prs
        'Suzuki is knowledgable (about it).'
    b. Suzuki-san ga   **o**kuwashii.
        S.-Suffix   Nom knowledgable.Prs
        'Mr. Suzuki (who is honorable) is knowledgable (about it).'

A handful of basic verbs have an irregular (or "suppletive") ARG1 honorific form; OSSHARU, for example, is an ARG1 honorific corresponding to IU 'say'. Some irregular ARG1 honorific verbs are not completely synonymous to corresponding non-honorifics; MESHIAGARU, for example, covers the meanings of both TABERU 'eat' and NOMU 'drink'.

(5) a. Suzuki ga   suteeki (#to wain) o   taberu.
        S.   Nom steak   and wine Acc eat.Prs
        'Suzuki will eat a steak (and some wine).'
    b. Suzuki ga   wain (#to suteeki) o   nomu.
        S.   Nom wine and steak   Acc drink.Prs
        'Suzuki will drink some wine (and a steak).'
    c. Suzuki-san ga   suteeki to wain o   meshiagaru.
        S.-Suffix   Nom steak   and wine Acc *meshiagaru*.Prs
        'Mr. Suzuki (who is honorable) will consume a steak and some wine.'

Some verbal honorifics in different classes (to be discussed below) exhibit the same feature; e.g., the ARG2 honorific UKAGAU covers the meanings of IKU 'go', KURU 'come', and KIKU 'listen, ask', and the ARG1 dishonorific/courtesy honorific MAIRU covers the meanings of IKU 'go' and KURU 'come'.

Corresponding to Oishi's (1975) "*kenjoogo* A", ARG2 honorifics elevate the referent of the second most prominent (second least oblique) argument. ARG2 honorific verbs typically have the form: "{*o*-V$_{stem}$(-*i*)/*go*-VN} *suru*" or {*o*-V$_{stem}$ (-*i*)/*go*-VN} *mooshiageru*". Literally, SURU means 'do'. MOOSHIAGERU, when used on its own, is an irregular ARG2 honorific corresponding to *iu* 'say'.

(6) a. Suzuki-san ni   fuutoo   o   **o**watashi **sita**.
        S.-Suffix   Dat envelope Acc *o*.hand   *suru*.Pst
        '(I) handed the envelope to Mr. Suzuki (who is honorable).'
    b. Suzuki-san o   **go**an'nai **mooshiageta**.
        S.-Suffix   Acc *go*.guide *mooshiageru*.Pst
        '(I) guided Mr. Suzuki (who is honorable).'

There are a handful of irregular ARG2 honorific verbs, such as MOOSHI-AGERU corresponding to IU 'say', ITADAKU corresponding to MORAU 'receive', and aforementioned UKAGAU. Some adjectives prefixed with *o*, such as OURAYA-MASHII '(be) envious (of)', can be used as ARG2 honorifics too.

Denotatum and possessor honorifics are nominals belonging to traditional *sonkeigo*. A denotatum honorific encodes respect toward its referent; some examples are KIDEN 'you (masculine)', HEIKA '(his/your/...) majesty', and KATA 'person' (as in *ano kata* 'that person'). A possessor honorific encodes respect toward the "possessor(s)" of its referent, where possession is to be taken broadly and as subsuming ownership, kinship, and creatorship. Often, the elevated individual (the possessor) is not explicitly mentioned but only is contextually understood. Possessor honorifics are often (though not always) formed with prefixal *o* or *go*. Some examples of possessor honorifics are OKURUMA 'car', GOSHISOKU 'son', GOCHOSHO 'book', and KISHA 'your company'.

Politeness honorifics, traditionally called *teineigo*, encode respect toward the audience. In contemporary Japanese, this class consists of (i) polite verbs with the component *mas* (which, arguably, are compound verbs with *mas* being a bound base), (ii) DESU, used either as a polite copula or an auxiliary that follows certain finite predicates, and (iii) GOZAIMASU, used either as a main verb meaning '(for a non-sentient entity to) exist', or an auxiliary following an infinitive copula or an infinitive adjective.

(7)   Banana ga   {aru   / arimasu   / gozaimasu}.
       banana Nom exist.Prs   exist.*mas*.Prs   *gozaimasu*.Prs
       'There is a banana.'

(8)   Kore wa banana {da   / desu   / de   gozaimasu}.
       this Th banana Cop.Prs *desu*.Prs Cop.Inf *gozaimasu*.Prs
       'This is a banana.'

2.2 Negative Honorifics

Negative honorifics, or dishonorifics, correspond to Oishi's (1975) *"kenjoogo* B". Oishi (1975: 88) characterizes their function to elevate the audience *by means of lowering the referent of the subject* (see also Kikuchi 1997).

The class of ARG1 dishonorifics consists of five verbs: (i) ITASU 'do', (ii) MAIRU 'go, come', (iii) ORU '(for a sentient entity to) exist', (iv) MOOSU 'say', and (v) ZONJIRU 'know'. ITASU may be used either as a main verb or as a light verb in combination with a verbal noun; MAIRU and ORU may be either used as a main verb or as an auxiliary. A key difference between ARG2 honorifics (*kenjoogo* A) and ARG1 dishonorifics (*kenjoogo* B) is that the latter do *not* require the presence of a non-subject complement referring to an individual or group to be elevated. Whereas (9a) with an ARG2 honorific is infelicitous in violation of the Ban on Self-Honorification (Sect. 4.2), (9b) with an ARG1 dishonorific is not.

(9) Ani   ga   watashi ni   soo {a. #mooshiagemashita /b.
     elder.brother Nom I   Dat so   *mooshiageru.mas*.Pst
     mooshimashita}.
     moosu.mas.Pst
     'My elder brother told me so.'

Denotatum/posessor dishonorifics are negative counterparts of denotatum/posessor honorifics. Denotatum dishonorifics include SHOOSHOKU 'I', WATASHI-ME 'I', and WATASHI-DOMO 'we (exclusive)'. Possessor dishonorifics include GUSOKU 'son', SETCHO 'book', and HEISHA 'my/our company'.

2.3 Hybrid Honorifics

The ARG1 dishonorific verbs, with the exception of ZONJIRU 'know', are said to have a separate use as courtesy honorifics (*teichoogo*), which do not lower the referent of the subject but only elevate the audience (Kikuchi 1997).

(10) (by a sports announcer)
      Sanbyaku-nin no   senshu   ga   sanka   itashimasu.
      300-Cl   Cop.Attr competitor Nom participate *itasu.mas*.Prs
      '300 competitors will participate (in this event).'

(11) (on the public address system at a railroad station)
      Mamonaku densha ga   mairimasu.
      soon   train Nom *mairu.mas*.Prs
      'A train will arrive soon.'

The functions of courtesy honorifics are quite similar to politeness honorifics; the only difference is that the former pose a (negative) constraint on the honorability of the referent of the subject, to the effect that it cannot be a (group) of individual(s) that is to be elevated even slightly. The speaker in (12), addressing a senior colleague, may use either (12a) or (12b), where IRASSHARU is an ARG1 honorific, depending on the relationship between them (e.g., their respective positions, social distance, etc.). (12a) is "less respectful" than (12b), but may sound "polite enough" in the context (see below for relevant discussion). (12c), on the other hand, is invariably odd in view of the standard norms.

(12) (to a senior colleague)
      a. Suzuki-san mo ikimasu   ka?
         S.-Suffix   also go.*mas*.Prs DP
         'Are you going too, Mr. Suzuki?'
      b. Suzuki-san mo   irasshaimasu   ka?
         S.-Suffix   Nom *irassharu.mas*.Prs DP
         '*idem*'
      c.#Suzuki-san mo   mairimasu   ka?
         S.-Suffix   Nom *mairu.mas*.Prs
         (*idem*)

Kikuchi (1997) considers that this feature of courtesy honorifics, which may be called the "upper-limit effect", to be a residue of their historical origins as dishonorifics.

The distinction between ARG1 dishonorifics and courtesy honorifics is rather subtle. One may hypothesize that ITASU, MOOSU, ORU, and MAIRU are invariably used as courtesy honorifics (this would imply that ZONJIRU is the only ARG1 dishonorific item). A major motivation to admit the ambiguity of ITASU, etc. is the factor of stylistic distribution. It appears that courtesy honorifics are stylistically more constrained than ARG1 dishonorifics, and characteristic to (though not limited to) formal public speech by announcers, MC's, etc. Kikuchi (1997: 273), in this connection, remarks that the usage of ITASU 'do', etc. as courtesy honorifics is less "typical" than that as ARG1 dishonorifics. The exact nature of the putative difference between ARG1 dishonorifics and courtesy honorifics in terms of stylistic niches is a matter that calls for systematic investigations in future research.

3   Features of the Japanese Honorific System

3.1   Gradience

Different honorific expressions are associated with different degrees of respect (Hasegawa 2015; Kikuchi 1997: 262–263, McCready *forthcoming*, among others); for example, (i) GOZAIMASU '(for a non-sentient entity to) exist' conveys a higher degree of respect than (truth-conditionally synonymous) ARIMASU, (ii) "{*o*-V/*go*-VN} *ni naru*" conveys a higher degree of respect than "V-(*r*)*areru*", and (iii) "{*o*-V/*go*-VN} *mooshiageru*" conveys a higher degree of respect than "{*o*-V/*go*-VN} *suru*" (Kikuchi 1997: 146, 296, 366).[4]

I assume the ranking of some representative (classes of) honorific expressions (in terms of the strength of honorification) shown in (13).

(13)   {V-MASU, N DESU} < {V-(R)ARERU, *(g)o* V(N) SURU} < *(g)o* V(N) *ni* NARU < {GOZAIMASU, *(g)o* V(N) MOOSHIAGERU}

I furthermore postulate that each honorific expression is associated with a honorific value—the degree of its "respectfulness", ranging from 1 (most respectful) to -1 (most disrespectful), with 0 being the neutral value. I tentatively assign (i) 0.2 to V-MASU and N DESU, (ii) 0.4 to V-(R)ARERU and *(g)o* V(N) SURU, (iii) 0.5 to (G)O V NI NARU, (iv) 0.6 to GOZAIMASU, and (v) the maximum value 1 to the class of honorifics called *saikoo keigo* (supreme honorifics) like ASOBASARERU 'do' (ARG1 honorific) and GYOKUON 'speech (of an emperor)' (possessor honorific). According to the present custom, supreme honorifics are used only when the members of the Japanese imperial family, or comparable "highest-ranked" individuals in non-Japanese societies, are involved. It is worth noting that the use of supreme honorifics has been in decline, especially after the World War II.

---

[4] A fuller account of honorification also needs to take into consideration the fact that different honorifics are compatible with different ranges of registers/styles. I put aside this matter in the current work.

3.2 Presuppositionality

Conventionally encoded meaning can be divided into proffered (or "at-issue") content and conventional implicature (CI). Here, CI is construed broadly and as an equivalent of Tonhauser et al.'s (2013) "projective content". Specifically, I assume the taxonomy/terminology of Oshima (2016), where conventional meaning is divided into (i) proffered content and (ii) CI, and the latter is divided into (ii-a) non-presuppositional CI and (ii-b) presuppositional CI. Presuppositional CI is what is simply called "presupposition" in much of the literature, and differs from non-presuppositional CI in being required to be taken for granted by the interlocutors, or at least be easily inferrable (accommodatable) from the audience's perspective, in the context of utterance.

Honorific meanings conveyed by honorifics are conventionally implicated, rather than proffered (Potts 2004; Kim 2007; McCready *forthcoming*). Furthermore, with data like (14), it can be shown that they are presuppositional; *omochi* DA and SARERU are ARG1 honorifics corresponding to *motte* IRU 'have, own', and SURU 'do', respectively.

(14)   (A and B work at the same hotel. A mentions a man who made a scene at a café across the street in the morning. B has seen the man, and realized that he was a professor of her college days.)

    A: Kimi wa sawagi   o   okoshita otoko o   mita   no?
       you   Th disturbance Acc cause.Pst man   Acc see.Pst DAux
       'Did you see the man who made the scene?'

    B: Ee, okane o   {motte   nai   / #**omochide** nai}
       yes, money Acc have.Ger Npfv.Neg.Prs   *omochida*.Inf NegAux.Prs
       noni   shokuji o   {shita / #**sareta**} yoo desu.
       although meal   Acc do.Pst   *sareru*.Pst Evid *desu*.Prs
       'Yes, from what I heard, he had a meal although he did not have money.'

                         (adapted from Oshima 2016: 56)

The use of the ARG1 honorifics in (14B) would be acceptable if B had informed A beforehand of the relation between her and the man in question.

As in Oshima (2006, 2016), I adopt a *pseudo-multidimensional* system of semantic representation, where proffered content and CI are represented within a single logical expression, but nevertheless contribute to the pragmatic effect of the utterance in distinct ways. In this system, two levels of truth values are distinguished. The first is the classic values of type t, 1 and 0, for logical formulas of the familiar kind; they will be referred to as *semantic truth values*. The second is the *pragmatic truth values* I and II, which are respectively concerned with "truth of proffered content" and "satisfaction of CI". The extension of a root declarative clause will be *a set of* pragmatic truth values, rather than an individual (semantic or pragmatic) value. The logical translations of clauses will involve a variant of Oshima's (2016) *transjunction* operator, defined in (15).

(15)   *The syntax and semantics of transjunction*
        syntax:
        If ϕ and ψ are expressions of type t ($\mathbf{D}_t = \{1, 0\}$), then $\langle\phi; \psi\rangle$ is an
        expression of type T ($\mathbf{D}_T = \wp(\{\text{I, II}\})$).
        semantics:
        a. $\text{I} \in [\![\langle\phi; \psi\rangle]\!]^{\text{c, w, g}}$ iff $[\![\phi]\!]^{\text{c, w, g}} = 1$.
        b. $\text{II} \in [\![\langle\phi; \psi\rangle]\!]^{\text{c, w, g}}$ iff $[\![\psi]\!]^{\text{c, w, g}} = 1$.

By way of exemplification, (16a), (16b), and (16c), respectively involving a
trivial CI, a non-presuppositional CI (the prejacent implication), and a presuppositional CI (the existential presupposition induced by *also*), will have logical
translations along the lines of (17a–c); "$\mathbf{CG}(^\wedge p)$" is to be read as "It is common
ground that p".

(16)   a.   I admire Liszt.
        b.   I only admire Liszt.
        c.   I also admire Liszt.

(17)   a. $\langle\mathbf{admire}(\mathbf{Speaker}, \mathbf{liszt}); \mathbf{T}\rangle$
        b. $\langle\neg\exists x[x \neq\mathbf{liszt}\ \&\ \mathbf{admire}(\mathbf{Speaker}, x)]; \mathbf{admire}(\mathbf{Speaker}, \mathbf{liszt})\rangle$
        c. $\langle\mathbf{admire}(\mathbf{Speaker}, \mathbf{liszt}); \mathbf{CG}(^\wedge[\exists x[x \neq\mathbf{liszt}\ \&$
             $\mathbf{admire}(\mathbf{Speaker}, x)]])\rangle$

See Oshima (2006) for a compositional analysis of how CI's induced at the lexical
level may be projected, filtered, or blocked as they form clauses with other
constituents and are embedded under different kinds of operators.

   The meanings of the ARG1 honorific *oyomi ni* NARU 'read' and the politeness
honorific GOZAIMASU '(for a non-sentient entity to) exist' can be approximated
as in (18a, b); note that the latter induces two presuppositions, one concerning
the honorability of the audience and the other the non-sentience of the referent
of the subject. **HON** represents a function that assigns to individuals honorific
values according to their honorability—the degrees of respect that the speaker
publicly acknowledge that they deserve; this function is indexical in nature,
varying across contexts of utterance (depending on who is speaking to whom,
etc.).

(18)   a. $\lambda y[\lambda x[\langle\mathbf{read}(x, y); \mathbf{CG}(^\wedge[\mathbf{HON}(x) \geq 0.5])\rangle]]$
        b. $\lambda x[\langle\mathbf{exist}(x); \mathbf{CG}(^\wedge[\neg\mathbf{sentient}(x)\ \&\ \mathbf{HON}(\mathbf{Audience}) \geq 0.6])\rangle]$

4   Basic Pragmatic Principles of Honorification

4.1   Maximization of Reverence

For a Japanese conversation to be felicitous, it is required that "due respect" be
expressed toward the individuals mentioned or evoked in the utterance as well as
toward the audience, and also that none of these individuals be excessively elevated ("overhonorified"). To illustrate, (19a) but not (19b) is appropriate when

the speaker is a high-school student and the hearer is his teacher; conversely, (19b) but not (19a) is appropriate when the interlocutors are high-school classmates.

(19)   Ame ga   {a. furimashita /b. futta}.
       rain Nom   fall.*mas*.Pst   fall.Pst
       'It rained.'

In a similar vein, (20b) is inappropriate if Abe is the academic supervisor of the interlocutors, and (20a) is inappropriate if Ito and the interlocutors are peer graduate students.

(20)   Abe-sensei ga   pasokon   o   {a. kawareta   /b. katta}.
       A.-teacher Nom personal.computer Acc   buy.*are*.Pst   buy.Pst
       'Professor Abe {(who is honorable)/∅} bought a personal computer.'

(21)   Ito(-san) ga   pasokon   o   {a. kawareta   /b. katta}.
       I.-Suffix Nom personal.computer Acc   buy.*are*.Pst   buy.Pst
       '(Ms.) Ito {(who is honorable)/∅} bought a personal computer.'

The fundamental principle accounting for such patterns can be formulated as in (22); the notion of "honorific variants" will be discussed presently.

(22)   **Reverence Maximization #1**: For any utterance u, each lexical item (word or multi-word unit) i involved in u must be chosen in such a way that i, among its honorific variants, expresses the highest degrees of reverence toward (i) the audience of u and (ii) the referents mentioned or evoked in u that do not exceed what these individuals deserve.

An exception to this principle is the exemption and avoidance of the use of (pseudo-)audience-oriented predicative honorifics in certain subordinate clauses. As detailed by Kikuchi (1997: 361–367), different types of subordinate clause impose different requirements as to the use of politeness honorifics. Suppose that the social relation between the interlocutors is such that the speaker is expected to use politeness honorifics in root environments. In clauses headed by *ga* 'though', the use of politeness honorifics is required in much the same way as in root clauses. In ones headed by *node* 'because', the use of politeness honorifics is possible, but the choice of neutral forms (the non-use of politeness honorifics) does not incur impoliteness and could be preferred. In relative clauses, the use of politeness honorifics is less typical and likely to be regarded as prolix.

(23)   (An office worker is speaking to a senior colleague.)
   a.   Ame ga   {furimashita / #futta} ga,   jikan-doori
        rain Nom fall.*mas*.Pst   fall.Pst though time-just.as
        owarimashita.
        finish.*mas*.Pst
        'Although it rained, (it) was finished as planned.'

b. Ame ga {(?)furimashita / futta} node, enki   shimashita.
    rain Nom fall.*mas*.Pst   fall.Pst because postpone do.*mas*.Pst
    'As it rained, (we) postponed (it).'

c. Ame ga {??furimashita / futta} hi wa getsuyoobi desu.
    rain Nom fall.*mas*.Pst   fall.Pst day Th Monday   *desu*.Prs
    'The day it rained is Monday.'

It appears that (i) ARG1 dishonorifics with pseudo audience-orientation (Sect. 4.3) and (ii) courtesy honorifics with dual orientation (Sect. 5) follow the same pattern as politeness honorifics, whereas the use of all other classes—ARG1, ARG2, denotatum and possessor honorifics and denotatum and possessor dishonorifics—is regulated in the same way (or at least in very similar ways) in root and subordinate clauses. I will not attempt here to formulate rules accounting for such complex patterns in non-root environments.

What counts as "honorific variants" of a lexical item is largely determined based on the relation of truth-conditional equivalence; any two items are honorific variants if they (i) are truth-conditionally equivalent but (ii) are different as to whether or not they have honorific meaning, or as to whom they (dis)honorify to what extent.

As noted above, however, some honorifics have wider truth-conditional meaning than their non-honorific "counterparts". IRU '(for a sentient entity to) exist', for example, does not have a truth-conditionally equivalent ARG1 honorific, *oi ni* NARU and IRARERU (as an honorific verb) being ill-formed. The irregular ARG1 honorific IRASSHARU covers its meaning, along with those of IKU 'go' and KURU 'come'. Crucially, utterance (24a) does not conform to the standard norms, contrasting with appropriate (24b).

(24)   (Abe is the academic supervisor of the speaker.)

a. #Abe-sensei wa ima Osaka ni   iru.
   A.-teacher Th now O.   Dat exist.Prs
   'Professor Abe is in Osaka now.'

b. Abe-sensei wa ima Osaka ni   irassharu.
    A.-teacher Th now O.   Dat *irassharu*.Prs
    'Professor Abe (who is honorable) is in Osaka now.'

Such observations imply that some lexical-item pairs where the less honorific member is hyponymous rather than synonymous to the more honorific, such as ⟨IRU, IRASSHARU⟩ and ⟨TABERU, MESHIAGARU⟩, may count as honorific variants of each other.

4.2 The Ban on Self-Honorification, Relativity, and the Dishonorification Constraint

One notable feature of the Japanese honorific system is that it is always inappropriate for the speaker to honorify himself; an utterance like (25) can only be taken to be jocular.

(25) #Watashi ga   okaki **ni naru**.
      I   Nom *o*.write *ni naru*.Prs
      'I (who is honorable) will write (it).'

Another, illustrated in (26), is its "relativity": one must not elevate members of his "micro-level community" (e.g., family, company) when talking to non-members ("outsiders").

(26) (Tanaka, an employee of a trading company, answers a phone call from another company. Yamada is Tanaka's superior.)

    a. Yamada wa niji   ni modorimasu.
        Y.   Top two.o'clock Dat return.*mas*.Prs
        'Yamada will be back at 2:00.'
    b. #Yamada-san wa niji   ni modoraremasu.
        Y.-Suffix   Top two.o'clock Dat return.*are.mas*.Prs
        (Mr. Yamada (who is honorable) will be back at 2:00.)

The speaker of (26), Tanaka, would avoid (26a) and might well use (26b) when talking to a colleague of her company—an "insider" of the relevant micro-level community.

Additionally, the target of dishonorification is limited to the speaker himself or the members of a micro-level community that includes the speaker and excludes the audience.

(27) {Watashi / otooto}   mo paatii ni shusseki itashimasu.
      I   younger.brother also party Dat attend *itasu.mas*.Prs
      '{I/my younger brother} will attend the party, too.'

(28) (to a colleague)

    a. Takahashi-san mo shusseki {suru / shimasu   / saremasu}?
        T.-Suffix   also attend do.Prs do.*mas*.Prs do.*are.mas*.Prs
        'Are (you) going to attend (it), Mr. Takahashi?'
    b. #Takahashi-san mo shusseki {itasu   / itashimasu}?
        T.-Suffix   also attend *itasu*.Prs *itasu.mas*.Prs

These features are accounted for by principles (29)–(31).

(29) **Ban on Self-Honorification**: In any context, the speaker's own honorific value cannot exceed 0.

(30) **Relativity**: In any context, for any micro-level community C such that the speaker belongs to and the audience does not belong to C, the honorific values of the members of C cannot exceed 0.

(31) **Dishonorification Constraint**: In any context, any individual can be assigned an honorific value smaller than 0 only if he or she belongs to a micro-level community that includes the speaker and excludes the audience.

4.3 Dishonorification as Honorification

Use of dishonorific expressions is motivated by a desire to express reverence toward the audience, rather than, say, a desire to express (self-)disdain (cf. pejoratives such as YAROO 'jerk'); (32b), which involves the denotatum dishonorific WATASHI-DOMO 'we (exclusive)' and the politeness honorific DESU (which is audience-oriented), illustrates that a dishonorific does not simply convey that the targeted individual is dishonorable.

(32)   a.   Watashi-tachi wa chikarabusoku {da/desu}   yo.
             I-Pl   Th inadequate   Cop.Prs/*desu*.Prs DP
             'We are not good enough.'
       b.   **Watashi-domo** wa chikarabusoku {#da/desu}   yo.
             I-Pl(dishonorific) Th inadequate   Cop.Prs/*desu*.Prs DP
             '*idem*'

To capture the audience-oriented effect of dishonorifics, I introduce the following principle.

(33)   **Inversion**: The degree of reverence that a lexical item i expresses toward the audience matches the highest of (i) the (positive) honorific value range attributed by i to the audience and (ii) the additive inverse of the (negative) honorific value range attributed by i to the speaker or a member of his/her micro-level community.

This guarantees that the presupposition induced by WATASHI-DOMO 'we (exclusive)', represented in (34a) with the tentative honorific value -0.6, is effectively equivalent to (34b), and the meaning of the ARG1 dishonorific ZONJIRU, represented in (35a) with the tentative honorific value -0.5, is effectively equivalent to (35b) (given (31) in conjunction with (33)).

(34)   a. $\mathbf{CG}(^\wedge[\mathbf{HON}(\mathbf{Speaker} \oplus X) \leq -0.6])$
       b. $\mathbf{CG}(^\wedge[\mathbf{HON}(\mathbf{Audience}) \geq 0.6])$

(35)   a. $\lambda y[\lambda x[\langle \mathbf{know}(x, y); \mathbf{CG}(^\wedge[\mathbf{HON}(x) \leq -0.5])\rangle]]$
       b. $\lambda y[\lambda x[\langle \mathbf{know}(x, y); \mathbf{CG}(^\wedge[\mathbf{HON}(\mathbf{Audience}) \geq 0.5])\rangle]]$

5   Dual-Orientation of Courtesy Honorifics

As discussed in Sect. 2.3, courtesy honorifics have a dual orientation, encoding (like politeness honorifics) respect toward the audience while implying the non-honorability of the referent of the subject. In other words, a courtesy honorific poses constraints on the honorific values of two parties. The meaning of ORU (for a sentient entity to) exist' as a courtesy honorific, for example, can be represented as in (36) (again, the honorific value 0.5 is tentative).

(36) $\lambda x[\langle \mathbf{exist}(x); \mathbf{CG}(^\wedge[\mathbf{sentient}(x) \,\&\, \mathbf{HON}(x) \leq 0 \,\&\, \mathbf{HON}(\mathbf{Audience}) \geq 0.5])\rangle]$

6   Non-redundancy of Iterated Honorification

Sometimes a lexical item (word or multi-word unit) may contain multiple features that honorify the same individual. In (37a), for example, the verb involves (i) the ARG1 honorific marker *are*, which elevates the referent of the subject, Tanaka, and (ii) the politeness honorific marker *mas*, which elevates the audience, who again is Tanaka. Interestingly, multiple occurrence of features honorifying the same target within a single word is not only permitted, but required in certain cases. Observe the infelicity of (37c), which involves only the honorific feature with a higher honorific value, *are*.

(37)   (Tanaka, an office worker, grabs a document on the desk. Eguchi, a
         younger colleague, says to her:)
   a.   Sore, moo   yomaremashita yo.
        that already read.*are.mas*.Pst DP
        'You read it already.'
   b.   Sore, moo   yomimashita yo.
        that already read.*mas*.Pst DP
   c.   #Sore, moo   yomareta   yo.
        that   already read.*are*.Pst DP

This is intriguing, because the meanings of (37a) and (37c), including the honorific content, are expected to be equivalent, the semantic contribution of *mas* being superfluous (cf. the redundancy of *big* in "??The statue is big and huge").

(38)   (37a): $\langle$**read**(tanaka, x); **CG**($^\wedge$[**HON**(tanaka) ≥ 0.2 &
         HON(tanaka) ≥ 0.4])$\rangle$
         (37b): $\langle$**read**(tanaka, x); **CG**($^\wedge$[**HON**(tanaka) ≥ 0.2])$\rangle$
         (37c): $\langle$**read**(tanaka, x); **CG**($^\wedge$[**HON**(tanaka) ≥ 0.4])$\rangle$

This observation motivates principle (39), which amounts to saying that when respect toward a certain party can be expressed within a single word with more than one type of honorific expression, it must.

(39)   **Reverence Maximization #2**: For any utterance u, each lexical item
         i involved in u must be chosen in such a way that i, among its honorific
         variants, expresses reverence toward the audience and the referents mentioned or evoked in u with the largest number of honorific feature types
         without expressing a degree of reverence that exceeds what they deserve.

"Honorific feature types" here refer to the nine types listed in (1). While (39) is formulated in a rather general way, cases where a single lexical item involves multiple honorific feature types targeting the same individual will be limited to a handful of types conforming to one of schemes (40a–c), all of which involves audience-oriented honorification (for independent reasons, there cannot be a lexical item that is both an ARG1 honorific and a possessor honorific, both an ARG1 honorific and an ARG2 honorific, etc.).

(40) a. {ARG1 honorific or ARG 2 honofiric} + politeness honorific

b. politeness honorific + {ARG1 dishonorific or courtesy honorific}

c. ARG 2 honorific + politeness honorific + {ARG1 dishonorific or courtesy honorific}

Yomaremashita in (37a) is an instance of (40a).

Principle (39) accounts for the constraint that ARG1 dishonorifics and courtesy honorifics are always used in combination with a politeness honorific, as illustrated in (41); *shusseki itashimasu* is an instance of (40b).

(41) Watashi mo shusseki {a. itashimau   /b. #itasu}.
I   also attend   *itasu.mas*.Prs /   *itasu*.Prs
'I will attend (it), too.'

The meaning of *shusseki itashimasu* regarded as involving (*itas*(*hi*) as) an ARG1 dishonorific (rather than courtesy honorific) component will be along the lines of (42a), which is effectively equivalent to (42b) because of (31) and (33).

(42) a. $\lambda y[\lambda x[\langle \textbf{attend}(x, y); \textbf{CG}(^\wedge[\textbf{HON}(x) \leq -0.5$ & $\textbf{HON}(\textbf{Audience}) \geq 0.2])\rangle]]$

b. $\lambda y[\lambda x[\langle \textbf{attend}(x, y); \textbf{CG}(^\wedge[\textbf{HON}(\textbf{Audience}) \geq 0.5$ & $\textbf{HON}(\textbf{Audience}) \geq 0.2])\rangle]]$

An example of (40c) is *o tetsudai itashimasu* '(I/he/...) will help (you/him/...), who is honorable)', whose meaning will be approximated as in (43) if the component *itas*(*hi*) is regarded an ARG1 dishonorific, and as in (44) if it is regarded a courtesy honorific.

(43) $\lambda y[\lambda x[\langle \textbf{help}(x, y); \textbf{CG}(^\wedge[\textbf{HON}(x) \leq -0.5$ & $\textbf{HON}(y) \geq 0.4$ & $\textbf{HON}(\textbf{Audience}) \geq 0.2])\rangle]]$

(44) $\lambda y[\lambda x[\langle \textbf{help}(x, y); \textbf{CG}(^\wedge[\textbf{HON}(x) \leq 0$ & $\textbf{HON}(y) \geq 0.4$ & $\textbf{HON}(\textbf{Audience}) \geq 0.2$ & $\textbf{HON}(\textbf{Audience}) \geq 0.5])\rangle]]$

(39) does not say anything about occurrence of multiple honorific features of the *same* type within a lexical item. While many verbs can be turned into an ARG1 honorific either with affix -(*r*)*are* or the combination of (*g*)*o* and NARU (see (3)), it is uncommon, and is discouraged by prescriptivism, to use both features on a single verb token.

(45) %Suzuki-san ga   **okaki ni narareru**.
S.-Suffix   Nom *o.write ni naru.are*.Prs
(Mr. Suzuki (who is honorable) will write (it).)

On the other hand, some combinations of an irregular ARG1 honorific verb and a regular (productive) ARG1 feature, and of an irregular ARG 2 honorific verb and a regular ARG2 feature, are allowed.

(46) a. Suzuki-san ga   suteeki o   **meshiagaru**.
S.-Suffix   Nom steak   Acc *meshiagaru*.Prs

'Mr. Suzuki (who is honorable) will consume a steak.'

   b. Suzuki-san ga   suteeki o   **omeshiagari ni naru**.
      S.-Suffix   Nom steak   Acc *o.meshiagaru ni naru*.Prs
      'Mr. Suzuki (who is honorable) will consume a steak.'

(47)   a. Watashi ga   Suzuki-san ni   **ukagau**.
      I   Nom S.-Suffix   Dat *ukagau*.Prs
      'I will ask Mr. Suzuki (who is honorable).'

   b. Watashi ga   Suzuki-san ni   **oukagai suru**.
      I   Nom S.-Suffix   Dat *o.ukagau suru*.Prs
      'I will ask Mr. Suzuki (who is honorable).'

Importantly, forms with multiple ARG1 or ARG2 honorific features, such as *okaki ni narareru* (if it is regarded as well-formed) *omeshiagari ni naru*, and *oukagai suru*, are used to convey a higher degree of reverence than their variants with just one. *Omeshiagari ni naru*, for example, is a honorific variant of *meshiagaru* associated with a(n even) higher honorific value (Hasegawa 2015: 263). Note that a variant of (39) that demands the largest number of honorific features (rather than honorific feature *types*) would exclude (46a) and (47a) along with (37c) and (41b), under the sensible assumptions that (i) MESHIAGARU is associated with at least as high an honorific value as *(g)o* V(N) *ni* NARU and (ii) UKAGAU is associated with at least as high an honorific value as *(g)o* V(N) *ni* SURU.

When multiple ARG1 or ARG2 honorific features targeting the same referent occur within a single word (as in (46b)/(47b)), their effects thus can be characterized as cumulative; given that this apparently is not a very systematic phenomenon, I refrain from positing an additional principle to account for it here.

7 Conclusion

This article presented a formal semantic analysis the meanings of classes of honorifics in Japanese, including ones that have hardly been addressed in the existing formal-semantic literature. It also discussed some essential discourse principles regulating the usage of Japanese honorifics. The social norms motivating and constraining the usage of honorifics are complex, involving a great deal of inter-speaker variation and affected by the factor of registers/styles; the framework illustrated above will hopefully contribute to future discussions of honorification from both language-specific and general-linguistic (typological) perspectives.

References

Comrie, B.: Linguistic politeness axes: speaker-addressee, speaker-referent, speaker-bystander. Pragmatic Microfiche 1.7:A3, Department of Linguistics, University of Oxford (1976)

Hasegawa, Y.: Japanese: A Linguistic Introduction. Cambrdige University Press, Cambridge (2015)

Kikuchi, Y.: Keigo [Honorifics]. Kodansha, Tokyo (1997)

Kim, J.B., Sells, P.: Korean honorificaiton: a kind of expressive meaning. J. East Asian Linguist. **16**, 303–336 (2007). https://doi.org/10.1007/s10831-007-9014-4

McCready, E.: Honorification and Social Meaning. Oxford University Press, Oxford (forthcoming)

Oishi, H.: Keigo [Honorifics]. Chikuma Shobo, Tokyo (1975)

Oshima, D.Y.: Perspectives in reported discourse. Ph.D. thesis, Stanford University, Stanford (2006)

Oshima, D.Y.: The meanings of perspectival verbs and their implications on the taxonomy of projective content/conventional implicature. Semant. Linguist. Theory (SALT) **26**, 43–60 (2016)

Potts, C., Kawahara, S.: Japanese honorifics as emotive definite descriptions. Semant. Linguist. Theory (SALT) **14**, 235–254 (2004)

Tonhauser, J., Beaver, D., Roberts, C., Simons, M.: Toward a taxonomy of projective content. Language **89**, 66–109 (2013). https://doi.org/10.1353/lan.2013.0001

On the Deliberative Use of the German Modal *sollte*

Frank Sode[1(✉)] and Ayaka Sugawara[2]

[1] Goethe University Frankfurt, Frankfurt, Germany
sode@em.uni-frankfurt.de
[2] Waseda University, Tokyo, Japan
ayakasug@waseda.jp

Abstract. This paper is about a particular use of the German modal *sollte* ('should') in the antecendent of conditionals as illustrated in (1)–(3). We call this use the "deliberative" use of *sollte*. We argue that on its deliberative use *sollte* doesn't behave as the weak necessity modal it is standardly assumed to be. The distributional facts suggest that the use conditions of *sollte*-antecendents are closely related to the use conditions of conditional antecendents with the complementizer *falls* ('in case'). Following a recent proposal by Hinterwimmer for *falls*, we propose that *sollte* in the antecendent of a conditional introduces a use condition that takes the truth of the antecendent proposition to be a truly open possibility against a given conversational background.

Keywords: Epistemic modals · Conditionals · Subjunctive mood

1 Introduction

The topic of this paper is the use of the German modal *sollte* in the antecendent of conditionals on a reading that we call "deliberative". This use is illustrated in (1)–(3).[1,2]

---

[1] We assume that everything we say in this paper holds in the same way for *wenn...sollte-* antecedents, as in (1) and (2), as for *sollte*-V1-antecedents, as in (3). Wherever we choose to illustrate a point with a *wenn...sollte-* antecedent, we might aswell have chosen a *sollte*-V1-antecedent and the other way around. We will refer to both types of antecedents as "*sollte*-antecedents".

[2] [4] report that "English *should* shows the same reading." As for example:

(i) If this should be proven to be correct, it would have major implications for particle physics.   http://news.mit.edu/2010/neutrinos-0812

We would like to thank the audiences at the Semantics and Pragmatics Workshop at Mie University, the Semantics Research Group Meeting at Keio University, the Oberseminar English Linguistics at Göttingen University and, in particular, Elin McCready, Shinya Okano, Jan Köpping, Osamu Sawada, Joe Tabolt, Hubert Truckenbrodt, Thomas Weskott and Ede Zimmermann for helpful discussions and comments. This work has been funded by the 2018 JSPS Summer Program.

K. Kojima et al. (Eds.): JSAI-isAI 2018 Workshops, LNAI 11717, pp. 341–356, 2019.
https://doi.org/10.1007/978-3-030-31605-1_25

(1)   Wenn dir das zu früh sein <u>sollte</u>, dann kannst du auch später
        If   you that too early be   should then can   you also later
        kommen.
        come
        'If that's too early for you, you can come later.'

(2)   Wenn es in Nordrhein-Westfalen   zu Neuwahlen   kommen <u>sollte</u>,
        If   it in North Rhine-Westphalia to new elections come   should
        dann hat die CDU gute Chancen auf einen Sieg.
        then has the CDU good chances for a   victory
        'If there happen to be new elections in North Rhine-Westphalia (= a
        German federal state), then the CDU (= a German political party) has
        a good chance of winning.'

(3)   Wenn der Innenminister   von den Zuständen an seiner
        If   the secretary of the Interior of   the state   at his
        Behörde gewußt haben <u>sollte</u>, dann muss er zurücktreten.
        office   known have   should then must he step down
        'If the secretary of the Interior was informed about the state of his office,
        he has to step down.'

What is interesting about these examples is that *sollte* doesn't seem to contribute
any additional modal meaning to the antecendents – or at least it doesn't seem
to contribute its usual interpretation as a (deontic[3] or epistemic) weak necessity
modal. The plot of the paper is as follows: First, we introduce some background
on the modal *sollte* and its interpretations as deontic and epistemic weak necessity modal. Second, we argue that the use under discussion is neither a deontic
use, nor a "conventional" epistemic use. We show that the use conditions of *sollte*
on the relevant reading are in most respects identical to the use conditions of
conditionals with the complementizer *falls* ('in case') on [2]'s account: the contribution of *should* to the antecendents of a conditional is a presupposition that
restricts its use to a conversational background in which the antecedent proposition is a truly open possibility. In the last two sections, we discuss occurences
of deliberative *sollte* in relative clauses and the relation of deliberative *sollte* to
its epistemic use.

As in German, one also finds conditional antecendents with *should* in first position.
More data from English can be found in Daan Van den Nest's dissertation:

(ii)   <u>Should</u> they use what is regarded as excessive or unnecessary force, they, too, might
        well become the targets of aggression.   Daan Van den Nest (2010)

[3] We use the term "deontic modal" here in a rather wide way corresponding to what
[6] calls a "priority modal".

2   Some Background on the German Modal *sollte*

sollte is an inflected form of the modal *sollen*. Its closest counterpart in English is *should*. Morphologically, the form *sollte* can either be the past tense form of *sollen* or its past subjunctive form (German: "Konjunktiv Präteritum" or "Konjunktiv II"). Usually it is assumed that the form of *sollte* in the use under discussion is its subjunctive form, see [4]. The subjunctive modal *sollte* is considered to be a weak necessity modal, see [4] for a detailed discussion and empirical tests that support this assessment. Accordingly, [4] propose the following classification of the German modal forms *muss* and *sollte* in agreement with the corresponding classification of the English modals *must* and *should*.

strong necessity	English must	German muss
weak necessity	English *should*	German *sollte*

Like other modal verbs in German (and English), *sollte* is polyfunctional, i.e., it can be used as a deontic modal, (4), or as an epistemic modal, (5).

(4)   Du solltest dir   die Hände waschen.
        you should REFL the hands wash.
        'You should wash your hands.'   deontic reading

Context: The doorbell rings.

(5)   Das sollte   die Post sein.
        this should the post be
        'This should be the mail.'   epistemic reading

3   The Deliberative Use is Not an Epistemic or Deontic Use

3.1   The Deliberative Use is Not a Special Case of a Deontic Use

The first question to ask is whether the deliberative use of *sollte* is a special case of an deontic use or an epistemic use of *sollte*. The first alternative of these is not very plausible to begin with. The closest we find to a deontic use of *sollte* in a conditional antecendent is a use that refers back to a given recommendation or a previous use of deontic *sollte*.

(6)   ?Wenn du besser den Bus nehmen solltest (wie es empfohlen   wird),
        If   you better the bus take   should (as it recommended is)
        dann steck dir   Kleingeld für den Fahrschein ein.
        then put   REFL change   for the ticket   in
        'If you are supposed to take the bus (as it was recommended to you),
        then think of some change for the ticket'

In any case, this is not the use that we are interested in.[4]

More evidence that the deliberative use is not a special case of a deontic use comes from the fact that we find deliberative uses of *sollte* in the antecendent of conditionals with progressive aspect and forms of the German "Perfekt" that are strongly marked on a deontic interpretation for *sollte* without an additional specification of a temporal reference point.

(7)   Du <u>solltest</u> { am Spülen   sein / gespült   haben }
       you should { at   washing the dished be / washed the dishes have   }
       #(wenn ich von der Arbeit zurückkomme).
       (when   I   from the work   come back)
       You should be washing the dishes / have washed the dishes #(when I come back from work).

(8)   Wenn du { am Spülen   sein / gespült   haben }
       if   you { at washing the dished be / washed the dishes have   }
       <u>solltest</u>, dann will   ich dich nicht weiter   stören.
       should then want I   you not   anymore bother
       'If you { are washing the dishes / have washed the dishes }, then I won't bother you anymore.'

3.2   The Deliberative Use is Not a Special Case of an Epistemic Use

In this section, we will present our reasons why we think that the deliberative use is not a special case of a use as an epistemic weak necessity modal. First, while other modals that allow for an epistemic use can be substituted for *sollte* in an underspecified context like in (9) (ignoring for the moment the subtle differences in conditions of use and meaning), these modals cannot be substituted for deliberative *sollte* as illustrated in (10) – irrespective of their modal strength in a corresponding context.[5]

---

[4] As in the example in (6), the comparative adverbials *besser* ('better') and *lieber* ('preferably') can in principle always accompany a deontic use of *sollte*. It cannot accompany the relevant deliberative use.

(i) Wenn das dir (*lieber/*besser) zu früh sein <u>sollte</u>, dann komm einfach später. If this should (*preferably/*better) be to early for you, then just come later.

[5] We don't want to say that modals that in principle do have epistemic interpretations never occur in the antecedent of conditionals, see [5] for a discussion. But these uses seem to be rare. The rareness of real epistemic readings of modals in the antecedent of conditionals is confirmed by a comprehensive corpus search in the DWDS subcorpus "DWDS-Kernkorpus (1900–1999)" (https://www.dwds.de/; date of search: October 06, 2018).

search string	results	relevant	epistemic	deliberative
"wenn #10 @muss ',"'	22	20	0	0
"wenn #10 @müsste ',"'	1	1	0	0
"wenn #10 @dürfte ',"'	49	39	0	0
"wenn #10 @sollte ',"'	1161	97 (of first 100)	0 (of first 100)	84 (of first 100)

(9)   Das $\left\{ \begin{array}{c} \text{sollte} \\ \text{muss} \\ \text{müsste} \\ \text{dürfte} \end{array} \right\}$ die Post sein.

       This   the mail be

'This MODAL be the mail.'

(10)   Wenn das die Post   sein $\left\{ \begin{array}{c} \text{sollte} \\ \text{\#muss} \\ \text{\#müsste} \\ \text{\#dürfte} \end{array} \right\}$, dann gib denen bitte

        If   that the postman be   then give them please

       das Paket.
       the parcel
       'If this MODAL be the mail, then please give them the parcel.'

Second, there clearly is no local interpretation of *sollte* in the sense of 'there is a weak epistemic necessity that p' as in the unembedded case.[6]

(11)   Das sollte die Post sein.
        'This should be the mail.'
        ⤳ There is a weak epistemic necessity that this is the mail.

(12)   Wenn das die Post sein sollte, dann gib denen bitte das Paket mit.
        'If this should be the mail, then please give them the parcel.'
        ⤳̸ If there is a weak epistemic necessity that this is the mail, then please
        give them the parcel.

That we don't find local epistemic interpretations for *sollte* doesn't already decisively show that *sollte* couldn't be interpreted epistemically. As [7] shows for the reportative use of the indicative form *soll*, we sometimes find global interpretations of the relevant modal element. Global uses can be paraphrased as parentheticals. The corresponding paraphrases would be as follows:

(13)   Wenn er schuldig gesprochen werden sollte, dann muss er zurücktreten.
        'If he should be found guilty, he has to step down.'
        ⤳ If he is found guilty – as it should be the case –, he has to step down.

(14)   Wenn der Innenminister   von den Zuständen an seiner
        If   the secretary of the Interior of   the state   at his
        Behörde gewußt haben sollte, dann muss er zurücktreten.
        office   known have   should then must he step down
        ⤳ If the secretary of the Interior was informed about the state of his
        office – as it should be the case –, he has to step down.

---

[6] The assumed paraphrase is of course a simplification. For concrete proposals of the meaning of English *should* as a weak epistemic necessity modal/normality modal: see [1] and [8]. The same point could be made if we were to assume a similar contribution for the German modal *sollte* on its epistemic use as [1] and [8] assume for *should*.

At first sight, this looks like a reasonable interpretation. But we also find examples of the following kind:

(15)   Der Richterspruch in der Sache wird für Mittwoch erwartet.
          'The verdict in this matter is expected for Wednesday.'
     a.   Sollte er schuldig gesprochen werden, dann muss er zurücktreten.
             'Should he be found guilty, then he has to step down.'
     b.   Sollte er nicht schuldig gesprochen werden, dann kann er im Amt
             bleiben.
             'Should it be the case that he is not found guilty, then he can stay
             in office.'

A paraphrase that assumes a global parenthetical interpretation results in a clash in the second conjunct as can be seen by the following paraphrse:

(16)   If he knew about it – *as it should be the case* –, he has to step down and
          if he didn't know about it, – #*as it should be the case* –, he can stay.

The given context indicates that the matter of whether the person under discussion is found guilty or not is not settled yet and therefore cannot be known. But still the interpretation of *should* is deliberative in the relevant sense. We take these examples to show that we do not have any commitment at all to the (global) truth of the proposition on a deliberative reading – not even a weak one.
     Other examples that can help to make the same point are examples with explicit parentheticals that deny any commitment, as in (17), uses with the focus sensitive particle *selbst* ('even') that indicates that the antecendent proposition is the least likely of the relevant propositions in the alternative set, as in (18), and the modal particle *doch* that indicates that the antecendent proposition is not in agreement with what was previously assumed or expected, as in (19).

(17)   And even if he should have done this (which seems to be impossible) he
          would be not as powerful as the living Shadow.   internet source

(18)   Selbst wenn er hier gewesen sein sollte, macht das keinen
          even   if   he here been   be   should makes this no
          Unterschied.
          difference
          'Even if he should have been here, it doesn't make a difference.'

(19)   Sollte   er doch   hier gewesen sein, dann nehme ich alles
          Should he PART here been   be   then take   I   everything
          zurück.
          back
          'Should he have been here afterall, I take everything back.'

It seems that the deliberative use in these examples marks that it an open question whether the antecedent proposition holds. We take this to show that the deliberative use is not a global epistemic use.[7]

4   The Use of Deliberative *sollte* is Not Simply a Way to Express Subjunctive Mood

If *sollte* on its deliberative use doesn't have its usual interpretation as a weak necessity modal, what does it contribute? [4] suggest that the use of *sollte* is maybe a way to express subjunctive mood (Konjunktiv). This would be in accordance with its characterization as "hypothetical" in reference grammars of German.

> "[German] reference grammars discuss a special use of *sollte* that often occurs in conditionals [...]:

(20)   Wenn es regnen sollte,   kommen wir sofort   zurück.
        If   it rain   SOLLTE come   we immediately back
        'If it should rain, we will come back right away.'

> The meaning contribution as hypothetical (Zifonun, Hoffmann and Strecker 1997b: 1893) might suggest that the Konjunktiv II is semantically interpreted here, while the stem of the modal is not semantically interpreted."

Here are some reasons why we think that the assumption that *sollte* is just a way to express subjunctive mood doesn't get the distributional facts right. First of all, substituting Konjunktiv for *sollte* doesn't always lead to an adequate paraphrase.

(21)   ??Wenn es regnen würde, kommen wir sofort zurück.
        (lit.:) 'If it WOULD rain, we will come back immediately.'

Second, usually we find matching mood between the antecedent and the consequent of conditionals.

---

[7] In a later paragraph, we will argue that certain occurences of *sollte* in relative clauses are also deliberative uses of *sollte*. With these examples, it can be clearly seen that the deliberative use of *sollte* is not an epistemic use since we also find clear cases of epistemic uses in (appositive) relative clauses.

(i)   Diejenigen, denen das zu früh sein <u>sollte</u>, können auch später kommen.
        The ones   who this too early be   should can   also later   come
        'If this should be too early for you, you can also come later.'

(ii)   Anna, der das zu früh sein <u>sollte</u>, kann auch später kommen.
        Anna who this too early be   should can   also later   come
        'Anna for who this should be too early can also come later.'

In contrast to (i), the reltative clause in (ii) clearly has an epistemic interpretation.

(22)   a.   Wenn es regnen <u>würde</u>,   dann <u>würden</u>   wir sofort
              if   it rain   will.SUBJ then will.SUBJ we immideately
              zurückkommen.
              back-come
        b.   Wenn es <u>regnet</u>,   dann <u>kommen</u>   wir sofort   zurück.
              if   it rain.IND then come.IND we immideately back

In the DWDS corpus search, we found for the first 84 occurences of deliberative *sollte* in the antecendent of a conditional 51 occurences of indicative mood
in the consequent (including 12 cases of reportative present subjunctive mood
that are not interpreted as conditional subjunctive mood), and 26 occurences of
conditional subjunctive mood (including 7 occurences of modal verbs in subjunctive mood); the rest being infinitival and imperative forms. So the combination
of deliberative *sollte* in the antecendent with indicative mood in the consequent
doesn't seem to be an exception from the rule.

Third – and this is the most important aspect – the use conditions of *sollte*-
antecedents are more restricted than the use conditions of plain subjunctive
antecedents. In fact, the use conditions of *sollte*-antecedents match the use conditions of conditional antecedents with the complementizer *falls* ('in case') in
German.[8]

5   *sollte*-antecendents and Degrees of Commitment

In this part of the paper, we are going to show that the use conditions of *sollte*-
antecendents are more narrow than the use conditions of subjunctive conditionals.
We will show this by testing whether the use of deliberative *sollte* is acceptable
against the background of a particular degree of commitment by the speaker
to the truth of the antecedent proposition. We consider the following range of
possible (modal) commitments of the speaker to the truth of the antecedent
proposition.

	$p \in$ *Common Ground* (factual)
range of possible (modal) commitments of the speaker to the truth of the antecendent proposition	p is a strong necessity p is a weak necessity p is a good possibility p is a better possibility than $\neg p$ p is as good a possibility as $\neg p$ p is a slight possibility
	$\neg p \in$ *Common Ground* (counterfactual)

This discussion follows a similar discussion in [2] for the German conditional
complementizer *falls*.

---

[8] For a detailed discussion of the use conditions of conditional antecedents with the
complementizer *falls* see [2].

5.1   Factual Conditionals

Conditionals with *sollte*-antecedents cannot be used as factual conditionals ('given (the fact) that'/'assuming that') – even if the consequent clause is in indicative mood. This is similar to *falls* according to [2].

(23)   According to the schedule, the train leaves at 8:00.

    a. Wenn der Zug um 8 Uhr abfährt, dann müssen wir spätestens
        if   the train at 8:00 leaves then must   we latest
        um 7.50 Uhr am   Bahnhof sein.
        at   7:50   at the station   be
        'If the train leaves at 8:00, we have to be at the station at 7:50.'

    b. ??<u>Sollte</u> der Zug um 8 Uhr abfahren, dann müssen wir spätestens
        should the train at 8:00 leave   then must   we latest
        um 7.50 Uhr am   Bahnhof sein.
        at   7:50   at the station   be
        'Should the train leave at 8:00, we have to be at the station at 7:50.'

$\times \neg p \in$ *Common Ground* (factual)
p is a strong necessity
p is a weak necessity
p is a good possibility
p is a better possibility than $\neg p$
p is as good a possibility as $\neg p$
p is a slight possibility
$\neg p \in$ *Common Ground* (counterfactual)

5.2   Strong Epistemic Necessity

Conditionals with *sollte*-antecedents cannot be used if the antecedent proposition is considered to be an epistemic necessity. We illustrate this point with epistemic *muss* ('must') in (24).

(24)   Anna muss da sein. Ihr Auto steht draußen.
    'Anna must be here. Her car is outside.'

    a. Wenn sie da   ist, dann bestimmt um ihre   Jacke abzuholen,
        if   she there be then certainly to of her jacket pick up
        die sie gestern   hier vergessen hat.
        that she yesterday here forgotten has
        'If she is here, then most likely she picks up her jacket that she
        forgot here yesterday.'

    b. ??<u>Sollte</u> sie da   sein, dann bestimmt um ihre   Jacke abzuholen,
        should she there be   then certainly to of her jacket pick up
        die sie gestern   hier vergessen hat.
        that she yesterday here forgotten has

'Should she be here, then most likely she picks up her jacket that
she forgot here yesterday.'

5.3   Circumstantial Necessity

Conditionals with *sollte*-antecendents cannot be used if the antecedent proposition is considered to be a circumstantial necessity – as for example with
promises:

(25)   Ich verspreche dir: Ich komme auf jeden Fall.
  'I promise you: I will definitely come.'
  a. Aber wenn ich komme, dann kommt Peter nicht.
    But if I come then comes Peter not
    'But if I will come, then Peter won't.'
  b. ??Aber <u>sollte</u> ich kommen, dann kommt Peter nicht.
    But *should* I come then comes Peter not
    'But should I come, then Peter won't.'

We assume that, given the promise, p is a circumstantial necessity, i.e., for all
future situations compatible with the (relevant) circumstances now (including
the promise) that are most normal: it is the case that p. Circumstantial necessity
associated with promises is in conflict with the use conditions of *sollte*.

×	$p \in Common\ Ground$ (factual)
×	p is a strong necessity
	p is a weak necessity
	p is a good possibility
	p is a better possibility than $\neg p$
	p is as good a possibility as $\neg p$
	p is a slight possibility
	$\neg p \in Common\ Ground$ (counterfactual)

5.4   Weak Epistemic Necessity

If the antecedent proposition is given in the discourse context as a weak epistemic necessity, introduced by the use of the weak epistemic necessity modal
müsste in the example in (26), then the use of *sollte* in the antecedent of the
conditional is possible.

(26)   Anna ist dienstags eigentlich immer da. Sie müsste da sein.
  'Anna is usually there on Tuesdays. She should be there.'
  a. Wenn sie da ist, dann frag sie doch nach deinem Buch.
    if she there be then ask her PRT for your book
    'If she is there, you should ask her for your book.'

b. <u>Sollte</u> sie da   sein, dann frag sie doch nach deinem Buch.
should she there be   then ask her PRT for   your   book
'If she should be there, you should ask her for your book.'

×	$p \in$ *Common Ground* (factual)
×	p is a strong necessity
✓	p is a weak necessity
	p is a good possibility
	p is a better possibility than $\neg p$
	p is as good a possibility as $\neg p$
	p is a slight possibility
	$\neg p \in$ *Common Ground* (counterfactual)

5.5   Varying Degrees of Possibility

The use of *sollte* as in (28) is fine against the background of discourse contexts in which the antecendent proposition is given as a possibility with varying degrees of commitment.

(27)   a. Es ist gut möglich, dass Anna da ist.
'There is a good possibility that Anna is here.'
        b. Es ist eher möglich, dass Anna da ist, als, dass sie nicht da ist.
'It is a better possibility that Anna is here than that she isn't.'
        c. Es ist genauso gut möglich, dass Anna da ist, wie, dass sie nicht da ist.
'It is as good a possibility that Anna is here than that she isn't.'
        d. Es besteht eine geringe Möglichkeit, dass Anna da ist.
'There is a slight possibility that Anna is here.'

(28)   <u>Sollte</u> sie da   sein, *sollten* wir bei ihr vorbeischauen.
should she there be   *should* we at her visit
'If she should be at home, we should drop by.'

×	$p \in$ *Common Ground* (factual)
×	p is a strong necessity
✓	p is a weak necessity
✓	p is a good possibility
✓	p is a better possibility than $\neg p$
✓	p is as good a possibility as $\neg p$
✓	p is a slight possibility
	$\neg p \in$ *Common Ground* (counterfactual)

5.6   Counterfactual Conditionals

sollte-antecedents cannot be used in counterfactual contexts for the antecedent-proposition.[9]

(29)   Damals kam es zu keiner Abstimmung.
'At that time there was no vote'

    a.   Aber wenn es zu einer Abstimmung gekommen wäre,
       but   if   it to a   vote   come   be.SUBJ
       hätte   er sich   ohnehin nicht beteiligt.
       have.SUBJ he REFL anyway not   participated
       'But if there had been a vote, he wouldn't have participated in it'

    b.   #Aber <u>sollte</u>   es zu einer Abstimmung gekommen sein,
       but   *should* it to a   vote   come   be.INF
       hätte   er sich   ohnehin nicht beteiligt.
       have.SUBJ he REFL anyway not   participated
       'But should there have been a vote, he wouldn't have participated in it'

× $p \in$ *Common Ground* (factual)
× p is a strong necessity
✓ p is a weak necessity
✓ p is a good possibility
✓ p is a better possibility than $\neg p$
✓ p is as good a possibility as $\neg p$
✓ p is a slight possibility
× $\neg p \in$ *Common Ground* (counterfactual)

    In summary: Our discussion of the data supports a similar conclusion as [2] reaches for *falls*-antecedents: Deliberative *sollte* seems to require that the

---

[9] Here is the only difference we found to the use conditions of *falls*-antecedents: Since *falls*-antecedents can in principle be marked with additional subjunctive mood, we find a difference in certain counterfactual contexts. Against the same background as (29), the *falls*-antecedent is fine:

(i)   Aber falls   es zu einer Abstimmung gekommen wäre,   hätte   er
      but   in case it to a   vote   come   be.SUBJ have.SUBJ he
      sich   ohnehin nicht beteiligt.
      REFL anyway not   participated
      'But if there had been a vote, he wouldn't have participated in it'

This example shows that Hinterwimmer's generalization that *falls*-antecedents cannot be used in counterfactual contexts for the antecendent proposition has to be modified. At the same time, it seems to be the right generalization for *sollte*-antecedents.

antecedent proposition is a "truly open possibility" against a given epistemic (or circumstantial) conversational background.[10]

6   The Proposal

We propose the following semantics for *sollte* in its deliberative use (here illustrated for the use in the antecendent of a conditional).[11]

(30) $[\![(\text{if } (\textbf{should}_{\text{DELIB}} \ \varphi)), (\textbf{then necessarily } \psi)]\!]^{w,f,g,\cdots} = 1$ iff
$[\![(\text{if } \varphi), (\textbf{then necessarily } \psi)]\!]^{w,f,g,\cdots}$, defined only if

    a. $[\![\varphi]\!]$ is a *simple possibility* in w with respect to f,

    b. $[\![\varphi]\!]$ is not a *human possibility* in w with respect to f and g.

f and g can – but don't have to – be the relevant conversational backgrounds for the interpretation of the conditional. g is a stereotypical ordering source[12] and f is either an epistemic conversational background or a circumstantial conversational background.

The meaning contribution of deliberative *sollte* is purely presuppositional. It presupposes that the antecendent proposition is a simple possibility with respect to the conversational background f in the world of the world of evaluation w and at the same time it must not be a human necessity – in the terminology of [3] – with respect to the modal base f and the ordering source g in the world of evaluation.[13]

7   Deliberative *sollte* in Relative Clauses

There is another context were we typically find deliberative readings for *sollte*: free relative clauses.

---

[10] [2]: "*falls* seems to require that the speaker considers the antecedent proposition to be a truly open possibility."

[11] This is very close in spirit to the proposal in [2] for *falls*.

[12] Hinterwimmer also assumes a stereotypical ordering source in the context of his proposal for *falls*.

[13] We use a syncategorematic meaning rule in (30-b) since this is the direct way to spell out our proposal. Here is the non-syncategorematic rule:

    (i) $[\![\textbf{should}_{\text{DELIB}}]\!]^{c,f,g}(p)(w) = 1$ iff $p(w)$, defined only if

        a. p is a *simple possibility* in c_w with respect to f,

        b. p is not a *human necessity* in c_w with respect to f and g,

        c. $w \neq c_w$;

    where c is the context of the local root clause/attitude.

This semantic rule gives us an interesting additional insight since it forces us to distinguish between the local world of evaluation and the local context world (for which we write "c_w"). This might have to be reconsidered in the light of the considerations at the end of this paper.

(31)   Wem das zu früh sein <u>sollte</u>, der kann auch später kommen.
          who this too early be   should the one can also   later   come
          (lit.:) 'If this should be too early for you, you can also come later.'

As already seen with conditional antecendents in (10), other modals that in
principle allow for epistemic interpretations cannot be substituted for *sollte*.

(32)   Wem das zu früh sein $\left\{\begin{array}{c} \text{sollte} \\ \#\text{muss} \\ \#\text{müsste} \\ \#\text{dürfte} \end{array}\right\}$, der kann auch später kommen.

          (lit.:) 'If this MODAL be too early for you, you can also come later.'

We also find deliberative readings for *sollte* in restrictive relative clauses to
universal quantifiers, (33), "generic" indefinites, (34) and plural definites, (35).

(33)   Aber wir waren entschlossen, jeden   zu befragen, der gewählt
          but we were   determined everyone to ask   who voted
          haben <u>sollte</u>.
          have   should
          (lit.:) 'We were determined to ask anyone who should have voted.'
          Die Zeit, 27.08.1976, Nr. 36

(34)   Einem Teilnehmer, dem das zu früh sein <u>sollte</u>, der   kann auch
          a   participant who this too early be   should the one can   also
          später kommen.
          later   come

(35)   Diejenigen,   denen das zu früh sein <u>sollte</u>, können auch später
          those (of you) who   this too early be   should can   also later
          kommen.
          come

Interestingly, all these sentences seem to have a modalized or generic interpretation. This is supported by the observation that with none of these sentences
there even has to be a single individual of which the main predication of the relative clause is true. The meaning of (32) can be paraphrased by the conditional
in (36).

(36)   Wenn das { jemandem / einem } zu früh sein sollte, dann kann
          if   that { someone   / one   } too late be   should then can
          der   auch später kommen.
          the one also later   come
          'If this should be too early for you, you can also come later.'

If (32) had the truth-conditions of (36), the fact that the main predication of
the relative clause doesn't have to be true of any individual would readily be
explained since the conditional in (36) gives wide scope to *sollte* with respect
to the existential quantifier *jemanden* ('someone')/the generic pronoun *einem*.

At this point, we don't have more to say about the use of deliberative *sollte* in relative clauses.

8   Conclusion

In this paper, we have discussed a particular use of the German modal *sollte* in the antecendent of conditionals that we called "deliberative". We presented arguments that the deliberative use of *sollte* is not a special case of a deontic use or an epistemic use of the modal *sollte*. By going through a range of contexts with varying degrees of (modal) commitment of the speaker to the truth of the antecendent proposition, we could show that the use of *sollte* marks the antecendent proposition as a truly open possibility against a given conversational background. The results are summarized again in the left table on the next page. We proposed that *sollte* on its deliberative use introduces a presupposition that restricts the use of the conditional to conversational backgrounds in which the proposition is given at least as a simple possibility and at most as a weak necessity.

In this final section, we want to take a step back and end with a few comments. As for the content of the presupposition: We are aware that the proposal is tailored to fit the observations and doesn't give us any deeper explanation. The main point of the proposal is to precisely illustrate the contrast between the deliberative use of *sollte* and its epistemic use. Secondly, we are aware that the status of the condition of use as a presupposition hasn't sufficiently been argued for. Since the use conditions of *sollte*-antecedents seemed to us to be similar to the use conditions of mood marking in conditionals and since mood marking is usually associated with a presupposition, we assumed that *sollte* contributes a presupposition, too. More interesting than the details of our proposal is a pattern that emerges from our generalizations and that might even shed new light on *sollte* (and English *should*) on its epistemic use: While the epistemic weak necessity reading of *sollte* is considered to be part of the asserted content and seems to be (mostly) restricted to syntactic root contexts, deliberative readings appear to be presuppositional and are restricted to non-root context.[14] The table summarizes this pattern.

	epistemic *sollte*	deliberative *sollte*
syntactic context	+root clause	−root clause
semantic level	contributes	contributes
	to the assertion	a presupposition

This pattern lets one wonder whether one should look out for a single *sollte* after all that flips its interpretation depending on its context of use.

---

[14] Deliberative *sollte* could be characterized as an anti-root-phenomenon. This is the reason why we introduced the condition that the local world of evaluation must be different from the world of the local root context in our definition, compare condition (i–c) of footnote 13 .

To end on a speculative note: If we were to assume that the common core to deliberative and epistemic *sollte* is the contribution *it is not the case that p is a strong necessity*, it would be intruiging to think of the assertion of *sollte* in a root context as coming with an exhaustification of the scale of graded modalities resulting in a reading as a weak necessity modal as suggested in the right table below. Since it is not at all clear how such an exhaustification should come about and what should account for its obligatoriness in root clauses, this is mere speculation at this point.

Deliberative *sollte*
× $p \in$ *Common Ground* (factual)
× p is a strong necessity
✓ p is a weak necessity
✓ p is a good possibility
✓ p is a better possibility than $\neg p$
✓ p is as good a possibility as $\neg p$
✓ p is a slight possibility
× $\neg p \in$ *Common Ground* (counterfactual)

Epistemic *sollte*
× $p \in$ *Common Ground* (factual)
× p is a strong necessity
✓ p is a weak necessity
⇑ p is a good possibility
⇑ p is a better possibility than $\neg p$
⇑ p is as good a possibility as $\neg p$
⇑ p is a slight possibility
× $\neg p \in$ *Common Ground* (counterfactual)

References

1. Copley, B.: What should should mean. Manuscript. CNRS (2006)
2. Hinterwimmer, S.: A comparison of the conditional complementizers if and falls, Wuppertaler Linguistisches Forum (WLF), Universität Wuppertal (2014)
3. Kratzer, A.: The notional category of modality. In: Eikmeyer, H.J., Rieser, H. (eds.) Words, Worlds, and Contexts, pp. 38–74. de Gruyter, Berlin (1981)
4. Matthewson, L., Truckenbrodt, H.: Modal flavour/modal force interactions in German: soll, sollte, muss and müsste. Linguist. Ber. **255**, 4–57 (2018)
5. Papafragou, A.: Epistemic modality and truth conditions. Lingua **116**, 1688–1702 (2006)
6. Portner, P.: Modality. Oxford Surveys in Semantics and Pragmatics. Oxford University Press, New York (2009)
7. Schenner, M.: Double face evidentials in German: Reportative 'sollen' and 'wollen' in embedded contexts. In: Groenn, A. (ed.) Proceedings of SuB12, pp. 552–566. ILOS, Oslo (2008)
8. Yalcin, S.: Modalities of normality. In: Charlow, N., Chrisman, M. (eds.) Deontic Modality, pp. 230–255. Oxford University Press, Oxford (2016)

Scalar Particles in Comparatives: A QUD Approach

Eri Tanaka[(⊠)]

Osaka University, 1-5, Machikaneyama, Toyonaka, Japan
eri-tana@let.osaka-u.ac.jp

Abstract. This paper deals with an interaction between modes of comparison and interpretations of scalar particle *mada* 'still' in Japanese. *Mada* is shown to have two interpretations in comparatives, additive and what I call *not-enough* readings. I argue that *mada*, as its counterparts in other languages do, induces a presupposition that a prejacent proposition is required to be more informative than an alternative one. Interacting with focus, different alternatives are computed, which, I claim, leads to these two different readings of the particle. Modes of comparison attested in the literature include explicit and contrastive comparisons. I show only the former can be associated with both of the additive and *not-enough* readings. I then propose to analyze the (un)availability of additive reading in two modes of comparison in terms of the contribution of the scalar particle to Question and Discussion (QUD). The additive reading does not conform to alternative questions, while the *not-enough* reading does.

Keywords: Scalar particles · Modes of comparison · QUD

1 Introduction

This paper discusses an interaction between types of comparatives and interpretations of scalar particle *mada* 'still' in Japanese. *Still*-type scalar particles crosslinguistically have been known to have several uses, including temporal, marginal, and additive uses [1,3,6]. I firstly observe that in comparatives, *mada* 'still' in Japanese exhibits what I call **not-enough reading**, in addition to **additive reading**. I then show that the *not enough* reading can be associated both with **explicit** and **contrastive** comparisons (EC and CC, hereafter, in the sense of [5,7,12]), while the **additive** one is disfavored by CC. I propose to analyze the contribution of scalar particle *mada* in terms of Question under Discussion (QUD) (in the sense of [9]), which solves the intriguing contribution of the scalar particle to a suitable question type for EC and CC.

I thank the audience at LENLES 15 for their invaluable comments on this paper. Usual disclaimers apply. This work was supported by JSPS Grant-in-Aid for Scientific Research (C) 17K02810.

K. Kojima et al. (Eds.): JSAI-isAI 2018 Workshops, LNAI 11717, pp. 357–371, 2019.
https://doi.org/10.1007/978-3-030-31605-1_26

2   Modes of Comparison and Interpretations of *mada*

It has been argued in the literature that in Japanese there are at least three modes of comparison: **explicit, implicit** and **contrastive** comparisons [7, 8, 12]. This paper focuses on two of them, EC and CC. These two comparison modes correspond to two morphologically different comparative constructions in Japanese.

(1)   This room is (slightly) larger than that one.

    a.   Explicit comparison (EC)
        *Kono heya-wa   ano heya-**yori** (wazukani) hiroi.*
        this   room-TOP that room-than (slightly) large

    b.   Contrastive comparison (CC)
        *Kono heya-**no-hoo**-ga   ano heya-**yori** (wazukani) hiroi.*
        this   room-GEN-hoo-NOM that room-than (slightly) large

(1a) is an example of EC, which is marked only by *yori* 'than', while (1b), an example of CC, has a comparative subject marked by *hoo* 'direction', in addition to *yori* marking on the comparative standard.

    From a semantic point of view, both of them allow for crisp judgment and modification by *wazukani* 'slightly', as observed by [7]. They do not convey any implication that either of the comparative subject and comparative standard reaches some contextually supplied degree of standard. Thus the continuation of "They are both rather small." to either of (1a) or (1b) does not cause a contradiction.

    Scalar particles like *mada* 'still' in comparatives alter this situation. In EC, *mada* induces an implication that the comparative standard (marked by *yori*) exceeds the contextually supplied degree of standard. Thus, in (2a), the sentence implies that "that room" is large. I call this reading **additive reading** of *mada*. Since under this reading the comparative standard is understood to exceed the contextual standard, the sentence sounds awkward with an individual usually taken to lack this property, as shown in (2b):

(2)   a.   **Additive reading**
        *Kono heya-wa   ano heya-yori **mada** hiroi.*
        this   room-TOP that room-than still   large
        "This room is still larger than that one."

    b.   *#Taro-wa ano jokki-yori mada se-ga   takai.*
        Taro-TOP that jocky-than still   height-NOM tall.
        "Taro is still larger than that jockey."

    In addition to additive reading, as indicated in (3a), ECs can be associated with what I call **not-enough** reading, which seems to be absent in its English counterpart. Under this reading, the sentence implies that both of "this room" and "that room" are not large (enough). The addition of a contrastive topic marker (indicated by capitalized *wa*) to the *yori* phrase facilitates this interpretation.[1] In this interpretation, both of the subject of a comparative sentence and the comparative standard are understood to have a lower degree than the contextual standard on the relevant scale. This requirement makes (3b) sound awkward:

(3)   a.   **Not-enough reading**
          *Kono heya-wa   ano heya-yori-(WA)   **mada** hiroi.*
          this   room-TOP that room-than-CONT still   large

          "This room is larger than that one, (although both of them are not large enough to live.)"

      b.   *#Taro-wa   ano   basukettobooru senshu-yori-(WA)   mada*
          Taro-TOP   that   basketball   player-than-(CONT)   still
           se-ga   takai.
          height-NOM tall.

          "Taro is taller than that basketball player, and both of them are not tall."

A comment on the additive reading of *mada* is in order. A reviewer doubts the robustness of this reading, observing that it is confined to temporal-spatial predicates. Six out of eight native Japanese speakers that I consulted (including myself) agree that non-temporal/spatial predicates also allow additive reading:[2]

(4)   a.   *Jiro-wa   kasikoi. Taro-wa   Jiro-yori mada kasikoi.*
          Jiro-TOP clever. Taro-TOP Jiro-than still   clever

          "Jiro is clever. Taro is still cleverer than Jiro."

      b.   *Jiro-no-heya-wa   hidoi.   Taro-no-heya-wa   sore-yori mada*
          Jiro-GEN-room-TOP terrible. Taro-GEN-room-TOP that-than still
           hidoi.
          terrible

          "Jiro's room is very untidy, and Taro's is still more untidy than that."

Thus it does not seem to be the case that the additive reading of *mada* is restricted to temporal/spatial predicates.

In contrast to EC, CC does not allow the additive reading of *mada*:

---

[1] A reviewer pointed out that the contrastive topic marker is obligatory for *not enough* reading in EC, at least to his/her ears, and suspected that there was some variation among native speakers. It doesn't seem to me that the contrastive topic marker is obligatory. I will be back to this point in Sect. 3.

[2] The predicates that I tested include: *yasui* 'cheap', *atsui*, 'hot', *kasikoi* 'clever', *muzukasii* 'difficult', and *hidoi* 'terrible'.

(5)   √*Not-enough* reading/*Additive reading

   a.   *Kono heya-**no-hoo**-ga*   *ano heya-yori* **mada** *hiroi.*
        this   room-GEN-hoo-NOM that room-than still   large

        "This room is larger than that one, although both are not large enough."

   b.   *Jiro-wa*   *kasikoi ga,* #*Taro-no-hoo-ga*   *Jiro-yori mada kasikoi.*
        Jiro-TOP clever   but Taro-GEN-hoo-NOM Jiro-than still   clever.

        "Jiro is clever and #Taro is clever than him (although they are both not clever."

   c.   #*Taro-no-hoo-ga*   *ano   basukettobooru senshu-yori   mada*
        Taro-GEN-hoo-NOM   that   basketball   player-than   still
           se-ga   *takai.*
        height-NOM   tall.

        "Taro is taller than that basketball player (although they are both not tall.)"

The infelicitous status of the examples in (5b) and (5c) testifies that CCs do not tolerate additive readings.

So the question is: why does CC exclude the additive reading of *mada*, when EC and CC exhibit a similar semantic behavior without the scalar particle?

3   The Presupposition of *mada* in Comparatives

Still-class scalar particles cross-linguistically have been treated as a presupposition trigger [1,3,6,15]. All the uses of this type of particles share the presupposition where the asserted part is preceded by an alternative one along some scale [1]. The temporal use of *still*, for example, presupposes that there is some preceding time to the evaluating time, at which the same event as the one in assertion holds.

(6)   a.   It is still raining.

      b.   Assertion: $[\![$it rains$]\!]$ is true at the speech time (t_0).

      c.   Presupposition: $\exists t'$. $t' < t_0 \wedge [\![$it rains$]\!]$ is true at t'

The presupposition in (6c) is too weak; there is almost always some time before the speech time at which "it is raining" is true. There should be some specific time (immediately before now, for example) when *it is raining* is true. To capture this, instead of existential quantification over the temporal variable, I assume that it is assigned its value from the context, following [1]:

(7) Presupposition of (6a): t*<t0 ∧ ⟦it rains⟧ is true at t*

I follow [1,3] and [15] in that *still*-type particles may be associated with different types (e.g., temporal intervals, individuals, degrees, and propositions). Assuming this, I propose that in comparatives, the precedence relation involved is **informativity** between two propositions, which is defined as asymmetric entailment relation (see also [15]):

(8) Let p and q be propositions. p is more informative than q iff p entails q but not vice versa.

I propose the denotation of *mada* as follows:

(9) ⟦mada⟧ = $\lambda C.\lambda p$: p* ∈ C ∧ p* is less informative than p. p = 1.

Given that *mada* takes a prejacent and a contextual variable, C, which is calculated as a (subset) of focus alternatives to the prejacent, as in the Alternative Semantics [10]. The starred proposition serves as a free variable whose domain is restricted to C. Thus the proposed semantics of *mada* is that it presupposes that a specific alternative proposition to the prejacent is less informative than it.

I assume the following LF for *mada* in comparatives. I also assume that gradable adjectives denote measure functions (of type $\langle e, d\rangle$, [4]) and that *yori* 'than' gives a comparative interpretation (see [13]).[3]

(10) a. LF: [$_{IP}$ mada p* [$_{IP}$ ∼C [$_{IP}$ this room [$_{DegP}$ [$_{yoriP}$ that room-yori] [$_{AP}$ large]]]]]

     b. ⟦hiroi 'large'⟧ = $\lambda x.$ size(x)   of type $\langle e, d\rangle$

     c. ⟦yori 'than'⟧ = $\lambda y. \lambda G_{\langle e,d\rangle}.\lambda x.$ G(x) > G(y).

     d. ⟦that room-yori hiroi⟧ = $\lambda x.$ size(x) > size(that room).

Let us first look at the case where the comparative standard is focused and how the computed presupposition gives rise to the **additive** reading of *mada*.

(11) **The comparative standard focused**

     a. Assertion: ⟦this room-TOP that room$_F$-yori hiroi⟧^{O} = size(this room) > size(that room)

     b. ⟦this room is that room$_F$-yori hiroi⟧^{F} ={ size(this room) > size(x) | x ∈ ALT(that room) }

     c. Presupposition:
         size(this room) > size(that room) is more informative than size(this room) > size(x), where x ∈ ALT(that room)

---

[3] I believe that nothing hinges on this choice of the measure function analysis over the standard degree predicate analysis (of type $\langle d, \langle e, t\rangle\rangle$). We can implement the same idea in terms of the latter approach to gradable adjectives.

Assuming that alternatives to "that room" are rooms A, B, and C. Then the alternative set will be {size(this room) > size(A), size(this room) > size(B), size(this room) > size(C), size(this room) > size(that room)}. To satisfy the presupposition in (11c), the alternative proposition has to be asymmetrically entailed by the prejacent.

(12) **Presupposition for the additive reading**

    a. Presupposition says: "This room is larger than that room" entails "This room is larger than room A/B/C".

    b. This relation holds iff "that room is larger than room A/B/C".

The presupposition is satisfied when one of the rooms is smaller than that room. Suppose that room A is smaller than that room. This proposition thus satisfies the presupposition.

Unfortunately, however, this in itself does not ensure that "that room is large."[4] I attribute the "exceeding the contextually given standard" component to the mirative effect of the particle [14]. In (3), for example, the use of the particle is accompanied by the expectation that Bill has left by the time of speaking, but the assertion is to make a point that this turns out to be false.

(13) a. Bill is still in Paris.

    b. Expectation: ⟦Bill is in Paris⟧ no longer holds at t0.

Applying this to the case at hand, I speculate that *mada* in comparatives has the following expectation:

(14) Expectation: p does not hold, because p* is less informative than p.

The speaker expects that "this room is larger than that room" will not hold, because "that room is larger than room A". To make sense of this expectation, room A should be considered to be (fairly) large, because if "that room" and room A are not particularly large, one would not expect that "this room" fails to exceed the size of "that room", and the effect of "surprise" will not arise. Thus the mirative component of *mada* (plus its presupposition) leads to the positive entailment of the comparative standard.

(15) a. Presupposition: That room is larger than room A.

    b. Expectation: That this room is larger than that room will not hold, because that room is larger than room A.

    c. Implication from presupposition and expectation: That room and room A are large.

---

[4] I thank Daisuke Bekki for bringing this issue for me at the conference.

When the comparative subject is focused, the **not enough** reading is obtained. The inference works in the same way as the one above:

(16) **The comparative subject focused**

   a.   Assertion: the same as (16a)

   b. $[\![$ this room$_F$ is that room-yori hiroi $]\!]^F$ = { largeness(x) > largeness(that room) | x ∈ ALT(this room) }

   c.   Presupposition:
        largeness(this room) > largeness(that room) is more informative than largeness(x) > largeness(that room), where x ∈ ALT(that room)

(17) Presupposition for **Not enough** reading

   a.   Presupposition says: "This room is larger than that room" entails "Room A is larger than that room".

   b.   This relation holds iff "This room is smaller than room A."

(18) a.   Expectation: That this room is larger than that room will not hold, under the context where that room is smaller than room A.

   b.   Implication from presupposition and expectation: This room and room A are both small.

One of the reviewers pointed out that the availability of **not enough** reading of the particle in EC is largely due to the contrastive topic marking on the comparative standard, observing that WA on the comparative standard is obligatory for the reading:

(19) **Not enough** reading (=(3a))
      *Kono heya-wa   ano heya-yori-(WA)   **mada** hiroi.*
      this   room-TOP that room-than-CONT   still   large

      "This room is larger than that one, (although both of them are not large enough to live.)"

Although I admit that WA facilitates the reading, I do not believe that the contrastive topic marker on the standard is indispensable. Rather, WA marking on the *yori*-phrase disambiguates the interpretations of *mada*.

   The contrastive topic on the comparative standard is considered to be a scalar use of the particle, as discussed in [11]. [11] contends that WA has both non-scalar and scalar uses and that the latter has the conventional implicature (CI) that is the mirror image of *even*. According to this analysis, it results in the implicature that the comparative standard has to be the one that does not reach the degree of standard of a gradable property, as evidenced by the following:

(20) a. *Taro-wa*   *ano* {*jokki-/#basukettobooru* *senshu-*}-*yori-WA*
           Taro-TOP   that {jockey/basketball   player}-than-CONT
           se-ga   *takai.*
           height-NOM tall.

           "Taro exceeds at least that {jockey/#basketball player} in height."

     b. $\exists x.\ x \in C \wedge x \neq$ that jockey $\wedge \neg(\text{height}(T) > \text{height}(x))$
         $\forall x.\ x \in C \wedge x \neq$ that jockey $\rightarrow$ unlikelihood$[(\text{height}(T) > \text{height}(x))$
         $>$ unlikelihood$[(\text{height}(T) > \text{height}(\text{that jockey}))]$

The CI in (20b) states that the unlikeliness of Taro's height exceeding the height of alternatives to the jockey is greater than the unlikeliness of Taro's height exceeding the jockey. This is satisfied if the jockey is considered to be shorter than alternatives. Note that in the case of contrastive topic WA, there is no restriction on the comparative subject. This is sharply contrasted with the case with **not enough reading** of *mada*.

Consider (20a) and (16) against two contexts given below. What is crucial about *mada* in **not enough reading** is the presence of presupposition that the comparative subject is short:

(21) *Taro-wa*   *ano jokki-yori*   **mada** *se-ga*   *takai.*
       Taro-TOP   that jockey-than   still   height-NOM tall

      "Taro is taller than that jockey (although both of them are not tall)."

(22) a. Context A: The interlocutors know that Taro is short.
          (20a): OK, (21): OK

      b. Context B: The interlocutors do not know how tall Taro is.
          (20a): OK, (21) #

Thus EC with WA-marking on *yori*-phrase is *compatible* with **not enough reading**, but it should not be the source of the reading.

Before moving on to the next section, let us examine another possibility that could explain the two different readings of *mada* in comparatives. I take up the analysis given to *still*-type particles by [1] here, and show that it does not predict the presupposition of *mada* in comparatives *unless it also incorporates the informativity scale in the presupposition.*

[1] takes *still*-type particles in English and German as multi-level items: it may take an individual, temporal, and propositional variable, depending on its position at LF. [1] proposes that the uses of *still*-type particles share (23a) as its semantics. EXH(austive)-operator in the sense of [2] is assumed to deal with the scalar implicature.

(23) a. $[\![\text{still}]\!] = \lambda S.\ \lambda x^*.\ \lambda x.\ \lambda P_{\langle x,t \rangle}: x^* < x \wedge P(x^*).\ P(x).$ (S refers to a relevant scale.)

      b. $[\![\text{EXH } \phi]\!] = 1$, iff $[\![\phi]\!] = 1 \wedge \forall q.\ q \in \text{ALT}(\phi) \wedge (\neg([\![\phi]\!]) \Rightarrow q) \rightarrow \neg q.$

Among the uses attested in [1], a possible candidate for *still/mada* in comparatives is **marginal** use, whose semantic/pragmatic contribution is given below:

(24)   a.   **Marginal use** of *still*
            Osnabruck is **still** in Lower-Saxony.

       b. $[\![(24a)]\!] = LS(O)$, defined if x* precedes Osnabruck on the path scale $\wedge\ LS(x^*)$.

       c. $[\![EXH\ (24b)]\!] = 1$, iff $LS(O) \wedge \forall q \in ALT(LS(O)) \wedge (LS(O) \not\Rightarrow q) \to \neg q$.

       d. $x^* < $ Osnabruck —) < Münster

The marginality of Osnabruck as a city in Lower-Saxony comes from the presupposition that there is a preceding city on the path scale and the scalar implicature (SI) given by EXH-operator that a city that proceeds Osanabruck is not in Lower-Saxony anymore.

Let us apply this semantics/pragmatics to the comparatives. Note that the relevant scale that determines the precedence relation between the alternative and the comparative standard/subject has to refer to the SI.

(25)   This room is **mada** larger than that one. (=(2a)/(3a))

(26)   **The comparative standard** is ordered; **additive reading**

       a.   PSP: x* precedes "that room" on a relevant scale $\wedge$ size(this room) $>$ size(x*)

       b.   SI: "this room" is not larger than rooms larger than "that room"

       c.   size(x*) $<$ size(that room)

(27)   **The comparative subject** is ordered; ***not-enough* reading**

       a.   PSP: x* precedes "this room" on a relevant scale $\wedge$ size(x*) $>$ size(this room)

       b.   SI: "The rooms smaller than "this room" is smaller than "that room"."

       c.   size(this room) $<$ size(x*)

In (26), for example, the relevant scale will consist of degrees that are less than the size of "this room"; if x precedes y on this scale, size(x) is less than size(y). Thus as shown in (26c), the alternatives are smaller than "that room", which would lead to the additive reading. The same reasoning is applied to (27) to get the *not-enough* reading.

In this reasoning, the contribution of SIs is indispensable. The SI associated with *mada* in general, however, seems to be cancellable (see [1]). Since the "marginality" component is indispensable to compute the ordering relation, it does not seem to be plausible to rely on SI to give an appropriate presupposition. Furthermore, *mada* in comparatives does not seem to induce a SI:

(28) Context: we share the following information: Taro's room is larger than Hanako's room. Hanako's room is large.

Kono   heya-wa   Hanako-no-heya-yori   mada hiroi   ga,
this   room-TOP   Hanako-GEN-room-than   still   large   but,
   Taro-no-heya-wa   kono heya-yori   hiroi/semai.
   Taro-GEN-room-CONT this room-than large/small

"This room is still larger than Hanako's, but Taro's is larger/smaller than this one."

(29) *Shiga-wa   mada Kansai-da   ga, Mie/#Osaka-wa Tookai-da.*
Shiga-TOP still   Kansai-COP but, Mie/Osaka-TOP Tookai-COP.

"Shiga prefecture is still in the Kansai area, but Mie/Osaka is in the Tookai area. "

In (3), one can "cancel" the supposed SI without any struggle to do so, while the marginal use (=(3)) cannot.

I thus believe that the informativity between the prejacent and an alternative proposition coupled with mirativity is a better way to capture the presupposition induced by *mada* in comparatives.

In the next section, I will turn to the puzzle of the incompatibility of additive reading with CC.

4   Analysis: A QUD Approach

4.1   Modes of Comparison and QUD

[7] argues that EC and CC differ in QUD articulated in the discourse. EC serves as an appropriate answer to a degree question, while CC to an alternative question. Neither of them is felicitous as an answer to a polar question:

(30) a. Degree question: How large is this room? –   √ EC (1a) / *CC (1b)

b. Polar question: Is this room large? –   *EC (1a) / *CC (1b)

c. Alternative question: Which room is larger, this one or that one? –
                            *EC (1a) / √CC (1b)

[7] proposes the following semantics and pragmatics of *hoo*: it presupposes that the number of the members in the comparison class is confined to two, and that one of them has to be the one marked by *hoo*. With this semantics and pragmatics, *hoo* conforms to an alternative question.

(31) ⟦ hoo ⟧ = λx: x ∈ CC ∧ $|CC|$ = 2. x. (where CC is a comparison class.)

[8] elaborates on the notion of comparison class involved in (31), because one can argue against this analysis on the basis of the following example, where the set of individuals included in the comparison class is not restricted to two:[5]

(32) *John-no-hoo-ga*   {*hoka-no*   *hito-tachi/Bill-ya   Mary*}-*yori*
      John-GEN-hoo-NOM {other-NOM person-PL/Bill-and Mary}-than
         se-ga   *takai.*
      height-NOM tall

      "John is taller than {the other people/Bill or Mary}."

(adapted from [8], 132)

[8] takes *hoka-no hito tachi* "other people" to denote a plural individual, and *John* is contrasted with this plural individual. In the same vein, I assume that *Bill-ya Mary* "Bill and Mary" denotes a sum of the two individuals.

4.2 *mada*-Comparatives and QUD

The addition of *mada* to EC expands the range of possible question-answer pairs. It makes it possible for a *mada*-comparative to be an answer to polar and alternative questions, in addition to a degree question. As an answer to an alternative question, however, only *not-enough* reading is possible.

In contrast to EC, *mada* does not alter the range of QUDs when it is combined with CC; it remains confined to an answer to an alternative question. Table 1 summarizes this situation:

Table 1. QUDs and *mada* + EC/CC

	Deg Q	Polar Q	Alt. Q
Additive	EC	EC	*
not-enough	EC	EC	EC, CC

EC with *mada* under the additive reading leads to a positive answer to the polar question in (30b) because of the presupposition conveyed by the particle: Since it is known that "that room" is large(er than other rooms) and "this room" is asserted to be larger than "that room", the speaker conveys the information that "this room" is large. The *not-enough* reading, on the other hand, provides us with a negative answer to the question. The presupposition here is that "this room" is not large, and this, together with the assertion, leads to the proposition that "both of the rooms are not large." This produces the negative answer to the polar question.

---

[5] I thank Hiroshi Mito and an anonymous reviewer of LENLS 15 for bringing up this problem.

(33) Is this room large? (=(30b))

    a. **Additive reading** → **positive** answer
       Assertion: This room is larger than that one.
       Presupposition: That room is larger than other rooms (or simply large).
       ⇒ This room is large.

    b. ***Not-enough* reading** → **negative** answer
       Assertion: This room is larger than that one.
       Presupposition: This room is not larger than other rooms (or simply not large).
       ⇒ Both of the rooms are not large.

Note that the positive answer-hood of *mada* + EC in additive reading is due to the comparison of the comparative subject with the comparative standard *and its alternatives*. In other words, the additive reading of *mada*-comparatives necessarily involves other entities than the comparative standard, when you make a comparison.

The *not-enough* reading, on the other hand, refers only to the comparative subject and its alternatives in answering the question. The comparison to the comparative standard is not indispensable in answering the polar question.

This difference in contribution to the QUD plays a crucial role in alternative questions. Only the *not-enough* reading is comfortable with alternative questions, as shown in Table 1, because the additive one necessarily includes the third party. In other words, under the *not-enough* reading, *mada* + EC may convey a relative comparison between the two individuals at the same time as it gives a negative answer to a polar question, while for the additive reading, *mada* + EC necessarily includes another comparison. The intuition behind this is corroborated by the following contrast:

(34) Which room is larger, this one or that one?

    a. *??Ano heya-wa   hiroi-shi, kono heya-wa   ano heya-yori*
       That   room-TOP large-and this room-TOP that room-than
       hiroi.
       large.
       "That room is large, and this room is larger than that."

    b. *Dochiramo hiroku-nai-ga, kono heya-wa   ano heya-yori hiroi.*
       either   large-not-but this room-TOP that room-than large.
       "Both of them are not large, but this one is larger than that."

(34a) does not fit with the alternative question in (34), because it necessarily compares "this room", "that room" and other rooms. On the other hand, (34b) can serve as an answer to the alternative question, because the comparison between "this room" and "that room" does not lead to another comparison regarding the size of the rooms.

That the different readings of *mada* with comparatives also correlates with the availability of binary comparison is indicated by the fact that EC with the *not-enough* reading of the particle comes to allow what [7] calls **judgment enforcer** (*dochiraka-to ieba* "if anything"), which is the hallmark of CC, as shown below:

(35) a. *Dochiraka-to-ieba,* {*??kono heya-wa/kono   heya-no-hoo-ga*}
          if-anything,   {this   room-TOP/this room-GEN-hoo-NOM}
             ano heya-yori hiroi.
             that room-than large

          "If anything, this room is {larger than that room/larger of the two}."

     b. [Context: There are two rooms, both of which are known to be small.]
          Dochiraka-to-ieba, {*kono   heya-wa/kono heya-no-hoo-ga*}
          if   anything, {this   room-TOP/this
             mada   *ano heya-yori hiroi.*
             room-GEN-hoo-NOM} still that   room-than

          "If anything, this room is larger than that one (, although both of them are rather small)."

The contrast given in (35a) is due to [7], where they argue that EC resists the judgment enforcer because *dochiraka-to-ieba* is an expression that requires a binary judgment and thus is not comfortable with an answer to a degree question.[6] (35b) shows that the addition of *mada* in *not enough* reading significantly improves the sentence, implying that the contribution of the particle resides in the alteration of the QUD.

4.3   CC and the Interpretations of *mada*

Let us turn to the question why CC does not accept the additive reading. I argue that in the case of CC, the additive reading leads to the presupposition failure.

Let us recall that according to [7], *hoo*-comparatives require the comparative subject marked by *hoo* be a member of the comparison class in question, and it also requires that the comparison class to have only two members:

(36) $[\![\,hoo\,]\!] = \lambda x: x \in CC \wedge |CC| = 2.\ x.$ (where CC is a comparison class.)
                                                                                    $= (31)$

Under the additive reading of *mada*, this presupposition fails because by making a comparison with the comparative standard, the alternative(s) to the standard is accommodated, which leads to a three (or more)-membered comparison class:

---

[6] One might doubt the reliability of the judgment reported regarding *dochiraka-to ieba*. I consulted eight people (including me) and three of them did not find difference in acceptability with (35a)–(35b). The rest of the people found that the EC in (35a) sounds weird with the judgment enforcer, while *mada* in *not-enough* reading improves it.

(37)   a.   = (5)
       *Kono heya-**no-hoo**-ga*   *ano heya-yori*   **mada** *hiroi.*
       this   room-GEN-hoo-NOM   that room-than   still   large

       "This room is larger than that one, although both are not large enough."

   b. $[\![(37a)]\!]$ = size(this room) > size(that room), defined if this room $\in CC \wedge |CC| = 2$.

   c.   Additive reading: CC ={ this room, that room, r* }, where r* is an alternative to "that room"

Here, the comparison class involves at least one alternative to *that room*, in addition to the comparative subject and the comparative standard. CC, which is marked by *hoo* in Japanese, contrasts *two* individuals, while the additive reading enforces it to have at least three.

The *not-enough* reading, on the other hand, does not lead to this presupposition failure: as discussed above, this reading puts two individuals (the comparative subject and the comparative standard) in the realm of *not Adj. enough* altogether. One can ask for a relative order of these individuals with respect to some gradable property that an adjective denotes. In other words, under the *not-enough* reading, one can answer an alternative question. Thus no presupposition failure results.

5   Conclusion

This paper presented the fact that modes of comparison affect the range of the interpretations of *mada* in Japanese. It proposes that this is induced by the (in)compatibility with the QUD, thereby contributing to the understanding of the interaction between pragmatic information conveyed by a specific syntactic/morphological construction and scalar particles.

References

1. Beck, S.: Discourse related readings of scalar particles. Proc. SALT **26**, 142–165 (2016). https://doi.org/10.3765/salt.v26i0.3783
2. Chierchia, G., Fox, D., Specter, B.: The grammatical view of scalar implicatures and the relationship between semantics and pragmatics. In: Maienborn, C., Portner, P., von Heusinger, K. (eds.) Semantics: An International Handbook of Natural Language Meaning, pp. 2297–2332. De Gruyter, Berlin (2011)
3. Ippolito, M.: On the meaning of some focus-sensitive particles. Nat. Lang. Seman. **15**, 1–34 (2007). https://doi.org/10.1007/s11050-007-9004-0
4. Kennedy, C.: Projecting the Adjective: The Syntax and Semantics of Gradability and Comparison. Garland, New York (1999)
5. Kennedy, C.: Vagueness and grammar: the semantics of relative and absolute gradable adjectives. Linguist. Philos. **30**, 1–45 (2007). https://doi.org/10.1007/s10988-006-9008-0

6. König, E.: Temporal and non-temporal uses of noch and schon in German. Linguist. Philos. **1**, 173–198 (1977)
7. Kubota, Y., Matsui, A.: Modes of comparison and question under discussion: evidence from 'contrastive comparison' in Japanese. Proc. SALT **20**, 57–75 (2010). https://doi.org/10.3765/salt.v20i0.2562
8. Matsui, A., Kubota, Y.: Comparatives and contrastiveness: the semantics and pragmatics of Japanese hoo comparatives. In: Proceedings of Formal Approaches to Japanese Linguistics, pp. 126–141 (2012)
9. Roberts, C.: Information structure in discourse: towards an integrated formal theory of pragmatics. Seman. Pragmatics **5**, 1–69 (1996/2012). https://doi.org/10.3765/sp.5.6. Article 6
10. Rooth, M.: A theory of focus interpretation. Nat. Lang. Seman. **1**(1), 75–116 (1992). https://doi.org/10.1007/BF02342617
11. Sawada, O.: The Japanese contrastive Wa: a mirror image of EVEN. BLS **34**(1), 281–292 (2008). https://doi.org/10.3765/bls.v34i1.3576
12. Sawada, O.: Pragmatic aspects of implicit comparison: an economy-based approach. J. Pragmatics **41**, 1079–1103 (2009). https://doi.org/10.1016/j.pragma.2008.12.004
13. Sawada, O., Grano, T.: Scale structure, coercion, and the interpretation of measure phrases in Japanese. Nat. Lang. Seman. **19**(2), 191–226 (2011). https://doi.org/10.1007/s11050-011-9070-1
14. Zeevat, H.: Expressing surprise by particles. Beyond expressives: explorations in use-conditional meaning, pp. 297–320 (2013)
15. Zhang, L., Ling, J.: Additive particles with a built-in Gricean pragmatics: the semantics of German noch, Chinese hái and Hungarian még. Proc. LSA **1**, 1–15 (2016). https://doi.org/10.3765/plsa.v1i0.3743. Article 22

Event Quantification in Infinitival Complements: A Free-Logic Approach

Yu Tomita[(✉)]

Department of Informatics, SOKENDAI (Graduate University for Advanced Studies),
Tokyo, Japan
tomita@nii.ac.jp

Abstract. In this paper, I argue that some infinitival complements can be analyzed as an argument of verbs, in the same way of perception verb analysis (Higginbotham 1983). Then, I consider an event quantification problem in infinitival complements, showing that quantificational event semantics (Champollion 2015) and free logic are the keys to solving it.

Keywords: Event semantics · Event quantification problem

1 Introduction

Some previous papers in (neo-) Davidsonian semantics (Higginbotham 1983; Parsons 1991) propose that an infinitival complement serves as an argument to perception verbs. I generalize this approach to some other infinitival complements. However, these previous studies do not consider the event quantification problem in infinitival complements. Champollion (2015) proposed that a sentence has a GQ type over events. In an opaque context, however, if an infinitival complement is regarded as a GQ-type argument, entailment relations wreak havoc, since all verbs contain an existential quantifier binding an event variable.

I will support Champollion's framework, admitting eventualities which do not exist and assuming that "existence of an eventuality" in some sense corresponds to a predicate or a property for an eventuality. This idea is adequately formalized by using free logic.

1.1 Entailment Relations in Event Semantics

In neo-Davidsonian semantics (Parsons 1990), the logical form of a sentence contains an event variable and an existential quantifier $\exists$ binding the variable (*event quantifier*). One of the virtues of the neo-Davidsonian framework is that this can adequately explain deductive relations among some sentences.

© Springer Nature Switzerland AG 2019
K. Kojima et al. (Eds.): JSAI-isAI 2018 Workshops, LNAI 11717, pp. 372–384, 2019.
https://doi.org/10.1007/978-3-030-31605-1_27

(1)   a.   Brutus stabbed Caesar violently yesterday.

    b.   Brutus stabbed Caesar violently.

    c.   Brutus stabbed Caesar yesterday.

    d.   Brutus stabbed Caesar.

(1a) entails both (1b) and (1c), and (1d) is entailed by all of them. Neo-Davidsonian logical form can capture these entailment relations by ordinary predicate logic. Here I use thematic role functions **ag** and **th** which take an event argument.

(2)   a. $\exists e.\textbf{stabbing}(e) \wedge \textbf{th}(e) = \textbf{c} \wedge \textbf{ag}(e) = \textbf{b} \wedge \textbf{violent}(e) \wedge \textbf{yesterday}(e)$

    b. $\exists e.\textbf{stabbing}(e) \wedge \textbf{th}(e) = \textbf{c} \wedge \textbf{ag}(e) = \textbf{b} \wedge \textbf{violent}(e)$

    c. $\exists e.\textbf{stabbing}(e) \wedge \textbf{th}(e) = \textbf{c} \wedge \textbf{ag}(e) = \textbf{b} \wedge \textbf{yesterday}(e)$

    d. $\exists e.\textbf{stabbing}(e) \wedge \textbf{th}(e) = \textbf{c} \wedge \textbf{ag}(e) = \textbf{b}$

It is apparent that (2a) entails (2b) and (2c), and so is that all of them entail (2d).

1.2   Scope Domain Principle

There are already ample debates on quantification in (neo-) Davidsonian event semantics. For example, take the sentence *Nobody stabbed Caesar*. This is not ambiguous with respect to scope order of *Nobody* binding z and the existential quantifier binding e.

(3)   Nobody stabbed Caesar.

    a. $\neg\exists z.[\textbf{person}(z) \wedge \exists e.[\textbf{stabbing}(e) \wedge \textbf{th}(e) = \textbf{c} \wedge \textbf{ag}(e) = z]]$
      (correct)

    b. $\exists e.[\neg\exists z.[\textbf{person}(z) \wedge \textbf{stabbing}(e) \wedge \textbf{th}(e) = \textbf{c} \wedge \textbf{ag}(e) = z]]$
      (incorrect)

In (3a), an existential quantifier which binds an event variable e takes scope under the quantificational argument *nobody*, whereas (3b) has an existential quantifier which takes the highest scope. (3a) is correctly inconsistent with (2d), just like our intuition for (3). However, (3b) is wrongly consistent with (2d), in that (3b) merely commits to the existence of some irrelevant event e, which is not a one of stabbing of Caesar by someone ($\exists z.[\textbf{person}(z) \wedge \textbf{stabbing}(e) \wedge \textbf{th}(e) = \textbf{c} \wedge \textbf{ag}(e) = z]$). Thus, (3b) is an incorrect description of the meaning of (3). However, most of the neo-Davidsonian framework assumes that the event variable is bound at sentence level, and quantificational NPs occur under the event quantifier.

    The first solution to this problem of quantifier scope is the mereological one, as proposed by Krifka (1989). He used subevents which the event argument in the clause consists of. This theory can explain the meaning of sentences like *three girls ate seven apples.* However, some papers (Champollion 2015, among others) pointed out that a mereological solution occasionally faces difficulties. I will not dwell on this theory here.

Landman (1996) suggested that the existential quantifier which binds an event argument obligatorily takes the lowest scope. Landman (1996, 2000) calls that constraint the *scope domain principle* as defined below:

(4)   Scope domain principle: Non-quantificational NPs can be entered into scope domains. Quantificational NPs cannot be entered into scope domains.

This constraint says, in other words, that all quantificational noun phrases such as *nobody* must take scope over and cannot take scope under the existential quantifier for the event argument in a clause.

There are already discussions on the solution to the *Event Quantification Problem (EQP)*, which forces quantificational noun phrases to take scope over event quantifiers (Champollion 2015; de Groote and Winter 2015; Luo and Soloviev 2017; Winter and Zwarts 2011)[1]. However, as far as I am aware, no one considers quantification in (infinitival) complements.

2   Problems: Nonexistent Events and Event Quantification

I here consider a semantics of infinitival complements.

One of the most popular semantic approaches to complement clauses assumes that a clause denotes a set of possible worlds. For example, an infinitival clause *2 (to) be a prime number* can be analyzed as the following formula.

(5)

This approach has some counterexamples, such as, a pair of sentences *Mary considered 2 to be a prime number* and *Mary considered 5 to be a prime number*. Although these two sentences have different infinitival complements respectively, their meaning is not distinguishable in the possible world framework.

(6)   a. $[\![2 \text{ to be a prime number}]\!] \rightsquigarrow \{w \mid 2 \text{ is a prime number in } w\}$

    b. $[\![5 \text{ to be a prime number}]\!] \rightsquigarrow \{w \mid 5 \text{ is a prime number in } w\}$

---

[1] Luo and Soloviev (2017) argues that Dependent Type Semantics (DTS) can provide an account for the EQP. They addressed a question about *why does the event quantifier take scope under all of the others* from a semantic point of view. In contrast, other studies (Champollion 2015; de Groote and Winter 2015; Winter and Zwarts 2011) proposed a solution for a problem about *how does the event quantifier take scope under all of the others*. In other words, strictly speaking, Luo and Soloviev (2017) considered a different question.

Since 2 and 5 are rigid designators and are prime in all possible worlds, (6a) and (6b) denote the same sets of possible worlds. Thus we cannot tell the semantic difference between (6a) and (6b). In contrast, Higginbotham (1983) and Parsons (1991) argued that perception verbs take an event argument of subordinate complements as their internal argument. In Higginbotham (1983), the (naked) infinitival complement covertly moves to the matrix position. Then, the trace in the complement position of perception verbs is interpreted as an event variable, being bound by the event quantifier in the moved complement. Parsons (1991) proposed that a sentence denotes an eventuality, and the truth condition of the sentence ϕ is given by $\mathbf{E!}(\phi)$. $\mathbf{E!}(t)$ is true iff t exists, iff t belongs to the class of existent entities. This means that a sentential denotation can become an event which does not exist.

2.1   First Tentative Approach: Parsons (1991)

Following Parsons (1991), I tentatively assume that sentences are symbolized as definite descriptions of eventualities, which have a type v. Then, the complements are distinguishable semantically.

(7)   a. $\iota e.[\mathbf{prime}(e) \wedge \mathbf{th}(e) = 2]$

     b. $\iota e.[\mathbf{prime}(e) \wedge \mathbf{th}(e) = 5]$

(7a) and (7b) denote an event of 2 being a prime number and an event of 5 being a prime number, respectively. They are distinguishable since $\mathbf{th}(e)$ has different values. Although this approach successfully solves the problem, Parsons (1991) does not consider the event quantification problem. Since he assume that a sentence denotes an eventuality, if an iota operator for an event variable is given to this infinitival complement, quantificational NPs such as *no student* cannot take scope over event arguments. For instance, although *no student left* means there is no event of leaving by students, this approach cannot give a correct denotation for this sentence.

2.2   Second Tentative Approach: Champollion (2015)

Champollion (2015) proposed an elegant framework which obeys (4). He assumes that all verbs contain an existential quantifier which binds an event variable.

(8)   a. $[\![\text{leave}]\!] \rightsquigarrow \lambda f.\exists e.[\mathbf{leaving}(e) \wedge f(e)]$

     b. $[\![\text{forbid}]\!] \rightsquigarrow \lambda f.\exists e.[\mathbf{forbidding}(e) \wedge f(e)]$

He also considers that thematic predicates are lexically separated ($[\mathbf{r}]$, where $\mathbf{r}$ is a thematic function, e.g., $\mathbf{ag}, \mathbf{th}, \mathbf{ex}, \dots$), assuming all NPs have a GQ type (over entities).

(9) $[\![NP + [\mathbf{r}]]\!] \rightsquigarrow \lambda N \lambda f.[[\![NP]\!](\lambda x.[N(\lambda e.\mathbf{r}(e) = x \wedge f(e)])])]$

The sentence denotes a GQ-type expression over events. Following Champollion (2015) straightforwardly, I assume that infinitival complements are treated as GQ arguments. Then they are analyzed just like NPs.

(10) $[\![every\ student\ (to)\ leave]\!]$
       $\rightsquigarrow \lambda f.\forall x.[\mathbf{student}(x) \rightarrow \exists e'.[\mathbf{leaving}(e') \wedge \mathbf{ag}(e') = x \wedge f(e')]]$

(10) has a GQ type over events ($\langle vt, t \rangle$). Thus (10) can be treated as a GQ argument of the verb. Now, with the sentential closure $\lambda e.\top$, the perceptual verb construction is analyzed as follows.

(11) $[\![Mary\ saw\ every\ student\ leave]\!](\lambda e.\top)$
       $\rightsquigarrow \forall x.[\mathbf{student}(x) \rightarrow \exists e'.[\exists e.[\mathbf{seeing}(e) \wedge \mathbf{leaving}(e')$
       $\wedge\ \mathbf{ag}(e') = x \wedge \mathbf{th}(e) = e' \wedge \mathbf{ag}(e) = \mathbf{m}]]]$

(11) satisfies the scope domain principle (4). One of the challenges for this approach is the factivity of embedded infinitives in opaque contexts. For instance, verbs which take an infinitive entail different consequences.

(12)   a.   Mary saw every student leave $\Rightarrow$ Every student left.

       b.   Mary forbade every student to leave. $\not\Rightarrow$ Every student left.

Interpretation of infinitival complements as GQ arguments is inconsistent with the entailment relations in (12b) because the Champollionian denotation for the infinitival complement *every student to leave* contains the existential quantifier which binds an event variable.

(13) $[\![(12b)]\!](\lambda e.\top)$
       $\rightsquigarrow \forall x.[\mathbf{student}(x) \rightarrow \exists e'.[\exists e.[\mathbf{forbidding}(e) \wedge \mathbf{leaving}(e')$
       $\wedge\ \mathbf{ag}(e') = x \wedge \mathbf{th}(e) = e' \wedge \mathbf{ex}(e) = \mathbf{m}]]]$

In (13), since the event variable for *leaving* is bound by the existential quantifier, this event must take place. I will modify Champollion's framework in a later section.

3   Free Logic

Free logic is an extension of the first-order system. In free logic, the quantificational domain contains entities which do not exist. Then, both universal and existential quantifiers are split into outer and inner quantifiers.

(14)   Existential quantifiers

       a. Σ: outer existential quantifier

       b. $\exists$: inner existential quantifier

(15)   Universal quantifiers

    a. Π: outer universal quantifier

    b. $\forall$: inner universal quantifier

These inner quantifiers are different from outer quantifiers in that the domain of quantification is restricted to a class of existing entities. Inner quantifiers can be defined in terms of the outer quantifiers and the existence predicate **E!**.

(16)   a. $\exists x.\phi(x) := \Sigma x.\mathbf{E!}(x) \wedge \phi(x)$

    b. $\forall x.\phi(x) := \Pi x.\mathbf{E!}(x) \rightarrow \phi(x)$

I argue that Parsons (1991) is compatible with quantificational event semantics if all verbs contain the outer existential quantifier instead of the inner one. Following this assumption, I support a quantificational event semantics with indirect evidence. I admit an eventuality which does not exist at the world and assume that "existence of an eventuality at the world" in some sense corresponds to a predicate or a property for an eventuality. I assume positive semantics, which allows some propositions of the form $P(a)$ to be true even if a does not exist. This idea is adequately formalized by using free logic. Although accepting nonexistent entities is severely criticized by Russell (1905) and Quine (1948), Parsons (1991) and I use the existence predicate for eventuality terms only. Thus, this assumption is outside the scope of their criticism.

4   Outer-Quantificational Event Semantics

I now modify quantificational event semantics using the outer existential quantifier and the existence predicate, generalizing approaches for perceptual reports (Higginbotham 1983; Parsons 1991) to other verbs which take an infinitival complement. A verbal denotation's existential quantifier is replaced with the outer one.

(17)   a. $[\![(\text{to}) \text{ leave}]\!] \rightsquigarrow \lambda f.\Sigma e.[\mathbf{leaving}(e) \wedge f(e)]$

    b. $[\![\text{forbid}]\!] \rightsquigarrow \lambda f.\Sigma e.[\mathbf{forbidding}(e) \wedge f(e)]$

    Now the meaning of (12b) is composed in the following way.

(18) $\lambda f. \forall x.[\mathbf{student}(x) \rightarrow \Sigma e'.[\Sigma e.[\mathbf{forbidding}(e) \wedge \mathbf{leaving}(e') \wedge \mathbf{ag}(e') = x \wedge \mathbf{cont}(e) = e' \wedge \mathbf{ag}(e) = \mathbf{m} \wedge f(e)]]]$

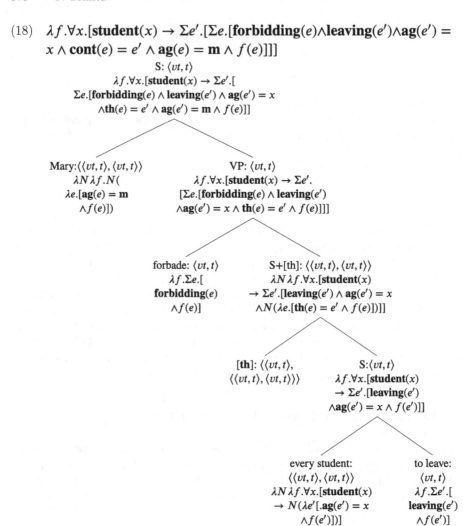

Instead of $\lambda e. \top$, the original sentential closure in Champollion (2015), I adopt **E!** as such closure.

(19) (18) **(E!)** $\rightsquigarrow \forall x.[\mathbf{student}(x) \rightarrow \Sigma e'.[\exists e.[\mathbf{forbidding}(e) \wedge \mathbf{leaving}(e') \wedge \mathbf{ag}(e') = x \wedge \mathbf{th}(e) = e' \wedge \mathbf{ag}(e) = \mathbf{m}]]]$

The truth condition of (18) is given by (19). Note that **E!** is applied to e but not to e', since the embedded infinitival clause is treated as an argument of the matrix verb. This does not entail, but is compatible with a situation in which *every student left* because (19) implies $\forall x.[\mathbf{student}(x) \rightarrow \Sigma e'.[\mathbf{leaving}(e') \wedge \mathbf{ag}(e') = x]]$, which does not commit to the existence of any leaving eventuality. Now, although the denotation for (12a) does not entail *every student left*, I argue that complements of perceptual verbs denote (20).

Table 1. Variants of neo-Davidsonian frameworks

	Sentential denotation type	Semantic closure	Scope domain principle	Nonexistent event
Landman (2000)	vt	$\lambda P.\exists e.P(e)$	✓	✗
Parsons (1991)	v	**E!**	✗	✓
Winter and Zwarts (2011)	$\langle\langle vt,t\rangle,t\rangle$	$\lambda P.\exists e.P(e)$	✓	✗
Champollion (2015)	$\langle vt,t\rangle$	$\lambda e.\top$	✓	✗
My proposal	$\langle vt,t\rangle$	**E!**	✓	✓

(20) $[\![\text{XP} + [\textbf{th}]]\!] \rightsquigarrow \lambda N\lambda f.[[\![\text{XP}]\!](\lambda x.[N(\lambda e.\textbf{th}(e) = x \wedge \textbf{E!}(x) \wedge f(e))])]$

Then (12a) entails *every student left* since **E!** applies to the embedded event.

Figure 1 shows the summary of neo-Davidsonian variants. This paper is considering both the event quantification problem and entailment relations with nonexistent events.

4.1   Limitations

This paper does not treat entailment of non-existence. For example, *Negotiation prevented a strike* entails there exists no eventuality of a strike (Condoravdi et al. 2001).

This paper (and Parsons's approach) cannot address the problem such as:

(21)   a.   Ralph considers the man in the brown hat to be a spy

b.   Ralph considers the man seen at the beach not to be a spy

In both sentences, *the man* denotes the same entity in context. However, both sentences can have different values (Quine 1956).

5   Concluding Remarks

Free logic can give a generalized treatment of infinitival complements in neo-Davidsonian semantics. As assumed in Champollion (2015), verbs contain an existential quantifier, but I argue that the domain of the quantifier contains nonexistent events. The proposed framework avoids the problem on scope domain principle and entailment relations with nonexistent events. If this approach is correct, it becomes plausible that infinitival complements are semantically regarded as an argument of attitude verbs, just like in the cases of a perception verb.

Acknowledgement. I am very grateful to Hitomi Hirayama, Makoto Kanazawa, and Chris Tancredi for their insightful discussion. I also thank two anonymous reviewers for their helpful comments. Needless to say, all remaining errors are my own.

A   Appendix: Formal Syntax for the Quantificational Event Semantics

In this appendix, I offer a simple grammar formalism which the quantificational event semantics is based on.

A.1   Directional Minimalist Grammar without MOVE

I introduce a (tiny) variant of *Directional Minimalist Grammars* (DMGs, Stabler 2011). Though the original DMGs have a MOVE operation, here I present a grammar formalism without MOVE to avoid unnecessary complexities. Similar approaches are adopted by Hunter (2010) and Tomita (2016).

Notations. Here I lay out formal notations which I use in this appendix.

A finite set of *phonological expressions* (or *strings*) V contains items such as Mary, forbade, (to) leave, ..., and the empty string ε. A set of *category features* B contains items such as c, d, v, ... This set determines a set of (right and left) selector features $B_= = \{$b= $\mid$ b $\in B\} \cup \{$=b $\mid$ b $\in B\}$. Both category and selector features are called *syntacitic features*. A set of sequences of syntacitic features Syn is defined as $B_=^* \times B$.

$$\frac{s:\text{b=},\phi \qquad t:\text{b}}{st:\phi}\ \text{MRG}_1$$

$$(s,t \in V^*, \text{b} \in B, \phi \in Syn)$$

$$\frac{t:\text{b} \qquad s:\text{=b},\phi}{ts:\phi}\ \text{MRG}_2$$

Fig. 1. Operation for DMGs

Grammar. The grammar formalism consists of a set of category features B, a set of phonological expressions V, and a finite set Lex, which consists of tuples of a phonological expression and a sequence of syntactic features, i.e., $Lex \subseteq V \times Syn$.

The grammar has a structure-building function called MERGE, which takes two expressions and combines them, concatenating two strings and saturating the leftmost selector feature with a corresponding category feature. This function is a union of two sub-operations, MRG$_1$ and MRG$_2$ shown in Fig. 1.

The set of well-formed expressions is a closure of expressions in Lex under MERGE. A derivation is completed when the only remaining feature in the well-formed expression is c.

A.2   Combination of the Grammar Formalism and Quantificational Event Semantics

On the semantic side of things, a minimalist expression is a sequence of pairs of both a syntactic feature and a semantic component. Following Hunter (2010) and Tomita (2016), I assume that the meaning of each verb consists of multiple semantic components.

First, verbal denotations are assigned to each category feature v in verbs.

(22)   Verbal denotation:

$$\mathcal{P}_{\mathbf{V}} := \lambda f.\Sigma e.\mathbf{V}(e) \wedge f(e)$$

where $\mathbf{V}$ is a verbal predicate constant (e.g. **stabbing**, **finding**,...) of type vt.

Second, a thematic predicate is assigned to each selector feature, being separated from the verbal denotation.

Table 2. A fragment for the free-logic approach

nominal elements	Mary	: $\langle d, \lambda k.k(\mathbf{m}) \rangle$
	someone	: $\langle d, \lambda k.\exists x.[\mathbf{person}(x) \wedge k(x)] \rangle$
	everyone	: $\langle d, \lambda k.\forall x.[\mathbf{person}(x) \rightarrow k(x)] \rangle$
verbal elements	(to) leave	: $\langle =d, \theta_{\mathbf{ag}} \rangle \langle v, \mathcal{P}_{\text{leaving}} \rangle$
	forbade	: $\langle v=, \theta_{\mathbf{th}} \rangle \langle =d, \theta_{\mathbf{ag}} \rangle \langle v, \mathcal{P}_{\text{forbidding}} \rangle$
	saw	: $\langle v=, \theta_{\mathbf{th}}^{\mathbf{E!}} \rangle \langle =d, \theta_{\mathbf{ex}} \rangle \langle v, \mathcal{P}_{\text{seeing}} \rangle$
functional elements	ε	: $\langle v=, I \rangle \langle c, \mathbf{E!} \rangle$

(23)   Thematic predicates:

$$\theta_{\mathbf{r}} := \lambda MNf.[M(\lambda x.[N(\lambda e.[\mathbf{r}(e) = x \wedge f(e)])])]$$

where $\mathbf{r}$ is a thematic role function of type ve such as $\mathbf{ag}$, $\mathbf{th}$,.... The leftmost selector feature in perceptual verbs is anntated with the different thematic predicate which contains the existence predicate.

(24)   Thematic predicates for perceptual verbs:

$$\theta_{\mathbf{th}}^{\mathbf{E!}} := \lambda MNf.[M(\lambda x.[N(\lambda e.[\mathbf{th}(e) = x \wedge \mathbf{E!}(x) \wedge f(e)])])]$$

A fragment of the grammar formalism with semantics is shown in Table 2.

Composition Scheme. The meaning of complex expressions (sentences and phrases) is composed via MERGE in derivations.

A composition scheme for MERGE is as follows. Along the lines of Tomita (2016), MERGE involves the functional application of an argument Q and a semantic component R assigned to the leftmost selector b= or =b. Then, this semantic component is applied to P, being assigned to the remaining category feature b'.

(25) Compositional scheme for MRG_1:

$$\frac{s:\langle \mathbf{b=}, R\rangle\langle \mathbf{f}_1, R_1\rangle \ldots \langle \mathbf{f}_n, R_n\rangle\langle \mathbf{b}', P\rangle \qquad t:\langle \mathbf{b}, Q\rangle}{st:\langle \mathbf{f}_1, R_1\rangle \ldots \langle \mathbf{f}_n, R_n\rangle\langle \mathbf{b}', R(Q)(P)\rangle} \; \text{MRG}_1$$

(26) Compositional scheme for MRG_2:

$$\frac{t:\langle \mathbf{b}, Q\rangle \qquad s:\langle \mathbf{=b}, R\rangle\langle \mathbf{f}_1, R_1\rangle \ldots \langle \mathbf{f}_n, R_n\rangle\langle \mathbf{b}', P\rangle}{ts:\langle \mathbf{f}_1, R_1\rangle \ldots \langle \mathbf{f}_n, R_n\rangle\langle \mathbf{b}', R(Q)(P)\rangle} \; \text{MRG}_2$$

where P, Q, R, R_i are semantic components, s and t range over sequences of strings in V^*, $\mathbf{b}$ and $\mathbf{b}'$ range over category features in B, and $\mathbf{f}_i$ ranges over selector features in $B_=$ for $1 \leq i \leq n$. Example derivations for *Mary saw everyone leave* and *Mary forbade everyone to leave* are shown in Figs. 2 and 3, respectively.

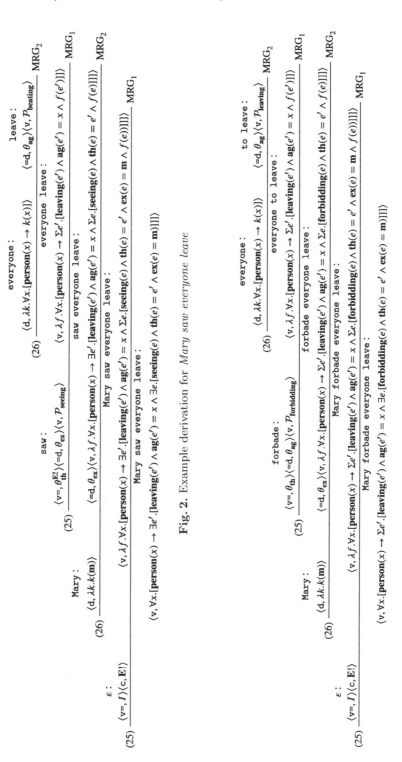

Fig. 2. Example derivation for *Mary saw everyone leave*

Fig. 3. Example derivation for *Mary forbade everyone to leave*

References

Champollion, L.: The interaction of compositional semantics and event semantics. Linguist. Philos. **38**(1), 31–66 (2015)

Condoravdi, C., Crouch, D., van den Berg, M.: Counting concepts. In: van Rooij, R., Stokhof, M. (eds.) Thirteenth Amsterdam Colloquium, pp. 67–72 (2001)

de Groote, P., Winter, Y.: A type-logical account of quantification in event semantics. In: Murata, T., Mineshima, K., Bekki, D. (eds.) JSAI-isAI 2014. LNCS (LNAI), vol. 9067, pp. 53–65. Springer, Heidelberg (2015). https://doi.org/10.1007/978-3-662-48119-6_5

Higginbotham, J.: The logic of perceptual reports: an extensional alternative to situation semantics. J. Philos. **80**(2), 100–127 (1983)

Hunter, T.: Deriving syntactic properties of arguments and adjuncts from Neo-Davidsonian semantics. In: Ebert, C., Jäger, G., Michaelis, J. (eds.) MOL 2007/2009. LNCS (LNAI), vol. 6149, pp. 103–116. Springer, Heidelberg (2010). https://doi.org/10.1007/978-3-642-14322-9_9

Krifka, M.: Nominal reference, temporal constitution and quantification in event semantics. In: Bartsch, R., van Benthem, J.F.A.K., Boas, P.V.E. (eds.) Semantics and contextual expression, vol. 75, pp. 75–115. Foris Publications, Dordrecht (1989)

Landman, F.: Plurality. In: Lappin, S. (ed.) Handbook of Contemporary Semantic Theory, pp. 425–457. Blackwell, Oxford (1996)

Landman, F.: Events and Plurality. Springer, Dordrecht (2000). https://doi.org/10.1007/978-94-011-4359-2

Luo, Z., Soloviev, S.: Dependent event types. In: Kennedy, J., de Queiroz, R.J. (eds.) Logic, Language, Information, and Computation, pp. 216–228. Springer, Berlin (2017)

Parsons, T.: Events in the Semantics of English: A Study in Subatomic Semantics. Current Studies in Linguistics. MIT Press, Cambridge (1990)

Parsons, T.: Atomic sentences as singular terms in free logic. In: Spohn, W., Van Fraassen, B.C., Skyrms, B. (eds.) Existence and Explanation. The University of Western Ontario Series in Philosophy of Science. A Series of Books in Philosophy of Science, Methodology, Epistemology, Logic, History of Science, and Related Fields, vol. 49, pp. 103–113. Springer, Dordrecht (1991). https://doi.org/10.1007/978-94-011-3244-2_8

Quine, W.V.O.: On what there is. Rev. Metaphys. **2**(1), 21–38 (1948)

Quine, W.V.O.: Quantifiers and propositional attitudes. J. Philos. **53**(5), 177–187 (1956)

Russell, B.: On denoting. Mind **14**(56), 479–493 (1905)

Stabler, E.P.: Computational perspectives on minimalism. In: Boeckx, C. (ed.) The Oxford Handbook of Linguistic Minimalism. Oxford University Press, Oxford (2011)

Tomita, Y.: Solving event quantification and free variable problems in semantics for minimalist grammars. In Park, J.C., Chung, J.-W. (eds.) Proceedings of the 30th Pacific Asia Conference on Language, Information and Computation: Oral Papers, Seoul, South Korea, pp. 219–227 (2016)

Winter, Y., Zwarts, J.: Event semantics and abstract categorial grammar. In: Kanazawa, M., Kornai, A., Kracht, M., Seki, H. (eds.) MOL 2011. LNCS (LNAI), vol. 6878, pp. 174–191. Springer, Heidelberg (2011). https://doi.org/10.1007/978-3-642-23211-4_11

A Probabilistic View on Erotetic Argumentation Within Language

Grégoire Winterstein[(✉)]

Département de Linguistique, Université du Québec à Montréal, Montreal, Canada
winterstein.gregoire@uqam.ca

Abstract. This paper deals with the phenomenon of erotetic argumentation, which is characterized by a speaker using premises to argue in favor of a question rather than a proposition as in standard cases of argumentation. We discuss some properties of erotetic argumentation and propose a Bayesian formalisation for these properties based on the idea that erotetic argumentation is marked by an increase of entropy rather than a decrease as in the standard cases. We then examine a series of natural language argumentative constructions (adversative conjunction, disjunction, epistemic modals and questions) and their (in)compatibility with erotetic argumentation. We conclude with a brief look at other types of semantic messages (imperatives and exclamatives) and the possibility of also targeting them as conclusions of an argument.

1 Introduction

This paper deals with *erotetic argumentation*. The term, due to Wiśniewski (1991), refers to cases in which an agent uses a set of premises in order to argue in favor of a conclusion in the form of a question. This contrasts with the usual cases of argumentation that target a proposition as their conclusion. A constructed example is given in (1) and a natural one, extracted from an interview, is in (2). In both cases, the last element in the list is the interrogative conclusion which arises from the preceding premises.

(1)   (Wiśniewski 1991).

    a.   Mary is married to Peter's father.

    b.   John is Peter's father or George is Peter's father.

    c.   ⤳ Who is Mary married to: John or George?

(2)   (retrieved from COCA, on Aug. 22, 2018)

    a.   It's thirty years since Overboard, which is the movie I personally have seen four hundred times. I love it. It's so funny and adorable. It's you and Goldie. If it's on TV, I always watch it. And now I hear they're making a remake.

The author would like to thank Jonathan Ginzburg, two anonymous reviewers and the audience of LENLS for their comments, insights and inspiration on this topic. All errors and inaccuracies remain of course my own responsibility.

K. Kojima et al. (Eds.): JSAI-isAI 2018 Workshops, LNAI 11717, pp. 385–400, 2019.
https://doi.org/10.1007/978-3-030-31605-1_28

b.   ⤳ So I ask you how do you improve upon perfection?

In contrast, a standard case of argumentation, using a proposition as its conclusion is shown in (3).

(3)   a.   This car is reliable and cheap.
       b.   ⤳ So you should buy it.

Argumentation studies have so far largely ignored cases of erotetic argumentation. This is largely because they traditionally consider argumentation as a means of persuasion, i.e. related to matters of truth and belief, which are characteristic of propositions rather than questions. This is for example obvious in the introduction of van Eemeren et al. (2014) where argumentation is defined as relative to a "standpoint", i.e. an opinion; or in works dealing with argumentative schemes (e.g. Walton et al. 2008) which treat argumentation in the perspective of AI and problem solving, and implicitly consider that conclusions can only be propositional.

To a degree, these approaches make sense. Since argumentation is about convincing, i.e. related to degrees of belief, it is hard to see how one could entertain beliefs about objects like questions, much less how one could be "convinced of a question". However, Wiśniewski (1991) has shown that, even from a strict logical point of view, one can define non-trivial notions and properties about erotetic argumentation that help capture part of what makes a sound erotetic argumentation. Besides this logical approach, one can also observe that erotetic arguments have the same linguistic characteristics as traditional arguments. Thus the example (2) uses the connective *so* which has been analyzed as indicating the conclusion of an argument (Carel and Ducrot 1999) in the framework of argumentation within language (*AwL*, see Anscombre and Ducrot 1983 or van Eemeren et al. 2014, chap. 9) which studies how natural language items encode argumentative constraints.

In this work we go over some of the general properties of erotetic argumentation and propose a (Bayesian) formalization for it (Sect. 2), then examine some linguistic markers showing how their semantics is compatible (or not) with an erotetic argumentation scheme (Sect. 3).

2   Properties of Erotetic Argumentation

2.1   Overview and Formalisation

An instance of argumentation is defined by a set of premises which are given as arguments in favor of a conclusion. For an argument to be successful, or cogent, accepting the premises entails accepting the conclusion, or at least getting more confident about the conclusion than before accepting the premises. The process by which the belief in the conclusion is affected by the premises and the validity of that process form the bulk of argumentation studies (van Eemeren et al. 2014).

Here we will take inspiration from the Bayesian approach to argumentation (Ramsey 1926; Carnap 1950; Merin 1999; Godden and Zenker 2016), which sees the relation of argumentation as a probabilistic one. Concretely, a set of premises R argues for (or *is relevant to*) a conclusion C if and only if the posterior belief in C is higher after accepting the content of R than the prior belief in C. Formally, we have:

(4) R is relevant to (argues for) C iff $P(C|R) > P(C)$

This approach has been used to describe how premises affect the belief in the conclusion, and to explain why argumentation schemes that are traditionally seen as fallacious can still be cogent (see e.g. Hahn and Oaksford 2006). Another use of the framework is as a way to formalize the insights of the theory of argumentation within language (Anscombre and Ducrot 1983) and capture the contribution of natural language argumentative markers (Merin 1999).

In the case of erotetic argumentation, we propose to adapt the approach along the following lines.

In keeping with traditional approaches, we assume that the denotation of a question is the Hamblin set of its congruent answers. This is simplificatory to a large extent, but will suffice here. Let's consider a set of premises R and a question Q meant to be the conclusion of the argument. The first properties we want to capture about erotetic argumentation are that (i) each possible answer to the target conclusion is supported by a subset of the premises; and (ii) all the propositions in the premises should play a role in leading to the conclusion, meaning each of them must be part of a subset of premises that is relevant to one of the answers to the conclusion. Note that we consider subsets of the premises rather than individual elements of the premises because some premises only bear some argumentative weight in combination with another proposition. For example in (1), the fact that Mary is married to Peter's father only becomes relevant to her being married to John or George after learning that one of them is Peter's father.

Formally, we write:

(5)   a. $\forall q \in Q : \exists R' \subseteq R : P(q|R') > P(q)$
        b. $\forall r \in R : \exists R' \subseteq R : [r \in R' \wedge \exists q \in Q : P(q|R') > P(q)]$

Note that standard cases of argumentation also obey the constraints in (5) though they are rarely spelt out explicitly. Formally, standard cases of argumentation as in (3) are such that the conclusion set only contains a single proposition C which represents the goal/conclusion of the speaker (i.e. $Q = \{C\}$, and thus $|Q| = 1$). In that case, the conditions in (5) amount to the definition of the relation of argumentation, i.e. that the premises should increase the belief in the conclusion, and that what counts as a premise in the argumentative scheme is an element that plays a role in increasing the belief in the conclusion.[1]

---

[1] The constraints in (5) also match how Merin (1999, fn. 30) describes the relation of being relevant to a question. His goal however is not to deal with erotetic argumentation, but with standard argumentation. His notion of being relevant to a question, is to be understood as being relevant to solve the question, rather than being about raising a question.

Since they also apply to standard argumentation, the two conditions of (5) are necessary, but not sufficient to characterize erotetic argumentation. An additional intuitive property of erotetic argumentation is that the question Q should be raised by the premises (or arise from them, see Wiśniewski 1991 for a discussion of the distinction). An intuitive way of making sense of that notion is to say that no answer to Q should be unilaterally favored by the premises R, i.e. should be less settled after accepting the premises than before. To rule out such cases, we assume that erotetic argumentation cases forbid a decrease in the *entropy* of the question Q, meaning that the premises should not decrease the uncertainty about an issue, rather than decrease it. Formally, we will say that a set of premises R erotetically argues for a conclusion Q if and only if the condition in (6) obtains.[2]

(6) $\text{Entropy}(Q|R) \geq \text{Entropy}(Q) \equiv$
$$- \sum_{q \in Q} P(q|R).log(P(q|R)) \geq - \sum_{q \in Q} P(q).log(P(q))$$

If one considers standard cases of argumentation, the entropy condition in (6) reduces to $-P(C|R).log(P(C|R)) \geq P(C).log(P(C))$ which is trivially false if $P(C|R) > P(C)$ and thus contradicts (5). This makes sense given our intuitive characterization of the difference between standard and erotetic argumentation. The former targets a proposition, and does not consider any alternative to determine whether a relation of argumentation holds. There is for example no minimum threshold of belief increase or belief target under which R would not be considered an argument (such things have been proposed, e.g. Godden and Zenker 2016, but do not affect whether an utterance linguistically argues towards a certain conclusion). As long as there is a positive change in the belief in C based on R, no matter how small, the relation of argumentation holds. In contrast, erotetic argumentation takes into account the presence of several propositions and their relative probabilities via the constraint in (6).

That being said, the proposed formalisation does not rule out that one and the same premise can be used for both standard and erotetic argumentation with the conclusion in the erotetic case being linked to that of the standard case. There have been proposals to see standard argumentation as involving a dichotomous issue formed by the conclusion and its negation: $\{C, \neg C\}$, (see a.o. Merin 1999; Winterstein and Schaden 2011). Standard cases of argumentation will select one element of the issue, say C, as their conclusion. However, if the condition in (6) holds with the set $\{C, \neg C\}$ as a conclusion, then the premise can also be used to erotetically argue in favor of the question $?C$. This case corresponds to situation in which the premises R offer some evidence for C in a way that both increases the belief in C but also increases the uncertainty about which of C or

---

[2] As mentioned above, the locution "raises the question" would be intuitively closer to the relation between premises and conclusion set in erotetic argumentation rather than "argues for", but we want to underline the similarities between all forms of argumentation.

$\neg C$ is the case. In practice, in the case of a dichotomous issue, this means that $0 < P(C) < P(C|R) < 0.5$.

To see how this works on a concrete case, imagine that in the context of elections between two candidates A and B, previous polls gave A as the winner with a score of 70% against 30% for B, i.e. $P(A) = 0.7$ and $P(B) = P(\neg A) = 0.3$. In that context new information as in (7) can be used to argue both in favor of B winning (standard argumentation), and for raising the question of who will win the election (erotetic argumentation) since the uncertainty about the winner has now increased.

(7)   A new poll is showing that voting intentions for candidate B have increased.

    a. $\rightsquigarrow$ Therefore candidate B might win.

    b. $\rightsquigarrow$ So who will win?

However, similar information about A can only give rise to a standard argumentation target, since the new information further decreases the uncertainty about the outcome of the election, i.e. lowers the entropy of the question (8).

(8)   A new poll is showing that voting intentions for candidate A increased.

    a. $\rightsquigarrow$ Therefore candidate A might win.

    b. $\not\rightsquigarrow$ So who will win?

2.2   Application

We can now deal with the examples given in the introduction of the paper. Starting with (1), we consider the three following atomic propositions:

(9)   a. $r_1 =$ Mary is married to Peter's father.
    b. $r_2 =$ John is Peter's father.
    c. $r_3 =$ George is Peter's father.

In (1), we consider that the assertion of $r_2 \lor r_3$ is such that it entails $P(r_2) \approx P(r_3) \approx 0.5$ in the absence of any additional information about the participants, i.e. the first premise is interpreted exhaustively (no other person is candidate to be Peter's father) without any bias towards John or George being the father. This is an idealization, but a valid one in the case of a constructed example like (1) since nothing is known about its various protagonists.

In combination with r_1, the information about r_2 and r_3 entails that the probability of Mary being married to John is roughly 0.5 (and the same for George). Thus, if one considers the set $\{J, G\}$, where $J =$ "*Mary is married to John*" and $G =$ "*Mary is married to George*", as the question being targeted, its entropy will increase given the premises since both conjuncts are given near equal probabilities, which maximizes the entropy of the question.

Note that in this example there is a decrease of the entropy of the question *Who is Mary married to?* after accepting the premises. This is because before accepting the premises, the set of potential candidates to be Mary's husband was potentially larger than just two individuals. Again, in the absence of any information about the candidates, we can attribute them the same probability to be married to Mary. Thus reducing the number of candidates to 2 will indeed decrease the entropy of the question. However the question we consider here is precisely *Is Mary married to John or George* (formally: $Q = \{J, G\}$), i.e. one that does not consider other potential candidates. In that case, whatever the values of $P(J)$ and $P(G)$ before accepting the premises, the entropy of Q will be maximal after accepting them, ensuring that it does not decrease.

The predictions change if one modifies the context of (1) by adding information according to which we know that Mary is married to either John, George or another third person, say Elliot, and that we know it is more likely for her to be married to John (e.g. with a probability of 50% against 25% for the other two). In that case the entropy of the question $\{J, G\}$ increases slightly after the premises. This is because the premise exclude Elliot being the father of Peter and thus Mary's husband, and because the members of the disjunction do not have equal weight. It is thus predicted that the new enriched context is less compatible with an erotetic argumentation scheme since it does not raise the target question as well as the original one.

Since the situation depicted in (1) and the modification we propose are rather cumbersome to express, we propose the case of (10) as another illustration of the same setup. It shares the characteristics of our modified (1) in what we hope is a more natural setting.

(10) a. Cameron always has some alcoholic drink at meals, with a strong preference for red wine over other drinks (e.g. white wine, beer, cocktails etc.)

   b. Today, Cameron ordered wine.

   c. $\overset{?}{\rightsquigarrow}$ So, did Cameron drink red or white wine?

In (10), the last question seems to be less natural to ask than in (1) since, given the context, it is very likely that Cameron ordered red wine. The additional information given in (10-b) actually further reinforces the belief that Cameron drank red wine, rather than cast doubt over it so the question in (10-c) does not seem warranted.

The case of (2) is in a way more straightforward. It essentially rests on the recognition of a number of underlying assumptions behind the speaker's assertions: e.g. that the remake of a movie attempts to improve on the original or that perfection is hard/impossible to improve on (which one could treat in terms of *topos* used in enthymematic situations Breitholtz and Cooper 2011; Breitholtz 2014). Once these are factored in, the problematic target issue naturally arise.

2.3   Related Approaches

In work related to this one, van Rooij (2003) investigates the link between the interpretation of questions and decision problems. He notes that whether an answer resolves a question is a contextual issue rather than a purely semantic matter (a point already made by, inter alia, Ginzburg 1995). van Rooij's point is that the semantics of questions is underspecified, and that it is the recognition of the *decision problem* that the speaker faces which will determine the proper meaning of a question, i.e. the relevant set of elements that compose that meaning (e.g. in terms of granularity). The right meaning for the question will be the one that help decide the problem in the most effective way, where effectiveness is measured via some utility function.

Here, we are concerned by how a decision problem gives rise to a question, which is a problem related to, but distinct from, the one discussed by van Rooij. He reconstructs the decision problem to clarify the meaning of the question. Our focus is on cases that make explicit the decision problem by putting forth a number of propositions that delimit a salient set of possibilities. Taken together these propositions are used as premises to justify asking the question corresponding to the set of open options.

Besides the fact that the elements in play are similar and comparable (questions, decisions problems and argumentative goals), the two approaches also have in common the determination of an element based on contextual cues and the semantic information conveyed by an utterance: the meaning of the question in the case of van Rooij, the argumentative goal in our case.

Formally speaking, van Rooij (2003) defines a decision problem as a probability measure that captures the beliefs of the speaker, to which are added a utility function representing the preferences of the speaker and a set of actions they consider. In the cases we have considered so far, and in many other instances of argumentation, the actions are actually about entertaining beliefs, and the decision problem is thus whether one should believe one proposition or another, and utility had no role to play (though one could imagine ways to factor it in, see Schaden and Winterstein 2019 for some potential applications).

We can however easily find cases that involve actions not related to beliefs and that support erotetic argumentative schemes such as (11).

(11)   I'm hungry, so where to go?

In (11), the speaker asks a question that is directly understood relative to the decision problem raised by their previous assertion: where should the speaker go to (satisfactorily) sate their hunger. One way to see how the question is formed by the assertion of the first part of (11) is to recognize that this first part can be used as a premise to argue in favor of going to several, mutually exclusive, places (12).

(12)   I'm hungry so...
    a.   ...I'll go to the burger place.
    b.   ...I'll go to the sushi place.
    c.   ...I'll go to the Chinese place.
    d.   etc.

Taken together the elements in (12-a)–(12-c) correspond to a question that can roughly be paraphrased as in the second part (11) by abstracting over all the possible places, thus giving the conclusion of the argument.

3   Linguistic Aspects of Erotetic Argumentation

In (5)–(6), we specified the constraints bearing on erotetic argumentation. Beyond constraints on the type of argumentation at hand, a discourse can also be subject to argumentative constraints stemming from the use of specific discursive markers. This is one key tenet of the approach of argumentation within language (*AwL*), which was formalised in Bayesian terms by Merin (1999). More generally, *AwL* makes the hypothesis that all discourse moves carry an argumentative potential that enters into consideration in their interpretation and is subject to the constraints conveyed by some markers and some more general argumentative discourse laws (Anscombre and Ducrot 1983). In this section, we show how the argumentative constraints we proposed for erotetic argumentation interact with those conveyed by adversative markers, disjunction and epistemic modals, then we discuss the argumentative orientation of questions themselves.

3.1   Adversative Conjunction

Adversative connectives such as *but* in English are described as connecting two premises that are in *argumentative opposition*. This means that the first conjunct in the conjunction needs to argue for some conclusion C such that the second conjunct argues against it (Anscombre and Ducrot 1977; Merin 1999; Winterstein 2012). In formal terms, this means that a conjunction of the form "R_1 *but* R_2" is felicitous if there exists a conclusion C such that:

(13) $P(C|R_1) > P(C)$ and $P(C|R_2) < P(C) \equiv P(\neg C|R_2) > P(\neg C)$

Therefore, adversative conjunction inherently refers to some decision problem related to which proposition to believe in. This is because it involves premises arguing for two complementary propositions which form the dichotomic issue: $?C = \{C, \neg C\}$ (where we shall call C the *pivot* of the coordination). Thus as long as the entropy condition of (6) is verified, it is predicted that an adversative conjunction offers an appropriate set of premises to argue in favor of asking $?C$.

Whether the entropy condition is verified depends on the use that is made of an adversative conjunction. One can distinguish between at least two such uses of relevance here.[3]

The first option, is to use an adversative marker like *but* to convey an *indirect opposition* between its conjuncts (Lakoff 1971; Winterstein 2010) (sometimes called argumentative uses). This use is characterized by the fact that the pivot

---

[3] We notably ignore the *corrective* uses of adversative markers which behave differently with regards to the argumentative properties of utterances, see e.g. Jasinskaja (2012) for details and discussions.

is different from both the first and second conjunct. An example is given in (14) where the two conjuncts are in indirect opposition and can be understood as arguing in favor/against a pivot conclusion such as *"I should buy the ring"*. As can be seen, the conjunction can be continued by explicitly asking about the pivot (14-b).

(14)   a.   This ring is nice but expensive.
        b.   So should I buy it?

This contrasts with the case of *direct opposition* (also called "denial of expectation" or "concession", cf. Lakoff 1971; Winter and Rimon 1994). In those cases the second conjunct directly denies the conclusion targeted by the first. In other terms this means that the second conjunct is the negation of the pivot. In that case it follows that after the conjunction is uttered, the issue $\{C, \neg C\}$ has been settled to $\neg C$ (assuming the information in the conjunction has been successfully grounded by all participants) and should thus not be compatible with an erotetic argumentation to $?C$. This is illustrated in (15), which shows that the direct opposition does not support erotetic argumentation in the same way as the indirect one.

(15)   #Cameron smokes, but they're in good health, so are they in good health?

In (15), the issue at hand is $C = $ *"Cameron is in good health"*, and the targeted erotetic goal is $?C = \{C, \neg C\}$. Given the second conjunct, the entropy of that latter question is null if one accepts both premises (since $P(C) \approx 1$) and therefore the entropy condition of (6) is violated. Of course this does not entail that direct opposition cases are incompatible with erotetic argumentation in general. One can use them to argue for questions other than a polar question about the pivot, for example about (possibly unstated) additional elements in the premises that led the first conjunct to argue for C:

(16)   Cameron smokes, but they're in good health, so is smoking really that bad?

As a final note on the topic, we will discuss a claim often made about adversative connectives regarding the strength of the second conjunct (already addressed by van Rooij 2004 though from a different perspective). Besides its argumentative orientation, an utterance also has an argumentative strength that measures how much it affects the belief in its conclusion. Authors such as Anscombre and Ducrot (1977) usually describe connectives like *but* (or its French equivalent *mais*) as encoding a strength constraint stating that the second conjunct is presented as being argumentatively stronger than the first, based on the fact that the premises in (14-a) cannot support a conclusion like $C = $ "I will buy the ring" (which the first conjunct argues for), whereas the opposite conclusion (supported by the second conjunct) is an option for continuation. This is taken to mean that the second conjunct "won" over the first one. However, in the light of (14) this seems empirically invalid. One can either conclude based on the second conjunct alone, or based on the information of both conjuncts taken together, which corresponds to the erotetic case. Thus rather than adding a strength constraint to the argumentative semantics of *but*, one can frame the impossibility of concluding to C as a problem related to the issue of the *accessibility* of discourse elements for subsequent attachment. More precisely we propose that it is related to the right-frontier constraint (see e.g. Asher and Lascarides 2003) that prevents an attachment to the sole left conjunct of (14-a) since the discourse relation of CONTRAST that connects the two conjuncts of *but* is a coordinating one (Asher and Vieu 2005). As illustrated on Fig. 1, where $\pi_1 = $ *This ring is nice* and $\pi_2 = $ *this ring is expensive*, the available sites for subsequent discursive attachment after uttering (14-a) are either π_2 or the pseudo-topic π_0 that subsumes the whole coordination. An erotetic argumentation targeting $?C$ will thus attach to π_0, bearing on both conjuncts to raise the question.

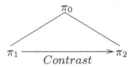

Fig. 1. A discourse structure for (14-a)

3.2   Markers of Uncertainty: Disjunction and Epistemic Modals

Other linguistic markers that also enjoy special links with erotetic argumentation are disjunctive markers and epistemic modals. This is because these markers inherently refer to the uncertainty of their complements: disjunctions offer an alternative between two possibly complementary options, and some epistemic modals indicate a belief than is less than certain.

We already approached the case of disjunction when discussing example (1) in Sect. 2.2. We showed how the use of disjunction can offer the proper ground for an erotetic argumentation to go through.

Epistemic modals, such as *might* or *maybe* are a more complex case. If one gives such markers a simple semantics that indicates that the degree of the belief of the speaker in their complement is between 0 and 1 (Yalcin 2010; Lassiter 2010), then it follows that the speaker also has a non-null belief in the complementary proposition of the proposition over which the modal scopes. Note that this only comes under the exhaustified reading of the modal, i.e. the one that arises after deriving a quantity conversational implicature on the basis of the literal meaning of the utterance and general principles of rational communication (Grice 1989; Geurts 2010). Under that reading, one expects a situation similar to the case of adversative conjunction mentioned above: the use of an epistemic modal should be compatible with an erotetic argumentation towards $?C$ where

C is the content of the prejacent of the modal. In practice, things are slightly more complex.

First, from a theoretical angle, the argumentative profile of an utterance seems independent of any not at-issue content conveyed by the utterance. In other words, any presupposed or implicated material will not take part in the argumentative reasoning process (see Winterstein 2013 for the case of Quantity implicatures, and Winterstein 2015 for conventional, not at-issue material). This suggests that the exhaustified reading of the modal could not be available to set the stage for an instance of erotetic argumentation.

Empirically, the situation seems to support this latter prediction: the first segment of an example like (17) does not appear to license concluding to a polar question about the prejacent of *might* (where the use of *so* is taken to be an indicator of the relation of argumentation as mentioned earlier).

(17)   ?Paul might come tonight, so will he?

One way to introduce such a question is to use an adversative connective rather than a consequence one as in (18).[4]

(18)   Paul might come tonight, (? so/but) will he?

In addition to the data in (17)–(18), we also observe that the same premise cannot be used to target a question formed on the basis of $\neg C$ rather than C (here we exclude the interpretation of *won't he* as a confirmation tag):

(19)   Paul might come tonight, (? so / ? but) won't he?

Formally speaking, given that the issue at hand is $\{C, \neg C\}$ one could think it equivalent to express it either as $?C$ or $?\neg C$. However, neither a concessive nor an adversative marker seem to be felicitous in that example. This, we argue, comes as the result of the argumentative properties of negation and polar questions. As defended in the context of *AwL*, argumentation is sensitive to the linguistic form of its elements (premises and conclusions) and not just to their content. This dovetails with a host of similar observations about the way natural language items behave argumentatively (Anscombre and Ducrot 1983; Winterstein 2010, 2017) and is thus not surprising in this particular light. In the next subsection, we discuss the argumentative profile of questions and use it to explain the facts about aversative coordination we just introduced.

3.3   The Argumentative Profile of Questions

Coming back to the case of (18), one way to approach the preference for using an adversative conjunction is to consider that polar questions themselves have

---

[4] Here, the second conjunct could be uttered by either the speaker of the first utterance or by the addressee, though the latter might be more natural. The possibility of having both utterances by the same speaker is related to the *polyphonous* nature of adversative conjunction which we will not discuss here (Ducrot 1984).

an argumentative orientation. Specifically, Anscombre and Ducrot (1983) show that a polar question of the form $?C$ argues in a way similar to the assertion of $\neg C$. This can be seen in example (20) (freely translated and adapted from Anscombre and Ducrot) where the first part can be justified by either a polar question $?C$ (20-a) or by the assertion of $\neg C$ (20-b) (i.e. the conclusion is given in the first part of (20) and (20-a) and (20-b) are two possible premises to justify it).[5]

(20)   You should not quit your job.
  a.   Will you be able to find something better?
  b.   You will not be able to find something better.

The case of (18) can then be explained on the grounds that modals conserve the argumentative orientation of their prejacent (Winterstein 2017), i.e. if an utterance R argues in favor of C then so will $\diamond R$. This is directly related to the aforementioned hypothesis that the argumentative profile of an utterance is solely based on its at-issue content. In the case at hand it means that the argumentative properties of a *might*-utterance are only based on the lower probability bound introduced by *might*.

Since a question of the form $?C$ argues in the same way as $\neg C$, the conditions for the use of an adversative connective are met in (18) (which has the general form $\diamond C$ *but* $?C$). If one postulates in addition that there is a pressure to use such connectives if their conditions of use are met (e.g. along the lines of a principle like maximize presupposition, see Heim 1990), then the preference for *but* is accounted for. What happens there is then not a case of erotetic argumentation similar to those we saw before (where $?C$ is the conclusion targeted by $\diamond C$), but is instead the balancing of two arguments via an adversative conjunction (one argument being in the form of an assertion, the other one in the form of a question).

Yet another way to frame the issue is by observing that the conclusion targeted by a set of premises cannot be expressed using a form that has an argumentative profile opposite to the premises, even though its probability is raised by the assertion of the premises. This can be seen in (21) where the first part entails that Lemmy was on time, yet does not allow to argue in favor of Lemmy being punctual. This can be attributed to the effect of *almost* which, in this case, constrains the argumentative possibilities of the utterance to those allowed by its prejacent, even though it conveys its negation (Jayez and Tovena 2008).

(21)   #Lemmy was almost late, so he is a punctual person.

---

[5] Note that the argumentative profile of polar questions is (at least partly) independent from the question of their bias. Thus, positive polar questions as in (20-b) are often taken to be unbiased (i.e. not favoring one answer over another), though they still argue in the same direction as the negative answer (though not necessarily in favor of the negative answer, which would correspond to a bias). A more thorough investigation of these interactions lies beyond the scope of this paper, but the case of Chinese languages, especially Cantonese, that have several particles to indicate various (un)biased questions (Yuan and Hara 2013; Hara 2014) would be a good testing ground for this matter.

4 Conclusion and Openings

To summarize, we have proposed a Bayesian treatment for cases of erotetic argumentation and linked that treatment to the argumentative semantics of different operators in natural language.

Beyond expanding the inventory of markers that are compatible with erotetic argumentation, another avenue for further research is to consider the argumentative status of other types of messages. So far we only considered assertions and questions, but it is customary to consider at least two other types of messages: imperatives and exclamatives (see e.g. Ginzburg and Sag 2000; Huddleston 2002). There is less consensus on the formal treatment of these objects, though there is agreement that they should not be seen as simple propositions or propositional abstracts.

Minimally, it seems that imperatives do have argumentative properties since one can for example argue in favor of an order (22).

(22)   (retrieved from COCA, on Aug. 22, 2018)
    a.   You're alive,
    b.   so shut up and keep playing.

So far, to our knowledge, nothing has been proposed to describe and explain the argumentative potential of imperatives, or their use in argumentative schemes, though they should be amenable to a probabilistic treatment as well.

Looking at corpora shows examples that can be analyzed as involving an exclamative target:

(23)   (retrieved from COCA, on Aug. 22, 2018)
    a.   And as this guy throws money out, he creates such a distraction for the folks on the street, just go running for it, right into the oncoming path of these vehicles that are in pursuit of this guy.
    b.   So what a dangerous situation!

(24)   (retrieved from COCA, on Aug. 22, 2018)
    a.   When anyone had a bad day, people would say they looked like Mr. Hong.
    b.   So what a suprise it was for us that after we sent a truckload of flour out to Myungi-col that Mr. Hong and three of his daughters showed up at the rectory and every one of them was smiling from ear to ear.

These latter observations are somewhat surprising and unexpected. This is because the nature of the message conveyed by exclamatives not only indicates that some property holds to a high degree, but also conveys what Marandin (2008) calls "ego-evidentiality", i.e. the indication that the information in the exclamative comes from immediate and direct knowledge of the speaker. Since that content is immediate, it should not need to be justified or argued for.

Doing so would intuitively go against what seem to be a core property of exclamatives. Similarly, the factive nature of exclamatives (Zanuttini and Portner 2003) frames their content as a not at-issue matter, and thus one that should not need (or even allow) justification. As we stand, we have no account for the exclamative examples we just presented, nor of the imperative ones. We leave these matters to future work, noting they imply a proper characterization of the type of semantic object denoted by these elements and how to assign an argumentative profile to these elements.

References

Anscombre, J.C., Ducrot, O.: Deux *mais* en français. Lingua **43**, 23–40 (1977)

Anscombre, J.C., Ducrot, O.: L'argumentation dans la langue. Pierre Mardaga, Liège, Bruxelles (1983)

Asher, N., Lascarides, A.: Logics of Conversation. Cambridge University Press, Cambridge (2003)

Asher, N., Vieu, L.: Subordinating and coordinating discourse relations. Lingua **115**, 591–610 (2005)

Breitholtz, E.: Reasoning with topoi – towards a rhetorical approach to non-monotonicity. In: Proceedings of the 50th Anniversary Convention of the AISB, pp. 190–198. AISB (2014)

Breitholtz, E., Cooper, R.: Enthymemes as rhetorical resources. In: Artstein, R., Core, M., DeVault, D., Georgila, K., Kaiser, E., Stent, A. (eds.) Proceedings of the 15th Workshop on the Semantics and Pragmatics of Dialogue (SemDial11), pp. 149–157 (2011)

Carel, M., Ducrot, O.: Le problème du paradoxe dans une sémantique argumentative. Langue Française **123**, 6–26 (1999)

Carnap, R.: Logical Foundations of Probability. University of Chicago Press, Chicago (1950)

Ducrot, O.: Le dire et le dit. Les Éditions de Minuit, Paris (1984)

van Eemeren, F.H., et al.: Handbook of Argumentation Theory. Springer, Dordrecht (2014). https://doi.org/10.1007/978-90-481-9473-5

Geurts, B.: Quantity Implicatures. Cambridge University Press, Cambridge (2010)

Ginzburg, J., Sag, I.A.: Interrogative Investigations: The Form, Meaning and Use of English Interrogatives. CSLI Lecture Notes, vol. 123. CSLI Publications, Stanford (2000)

Ginzburg, J.: Resolving questions. Linguist. Philos. **18**, 459–527 (1995)

Godden, D., Zenker, F.: A probabilistic analysis of argument cogency. Synthese **195**, 1715–1740 (2016)

Grice, H.P.: Studies in the Way of Words. Harvard University Press, Cambridge (1989)

Hahn, U., Oaksford, M.: A Bayesian approach to informal argument fallacies. Synthese **152**, 207–236 (2006)

Hara, Y.: Semantics and pragmatics of cantonese polar questions: an inquisitive approach. In: Aroonmanakun, W., Boonkwan, P., Supnithi, T. (eds.) Proceedings of PACLIC, vol. 28, pp. 605–614. Phuket, Thailand (2014)

Heim, I.: Artikel und Definitheit. In: Stechow, A.V., Wunderlich, D. (eds.) Handbuch der Semantik, pp. 487–535. de Gruyter, Berlin (1990)

Huddleston, R.: Clause type and illocutionary force. In: Huddleston, R., Pullum, G.K. (eds.) The Cambridge Grammar of the English Language, pp. 851–945. Cambridge University Press, Cambridge (2002)

Jasinskaja, K.: Correction by adversative and additive markers. Lingua **122**(15), 1899–1918 (2012)

Jayez, J., Tovena, L.: Presque and almost: how argumentation derives from comparative meaning. In: Bonami, O., Hofherr, P.C. (eds.) Empirical Issues in Syntax and Semantics, vol. 7, pp. 1–23. CNRS, Paris (2008)

Lakoff, R.T.: If's, and's and buts about conjunction. In: Fillmore, C.J., Langendoen, D.T. (eds.) Studies in Linguistic Semantics, pp. 114–149. de Gruyter, New York (1971)

Lassiter, D.: Gradable epistemic modals, probability, and scale structure. In: Li, N., Lutz, D. (eds.) Semantics and Linguistic Theory (SALT), vol. 20, pp. 197–215. eLanguage (2010)

Marandin, J.M.: The exclamative clause type in French. In: Müller, S. (ed.) Proceedings of the 15th international HPSG Conference, pp. 436–456 (2008)

Merin, A.: Information, relevance and social decision-making. In: Moss, L., Ginzburg, J., de Rijke, M. (eds.) Logic, Language, and computation, vol. 2, pp. 179–221. CSLI Publications, Stanford (1999)

Ramsey, F.P.: Truth and probability. In: Braithwaite, R. (ed.) The Foundations of Mathematics and other Logical Essays, chap. VII, pp. 156–198. Kegan, Paul, Trench, Trubner & Co., London (1926)

van Rooij, R.: Questioning to resolve decision problems. Linguist. Philos. **26**, 727–763 (2003)

van Rooij, R.: Cooperative versus argumentative communication. Philosophia Scientae **2**(8), 195–209 (2004)

Schaden, G., Winterstein, G.: (Strategic) Miscommunication on the Hearer Side, March 2019. Presentation at the Jahrestagung der Deutschen Gesellschaft für Sprachwissenschaft; Workshop 13: Post-Truth

Walton, D.N., Reed, C., Macagno, F.: Argumentation Schemes. Cambridge University Press, Cambridge (2008)

Wiśniewski, A.: Erotetic arguments: a preliminary analysis. Stud. Logica **50**(2), 261–274 (1991)

Winter, Y., Rimon, M.: Contrast and implication in natural language. J. Semant. **11**, 365–406 (1994)

Winterstein, G.: La dimension probabiliste des marqueurs de discours. Nouvelles perspectives sur l'argumentation dans la langue. Ph.D. thesis, Université Paris Diderot-Paris 7 (2010)

Winterstein, G.: What *but*-sentences argue for: a modern argumentative analysis of but. Lingua **122**(15), 1864–1885 (2012)

Winterstein, G.: The independence of quantity implicatures and adversative relations. Lingua **132**, 67–84 (2013)

Winterstein, G.: Layered meanings and Bayesian argumentation: the case of exclusives. In: Zeevat, H., Schmitz, H.-C. (eds.) Bayesian Natural Language Semantics and Pragmatics. LCM, vol. 2, pp. 179–200. Springer, Cham (2015). https://doi.org/10.1007/978-3-319-17064-0_8

Winterstein, G.: Perspectives on Argumentation within Language. Theoretical, Processing, Computational and Social aspects. Ph.D. thesis, Université Paris Diderot-Paris 7 (2017). Habilitation à diriger les recherches

Winterstein, G., Schaden, G.: Relevance and utility in an argumentative framework: an application to the accommodation of discourse topics. In: Lecomte, A., Tronçon, S. (eds.) Ludics, Dialogue and Interaction. LNCS (LNAI), vol. 6505, pp. 134–146. Springer, Heidelberg (2011). https://doi.org/10.1007/978-3-642-19211-1_8

Yalcin, S.: Probability operators. Philosophy Compass **5**(11), 916–937 (2010)

Yuan, M., Hara, Y.: Questioning and asserting at the same time: the l% tone in a-not-a questions. In: Aloni, M., Franke, M., Roelofsen, F. (eds.) Proceedings of the 19th Amsterdam Colloquium, pp. 265–272 (2013)

Zanuttini, R., Portner, P.: Exclamative clauses: at the syntax-semantics interface. Language **79**(1), 39–81 (2003)

LENLS 14

Logic and Engineering of Natural Language Semantics (LENLS 14)

Katsuhiko Sano

Department of Philosophy and Ethics, Faculty of Humanities
and Human Sciences, Hokkaido University, Nishi 7 Chome, Kita 10 Jo, Kita-ku,
Sapporo, Hokkaido 060-0810, Japan
v-sano@let.hokudai.ac.jp

1 The Workshop

The international workshop Logic and Engineering of Natural Language Semantics (LENLS) started in 2005. Its purpose is to provide a venue for researchers working on natural language semantics and pragmatics, (formal) philosophy, logic, artificial intelligence, and computational linguistics together for discussion and interdisciplinary communication. Over the lifespan of the workshop, whose 14th iteration was held at JSAI-isAI 2017 during November 13–15, 2017, many researchers have presented their work, and the workshop has become recognized internationally in the semantics pragmatics community. LENLS 14 had 3 one-hour invited lectures and 27 thirty-minute submitted talks selected by the Program Committee (the total number of the submission was 36, which is the largest since LENLS 8, according to the EasyChair record). The number of participants was about 50. The invited speakers were Craige Roberts (The Ohio State University, USA), Ivano Ciardelli (Munich Center for Mathematical Philosophy, LMU München, Germany), and Shoichi Takahashi (Aoyama Gakuin University, Japan). Topics discussed by the submitted papers raised issues from syntax-semantics-pragmatics interface, morpho-semantic interfaces, semantics of conditionals, semantics of emotions, type theory, semantics of expressives, categorical grammar, attitude verbs and evidentials, among many others. As the reader can see from this volume, a wide range of topics is characteristic of LENLS. The two selected papers appearing in this volume, "Quality as a Speech-Act CI and Presuppositions" by Lukas Rieser and "Explaining Prefix Contributions in Russian using Frame Semantics and RSA" by Yulia Zinova, were supposed to be included in the post proceedings of LENLS 14. We hope to keep the tradition of LENLS in future to promote international researches in the semantics-pragmatics community.

Quality as a Speech-Act CI
and Presuppositions

Lukas Rieser[(✉)]

Yamagata University, Yamagata, Japan
lukasjrieser@gmail.com

Abstract. In this paper, I propose a novel account of Gricean Quality
[3] in terms of conventional implicatures (CIs) that speech acts give rise
to. This view of Quality as a speech-act CI leads to a novel view of the
relation between Quality CIs and CIs arising on the prejacent rather than
the speech-act level of utterance meaning, as triggered by expressives and
parentheticals [13]. It also sheds light on the interaction of (Quality) CIs
and presuppositions, which I take to be properties of propositions. On my
view, utterance felicity is determined by both speech-act CIs differing by
utterance type and prejacent CIs. Building on Grice's maxims of Quality, I propose speech-act CIs for three types of utterances differentiated
by interrogative vs. assertive force and speaker- vs. addressee-orientation
and predict the effect of presuppositions on utterance felicity by their
interaction with the use-conditional evaluability of speech-act CIs, and,
in some cases, prejacent CIs.

1 Truth- and Use-Conditional Meaning

I propose to capture utterance felicity, and thus utterance meaning, in terms of
use conditions, where the use-conditional meaning of an utterance is characterized by a set of propositions, which, when true, make the utterance felicitous—see
for instance Gutzmann (2015) [6] for extensive discussion of formal approaches
to the basic idea of use-conditional meaning formulated by Kaplan (1999) [8].
Formally, I build on my own analysis of speech-act types and utterance felicity
in Rieser (2017) [15] for the formal implementation of speech-act CIs, which in
turn builds on Potts (2005) [13] framework of feature semantics with extensions
by Gutzmann, which I rely on for both the basic definition of CIs and the formal
implementation of prejacent CIs, and extensions due to McCready (2015) [12],
which I use to implement the analysis of Quality as a speech-act CI.

1.1 Utterance Felicity and Conveyed Utterance Meaning

The felicity conditions of an utterance are determined by the set of propositions
in its expressive meaning dimension, that is by its use-conditional meaning. The
expressive meaning dimension of an utterance can also be thought of as the set of
its CIs, containing both prejacent CIs and speech-act CIs. Prejacent CIs are those

© Springer Nature Switzerland AG 2019
K. Kojima et al. (Eds.): JSAI-isAI 2018 Workshops, LNAI 11717, pp. 403–415, 2019.
https://doi.org/10.1007/978-3-030-31605-1_29

conventional implicatures that arise from triggers contained in the prejacent of a speech act, such as lexical CI-triggers like expressives or parentheticals, *cf.* Potts (2015) [14]. Speech-act CIs, on the other hand, arise from the respective speech act that is performed in the utterance. As mentiI also refer to the two types of CIs contained in the CI set as the prejacent and speech-act levels of utterance meaning, respectively. I claim that the conveyed meaning of an utterance is determined by these two levels of meaning taken together. This means that it is an utterance's use-conditional or expressive content, rather than its truth-conditional or descriptive content is what determines the meaning it conveys. This claim is based on the assumption that an utterance conveys information about its speaker's mental state via observer (addressee) reasoning based on the assumption that the utterance is felicitous.[1] As utterance felicity is thus determined by the truth or falsity of the CIs (both prejacent and speech-act) it gives rise to, and as these are only indirectly connected to the truth or falsity of the utterance's descriptive content, I thus claim that an utterance's use-conditional meaning fully captures its conveyed meaning.

1.2 Felicity and the Expressive/Descriptive Distinction

To illustrate the relation between truth- and use-conditional meaning on one hand, and the descriptive and expressive dimensions of utterance meaning on the other, consider example (1) of an assertion of a prejacent proposition $\varphi =$ "Ash is home" without CI-triggers.

(1)   Ash is home.

(1) is intuitively judged a "true" assertion when φ holds at the utterance world, but as "false" when this is not the case. That is, the perceived truth or falsity of the assertion depends on the valuation of φ at the world (and time) of utterance. I claim that the question of whether or not (1) is a felicitous assertion of φ, however, depends not directly on the truth or falsity of φ at the utterance world, but rather on whether or not the originator of the utterance, *i.e.* the speaker believes φ to be true and has adequate (in the Gricean spirit) evidence to back up this belief. The prejacent proposition φ is the utterance's descriptive content, with which in the case of (1) the speech act of assertion is performed, so that utterance felicity is closely linked to the truth of φ. However, this is, for instance, not the case in questions, where utterance felicity is independent of the truth of the prejacent proposition, even though it has the same descriptive content as an assertion. As an intuitive test, an utterance's descriptive content is the proposition φ on which the perceived truth or falsity of assertion depends. This is because, in the case of assertions, the descriptive content influences utterance meaning in form of quality CIs, as will be discussed in the analysis further below.

Other than the prejacent proposition or descriptive content of an utterance, prejacent CI-triggers are part of an utterance's prejacent as opposed to being part

---

[1] See Rieser (2017) [15] for more discussion on the role of addressee reasoning in the derivation of conveyed utterance meaning.

of or modifying the speech act itself. However, they directly influence whether or not it is judged as "felicitous" or "infelicitous", that is they are part of the expressive meaning and do not influence, for instance, whether or not an assertion is intuitively judged as "true" or "false". Prejacent CIs thus contribute to the utterance's use-conditional meaning, and together with speech-act CIs that arise from the speech act proper (see next section) constitute an utterance's expressive content, which I claim to be its conveyed meaning. Prejacent CI-triggers include parentheticals or expressives such as the negatively connotated *cur* vs. the attitude-neutral[2] *dog*, *cf.* Gutzmann (2015) [6]. As for the relation between truth- and use conditions in (prejacent) CIs, the meaning of *cur* can be captured by a paraphrase on the lines of "the speaker has a negative attitude towards the dog referred to", which needs to be *true* at the utterance world in order for the utterance (of any illocutionary force) hosting *cur* to be *felicitous*—the paraphrase of *cur*'s expressive meaning is part of the expressive as opposed to the descriptive dimension of utterance meaning as its truth *directly* influences felicity, regardless of utterance or speech-act type (assertion, question, etc.).

2   Speech-Act CIs and Utterance Felicity

The main focus of this paper, however, are not prejacent CIs as outlined above and much discussed in previous research, but speech-act CIs, in particular those that arise as Gricean Quality implicatures[3]. Since speech-act CIs are, in contrast to prejacent CIs, *necessarily* part of any utterance's meaning, as whenever an utterance is made a speech act is performed and every speech act gives rise to speech-act CIs on my view, I take them to be the primary determinant of the felicity or infelicity of any given utterance. What I propose is that illocutionary force (which on my view arises from force such as assertive or interrogative together with sentence-final intonation) is a CI-trigger on the speech-act level of utterance meaning that gives rise to speech-act rather than prejacent CIs as CI-triggers on the prejacent level of utterance meaning do. In this section, I first briefly return to prejacent CIs in order to set the stage for the subsequent discussion of the speech-act CIs of assertions as well as other speech acts, concretely rising declaratives and rising interrogatives or questions. In the next section, I move on to discuss the interaction of utterance felicity and presuppositions.

2.1   Prejacent CIs and Utterance Felicity

Parallel to prejacent CIs arising from triggers such as expressives and parentheticals, expressive meaning arising on the speech-act level, *i.e.* speech-act CIs can be paraphrased in terms of use-conditional propositions. Both can thus be captured within the same form and framework, an analysis I sketch in the following

---

[2] Ignoring the possible use of either as a derogatory term when referring to a person.
[3] For more detailed discussion on the basic idea of Gricean implicatures as CIs see McCready (2015) [12] and Rieser (2017) [15].

section. To illustrate how speech-act CIs differ by illocutionary force or utterance type and to demonstrate how they differ from prejacent CIs, consider the example of an assertion (or, on my compositional view of illocutionary force, of a final falling declarative) in (2), a variant of (1) to which a prejacent CI-trigger has been added.

(2)   Ash, that bastard, is home.

The descriptive content of the utterance is $\varphi =$ "Ash is home", just as in (1) above. On top of this, the parenthetical "that bastard" with the lexical CI-trigger "bastard" adds expressive content I label ψ, which can be paraphrased on the lines of "the speaker has a negative attitude towards Ash" (I choose this example to represent both of the prejacent CI-triggers mentioned above—expressives and parentheticals). Crucially, ψ has no bearing on the truth conditions of φ, and does not influence whether assertion of φ is judged "true" but rather adds directly to the use, or felicity, conditions of the utterance. While both φ and ψ need to be true for felicitous assertion of φ, the intuition is that if ψ is false, *i.e.* if the speaker does not have a negative attitude towards Ash, this does not make (2) "false", but rather "infelicitous". This is in contrast to φ, the truth or falsity of which determines thee perceived truth or falsity of the assertion.

2.2 Descriptive Content and Felicity of Assertion

This leads to the following question: if not only expressive content such as ψ, but also φ, the propositional content or prejacent that constitutes the descriptive content of (2), should intuitively hold for assertion to be felicitous, how exactly does the truth or falsity of φ relate to the utterance's felicity? A straightforward assumption might be to assume that φ needs to be true in order for the utterance to be felicitous. To my intuition, however, this is not necessarily the case, as if the speaker of (2) has sufficient grounds to believe φ and does not entertain a belief to the contrary, the utterance could reasonably be judged felicitous even if Ash, in fact, is not home.[4] This directly relates felicity of assertion to the two specific Gricean maxims of Quality—when they are satisfied, the utterance is felicitous.

The use-conditional propositions (3) and (4) represent the first and second maxims of Quality, respectively. I claim that they need to be true in order for assertion to be felicitous and are thus relating the truth or falsity of its descriptive content to felicity by way of use-conditional propositions.

(3)   The speaker does not believe φ to be false.

---

[4] I am not claiming that when the speaker of an assertion believes the prejacent proposition to be true, but it is in fact false, there is *nothing* wrong with this assertion. It seems, however, quite clear to me that there is *something else* wrong when the speaker actually believes the prejacent to be false or has no sufficient grounds to assert it. The latter is the kind of badness (Gricean in spirit) I seek to capture—see Jary (2010) [7] for an overview of alternative views.

(4)   The speaker has evidence to back up commitment to φ by assertion.

The basic assumption for my proposal is that the use-conditional propositions (3) and (4) are added to the expressive meaning of (2) as speech-act CIs from assertive force, much like the prejacent-CI ψ is added by the parenthetical "that bastard". It should be noted here that when (3) and (4) hold, it can be concluded that (5) holds as well.

(5)   The speaker believes φ to be true.

While accounting for the modification of Quality II, *i.e.* (4) by speech-act modifiers such as evidentials makes both (3) and (4) necessary, for the proposal below it is sufficient to assume that Quality gives rise to (5), directly committing the speaker to the prejacent. (5) also accounts for the most basic intuition on felicitous assertion that the speaker needs to believe the prejacent to be true (also reflected in Grice's general maxim of Quality "Try to make your contribution one that is true").

2.3   Felicity of Other Utterance Types

Next, what about speech acts other than assertions, specifically such with final rising intonation, which are not readily accounted for with Gricean maxims? When they have the same prejacent proposition, their descriptive meaning ought to be the same, but it relates differently to their felicity, *i.e.* must enter expressive meaning in a way that differs from assertion. Consider the example of a rising declarative (RD) in (6) and the question, or rising interrogative, in (7) below.

(6)   Ash, that bastard, is home?

(7)   Is Ash, that bastard, home?

Both (6) and (7) share their prejacent proposition φ with the assertion, or falling declarative, in (2), and the parenthetical contributes the same use-conditional proposition ψ.

I claim that the difference in felicity to (2) can be straightforwardly explained by different CIs arising from rising declarative and rising interrogative force. First, I propose that use-conditional propositions (8) and (9) become part of expressive meaning of RDs as speech-act CIs.

(8)   The speaker does not assume the addressee believes φ to be false.

(9)   The speaker has evidence to back up commitment of the addressee to φ.

This is based on the assumption that from rising declaratives, (indirect) commitment of the addressee by the speaker arises, as paraphrased in (10). Similar assumptions also underlie the RD-analyses of Gunlogson (2003) [5] and Davis (2011) [2], also compatible with analyses of RDs as "monopolar questions" like that in Krifka (2015) [11].

(10)   The speaker assumes the addressee believes φ to be true.

This reflects the intuition that by uttering a rising declarative, the speaker commits to a higher-order belief over addressee belief based on evidence not for the prejacent proposition itself, but for the addressee believing that this is the case.

The second type of speech act with rising intonation I discuss are rising interrogatives, or canonical (addressee-oriented) questions. Categorizing speech acts by sentence type (declarative or interrogative) and sentence-final intonation (rising and falling), questions differ from assertions in both categories. I first propose that both falling and rising interrogatives give rise to a speech-act CI as paraphrased in (11).

(11)   The speaker does not believe φ to be true.

Clearly, this can not account for all things that questions do but rather gives the bare-bones condition which needs to satisfied in any case where a rising (or other) interrogative is uttered, in the case of canonical, information-seeking questions corresponding to Searle's (1969) [18] condition that the speaker "not know the answer". Furthermore, rising interrogatives plausibly give rise to the implicature that the speaker does *not* commit the addressee to a belief regarding the prejacent, *cf.* Rieser (2017) [15]. The problem of what the effect of questions on the utterance context and thus the discourse is relates to their information-seeking function and been discussed in a large body of research—for recent theories, see, for instance, the inquisitive approach differentiating between inquisitive and assertive update see Groenendijk and Roelofsen (2009) [4] and Ciardelli and Roelofsen (2011) [1], or Krifka (2015) [11] for the commitment space approach on which questions are assumed to constrain possible continuations of the discourse. For the purposes of the discussion in this paper, however, it will be sufficient to consider the felicity condition on questions paraphrased in (11), which needs to be satisfied in order for any interrogative to be felicitously uttered.

Summing up, the descriptive content of an utterance links to different use-conditions depending on which speech-act CIs are associated with sentence type and sentence-final intonation (illocutionary force). Prejacent CI-triggers such as parentheticals and expressives, on the other hand, gives rise to the same CI regardless of utterance type: all of the assertion (2), the RD (6), and the question (7) require ψ = "the speaker has a negative attitude towards Ash" to hold to be felicitously uttered.

3   CIs and Presuppositions

While the discussion of how similar or different (prejacent-level) CIs and presuppositions are is ongoing—*cf.* Potts (2015) [14] and references therein for an overview, Karttunen and Zaenen (2005) [10] and Karttunen (2016) [9] for discussion highly relevant to this paper—their similarities are conspicuous enough to make the distinction somewhat fuzzy. In this section, I discuss the effect of presuppositions on utterance felicity the view from my theory of CIs on both the prejacent and the speech-act levels.

3.1   How Presuppositional Are CIs?

On my view, CIs (both speech-act and prejacent) are "presuppositional" in that they constitute conditions that need to be satisfied before an utterance is made, *i.e.* the use-conditional propositions representing them need to hold of the world at utterance time in order for a speech act to be performed felicitously. Presuppositions, on the other hand, need to be satisfied in order for truth of another proposition to be evaluable. In other words, presuppositions are properties of propositions, but in principle independent of speech acts—only when a speech act with a prejacent that contains a presupposition trigger is performed do presuppositions become conditions on utterance felicity.

To illustrate the relation between utterance felicity and presuppositions, consider the following three examples of assertions. (12) contains a presupposition trigger ("the king of France" after Russell's classic example [17]), (13) a CI-trigger ("that bastard", the same parenthetical as in the examples before), and (14) both a presupposition trigger and a CI-trigger.

(12)   Ash, that bastard, is home.

(13)   The king of France is home.

(14)   The king of France, that bastard, is home.

Example (12), repeated from (2), is an assertion with a parenthetical giving rise to the prejacent CI $\psi =$ "the speaker has a negative attitude towards Ash", which needs to be true for assertion of $\varphi =$ "Ash is home" to be felicitous.

As example (13) contains no CI-triggers, no expressive content arises on the prejacent level, but the asserted proposition $\varphi' =$ "the king of France is home" contains the presupposition trigger "the king of France" so that the truth of φ' can not be judged when the presupposition $\pi =$ "there is a (unique) king of France" is not true. This has an effect on the felicity of (13) as the CI-triggering parenthetical does, for (2), but only via speech-act CIs—the truth or falsity of any proposition on speaker belief or evidence regarding φ' (*i.e.* that of the use-conditional properties reflecting the two specific maxims of Quality) can only be judged when π holds, or, more precisely, when the first-order agent within the speech-act CI believes that π holds (more on this shortly).

Finally, in (14), the prejacent CI $\psi' =$ "The speaker has a negative attitude towards the king of France" is introduced to the expressive dimension of meaning in addition to the presupposition π. Note that in this particular case there is an interesting interaction between presupposition and CI: the truth of ψ can only be judged when π holds, thus π influences not only the evaluability of the use-conditional propositions representing speech-act CIs, but also of ψ' representing the prejacent CI. In this sense, presuppositions have a more global effect on the utterance's meaning than prejacent CIs as they are a property of, rather than an expressive addition to, the descriptive content.

Table 1 sums up the discussion above: The expressive meaning of assertion of a prejacent proposition with the descriptive content φ containing a CI trigger consists of the use-conditional propositions from Gricean Quality, for assertion written with $\Box$ for doxastic necessity as $\Box_S\varphi$ for "the speaker believes φ to be true", *i.e.* the paraphrase of commitment from assertion, and the use-conditional proposition ψ representing the prejacent CI. When there is a presupposition trigger, but no CI trigger in the prejacent, the expressive meaning consists of the propositions from Gricean Quality that are only evaluable when the presupposition π holds, written as $\Box_S\varphi'_\pi$. Finally, with both presupposition trigger and (parenthetical) CI-trigger, the evaluation of ψ' also presupposes π in the example at hand, written here as ψ'_π.

Table 1. Expressive meaning of assertions with CIs and presuppositions

	(12)	(13)	(14)
Presupposition	None	π	π
Prejacent CI	ψ	None	ψ'
Expressive meaning	$\Box_S\varphi, \psi$	$\Box_S\varphi'_\pi$	$\Box_S\varphi'_\pi, \psi'_\pi$

To conclude, presuppositions differ from prejacent CIs in that they are required to be true for felicity to be evaluated, but their truth is merely a prerequisite for felicity and does not guarantee felicitous utterance. Furthermore, while presuppositions potentially interact with prejacent CIs as in (14), this is only the case because the CI-trigger is a parenthetical apposed to the presupposition trigger, and they are in principle independent. Next, I turn to the difference between speech-act CIs and prejacent CIs and their relation to presuppositions.

3.2   Speech-Act CIs vs. Prejacent CIs and Presuppositions

Presuppositions are properties of propositions which indirectly influence speech act felicity by the effect they have on speech-act CIs, but do not vary with the type of speech act they are used in—while the speech-act CIs are different for each utterance type, their evaluability depends on the truth of the original presupposition. This invariability across speech-act type is a property they share with prejacent CIs (*i.e.* CIs after Potts' definition) which directly add felicity requirements to the expressive dimension, but there is a small yet crucial difference. As the effect of presuppositions on utterance felicity is mediated by speech-act CIs, intonation can shift the first-order agent of belief within the use-conditional proposition representing Gricean quality.

Speech-act CIs depend on the type of speech act they arise from. Therefore, the difference between prejacent CIs and speech-act CIs lies in the way that they interact with different speech-act types, as the following examples illustrate.

(15)   The king of France is home?

(16)   The king of France, that bastard, is home?

(17)   Is the king of France home?

(18)   Is the king of France, that bastard, home?

A prejacent CI ψ' conveying the speaker's negative attitude towards the king of France equally arises from the versions of the rising declarative in (16) and the rising interrogative in (18) just as from the assertion (14) as all contain the same CI trigger. The presupposition π of the prejacent proposition with descriptive content φ' in both (15) and (17), on the other hand, has quite different effects in the two examples due to their different speech-act CIs.

First, felicity of the RDs (15) and (16) depends on whether the (use-conditional) propositions in (19) and (20) representing the first and second maxims of quality.

(19) S believes that A does not believe the king of France isn't home.

(20) S has sufficient evidence to commit A to the king of France being home.

When (19) and (20) are satisfied, this allows an observer to infer that (21), the paraphrase for commitment from the RD (15), holds. In the discussion, I will henceforth only mention commitment for ease of exposition.

(21) S assumes A believes the king of France is home.

What is the role in determining utterance felicity of the presupposition π that the evaluability of φ depends on? Note that in order for the truth of (21) to be evaluable, the speaker must have sufficient grounds to believe that the addressee believes π, *i.e.* that there is a king of France. However, the speaker does not necessarily have to believe this as well. I contend that a reading on which the speaker does not believe π is, while not necessarily the standard interpretation, available for (15), the RD without the parenthetical—"The king of France is home?" can felicitously be followed by an assertion "There is no king of France!". Note that this reading does not appear to be available for (16), the version of (15) with the parenthetical CI trigger, which is predicted due to the prejacent CI, that is the use-conditional presupposition ψ' on the use-conditional level requiring that the speaker has a negative attitude towards the king of France requires that the speaker believe π to be evaluated.

The case of the question in (17) is different in that no reference to addressee belief arises from the speech-act CIs that needs to be satisfied for felicitous performance of an interrogative speech act, given in (22).

(22)   The speaker does not believe that the king of France is home.

Crucially, there is no requirement for the speaker to believe the prejacent proposition φ' to be false, which would require the truth of π to be evaluable, so that a version of (17) without the parenthetical would not be infelicitous if the speaker did not believe that there is a king of France. However, it is still intuitively a requirement for felicity of the question that the speaker believes so (a long-standing and widely accepted observation on presupposition projection), which I take to be due to the fact that presupposition failure would affect a potential answer to the question. In other words, the partition introduced by the question would be bad as it rests on a foul premise, thus the speaker is required to believe π for felicitous utterance of a question with the prejacent φ', the evaluability of which depends on the truth of π. While this cannot be fully captured without a dynamic and possibly an inquisitive framework, the badness of (17) in case the speaker does not believe π drastically increases with the parenthetical, as the evaluability of ψ' depends on the truth of π.

Table 2 sums up the expressive meaning of utterances with final rising intonation with presuppositions and with or without CI triggers. The speech-act CIs of the respective utterance types are written in form of belief propositions, where $\square$ stands for doxastic necessity, $\lozenge$ for doxastic possibility, $\square_x\square_y\varphi$ for "x believes (or assumes) that y believes φ", and $\lozenge_x\neg\varphi$ for "x does not believe φ to be true". As above, S stands for the speaker, A for the addressee.

Table 2. Expressive meaning of RDs and questions with CIs and presuppositions

	(15)	(16)	(17)	(18)
Force	DECL↑	DECL↑	INT↑	INT↑
Presupposition	π	π	π	π
Prejacent CI	None	ψ'	None	ψ'
Expressive meaning	$\square_S\square_A\varphi'_\pi$	$\square_S\square_A\varphi'_\pi, \psi'_\pi$	$\lozenge_S\neg\varphi'_\pi$	$\lozenge_S\neg\varphi'_\pi, \psi'_\pi$

The discussion so far shows how presuppositions interact with utterance felicity depending on utterance or speech-act type on my view. First, in the case of rising declaratives, the requirement from a presupposition π is that the speaker assume the addressee believe π to be true. Next, in the case of rising interrogatives or questions, there is not necessarily a requirement that the speaker believe π, while there is potentially a requirement that the speaker believe the addressee to believe π, as otherwise the question could not be answered felicitously. Prejacent CIs differ clearly from presuppositions in that the speaker is always required to believe them, as well as the presupposition triggered by the phrase they are apposed to in case of the examples at hand, in order for the utterance to be felicitous.

4   Formal Implementation in Use-Conditional Semantics

In this section, I sketch an implementation of the proposal outlined above in a feature-semantics framework fundamentally based on Potts (2005) [13] analysis as further developed by McCready (2015) [12] (building on a number of previous innovations, see references therein). McCready's crucial innovation for this project is that of an utterance-type in the expressive dimension—in my proposal, speech-acts are of this type and thus gives rise to speech-act CIs in the expressive dimension, while descriptive content and prejacent CIs come about as usual. Also see Rieser (2017) [16] for an earlier version of this formal framework applied to non-canonical conditionals I take to restrict the modal base of speaker belief on the speech-act level, *i.e.* to operate on speech-act CIs in the terms of the present paper.

In the remainder of this section, I thus propose an account of Gricean Quality implicatures as speech-act CIs compatible with extant use-conditional theories of conventional implicature. Viewing presuppositions simply as conditions on the (truth-conditional) evaluability of propositions within this proposal finally sheds new light on the relation between CIs and presuppositions.

4.1   Utterance Lifting and Speech-Act Level Meaning

To account for utterance modifiers such as Quality and Relevance hedges that operate on Gricean CIs, McCready (2015) [12] introduces an operation *utterance lifting* (UL), which moves descriptive content into the expressive domain. I take UL to generate a set of propositions as speech-act CIs, depending on illocutionary force. (23) shows my version of UL, writing $\mathcal{A}$ for a speech act, t^a and t^c for truth- and use-conditional propositions respectively, and u^c for the aforementioned utterance type that I will use for speech-acts that generate the use-conditional propositions determining utterance felicity.

(23) $\text{UL}^{\mathcal{A}} = \lambda\varphi.\mathcal{A}(\varphi) : <t^a, u^c>$

This is a type-shifting operation, by which the descriptive content φ of an utterance is moved to the expressive domain, where a speech act $\mathcal{A}$ is applied to φ, generating a characteristic set of use-conditional propositions (speech-act CIs) for each utterance type or illocutionary force (*i.e.* combination of sentence type and final intonation). Following the convention $\langle \tau^a, \tau^c \rangle$, writing truth-conditional types on the left, use-conditional types on the right, (24) shows the result of UL, where $U^{\mathcal{A}}$ represents the set of speech-act CIs of type t^c resulting from application of $\mathcal{A}$ to φ.

(24) $\langle \varphi, \mathcal{A}(\varphi) \rangle = \langle \varphi, U^{\mathcal{A}} \rangle$

4.2   Quality Implicatures as Speech-Act CIs

Representations showing the characteristic use-conditional propositions $U^{\mathcal{A}5}$ in the expressive dimension for assertion (falling declarative, DEC ↓), rising declarative (DEC ↑), and question (rising interrogative, INT ↑) with the prejacent φ are shown in (25) through (27) below, representing the speech-act CIs (in the case of the declaratives, the commitments that follow from them) introduced above to capture Quality implicatures. $\Box_x\varphi$ and $\Diamond_x\varphi$ stand for doxastic necessity and possibility relative to agent x's beliefs. The descriptive content of the prejacent proposition is given as φ, and the prejacent contains neither presupposition nor CI-triggers.

---

[5] Here, I show speech-act CIs from Quality only, which are not necessarily the only members of $U^{\mathcal{A}}$, but the only ones that matter for the discussion in this paper.

(25) $\text{DEC}{\downarrow}(\varphi)=\langle\varphi,\Box_S\varphi\rangle$

(26) $\text{DEC}{\uparrow}(\varphi)=\langle\varphi,\Box_S\Box_A\varphi\rangle$

(27) $\text{INT}{\uparrow}(\varphi)=\langle\varphi,\Diamond_S\neg\varphi\rangle$

This implements the basic claims on speech-act CIs from the discussion in the previous sections. First, with an assertion, the speaker commits to the descriptive content—the utterance is only felicitous if the speaker believes φ to be true. This is not to say that the goodness of assertion does not suffer when this belief is false, but I defend that this does not matter for Gricean Quality. Next, with a rising declarative, the speaker indirectly commits the addressee, that is the RD is felicitous if the speaker assumes that the addressee believes φ. Finally, a question only requires the speaker to not believe the prejacent φ to be true.

4.3 Prejacent CIs

Innovations regarding speech-act CIs notwithstanding, prejacent CIs behave in the usual way, so that when an expressive contributes ψ to the expressive dimension as in the examples containing the CI trigger "that bastard", this simply adds the use-conditional proposition ψ (that the speaker has a negative attitude towards the referent of the phrase ψ is apposed to) to the expressive dimension, regardless of illocutionary force. The according meanings of the descriptive and expressive dimensions, *i.e.* of the truth- and use-conditions defining assertion, RD, and question after UL and application of the respective $\mathcal{A}$ to φ are represented in (28) through (30), capturing the felicity conditions of three utterance types according to the present proposal.

(28) $\text{DEC}{\downarrow}(\varphi')=\langle\varphi,\psi\wedge\Box_S\varphi\rangle$

(29) $\text{DEC}{\uparrow}(\varphi')=\langle\varphi,\psi\wedge\Box_S\Box_A\varphi\rangle$

(30) $\text{INT}{\uparrow}(\varphi')=\langle\varphi,\psi\wedge\Diamond_S\neg\varphi\rangle$

This simply shows that prejacent CIs enter expressive meaning directly and regardless of speech-act type.

4.4 Presuppositions

When the prejacent proposition φ' additionally contains a presupposition trigger that requires the presupposition π to be true for the truth of φ to be evaluable, this has roughly the following effects (I refer to the discussion in Sect. 3 for more details).

  In the case of the declaratives, the condition for π is effectively the same as for the prejacent propositions: the speaker is required to believe π, or to assume that the addressee does ($\Box_S\pi$ and $\Box_S\Box_A\pi$, respectively). Recall that I have argued that commitment arises from the satisfaction of the two maxims of quality, and assumed commitment to arise as a speech-act CI as a simplification. This does not go for presuppositions, which explains that they are not affected by utterance modifiers that target quality.

In the case of questions, on the other hand, similar implicatures may arise from presuppositions, but then depend on the information-seeking function of the question—an answer is not possible if the presupposition is not believed by the addressee, and can not be accepted by a speaker that does not believe the presupposition. Crucially, however, prejacent CIs which carry presuppositions, as the parentheticals apposed to presupposition triggers in the examples given above, strengthen the presuppositions of questions, which is predicted by the current proposal.

References

1. Ciardelli, I., Roelofsen, F.: Inquisitive logic. J. Philos. Logic **40**(1), 55–94 (2011)
2. Davis, C.: Constraining interpretation: sentence final particles in Japanese. Ph.D. thesis, University of Massachusets, Amherst (2011)
3. Grice, H.P.: Logic and conversation. In: Cole, P., Morgan, J.L. (eds.) Syntax and Semantics, Speech Acts, vol. 3, pp. 41–58. Academic Press, New York (1975)
4. Groenendijk, J., Roelofsen, F.: Inquisitive semantics and pragmatics. In: Proceedings of SPR, vol. 9, pp. 41–72 (2009)
5. Gunlogson, C.: True to form: rising and falling declaratives as questions in English. Ph.D. thesis, UCSC (2003)
6. Gutzmann, D.: Use-Conditional Meaning: Studies in Multidimensional Semantics. Oxford Unviersity Press, Oxford (2015)
7. Jary, M.: Assertion. Springer, Boston (2010). https://doi.org/10.1057/9780230274617
8. Kaplan, D.: The meaning of ouch and oops. In: Cornell Conference on Context Dependency (1999)
9. Karttunen, L.: Presupposition: what went wrong? In: Semantics and Linguistic Theory, vol. 26, pp. 705–731 (2016)
10. Karttunen, L., Zaenen, A.: Veridicity. In: Katz, G., Pustejovsky, J., Schilder, F. (eds.) Annotating, Extracting and Reasoning about Time and Events (2005). http://drops.dagstuhl.de/opus/volltexte/2005/314
11. Krifka, M.: Bias in commitment space semantics: declarative questions, negated questions, and question tags. In: Proceedings of Semantics and Lingustic Theory (SALT), pp. 328–345 (2015)
12. McCready, E.: Reliability in Pragmatics. Oxford University Press, Oxford (2015)
13. Potts, C.: The Logic of Conversational Implicatures. Oxford University Press, Oxford (2005)
14. Potts, C.: Presupposition and implicature. In: Lappin, S., Fox, C. (eds.) The Handbook of Contemporary Semantic Theory, vol. 2, pp. 168–202. Wiley (2015)
15. Rieser, L.: Belief States and Evidence in Speech Acts: The Japanese Sentence Final Particle no. Ph.D. thesis, Kyoto University (2017)
16. Rieser, Lukas: Truth conditionals and use conditionals: an expressive modal analysis. In: Kurahashi, Setsuya, Ohta, Yuiko, Arai, Sachiyo, Satoh, Ken, Bekki, Daisuke (eds.) JSAI-isAI 2016. LNCS (LNAI), vol. 10247, pp. 108–122. Springer, Cham (2017). https://doi.org/10.1007/978-3-319-61572-1_8
17. Russell, B.: On denoting. Mind **14**(56), 479–493 (1905)
18. Searle, J.R.: Speech Acts. Cambridge University Press, Cambridge (1969)

Explaining Prefix Contributions in Russian Using Frame Semantics and RSA

Yulia Zinova[(✉)]

Heinrich Heine University, Düsseldorf, Germany
zinova@phil.hhu.de

Abstract. Variability in the interpretation of Russian verbal prefixes is traditionally regarded as an issue of lexical semantics. Grammars and dictionaries list
different usages that are possible for each prefix without explaining when and
why particular usages are realised. For a limited amount of prefixed verbs further
information can be found in the dictionaries, but often even this is not enough for
a precise interpretation. In Zinova (2017) I proposed a Frame semantic analysis
that allows to compositionally construct the meaning of a complex verb. In this
paper I make a further step towards a computational account of the pragmatic
component of the system that would allow to predict the final interpretation of
a given verb. I claim that the competition between various verbs derived from
the same stem is an important part of the prefixation system that ensures its flexibility and leads to what on the surface looks like lexical ambiguity. The final
interpretation of a verb depends on the availability of alternative expressions.

Keywords: Russian · Frame Semantics · Lexical semantics · Pragmatic
competition · RSA · Verbal prefixation

1 Introduction

Russian verbal derivational morphology is extremely rich. One stem can serve as a base
for deriving hundreds of verbs via prefixation and suffixation. This is due to the large
number of prefixes (Švedova 1982, p. 353 lists 28, most of them have productive usages)
as well as their polysemy (e.g., the prefix *pere-* has 10 usages according to Švedova
1982, pp. 363–364), and the possibility of stacking. In addition to this, at some stages
of the derivation (once per derivation) the imperfective suffix can be attached to the
verb. As only a small part of all possible complex verbs is present in the dictionaries, a
computational approach is necessary in order to predict the existence and properties of
complex verbs.

In Zinova (2017) I have proposed an account that provides a basis for such an
approach. It is based on Frame Semantics (Fillmore 1982) in combination with Tree
Adjoining Grammars (Joshi 1985, 1987; Joshi and Schabes 1997) as formalized in
Kallmeyer and Osswald (2013). In this framework I model the derivation of complex
verbs. The key feature of a Frame Semantics–TAG combination is that it allows for a
semantically driven analysis of derivational morphology paired with a high decomposition level. An important property of the approach offered in Zinova (2017) is underspec-
ification of prefix contributions. Most of it is then resolved when the prefix is combined

© Springer Nature Switzerland AG 2019
K. Kojima et al. (Eds.): JSAI-isAI 2018 Workshops, LNAI 11717, pp. 416–431, 2019.
https://doi.org/10.1007/978-3-030-31605-1_30

with the verbal stem, but the resulting interpretation is often not as precise as the one listed in the dictionaries. In this paper I show some cases when such a mismatch is observed and propose how this gap can be put in place by using pragmatic competition between various verbs. In particular, I claim that whenever the general meaning of the prefix is underspecified, the interpretation of a particular verb gets settled in the optimal way. With respect to the prefixation system this means that for the range of the prefixed verbs derived form one root their interpretation is adjusted in a way that allows to most efficiently cover the range of meanings a speaker may want to express.

I propose to use underspecified semantics and probabilistic pragmatic modelling to explain the flexibility of prefix contributions in combination with distinct stems. The main idea behind this proposal is inspired by game theory and optimality theory principles: whenever the semantics of two or more lexical items (prefixed verbs formed from the same stem in our case) overlaps, their usage gets restricted in such a way that the uncertainty of the listener is minimized. This line of reasoning follows the recent research on vague language usage, see, e.g., van Deemter (2009) and references therein.

The rest of the paper is structured as follows: in Sect. 2 I provide data that evidences the competition in Russian verbal prefixation system in general. In Sect. 3 a particular example (four perfective verbs derived from the base verb *zimovat'* 'to spend winter time') is considered: I provide frame representations for the respective components and show how they are combined in order to obtain the representations of the complex verbs. In Sect. 4 I show how pragmatic competition functions when the information from the frame representations is transferred to the pragmatic competition module.

2   Competition Within the Prefixation System

Let us start by considering three Russian verbal prefixes: *na-*, *po-*, and *pere-*. When a large enough set of data is analysed (as is done, e.g., in Kagan 2015 or Zinova 2017), one comes to the following conclusion with respect to the semantics of the verbs derived using these prefixes.

1. Verbs prefixed with *na-* or *po-* can refer to events that culminate when the expected/standard degree is reached.
2. Verbs prefixed with *na-* can denote events that culminate at the degree higher than the expected degree.
3. Verbs prefixed with *po-* may refer to events that culminate without reaching the standard degree.
4. Verbs prefixed with *pere-* denote events that culminate at or above the standard degree.

When a *pere-*prefixed verb denotes an event that culminates above the standard degree, the usage of the prefix is called *excessive*. Let us consider verbs that contain the prefix *pere-* in such a usage. It turns out that there is always another verb derived from the same base, that is used as a neutral perfective. Under *neutral perfective* I mean either a verb that refers to an action performed until the normal/standard/appropriate degree,[1]

---

[1] These verbs would constitute aspectual pairs with the imperfective source verbs on the pair-based accounts of Russian verbal system. Janda (2007) calls such verbs Natural Perfectives.

or a verb that denotes an action that lasted for some non-specified time.[2] For example, if the verb *gret'* 'to heat' is prefixed with *pere-*, the resulting verb *peregret'* means 'to overheat'. The same verb can be prefixed with *na-* and the resulting verb *nagret'* means 'to warm up (until the desired temperature)'. In addition, the verb *pogret'* 'to heat' means warming up without necessarily reaching some particular temperature. In this case both *nagret'* 'to warm up' and *pogret'* 'to heat' are neutral perfectives, only with respect to different scales. More pairs and triples are provided in the Table 1. Let us explore them.

Table 1. Distribution of excess-denoting and neutral perfectives across verbal bases and prefixes

Source verb	Translation	"Excess"	Neutral	Other competing verbs
zanimat'sja	'to study'	*perezanimat'sja*	*pozanimat'sja*	
platit'	'to pay'	*pereplatit'*	*zaplatit'*	*oplatit'$_{trans}$* 'to pay for smth'
rabotat'	'to work'	*pererabotat'*	*porabotat'*	*otrabotat'$_{trans}$* 'to work in compensation of smth'
xvalit'	'to praise'	*perexvalit'*	*poxvalit'*	
žarit'	'to fry'	*perežarit'*	*požarit'*	*prožarit'* 'to fry thoroughly,' *nažarit'* 'to fry a lot of'
gret'	'to heat'	*peregret'*	*nagret'*	*pogret'* 'to heat,' *progret'* 'to heat through'
kormit'	'to feed'	*perekormit'*	*nakormit'*	*pokormit'* 'to feed'
trenirovat'	'to train'	*peretrenirovat'*	*natrenirovat'*	*potrenirovat'* 'to train for some time'

The upper third of the table contains three intransitive verbs. The prefix that is used to form a neutral perfective depends on the scale lexicalized by the verb. If there is no scale except for the time scale, the prefix *po-* is used. If there is a scale that allows for the attachment of the resultative *za-*, it may be the option. The lines in the middle third of the table are occupied by two transitive verbs that denote events that are by default measured according to these verbs' internal scales and do not rely on the information coming from the verbal arguments. These verbs form neutral perfectives using the prefix *po-*. In the bottom third the other type of transitive verbs is represented: for them the standard is determined for the pairs of event types and undergoers. In such a case it is the *na-*prefixed verb that refers to the situation of reaching the standard. The attachment

---

[2] Such verbs fall in the Complex Act Perfectives class in the account by Janda (2007).

of the prefix *po-* is also possible, but now the *po*-prefixed verbs tend to refer to events in course of which the standard value is not reached.

What we see is that even if the range of prefixes that two verbs can attach is the same, as for the verbs *žarit'* 'to fry' and *gret'* 'to heat', the semantic contribution of these prefixes may be different. While both *perežarit'* 'to burn by frying' and *peregret'* 'to overheat' have the meaning of excess, the role of the prefix *na-* in the verbs *nažarit'* 'to fry a lot of' and *nagret'* 'to heat' seems to be not the same. In what follows we will explore and fully model a particular example that will allow to shed some light on how these differences in the final semantic contribution can be explained using pragmatic competition principles.

3 Proposal

3.1 Data

Let us discuss and model a rather simple and clear example. Consider the verb *zimovat'* 'to spend winter time'. The OSLIN database[3] of verbal aspect provides the following list of the verbs derived from it: *vyzimovat'* 'to survive the winter' (usually about the plants), *dozimovat'* 'to spend the rest of the winter', *zazimovat'* 'to stay for the winter', *otzimovat'* 'to finish spending the winter', *perezimovat'* 'to spend the winter', *pozimovat'* 'to spend some winter time', *prozimovat'* 'to spend the winter time'.

However, out of these seven verbs only four are commonly used in contemporary texts, as evidenced by the data in Russian National Corpora[4]. These are (1) *pozimovat'* 'to spend some winter time' that describes a finished event of staying in some particular place without imposing further restrictions on the start and the end of the stay, ex. (1); (2) *zazimovat'* 'to stay for the winter' that establishes a connection between the start of staying somewhere and the beginning of the winter, ex. (2); (3) *dozimovat'* 'to spend the rest of the winter' that fixes the end point of the stay to be the end of the winter, ex. (3); and (4) *perezimovat'* 'to spend the winter' that relates both the start and the end points of the stay to the beginning and the end of the winter, respectively, ex. (4).

(1) Ix   by k nam na severa,   čtoby pozimovali   v svoix kartočnyx
     they   to us on north.PL.PREP, that   po.winter.PST.PL in their card
     domikax.
     house.PL.PREP
     'I would like to see them spending winter time here in the north in their houses
     of cards.'   (doskapozorakomi.ru)

(2) Èkspedicija   zazimovala   na Novoj Zemle.
     expedition.SG.NOM za.winter.PST.SG.F on Novaya Zemlya
     'The expedition stayed on the Novaya Zemlya for the winter.'   (Ušakov 1940)

---

[3] Open Source Lexical Information Network, available online at http://ru.oslin.org/index.php?
action=aspect.

[4] Available online at ruscorpora.ru.

(3) Dozimuem   na korable vo l'dax.
     do.winter.PRES.PL.1 on ship   in ice.PL.PREP
     'We will spend the rest of the winter on a ship in the ices.'   (Ušakov 1940)

(4) Perezimovat' v derevne.
     pere.winter.INF in village.SG.PREP
     'To spend the winter in a village.'   (Ušakov 1940)

What is special about the verb *zimovat'* 'to spend winter time' and makes this case more transparent than the others is that it (1) refers to a specific scale – the scale of spending winter time and that (2) this scale has a clear structure: it is a closed scale with two distinguished points (winter start and winter end). Due to this, a natural set of situations that one may want to refer to with respect to spending winter time contains four elements (Table 2):

1. spending one whole winter (t_1);
2. spending an initial part of the winter (t_2);
3. spending a final part of the winter (t_3);
4. spending some time of the winter without bounding the event duration to the duration of the winter (t_4).

Table 2. The domain of terminated events related to spending the winter

	event start = winter start	event end = winter end
t_1	+	+
t_2	+	−
t_3	−	+
t_4	−	−

Note that the four perfective verbs that are related to spending winter time situations cover the corresponding domain of the events. One possible explanation would be that selected prefixes refer exactly to the corresponding configurations. The other option that I argue for in this paper is that the contribution of prefixes is broader and gets restricted and shaped to cover the situations a speaker may naturally want to refer to.

3.2 Frame Semantic Representations

The idea of using frame representations in linguistic semantics and cognitive psychology has been put forward by Fillmore (1982) and Barsalou (1992), among others. The main ideas that motivate the use of frames as a general semantic and conceptual representation format can be summarized as follows (cf. Löbner 2014):

- conceptual-semantic entities can be described by types and attributes;
- attributes are functional relations, i.e., each attribute assigns a unique value to its carrier;

- attribute values can be also characterized by types and attributes (recursion);
- attribute values may be connected by additional relational constraints (Barsalou 1992) such as spatial configurations or ordering relations.

A number of recent studies offer further formalization of the frame theory (Petersen 2007; Petersen and Osswald 2009; Kallmeyer and Osswald 2012, 2013; Kallmeyer et al. 2015; Löebner 2014, among others). This paper is based on the formalization provided in Kallmeyer and Osswald 2013. Frames in the sense of Kallmeyer and Osswald (2013) are finite relational structures in which attributes correspond to functional relations. The members of the underlying set are referred to as the *nodes* of the frame.

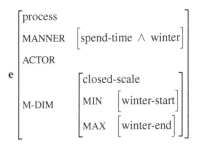

Fig. 1. Frame representation of the verb *zimovat'* 'to spend winter time'

An important restriction is that any frame must have a *functional backbone*. This means that every node has to be accessible via attributes from at least one of the *base nodes*: nodes that carry *base labels*. Importantly, feature structures may have multiple base nodes. In such a case often some nodes that are accessible from different base nodes are connected by a relation. Base labels serve as unique identifiers, that is, a given base label cannot be assigned to more than one node. Due to the functional backbone requirement, every node of the frame can be addressed by a base label plus a (possibly empty) finite sequence of attributes.

Let us start with a frame representation of the base verb *zimovat'* 'to spend winter time'. As shown on Fig. 1, this verb refers to a process (the type of the hole frame with the base node e). It has three attributes: MANNER that is of type *spend-time* ∧ *winter*, ACTOR, and a measure dimension that is of type *closed-scale* and has the start of the winter as its minimum point and the end of the winter as its maximum point.[5]

Now we will explore the semantics of the four prefixes that are used to derive verbs from the *zimovat'* 'to spend winter time' stem: *po-*, *pere-*, *do-*, and *za-*. The contribution of the prefix *po-* can be represented by the frame on the left side of Fig. 2 (following Zinova 2017). This frame encodes the following information: first, the type of the frame

---

[5] Please note that representing the contribution of the base verb is not the primary goal of this paper and there may be better and more accurate solutions for this.

is *bounded-event*; second, the measure dimension of the event (M-DIM) is of type *scale*;[6] third, the event has an initial (INIT) and a final (FIN) stages that are associated with some degrees. It is left implicit that these degrees have to be degrees on the scale that is the measure dimension of the event. Overall, this is a highly underspecified representation that reflects that the prefix *po-* contributes a rather limited amount of information. While it is often considered that *po-* has an additional delimitative usage that allows to derive interpretations related to small quantity or time (Filip 2000; Kagan 2015), I claim that it is not necessary to postulate in in addition to the proposed semantic representation, as in what follows we will derive such a contribution via pragmatic competition.

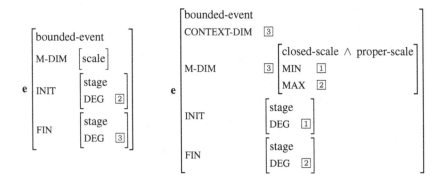

Fig. 2. Frame representations of the prefixes *po-* (left) and *pere-* (right) following Zinova 2017

At the same time, most verbs can attach prefixes that are more restrictive with respect to the identification of the initial and final stages of the event than *po-*. For example, the prefix *pere-*, as shown on right side of Fig. 2, provides information about both endpoints of the event. First, it states that the degree associated with the initial stage of the event (INIT.DEG) is the minimum degree on the relevant scale (M-DIM.MIN). Second, the degree associated with the final stage (FIN.DEG) is the maximum degree on the same scale (M-DIM.MAX). In addition to this, the prefix *pere-* limits the type of the measure dimension to proper scales. According to Zinova (2017, p. 223), proper scales are scales that impose an additional restriction on the event: if the measure dimension of the event is of type *proper-scale*, for each point of the scale there must be an event stage that is characterized exactly by this point (injection between stages and degrees on the scale). When such a requirement is absent, the scale may also be of type *measure of change*. This notion is adopted from Kennedy and Levin (2008) and Kennedy (2012).

The representation of the prefix *do-* is more complex. According to Kagan (2015), the prefix *do-* has completive or additive semantics: it can refer to the terminal part of

---

[6] Note that in Zinova (Zinova 2017) the frame for the prefix *po-* is associated with an additional restriction that the measure dimension (M-DIM) is the verbal dimension (VERB-DIM). This restriction is removed here.

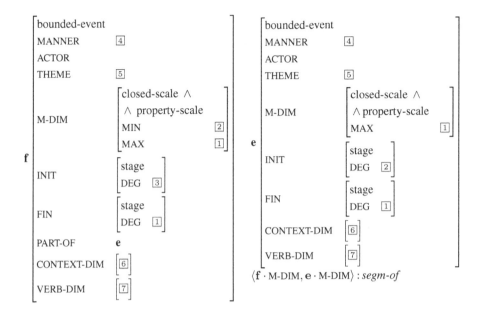

Fig. 3. Frame representation of the prefix *do-*

the event or to an event that can be seen as a continuation of another event. The frame that implements this semantic contribution is shown on Fig. 3.

In essence, the prefix *do-* introduces a new event that is a part of an event referred to by the base verb (the frame with the base label **e** will be unified with the frame representation of the base verb). This new event copies the MANNER and the THEME of the old one as well as the types of all the measure dimensions. The new measure dimension is defined on the basis of the old initial and final stages: for the base verb, the degree of the final stage (**e**.FIN.DEG) is the MAX of the M-DIM and this is also true for the new event. At the same time the MIN of the new event measure dimension is the degree of the initial stage of the base event (**e**.INIT.DEG). This is often (in case the derivation base verb does not contain further prefixes, as in the example considered in this paper) the minimum of the measure dimension of the event. Last, but not least, the degree of the initial stage of the new event is some degree on the corresponding measure dimension scale, but not necessarily its minimum. This ensures that the new event refers to some final segment of the old one, not excluding the possibility of the two events being equal.

Note that attributes in Frame semantics are functional, so the attribute PART-OF has to satisfy this restriction as well, that is why the value of this attribute is defined as the maximum event that the event in question is part of. In particular, it would be an event that proceeds from the minimum to the maximum degree on the relevant scale (provided by the M-DIM attribute). The scale has to be closed in order for the value of the PART-OF attribute to be defined.

The last prefix that is relevant for the discussed case is *za-*. The basic frame that I propose in order to represent its general semantic contribution is provided on Fig. 4. Informally it can be read in the following way: suppose the derivational base denotes some event **e** that has as its measure dimension a scale of type *proper-scale*. Then the verb prefixed with *za-* denotes another event of type *transition*. A transition is in general characterized by its anterior and posterior states. In this case we are interested in the posterior state that has to be a segment of the event denoted by the derivation base. What we also know is that the scale in the measure dimension of the posterior state of the transition event corresponds to some initial segment of the scale in the measure dimension of the event denoted by the derivational base. The identity of two attributes VERB-DIM and M-DIM of the event frame on Fig. 4 ensures that the measure dimension of the event is determined by the verb.

3.3 Representations of Prefixed Verbs

The next step is combining the representation of the base verb with the representations of the prefixes. This is done via the unification of the corresponding frames. When the frame for the verb (Fig. 1) is unified with the frame for the prefix *po-* (left side of Fig. 2), the frame on the left side of Fig. 5 is obtained. This resulting frame description refers to a bounded process of spending winter time that starts at some degree of the closed scale referring to winter time and ends at some other degree on the same scale. No further information is provided, so it is not excluded that these degrees can also be the minimum and the maximum of the scale.

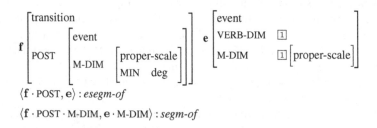

$$\langle \mathbf{f} \cdot \text{POST}, \mathbf{e} \rangle : esegm\text{-}of$$

$$\langle \mathbf{f} \cdot \text{POST} \cdot \text{M-DIM}, \mathbf{e} \cdot \text{M-DIM} \rangle : segm\text{-}of$$

Fig. 4. Representation of the contribution of the prefix *za-*

The second prefix we were considering is *pere-*. When its representation (see right side of Fig. 2) is unified with the representation of the verb *zimovat'* 'to spend winter time' (Fig. 1), the resulting frame (right side of Fig. 5) refers to a bounded event of spending winter time with the degree of the initial stage of the event being the minimum of the measure dimension scale (winter start) and the degree of the final stage of the event being the maximum of the measure dimension scale (winter end). Simply put, the obtained representation of the prefixed verb *perezimovat'* denotes an event of spending the whole winter (from the winter start to the winter end).

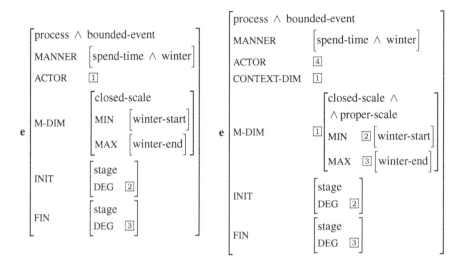

Fig. 5. Frame representations of the verb *pozimovat'* 'to spend some winter time' (left) and of the verb *perezimovat'* 'to spend the winter' (right)

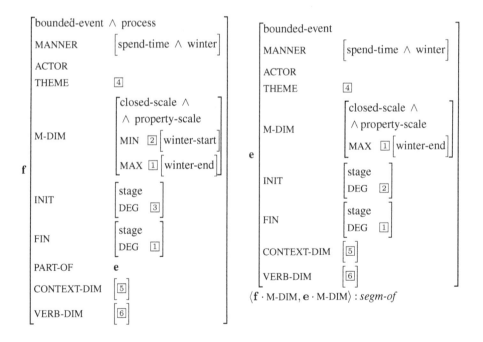

Fig. 6. Frame representation of the verb *dozimovat'* 'to finish spending the winter'

The next prefix is *do-*. To obtain the representation of the prefixed verb *dozimovat'* 'to finish spending winter time', the frame for the base verb (Fig. 1) has to be unified with the frame for the event with the base label **e** on Fig. 3. The resulting frame is shown on Fig. 6, whereby the prefixed verb refers to the event labelled by **f**. It is again a bounded process of spending winter time such that the degree of the final stage is the maximum of the measure dimension (winter end), but the degree of the initial stage may be any point on the same scale.

The last combination is that of the prefix *za-* (Fig. 4) with the same base verb (Fig. 1). The resulting frame, shown on Fig. 7, refers to a transition event such that its posterior stage is an event of spending winter time that necessarily includes the start of the winter. There is no information about how the situation developed apart from that.

4   Pragmatic Competition

Now, given the situations specified in Table 2 and the restrictions imposed by particular prefixes, possible interpretations of prefixed verbs are shown on Fig. 8: the verb *pozimovat'* 'to spend some winter time' can refer to any of the situations t_1–t_4, the verb *zazimovat'* 'to stay for the winter' can refer to t_1 and t_2, *dozimovat'* 'to spend the rest of the winter' – to t_1 and t_3, and *perezimovat'* 'to spend the winter' – only to t_1. In such a configuration, however, it follows from basic pragmatic and game-theoretic principles that the usage of the *za-*, *do-*, and *po-*prefixed verbs would be restricted to the situations t_2, t_3, and t_4, respectively: one can use, e.g., Gricean principles (Grice 1975), Game theory (Benz *et al.* 2006; Jäger 2008), or Optimality Theory (Blutner 2000; Dekker and Van Rooy 2000; Franke and Jäger 2012).

As a further step, I propose to implement such an approach using the Rational Speech Act model (RSA, Goodman and Frank 2016, Goodman and Tenenbaum 2016). The RSA model is an implementation of a social cognition approach to the understanding of utterances. It is based on Gricean ideas that speakers are cooperative and aim to produce utterances balancing between being informative and yet saving effort. A (pragmatic) listener then interprets the utterance by inferring what a speaker must have meant, given the expression they uttered (Bayesian inference). An advantage of this approach is that its output is a probability distribution that can be experimentally tested.

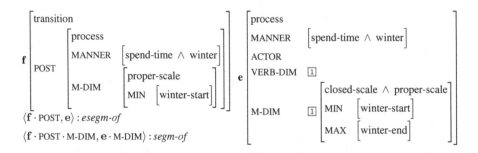

Fig. 7. Representation of the prefixed verb *zazimovat'* 'to stay for the winter'

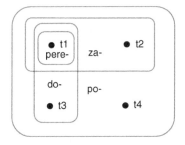

Fig. 8. Possible interpretations of the verbs derived from *zimovat'* 'to spend the winter', see also Table 2

For the implementation I use a probabilistic programming language (WebPPL[7]) with a basic three-layered RSA model. This model includes (i) a literal listener that interprets the utterance according to the provided literal semantics; (ii) a pragmatic speaker that selects an utterance from the available options based on the probability of the literal listener inferring the desired state of the world; (iii) a pragmatic speaker that interprets the utterance by reasoning about the pragmatic speaker. Six things need to be provided as an input to the model:

1. the world model;
2. probability distribution over possible world states;
3. set of alternative utterances;
4. their probabilities;
5. a meaning function from utterances to states;
6. a value of the optimality parameter.

Let us go through the list. First is the world model that in our case it contains four states that are shown in Table 2. This is a motivated by the structure of the scale the event relates to.

Next is the probability distribution over different states. In the implementation provided here I have assumed a flat prior over four world states which means that they are supposed to be equally likely. In order to later test the predictions of the model against speakers' intuitions the prior has to be either estimated from the data or the experimental design should allow for a prior setup.

I assume that the set of alternative utterances in case of a context-free setup is the set of all prefixed verbs formed from the same stem.[8] Such a set, however, can be very large, so an additional assumption I adopt here is to limit the set of alternatives to the verbs that have the same or smaller degree of morphological complexity with respect to the target verb. If more complex verbs are to be added, they would probably be associated with higher cost and thus lower prior probability. For the verbs of the same complexity (like in our example) I assume a flat probability distribution.

---

[7] https://probmods.org/.
[8] The question of competition between verbs that have different stems but are semantically close is left for future work.

Manipulating both priors (state prior and utterance prior) will lead to different probability distributions with respect to the interpretation of the individual prefixed verbs. For this reason the output of the model I show in this paper is not yet suitable for a comparison with experimental data for speakers' beliefs about the world after they have heard the utterance.

The next important piece of information is the meaning function that maps utterances to states. It comes more or less directly from the frame representations. Two parameters are set up: event start and event end. Both of them can get as a value any point other than winter start and winter end (value *some* in the code) or the respective endpoint of the scale (*winter_start* or *winter_end*).

The last parameter that has to be set is alpha, the optimality parameter. In the current implementation, the value of alpha is 1[9].

The graph on the left side of Fig. 9 represents the literal listener's probability distributions over the four possible situations (left to right: spending some winter time, spending time from winter start until some point, spending time from some point until the winter end, spending the whole winter). As the *po*-prefixed verb can refer to any of the situations, the distribution that the literal listener obtains corresponds to the prior distribution (in this case a uniform one).

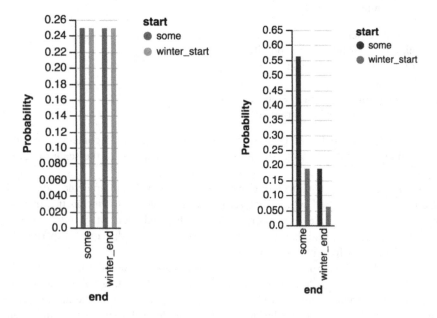

Fig. 9. RSA model output

---

[9] This is an arbitrary selected value. By varying this parameter one can model different behaviour: more or less dependent on the rational considerations. If alpha equals zero, pragmatic listener's behaviour will not differ from that of a literal listener.

Given this model the verb *pozimovat'* is interpreted by a pragmatic listener as 'spend some but not all winter time' with the probability almost 0.55, as shown on the right side of Fig. 8. The same verb can still be used to refer to the situations t_2 and t_3 (with probability a bit below 0.2) or t_4 (very low probability).

5 Results and Future Work

In sum, in this paper I have shown how underspecified semantics coordinated with pragmatic competition allows to explain the observed inference of 'low intensity' or 'short duration' of the *po*-prefixed verbs by the competition between various perfective verbs derived from the same derivational base. Simply put, when the semantics of several prefixed verbs overlaps, the usage of the *po*-prefixed verb gets restricted to the 'low degree' situations.

In future work I plan continue implementation within the RSA framework parallel to the experimental work that would allow to verify not only the qualitative, but also the quantitative predictions of the proposed approach. In course of this work, not only the final interpretations, but also the priors have to be tested and acquired from the data.

Another question that has to be addressed is whether the competition I have outlined here takes place every time a speaker produces and a listener hears an utterance (as shown above) or it is an evolutionary process.

A RSA code

```
// possible states of the world //
var worldPrior = function() {
  return categorical({ps: [1, 2, 4, 2],
    vs: [{start: "winter_start", end: "winter_end"},
        {start: "some", end: "winter_end"},
        {start: "some", end: "some"},
        {start: "winter_start", end: "some"},]})}

// possible one-word utterances //
var utterances = ["zazimovat","pozimovat","perezimovat","dozimovat"]
// possible preferences of utterances//
var utterancePrior = function() {
  return categorical({ps: [1, 1, 1, 1], vs: utterances})}
// meaning function to interpret the utterances//
var meaning = function(utterance, world){
  return utterance == "zazimovat" ? "winter_start"==world.start :
  utterance == "perezimovat" ? "winter_start"==world.start
  && "winter_end"==world.end :
  utterance == "dozimovat" ? "winter_end"==world.end : true}

// literal listener //
var literalListener = function(utterance){
  Infer({method:"enumerate"}, function(){
    var world = worldPrior();
    var uttTruthVal = meaning(utterance, world);
```

```
    condition(uttTruthVal == true)
    return world})}

// define speaker optimality //
var alpha = 1
// pragmatic speaker //
var speaker = function(world){
  Infer({method:"enumerate"}, function(){
    var utterance = utterancePrior();
    factor(alpha * literalListener(utterance).score(world))
    return utterance})}

// pragmatic listener //
var pragmaticListener = function(utterance){
  Infer({method:"enumerate"}, function(){
    var world = worldPrior();
    observe(speaker(world), utterance)
    return world})}
```

References

Barsalou, L.W.: Frames, concepts, and conceptual fields. In: Lehrer, A., Kittay, E.F. (eds.) Frames, Fields, and Contrasts, New Essays in Semantic and Lexical Organization, pp. 21–74. Lawrence Erlbaum Associates, Hillsdale (1992). Chapter 1

Benz, A., Jäger, G., Van Rooij, R.: An introduction to game theory for linguists. In: Benz, A., Jäger, G., Van Rooij, R. (eds.) Game Theory and Pragmatics, pp. 1–82. Springer, London (2006). https://doi.org/10.1057/9780230285897_1

Blutner, R.: Some aspects of optimality in natural language interpretation. J. Semant. **17**(3), 189–216 (2000)

Dekker, P., Van Rooy, R.: Bi-directional optimality theory: an application of game theory. J. Semant. **17**(3), 217–242 (2000)

Filip, H.: The quantization puzzle. Events as Grammatical Objects, pp. 3–60. CSLI Press, Stanford (2000)

Fillmore, C.J.: Frame semantics. Linguistics in the Morning Calm, pp. 111–137. Hanshin Publishing Co., Seoul (1982)

Franke, M., Jäger, G.: Bidirectional optimization from reasoning and learning in games. J. Logic Lang. Inf. **21**(1), 117–139 (2012)

Goodman, N.D., Frank, M.C.: Pragmatic language interpretation as probabilistic inference. Trends Cogn. Sci. **20**, 818–829 (2016)

Goodman, N.D., Tenenbaum, J.B.: Probabilistic Models of Cognition (2016). http://probmods. org/. Accessed 2 Mar 2018

Grice, H.P.: Logic and conversation. In: Cole, P., Morgan, J.L. (eds.) Syntax and Semantics 3: Speech Acts, pp. 41–58. Academic Press, New York (1975)

Jäger, G.: Applications of game theory in linguistics. Lang. Linguist. Compass **2**(3), 406–421 (2008)

Janda, L.A.: Aspectual clusters of Russian verbs. Stud. Lang. **31**(3), 607–648 (2007)

Joshi, A.K.: Tree adjoining grammars: how much context-sensitivity is required to provide reasonable structural descriptions? In: Dowty, D., Karttunen, D., Zwicky, A. (eds.) Natural Language Parsing, pp. 206–250. Cambridge University Press (1985)

Joshi, A.K.: An introduction to tree adjoining grammars. In: Manaster-Ramer, A. (ed.) Mathematics of Language, pp. 87–114. John Benjamins, Amsterdam (1987)

Joshi, A.K., Schabes, Y.: Tree-adjoining grammars. In: Rozenberg, G., Salomaa, A. (eds.) Handbook of Formal Languages, pp. 69–123. Springer, Heidelberg (1997). https://doi.org/10.1007/978-3-642-59126-6_2

Kagan, O.: Scalarity in the Verbal Domain: The Case of Verbal Prefixation in Russian. Cambridge University Press, Cambridge (2015)

Kallmeyer, L., Osswald, R.: A frame-based semantics of the dative alternation in lexicalized tree adjoining grammars. Submitted to Empirical Issues in Syntax and Semantics 9 (2012)

Kallmeyer, L., Osswald, R.: Syntax-driven semantic frame composition in lexicalized tree adjoining grammars. J. Lang. Model. **1**(2), 267–330 (2013)

Kallmeyer, L., Osswald, R., Pogodalla, S.: Progression and iteration in event semantics-an LTAG analysis using hybrid logic and frame semantics. In: Colloque de Syntaxe et Sémantique à Paris (CSSP 2015) (2015)

Kennedy, C.: The composition of incremental change. In: Demonte, V., McNally, L. (eds.) Telicity, Change, State: A Cross-categorical View of Event Structure. Oxford University Press, Oxford (2012)

Kennedy, C., Levin, B.: Measure of change: the adjectival core of degree achievements. In: McNally, L., Kennedy, C. (eds.) Adjectives and Adverbs: Syntax, Semantics, and Discourse. Oxford University Press, Oxford (2008)

Löbner, S.: Evidence for frames from human language. In: Gamerschlag, T., Gerland, D., Osswald, R., Petersen, W. (eds.) Frames and Concept Types. SLP, vol. 94, pp. 23–67. Springer, Cham (2014). https://doi.org/10.1007/978-3-319-01541-5_2

Petersen, W.: Representation of concepts as frames. In: The Baltic International Yearbook of Cognition, Logic and Communication, vol. 2, pp. 151–170 (2007)

Petersen, W., Osswald, T.: A formal interpretation of frame composition. In: Proceedings of the Second Conference on Concept Types and Frames, Düsseldorf (2009, to appear)

Ušakov, D.N., (ed.): Tolkovyj slovar' russkogo jazyka. [Explanatory Dictionary of the Russian Language.]. Izdatel'stvo Akademii Nauk SSSR, Moscow (1935–1940)

van Deemter, K.: Utility and language generation: the case of vagueness. J. Philos. Logic **38**(6), 607 (2009)

Švedova, N.J.: Russkaja Grammatika, vol. 1. Nauka, Moscow (1982)

Zinova, Y.: Russian verbal prefixation. Ph.D. thesis, Heinrich-Heine University, Düsseldorf (2017)

SKL 2018

5th International Workshop on Skill Science (SKL 2018)

Tsutomu Fujinami

Japan Advanced Institute of Science and Technology, 1-1 Asahidai, Nomi, Ishikawa 923-1292, Japan

1 Aims and Scope

Human skills involve well-attuned perception and fine motor control, often accompanied by thoughtful planning. The involvement of body, environment, and tools mediating them makes the study of skills unique among researches of human intelligence. The symposium invited researchers who investigate human skill. The study of skills requires various disciplines to collaborate with each other because the meaning of skills is not determined solely by effciency, but also by considering quality. Quality resides in person and often needs to be transferred through the master-apprentice relationship. The procedure of validation is strict, but can be more complex than scientific activities, where everything needs to be described by referring to evidences. We are keen to discuss the theoretical foundations of skill science as well as practical and engineering issues in the study.

2 Topics

We invited wide ranges of investigation into human skills, from science and engineering to sports, art, craftsmanship, and whatever concerns cultivating human possibilities. 15 pieces of work were presented at the workshop, including an invited lecture. Five selected pieces of work are included in this issue from our workshop. Two articles explain how we can collect data of motions using widely available technologies to analyze the quality of motor control. The third article investigates the perception of music. The study shows how different trainings in jazz and classic music may lead to different perceptions of music. The fourth article proposes a method to evaluate the balance control of the elderly, and the fifth article investigates whether playing computer games helps us to improve our cognitive capability. We are pleased to see that our study extends its domains to address important issues such as our physical or mental health. The workshop organizer is honored to present these reports and hopes that the reader will find them interesting and will be stimulated to look into the field of Skill Science.

Prediction of Basketball Free Throw Shooting by OpenPose

Masato Nakai[✉], Yoshihiko Tsunoda, Hisashi Hayashi, and Hideki Murakoshi

School of Industrial Technology, Advanced Institute of Industrial Technology,
1-10-40, Higashiooi, Shinagawa-Ku, Tokyo 140-0011, Japan
{b1617mn,b1613yt,hayashi-hisashi,hm}@aiit.ac.jp

Abstract. OpenPose, which is developed by Carnegie Mellon University (CMU) presented in CVPR 2017, takes in real-time motion images via a simple web camera and is capable of recognizing skeletons of multiple persons in these images. It also generates recognized skeleton point coordinates to files. OpenPose is featured by CMU's original top-down method for real-time recognition and it is open online especially for research purposes. Thus we aimed to build a posture analysis model using OpenPose skeletal recognition data and verifying the practicality of OpenPose by verifying the accuracy of the model. As a posture analysis model, we adopted a logistic regression model that predicts the shooting probability of the basketball free throw with skeleton posture data as explanatory variables and the fact whether the ball enters the basket or not as a binary target variable. As the result, sufficiently significant prediction accuracy was obtained. Therefore, posture analysis using OpenPose has been verified to be practical with our model. We consider that with many skeleton data which are easily provided by a simple web camera, OpenPose makes statistical diagnostic approach possible. We also consider it could lower costs (in both financial and time-wise) of such an analysis which has previously required more equipments and more time for preparation regarding motion capture analysis systems.

Keywords: OpenPose · Logistic regression ·
Basketball shooting prediction · Posture diagnosis

1 Introduction

A large number of various human posture data with high precision are required to improve performance in statistical posture analysis. However, we found that there are not enough posture data available, because of complexity for acquiring posture data. In order to acquire whole posture data as a time-series, there are two major methods. One is video motion analysis (manual marking) and the

K. Kojima et al. (Eds.): JSAI-isAI 2018 Workshops, LNAI 11717, pp. 435–446, 2019.
https://doi.org/10.1007/978-3-030-31605-1_31

other is motion capture analysis. Video motion analysis is very laborious, because we have to divide video into photographs and mark annotations on the pose images. Motion capture analysis is necessary to attach so many sensors on limbs that acquisition of data is complicated in operation. At CVPR 2017 conference, Carnegie Mellon University (CMU) presented OpenPose [1][1] which can recognize skeletons of multiple players in real-time, using a simple web camera, as shown in Fig. 1. OpenPose adopts unique top-down position recognition using Deep Learning and also the unique algorithm as affiliation recognition of body parts by PAF (Part Affinity Fields) [2]. As a result, in the moving skeletal pictures generated by OpenPose, the skeleton marks are shown and overlapped well with the figure of people. And it seems that recognition accuracy is very high even for various people in various environments.

Although Results of OpenPose's paper [2] said that OpenPose had achieved State-of-the-Arts in the COCO2016 keypoints challenge [3], we decided to evaluate the performance of OpenPose on our own in two aspects. At first we evaluated the correspondence between the actual body positions and the output data generated by OpenPose. As a result of column (actual/openPose rate) in Fig. 2, we found that the CV (Coefficient of Variation: std/mean) of rates of the distance from the neck of OpenPose to the actual body was 0.08. For example, since a neck is wide in the range of several cm, measurement errors can not be avoided to measure actual distance from the neck to each part. We estimate that CV shows acceptable accuracy. So we can evaluate that OpenPose recognizes body points in a static pose.

However the skeletal recognition of OpenPose in dynamic motion is not clear. In order to evaluate OpenPose's performance in a dynamic motion, next we decided to build a basketball shooting prediction model using real-time skeletal data generated by OpenPose. The "OpenPose's performance" we aim to clarify includes the accuracy of dynamic recognition and usefulness as a dynamic data generator with the accuracy of our shooting prediction model using dynamic data generated by OpenPose.

As a result, we found that the free throw prediction model indicated sufficiently significant accuracy. Thus, we found that OpenPose is a convenient and practical generator of posture data.

The rest of the paper is as follows. In Sect. 2, we briefly review previous dynamic posture analysis models. In Sect. 3, we show our experimental methods and selection of the prediction model. In Sect. 4, we show experimental result and estimation the accuracy of prediction. In Sect. 5, we conclude this paper. In Sect. 6, we present future works.

---

[1] OpenPose realizes three-dimensional acquisition by stereo (compound eye) camera in March 2017, but in this research, OpenPose of 2D position recognition version using monocular Web camera is used because of easy operation and sufficient use frequency.

Fig. 1. OpenPose

no	name	openPose x	openPose y	Distance from no.1	Actual distance (cm)	actual/openPose rate
0	nose	1114.4	722.1	147.67	20	0.13544
1	neck	1262.0	726.4	0.00		
2	R.shoulder	1266.3	861.2	134.86	18	0.13347
3	R.elbow	1316.9	1076.4	354.34	48	0.13546
4	R.wrist	1333.9	1266.3	544.67	64	0.11750
5	L.shoulder	1249.4	616.5	110.62	18	0.16272
6	L.elbow	1283.1	409.8	317.29	48	0.15128
7	L.wrist	1296.0	215.8	511.67	64	0.12508
8	R.hip	1684.0	793.7	427.30	60	0.14042
9	R.knee	1975.1	785.3	715.54	98	0.13696
10	R.ankle	2270.4	785.2	1010.12	136	0.13464
11	L.hip	1700.9	646.0	446.22	60	0.13446
12	L.knee	1992.0	629.1	736.48	98	0.13306
13	L.ankle	2262.1	624.9	1005.23	136	0.13529
					mean	0.13660
					std	0.01097
					std/mean	0.08034

Fig. 2. Comparison of distance from neck between OpenPose and actual body positions, Column Distance from no. 1 is the distance from neck to each point of OpenPose. Column actual/openPose rate is actual distance divided by Distance from no. 1

2   Previous Research for Posture Analysis

As a previous analysis of sports motion, there is a method called video motion analysis which divides video into photographs and marks points manually on the pose image for annotation [4]. As a direct sampling posture data, motion capture is used to collect data from sensors on body and limbs [5]. However, these methods are so expensive to collect data that statistical models such as regression could not be applied. MicroSoft KINECT, which is not sold as of early 2018, can easily take 3D posture data, but the sensing range is very narrow and the recognition accuracy of skeletal points are somewhat lower [6].

On the other hand, as a statistical approach, it is realized that winning prediction of basketball game was modeled by logistic regression using records which include the winning/losing results and the frequency of shooting and robbing the ball in the game [7].

As a time-series analysis for motions, there is a research that tries to transfer abstracted motions from a human to a robot with hidden variables estimated by Hidden Markov and reversely predict the next action of the robot from estimated hidden variables [8]. However, our shooting prediction of basketball free throw is not a general time-series model that predicts the next action from the last time-series of motions because our model predicts a result whether to shoot in the basket or not rather than an action. The number of persons monitored in this experiment was limited to 51. We adopted a logistic regression [9] using the features which are composed with the positions at the start and the end or their difference, velocity and acceleration between start and end positions extracted from a time-series of the free throw motions.

3   Method

3.1   Subject of Experiment

In order to construct the shooting prediction model of basketball free throw, we took movies of basketball free throw motions with a full hi-vision video camera. For subject of experiment, we used 51 records which were obtained by two or three trials of various skill levels of 23 persons of a high-school basketball team and some members of an exchange student basketball circle. We generated their skeletal data by OpenPose from the movies. In this experiment, 20 out of 51 records succeeded in the free throw.

3.2   Output of OpenPose

The version of OpenPose (see Footnote 1) adopted in this paper is for 2 dimensional skeleton recognition, and the skeletal coordinates of 18 points (COCO keypoints [2]) as shown in Fig. 3 are outputted to files in about 10 to 20 frames per second depending on a computer performance[2] and connected as shown in Fig. 4 to make time-series data. A skeletal coordinate is composed of 3 values which are x as horizontal, y as vertical and p as confidence probability. We ignored low confident coordinates with less than 0.7 confidence probability.

Though we used only skeletal data for prediction of shooting model, OpenPose can recognize also hands and faces as shown in Fig. 5 and outputs each recognized data to each file.

---

[2] Our experimental machine is CPU: AMD Ryzen 7 1800X, MEMORY: 16 GB, GPU: NVidia GeForce GTX 1080ti, OS: Ubuntu 14.04 LTS, CUDA version: 8.0, cuDNN version: 5.1 for CUDA8.0.

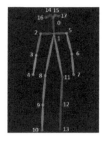

Fig. 3. Skeleton points of OpenPose cited from [1]

Fig. 4. Connection of frames

Fig. 5. Recognized finger and face points of OpenPose (cited from [1])

3.3 Statistical Model

The shooting prediction model is a binary prediction as to whether to enter the basket or not. As major binary prediction models, there are logistic regression, SVM [10] and Xgboost [11]. The SVM using the kernel method is a nonlinear model which may make high accuracy but cannot calculate the shooting probability because SVM maps data space to higher dimensional space. Xgboost using the stochastic gradient method that has a high reputation for accuracy and robustness is not adequate for a diagnostic model because this model cannot indicate explicitly the degree of importance of explanatory variables. So we adopted a logistic regression model that is easy to interpret and commonly used.

Probability of logistic regression is as follows using α, β and features. The relationship between Z value and probability is shown in Fig. 6. Regression intercept α and coefficients β are calculated by multivariate logistic binary regression on Maximum Likelihood whose partial difference can be solved by Newton-Raphson method [9] because of no local minimum in this optimization.

$$\mathcal{Z} = \alpha + \sum_{i=1}^{n} \beta_i \cdot feature_i \tag{1}$$

$$probability = \frac{1}{1 + \exp(-\mathcal{Z})} \tag{2}$$

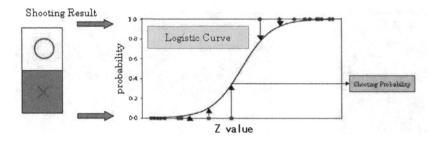

Fig. 6. Logistic regression

3.4 Variables of Logistic Regression

The explanatory variables of the logistic regression model are features calculated from the time-series data. Features include the positions of skeletal points, moving speed, acceleration, etc. The target variable is the fact whether the ball enters the basket or not In the time-series data, as shown in Fig. 7, everyone bent knees at the start of the throw and lifted hands to the highest level upon completion of the throw. So we decided to define the interval of a free throw between the time when the knees were bent the most at the start and the time when the hands were lifted to the highest physical point at the end. All the coordinate positions were relative from the neck point.

Fig. 7. Posture of start and end

4   Results

4.1   Accuracy of Logistic Regression

In general, the precision of the logistic regression model is expressed in the pareto diagram as shown in Fig. 8. In this diagram, the horizontal axis shows the composition rate of all the members in descending order of shooting probability predicted by the logistic regression, and the vertical axis shows the composition rate of the number of people who succeeded in free throw. About 40% people succeeded at this experiment. Red dots in Fig. 8 indicate composition rate of accumulated people who shot in basket. For example, if a player with a high shooting probability at 5% point of composition rate in descending order of the probability and this success shoot is at the fourth among the total 100 success shoot, the red dot is marked at (0.05, 0.04). If the model was perfect, it would be represented by the line of the perfect model with descending order of shooting probability, and if the shooting probability of the model was uncorrelated with the actual shooting in basket, it would be the line of the uncorrelated model. The accuracy of logistic regression model is indicated by the ratio of the area A of the cumulative curve shown in Fig. 9. This figure shows that sufficiently significant accuracy AR (AccuracyRatio) = 41% was obtained. We also discuss this AR value in more detail in Appendix.

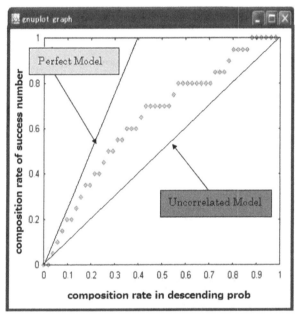

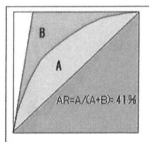

Fig. 8. Parete figure   **Fig. 9.** Area of AR value

4.2   Interpretation of Significant Features in Logistic Regression

As a result, significant features that make the high shooting probability in the logistic regression were shown in Fig. 10. The shooting probability becomes higher when the blue color features are larger. The shooting probability also becomes higher when the red color features get smaller. From this result, the followings were found out. It shows that the shooting probability is higher if the bend of the knees is increased and knees are pulled quickly and at the same time the ball is pulled back and thrown over head. This motion uses the force of the knees' extension and the centrifugal force created when throwing the ball overhead.

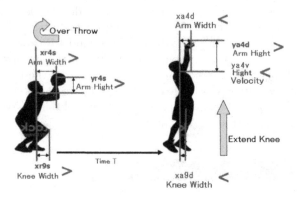

Fig. 10. Relation for shooting probability and features

4.3   Real Time Diagnosis

The diagnostic system using OpenPose can display the shooting probability in real-time as shown in Fig. 11 and even if there are not any basket and ball, it becomes possible to judge the skill level directly just by gesture.

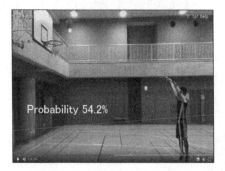

Fig. 11. Real time diagnosis by OpenPose

4.4   Posture Diagnosis

By comparing feature quantities between a beginner (a person with low shooting probability) and an expert (a person with high shooting probability), it is possible to diagnose the amount of correction for beginner's postures. In the example of Fig. 12, one of the remarkable differences between the beginner and the expert is the position of the arm at the start in this experiment. The beginner pushed the ball from the chest, but the expert put the ball in front of the head and threw the ball over head. In this case, it is necessary to teach the beginner the form of overhead throwing.

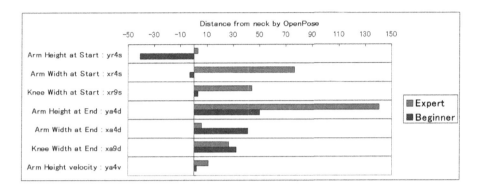

Fig. 12. Comparison of features between the beginner and the expert. Horizontal axis represents significant feature value in Fig. 10.

Next we tried to analyze the sensitivity. As the result in Table 1, improvement of shooting probability was obtained when the beginner's pose improves 2.0 (about 1 cm) at each feature.

Table 1. Sensitivity analysis, Column inc(%) shows incremental of shooting probability

Name	Val	yr4s	xr4s	xr9s	ya4d	xa4d	xa9d	xa4v	prob(%)	inc(%)
Arm Height at START	yr4s	2.0	0.0	0.0	0.0	0.0	0.0	0.0	6.44	0.20
Arm Width at START	xr4s	0.0	2.0	0.0	0.0	0.0	0.0	0.0	6.27	0.03
Knee Width at START	xr9s	0.0	0.0	2.0	0.0	0.0	0.0	0.0	6.41	0.16
Arm Height at END	ya4d	0.0	0.0	0.0	2.0	0.0	0.0	0.0	6.47	0.22
Arm Width at END	xa4d	0.0	0.0	0.0	0.0	−2.0	0.0	0.0	6.41	0.16
Knee Width at END	xa9d	0.0	0.0	0.0	0.0	0.0	−2.0	0.0	6.76	0.52
Arm Height Velocity	ya4v	0.0	0.0	0.0	0.0	0.0	0.0	−2.0	6.70	0.46
ALL		2.0	2.0	2.0	2.0	−2.0	−2.0	−2.0	8.55	2.31

5   Conclusion

We evaluated the performance of OpenPose. At first, we evaluated the correspondence between the actual body positions and the output data generated by OpenPose in the static conditions. Next, for evaluating OpenPose in the dynamic conditions, we built a basketball free throw prediction model by a logistic regression model. We found out the followings.

1. The skeletal data recognized by OpenPose are found to be highly applicable with sufficient accuracy.
2. In the previous posture diagnosis, data are generated by marking on a picture frame from a video stream or collected sensor signals by motion capture on the human parts. These methods are so expensive for data collection that statistical models could not be introduced. On the other hand, OpenPose can easily collect accurate data by using a simple web camera, it made it possible to obtain more accurate posture diagnosis by collecting more data.

6   Future Works

The data of basketball free throw in this experiment were taken from one side only by a web camera, so it was suitable to analyze with 2 dimensional data provided by OpenPose. However 3 dimensional motion data could bring better analysis in many occasions in general sports motion analysis field. So use of 3 dimensional OpenPose or expand 2D data generated by 2D OpenPose to 3D data [12] could be demanded. Also instead of the regression model, we would like to challenge a motion analysis by time series models reflecting correlation between the skeleton points using many data generated by OpenPose.

Acknowledgment. We would like to thank Basketball Club Team of Tokyo Metropolitan College of Technology and the Exchange Students Basketball Community at Tokyo International Exchange Center by JASSO (Japan Student Services Organization) for their cooperation in our taking movies of their basketball free throw. We would like to special thank to Dr. Atushi Shibata of AIIT for provision of experimental computation environment.

A   Appendix: Discussion on the AR Value

In order to consider obtained our AR value in this experiment, we compared NBA (National Basketball Association) Free Throw data [13]. Figure 13 shows the histogram of free throw success rate of NBA's 238 players who threw more than 5 times last year. As shown in Table 2, we generated simulation data according to the number of NBA histogram. These data are consisted of the level and the binary flag in each record. The level is set according to the success rate, but the success rate less than 0.5 was compiled to level 4 because of very few people. The binary flag is set randomly according to the success rate. But we generated 2380 records by multiplying the number by 10 to avoid bias of the random.

We made logistic regression using the binary flag as a target variable and the level[3] as a explanatory variable to obtain the AR value. As the result we obtain AR = 35%. In this simulation, even if the level as a explanatory variable has a strong correlation with the success rate explicitly, the AR was only 35%.

---

[3] Since many same records are generated according to this table, we added a small perturbation of $\mathcal{N}(0, 0.01)$ to level value to avoid rank deficient by same records. For example 7.0026 at level 7.

We thought that the low AR value is due to the relatively small number of people at high and low levels. Because we obtained AR = 60% in the case of same number at each level in our simulation. Assuming expert or beginner players were somewhat few in our experiment, our experiment AR = 41% can be considered as sufficiently significant accuracy.

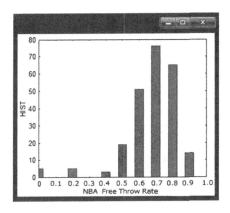

Fig. 13. Histogram of NBA Free Throw success rate

Table 2. Simulation data for AR

Level	Number	Success rate
9	140	0.9
8	650	0.8
7	760	0.7
6	510	0.6
5	190	0.5
4	130	0.25

References

1. CMU-Perceptual-Computing-Lab. https://github.com/CMU-Perceptual-Computing-Lab/openpose
2. Cao, Z., Simon, T., Wei, S., Sheikh, Y.: Realtime multi-person 2D pose estimation using part affinity fields. In: CVPR 2017 (2017)
3. MSCOCO keypoint evaluation metric. http://mscoco.org/dataset/#keypoints-eval
4. Hulka, K., Cuberek, R., Svoboda, Z.: Time-motion analysis of basketball players: a reliability assessment of Video Manual Motion Tracker 1.0 software. J. Sports Sci. **32**(1), 53–59 (2013)

5. Wang, X.: An optimization method of basketball teaching and training system design based on motion capture technology (2017)

6. Dutta, T.: Evaluation of the Kinect sensor for 3-D kinematic measurement in the workplace. Appl. Ergon. **43**(4), 645–649 (2012)

7. Shanahan, J.K.: A model for predicting the probability of a win in basketball. University of Iowa (1984)

8. Inamura, T., Nakamura, Y., Toshima, I.: Embodied symbol emergence based on mimesis theory. Int. J. Robot. Res. **23**(4), 363–377 (2004)

9. Bishop, C.M.: Pattern Recognition and Machine Learning. Springer, New York (2006). 4.3.2 Logistic regression

10. Platt, J.C.: Fast training of support vector machines using sequential minimal optimization (1999)

11. Chen, T., Guestrin, C.: XGBoost: a scalable tree boosting system. arXiv:2016.02754 (2016)

12. Kudo, Y., Ogaki, K., Matusi, Y., Odagiri, Y.: Unsupervised adversarial learning of 3D human pose from 2D joint locations. arXiv:1803.08244 (2018)

13. ESPN Western Conference Player Free-Throw Shooting Statistics - 2018–19. http://www.espn.com/nba/statistics/player/_/stat/free-throws/sort/freeThrow-Pct/league/west/qualified/false/order/false

Constraints on Joint Degrees of Freedom Affect Human Postural Dynamics: A Pilot Study

Kentaro Kodama[1]([envelope]), Kazuhiro Yasuda[2], and Hideo Yamagiwa[3]

[1] Kanagawa University, 3-27-1, Rokkakubashi, Kanagawa-ku, Yokohama-shi, Kanagawa, Japan
kkodama@kanagawa-u.ac.jp
[2] Waseda University, 3-4-1 Okubo, Shinjuku-ku, Tokyo, Japan
kazuhiro-yasuda@aoni.waseda.jp
[3] Tokyo Metropolitan Tobu Medical Center, 3-3-25, Shinsuna, Koto-ku, Tokyo, Japan
somatolearning@gmail.com

Abstract. This study aimed to investigate the direct relationship between the joint degrees of freedom (DoF) of human movement system and its postural dynamics. In our pilot experiment we fixed the join DoF (knee and ankle) to constrain the functional DoFs (one for knee, two for ankle). Young healthy participants were required to perform the single-leg standing task with their dominant leg fixed. The center of pressure (COP) trajectory data were measured and analyzed using linear and nonlinear methods to assess *static* and *dynamic* property of their postural dynamics. Results of comparing across conditions (normal no-fixation, ankle and knee fixation condition) revealed that *static* measure (COP trajectory length) did not differ significantly. However, *dynamic* measures (sample entropy and the fractal scaling exponent) significantly differed. The ankle joint fixation affected sample entropy decline (losing efficiency of postural control) and the scaling behavior (weakening the anti-persistent postural control process) in the mediolateral direction. These results seemed to agree with the notion of the loss of complexity framework.

Keywords: Loss of complexity · Freezing degrees of freedom · Single-leg standing · Entropy analysis · Fractal analysis

1 Introduction

1.1 Adaptability/Flexibility as an Embodied Skill

Adaptability and flexibility can be considered unique abilities of human beings or living organisms in contrast to traditional robots or artificial intelligence (AI). These abilities enable living systems to adapt flexibly to their environment which can vary dynamically. In the AI research field, such a dynamic ability to respond to dynamic situations and behave flexibly is considered an essential feature of *intelligence* (Suwa 2013). It is also related to another important concept *embodiment*. The living body consists of perception and action systems that have dynamic real-time interactions with their environment (Gibson 1966). Authors have called such an embodied skill *dynamic*

© Springer Nature Switzerland AG 2019
K. Kojima et al. (Eds.): JSAI-isAI 2018 Workshops, LNAI 11717, pp. 447–460, 2019.
https://doi.org/10.1007/978-3-030-31605-1_32

embodied adaptability and it is supposed to be a characteristic property of living systems, which differ from traditional robots or AI (Kodama et al. 2017). Although these artificial systems are good at repeating the same movement or process in the same way, living systems are not; however, they perform the same task in a variety of the different ways. Such variability is an important feature of human skilled performance particularly in terms of adaptable/flexible behavior (Bernstein 1967; Kudo and Ohtsuki 2008).

For example, Nonaka (2013) investigated skilled coordinated behavior of an exceptional tetraplegic individual who has practiced Japanese calligraphy with a mouth-held brush (Nonaka 2013). The author showed evidence that joint configuration variances at different phases of writing were structured so as to maintain some important task variables across different realizations of the writing task; moreover compensatory coupling between joint variables contributed to the observed structure of joint configuration variance (Nonaka 2013). In another study, he and his colleague compared flexible bead-making behavior of bead craftsmen with different skill levels (Nonaka and Bril 2014). As a result, they found that the highly skilled craftsman had rich flexibility and exquisite context sensitivity as well as the largest interstroke variability in the coordination of movement (Nonaka and Bril 2012, 2014). Ito and her colleagues examined the role of postural control in a skilled task that requires perceptual-motor coordination of expert *Kendama* players (Ito et al. 2011). They revealed the importance of flexibility of knee movement to support dynamical coordination between body movement and the moving ball and the stability of the strong coupling of the head and the ball (Ito et al. 2011). Then how can adaptability/flexibility be realized and how can variability of observed data be explained?

1.2   Degree of Freedom and Complex Systems

In human movement science and skill science research fields, it is said that the functional degrees of freedom (DoF) can provide the human movement system with the foundation of adaptive/flexible or skilled behavior. The human body has many multifarious DoFs, from the microscopic cell level to macroscopic joint level (Bernstein 1967; Turvey 1990). The DoF problem suggested that the large number of controllable DoFs poses a computational burden to the central nervous system, if we assume a computational model (Turvey 1990). This indicates the difficulty of the unidirectional top-down motor control model using computer metaphor. Bernstein, who proposed the DoF problem, supposed that each component (DoF) is coordinated and coupled with other components to organize a functional unit (*synergy*) rather than being controlled separately (Bernstein 1967). Bernstein attempted to solve the DoF problem with the idea of synergy. Such coupled components are not organized in non-directional or random ways, but in sensitive and flexible way to achieve a specific task in a specific situation/environment (Bernstein 1996).

Although the DoF problem is actually a problem from the viewpoint of the computational model (top-down motor control model), it is also possible to consider redundant DoFs as a benefit to enable movement systems to behave adaptably/flexibly. The human body has an intrinsic fluctuation derived from a physiological mechanism and is exposed to external perturbation from its environment or own body movement.

However, if the system has redundant DoFs and an ability to freeze and release them quickly, it might realize stable behavior in an adaptive/flexible way against intrinsic fluctuation or external perturbation (Kodama and Aoyama 2017).

After Bernstein's proposal of the DoF problem and the idea of synergy, the self-organization theory (Haken 1978; Nicolis and Prigogine 1977) was applied to human movement studies to understand emergent properties of a human movement system. It is called the *dynamical systems approach* (DSA) and has been widely applied to human movement science areas. Compared to the traditional approach to motor behavior assuming internal computation, DSA focuses more on interactions between the body (including brain), environment, and task (Davids et al. 2003). While the traditional top-down motor control model supposes a dominant central system (i.e., brain) and focuses on its component, DSA focuses on the interaction among system's component (Van Orden et al. 2003). Complex systems consist of a large number of interacting components (DoF); the emergent behavior of the system is self-organized and can be difficult to anticipate from dynamics of the individual components (Boccara 2003). Their emergent behavior does not result from the existence of a central controller like brain (Boccara 2003).

1.3 Loss of Complexity Hypothesis

The perspective of the self-organizing theory provides new insight and a useful framework for not only human movement science and skill science, but also the clinical and therapeutic research fields. The *loss of complexity* (LoC) *hypothesis* is a broad theoretical perspective applied widely to physiological and behavioral processes (Lipsitz and Goldberger 1992). According to the hypothesis, the age- and/or disease-related changing process can be defined by a progressive LoC within the dynamics of physiologic outputs (e.g., physiological and behavioral data) (Manor and Lipsitz 2013). In other words, LoC leads to an impaired ability to adapt to stressors or perturbation (Lipsitz and Goldberger 1992). It is supposed to be due to a loss or impairment of functional components, and/or altered nonlinear coupling between these components (Lipsitz and Goldberger 1992). Thus, the hypothesis assumes that a system's adaptive/flexible function relates to its complexity and is observed in the dynamics of the system's output behavior (e.g., physiological and behavioral times series data). Moreover, these dynamics are characterized by the amount of regularity/predictability or the presence of fractal scaling in the dynamics (Lipsitz and Goldberger 1992; Stergiou 2016).

For postural balance studies, the LoC hypothesis has been applied and the center of pressure (COP) fluctuation is supposed to relate to the adaptive/flexible function of the postural system. For example, the postural dynamics of healthy young and healthy elderly people have high complexity than that of elderly people who have a history of falls (Costa et al. 2007). Parkinson's disease patients also show lower flexibility in terms of deterministic structure of the COP dynamics than healthy participants (Schmit et al. 2006). Sensory impairments contributed to a decreased COP complexity, which reflected a reduced adaptive capacity of the postural control system (Manor et al. 2010).

Those postural balance studies applied nonlinear analysis methods like *entropy analysis* and *fractal analysis* to COP time series data. To assess the complexity of the system, a *dynamic* measure based on the idea of *entropy* derived from information theory has been also applied to biological and physiological data. Entropy refers to the rate of information generation by a system. While repeating systems generate less new information, systems with varying complexly generate new (non-redundant) information when the system visits new states. Generally, high entropy means relatively irregular and complex variability. In contrast, low entropy means regular and predictable behavior. According to the LoC hypothesis, healthy systems are characterized by an irregular/complex variability, whereas disease or aging is associated with regularity/predictability and less complexity (Donker et al. 2007; Goldberger et al. 2002; Pincus 1991). Fractal analysis is a time series analysis that obtains a *dynamic* measure. It can evaluate the temporal correlation of a time series (Brown and Liebovitch 2010). Such a property is called a fractal property and indicates that fluctuations in the time series extend across many time scales (Eke et al. 2002). Such relative independence of the underlying processes at different time scales suggests that $1/f$ noise renders the system more stable and more adaptive to internal and external perturbations (Delignières et al. 2005). Thus, fractal property is considered a *dynamic* measure and is associated with health/pathology (Lipsitz and Goldberger 1992) and flexibility/adaptability (Hausdorff 2009).

It is supposed that the LoC relates to a decline in the capability to reorganize the interactions between its components (its functional DoF) to adjust the degree of unpredictability of behavioral fluctuations to meet task demands (Sleimen-malkoun et al. 2014). Aging and/or disease are involved in change in coupling between components (DoFs) and the decrease in interaction between them. In other words, systems with less interaction between their components and few functional DoFs tend to behave regularly and their dynamics lose dimensionality or complexity (Sleimen-malkoun et al. 2014). However, most previous studies have investigated the relationship between DoF and system dynamics by comparing particular populations such as elderly/impaired people with healthy young people. In these cases, it is difficult to reveal the direct relationship between the DoF and system dynamics because other factors derived from aging and/or disease cannot be ignored.

1.4   Our Research Aims

As an exploratory investigation, our pilot study manipulated the DoF of a human movement system as an independent variable using a within-subjects design, because previous studies suggested that systems with few DoFs tend to behave regularly and their dynamics lose complexity (Sleimen-malkoun et al. 2014). We focused on a joint DoF (e.g., range of motion) because it can be considered as a DoF of a system and is easy to be manipulated experimentally. Then, we hypothesized that human postural system might lose more complexity in the less DoF condition and compared different DoF conditions within subjects. We fixed and constrained the ankle joint (two DoFs) and knee joint (one DoF) of the dominant leg and required young healthy participants to perform single-leg standing task by their dominant legs; each condition was compared to the no-fixation normal condition. The COP trajectory data were measured and analyzed by linear and nonlinear methods to assess a *static* and *dynamic* properties of the postural dynamics.

In general context of motor control studies, static/dynamic balancing ability is defined based on the relationship between the center of mass and the base of support (e.g., Guskiewicz and Perrin 1996). However, the present study defined *static* and *dynamic* balancing ability differently from the general meaning. In this article, we define *static* balancing as postural strategy which is characterized as minimization of the COP trajectory length or sway area because these traditional measures regard smaller length/area as more stable balancing. These measures can be calculated usually by linear method. On the other hand, *dynamic* balancing is defined not necessarily as minimization of postural sway. Such a dynamic property can be assessed by nonlinear methods (e.g., SampEn for assessment in terms of stochastic predictability or regularity, DFA for assessment in terms of multiscale dynamics).

Then, the direct relationship between the DoF and COP dynamics was investigated. Such an investigation may lead to deeper understanding of their relationship and provide an experimental evidence of the LoC hypothesis. As reviewed briefly above, many previous studies based on the LoC hypothesis have suggested that the complexity of system can reflect the health status of the system and it might relate to its DoF (e.g., Lipsitz and Goldberger 1992; Manor and Lipsitz 2013; Sleimen-malkoun et al. 2014). Therefore, investigating the direct relationship between the complexity and the DoF of the system can lead to assessment of health status of people who are elderly or with physical impairments, and these studies can provide medical and clinical fields with ways to predict some risks (e.g., fall risk) in those people. We believe that the LoC hypothesis and its analytical framework can help assess individuals with physical impairments and elderly people and prevent their risks.

2   Method

2.1   Participants

Six healthy male participants (average = 23.50 (SD = 4.68) years, all right-handed) were recruited to join the experiment. The experimental procedures were approved by the research ethics committee of Kanagawa University, where the experiment was conducted. Each participant provided informed consent for participation in this study.

2.2   Apparatus

Joint fixation equipment (REAQER ankle supporter, REAQER knee supporter, Fig. 1) were used to fix the ankle and knee joints. The center of pressure (COP) trajectories were measured using a force plate (Leptrino CFP600YA302US, sample rate = 200 Hz). To process and analyze COP data, MATLAB (R2017b, MathWorks) and RStudio (Version 1.1.423) were used to process and analyze the COP data.

2.3   Procedure

In the current pilot experiment, three conditions were compared, namely, the normal condition (no joint fixation), ankle condition (ankle joint fixation), and knee condition

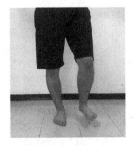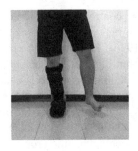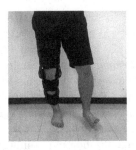

Fig. 1. Experimental conditions and joint fixation equipment (Left: Normal condition, Middle: Ankle condition, Right: Knee condition).

(knee joint fixation) as shown in Fig. 1. Under the joint fixation conditions, each joint of the dominant leg (i.e., right leg) of each participant was fixed using the equipment. Each participant was asked to maintain single-leg standing with their dominant leg for 35-s. After conducting the normal condition task first as a baseline condition, the ankle and knee condition tasks were counterbalanced between the participants. Under each condition, they were required to repeat a 35-s trial four times with 30-s interval between trials, and with 3-min rest between conditions.

2.4   Data Analysis

After measuring the COP trajectory data, we removed the initial 5-s data and analyzed the remaining 30-s of time series data of the COP in the mediolateral (ML) and anteroposterior (AP) directions. Before performing the following time series analyses, all COP data were smoothed by a 10-Hz low-pass filter (4th order Butterworth filter).

To assess postural stability, the COP trajectory length was calculated and regarded as a *static* measure (Horak 989; Shumway-Cook and Woollacott 2013). This measure defines shorter trajectory length as less movement (less postural sway) and it means more stable posture. In this sense, we interpret this as a *static* measure.

By contrast, to evaluate dynamic postural stability, we also applied nonlinear time series analyses, *sample entropy* (SampEn; Richman and Moorman 2000) and *detrended fluctuation analysis* (DFA; Peng et al. 1994). *Sample entropy* analysis is a method with which to quantify the complexity or irregularity of a time series (Richman et al. 2000). Sample entropy (SampEn) indexes the (ir)regularity of a time series and is used to analyze the dynamics of complex systems. While a smaller sample entropy means greater regularity, a larger sample entropy indicates relatively irregular or complex dynamics. For a given embedding dimension m, tolerance r, and number of data points N, SampEn is the negative logarithm of the probability that if two sets of simultaneous data points of length m have distance $< r$ then two sets of simultaneous data points of length $m + 1$ also have distance $< r$ (Stergiou 2016). DFA is a fractal analysis for nonlinear time series data, and has been used to assess a system's scaling behavior (Roerdink et al. 2006) and adaptability/flexibility (Hausdorff 2009) in terms of temporal correlation in time series data (Brown and Liebovitch 2010). DFA calculates the scaling exponent α as the slope of the log-log plot of fluctuation vs. time scale. A linear relationship on a log-log plot indicates the presence of scaling. The DFA scaling exponent α is interpreted as an estimation of the Hurst exponent H, and is related to H as follows (Delignières et al. 2011): if $0 < \alpha < 1$, then $H = \alpha$; if $1 < \alpha < 2$, then $H = \alpha - 1$. H can be interpreted for the time series as follows: if $0 < H < 0.5$, the time series is anti-persistent; if $H = 0.5$, it is uncorrelated (*white noise*); if $0.5 < H < 1$, it is persistent; if $H = 1$, it is considered $1/f$ *noise* (Delignières et al. 2011). SampEn was performed using the R package '*pracma*' (Borchers 2018) with input parameters, embedding dimension $m = 3$ and a ratio of standard deviation of the data of $r = 0.2$ (we confirmed both embedding dimensions 2 and 3, and found that $m = 2$ was an insufficient dimension, whereas $m = 3$ provided us with robust results). DFA was performed using the R package '*nonlinearTseries*' (Constantino et al. 2015).

3 Result

3.1 COP Trajectory Length

Figure 2 shows the mean COP trajectory length for each condition (left: normal condition; center: ankle condition; right: the knee condition; error bar: standard deviation). The mean value was 1393.61 (SD = 228.82) [mm] in the normal condition, 1507.60 (SD = 210.93) [mm] in the ankle condition, and 1471.48 (SD = 350.43) [mm] in the knee condition. The results seem to indicate that postural sway is the smallest in the normal condition, which is the largest DoF condition. However, the result of one-way ANOVA revealed no significant differences between the conditions ($F(2, 5) = 0.995$, $p = 0.404$, *N.S.*).

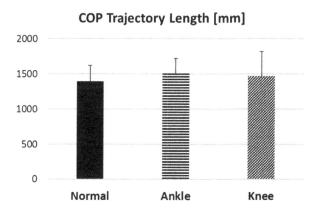

Fig. 2. COP trajectory length [mm] (Left: Normal condition; Center: Ankle condition; Right: Knee condition).

3.2 Sample Entropy

Figure 3 represents the mean SampEn for each condition in the ML and AP directions respectively (left: normal condition; center: ankle condition; right: the knee condition;

error bar: standard deviation). In the ML direction, the mean value was 0.117 (SD = 0.023) in the normal condition, 0.095 (SD = 0.018) in the ankle condition, and 0.116 (SD = 0.025) in the knee condition. In the AP direction, the mean value was 0.073 (SD = 0.026) in the normal condition, 0.076 (SD = 0.026) in the ankle condition, and 0.074 (SD = 0.026) in the knee condition. To compare these values statistically, one-way ANOVA was conducted for each SampEn of both the ML and AP directions. The results show that we found the significant main effect on SampEn only in the ML direction $(F(2, 5) = 4.295, p < 0.05)$. Because of multiple comparisons (Ryan's method), significant differences were found between the ankle and normal conditions $(t(5) = 2.616, p < 0.05)$, and between the ankle and knee conditions $(t(5) = 2.453, p < 0.05)$. These results indicate that SampEn was larger in the ankle condition than in the other conditions in the ML direction. In contrast, there was no significant main effect in the AP direction $(F(2, 5) = 0.071, p = 0.931, N.S.)$.

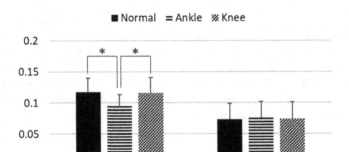

Fig. 3. Sample Entropy (Left side x-axis ML direction, Right side: y-axis AP direction, in each side, Left: Normal condition, Middle: Ankle condition, Right: Knee condition).

3.3 DFA Scaling Exponent α

Figure 4 displays the mean DFA scaling exponent for each condition in the ML and AP directions, respectively (left: normal condition; center: ankle condition; right: the knee condition; error bar: standard deviation). In the ML direction, the mean value was 1.17 (SD = 0.07) in the normal condition, 1.25 (SD = 0.05) in the ankle condition, and 1.18 (SD = 0.06) in the knee condition. In the AP direction, the mean value was 1.30 (SD = 0.09) in the normal condition, 1.31 (SD = 0.09) in the ankle condition, and 1.30 (SD = 0.10) in the knee condition. To compare these values statistically, one-way ANOVA was conducted for each scaling exponent α of both the ML and AP directions. The results show that we found the significant main effect on the scaling exponent α only in the ML direction $(F(2, 5) = 0.011, p < 0.05)$. Because of multiple comparisons (Ryan's method), significant differences were found between the ankle and normal conditions $(t(5) = 2.833, p < 0.05)$, and between the ankle and knee conditions

($t(5) = 2.415$, $p < 0.05$). These results indicate that the scaling exponent α was larger in the ankle condition than in the other conditions in the ML direction. In contrast, there was no significant main effect in the AP direction ($F(2, 5) = 0.081$, $p = 0.922$, N.S.).

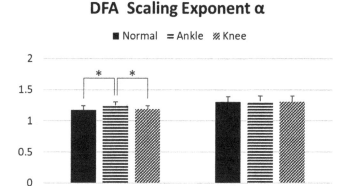

Fig. 4. DFA scaling exponent α (Left side x-axis ML direction, Right side: y-axis AP direction, in each side, Left: Normal condition, Middle: Ankle condition, Right: Knee condition).

4 Discussion

4.1 COP Trajectory Length

COP trajectory length can be interpreted as a *static* measure because it indicates how much postural sway is observed and it is defined as less movement or more stable sway. As a result of COP trajectory length analysis, we could not find any significant differences between the conditions in terms of the quantity of postural sway. This implies that the joint fixation did not affect the *static* measure (i.e., how much posture fluctuate) in the case of our pilot study.

4.2 Sample Entropy

A high SampEn indicates relatively low regularity or high complexity, while low SampEn means relatively high regularity or predictability. In the current data, postural sway was more regular in the ML direction in the ankle condition than the other two conditions. The result suggests that low SampEn (more regular postural sway) in the ankle condition was interpreted as an increase in the effectiveness of postural control in the ML direction in terms of amount of attention or cognitive involvement (Donker et al. 2007). Some previous studies argued that postural sway regularity is positively correlated with the degree of cognitive involvement in postural control (Donker et al. 2007; Roerdink et al. 2006). Actually, some participants reported that it was more difficult to perform the single-leg standing task in the ankle condition than in other two conditions. We guess that such a difficulty leaded to more attention to postural control and more regular postural sway in the ankle condition.

4.3 DFA Scaling Exponent α

The DFA scaling exponent is interpreted as follows: if $\alpha = 1$, then the time series is considered $1/f$ noise; if $\alpha = 1.5$, indicates Brownian motion. For $1 < \alpha < 1.5$, the time series has correlation, but lose fractality and ceases to be a power-law relation (Peng et al. 1995). In the current data, the DFA scaling exponents were ranged between 1 and 1.5. Within this range, the scaling exponent α is related to the Hurst exponent H as $H = \alpha - 1$, then $0 < H < 0.5$, the time series has anti-persistent dynamics (Delignières et al. 2011). This implies that an increasing trend in the past is likely to be followed by a decreasing trend (an anti-persistent correlation process) (Delignières et al. 2011). Comparing our results across conditions, α was higher in the ankle condition than other two conditions in the ML direction. This means that the anti-persistent process that regulates single-leg standing posture in the ML direction weakened when the ankle joint was fixed. Two DoF fixation of the ankle joint might weaken the anti-persistent postural control process.

4.4 General Discussion

COP trajectory length can be interpreted as a *static* measure because it indicates how much postural sway (i.e., the quantity of postural sway) is observed and it is defined as less movement or more stable sway. In the current pilot experiment, we could not find any significant differences between the conditions in terms of the quantity of postural sway. This means that joint fixation did not affect the static balancing ability of single-leg standing. In contrast, SampEn and the DFA scaling exponent α can be considered *dynamic* measures because they quantify how the posture fluctuated in terms of temporal pattern complexity or temporal correlation of the time series data. Our results suggest that postural sway during the single-leg standing task had less irregular/complex fluctuation and a weaker anti-persistent process in the ML direction in the ankle condition than in the other two conditions.

The single-leg standing task requires postural control based on foot function using ankle joint movement (King and Zatsiorsky 2002). The ankle joint fixation seemed to constrain the mobility of the foot movement and postural control in the ML direction, whereas the knee joint fixation did not affect the postural dynamics because the knee joint has only one DoF (flexion-extension) and is not involved in postural control in the ML direction. In terms of functional DoF, the knee joint has one DoF and the ankle joint has two DoFs, therefore our results of fractal analysis show that the ankle joint fixation might cause less fractality. On the other hand, the results of entropy analysis suggest that the ankle joint fixation might cause relatively regular postural sway (low sample entropy); in other words, it might evoke a LoC in the postural dynamics in the ML direction. This notion also seems to agree with the LoC hypothesis (Sleimenmalkoun et al. 2014).

4.5   Future Directions

The present article reports only the results of the pilot experiment (N = 6). We should collect more data and confirm whether a similar tendency can be found in the future. In addition, we also plan to investigate not only single-leg standing with the dominant leg, but also other balancing tasks. In terms of data analysis, other methods should be conducted to quantify complexity, adaptability/flexibility, and dimensionality (Bravi et al. 2011; Cavanaugh et al. 2005; Hidaka and Kashyap 2013), and associate them with empirical data of previous studies.

As discussed, our results should be explained from kinematic or biomechanical perspective in more detail to understand the relationship between the functional DoF (and its fixation) and the system dynamics in terms of complexity and adaptability/flexibility. Further experimental studies regarding the effects of the freeze and release of DoF on the *static* and *dynamic* properties of system dynamics may lead to a deeper understanding the direct relationship between them and to obtaining empirical evidence on the LoC hypothesis. We also expect that such experimental strategies can provide more applied research on not only the clinical assessment of the fall risk of elderly/impaired people, but also practical evaluation of sports skills or dexterous performances of athletes with further validity of quantification and evaluation using various data analytical methods.

5   Conclusion

This article reported the results of our pilot experiment to investigate the direct relationship between the joint DoF of the human movement system and its postural dynamics. In the experiment we manipulated the join DoFs (knee and ankle) with joint fixation equipment. Young healthy participants were required to maintain single-leg standing with their dominant leg fixed. The COP time series data were measured and analyzed by linear and nonlinear methods to assess the *static* and *dynamic* properties of their postural dynamics. The results of comparing across conditions (normal no-fixation, and ankle and knee fixation condition) show that the *static* measure (COP trajectory length) did not significantly differ across conditions; however, the *dynamic* measures (sample entropy and DFA scaling exponent) differed significantly. The ankle joint fixation (two DoFs constrained condition) affected a sample entropy decline which indicated the losing efficiency of postural control requiring an amount of attention (cognitive involvement), and the scaling behavior leading to weakening of the anti-persistent postural control process. These results of *dynamic* measures seem to agree with the previous studies' insight within the LoC framework that suggests that less functional DoF might lead to loss of complexity or adaptability/flexibility of the system behavior.

Acknowledgement. This work was supported by Kanagawa University Grant for Joint Research.

References

Bernstein, N.A.: The Co-ordination and Regulation of Movements. Pergamon Press Ltd., New York (1967)

Bernstein, N.A.: Dexterity and Its Development. Psychology Press, London (1996)

Boccara, N.: Modeling Complex Systems, 1st edn. Springer, New York (2003). https://doi.org/10.1007/b97378

Borchers, H.W.: Package "pracma" (2018). https://cran.r-project.org/web/packages/pracma/pracma.pdf

Bravi, A., Longtin, A., Seely, A.J., Ca, B.: Review and classification of variability analysis techniques with clinical applications. BioMed. Eng. OnLine **10**(October), 90 (2011). https://doi.org/10.1186/1475-925X-10-90

Brown, C.T., Liebovitch, L.S.: Fractal Analysis. SAGE Publications, London (2010). https://uk.sagepub.com/en-gb/asi/fractal-analysis/book233383

Cavanaugh, J.T., Guskiewicz, K.M., Stergiou, N.: A nonlinear dynamic approach for evaluating postural control: new directions for the management of sport-related cerebral concussion. Sports Med. **35**(11), 935–950 (2005). https://doi.org/0112-1642/05/011-0935

Constantino, M., Garcia, A., Constantino, A., Sawitzki, G.: Package "nonlinearTseries" (2015). https://cran.r-project.org/web/packages/nonlinearTseries/nonlinearTseries.pdf

Costa, M., et al.: Noise and poise: enhancement of postural complexity in the elderly with a stochastic-resonance-based therapy. Europhys. Lett. **77**, 68008 (2007). https://doi.org/10.1209/0295-5075/77/68008

Davids, K., Glazier, P., Araújo, D., Bartlett, R.: Movement systems as dynamical systems: the functional role of variability and its implications for sports medicine. Sports Med. **33**(4), 245–260 (2003). https://doi.org/10.2165/00007256-200333040-00001

Delignières, D., Torre, K., Bernard, P.-L.: Transition from persistent to anti-persistent correlations in postural sway indicates velocity-based control. PLoS Comput. Biol. **7**(2), e1001089 (2011). https://doi.org/10.1371/journal.pcbi.1001089

Delignières, D., Torre, K., Lemoine, L.: Methodological issues in the application of monofractal analyses in psychological and behavioral research. Nonlinear Dyn. Psychol. Life Sci. **9**(4), 451–477 (2005). https://doi.org/10.1093/beheco/aru014

Donker, S.F., Roerdink, M., Greven, A.J., Beek, P.J.: Regularity of center-of-pressure trajectories depends on the amount of attention invested in postural control. Exp. Brain Res. **181**(1), 1–11 (2007). https://doi.org/10.1007/s00221-007-0905-4

Eke, A., Herman, P., Kocsis, L., Kozak, L.R.: Fractal characterization of complexity in temporal physiological signals. Physiol. Meas. **23**(1), R1–R38 (2002). https://doi.org/10.1088/0967-3334/23/1/201

Gibson, J.J.: The Senses Considered as Perceptual Systems. Praeger, New York (1966)

Goldberger, A.L., Amaral, L.A.N., Hausdorff, J.M., Ivanov, P.C., Peng, C., Stanley, H.E.: Fractal dynamics in physiology: alterations with disease and aging. Proc. Nat. Acad. Sci. **99** (Supplement 1), 2466–2472 (2002). https://doi.org/10.1073/pnas.012579499

Guskiewicz, K.M., Perrin, D.H.: Research and clinical applications of assessing balance. J. Sport Rehabil. **5**(1), 45–63 (1996). https://doi.org/10.1123/jsr.5.1.45

Haken, H.: Synergetics: An Introduction: Nonequilibrium Phase Transitions and Self-Organization in Physics, Chemistry and Biology. Springer, Heidelberg (1978). https://doi.org/10.1007/978-3-642-96469-5. https://books.google.co.jp/books/about/Synergetics.html?id=z9PuAAAAMAAJ&pgis=1

Hausdorff, J.M.: Gait dynamics in Parkinson's disease: common and distinct behavior among stride length, gait variability, and fractal-like scaling. Chaos **19**(2) (2009). https://doi.org/10.1063/1.3147408

Hidaka, S., Kashyap, N.: On the estimation of pointwise dimension (2013). http://arxiv.org/abs/1312.2298

Horak, F.: Components of postural dyscontrol in the elderly: a review. Neurobiol. Aging **10**(6), 727–738 (1989). https://doi.org/10.1016/0197-4580(89)90010-9

Ito, M., Mishima, H., Sasaki, M.: The dynamical stability of visual coupling and knee flexibility in skilled kendama players, pp. 308–332 (2011). https://doi.org/10.1080/10407413.2011.617669

King, D.L., Zatsiorsky, V.M.: Periods of extreme ankle displacement during one-legged standing. Gait & Posture **15**(2), 172–179 (2002). https://doi.org/10.1016/S0966-6362(01)00189-8

Kodama, K., Aoyama, K.: Foundation of ecological approach. In: Rehabilitation Based on Perception. CBR (2017)

Kodama, K., Kikuchi, Y., Yamagiwa, H.: Whole-body coordination skill for dynamic balancing on a slackline. In: Otake, M., Kurahashi, S., Ota, Y., Satoh, K., Bekki, D. (eds.) New Frontiers in Artificial Intelligence, JSAI-isAI 2015. Lecture Notes in Computer Science, vol. 10091, pp. 528–546. Springer, Cham (2017). https://doi.org/10.1007/978-3-319-50953-2_39

Kudo, K., Ohtsuki, T.: Adaptive variability in skilled human movements. Trans. Jpn. Soc. Artif. Intell. **23**(3), 151–162 (2008). https://www.jstage.jst.go.jp/article/tjsai/23/3/23_3_151/_pdf

Lipsitz, L.A., Goldberger, A.L.: Loss of "Complexity" and Aging. JAMA **267**(13), 1806 (1992). https://doi.org/10.1001/jama.1992.03480130122036

Manor, B., et al.: Physiological complexity and system adaptability: evidence from postural control dynamics of older adults. J. Appl. Physiol. **109**(6), 1786–1791 (2010). https://doi.org/10.1152/japplphysiol.00390.2010

Manor, B., Lipsitz, L.A.: Physiologic complexity and aging: Implications for physical function and rehabilitation. Prog. Neuropsychopharmacol. Biol. Psychiatry **45**(617), 287–293 (2013). https://doi.org/10.1016/j.pnpbp.2012.08.020

Nicolis, G., Prigogine, I.: Self-organization in nonequilibrium systems: from dissipative structures to order through fluctuations. Wiley (1977). https://books.google.com/books?id=mZkQAQAAIAAJ&pgis=1

Nonaka, T.: Motor variability but functional specificity: the case of a C4 tetraplegic mouth calligrapher. Ecol. Psychol. **25**(2), 131–154 (2013). https://doi.org/10.1080/10407413.2013.780492

Nonaka, T., Bril, B.: Nesting of asymmetric functions in skilled bimanual action: dynamics of hammering behavior of bead craftsmen. Hum. Mov. Sci. **31**(1), 55–77 (2012). https://doi.org/10.1016/j.humov.2010.08.013

Nonaka, T., Bril, B.: Fractal dynamics in dexterous tool use: the case of hammering behavior of bead craftsmen. J. Exp. Psychol. Hum. Percept. Perform. **40**(1), 218–231 (2014). https://doi.org/10.1037/a0033277

Peng, C., Buldyrev, S.V., Havlin, S., Simons, M., Stanley, H.E., Goldberger, A.L.: Mosaic organization of DNA nucleotides. Phys. Rev. E **49**(2), 1685–1689 (1994). https://doi.org/10.1103/PhysRevE.49.1685

Peng, C., Havlin, S., Stanley, H.E., Goldberger, A.L.: Quantification of scaling exponents and crossover phenomena in nonstationary heartbeat time series. Chaos **5**(1), 82–87 (1995). https://doi.org/10.1063/1.166141

Pincus, S.M.: Approximate entropy as a measure of system complexity. Mathematics **88**(March), 2297–2301 (1991). https://doi.org/10.1073/pnas.88.6.2297

Richman, J.S., Moorman, J.R.: Physiological time-series analysis using approximate entropy and sample entropy. Am. J. Physiol. Heart Circ. Physiol. **278**(6), H2039–H2049 (2000). https://doi.org/10.1103/physreva.29.975

Roerdink, M., De Haart, M., Daffertshofer, A., Donker, S.F., Geurts, A.C.H., Beek, P.J.: Dynamical structure of center-of-pressure trajectories in patients recovering from stroke. Exp. Brain Res. **174**(2), 256–269 (2006). https://doi.org/10.1007/s00221-006-0441-7

Schmit, J.M., et al.: Deterministic center of pressure patterns characterize postural instability in Parkinson's disease. Exp. Brain Res. **168**(3), 357–367 (2006). https://doi.org/10.1007/s00221-005-0094-y

Shumway-Cook, A., Woollacott, M.H.: Motor control: translating research into clinical practice. Lippincott Williams & Wilkins (2013). https://books.google.com/books?id=BJcL3enz3xMC&pgis=1

Sleimen-malkoun, R., Temprado, J., Hong, S.L.: Aging induced loss of complexity and dedifferentiation: consequences for coordination dynamics within and between brain, muscular and behavioral levels. Front. Aging Neurosci. **6**(June), 1–17 (2014). https://doi.org/10.3389/fnagi.2014.00140

Stergiou, N.: Nonlinear Analysis for Human Movement Variability. CRC Press, Boca Raton (2016)

Suwa, M.: Story-telling and encouragement as a research environment - what is "researchers learn from one another"? Artif. Intell. **28**(5), 695–701 (2013)

Turvey, M.T.: Coordination. Am. Psychol. **45**(8), 938–953 (1990)

Van Orden, G.C., Holden, J.G., Turvey, M.T.: Self-organization of cognitive performance. J. Exp. Psychol. Gen. **132**(3), 331–350 (2003). https://doi.org/10.1037/0096-3445.132.3.331

Effects of the Difference in Accented Beat Between Jazz and Classical Music Styles Through Sight-Reading of a Jazz Ad-Lib Solo

Daichi Ando[✉]

Tokyo Metropolitan University, Hachioji, Japan
dandou@tmu.ac.jp

Abstract. The author conducted a survey to determine classical music performers' rhythm and phrase recognition scores based on sight-reading of a jazz ad-lib solo. Classical music performers generally take the 1st and 3rd quarter as accented beats when performing 4/4 beat phrases. However, jazz performers generate their ad-lib phrases, taking the 2nd and 4th quarter as accented beats. Thus, for the classical music performers, sight-reading of a generated jazz phrase is difficult.

In this paper, the author reports the findings of a survey conducted to determine the processes undertaken by classical music performers during sight-reading of jazz blues ad-lib phrases while interchanging the accented beats. The targeted ad-lib phrase is Charlie Parker's blues solo which was given a musical notated score. For the first time, the performers were to sight-read the target ad-lib phrase, counting off beat (2nd and 4th quarter) as accented beat, according to the jazz style. The second time, the performers did a similar sight-reading, counting on beat (1st and 3rd quarter) as accented beat, according to a normal classical style. For the third time, the performers did the sight-reading while counting all quarters. The performers recorded the stumbling phrases for each of their attempted varied counts. As a result, most performers recorded different stumbling phrases of both the jazz and classical counting styles. These results indicate that the difference in beat counting and accented beat, between the classical music and jazz style, affected their recognition of the ad-lib phrases.

Keywords: Musical recognition · Jazz ad-lib performance

1 Introduction

1.1 Motivation

It is very difficult for an audience to observe how the performers on the stage recognize their musical expression. In this paper, we discuss the recognition of the phrase and its rhythm by the difference in position of accented beats between

© Springer Nature Switzerland AG 2019
K. Kojima et al. (Eds.): JSAI-isAI 2018 Workshops, LNAI 11717, pp. 461–467, 2019.
https://doi.org/10.1007/978-3-030-31605-1_33

jazz and classical music styles, based on interviews conducted with classical music performers playing a jazz ad-lib solo.

Butterfield discussed a typical element of the jazz rhythm, "Swing" [1,2]. However, "Swing" alone is not a typical rhythm in jazz as compared to classical music. The author presumes that it is important for jazz learners to be sensitive to the difference in accented beats between classical music and jazz in order to acquire the likelihood of jazz improvisation. The author expects that the problem of internalization of rhythm, due to differences in the accented beat, may be referred to as "Groove" in music cognition and perception research. Stupacher et al. conducted general discussions of "Groove" based on quantitative experiments from the viewpoint of brain and cognitive sciences [4]. However, the author was of the opinion that these experiments and discussions are not from a music, musical theory, nor music educational perspective but are rather from the perspectives of actual jazz learners.

"Jazz" is mainly performed by trained jazz musicians capable of ad-lib performances; however, jazz works are also performed in concerts of other music genres other than jazz ad-lib performances. In such a case, it is common to observe classical performers play copies of jazz ad-lib solos with notated scores. In a classical music player's performance, the copied ad-lib solo phrases are noted in scores; however, it is generally stated that the "Groove" is different from the original performance of the copied ad-lib solo. For the purpose of applying the actual performance, we should clarify the problem associated with "Groove" when classical musicians copy jazz ad-lib solos on a score basis.

In this paper, the author reports an experiment which was conducted to establish the issues associated with rhythm cognition caused by accented beats when classical music performers copy jazz ad-lib solos on a score basis, and subsequently, discusses the results.

1.2 Effects of Difference of Accented Beat Between Jazz and Classical Music

Figure 1 indicates Charlie Parker's own ad-lib solo in *Now's the Time* [3]. From a rhythmic point of view, the author predicts that the classical music performers cannot easily internalize this ad-lib phrase as compared to general classical music pieces. Figure 2 indicate several red square frames which represent "stucked places" when the author, who studied classical music singing in a music academy as a major, actually practiced this ad-lib phrase. "stucked place" means that the author failed to internalize the phrase.

The author observed that certain types of phrases were confusing to the author in terms of rhythm cognition. In classical music, we feel the accented beat in the 1st and 3rd quarter. On the other hand, in jazz, we feel the accented beat in the 2nd and 4th quarter. Thus, the author is accustomed to taking accented beats in the 1st and 3rd quarter, from the experience of learning classical music phrasing. Therefore, the author naturally takes the count at the 1st and 3rd quarter when sight-reading the scores. On the other hand, it is generally stated that we should feel the accented beat in the 2nd and 4th quarter when performing jazz.

The Charlie Parker's ad-lib solo has a lot of phrases with a rhythm deviated from anacrusis and a beat which is difficult to understand in the context of classical music.

Let us discuss about the author's "stucked places." Fig. 3 indicates bars 29–30 of the Fig. 2, the first "stucked place." Such melodies cannot be observed much with the classical music accented beats. In general, the classical music accented beats generate a melody as indicated in the Fig. 4. In the head of bar 30, the chord tone (B-flat) has an accented beat and sufficient duration. Also, Fig. 5 indicates the author's second "stucked place," bar 32–33, which can be translated to a classical music accented beat as shown in the Fig. 6. Note: In the first note of bar 33, the root note of the chord tone has a longer duration. Similarly, Fig. 7 indicates the author's third "stucked place," bar 53–54. When this is converted according to a classical music's strong beat, it becomes as shown in Fig. 8. Focusing on the head of bar 54, the two sounds of the head (G and B flat) have short durations, but can be regarded as an accessory embellishing note. It is common for such embellishing note movement to be at the beginning of bars. The author internalizes the sense that it can naturally transform melodies into classical music accented beats as indicated in Figs. 4, 6, and 8. The author predicts that the sense of the classical music accented beat is the cause of the confusion. From a musical point of view, to begin with, these phrases were composed and played by Charlie Parker himself with a sense of jazz accented beats. Consequently, it is musically unnatural for us to perform the phrases with a classical music accented beat.

In order to solve this, the author performed sight-reading practice initially counting every quarter, then gradually changing over to counting 2nd and 4th quarters. This made it possible for the author to sight-read the phrases naturally, though gradually and imperfectly. Note: However, the author concluded that the sensation is still wrong as usual with regards to bar 29–30. The result of this practice indicates that internalization of the accented beat position is not complete but mostly changeable through the counting beat, thereby, facilitating the internalization of the phrase.

Based on what has been mentioned, the author formulates the hypothesis that when classical music performers sight-read jazz ad-lib solo phrases, the difference in position of the accent beat generated by counting affects the difficulty of internalizing the phrases.

2   Experimental Detail and Result

As mentioned earlier, the motivation of this research is to gain appropriate knowledge of the actual practical music situation. From a practical perspective, the author set the experiment assuming that the classical music performers sight-read a jazz ad-lib solo with noted scores as their repertoires during concerts.

If the hypothesis given in the previous section is correct, we can observe the differences in a musician's recognition as they change the count from jazz to classical music counting style as they sight-read the jazz phrases. Therefore, the author performed the following experiment.

Fig. 1. Charlie Parker *Now's the Time* Ad-lib Solo in *Charlie Parker Bee Boppers* (1945)

Fig. 2. "Stucked places" of the author

Fig. 3. The author's "stucked place" 1, bars 29–30.

Fig. 4. An example of correcting Fig. 3 the classical music accented beat naturally.

Fig. 5. Stacked place of the author 1, the bars 32–33.

Fig. 6. An example of correcting Fig. 5 the classical music accented beat naturally.

Fig. 7. Stucked place of the author 3, the bars 53–54.

Fig. 8. An example of correcting Fig. 5 the classical music accented beat naturally.

There were 4 subjects, classical saxophone performers. Two subjects had master's degrees and the other two had undergraduate degrees from a music college. Experimental instruction, including the score, was sent to subjects by e-mail as indicated in Fig. 1. The experimental instruction was as follows:

Please sight-read this score. You can either use or not use your instruments. The instruction sets limit the counting of beats during sight-reading. Please do not use a metronome while counting the beat, independently.
1. 2 counts for a bar (2nd and 4th quarter)
2. 2 counts for a bar (1st and 3rd quarter)
3. 4 counts for a bar (every quarter)
First, please sight-read while taking the count, as indicated by 1 (2nd and 4th quarter). Please write down your "stucked places." The sight-reading is to be done once or twice.
Second, please sight-read while taking the count, as indicated by 2 (1st and 3rd quarter). Please write down your "stucked places" as well.
Finally, please sight-read while taking the count, as indicated by 3 (every quarter). Please write down your "stucked places" as well.

Figures 9, 10, 11, 12 are results of subjects 1, 2, 3, and 4. Gray squares mean "stucked places" as counted during style 1 (2nd and 4th quarters, jazz style), blue squares mean "stucked places" as counted in style 2 (1st and 3rd quarters), and red squares mean "stucked places" as counted in style 3 (every quarter).

Only test subject 1's (Fig. 9) "stucked places" as counted in style 1 (2nd and 4th quarter) improved in count style 2 (1st and 3rd quarter) and 3 (every quarter). On the other hand, subjects 2 (Fig. 10), 3 (Fig. 11), and 4 (Fig. 12) had different "stucked places" for count style 1 (2nd and 4th quarters) and 2 (1st and third quarters), respectively.

3   Discussion

3.1   Differences Depend on the Accented Beat

The result indicate that, in subjects 2, 3, and 4, the "stucked places" were different depending on the difference in position between the jazz and the classical music styles of accented beat, as observed. This result suggests that the internalization of the phrase's rhythm may be affected by the location of the accented beat. This fact affirms the hypothesis to some extent in the sense that "differences of accented beat internalized by counting affect the internalizing rhythm recognition of jazz ad-lib phrases."

3.2   Triplet Notes with Anacrusis in Loose Rhythm Fluctuation

Three out of 4 subjects answered that they were stuck at bar 28 and 51. Subjects 1 and 3 were stuck at bar 28 according to counting style 1 (2nd and 4th quarter), while subject 2 was stuck at the same bar with regards to counting style 2 (1st

Fig. 9. Subject 1   **Fig. 10.** Subject 2

Fig. 11. Subject 1   **Fig. 12.** Subject 2

and 3rd quarter). Subjects 3 and 4 were both stuck at bar 51 according to both counting styles 1 and 2. Note that in the shape of both notes of bar 28 and 51, the bar's start point is not a note-on, subsequently, a phrase which begins at the eighth off beat in the 2nd quarter includes triplets and 16th notes. In jazz, the 2nd quarter is an accented beat while in classical music, the 2nd quarter is an up-beat. Also, Charlie Parker performed this phrase's rhythm note just in time, accompanied by a rather loose rhythm fluctuation in his CD [3]. The author predicts that the rather loose rhythm fluctuation is due to the difference in accented beat, and hence, the difference between jazz and classical performers' rhythm cognition, thus, this phrase arises from the sense of jazz style rhythm and is difficult for classical music players to easily grasp.

4 Conclusion

In this paper, the author predicted that the difference in the accented beat between jazz and classical music might have an influence in cognition of phrases, and subsequently, performed an experiment by allowing actual classical music performers to sight-read jazz ad-lib solo phrases while interchanging the accented beat from classical music to jazz style. The result suggested that the difference in the accented beat has an influence on cognition of jazz phrases. The results of the experiment indicated that the author's hypothesis was possibly correct.

References

1. Butterfield, M.W.: Participatory discrepancies and the perception of beats in jazz. Music Percept. Interdisc. J. **27**(3), 157–176 (2010)
2. Butterfield, M.W.: Why do jazz musicians swing their eighth notes? Music Theory Spectrum **33**(1), 3–26 (2011)
3. Parker, C.: Now's the time in Charlie Parker Bee Boppers. CD (1945)
4. Stupacher, J., Hove, M.J., Novembre, G., Schütz-Bosbachch, S., Keller, P.E.: Musical groove modulates motor cortex excitability: a TMS investigation. Brain Cogn. **82**(2), 127–136 (2013)

Detecting Freezing-of-Gait Symptom in Parkinson's Disease by Analyzing Vertical Motion from Force Plate

Dinh-Khiet Le[1][(✉)], Takuma Torii[1], Tsutomu Fujinami[1], Wannipat Buated[2], and Praween Lolekha[3]

[1] Japan Advanced Institute of Science and Technology,
1-1 Asahidai, Nomi, Ishikawa 923-1292, Japan
ledinhkhiet1804@gmail.com
[2] Department of Physical Therapy, Faculty of Allied Health Sciences,
Thammasat University, Bangkok, Thailand
[3] Neurology Division, Department of Internal Medicine, Faculty of Medicine,
Thammasat University, Bangkok, Thailand

Abstract. Introduction: Freezing of Gait (FoG) is a common symptom in Parkinson's Disease (PD), which has impact on the gait pattern and relevant to risk of falls. Data-driven approach to FoG detection would allow systematic assessment of patient's condition and objective evaluation of the clinical effects on treatments. Many researchers recently studied FoG in PD by analyzing patient's center of pressure dynamics in term of various features such as path-length. **Objective:** In this research, we attempt to automatically classify two groups of PD patients that with and without FoG by considering standing balance ability during cognitive loading tasks. **Methods:** The dataset consists of sixty PD patients (Hoehn and Yahr stages 1–3) were collected from Thammasat University Hospital, Thailand. The participants were categorized either to be FoG or non-FoG according to the Freezing of Gait-Questionnaire (FoG-Q) scores. Their postural balance ability was measured with Nintendo Balance board which produces a time-series of center of pressure along with the value of changing weight. We turn to a new kind of feature named "Fluctuation of Vertical Acceleration" (FVA) which informs us the acceleration due to the body's up-down motion and use comparative analysis to analyze the postural control function activities in cognitive loading tasks of all patients, FoG and non FoG groups. **Results:** Significant increases of the FVA were observed when applying cognitive loading ($p < 0.001$) in all cases (considering all data or each subgroup). The FVA also increased between the rest state and the other rest state after a cognitive loading task ($p < 0.001$). The difference between FoG and non FoG was observed by using FVA ($p < 0.05$). The test results when using FVA are in line with using other features extracted from the trajectory of center of pressure (such as path-length). **Conclusions:** The new simple feature, FVA, seems to reflect well postural control activities in people with PD, especially recognizing the change in a cognitive loading task. In addition, based on the postural control function, indirectly through the FVA, we are possible to classify automatically PD patients into the FoG or the non-FoG group.

© Springer Nature Switzerland AG 2019
K. Kojima et al. (Eds.): JSAI-isAI 2018 Workshops, LNAI 11717, pp. 468–477, 2019.
https://doi.org/10.1007/978-3-030-31605-1_34

Keywords: Parkinson's disease · Postural control · Cognitive loading · Freezing of gait

1   Introduction

Freezing-of-gait (FoG) is a common clinical symptom in Parkinson's disease [2] (PD), observed as inability to start doing a motion and shaking/shuffling gait in a motion [9,13]. FoG is usually found in PD patients in the advanced stages, but recently FoG has been reported in the early stages as well. Approximately 44–53% of PD patients have the symptom of FoG [6,12] and the percentage increases up to 80% of PD patients in the advanced stages [10,19]. PD patients with FoG often have significant changes in their gait progression, decreased foot length, and tremors in FoG attacks [13]. Due to these changes, a basic risk for PD patients with FoG is falling over [1,15,16] and so PD patients with FoG are exposed to high risk of fatal accidents, such as fractures or immobility [3]. Therefore, early detection of FoG symptom among PD patients is helpful to prevent them from such accidents, as well as to improve their quality of life.

The mechanism of FoG is yet not entirely understood up to now. Currently, with or without FoG is classified by clinical assessment but often detected after accidents. Recent researches have attempted to elucidate procedures of FoG assessments by incorporating recent findings on the relationship between FoG and other factors. In bio-mechanical approach, Pelykh et al. [17] and Buated et al. [4] characterized the postural control ability of PD patients during cognitive loading tasks by analyzing their center-of-pressure time series. Both studies showed reduced postural control during cognitive loading tasks in both FoG and non-FoG groups; However, no significant difference between groups was reported. Onell et al. [14] reported that the vertical acceleration amplitude in the vertical direction motion increased in cerebrovascular disease patients during quite standing compared with controls. Similarly, Minamisawa et al. [18] reported the relevant of temporal fluctuation of the vertical ground reaction force during quite stance with PD. In clinical approach, Duncan et al. [8] invented the sub-clinical screening test, called the BESTest, to examine some difference between FoG and non-FoG and obtained high reliability ($p < 0.001$). However, a shortcoming of this test is taking longer than 30 min, and expert factors will be cause of limitations in clinical application to a large number of patients.

In this study, our objective is to detect the freezing-of-gait (FoG) symptom in Parkinson's disease (PD) patients based on physical or bio-mechanical data. For this objective, we develop a new statistical feature (or factor) for automatically detecting the FoG symptom of PD patients and easily applicable in clinical assessments. To test our proposed feature, including the standard path length, we analyzed the center-of-pressure time series under cognitive loading tasks.

2   Methodology

2.1   Participants

We briefly describe our data, originally collected by our colleagues [4]. See Buated et al. [4] for details.

60 PD patients included in the present study had the following: 24 males and 36 females, aged 66.48 ± 10.32 years, duration of the disease 5.31 ± 3.42 years, age of onset 61.27 ± 10.96 years, Hoehn & Yahr stage [11] 1–3 and collected in Thammasat Hospital, Thailand. The patients with other problems, i.e., vascular parkinsonism, parkinsonims plus, drug-induced parkinsonism, motor weakness such as severe sensory neuropathy and cerebellar ataxia, unable to stand without support, partial or complete blindness, psychological problems, postural hypotension, or severe dyskinesia were excluded. All participants with Parkinson's disease were examined during the on-time medication without presenting excessive rigidity, bradykinesia, or tremor and they can stand for 3 min without support; Their center-of-pressure time series data were collected as a physical data.

2.2   Apparatus and Procedures

Center-of-pressure (CoP) time series were recorded using a force place, called Nintendo Wii Balance Board [5], which is a platform for measuring distribution of weight bearing of the subject on it. A recorded data consists of the relative positions of the center-of-pressure (CoP) along the medial-lateral (x) and anterior-posterior (y) dimensions, on the two dimensional surface of the Wii Balance Board, with timestamps 1 ms. In addition, as a force plate, this Wii Balance Board can record the additional dimension that the vertical force exert on the plate, we refer, 'weight', which measured in unit converted to kilogram [kg]. More specifically, the initial force unit is newton [N], but for convenience, people often convert into kilograms [kg] by dividing by the gravitational acceleration $g = 9.8 (\mathrm{m/s}^2)$.

Each patient was instructed first to stand upright on the balance board, looking horizontally to a marker on the wall at 3 m apart, and then to follow the four instructions: (1) Before I: Keep standing for 30 s; (2) Reading (RE): Keep standing with reading a pre-prepared material, such as, "One", "Two", etc., for 30 s; (3) Before II: Keep standing for 30 s; and (4) Counting Backward (CB): Keep standing with counting backward, such as, count from ten to one, for 30 s.

3   Features for Postural Instability

In this section, we described the newly proposed statistical feature, called Fluctuation of Vertical Acceleration (FVA), as well as the clinical standard, known as path length.

3.1   Path Length

Path length is simply the total length of a CoP path. Given time series of CoP $(x(t), y(t))$ at time frame t, it was calculated by summing up the distances between consecutive data points [7], i.e.,

$$\text{PathLength} := \sum_t \sqrt{[x(t+1) - x(t)]^2 + [y(t+1) - y(t)]^2} \qquad (1)$$

3.2   Fluctuation of Vertical Acceleration (FVA)

We derive a new statistical feature, we name it, Fluctuation of Vertical Acceleration (FVA). As we have described, the Wii Balance Board can record the interaction force between force plate and other object put on it. In this study, this force is called "weight", meaning the total force that patient impacts on the plate. According to Newton's second law in physics, force is directly related to mass, motion and acceleration. Similarly, in this case, weight is directly related to the patient's vertical movement. This is also the reason for why weight can change over time.

Because the weight amplitude is strongly influenced by body mass, we remove this factor by considering only the acceleration (also meaning normalized weight by dividing the body mass). We then postulate that the postural instability can be characterized by the fluctuation of the acceleration, which formed as below.

According to the Newton's second law, the weight $\bar{w}$ on Earth at the rest state is the body mass m times gravitational constant g: $\bar{w} = mg$. In addition to this, the weight $w(t)$ measured by the balance board at time t can include the additional factor due to the acceleration (or force) approximately along the vertical $a_z(t)$: $w(t) = mg + ma_z(t)$. Then, from recorded time series $w(t)$, we can extract the vertical acceleration at time t by

$$a_z(t) = \frac{w(t) - \bar{w}}{m}. \qquad (2)$$

Taking the ratio gives a quantity independent of the body mass m as

$$\frac{a_z(t)}{g} = \frac{w(t)}{\bar{w}} - 1. \qquad (3)$$

which is in units of percent [%]. The value of $\bar{w}$, the weight at no motion, can be measured by a weight scale at home or estimated by the average over time $\bar{w} = (1/T) \sum_t w(t)$. Finally, our new feature, Fluctuation of Vertical Acceleration (FVA), is defined as its deviation from the mean

$$\text{FVA} = \text{std}\left(\frac{a_z(t)}{g}\right) \times 100, \qquad (4)$$

where the $\text{std}(\cdot)$ operator calculates the standard deviation.

3.3 Visualization of Features

Figure 1(a) visualized a CoP path of a patient. Four colors, green, red, yellow, and blue, were used for the four conditions, i.e., Before I, Reading, Before II, Counting Backward, respectively. In Fig. 1(b), we showed the time series of Vertical Acceleration (VA), calculated by using Eq. (3). Our new feature, Fluctuation of Vertical Acceleration (FVA), Eq. (4), characterizes the variation of Vertical Acceleration in Fig. 1(b). As we can see, the variation of the first and third tasks seem lower than two remaining tasks.

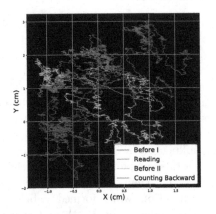 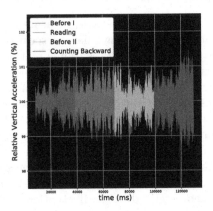

(a) Center-of-Pressure path   (b) Vertical Acceleration (VA)

Fig. 1. (a) A visualization of a patient's center-of-pressure data. The green, red, yellow, and blue colors corresponds to the four conditions: Before I, Reading, Before II, Counting Backward. (b) Part of the new feature, Vertical Acceleration, in Eq. (3). (Color figure online)

4 Results

4.1 Data Processing

In our data analyses, for each PD patient's CoP path, we calculated two feature statistics, Path Length (PL) and Fluctuation of Vertical Acceleration (FVA), for four data segments corresponding to the four conditions of our data recording: i.e., Before I, Reading, Before II, and Counting Backward. In some analyses, we also used two combined features, difference in the values of each feature (FVA or PL) between Before I and Reading and between Before II and Counting Backward. Resulting, we obtained $4 \times 2 = 8$ features, or $4 \times 2 + 4$ features for each PD patients.

PD patients were classified into two groups, FoG and non-FoG, based on FoG-Q scores, FoG-Q ≥ 6 for FoG (n $= 39$) and the rest for non-FoG (n $= 21$). See Buated et al. [4] for details.

Table 1 is the summary of two kinds of feature statistics for all combinations of the four conditions times three subsets of data. Each cell of Table 1 contains $\mu \pm \sigma$ as the mean μ and the standard deviation σ. In most cases, the mean values increase from non-FoG to FoG and from Before I, Before II, RE, to CB, orderly.

Table 1. The average and standard deviation of FVA and path length in the dataset. RE = Reading; CB = Counting Backward; FVA: unit in percent; Path length: unit in centimeter

Feature task	FVA			Path length		
	All data	FoG	non-FoG	All data	FoG	non-FoG
Before I	0.23 ± 0.18	0.25 ± 0.21	0.19 ± 0.08	81 ± 33	85 ± 39	73 ± 14
RE	0.32 ± 0.32	0.36 ± 0.39	0.23 ± 0.07	93 ± 58	100 ± 70	79 ± 16
Before II	0.27 ± 0.28	0.32 ± 0.34	0.20 ± 0.06	89 ± 47	95 ± 56	77 ± 17
CB	0.41 ± 0.54	0.48 ± 0.65	0.28 ± 0.12	109 ± 82	121 ± 98	87 ± 24

4.2 Goals and Procedures of Statistical Analysis

In this study, we set two goals for analysis. Firstly, we analyze the effects of the cognitive loading tasks (Reading and Counting Backward) on postural control by comparing them from the preceding rest conditions (Before I and Before II), within the groups. Because we will compare two related samples, and have no assumption or prior about their distribution, so we employ a non parametric statistical hypothesis test that the Wilcoxon singed-rank test to analyze the differences. The significant of difference will shown by the p-value.

Secondly, to demonstrate the ability of the new feature for detection of FoG in PD patients, we compared the effects on postural control between the groups, the FoG and non-FoG group. In this test, we compare two independent samples without the assumption or prior about their distribution. We want to determine a randomly selected value from one sample will be less than or greater than a randomly selected value from a second sample. So, we employ a non parametric statistical hypothesis test that the Mann-Whitney U test to compare two samples. The p-value is also selected to assess the significant.

4.3 Impact of Cognitive Loading on Postural Control

The results of empirical data analysis showed in Table 2. Each cell contains the p-values of Wilcoxon signed-rank statistics in comparison between the conditions. We observed that both FVA and PL produced the significant influence (mostly $p \leq 0.01$) of cognitive loading on posture control. This is the necessary condition to consider using them for the next step detecting FoG.

We visualized the influence of the cognitive loading tasks, within the groups, shown in Fig. 2. Figure 2 shows the FVA's of all patients, their $ID = 0, 1, 2, \ldots, 59$, separately, along the horizontal axis of each figure. The bottom figure includes all four conditions, i.e., Before I (green), Reading (red), Before II (yellow), and Counting Backward (blue). The top-left includes only Before I (green) and Reading (red) and the top-right includes only Before II (yellow) and Counting Backward (blue). We also observed the increases in FVA's clearly from Before I (green) to Reading (red), and from Before II (yellow) to Counting Backward (blue). In overview, we can see the magnitude of FVA in the Reading and Counting Backward tasks almost larger than the Before I and Before II tasks. This is the evidence for the effect of cognitive loading on the postural stability in the visualization.

Table 2. Results (p-values) of Wilcoxon signed-rank test between the experimental conditions. RE = Reading, CB = Counting Backward

Task		FVA			Path length		
A	B	All data	FoG	non-FoG	All data	FoG	non-FoG
Before I	RE	<0.001	<0.001	<0.001	<0.001	<0.001	<0.001
Before II	CB	<0.001	<0.001	<0.001	<0.001	<0.001	<0.001
Before II	RE	<0.001	0.002	<0.001	0.010	0.044	0.120
RE	CB	<0.001	0.035	0.021	0.002	0.008	0.010
Before I	Before II	<0.001	0.001	0.01	0.003	0.01	0.006

4.4   Comparison Between the FoG and non-FoG Group

Next, we examined differences between the FoG and non-FoG group. In this analysis, we used the combined features, described in the section of data processing, denoted by Δ(Before I, RE) for the difference in a feature between the Before I and Reading condition, and Δ(Before II, CB) between the Before II and Counting Backward condition. These two features are used for the purpose of considering whether there is a difference in the response of two groups of patients to the cognitive process.

The test results, with p-values of the Mann-Whitney U test, shown in Table 3 indicated that the significant differences between the two groups, which observed with different type of features (FVA and PL), are different. The significant difference level of FVA was seemly smaller than of PL. The difference between FoG and non FoG was observed with p-value less than 0.05 in the Before II and using FVA. This result support for the idea that by using FVA, we can easily observe the difference between FoG and non FoG, based on that, automatically detecting FoG in PD patients.

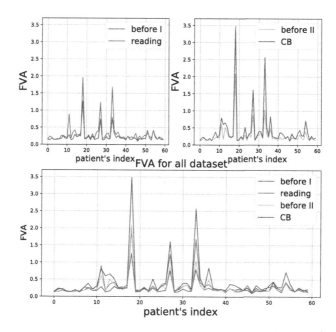

Fig. 2. The Cognitive loading tasks tend to show larger individual variation in FVA

We can also confirm visually the results of statistical tests in Fig. 3. Figure 3, the left two figures compare the impacts of the Reading task and the right two figures compare the impacts of the Counting Backward task. The bottom two figures contain the FVA's of PD patients with non-FoG and the top two figures contain the FVA's of PD patients with FoG. From these figures, we observed that the patients with FoG tend to show larger individual variation in FVA, in both the cognitive loading tasks, that was as an evidence for thinking about the difference between two groups.

Table 3. Results (p-values) of the Mann-Whitney U test between the FoG and non-FoG group. RE = Reading and CB = Counting Backward. Δ(Before I, RE) = change from Before I to Reading. Δ(Before II, CB) = change from Before II to Counting Backward.

Task	FVA	Path length
Before I	0.18	0.28
RE	0.11	0.28
Before II	0.03	0.22
CB	0.31	0.33
Δ(Before I, RE)	0.08	0.31
Δ(Before II, CB)	0.32	0.41

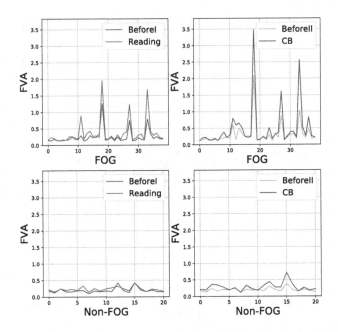

Fig. 3. The patients with FoG tend to show larger individual variation in FVA, in both the cognitive loading tasks

5   Discussion

In this paper, we tried to detect the freezing-of-gait (FoG) symptom in Parkinson's disease (PD) patients based on physical or bio-mechanical data. In our data analysis, in addition to the standard Path Length (PL), we evaluated our newly proposed feature, called Fluctuation of Vertical Acceleration (FVA). Our results suggest that both PL and FVA can work for detecting the effect of cognitive loading on the postural control. The difference between FoG and non FoG groups was observed with p-value less than 0.05 by using FVA.

In addition, the FVA was based on the one-dimension time series, which formed by measuring the weight along the vertical axis, it is not only easily to set up in the practice (can use only one weight sensor) but also interpret easier than others in multi-dimensions. So, this thing therefore suggests that we can develop some experimental schemes suitable for FVA, which can be helpful for earlier defection of the FoG symptom. One of our future works is to develop such experimental schemes, toward data-driven clinical assessments, to help people with the freezing-of-gait symptom in Parkinson's disease patients.

References

1. Allen, N., Schwarzel, A., Canning, C.: Recurrent falls in Parkinson's disease: a systematic review. Parkinson's Dis. **2013**, 906247 (2013)

2. Bloem, B., Hausdorff, J., Visser, J., Giladi, N.: Falls and freezing of gait in Parkinson's disease: a review of two interconnected, episodic phenomena. Mov. Disord. **19**, 871–884 (2004)

3. Bloem, B., Steijns, J., Smits-Engelsman, B.: An update on fall. Curr. Opin. Neurol. **16**, 15–26 (2003)

4. Buated, W., Lolekha, P., Hidaka, S., Fujinami, T.: Impact of cognitive loading on postural control in Parkinson's disease with freezing of gait. Gerontol. Geriatr. Med. **2**, 1–8 (2016)

5. Clark, R., Bryant, A., Pua, Y., McCrory, P., Bennell, K., Hunt, M.: Validity and reliability of the Nintendo Wii Balance Board for assessment of standing balance. Gait Postural **31**, 307–310 (2010)

6. Contreras, A., Grandas, F.: Risk factors for freezing of gait in Parkinson's disease. J. Neurol. Sci. **320**, 66–71 (2012)

7. Donker, S., Roerdink, M., Greven, A., Beek, P.: Regularity of center-of-pressure trajectories depends on the amount of attention invested in postural control. Exp. Brain Res. **181**, 1–11 (2007)

8. Duncan, R., et al.: Balance differences in people with Parkinson's disease with and without freezing of gait. Gait Posture **42**(3), 306–309 (2015)

9. Giladi, N., Nieuwboer, A.: Understanding and treating freezing of gait in Parkinsonism, proposed working definition, and setting the stage. Mov. Disord. **23**, S423–425 (2008)

10. Hely, M., Reid, W., Adena, M., Halliday, G., Morris, J.: The Sydney multicenter study of Parkinson's disease: the inevitability of dementia at 20 years. Mov. Disord. **23**, 837–844 (2008)

11. Hoehn, M., Yahr, M.: Parkinsonism: onset, progression and mortality. Neurology **17**, 427–442 (1967)

12. Giladi, N., Treves, T., Shabta, H., Orlov, Y., Kandinov, B., et al.: Freezing of gait in patients with advanced Parkinson's disease. J. Neural Transm. **108**, 53–61 (2001)

13. Nutt, J., Bloem, B., Giladi, N., Hallett, M., Horak, F., Nieuwboer, A.: Freezing of gait: moving forward on a mysterious clinical phenomenon. J. Neurol. Sci. **10**, 734–744 (2011)

14. Onell, A.: The vertical ground reaction force for analysis of balance? Gait Postural **12**, 7–13 (2000)

15. Paul, S., et al.: Risk factors for frequent falls in people with Parkinson's disease. J. Parkinson's Dis. **4**, 699–703 (2014)

16. Paul, S., Sherrington, C., Canning, C., Fung, V., Close, J., Lord, S.: The relative contribution of physical and cognitive fall risk factors in people with Parkinson's disease: a large prospective cohort study. Neurorehabilitation Neural Repair **28**, 282–290 (2013)

17. Pelykh, O., Klein, A., Botzel, K., Kosutzka, Z., Ilmberger, J.: Dynamic of postural control in Parkinson patients with and without symtoms of freezing of gait. Gait Postural **42**, 246–250 (2015)

18. Minamisawa, T., Sawahata, H., Takakura, K.: Characteristics of temporal fluctuation of the vertical ground reaction force during quiet stance in Parkinson's disease. Gait Postural **35**(2), 308–311 (2012)

19. Tan, D., McGinley, J., Danoudis, M., Lansek, R., Morris, M.: Freezing of gait and activity limitations in people with Parkinson's disease. Arch. Phys. Med. Rehabil. **92**, 1159–1165 (2011)

Effects of Casual Computer Game on Cognitive Performance Through Hemodynamic Signals

Phetnidda Ouankhamchan[✉] and Tsutomu Fujinami

Japan Advanced Institute of Science and Technology,
1-1 Asahidai, Nomi, Ishikawa 923-1292, Japan
s1720405@jaist.ac.jp

Abstract. Slowing cognitive decline is important in our aging society. Computer games are assumed to increase brain activity. There are many types of computer games in which each of them potentially has different effect on brain activity. We present how playing a casual color-matching puzzle game changes cognitive performance through scores of a cognitive neuropsychological test involving seven participants. The results indicate that the puzzle game improves spatial imaging, speed perception, and working memory but hampers in attention. Meanwhile, it has been claimed that brain activity can be studied with signals received from the brain. We discuss the changes found in hemodynamics signals collected from a wearable functional near-infrared spectroscopy device. We found that the puzzle game improved cognitive performance on average by referring to the median of max-min normalized in terms of oxygenated hemoglobin and deoxygenated hemoglobin along with smaller variation in brain activity through the power spectral density after playing the casual puzzle game. The results indicate that the game has a positive effect on cognitive performance by relieving the players from mental workload. The classification of cognitive performance obtained from a support vector machine indicates that we may understand the changes in cognitive performance from features identified from hemoglobin concentration changes.

Keywords: Cognitive performance · fNIRS ·
Oxygenated hemoglobin signals · Deoxygenated hemoglobin signals ·
Stroop task · Mental rotation task · Power spectral density ·
Normalization · SVM classification

1 Introduction

Cognitive performance often declines among the elderly, but it sometimes can occur in younger adults [1]. Enhancing cognitive performance is essential to slow the process of cognitive decline.

Affectivity is associated with cognitive performance in the bi-direction. Previous studies found that individuals with severe cognitive impairment have strong

© Springer Nature Switzerland AG 2019
K. Kojima et al. (Eds.): JSAI-isAI 2018 Workshops, LNAI 11717, pp. 478–492, 2019.
https://doi.org/10.1007/978-3-030-31605-1_35

affective bias in perceiving emotions [2,3]. Conversely, emotion affects the cognitive process. Negative affectivity, such as perceived stress and depression, results in a rapid decline in cognitive performance among the elderly [4,5]. It is also known that activities stimulating positive valence and arousal enhance cognitive performance such as executive function and working memory [6]. We investigated activities that stimulate the brain to improve cognitive performance.

1.1 Computer Game as a Tool for Cognitive and Mental Activities

Computer games are designed to include several elements that stimulate our mind for entertainment and mental fitness at different levels of valence and arousal. Some claim that computer games enhance cognitive performance [7], but their effects might vary depending on the type of game. Previous studies showed that the brain becomes more active after playing video action games [8]. It is known that other types of computer games, such as puzzles, enable the player to think logically to solve the puzzle. Previous studies found evidence supporting a hypothesis that mental rotation tasks for solving puzzles enhance cognitive performance [9]. "Tetris" is such a puzzle for which the player has to rotate in their minds the images of falling items on display to fit them into matching holes.

We are also interested in color-matching tasks for solving puzzles in addition to metal rotation tasks. Some argue that color has positive effects on enhancing memory and attention [10,11]. "Candy crush" is a computer puzzle game designed considering the logical complexity of color matching. King Digital Entertainment reported in 2014 that more than 93 million people had played the game daily [12]. We investigated the effects of "Candy Crush" on players in terms of cognitive performance to see how the popular puzzle game enhances cognitive performance and report evidence suggesting that playing computer games may slow the early stages of cognitive decline along with having a therapeutic effect.

1.2 Brain Signals as Measurement of Emotional and Cognitive Activities

The phenomena associated with affections and cognitions are studied in neuroscience with objective measurement of brain signals such as through electroencephalogram (EEG), functional magnetic resonance imaging (fMRI), and functional near-infrared spectroscopy (fNIRS). EEG components are investigated as biomarkers of brain disorders [14], and these markers help researchers understand the emotional statue of subjects [13]. Along with the potentials measured from the electric activity in the brain, another type of signal is detected by sensing the metabolism in the brain and serves an important source of information to monitor brain activities. fMRI and fNIRS are well known as means of monitoring the blood flow in the brain and enable the development of brain computer interfaces (BCIs) by measuring the blood oxygenation level-dependent (BOLD). Studies using fMRI discovered that the cognitive performance among

Alzheimer patients can be measured by referring to the changes found in magnetic properties associated with oxygenated hemoglobin (oxy-Hb) and deoxygenated hemoglobin (deoxy-Hb) during brain activity [15,16]. fNIRS provides the same bio-markers as fMRI does, but it is based on a different principle known as absorption of near-infrared light and is often used in BCI studies for observing brain activities. Some use fNIRS to investigate the changes in hemoglobin in the brain to assess the level of workload for mental tasks [17], while others use it to observe the changes in hemoglobin for diagnosing the early stages of mild cognitive impairment [18].

fNIRS is a non-invasive optical neuroimaging technique and has advantages of portability and lower cost over fMRI. Due to its convenience, fNIRS has been used more often recently for the study of BCI and related studies. We thus adopted fNIRS to investigate the effects of a computer-based color-matching puzzle game on cognitive performance, observing the metabolic response through oxy-Hb and deoxy-Hb hemodynamic concentration changes in the cerebral frontal cortex of the brain.

1.3 Hypothesis

Computer-based puzzle games are easy to play and addictive. Evidence suggests that color-matching games benefit players in terms of cognitive performance by forcing them to remember colors. Our first hypothesis is as follows: color-matching games may help players improve performance on cognitive tests. The cognitive tasks adopted for our investigation of cognitive performance assess the flexibility in cognition through the Stroop task, a mental rotation task to test visuo-spatial capability, a pair association task to test memory capacity, and a different-item-finding task to test attention.

While the brain is activated, regional blood flow increases, resulting in changes in concentrations of oxy-Hb and deoxy-Hb [19]. However, puzzle games might reduce mental work load to some extent if the person enjoys playing the game. Reducing work load in the brain might lead to lower changes in BOLD. In this study, we investigated the differences in oxy-Hb and deoxy-Hb before and after participants played a color-matching puzzle game while they were engaged in cognitive tasks. We hypothesize that the effects of playing this computer game decrease concentration in hemoglobin signals when players show improvements in performing cognitive tasks.

2 Method

2.1 Participants

We initially recruited seven participants (three male and four female) who were all students at Japan Advanced Institute of Science and Technology. They were healthy without any clinical history related to brain, neurological, psychiatric, and cardiovascular disorders. Their mean age was 27 ± 3.8. We followed the standard procedure in collecting data, that is, participants were well informed of the experiment and agreed to take part.

2.2 Neuropsychological Testing

Neuropsychological testing is a performance-based method for assessing a wide range of cognitive functions and abilities. We adopted the Stroop task and mental rotation task for our neuropsychological study.

The Stroop task was originally developed in 1993 [20]. It has been used widely for various research purposes in cognitive psychology [22,23]. These studies used the Stroop task to measure the speed of perceptual processing. We used Psy-Toolkit "psytoolkit.org/" [24,25] to implement a computer-based Stroop task for our experiment. We also examined the visuo-spatial capability of each participant before and after playing a puzzle game involving a mental rotation task, the concept of which was first proposed in 1971 by Shepard and Metzler [26]. We asked the participants to rotate mental representatives of two-dimensional objects.

Additional tests of attention and memory were also carried out. We adopted an associated pair-matching game for testing memory. This game allowed the participants five seconds to remember nine positions of three pairs of pictures. The participants were then asked to associate each picture with its matching pair on a correct position. We also asked them to find a unique item in a group for testing their attention. We showed them sets of pictures and asked them to identify a unique picture for each set.

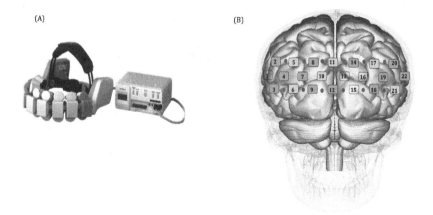

Fig. 1. (A) fNIRS WOT 220 head set with portable control box equipped with (B) 22 channels to simultaneously measure signals of hemoglobin concentration changes on cerebral prefrontal cortex. Head set was placed on forehead, where channel 12 was in the middle and far from the nose root point in crossing mark in (B) with appropriate distance regarding 10–20 system of electrode placement [28]. Eight light sources were presented as red dots, while photon detectors were presented as blue dots. Highlighted squares with green represent channels detecting stable signals of time-series. Signals presented in yellow were unstable and transparent squares indicate channels that had obstacles due to individuals' physical conditions such as head shape and hair interference.(Color figure online)

2.3   Optical Topography fNIRS Device

We asked each participant to sit in front of a computer display. Throughout the experiment, the fNIRS WOT 220 head set with portable control box equipped with 22 channels (as shown in Fig. 1) is placed that covering subject's forehead to measure blood hemoglobin concentration changes on cerebral prefrontal cortex. Each participant was instructed not to lower or raise his/her head while wearing the fNIRS device for each session so as not to produce noise. As shown in Fig. 2, the experiment involved three main sessions: pre-neuropsychological test of cognitive performance before playing the puzzle game (pre-session), the puzzle game playing, and post-neuropsychological test after playing it (post-session).

The neuropsychological test involved four cognitive tasks, i.e., the Stroop, mental rotation, pair-matching, and different-item finding for both pre and post sessions. Each task for each session was set for 75 s with 5 s for a rest. The puzzle game used for this experiment was "Candy Crush Soda Sugar". Each participant was asked to play this puzzle game for 20 min on a "MultiTaction" device with Windows operating system and a 55-in. (16:9) Full HD 1920 × 1080 display (Fig. 2) The participants were asked to calm themselves down between sessions by closing their eyes and deep inhaling-exhaling for three times.

The experiment was carried out in a quiet room with only the participants and a researcher to minimize interruption by external factors.

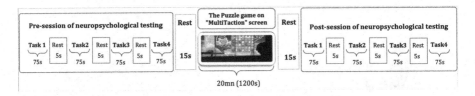

Fig. 2. Overview of experimental setting

3   Data Acquisition

3.1   Data of Cerebral Blood Flow

We collected the data of cerebral blood flow including changes in concentrations oxy-Hb and deoxy-Hb signals with the fNIRS WOT-220 HITACHI device.

(1) Removing noise and artifacts: Sample data of 75 s were selected for each task in the pre and post sessions of neuropsychological testing. The hemoglobin signals during the rest periods were excluded from the analysis.
(2) Selecting target channels: Evidence has shown that the lateral part of the prefrontal cortex (PFC) is critically involved in broad aspects of executive cognitive behavior control [30] and working memory related to the process of information manipulation [29]. The PFC plays a role in visual attention and complex cognitive tasks, and lesions in this brain area leads to deficits

in attention and working memory [31]. The cognitive tasks and videogames used for the experiment require some level of attention and working memory related to reasoning as well as cognitive flexibility to complete the assigned tasks. We thus initially focused on channels 1–7 for the right lateral PFC and channels 16–22 for the left lateral PFC to monitor the performance of cognitive function related to working memory and visual attention. Due to the interference of hair and other physical conditions peculiar to each participant, data obtained from some channels were excluded from consideration due to their low quality. We ended up focusing on channels 3 and 4 for the right PFC together with channels 19 and 21 for the left PFC. Figure 3 Illustrates the hemodynamic signals collected from participant C using a max-min approach.

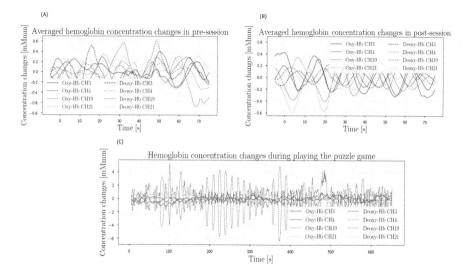

Fig. 3. Average hemoglobin concentration changes from target channels (Channels 3, 4, 19, and 21) during experiment from participant C. Warm colors indicate changes in oxy-Hb concentration while cool colors indicate changes in deoxy-Hb concentration. Average concentration changes in oxy-Hb and deoxy-Hb through four tasks in pre-session of neuropsychological tests are illustrated in (A) and those in post-session in (B). (C) Graph showing hemoglobin concentration changes while playing game for 10 min.

3.2   Normalization on fNIRS Hemodynamic Signals

The oxy-Hb and deoxy-Hb signals in channel-n of participant i were normalized with the max-min normalization approach with the following equation

$$OxyHb'_{i_n} = \frac{OxyHb_{i_n} - min(i_n)}{max(i_n) - min(i_n)}$$

where $min(i_n)$ is the minimum value and $max(i_n)$ is the maximum value of an oxy-Hb signal in channel-n of participant i throughout both neuropsychological test sessions (pre-session and post-session).

The frequency distribution of hemoglobin signals do not follow the normal distribution found in other types of brain signals, such as EEG, but does follow the skew distribution where the mean is greater than median. Median becomes an appropriate parameter to present the central tendency of the brain signal. We computed the medians of the normalized oxy-Hb and deoxy-Hb signals to measure the central tendency of hemoglobin concentration changes as a basic feature of hemoglobin signals during cognitive performance in pre- and post-sessions.

Each signal is considered a vector V that contains k components (with k length). The median each normalized signal was generated by sorting the data component of each signal in ascending order then, the middle value of a signal was $\frac{(k+1)}{2}^{th}$ when k length was an odd number. The median of a signal was subsequently computed by the average of two middle values when k length was an even number.

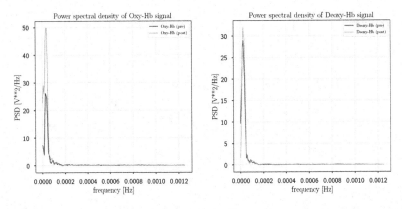

Fig. 4. Example of PSDs of fNIRS channel 3 from participant C during sessions of cognitive tasks. Left figure presents PSDs of oxy-Hb signals, while right figure shows those of deoxy-Hb signals. Dark colors indicate fNIRS hemodynamic signals from pre-session, and light colors indicate those from post-session.

3.3   Power Spectral Density of fNIRS Hemodynamic Signal

The power spectral density (PSD) is the other feature of signals considered in this study. PSD is a point estimation of the energy variation in time series as a frequency function. We computed the PSDs based on Welch's method [32] to extract the strongest variance in target hemodynamic oxy-Hb and deoxy-Hb signals derived from each participant. The PSDs were determined by an average of the windowed periodogram [33]. Regarding the Welch method, the original sequence signal is divided in multiple overlapping segments. Then an array for each segment $(1, ..., k)$ is computed in which each element is an average of the corresponding elements of all divided segments as

$$PSD_x(v) = \frac{1}{k} \sum_{k=1}^{k} \left(\frac{1}{W} \mid x_k(v)^2 \mid \right)$$

where $x_k(v)^2$ is a discrete Fourier transform [33] and W is the sum of squared window functions.

Two signals are similar when they have similar energy variation. We computed PSDs to extract the maximum energy as the strongest variance in the signals during pre- and post-sessions to investigate the difference between them. We implemented the PSDs on python with a library called SciPy. An example of the PSDs generated from oxy-Hb and deoxy-Hb signals retrieved from channel 3 during pre- and post-sessions of cognitive tasks for participant C are shown in Fig. 4.

4   Results and Discussion

4.1   Cognitive Performance Through Neuropsychological Testing

Table 1. Changes in cognitive performance on cognitive tasks through neuropsychological test after playing puzzle game. + indicates improvement with better neuropsychological test scores, and − indicates opposite. △ denotes no changes in performance when participant maintained same scores in pre and post-sessions.

Task	A	B	C	D	E	F	G
Task1: Stroop task	+	+	−	−	−	+	+
Task2: Mental rotation	△	+	+	+	△	+	+
Task3: Associate pair matching task	−	−	+	−	−	+	+
Task4: Different-item finding task	−	−	+	−	−	+	−

With the evidence shown in Table 1, (1) all participants exhibited positive changes in visuo-spatialization capability; the scores from five participants for the mental rotation task increased, while the other two participants maintained the same scores. (2) 60% of participants showed lower scores for the Stroop task after playing the puzzle game. The score for the Stroop task known as Stroop effect was computed from the difference between the average speed in correct trials of incongruence and those of congruence. The lower scores for the Stroop task indicate that individuals were faster in naming the color of a word [37]. The color Stroop and mental rotation tasks are likely to have similar cognitive requirement to a color-matching game. Playing such a game could enhance cognitive functions related to cognitive flexibility in terms of speed of perception information and visuo-spatialization. (3) The capacity of short-term memory of four participants through the associated pair-matching task was, in contrast, declined when the participants could not remember the positions of a pair of pictures distributed on the screen. The overall memory performance through task 3 improved when comparing the data between pre- and post-sessions when the statistical mean score increasingly changed from 4.41% (Table 2). (4) Visual attention for finding unique pictures decreased when five participants produced lower scores of finding the different items under the same conditions of time and level of picture complexity.

As Table 2 showing an averaged scores for all participants on each task, playing the puzzle game had positive effects on speed in perceptual processing, visuospatial capability, and memory-process activation. Yet, these parameters obviously illustrate the reduced capacity of attention during cognitive performance after playing the puzzle game. The color-matching puzzle game includes a vivid color matrix that might have caused participants visual fatigue, which degraded visual attention ability in finding unique items from the given sets of pictures.

Table 2. Comparison of cognitive performances of all participants between pre- and post-sessions with fundamental statistic parameters

Task	Pre-session		Post-session	
	Mean	(std)	Mean	(std)
Task1: Stroop task (ms)	124	(99.61)	74.43	(71.11)
Task2: Mental rotation (% of correct response)	0.8	(0.11)	0.97	(0.05)
Task3: Associate pair matching task (% of correct response)	0.68	(0.15)	0.71	(0.064)
Task4: Different-item finding task (correct response)	10.38	(8.39)	7.48	(5.00)

4.2   Changes in Hemodynamic Concentration Signals

The oxy-Hb and deoxy-Hb signals are different entities, helping us to understand the meaning of changes found in hemoglobin concentration during brain activity.

Figures 3(A) and (B) show the averages of target oxy-Hb and deoxy-Hb signals during the four tasks (75 s per task) of neuropsychological testing when participants were engaged in the tasks for the pre- and post-sessions. The hemodynamic signals from the target channels in the post-session exhibited a larger variance than those in the pre-session. We also observed that participants showed the highest variation in hemodynamic concentration when playing the game (Fig. 3(C)). This might suggest that the brain was highly activated when a participant was attempting to solve the puzzle and from the effects of entertainment factors such as colors, game sounds, and excitement. However, it is beyond the scope of this study to investigate brain activities while participants are engaged in casual computer games. By plotting the median and other statistical characteristics of data normalized with the max-min approach, we observed larger variations among the oxy-Hb signals than among the deoxy-Hb signals, as shown in Fig. 5. The oxy-Hb signals showed larger max values of the variation (>5 mMmm), while deoxy-Hb showed lower max values of variation (<2 mMmm). These results are consistent with existing theories such as that by

Sevick et al. [34], who reported that an oxy-Hb signal reflects the amount of oxygen contained in the blood in the brain tissue while the deoxy-Hb signal is linked to the amount of oxygen absorbed in the brain neuron tissue.

We investigated the changes in hemoglobin concentration while the brain is active to deal with the cognitive tasks by looking into the PSD peaks of oxy-Hb and deoxy-Hb signals and the medians of normalized oxy-Hb and deoxy-Hb signals.

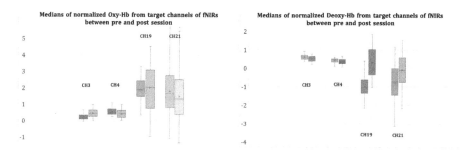

Fig. 5. Medians of normalized oxy-Hb and deoxy-Hb signals from fNIRS target channels. Left figure shows medians of normalized oxy-Hb, while right figure shows those of normalized deoxy-Hb. The values on vertical axes of both figures represent level of hemoglobin-concentration changes in millimolar-millimeter ($mMmm$). In each figure, left bars of each pair represent medians of signals during cognitive tasks in pre-session, while right bars of each pair are those of signals during cognitive tasks in post-session.

(a) Changes through medians of normalized signals

The median of each normalized hemodynamic signal represents the central tendency of signal data and is considered a parameter for comparing brain activity before and after playing a computer game by referring to hemodynamic signals. Figure 5 shows that the means of signals from all channels are higher than the medians. We can infer based on these results that the data distribution of these fNIRS hemodynamic signals are skewed to the right. Thus, we consider the median as an appropriate parameter for representing the central tendency of these signal data.

The changes in the medians of fNIRS in pre- and post-sessions of cognitive performance of a single participant (participant C) are shown in Fig. 5. The medians of oxy-Hb signals from channels 3 and 19 in the post-session were larger than those in the pre-session, while oxy-Hb signals from channels 4 and 21 exhibited lower medians in the post-session on cognitive performance. Different from the median changes in the deoxy-Hb signals shown in the right figure of Fig. 5, the medians of the deoxy-Hb signals from channels 3 and 4 on the right-PFC decreased in the post-session compared to those in the pre-session, but median changes in the deoxy-Hb signals from channels 19 and 21 on the left-PFC significantly increased. This means that after playing the game, the neuron tissues of participant C's left-PFC absorbed more oxygen than the neuron tissues of the right-PFC.

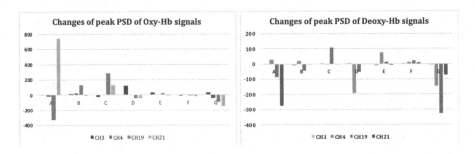

Fig. 6. Changes in brain activation through PSDs of signals from target channels derived from all participants.

(b) Changes through power spectral density

The PSD is one important feature to investigate the differences between signals. Two signals with varying energy variation indicate the differences between them. Thus, the PSDs of both oxy-Hb and deoxy-Hb signals were also investigated for observing the changes in hemodynamic signals between pre- and post-sessions. The sample visualization of PSDs from participant C in channel 3 shown in Fig. 4 seems to point to a higher PSD peak when he was engaged in the cognitive tasks after playing the game. Figure 6 shows clear changes in the PSD peaks, where each PSD in the post-session was subtracted by one in the pre-session for each channel. The energy variation in changes through the PSD of oxy-Hb signals seemed to vary across participants. Participants F and G, who performed better on tasks 1–3 of neuropsychological testing in the post-session compared to the pre-session (refer to Table 1), had reduced PSDs of oxy-Hb signals from the left-PFC at channels 19 and 21. Changes in the PSDs of deoxy-Hb signals from all channels of participant F, who performed better on all cognitive tasks in the post-session, represent positive changes.

Previous studies based on fNIRS-based signals indicated that healthy people show a higher level of brain activity during a mental task than schizophrenic patients [36]. Another study on the effects of mental workload at different levels induced the brain activations in medium and difficult mental tasks induced higher activities than easy tasks [35]. Through our case study with healthy participants, we found that the changes in hemoglobin concentration through middle values and PSD slightly decreased in oxy-Hb and increased in deoxy-Hb for participants whose cognitive performance concerning the mental rotation and Stroop tasks gradually improved. This might suggest the relieving of workload on brain function after playing puzzle games.

(c) Effects of the casual color-matching puzzle game on cognitive performance

By investigating changes of PSD and median, we learnt that the median changes in normalized hemoglobin signals and PSD can only indicate changes in brain activation before and after playing a puzzle game. We implemented a classification task to examine the relationship between the cognitive performance and the hemoglobin-concentration changes. We used principal component analysis

(PCA) to reduce the number of features by selecting the most influential signals with a support vector machine (SVM) that classifies which participants performed better in the cognitive neuropsychological tasks after playing the casual puzzle game. The result indicates the relation between the hemoglobin responses through fNIRS oxy-Hb and deoxy-Hb and the changes in cognitive performance from playing the puzzle game. Figure 7 shows sample data aligning near the SVM decision boundary. By adjusting the SVM model with a kernel function and its parameter of margin maximization, both median and PSD-based approaches represent appropriate features to explain the types of cognitive performance (class 1 if a participant with better performance means cognitive scores (Table 1) equal or higher than 50%, 0 otherwise) based on hemoglobin responses.

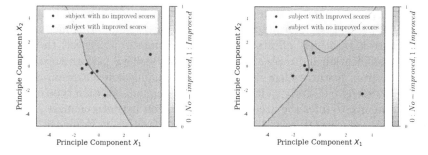

Fig. 7. Visualization of SVM classification through adjusting kernel and parameters for cognitive-performance classification based on features of hemodynamic signals. SVM with median-based approach is shown in (A), and PSD-based approach is shown in (B)

There were limitations to this study. The analysis results from using only an SVM visualizes the relation between the brain's hemodynamic response and its activity after playing a game, though this is not clear. This study required a larger number of samples. Our study was also limited to the investigation of fNIRS signals for four cognitive tasks. Each cognitive task, i.e., the mental rotation task, Stroop task, associated pair-matching task, and different item-finding task, has its own characteristics and might require a different pattern of hemoglobin concentration for activating the brain. Investigating changes in signals reflecting the hemoglobin concentration in a particular domain of cognitive function through each task of the cognitive neuropsychological test would produce meaningful results. Figure 3 shows subjects had more highly activated brain during playing the puzzle game than during the performance of cognitive neuropsychological task. Brain activity, however, was only investigated through the comparison of before and after the game play. The activity for a cognitive neuropsychological task before and after engaging in other types of activity should have been taken into account to validate the effects of this computer game. These limitations should be addressed for future work.

5   Conclusion

We investigated the differences between cognitive performances before and after playing a color-matching puzzle on a computer. The results suggest the positive effect of playing the puzzle game called "candy-crush" on the activation of cognitive functions [of speed of cognitive perception, visuo-spatial ability, and memory. It is however not clear whether the ability of quickly moving eyes decreases due to visual fatigue. In this study, investigation of objective index to evaluate visual fatigue is yet included. We then investigated whether changes in brain activity could be understood by referring to changes in hemoglobin concentration responses after playing this game. The features such as median of max-min normalized hemoglobin signals and power spectral density of hemoglobin signals show the differences in brain activity, in which oxy-Hb and deoxy-Hb signals after playing the game decreased with smaller variations compared with those before playing it. This suggests that playing such a game helps in lowering mental workload because it positively affects cognitive performance. Moreover, the results of SVM classification indicates that changes in cognitive performance can be understood from features identified from hemodynamic-concentration changes. We plan to extend our study to involve more participants for each type of cognitive performance to infer the accuracy of the relation between changes found in hemodynamic concentration and improvement in cognitive performance. We will consider other features for statistical machine learning to interpret the changes in fNIRS of oxy-Hb and deoxy-Hb signals regarding cognitive performance.

References

1. Salthouse, T.A.: When does age-related cognitive decline begin? Neurobiol. Aging **30**(4), 507–514 (2009)
2. Kensinger, E.A., Brierley, B., Medford, N., Growdon, J.H., Corkin, S.: Effects of normal aging and Alzheimer's disease on emotional memory. Emotion **2**(2), 118 (2002)
3. Weiss, E.M., et al.: Impairment in emotion recognition abilities in patients with mild cognitive impairment, early and moderate Alzheimer disease compared with healthy comparison subjects. Am. J. Geriatr. Psychiatry **16**(12), 974–980 (2008)
4. Turner, A.D., James, B.D., Capuano, A.W., Aggarwal, N.T., Barnes, L.L.: Perceived stress and cognitive decline in different cognitive domains in a cohort of older African Americans. Am. J. Geriatr. Psychiatry **25**(1), 25–34 (2017)
5. Hammar, A., Ardal, G.: Cognitive functioning in major depression-a summary. Front. Hum. Neurosci. **3**, 26 (2009)
6. Esmaeili, M.T., Karimi, M., Tabatabaie, K.R., Moradi, A., Farahini, N.: The effect of positive arousal on working memory. Procedia Soc. Behav. Sci. **30**, 1457–1460 (2011)
7. Huang, V., Young, M., Fiocco, A.J.: The association between video game play and cognitive function: does gaming platform matter? Cyberpsychology Behav. Soc. Netw. **20**(11), 689–694 (2017)
8. Chandra, S., Sharma, G., Salam, A.A., Jha, D., Mittal, A.P.: Playing action video games a key to cognitive enhancement. Procedia Comput. Sci. **84**, 115–122 (2016)

9. De Lisi, R., Cammarano, D.M.: Computer experience and gender differences in undergraduate mental rotation performance. Comput. Hum. Behav. **12**(3), 351–361 (1996)

10. Dzulkifli, M.A., Mustafar, M.F.: The influence of colour on memory performance: a review. Malays. J. Med. Sci. MJMS **20**(2), 3–9 (2013)

11. Xia, T., Song, L., Wang, T.T., Tan, L., Mo, L.: Exploring the effect of red and blue on cognitive task performances. Front. Psychol. **7**, 784 (2016). https://doi.org/10.3389/fpsyg.2016.00784

12. Dredge, S.: Why is Candy Crush Saga so popular? 26 March 2014. https://www.theguardian.com/technology/2014/mar/26/candy-crush-saga-king-why-popular

13. Lee, Y.Y., Hsieh, S.: Classifying different emotional states by means of EEG-based functional connectivity patterns. PloS one **9**(4), e95415 (2014)

14. Al-Qazzaz, N.K., et al.: Role of EEG as biomarker in the early detection and classification of dementia. Sci. World J. **2014** (2014). Article no. 906038

15. Yin, C., Li, S., Zhao, W., Feng, J.: Brain imaging of mild cognitive impairment and Alzheimer's disease. Neural Regeneration Res. **8**(5), 435 (2013)

16. Sirály, E., et al.: Monitoring the early signs of cognitive decline in elderly by computer games: an MRI study. Plos One **10**(2), e0117918 (2015)

17. Peck, E.M., Afergan, D., Yuksel, B.F., Lalooses, F., Jacob, R.J.K.: Using fNIRS to measure mental workload in the real world. In: Fairclough, S.H., Gilleade, K. (eds.) Advances in Physiological Computing. HIS, pp. 117–139. Springer, London (2014). https://doi.org/10.1007/978-1-4471-6392-3_6

18. Kato, S., Endo, H., Nagata, R., Sakuma, T., Watanabe, K.: Early detection of mild cognitive impairment and mild Alzheimer's disease in elderly using CBF activation during verbally-based cognitive tests. In: Proceedings of the International Joint (2014)

19. Seiyama, A., et al.: Circulatory basis of fMRI signals: relationship between changes in the hemodynamic parameters and BOLD signal intensity. NeuroImage **21**(4), 1204–1214 (2004)

20. Stroop, J.R.: Studies of interference in serial verbal reactions. J. Exp. Psychol. **18**(6), 643–662 (1935)

21. Koss, E., Ober, B.A., Delis, D.C., Friedland, R.P.: The Stroop color-word test: indicator of dementia severity. Int. J. Neurosci. **24**(1), 53–61 (1984)

22. Zahedi, A., Stuermer, B., Hatami, J., Rostami, R., Sommer, W.: Eliminating Stroop effects with post-hypnotic instructions: brain mechanisms inferred from EEG. Neuropsychologia **96**, 70–77 (2017)

23. Sisco, S.M., Slonena, E., Okun, M.S., Bowers, D., Price, C.C.: Parkinson's disease and the Stroop color word test: processing speed and interference algorithms. Clin. Neuropsychologist **30**(7), 1104–1117 (2016)

24. Stoet, G.: PsyToolkit: a software package for programming psychological experiments using Linux. Behav. Res. Methods **42**(4), 1096–1104 (2010)

25. Stoet, G.: PsyToolkit: a novel web-based method for running online questionnaires and reaction-time experiments. Teach. Psychol. **44**(1), 24–31 (2017)

26. Shepard, R.N., Metzler, J.: Mental rotation of three-dimensional objects. Science **171**(3972), 701–703 (1971)

27. Atsumori, H., et al.: Development of wearable optical topography system for mapping the prefrontal cortex activation. Rev. Sci. Instrum. **80**(4), 043704 (2009)

28. Homan, R.W., Herman, J., Purdy, P.: Cerebral location of international 10–20 system electrode placement. Electroencephalogr. Clin. Neurophysiol. **66**(4), 376–382 (1987)

29. D'Esposito, M., Postle, B.R., Rypma, B.: Prefrontal cortical contributions to working memory: evidence from event-related fMRI studies. In: Schneider, W.X., Owen, A.M., Duncan, J. (eds.) Executive Control and the Frontal Lobe: Current issues, pp. 3–11. Springer, Heidelberg (2000). https://doi.org/10.1007/978-3-642-59794-7_2

30. Wagner, A.D., Maril, A., Bjork, R.A., Schacter, D.L.: Prefrontal contributions to executive control: fMRI evidence for functional distinctions within lateral prefrontal cortex. Neuroimage **14**(6), 1337–1347 (2001)

31. Voytek, B., Knight, R.T.: Prefrontal cortex and basal ganglia contributions to visual working memory. Proc. Nat. Acad. Sci. **107**(42), 18167–18172 (2010)

32. Welch, P.: The use of fast Fourier transform for the estimation of power spectra: a method based on time averaging over short, modified periodograms. IEEE Trans. Audio Electroacoust. **15**(2), 70–73 (1967)

33. Stoica, P., Moses, R.L.: Spectral analysis of signals (2005)

34. Sevick, E.M., Chance, B., Leigh, J., Nioka, S., Maris, M.: Quantitation of time- and frequency-resolved optical spectra for the determination of tissue oxygenation. Anal. Biochem. **195**(2), 330–351 (1991)

35. Nakagawa, T., Kamei, Y., Uwano, H., Monden, A., Matsumoto, K., German, D.M.: Quantifying programmers' mental workload during program comprehension based on cerebral blood flow measurement: a controlled experiment. In: Companion Proceedings of the 36th International Conference on Software Engineering, pp. 448–451. ACM (2014)

36. Fujiki, R., et al.: Single event-related changes in cerebral oxygenated hemoglobin using word game in schizophrenia. Neuropsychiatric Dis. Treat. **10**, 2353 (2014)

37. Bujarski, S.J., Mischel, E., Dutton, C., Steele, J.S., Cisler, J.: The elicitation and assessment of emotional responding. In: Sleep and Affect, pp. 91–118 (2015)

Author Index

Printed in the United States
By Bookmasters